GARDENS OF EDEN

Recreation·

Everything but *Mountain Climbing!* This tells the Story of the Wonderful Recreative Features of

Brightwaters

Nowhere on Earth is there Opportunity for a greater Variety of Outdoor Sports and Pleasures than in this Beautiful

Arcadia

of Spring Lakes, Pine Woods and Sea Shore·

8. Title page from a Brightwaters promotional booklet, ca. 1908. Bay Shore Historical Society

GARDENS OF EDEN

LONG ISLAND'S EARLY TWENTIETH-CENTURY PLANNED COMMUNITIES

EDITED BY ROBERT B. MacKAY

W.W. NORTON & COMPANY

NEW YORK • LONDON

For information about permission to reproduce selections from this book, write to
Permissions, W. W. Norton & Company, Inc., 500 Fifth Avenue, New York, NY 10110

For information about special discounts for bulk purchases, please contact
W. W. Norton Special Sales at specialsales@wwnorton.com or 800-233-4830

Manufacturing by Walsworth Publishing Company
Book design by Abigail Sturges Graphic Design
Production manager: Christine Critelli

Library of Congress Cataloging-in-Publication Data

Gardens of eden : Long Island's early twentieth-century planned
communities / edited by Robert B. MacKay. — First edition.
    pages cm
Includes bibliographical references and index.
ISBN 978-0-393-73321-1 (hardcover : alk. paper)
1. Planned communities—New York (State)—Long Island—History—20th century. 2. Garden
cities—New York (State)—Long Island—History—20th century. 3.City planning—New York
(State)—Long Island—History—20th century. I. MacKay, Robert B.
HT169.57.U62L6643 2015
307.76´80974721—dc23
                    2015000169

W. W. Norton & Company, Inc., 500 Fifth Avenue, New York, N.Y. 10110
                    www.wwnorton.com
W. W. Norton & Company Ltd., Castle House, 75/76 Wells Street, London W1T 3QT

1 2 3 4 5 6 7 8 9 0

CONTENTS

Preface and Acknowledgments   7
Robert B. MacKay

1   The Residential Park Phenomenon on Long Island   10
Robert B. MacKay

2   Garden City: American Versions of Utopia   22
Richard Guy Wilson

3   A Modern Venice: H. O. Havemeyer's Bayberry Point   46
Anne Walker

4   For Teachers Only: Plandome and Its Companions   52
Robert B. MacKay

5   From Flatbush to the Shinnecock Hills: Dean Alvord's Idea   58
Robert B. MacKay

6   Mrs. Marsh's Bellerose   72
Virginia L. Bartos

7   Kensington and Douglas Manor: The Rickert-Finlay Realty Company   78
Kevin Wolfe

8   Long Beach: Senator William H. Reynolds's City by the Sea   100
Anthony W. Robins

9   The Thousand-Acre City by the Sea: T. B. Ackerson's Brightwaters   116
Richard F. Welch

10   Great Neck Estates: Harvey Stewart McKnight and   130
the McKnight Realty Company, 1907–1916
Ellen Fletcher Russell and Sargent Russell

11   Paul V. Shields at Great Neck: Great Neck Villa and Grenwolde   140
Ellen Fletcher Russell and Sargent Russell

12   Carl Graham Fisher and Montauk Beach: "I just have to see   148
the dirt fly!"
Ellen Fletcher Russell and Sargent Russell

13   Robert Burton's Woodmere   168
Millicent D. Vollono

14   The Grand Scheme: Felix Isman, Ernestus Gulick,   180
      and the Creation of Jamaica Estates
      Carl Ballenas and the Aquinas Honor Society

15   Robert Weeks de Forest: Forest Hills Gardens and Munsey Park   186
      Virginia L. Bartos

16   Hapgood's Shoreham: Arts and Crafts by the Sea   198
      Mary Ann Oberdorf and Joseph Falco

17   Beacon Hill: A Gem in the Diadem   212
      Lynn Stowell Pearson

18   Surf and Controversy: Realty Associates & Neponsit   222
      Robert B. MacKay

19   Gondolas in Copiague: Victor Pisani, Isaac Meister,   228
      and the Creation of American Venice, 1925–1929
      Mary Cascone

20   Old Field South   240
      Richard F. Welch

21   What If? Planned Communities That Might Have Been   246
      Robert B. MacKay

      Notes   252
      Selected Bibliography   279
      Index   282

PREFACE
AND ACKNOWLEDGMENTS

Long Island is full of stories and one of the most fascinating concerns the two distinct housing phenomena at the dawn of the twentieth century. The Society for the Preservation of Long Island Antiquities (SPLIA) covered the first phenomenon in *Long Island Country Houses and Their Architects 1860–1940,* published by W. W. Norton in 1997. The country houses, built for the new captains of finance and industry, as well as for New York's old moneyed class, were easily identified as they were built for seasonal living beyond the limits of existing towns, designed by architects for owners who, with few exceptions, had no previous connection with the region. In this book, we are focusing on the second phenomenon, the "residential parks," as they were known, or garden suburbs, as we might call them, built by developers for people of more modest means seeking to escape the city. Isaac Hicks, the Quaker nurseryman from Westbury, put his finger on it when he observed at the turn of the twentieth century that while agrarian communities were rapidly vanishing, "great wealthy ones continually come," and "a large number of small ones come too."[1]

Indeed, at that time, ads for these comprehensively planned communities began appearing in *Country Life in America* and other publications, and some of the same architects and landscape architects who had designed the large country houses were involved. Discussion of these new communities, however, was judged to be beyond the scope of the *Country Houses* book, with the exception of C. P. H. Gilbert's work at the North Country Colony, an enclave in Glen Cove, and Grosvenor Atterbury's Bayberry Point in Islip, a summer colony for H. O. Havemeyer.

Now we turn to this lesser-known story, these gardens of Eden of the Progressive Era, and find, as is so often the case with things that happen first on Long Island, a tale of great consequence. It introduces figures in Long Island history who have either been overlooked or have received scant attention in the past: community builders who were visionaries, realtors, and financiers intent on transforming their industries; publishers and railroad executives who saw possibilities in the phenomenon; and residents who were intrepid pioneers. All were risk takers who, in the interest of a new lifestyle, were willing to live in a region where paved roads, shopping centers, and even service stations were still well into the future. A region so distant and unknown, in fact, that one builder would not reveal the location of his first project east of the city line until he had sold a sufficient number of plots to assure the public that it wasn't folly. The story also reveals a great deal about the origins of the Long Island we live in today and the influence it has had on the nation. This region of so many separate realities, this land of innumerable residential enclaves, was formed by events that took place at the turn of the twentieth century. "This is Long Island's story," observes Dr. Virginia Bartos, who oversaw Long Island for the state agency administering the National Register of Historic Places.

It is a story of such magnitude that what is presented here only introduces the subject and is not intended to be comprehensive. We focus on some of the most significant residential parks of the pre–World War I era and a handful of interesting projects from the 1920s, when the number of new subdivisions on Long Island expanded exponentially. Left for future scholarship are dozens of others. In Queens, Hollis Park Gardens, and William Ziegler's Realty Trust project at Whitestone, Malba-on-the-Sound, are also deserving of study. Farther east, LaMarcus Adna Thompson, the man who helped perfect the roller coaster, developed a small but distinctive project at Sea Cliff called Thompson Park. Wampage Shores at Sands Point intrigued us and could have amounted to much more had it not been for the untimely death of its developer, S. Osgood Pell. Kew Gardens and Baxter Estates (Port Washington) had some of the characteristics we were looking for, and two South Shore projects from the 1920s, seriously considered for inclusion, were movie magnate William Fox's Biltmore Shores and George J. Brown's Amity Harbor, the latter planned as "a home for the white-collar man, with a car in the front and a boat in the rear."[2] Abraham Levitt's Strathmores of the 1930s is beyond the time frame of this study but has recently been the subject of a wonderful chapter by Richard Longstreth in *Second Suburb: Levittown, Pennsylvania*.[3] It is important to note that as a young attorney, Levitt (1880–1962) focused on real estate law in Brooklyn just when Flatbush was emerging as a cradle of suburbia. His later emphasis on landscaping, covenants, and other measures aimed at creating a sense of community for his projects must have been influenced by what he observed early in his career in his native borough. Long before the post–World War II subdivisions that rolled out like a carpet down the spine of Long Island, Levitt was an innovator.

Richard Guy Wilson, Commonwealth Professor of Architectural History at the University of Virginia and a collaborator on past SPLIA projects, starts us off by exploring the origins of an ideal American way of life as reflected in Garden City's evolution from A. T. Stewart's Garden of Eden to a suburban utopia of the twentieth century. Along the way, he profiles the creation of such seminal communities as Llewellyn Park, New Jersey, generally considered to be the country's first planned garden suburb, and Riverside, Illinois, the model suburb near Chicago designed by Frederick Law Olmsted and Calvert Vaux, whose remarkable web of curvilinear streets became one of the most recognizable features of residential parks across the country.

For all of Garden City's significance on the national level, however, the suburban phenomenon that manifested itself on Long Island at the outset of the twentieth century first appeared in the cornfields of Flatbush. Sparked by transportation improvements and a new lifestyle, it moved from west to east and is the subject of my chapter "From Flatbush to the Shinnecock Hills: Dean Alvord's Idea."

The chapters on individual developers and their communities, which comprise the greater part of this study, are the work of many hands.

Mary Cascone, historian for the Town of Babylon; Millicent Vollono, curator of the local history collection at the Hewlett-Woodmere Public Library; Shoreham Village historian Mary Ann Oberdorf and Joe Falco; Carl Ballenas, director of the Aquinas Honor Society at the Immaculate Conception School of Jamaica Estates;[4] and Kevin Wolfe, Douglas Manor's historian, are all authors of books about their communities. Here they are responsible for the chapters on American Venice in Copiague, Woodmere, Shoreham, Jamaica Estates, and Douglas Manor, respectively.

Lynn Stowell Pearson and Ellen Fletcher Russell, former residents of North Hempstead, meticulously researched their subjects among the home colonies of Great Neck and Port Washington. Dr. Virginia Bartos returns to familiar territory in illuminating the interesting stories of Helen Marsh's Bellerose and Robert de Forest's communities.

Anthony W. Robins, former director of Education and Programs at the Municipal Arts Society, who has done so much to document New York City's architecture and shape strategies for the preservation of its early twentieth-century theaters, profiles one of era's most colorful real estate impresarios, a truly theatrical character, ex-Senator William H. "Billy" Reynolds, whose career began well to the west of his final projects at Long Beach and Lido Beach. Anne Walker, co-author of *The Architecture of Grosvenor Atterbury* and other monographs, profiles Atterbury's Bayberry Point project. Long Island historian Richard Welch focuses on two remarkable Suffolk communities, Ackerson's Brightwaters and Ward Melville's Old Field South.

Our hats are off to many village, town, and city historians who have facilitated our research, including Nancy Orth of Belle Terre, Kenneth Brady of Port Jefferson, Scott Wilson of Plandome, Robert Sargent of Roslyn Estates, Ilse Kagan of Great Neck Estates, Zachary Studenroth of Southampton, Robert Hughes of Huntington, Howard Kroplick of North Hempstead, Roberta Fiore of Long Beach, and the Office of Historic Services, Town of Babylon. We would also like to thank Eric Huber, image archivist at the Long Island

Division of the Queens Borough Public Library. Jim McNamara, John Santos, Ian Zwerdling, and many others generously lent images from their personal collections. Special thanks are also due to Kristen J. Nyitray, head of Special Collections and University Archives at SUNY Stony Brook; George W. Fisher, archivist, Nassau County Department of Parks, Recreation and Museums Photo Archives Center; the Brooklyn Room at the Brooklyn Public Library; Julie May, photographic archivist at the Brooklyn Historical Society; Bill Keeler and the staff of the Rochester Historical Society; Jonathan Aubrey, local history librarian at the Great Neck Library; Elly Shodell, Local History Center director and Dan Chuzmir of the Port Washington Public Library; Robin Strong at Montauk Library; and the Hewlett-Woodmere Public Library. Carol Stern and Elizabeth Cameron of the Glen Cove Public Library assisted our project. We are also grateful to Karen Martin of the Three Village Historical Society, Chris Bain of the Cow Neck Peninsula Historical Society, the Amity Historical Society, the Lindenhurst Historical Society, the Douglaston and Little Neck Historical Society, the Douglas Manor Association, and the Jamaica Estates Association. We gratefully acknowledge images obtained from the New York Public Library; Frederick Law Olmsted National Historic Site; David M. Rubenstein Rare Books & Manuscript Library at Duke University; and the Frank Lloyd Wright Foundation.

This work, long in the planning, would not have been possible without the advice, assistance, and encouragement of many intrigued by its subject. The Gerry Charitable Trust was generous in its support; its late chairman, Huyler C. Held, remembered his grandparents who resided in Garden City and knew one of the principal figures in its development, Gage E. Tarbell. Indeed, personal history linked many of the participants. SPLIA's former president, Paul Vermylen, grew up in Shoreham; Trustee Council member Greg Riley, in Kensington; and Sandy Branciforte, authors' liaison for the project, lives just down the road from Roslyn Estates. My maternal grandfather, a Brooklyn physician, thought about moving to Forest Hills Gardens before settling in Plandome. Alexandra Wolfe, the Society's current director, is a resident of Douglas Manor, where her husband, Kevin, is village historian and author of that community's wonderful history, *This Salubrious Spot: The First 100 Years at Douglas Manor 1906–2006*.

Robert B. MacKay

1

THE RESIDENTIAL PARK PHENOMENON ON LONG ISLAND

ROBERT B. MacKAY

"Why should they have all the garden suburbs on Long Island?" asks Carol Kennicott in Sinclair Lewis's *Main Street*.[1] more than three dozen "residential parks," or early planned communities, were created in Brooklyn and east through Queens, Nassau, and Suffolk counties. Lewis, whose own bungalow on Vanderventer Avenue in Port Washington[2] was not far from the Tuxill Realty Company's posh Beacon Hill, would have known many of them. On his commute on the Long Island Railroad (hereafter L.I.R.R.), he passed by Plandome Park, which Frances Hodgson Burnett of *Little Lord Fauntleroy* fame found ideal, as well as Roslyn Estates, Christopher Morley's "rustic Nirvana," which he referred to as "Salamis" in his writings, for fear that the public would discover "our little world was there."[3] Farther west was Great Neck Estates, where F. Scott Fitzgerald resided while writing *The Great Gatsby*; Douglas Manor, home in the twenties to the young dancer Ginger Rogers; and Forest Hills Gardens, one of the most celebrated planned communities in America, an acknowledged masterpiece of planning, design, and construction.[4]

"The residential park, laid out and developed idealistically," the *New York Times* reported in 1908, "where the developer is prepared to preserve and enhance the natural qualities of a site, has become the most pleasing and attractive feature of the building up of Long Island as a land of homes."[5] Driving the transformation was a host of factors, not the least of which was the appeal of the countryside and leisure pursuits as an antidote to the increasing complexities of urban life. P. G. Wodehouse even put it to words and Jerome Kern provided the score for a 1917 musical:

> Oh, let us fly without delay
> Into the country far away,
> Where, free from all this care and strife,
> We'll go and live the simple life. . . .
> Let's build a little bungalow in Quogue
> In Yaphank or in Hicksville or Patchogue.[6]

The residential park phenomenon unfolding here at the outset of the twentieth century combined the growing interest in landscape architecture with concepts introduced by the Garden City movement in England to create something entirely new, entirely American. Variously referred to at the time as "residential parks," "garden suburbs," "home colonies," and yet other terms, these early planned communities rose in previously undeveloped areas, were characterized by significant investment in landscaping and infrastructure, conformed to restrictions that were determined before construction, and benefited from the emergence of new methods of financing. In requiring homeowners to relinquish property rights through deed stipulation for the good of the community, they were the antithesis of the speculative "land booming" schemes that were then prevalent. And finally, in answer to Kennicott's question, these garden sub-

"The Mirage on the Desert." Brooklyn Daily Eagle, June 8, 1907

urbs developed apace with the country house boom because a sea change in transportation, recreation, and lifestyle so transformed Long Island that the *Brooklyn Daily Eagle* commented, "It was as if the region had been touched by magic, a new version of the sleeping princess."[7]

At the close of the nineteenth century, Long Island had been *terra incognita*, a place apart. "So few people know the North Shore," lamented the architect Robert Gibson.[8] Part of the problem, despite the extension of the L.I.R.R.'s lines, continued to be transportation. The only East River span was the Brooklyn Bridge, well south of midtown Manhattan, and ferry bottlenecks still made the prospect of commuting a challenge. Solutions would have to await the twentieth century. Yet changes were occurring that presaged the explosive growth of residential parks in the early twentieth century. Salaries of white-collar workers rose by a third between 1890 and 1910, fostering a consumer culture that embraced leisure and sparked a revolution in recreation at the outset of the Progressive Era.

Cradle of Recreation

"As leisure time increased," historian Kenneth T. Jackson has noted, "compulsive play became an accepted alternative to compulsive work."[9] Manhattan's captains of finance and industry, and their well-heeled sons, soon discovered that "there was hardly a diversion of the sportsman short of big

game hunting that cannot be enjoyed somewhere on Long Island," as the *Brooklyn Daily Eagle* observed in 1915.[10] Long Island was simply "a paradise for equestrians," wrote Paul D. Cravath in *Country Life in America* in 1913.[11] In summer colonies along the North Shore, young men who considered it "a matter of personal pride to scrape, paint, rig and sail their own boats,"[12] organized the Seawanhaka Corinthian Yacht Club (1871), the first of dozens of similar clubs that would ring the Island, "fostered by conditions as favorable as may anywhere by found."[13] And interest in golf exploded in the 1890s; Shinnecock Hills Golf Club (1891–92), the first professionally designed course in the country to be built in conjunction with a clubhouse, was quickly followed by many more.[14] By 1907, all of Long Island was simply "dotted with them."[15] In short, the Island boasted the greatest concentration of golf courses in America. Myriad other pastimes, including polo, tennis, cycling, aviation, motoring, and farther east, fishing and hunting, also contributed to turning Long Island into a playground. It was "the ideal place," Garden City Estates' Gage E. Tarbell thought, for those with a "passion for outdoor life," a lifestyle that he and fellow community builders realized they could market to the rich and the not quite as rich alike. "The great level stretches are especially suited for modern sports."[16] Recreation was as important to the development of residential parks as it was in sparking the region's country house phenomenon.

A Revolution in Transportation

For those who wished to participate in these new pastimes and longed for their growing families to experience suburban living, the open sesame came in 1900 with the Pennsylvania Railroad's acquisition of the L.I.R.R. and its commitment to build the East River tunnels, which opened in 1910.[17] Here, finally, was the critical link tying the Long Island system, which was largely complete after the North Shore Division was extended from Great Neck to Port Washington in 1898, to the huge new terminal in the heart of Manhattan, Pennsylvania Station. The next year, the L.I.R.R. carried 33,867,228 passengers, a figure that more than tripled by its peak year in 1929. Thanks to the "Pennsy," new equipment and extensive electrification of the tracks in Brooklyn and Queens in the decades leading up to World War I added to the system's effectiveness, and in 1915, when the Interborough Rapid Transit Subway (hereafter IRT) reached Long Island City, where it connected to the L.I.R.R. at Jackson Avenue, and was extended to Queens Plaza the following year, the number of options increased.

Developing apace with the improvements in rail transportation were those in auto travel. The completion of the East River bridges, particularly the Queensboro, or 59th Street, Bridge in 1909, heralded a new era of accessibility. The Jamaica Estates Company, for example, launched their new community the following year, when Queens Boulevard was laid out from the new bridge to Jamaica, but the impact of the new span was hardly limited to Queens. For those heading to the North Shore via Routes 25 and 25A or to the east via William K. Vanderbilt Jr.'s new Long Island Motor Parkway (1906, the first limited-access highway), the savings in time and the possibilities presented were almost beyond comprehension. Even before the opening of the Queensboro Bridge, A. R. Pardington, the Motor Parkway's chief engineer, writing in *Harper's Weekly,* crowed:

> Think of the time it will save the busy man of affairs, who likes to crowd into each day a bit of relaxation. He will leave downtown at three o'clock

in the afternoon, take the subway to a garage within striking distance of the new Blackwell's Island–East River Bridge. In twenty minutes, a 60-horse-power car will have him at the western terminus of the Motor Parkway. Here a card of admission passes him through the gates, speed limits are left behind, the great white way is before him.[18]

The prescient Pardington, who had also organized the Long Island Automobile Club and served as contest chair for the American Automobile Association, was well aware that by 1907, the automobile was becoming a necessity. By 1910, there were some 458,500 registered motor vehicles in the United States and production of the Model T, introduced two years earlier by Henry Ford, had reached 32,053 cars per annum on its way to 734,811 in 1916. What Pardington foresaw, and developers of residential parks were quick to appreciate, were the intermodal opportunities that car, train, and subway travel afforded Long Island.

The Developers

Bodacious and self-confident in the face of great risk and passionate about their plans, many of the remarkable developers behind the residential-park phenomenon apparently possessed the qualities attributed to Long Beach creator, State Senator William H. "Billy" Reynolds, a fabulous character who had the ability of talking "people into doing things they never intended to do."[19] "These men have not been afraid," wrote architect John J. Petit in 1908, "they have dared to depart from the order of things."[20] The visionaries also shared other characteristics. First, most of them had cut their teeth elsewhere[21] or had learned their trade through earlier projects in Brooklyn (particularly Flatbush) and Queens. Most knew one another, had offices within a few blocks of Penn Station, and were involved in the trade association Real Estate Exchange of Long Island, which disseminated information and advocated for the East River tunnels.[22] In fact, in the relatively small world of suburban development, they often made use of the same architects and realtors, sought capital from the same investors, and even sold one another tracts to concentrate on more promising prospects. The majority resided in the communities they built. All were avid recreationalists in their own right, interested in "automobiling" and the possibilities inherent in the emergence of the combustion engine. Dean Alvord, one of the region's most prolific community builders, had been an original promoter of William K. Vanderbilt Jr.'s Long Island Motor Parkway and became actively involved in acquiring the right-of-way. Frank Bailey, the real estate financier and personi-

"Looking over the property." Brooklyn Daily Eagle, June 27, 1909

fication of Toad in Kenneth Grahame's *The Wind in the Willows*, terrorized Brooklyn in his "motor," the "Scarlet Scooter."[24] In 1915, Bailey joined Carl Fisher, the developer of Montauk and founder of the Indianapolis Speedway, on the board of a new corporation intent on bringing automobile racing to the site of the old Coney Island Jockey Club track at Sheepshead Bay.[24] The leisure pursuits these community builders embraced mirrored Long Island's remarkable variety, and, as participants in the country life experiment, they were also advocates of the new lifestyle.[25] Many were adherents of City Beautiful, the beautification movement that swept the country around the turn of the century, linking quality of life and social harmony with careful planning and architectural achievement. The dream was dramatically given its first expression in 1893 in the "White City," as the architecture at the

Frank Bailey in his 1909 Packard, the "Scarlet Scooter," in Prospect Park. Brooklyn Historical Society

World Columbian Exposition in Chicago came to be known. Certainly Forest Hills Gardens' creators had the credentials. Robert W. de Forest, a trustee of the Russell Sage Foundation, shared Mrs. Sage's concern for improving housing for the working class. Frederick Law Olmsted Jr. (1870–1957), the landscape architect who had spent a college summer as assistant to Daniel H. Burnham in the planning of the White City, was already on the path to becoming the nation's champion of city planning, and his collaborator, architect and housing reform advocate Grosvenor Atterbury (1869–1956), were the perfect team for the experiment at Forest Hills. Frank Bailey, whose eleemosynary interests were myriad, was continually involved in efforts to build his city's cultural primacy.[26] The donor of Prospect Park's Bailey Fountain, he was interested in civic improvement and the development of parks, a concern shared by Timothy L. Woodruff, whose political career began with his appointment as Brooklyn's Park Commissioner in 1896. Dean Alvord, a member of the Municipal Arts Society who was interested in how landscape architecture could improve real estate development, was also on the bandwagon. He addressed Brooklyn's Municipal Club on how that city could become a "City Beautiful"; the prizes he offered for "the best ordered and most beautiful front and back yards"[27] were exactly what the movement's village improvement advocates, such as Jesse Good and the National League of Improve-

ment Associations, were urging.[28] They were all on the same progressive page, avid modernists, believers in the power of change when it came to science, technology, and education. Even Senator Reynolds, the politician developer, seems to have been touched by the progressive spirit. His short-lived Coney Island amusement park, "Dreamland" (1904–11), was the New York area's greatest evocation of the White City. Its inspiring architecture, white towers, wide avenues, and inclusion of educational exhibits adhered to the movement's principles and were aimed at an audience Coney Island had yet to embrace—the middle class.

Though many of Long Island's community builders and architects undoubtedly believed they were creating a framework for a better society, they were also businessmen attuned to marketplace realities. They had grasped the sea change in the public's attitude that favored a collective approach toward amenities and security, understood the value of marketing and the appeal of exclusivity, and, like today's green developers, were offering the public what it sought.

Envisioning the Residential Park

What the public did not want, Alvord contended, was the commonplace, the sort of development where "streets are run at exact angles and lots subdivided with mathematical precision: where cement sidewalks and rows of saplings crisscross the landscape into checkerboard regularity and monotony and where the home builder has no chance to impart individuality to his property."[29] Writing in *Country Life in America*, renowned architect John M. Carrère agreed. Inveighing against "rule of thumb street arrangements," Carrère thought that to improve suburban development, the most important step was for municipalities and community builders to abandon the grid and uniform lot size for a less formal and "more thoughtful and artistic" result. And in the closing decades of the nineteenth century, something different began to rise out of the cornfields of Flatbush.[30] Olmsted and Vaux's magnificent Prospect Park, begun in 1866, and the two parkways, Eastern and Ocean, radiating from it, coupled with rail improvements,[31] drew attention to the old farming town as Brooklyn expanded toward the sea. In 1886, Richard Ficken (d. 1907) purchased property and began his seminal development of single-family, freestanding houses, Tennis Court. By building in an area with defined boundaries, where construction could be regulated, and by linking his project to a recreational amenity, the Knickerbocker Field Club, organized in 1889 on land he leased to lawn tennis enthusiasts, Ficken not only broke new ground but also fashioned a new lifestyle. In 1891, *Brooklyn Life* commented that "one of the chief charms of the club is the presence of women as members" and that the "courts are usually well patronized by both sexes," while on Saturday evenings, "music and dancing serve to pass away the time."[32] Henceforth, Flatbush became a suburban incubator, as entire neighborhoods, including Ditmas Park, Fiske Terrace, and Prospect Park South, arose, creating, in the opinion of John J. Petit, a residential section above all others.[33] Prospect Park South—Dean Alvord's *rus in urbe*, an attempt "to create a rural park within the limitations of the conventional city block,"[34] proved to be Flatbush's greatest tastemaker. Yet for all of Prospect Park South's inventiveness, it was still constrained by Flatbush's unrelieved topography and the city street grid. Long Island would not have a community in the tradition of Llewellyn Park, New Jersey, or Riverside, Illinois, until after the turn of the century, but change was already apparent east of the city line. Cottage colonies, often organized as syndicated real estate developments for summer residents and offering protected sites for country houses, began to appear at the century's close. Wave Crest at Far Rockaway (ca. 1880), Bay Crest at Huntington Bay (1888), Sea Gate at Coney Island's western extremity (1892), and Glen Cove's North Country Colony (1893) exhibited some of the controls and features that were to characterize the appearance of the Long Island residential parks

that arose in the early twentieth century, the organizational underpinnings of which lay in the restrictions attached to their deeds.

Carefully Crafted Restrictions

As a wedge against the unexpected, deed restrictions ensured development by plan, enhanced property values, and became an important promotional tool. In the age before zoning (even New York City did not have an ordinance until 1916), these "voluntary private contracts," as real estate expert Marc Weiss notes, went beyond the policing power of public regulations and "constituted a very significant abridgement of private property rights,"[35] yet many homeowners were ready to relinquish those rights in the interest of maintaining neighborhood character. Community builders emphasized the presence of restrictions governing the character and quality of their projects in their advertisements and brochures. The setbacks and lot dimensions of the single-family detached dwellings they built were predetermined, as were their size, height, cost, and, at times, even their architectural style and landscaping. Nonconforming activities, such as commerce, were prohibited in these stipulations, which exercised broad control over design and land-use matters. Restrictions on race and religion were also included in some instances. Edward Bouton, developer of Baltimore's Roland Park, advised the Sage Foundation that whether Forest Hills Gardens was to be Jewish or Gentile was a commercial decision without prejudice, and William J. Levitt, whose grandfather had been a rabbi, is said to have restricted Jews from his upscale pre–World War II Strathmore developments on the North Shore.[36] "It is a complex task," Dolores Hayden observes, "to unravel the racism and snobbery of certain picturesque enclaves from the positive aspects of these communities."[37]

Time limitations were placed on these controls. "All restrictions run to January 1, 1930," the 1910 Jamaica Estates prospectus declared. As expiration dates neared, many communities east of the city line sought to incorporate as villages so that concerned residents could exercise zoning and police

View of Prospect Park South. Society for the Preservation of Long Island Antiquities

15

controls. Yet, despite limitations, the use of restrictions became widespread. The National Conference on City Planning supported their use in 1916 at a meeting attended by such planned-community luminaries as J. C. Nichols (1880–1949), developer of Kansas City's Country Club District, John Nolen (1869–1937), and F. L. Olmsted Jr. By the late 1920s, the application of these controls had become a science. Helen C. Monchow's *Use of Deed Restrictions in Subdivision Development* (1928), as David L. Ames and Linda F. McClelland note, was endorsed by the President's Conference on House Building in 1931 as "the principal means for ensuring neighborhood stability, maintaining real estate values, and protecting residential neighborhoods from non-conforming industrial or commercial activities."[38]

Enhanced Real Estate Transactions

New methods of transferring and financing real estate were also facilitating the spread of planned communities as the twentieth century dawned. The appearance of title guarantee companies, insuring the validity of titles and creating local index systems for real estate records, streamlined the complex process of title searching, formerly the domain of real estate lawyers. Property titles could be examined faster and at a fraction of the expense previously required. In the New York area, the principal innovator was the Title Guarantee and Trust Company, formed in 1883, which could also loan money on mortgages. For the next half century, Title Guarantee enjoyed a near hegemony on major transactions. In 1898, it provided the Garden City Company with the capital that launched the second stage of that fabled community's existence and was also a factor in the early success of the McKnight brothers, creators of Great Neck Estates.[39] Sensing opportunity as the real estate field expanded, the company formed a subsidiary in 1892 to accept and sell mortgages, guaranteeing their payment at the same time as the parent company held the titles, and thus financing property from the beginning of the development process through its sale. The Bond and Mortgage Company proved to be the trendsetter among the era's other mortgage providers, as it came to "control a vital bottleneck by serving as intermediary between those who wished to invest and those who wished to build."[40] These investor-friendly innovations unleashed a flood of new capital and proved to be particularly consequential to developments in Brooklyn and on Long Island.

At the center of this revolution in real estate practices was the remarkable financier Frank Bailey (1865–1953), whose Lattingtown estate, Munnysunk, is today's Bailey Arboretum. Described as a "frictionless logic machine,"[41] Bailey, at the peak of

his career, served as president of both Title Guarantee and Realty Associates, which he formed in 1901 with his partner in many Brooklyn projects, Senator Reynolds, and associates from the title company. Realty Associates became one of the largest lending institutions in the country and a significant producer of moderately priced housing.

For all the progress, however, home building was to remain a volatile enterprise. Home ownership was beyond the grasp of most Americans during the first four decades of the twentieth century, and those who did own often had to juggle two, even three mortgages of short duration. Munsey Park's purchase terms, for example, required, for title, a down payment of 15 percent, a five-year first mortgage at 6 percent, payable semi-annually, and a second mortgage at 10 percent, payable quarterly.[42] Such arrangements necessitated frequent refinancing and left homeowners vulnerable when real estate values declined during recessions. Long Island was particularly hard hit by the Panic of 1907 and the speculative craze surrounding the opening of the Pennsylvania Railroad tunnels in 1910, which peaked in 1912, a record year for building starts that would not be exceeded until 1922.[43] "Hundreds who invested on top of the wave and have been unable to meet the heavy carrying charge, are ruined," reported the *Brooklyn Daily Eagle* in 1913.[44] Bankruptcy became another shared characteristic of the community builders. Among those who lost their shirts were Dean Alvord, who departed for the then-remote west coast of Florida after the collapse of his companies that year, and Shoreham's Herbert J. Hapgood, who hightailed it all the way to Australia, never to return. "It is our policy not to aid in building operations which can neither be rented nor sold," cautioned Bailey in 1915.[45] Though the deduction of interest on home mortgages had made its appearance in the federal tax code of 1913, home financing was not to find its safety net until the 1930s. In the face of an unprecedented number of foreclosures, a series of federal laws and the creation of the Federal Housing Administration provided insurance for privately financed mortgages and subdivisions, transforming the industry.

Architecture

The architecture of the planned communities is an unexpected testament to the many forms that the American dream of home ownership could take. Enlivened by a potpourri of period architectural styles and an array of new building materials, the visual appeal of the houses in these communities remains undiminished, even a century after their creation.

At Great Neck Estates, Frank Lloyd Wright's only Long Island commission stands across the street from an Arts and Crafts house designed by Gustav Stickley's Craftsman Architectural Department.[46] Elsewhere, the Colonial, Georgian, and Tudor idioms that so dominated the country house phenomenon on Long Island were juxtaposed to the Mediterranean, Spanish, and Moorish styles. The latter were much in vogue due to their adaptability to hollow-tile construction, which was then making its appearance along with an array of new roofing materials.[47] The popularity of the Colonial Revival and Craftsman styles reflected the Progressive Era's reaction to Victorian excesses, emphasis on craftsmanship, and preference for hand-wrought materials. Building fairs, such as the 1910 Real Estate and Ideal Homes Exposition at Madison Square Garden, drew attention to these developments with exhibits ranging from architects' models to entire buildings. Natco (the National Fireproofing Company) erected a hollow-tile house at the expo with a stucco exterior and Ludowici tile barrel roof, assuring visitors that its hollow terra-cotta blocks could not burn and were cooler in summer and warmer in winter, a claim echoed by the Atlas Portland Cement Company, whose product was used for the stucco exteriors and deemed to be maintenance-free and color permanent. The *Brooklyn Daily Eagle*, whose publisher, Herbert F. Gunnison (1858–1932), resided in Prospect Park South and was cognizant of the paper's substantial revenue from this industry, had its own booth at the expo and disseminated information on real estate topics.

The architects of the residential parks included such well-known country house designers as Albro & Lindberg, Grosvenor Atterbury, Bradley Delehanty, Aymar Embury II, Wilson Eyre, C. P. H. Gilbert, Robert W. Gibson, Peabody, Wilson & Brown, and Frederick J. Sterner, but most were less well known.[48] Several communities had official supervisory architects such as Fred Briggs for the Plandome Land Company. Among the many practitioners with multiple commissions in a single community was Josephine Wright Chapman, one of the nation's first successful women architects, who designed eight houses at Douglas Manor.[49] Many hands, however, were responsible for the appearance of most planned communities. Kevin Wolfe, author of *This Salubrious Spot*, a history of Douglas Manor, has established that fourteen architects were among that community's first residents and responsible for sixty houses built there.

No architectural firm, however, was more closely associated with the residential-park phenomenon than Kirby, Petit & Green (ca. 1904–9), later Kirby & Petit (1909–15), whose clients included many of the community builders profiled in this study.[50] The

versatile, stylistically fluent partnership was headed by Henry P. Kirby (1853–1915), a twenty-year veteran of the drafting department of George B. Post's office who had trained at the École des Beaux-Arts in Paris, although John J. Petit (1870–1923), his junior partner, proved to be more prominent with respect to the residential parks. First working for Richard Ficken at Tennis Court and for other Flatbush developers, Petit became Alvord's principal architect for Prospect Park South, where he was responsible for at least fifteen houses, including the developer's own home on Albemarle and, with the assistance of three Japanese artisans, the celebrated pagoda-inspired Japanese house on Buckingham Road (1902–3). "He caught the real spirit of the enterprise at the outset," the developer noted, and "contributed his full share to its artistic development."[51] At the same time and a few miles to the south, Kirby, Petit & Green were engaged in an even more fanciful project—the design of Dreamland, the marvelous amusement park at Coney Island for ex-Senator Reynolds, who would become one of the firm's most important clients. At Reynolds's "American Riviera" in Long Beach, Petit is credited with at least the first five houses in the "Estates" section. In 1907, the firm designed the impressive stone entrance lodge at Jamaica Estates, and the same year, "attractive landscape effects" and some of the first residences at Garden City Estates. Next came Belle Terre, Alvord's "Tuxedo Park of Long Island," where their credits included the gatehouse, picturesque pergolas, and clubhouse (1910). At the outset of the century's second decade, the firm was at work at Neponsit, the fashionable residential enclave on the Rockaway peninsula, where the *Brooklyn Times* reported they were responsible for an ornamental gateway and many of the houses.[54] Given Petit's substantial contributions to the residential parks, it is somewhat surprising that more is not known about him. Whereas in the first decade of the century, newspaper accounts record his rather active social life,[55] following Kirby's death in 1915 and the completion of a country house commission for Frank Nelson Doubleday,[56] Petit's activities are no longer mentioned in the press. Just what befell this talented practitioner has long been a mystery. A recently discovered obituary, however, suggests that the breakup of the firm after Kirby's demise freed the architect to pursue a new career in interior design, specializing in restaurants and hotel makeovers.[57]

Landscape Architects and a Vision of Venice

Though landscape architects were involved in only a small percentage of the country houses that were appearing on Long Island at the outset of the twentieth century, they were fundamental to the residential-park phenomenon.[58] The early practitioners possessed a range of backgrounds typical of a new and emerging field. Among the older hands were civil engineers such as Gustav A. Roullier (1849–1910), who was responsible for Plandome, and Major Clemens T. Barrett (1840–1906), the designer of Woodmere, whose career mixed landscape architecture with sanitary engineering. A number of young professionals also received their first opportunities. Robert Anderson Pope, a landscape architect and student of Frederick Law Olmsted Jr., won the competition for Great Neck Estates, while Port Jefferson's E. Post Tooker had the opportunity to assist Charles W. Leavitt Jr. (1871–1928) at Belle Terre. Major figures were also involved: Nathan F. Barrett, designer of Pullman, Illinois, was responsible for Bayberry Point; John Charles Olmsted and Downing Vaux collaborated on a plan for Alvord's Shinnecock Hills project; and Frederick Law Olmsted Jr. was famed for his design at Forest Hills Gardens.

No landscape practitioner, however, was more involved with the residential-park phenomenon on Long Island than Leavitt. Already an experienced civil engineer before opening his own office in New York in 1897, he preferred the title "landscape engineer" and quickly built a successful practice specializing in city planning, parks, parkways, racetracks, estates, and subdivisions. No challenge was too great for this perfectionist, whose practice here

and abroad was both diverse and distinguished. His residential park work on Long Island included Long Beach, Jamaica Estates, Garden City, and Belle Terre.

Planted or "parked" medians (also referred to in period as "parking") [fig. 8] were a common landscaping feature of Long Island's residential parks, and winding drives in the Riverside tradition were prevalent on the North Shore, but on the South Shore, landscape designers took their cue from Venice. Although achieving fame by amassing a fortune and spending conspicuously, as Brendan Gill reminded us, was characteristic of both Venice during the Renaissance and New York at the turn of the twentieth century, topography appears to have been a more important determinant on the South Shore. With a tide fall of only a foot vis-à-vis seven feet on the North Shore, the bay front of the Great South Bay could be easily dredged and its wetlands filled. Canalizing was the obvious means of increasing the number and value of waterfront lots, and Venice provided the familiar, if trite, theme. "The Canals of Venice" was a popular attraction at Reynolds's Dreamland, and perhaps it's not surprising that H. O. Havemeyer's Bayberry Point, T. B. Ackerson's Brightwaters, Isaac Meister and Victor Pisani's American Venice, and other South Shore planned communities featured *canalizzazione*. Ackerson's mission was "to make

Parked median at Fiske Terrace. Society for the Preservation of Long Island Antiquities

Postcard showing a Moorish-style house at Bayberry Point, Bay Shore. Society for the Preservation of Long Island Antiquities

Grand Venetian Yacht Harbor at Brightwaters. "Brightwaters" brochure. Courtesy Queens Borough Public Library, Archives

Brightwaters as near like Venice as possible."[59] His Venetian Canal and Yacht Harbor, terminating in a grand plaza, was his way of linking Islip with the Queen of the Adriatic, but the phenomenon was perhaps most fully realized at American Venice in Copiague, where the developers went so far as to order gondolas directly from Italy.

Landscape architecture imbued the residential parks with character and individuality, and the thoughtful landscaping of individual lots proved to be a hedge, over time, against depreciation.

Amenities

Amenities were joined at the hip to the planned-community phenomenon. Beginning with the Knickerbocker Field Club, whose facilities were open not only to the residents of Ficken's Tennis Court but also to those of Alvord's adjacent Prospect Park South, a casino or clubhouse was a requisite. As Ellis P. Butler quipped in "The Adventures of a Suburbanite" (1910): "I have often noticed three things: I have noticed that a boy is never really happy until he owns a dog; I have noticed that a flat-dweller is never content until he owns a phonograph; but above all I have noticed that the commuter—the man that lives in the sweet-scented, tree-embowered suburbs—is restless and uneasy until he joins the Country Club."[60] In *The American Scene* (1907), Henry James describes the country club phenomenon as culturally legitimizing and thoroughly American, "a complete product of the social soil and air which alone have made it possible."[61]

Country clubs developed informally at first, but as Nicholas Bloom notes, by the turn of the twentieth century, developers "consciously shaped many new suburbs around country clubs,"[62] and they became essential elements of the suburban lifestyle. A 1908 brochure for the Garden City Estates Club House boasts that it is "replete with enjoyable features, such as are found in most of the metropolitan clubs" and "with its tennis courts and croquet grounds [it] is conducted for the benefit of the residents and their friends."[63] Just how to conduct the relationship between homeowners and clubs proved quite variable. At Tuxedo Park, where the association was at liberty to sell to non-members, it was advisable to join the club before acquiring a house, whereas at Alvord's Belle Terre Club, membership was a requisite for anyone interested in buying property. Elsewhere, membership was given to every purchaser. That was the case at Douglas Manor, where management of the club was the domain of the residents' association, and the developers relinquished control of the association after the first year. Whatever the formula, clubs flourished, fostering sociability, community identity, and family interaction.

Water sports and activities served as the promotional hook for many of the early communities such as Brightwaters, whose ads often started with "boating, bathing, and fishing" and the dimensions of its "Venetian Yacht Harbor." Kensington's "waterfront park" offered a bathing beach, a dock for yachts, and a large swimming pool "supplied by a flowing artisan well."[64] Soon, however, golf became the sine qua non of ambitious projects. It was no longer sufficient, as Kensington's developers had hoped, for a golf course to be within a few minutes' walk of the community. Courses had to be integral. Alvord, for example, had relied solely on the picturesque attributes of his first project east of the city line, Roslyn Estates, but recognized the trend in planning for his next endeavor, Belle Terre, which featured a nine-hole course. By the 1920s, eighteen

holes became the norm at Great Neck Estates, Lido Beach, Munsey Park, Montauk, Belle Terre, Biltmore Shores (as planned), and around Garden City, where links seemed to expand exponentially.[65] In this final phase, the planned community doubled as a destination resort, and brochures emphasized a kaleidoscope of leisure pursuits. Public attention was riveted to such wonders as Reynolds's and Fisher's posh Schulze & Weaver–designed hotels, the Lido Golf Club and Montauk Manor, respectively. Not to mention such remarkable facilities as the latter's vast Montauk Tennis Auditorium (1928–29), which could seat six thousand and also be used for theatricals and boxing matches.

Home Rule

The residential parks helped spark the incorporated village movement, and by the end of the twentieth century there were a hundred home-rule hamlets east of the city line, the greatest concentration in the state. "I never knew a village that would disincorporate," noted Great Neck Estates creator Stewart McKnight, who felt strongly that every community should do so as a hedge against encroachments and municipal consolidation.[66] The impetus behind these incorporations were the residents' associations, which were often created by the developers themselves. The Douglas Manor Association, for example, formed in 1906 by the developers Rickert and Finlay, is now in its second century of existence, continuing its mission to provide "sociability and an enhanced natural setting,"[67] as does the almost as venerable Association of Roslyn Estates (1911), the oldest residents' association in Nassau County.

The motivations for residents to form associations or take the further step of incorporating included the expiration of deed restrictions and developers' financial difficulties. T. B. Ackerson's financial problems were the catalyst for Brightwaters to incorporate as a village in 1916; the Jamaica Estates Company's bankruptcy in the 1920s and the

realization that covenants under which residents had purchased their property would expire in 1929 led to the formation of the Jamaica Estates Association that year. If Jamaica Estates had not formed its association, which successfully lobbied the city's Board of Estimate to place a large portion of the community under the most restrictive (F-zone) zoning, apartment buildings and multifamily houses would have been permitted. The association also soon found itself engaged in efforts to mitigate a tsunami of Robert Moses–era parkway projects, including the Grand Central, which cut through the center of the community.

East of the city line, where it was possible for communities to incorporate under state law as villages, few did, with the exception of the major towns, until Great Neck Estates and Plandome incorporated in 1911. Over the next several decades, many of the municipalities to achieve village status on Long Island were planned communities.[68] Incorporation brought with it both police and zoning powers, which, as had been the case with deed restrictions, proved a useful tool in managing the process of development.

Conclusion

By the eve of World War I, residential parks had appeared outside of many American cities, but on Long Island they were a phenomenon whose influence was at once widespread, profound, and enduring. They helped not only to pave the way for the acceptance of community-planning principles but also to popularize the model of the well-located, readily accessible, appropriately restricted, and thoughtfully landscaped curvilinear suburb. The Regional Plan for New York, sponsored by the Russell Sage Foundation in the 1920s, included these concepts, which were in turn adopted by the President's Conference on Home Building and Home Ownership in 1931. The Federal Housing Administration (FHA) standards of the 1930s would dictate much of the appearance of subdivisions after the

World War II, as neighborhood planning became institutionalized. Nassau and a good part of Suffolk County developed much as the Regional Plan's director, Thomas Adams, envisioned in 1931, when he called on citizens to "break down the barriers of home ownership and cover the fields of Nassau."[69] Between 1950 and 1960, the county's population almost doubled, reaching 1.3 million and triggering a reaction to what many felt was the "monotonous ugliness of most of our suburbia," as Peter Blake put it in his 1964 diatribe *God's Own Junkyard*.[70] For Blake, the culprits were developers who had become nothing more than manufacturers of a mass-produced product, as well as architects and planners who had advocated a form of Garden City development in which every family would have their house "smack in the center" of their plot and be constrained by a "bureaucratic strait jacket" on the planning, design, and landscape of suburbia imposed by the FHA and other government agencies. A generation later, in *The Geography of Nowhere*, suburbia's uber critic, James Howard Kunstler, lamented that the shortcomings of the early planned communities had "become embedded into a universal pattern."[71] What's missing from the "debased modern variants," Kunstler has long argued, is sense of place.[72] Riverside, he notes, may be, in the broader schematic sense, the father of the postwar suburb in all of its artificialness and curvy street conformity, yet a closer look reveals that its defining features and attention to detail continue to make it a most ambient and distinctive community. Here on Long Island, the early planned communities, a century after their creation, also exude a strong sense of place. The mature landscapes, provision for public spaces, tapestry of architectural styles, civic involvement, and amenities give each enclave its own enduring identity. Time has made some changes, of course; infill housing and unsympathetic renovations have occurred where architectural review has not been exercised. However, encountering Prospect Park South, after passing through blocks of nondescript apartment buildings, winding through Shoreham under a verdant canopy, or savoring the kaleidoscope of architectural styles at Roslyn Estates or Belle Terre is to realize that these are cultural environments worth caring about and saving. "Today," writes the National Trust for Historic Preservation's former president Richard Moe, historic preservation is "about people and the places they care about—where they live, work, shop, worship and celebrate." Long Island's planned communities of the Progressive Era are such places. A century after their creation they continue to be our Gardens of Eden.

2
GARDEN CITY

AMERICAN VERSIONS OF UTOPIA

RICHARD GUY WILSON

Garden City, Long Island, an early planned community, illuminates changing American attitudes toward a utopian, or ideal, way of life. Founded by A. T. Stewart in 1869 and laid out shortly thereafter, the community evolved between the 1870s and the 1920s, demonstrating a variety of attempts to create the ultimate American community. Described as a "Garden of Eden" soon after being created, it successively became a cathedral town, a sporting and recreational utopia, and finally a suburban utopia emulating in several ways the English Garden City movement, the roots of which, ironically, may have been sown in Garden City, Long Island.

Sources of Utopia and Garden of Eden

Early writings about Garden City describe it as "The Eden of Long Island," because of its layout, the verdant rows of trees—some 45,000 in number—lining its roads, and its architecture.[1] As one writer gushed: "a township of beautiful and healthful homes; with parks, gardens, and public buildings for educational purposes and for those of amusement."[2] Even as late as 1903 a historian characterized it as "model community, a little republic, . . . a garden spot—a veritable Eden."[3] Such glowing accounts suggest that it was born of a utopian vision.

The history of the concept of a utopian way of life is long and complicated; however, its origin is generally credited to Sir Thomas More's 1516 book

Utopia, which envisioned a fictional community of peace and harmony and public ownership (no private property) located on an island in the Atlantic Ocean.[4] More derived the word *utopia* from the Greek, which has multiple meanings, including "no place," though the most popular is certainly "good place" or "ideal place." Although Sir Thomas More coined the term, the concept of an ideal community can be traced back to Plato's *Republic* (ca. 300 BC) and even further, to the Bible, in such passages as the description of the Garden of Eden in Genesis and in references to ideal gardens and cities found in books such as Ezekiel and Psalms.[5] During the Renaissance, various treatises, including those by architects Vincenzo Scamozzi, Pietro di Giacomo Cataneo, and Filarete, embraced the notion of ideal, or utopian, cities, depicting them with highly organized, radial plans. Painters, too, from Lucas Cranach to Thomas Cole, have depicted their visions of Eden or arcadia (which at times is a synonym). One of the earliest North American expressions of the concept of an ideal city was John Winthrop's 1630 proclamation of a "City upon a hill" as his ship approached the coast of Massachusetts, not far from where Boston would be founded.[6] The cities of Philadelphia (1682) and Savannah (1734) were laid out with elements of an ideal city, including a strict grid of streets interspersed with squares and open spaces.

During the first half of the nineteenth century, attempts to create ideal cities or towns flourished,

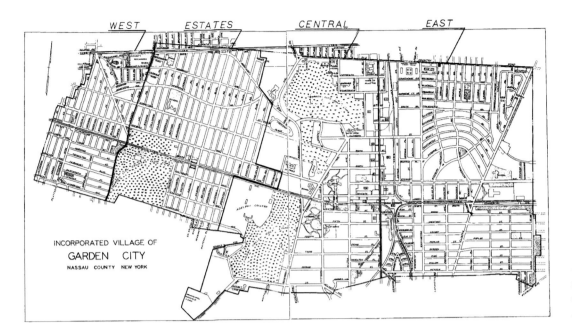

including the various Shaker settlements in New York State, New England, Kentucky, and elsewhere. In Ohio, members of the German Society of Separatists founded Zoar in 1817; a flower garden at its center, with a towering tree representing Jesus, was based on the Book of Revelation. In southern Indiana, Welshman Robert Owen, founder of the utopian New Lanark in Scotland, took over a recently established town, which he renamed New Harmony, with the intention of creating an ideal community based on socialist principles. Though New Harmony ultimately failed, it attracted considerable attention. In France, Charles Fourier's socialist concept of fair and just worker compensation through "phalanxes," or ideal communities for working and living, became widely influential. Fourier developed a considerable following in the United States as well; phalanxes were established in upstate New York (1830s) and Monmouth County, New Jersey (1843–56). Another variation on the concept of the ideal community was John Humphrey Noyes's Oneida, New York, a socialist community that existed from 1848 to 1881; among its tenets was a belief in "free love." American religious enthusiasm spawned yet another variation on the quest for an ideal way of life, the camp meeting movement, wherein families would leave the city for a few weeks or longer during the summer and experience religious revivalism at a rural site. Initially, in the 1820s and '30s, families lived in tents, but by the 1860s, permanent houses began to sprout up at Wesleyan Grove on Martha's Vineyard and elsewhere. Camp meeting grounds were particularly popular after the Civil War.[7]

Religion certainly played a role in utopian schemes, as did various forms of socialism, but also driving the quest for a new way of life was the growth of large industrial cities. During the nineteenth century, the Industrial Revolution in both the United States and Europe, and the consequent relocation of people from rural areas to the city, resulted in crowded and unspeakable living conditions. A return to nature became the new ideal, and in the United States a number of artists, landscape designers, philosophers, and poets such as Thomas Cole, Andrew Jackson Downing, Ralph Waldo Emerson, Henry David Thoreau, and William Cullen Bryant espoused the country life as the way to achieve respite from the close quarters, violence, smoke, pollution, foul water, trash, and dung-filled streets of the city.

By the mid-nineteenth century, the concept of the American family residing in a house located in nature began to emerge as the national ideal. Andrew Jackson Downing's books, such as *Country Residences* (1842), played a role in fostering this concept, as did Catharine Beecher and Harriet Beecher Stowe's immensely popular *The American Woman's Home* (1869) and countless Currier & Ives prints of American homes in the country and on the farm, including two of the all-time favorites: *Home Sweet Home* and *God Bless Our Home*.[8]

23

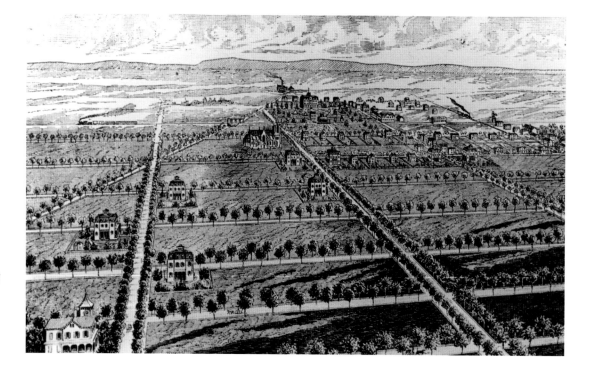

There is one other community type that also emerged in these years: the mill village, or factory town. It never gained any popularity but needs to be noted here. In Lowell, Massachusetts, and many other places, factory owners constructed housing for the mill workers and strictly controlled their lives, even requiring attendance at church on Sundays. The workers—men and women alike—paid the company for their accommodations (and in some cases food). Though neither ideal nor utopian, some elements of this type of community made their way into Stewart's Garden City.

The desire to escape from the city and live in the country resulted in the development of the *rus in urbe*, or "country in the city"—the garden suburb. Llewellyn Park, located in West Orange, New Jersey, about twelve miles from lower Manhattan, is considered the United States' first planned garden suburb. Llewellyn Haskell, a wealthy man who made his fortune in pharmaceuticals, was a follower of Fourier and a Swedenborgian Perfectionist. He was deeply involved in New York intellectual life, a friend of the recently deceased Downing, and a major supporter of Central Park, which began to be built in 1857. Work on Llewellyn Park, designed by Alexander Jackson Davis, began earlier, in 1853. It initially encompassed about 350 acres (growing to more than 500 acres) on a hillside. Davis laid out roads following the contours of the site and placed a large park along a stream in the center. Houses were located on substantial plots, and Haskell spent much money on landscaping and plantings. By 1857, when it began to be occupied, Llewellyn Park had attracted considerable attention in the New York and national press and was known for its intellectual climate and progressive ideals.[9]

In 1868–69 the partnership of Frederick Law Olmsted, Calvert Vaux, and Frederick Withers designed a large suburb of 1,600 acres at Riverside, Illinois. All three had worked on Central Park and were then involved in the design of several other parks, including Prospect in Brooklyn. Located nine miles west of downtown Chicago at a curve in the Des Plaines River, the Riverside site was crossed by the Burlington and Quincy Railroad and hence afforded easy transit into the city. Certainly, idealistic notions about lifestyle and escaping the horrid conditions of Chicago were central to the developer, Emery E. Childs, who set up the Riverside Improvement Company, but he and his partners also intended to make a profit from the sale of the lots. The Olmsted, Vaux & Withers firm laid out the site with curving streets, a large park along the river, and a broad boulevard—known as Long Common—for travel, walking, and contemplation. Extensive plantings of trees and shrubs were brought in, a hotel where prospective house buyers could stay was erected at the river, and a small town center with stores and a railroad station were built. Houses were to be situated well back from the street, and at least two trees would shield each one. Initially, a few houses were constructed after designs by Vaux, Withers, William Le Baron Jenney, and others, but the project floundered in the wake of the severe economic depression that began in 1871 and the Chicago fires of 1871 and 1874. The Riverside Improvement Company went bankrupt. When the economy recovered in the 1880s and 1890s, Riverside evolved into an upper-middle-class suburb.[10]

A. T. Stewart's plans for Garden City took shape in 1869, contemporaneous with those for

Riverside. It is important to note that the quest for a utopian community was still ongoing, and several books influenced the later development of Garden City. One was Edward Bellamy's *Looking Backward, 2000–1887* (1888), which envisioned future cities of skyscrapers, with all services underground. According to Bellamy, the future would be a state-controlled economy with huge, nationalized factories. The book became a bestseller, and clubs sprang up to advance his vision. But Bellamy's futuristic view of giant metropolises also elicited strong rebuttals, the most famous of which was perhaps William Morris's *News from Nowhere* (1890). In this work, Morris, founder of the Arts & Crafts movement and a socialist pioneer, envisioned the future as a post-revolutionary agrarian socialist society in which there are no cities and no private property. The people live in the countryside in harmony with nature, taking pleasure in their work—handmade, rather than industrial production. Out of this sprang Ebenezer Howard's concept of ideal small towns that combined the benefits of both city and country, which he espoused in *To-morrow: A Peaceful Path to Real Reform* (1898), subsequently retitled and published many times as *Garden Cities of To-morrow* (1902). Howard's ideas engendered the Garden City movement, and two cities in England—Letchworth and Welwyn—were built according to Howard's principles. In the United States, cities such as Forest Hills Gardens and Sunnyside Gardens, Queens; Radburn, New Jersey; and Greenbelt, Maryland, were also influenced by his ideas. Howard spent the years 1871–75 in the United States, first in Nebraska and then Chicago. Scholars have suggested that his concept of the garden city had its roots in Riverside, Illinois, but the name he chose and the extensive publicity that Garden City, Long Island, was receiving at the time make it a possible inspiration for his ideas.[11] Indeed, there are some similarities between Howard's schematic layout and Garden City's layout and park-like areas.

Stewart's Garden of Eden, 1869–1876

A. T. Stewart's concept of a garden city located between twelve and eighteen miles from Manhattan adheres in many ways to the utopian ideals that guided much of mid-nineteenth-century American suburban planning. Stewart was a very private individual and never wrote explicitly about his intentions, but there can be no doubt that he intended Garden City to be a restful place located in the countryside with plenty of parkland and trees and plantings. He also saw it as a real estate venture for which he would receive a return on his investment. He would control it and own the property, which would be leased or rented.

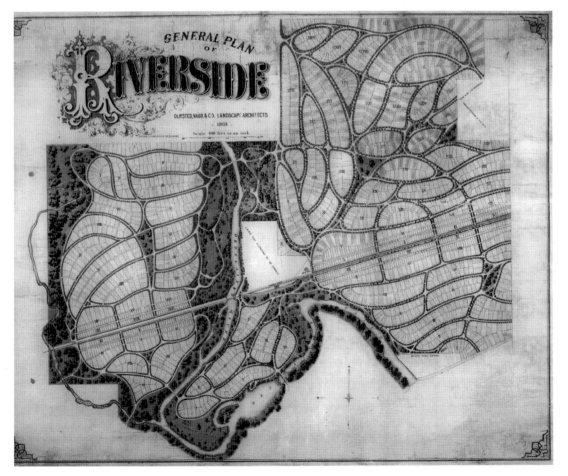

General plan of Riverside, 1809, Olmsted, Vaux & Co., landscape architects. Historian's office, Village of Riverside, Illinois

Portrait of Alexander Turney Stewart, by T. P Rossiter, 1860. Village of Garden City, NY, Archives Collection

Portrait of Cornelia Clinch Stewart, by E. D. Marchant, 1844. Village of Garden City, NY, Archives Collection

Alexander Turney Stewart (1801–1876) was born into a Scottish family of some financial means (he inherited $10,000 in 1822) in Lisburn, Ireland, and received an upper-middle-class education in Scotland.[12] He first visited New York in 1818; returning in 1823 with his patrimony, he set up a dry goods shop on lower Broadway. A canny merchant, he prospered and expanded his sales into other areas, founding what can be considered the first American department store. Money flowed in, and in 1848 he built a large white marble store in the Italian Renaissance style designed by Trench and Snook at Broadway and Chambers streets, in the block north of City Hall. Success and money continued to flow in, and in 1862 he constructed his "Iron Palace," designed by John Kellum, a vast, cast-iron, six-story structure on a full city block further north, bounded by Broadway and Fourth Avenue and 9th and 10th streets. The land and structure cost a reported $2,750,000, and it was the largest retail store in the world, with more than two thousand employees. He owned mills in Massachusetts, supply houses abroad, including one in India, and huge swaths of real estate, including hotels in New York and Saratoga Springs. By 1869 A. T. Stewart was one of the richest individuals in the United States, some claiming he ranked in the top three.[13]

In 1825, Stewart married Cornelia Clinch (1803–1886), the daughter of a prosperous ship chandler. The marriage was by all accounts happy, except that their two children died at birth. Lacking an heir, Stewart took under his wing a lawyer, Henry Hilton (1824–1899), who was related by marriage to Mrs. Stewart. Hilton went on to play a major role in Garden City. Seeking other outlets, Stewart, who was raised as a Quaker, embraced his wife's Episcopal orientation and became very involved with St. Mark's Church in-the-Bowery.[14] The Stewarts' interests included art collecting, and during their frequent trips to Europe they amassed a huge collection of nineteenth-century paintings, statuary, books, and decorative art. To showcase their collection they commissioned John Kellum to design a vast Second Empire mansard-roofed white "Marble Palace" (1864–69), which stood on the northwest corner of Fifth Avenue and 34th Street. One of the first of the dwellings that came to be called "Millionaires Row," the house was well known and published.[15] Although Stewart was not considered a "great" philanthropist, he did contribute money and provisions to the Irish during the great potato famine and transported some survivors to the United States.[16] In 1871, he supported textile workers in Paris and contributed money to Chicago after the great fire. An abolitionist and a major advocate for the Union cause during the Civil War, he met Lincoln, supported U. S. Grant's nomination for president, and lobbied successfully for the Republican Convention to meet in New York City in 1868. As a result, Grant nominated Stewart to be secretary of the treasury, but his business interests came into conflict and he had to decline. As a prominent figure in the city, he became involved in some of the Tweed Ring's schemes and his reputation was somewhat tarnished.

In mid-1869, just as Stewart and his wife were moving into their Fifth Avenue Marble Palace, John Kellum, his architect, informed him that a huge tract of land located between twelve and eighteen miles from New York was available for purchase. Negotiations took place with the Town of Hempstead and after a vote it was announced in mid-July that A. T. Stewart had purchased 7,170 acres of land at the price of $394,350. Soon thereafter he added another 2,000+ acres and set to work creating a model town. *Harper's Weekly* reported that Stewart intended to spend between $6 and 10 million and commented, "This design is so gigantic that it throws into the shade every attempt of the kind hitherto made." The writer, searching for metaphors, claimed, "Hempstead Plains, hitherto a desert, will be made to blossom as the rose."[17]

The initial architect and designer of Garden City was John Kellum (1809–1871), who had grown up in the Hempstead area of Long Island. Kellum began his career as a carpenter, which was common for most American architects, as no architecture schools existed until the Massachusetts Institute of Technology created a program in 1865. Kellum worked with Gamaliel King, a successful commercial architect. Together they designed many of the cast-iron buildings that transformed the commercial architecture of New York. Kellum designed a building for the New York Stock Exchange (demolished), several hotels, the New York Herald Building (demolished), and the New York County Courthouse, located behind City Hall, the construction of which became notorious for the "kickbacks" involving the Tweed Ring. Kellum and Stewart had developed a close relationship during the design and construction of the Iron and Marble palaces, and they worked together on the design of Garden City.

Assisting Kellum on the project were several individuals who took on important roles, especially after Kellum died in late June 1871. Delameter S. Denton was an engineer who had worked with Kellum and took charge of much of the surveying, grading, water system, and other tasks. Assisting him was Samuel Hendrickson, who also surveyed and worked on engineering projects. Benjamin Fowler of Flushing was in charge of the building operations and contributed some architectural designs after 1871. James H. L'Hommedieu of Great Neck oversaw construction after Kellum's death and played a design role. Robert Stewart, a New York architect who had connections to Kellum, took on a major role in the design of the hotel.

Of Stewart's vast landholdings in the Hempstead Plains, which lay north of the Village of Hempstead, west of Bethpage and Hicksville villages, and east of Brushville (Floral Park),[18] only five hundred were initially devoted to the new city; in time more acreage was added. The remaining land was allocated to farming, and Stewart established a brick factory in Bethpage to provide materials for the expected new construction.

Transportation posed a major problem for the builders. The Long Island Railroad's line ran to the north of Stewart's tract, so building materials could not be delivered directly to the site by rail. Stewart resolved to construct his own line, the Central Railroad of Long Island, which would run right through the proposed village and connect to Bethpage Village and the brickworks. But the Long Island Railroad eventually gave in and established a north–south branch that ran through the site. Transportation across the East River to Manhattan was also a problem until the Brooklyn Bridge opened in 1883. Before then, ferries were the only means of transport across the East River between Manhattan and Brooklyn; Stewart set up a dedicated ferry line to Garden City.

Garden City Master Plan, 1873. Village of Garden City, NY, Archives Collection

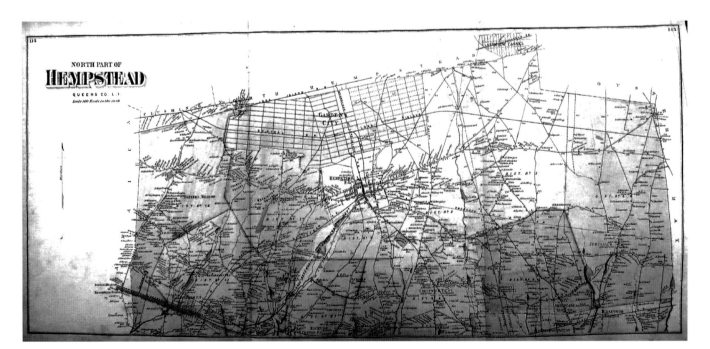

First house, 1870, John Kellum, architect. Village of Garden City, NY, Archives Collection

Brick Disciple house, ca.1875, John Kellum, architect. Village of Garden City, NY, Archives Collection

Garden City was laid out in late 1869 and early 1870. The basic plan, apparently a collaboration between Kellum and Stewart, was a grid, a time-honored layout in both Europe and North America. But in this case the grid had two sections, with the western portion on the standard north–south, east–west orientation, and the center—which became the center of the town—and the eastern portion at an angle. This shift in the grid was necessary to accommodate the preexisting roads and new railroad lines on the site, as well as its topography and drainage. Later, in the 1910s, some curvilinear streets were inserted into the eastern section.

Several other issues had to be addressed, including the relocation of a small cemetery and the Queens County Fairgrounds, which was awkwardly situated, as well as the closing of a small racetrack. Once these tasks were accomplished, Kellum laid out the town. Avenues (which ran north–south—the names were later changed), streets (east–west, names all changed), and parks were delineated. Initially, the parks were between 50 and 150 acres, but in time they were enlarged. On average, each

Apostle house, 1877, John Kellum, architect. Village of Garden City, NY, Archives Collection

Smaller, or "worker" house, ca. 1871–75, John Kellum, architect. Village of Garden City, NY, Archives Collection

block measured between 1,000 and 1,500 feet long by 500 feet wide. The size varied slightly, depending on the topography. On each block the corner lot measured 250 x 250 feet; intermediate lots were 200 x 200 feet. Houses were to be set back 75 feet from the street or avenue. The major avenues were 100 feet wide; the smaller streets were 50 feet wide, with 15 feet on either side for shade trees and sidewalks.

More than 200 local workmen began grading and by mid-summer 1870, sightseers arrived to view the work in progress. By September 1870, 120 acres were ready for development and 16 miles of streets and avenues lined with picket fences crisscrossed the new town. In the leveling process, a depression was created that became a small lake. Kellum personally oversaw the planting of trees. From nurseries in Flushing and elsewhere, young trees were loaded on railcars, brought to the site, and planted. Locusts were popular, and more than 6,500 sugar maples were imported.

Houses began to be constructed in 1870. At his offices in Hempstead, Kellum reportedly displayed designs for more than three hundred "villas" rang-

ing in construction cost from $2,000 to $20,000. All were to have gardens. Water and gas were to be provided by the town; as an advertisement from about 1874 claimed, the houses would be equipped with "gas fixtures, hot-air furnaces, ranges, baths, water closets, etc."[19] Over the next several years a variety of houses scattered about the town were completed. The largest—later named "Disciple" houses because of the cathedral—had huge mansard roofs, stood four stories tall, and encompassed about 3,500 square feet, plus stables and other outbuildings. Most were of brick, though a few were of wood, and they cost about $17,000 to construct. The rent was $1,200 a year, later reduced to $1,000. Next in size, at about 2,000 square feet, were the "Apostle" houses, a few of brick but most of wood. Stylistically, they were more varied, with roofs ranging from mansard to gabled, and sporting different ornamental details. Their construction cost was between $3,500 and $4,500 and their annual rent was $500–850 (it changed over time). These houses [figs. 7–10] were three and four stories tall with between ten and fourteen rooms. At the bottom end was a group of dwellings sometimes called "worker" houses, which cost between $1,600 and $2,500 to build. Constructed out of wood, these houses encompassed about 1,000 square feet, had seven to ten rooms, and rented for $250–400 per year. By 1874, at least 35 houses had been built, and by 1876, 109 houses were reportedly finished and ready for occupancy.[20]

At about the same time, work got under way on Garden City's grand hotel, which was also to serve as the residence for Mr. and Mrs. Stewart. The original design of the hotel was Kellum's, but Robert Stewart took it over after his death. The initial scheme was very large, but the economic recession of 1871 caused it to be scaled back to a four-story brick structure with a large entrance tower and a mansard roof. Cast iron was used on the interior. As the hotel went up on the town's flat plain, it looked isolated, so houses and stores were built in the area surrounding it. This became the heart of the town and remains so today. A small railroad station was built and a large, impressive, mansard-roofed "estate" office for the management of the town went up near the hotel, which opened to much fanfare on July 30, 1874, with reports on the magnificent carpets, black walnut paneling, and marble mantels.

To supply the village with water, a great well fifty feet in diameter—at the time the largest on Long Island—was dug and a waterworks pumping station was built. Water mains were laid throughout the town and a gasworks was constructed just west of the waterworks building. As in any city, trash removal and sewage were major concerns. One newspaper claimed that "the sanitary arrangements of Garden City are admirable" and that New York City should follow the example set out on Long Island. Solid refuse was collected daily on carts.[21] At first the hotel and houses employed cesspools, but in 1878 construction began on a sewage disposal plant with large settling basins at the south end of the village. Sewer lines were laid through the village and Garden City enjoyed the distinction of having one of the finest sewage systems in the country.[22]

In general, the press about Stewart's Garden City was extremely positive, but some criticisms

Waterworks, 1876. M. H. Smith, *Garden City, Long Island in Early Photographs, 1869–1919* (New York: Dover Publications, 1987)

were reported. The local *Flushing Journal* noted in August 1873: "Not-withstanding its beautiful villas and handsomely laid-out streets, it has no inhabitants . . ."[23] A major advertisement appeared in New York newspapers in January 1874: "To let— 25 dwellings at Garden City, 18 miles distant on Central Railroad of Long Island. Rents from $150 to $800."[24] By March 1874, only six houses had been rented and most of those were occupied only during the summer. Stewart was not deterred, and in the course of that year more than 27,000 trees and shrubs were planted and more houses built. To spur housing and business development, Stewart hired an estate manager, William R. Hinsdale, not only to oversee construction in the town but also to run the vast farm acreage beyond it.

Views of Garden City from the mid-1870s show a flat plain with streets laid out, picket fences, trees lining the streets, and a smattering of houses

across the site, with a concentration around the hotel. In the distance trains can be seen chugging through.

Stewart intended Garden City to be strictly regulated and controlled. He would permit the community to enact its own laws, but he or his company would retain ownership of all the land, and the houses would be leased and/or rented, not privately owned.[25] In this regard, his vision was of an upscale factory town in which the proprietor controlled all. His intention to control the town came under scrutiny, and as a New York newspaper noted: "He is attempting a daring experiment, nothing less than a community . . . [with] all the appliances of municipal life, without a single other person having an interest in a foot of the whole domain. He proposes to be landlord, mayor, and alderman, in fact the whole community. . . . This may succeed but it would be a miracle should it do so."[26]

Panoramic photograph of Garden City, 1878. Village of Garden City, NY, Archives Collection

In mid-March 1876 A. T. Stewart contracted a severe cold, which led to other complications, and on April 10 he died. The funeral three days later was a massive affair: flags flew at half mast, the streets were lined with people, and a procession of 150 carriages made its way down Broadway to the interment at St. Mark's Church in-the-Bowery. A few days after the service the announcement came that Mrs. (Cornelia Clinch) Stewart, who had inherited his entire estate, had transferred full power of attorney to Judge Henry Hilton and William Libby. Hilton had been Stewart's protégé in many ways and he now was in charge of about $25 million worth of assets, including Garden City.

As noted, A. T. Stewart never wrote anything (at least that has survived) about his vision for Garden City. Though he certainly saw it as an investment with some return, his continuing to build despite sluggish sales suggests that his vision went beyond mere real estate. He wanted to create a special place for people to live.

Cathedral City, 1876–1893

Although Mrs. Stewart turned over the management of the department stores and various other properties to Henry Hilton, for her, Garden City was A. T. Stewart's real legacy and contribution, and she gave it her full attention. The result was a shift in focus away from building nice houses to rent to the creation of a religious and educational community. The implications were not lost on observers; in 1885, *Harper's Weekly* claimed that Mrs. Stewart wanted to make "Garden City a great educational centre—a sort of American Oxford."[27]

Though A. T. Stewart had a strong affiliation with the Episcopal Church in New York City, Garden City initially had no church. In 1874, the year of the first (minimal) occupancy of the village, there is no record of any church services. In May 1875, Stewart gave permission for Episcopal services to be held at the meeting hall and shortly thereafter the Methodists of nearby Hempstead began holding services on alternate Sundays.

On May 15, 1876, a little more than a month after Stewart's burial, Mrs. Stewart and Judge Hilton visited Garden City to choose a location for a large, white marble, Gothic-style Episcopal church. By late July, a sixty-acre site a few blocks southwest of downtown had been selected and work commenced. As a Long Island historian wrote twenty-eight years later: "[T]he cathedral, the school and bishop's palace were her free offering to the Diocese, and all she asked in return was that the group of buildings should become the Seat of the Bishop of Long Island and that the crypt in the cathedral be the resting place of her husband."[28]

The idea of an Episcopal cathedral located in Garden City was both new and somewhat controversial. In the 1840s the Episcopal Church of America began to undergo a transformation as some parishes and dioceses embraced elements of the Ecclesiological, or High Church, movement in England. Depending on the location and the personnel in charge, the Protestant tradition of the Episcopal Church of the seventeenth and eighteenth centuries was discarded in favor of a return to liturgy, processions, and elaborate buildings with stained-glass windows that in their Gothic dress recalled the Middle Ages prior to the Anglican Church's split with Rome. The transference of these ideas and forms from England to the United States was not universal, and some dioceses (such as Virginia and North Carolina) remained resolutely "low church" and non–Gothic Revival until the 1890s, while others such as New York were fervent supporters and leaders. The "new" style for Episcopal churches became some version of the medieval, with English Decorated and Perpendicular the most popular. Part of the new High Church movement involved the introduction of bishops and cathedrals.

Long Island had become a diocese only eight years earlier, in 1869, with the bishop's seat located in Brooklyn. In the spring of 1877, Mrs. Stewart wrote Bishop A. N. Littlejohn, D. D., with an offer: she would build a cathedral for the diocese, and the see of the bishopric would be transferred to Garden City. Needless to say, there was opposition from Episcopal parishes in Brooklyn, Queens, and other areas close to the city, but Littlejohn, who was frustrated in his search for an appropriate cathedral, prevailed and accepted her offer. Mrs. Stewart also offered to establish schools for boys and girls, making Garden City America's only cathedral town. Certainly the vision of a giant cathedral rising amid the green fields of Long Island surrounded by trees called to mind Ely and Canterbury and John Constable's paintings of Salisbury Cathedral.

Construction had already begun on the church, which was named Cathedral of the Incarnation. A formal ceremony for the groundbreaking, presided over by Judge Henry Hilton, had taken place in 1876. On June 28, 1877, in the presence of a crowd estimated at several thousand, many of whom came out in three trainloads from Manhattan and Brooklyn, Bishop Littlejohn formally laid the cornerstone. Almost a year and a half later, in November 1878, came the shocking news that "fiends has stolen his [A. T. Stewart's] lifeless corpse from the church-yard of St. Mark's in the Bowerie [*sic*], where it had been deposited temporarily," until it could be reinterred in the completed cathedral in Garden City.[30] The body snatching and the criminals' demand for payment for its return made national news. Exactly what transpired and whether Stewart's body was ever recovered remains a mystery, but Mrs. Stewart was apparently convinced by Judge Hilton that the stolen corpse had been recovered, and A. T. Stewart presumably rests today in the cathedral's crypt.[31]

Mrs. Stewart's original idea for a white marble cathedral underwent some changes. The prominent English-born New York architect Henry G. Harrison (1813–1895) was commissioned to design it. Well known in Episcopal circles, Harrison was concurrently designing other churches, including an Episcopal cathedral in Omaha. The builder, James L'Hommedieu, who had done most of the construction in Garden City, purchased an interest in a large rock quarry in Belleville, New Jersey, which supplied the sandstone for the church. Thus, white marble became brownstone. Harrison's original design was reputedly for a much larger building, but according to some accounts, when Judge Hilton saw the plans he crossed out the extended transept arms with a red crayon.[32]

Even without the extended transepts, Henry Harrison designed an immense cruciform cathedral in the English Decorated Gothic idiom; it measured 175 feet long and 96 feet wide. The interior reached a height of 53 feet; the aisles were 27 feet high and 12 feet wide. The chancel was suitably deep and impressive, in accord with the High Church orientation of the cathedral. A giant crypt lay beneath it, intended as the Stewarts' final resting place. The bell tower stood at 80 feet and was crowned by a 130-foot spire, for a total height of 210 feet. The cathedral dominated the landscape and could be seen from as far away as the East River and the North Shore of Long Island. The press praised its "architectural perfection . . . comparing favorably with the best cathedrals in Europe."[33] When completed, it was certainly the largest Episcopal cathedral in the country.

The basement and foundations were of granite; the main structure, of the New Jersey brownstone. It was elaborately decorated on the exterior with carved finials, gargoyles, door surrounds, and other elements. Flying buttresses added to the visual excitement, though they were not really functional. What makes the Cathedral of the Incarnation particularly unique is the employment of cast iron for the columns on the main floor and in the crypt. Cast-iron staircases connect the levels. The interior was decorated with a marble floor and Minton tiles and plenty of wood tracery. The English firm of Clayton and Bell produced seventy-two stained-glass windows for the nave, chancel, aisles, and transepts. The elaborate decoration continued in the crypt and undercroft with tiles, paneling, carv-

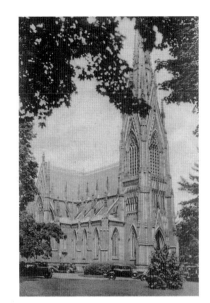

14. Cathedral of the Incarnation, 1877–85, Henry G. Harrison, architect. Society for the Preservation of Long Island Antiquities

ing, and thirteen stained-glass windows from Heaton, Butler and Bayne of London.

On June 2, 1885, at the consecration service for the completed cathedral, Mrs. Stewart presented Bishop Littlejohn with the deed to the building, the Bishop's See house, and two schools, St. Paul's and St. Mary's. On October 17, 1886, Mrs. Stewart passed away and joined—she hoped—her husband in the cathedral's crypt.

The Bishop's See house, located next door to the cathedral, and the two schools were designed by Edward H. Harris (1839–1919?), a prominent New York architect who trained at MIT. Harris also insinuated himself into aspects of the cathedral's construction, much to Harrison's annoyance. The Bishop's See house, built 1879–84, was a giant structure containing thirty-two rooms, located in the cathedral's park. Although nominally in the Second Empire mode with an enormous mansard roof capping the three stories below, the red brick walls and light-colored stone trim created a polychrome effect more English than French. From the large porte cochere, the visitor entered a large hall with stained-glass windows and progressed into rooms with Santo Domingo mahogany furniture, black walnut wall paneling, tapestries, plush silk sofas, and other opulent decoration and furnishings. The stable to the rear contained six stalls and quarters for the coachman.[34] Obviously, Bishop Littlejohn would live well.

St. Paul's School for boys (1879–83) was equally large, indeed mammoth for its time. The school, run by the Episcopal Church, had existed for a few years in Glen Cove, but in 1877, when Mrs. Stewart announced her gift, it was transferred to Garden City. Students took up residence in several unoccupied houses until the new building was completed. The cornerstone ceremony, as to be expected, was imposing, with plenty of onlookers as the bishop and Mrs. Stewart carried out their tasks.

St. Paul's red brick facades, light-colored stone trim, and succession of mansard roofs competed with the massive bell and clock tower at the end of one wing. The main elevation was three hundred feet long and contained a variety of pavilions. The overall plan was a giant E shape, the central wing of which was occupied by the two-story chapel, which seated five hundred and featured Clayton and Bell stained-glass windows. Designed to board more than two hundred young men plus the faculty, it boasted two elevators (unusual for the time), an armory (as initially many of the students were cadets), an art gallery, a library, and many other facilities. The school struggled for pupils at first, but by the late 1880s it was doing well and gained a reputation as a first-class place for the education of young men. In addition to the usual academic subjects, St. Paul's had a boys' choir, which was an essential part of High Church services, and it performed for years.

St. Mary's Cathedral School for girls was the last of Mrs. Stewart's notable contributions to Garden City. A very small private girl's school, Mrs. Scovel's "Young Ladies Seminary," had opened in Garden City in late 1875 but closed two years later because of economic issues. In 1877, Bishop Littlejohn announced that the church would start St. Mary's; initially it occupied a house and expanded to two houses by the next year. In 1880 the site for the school was selected in a park east of and across from the cathedral. E. H. Harris drew up the plans for St. Mary's in early 1881, but because of Judge Hilton's mismanagement of funds, Mrs. Stewart was experiencing financial difficulties, and construction was delayed. Mrs. Stewart did leave funds for the school in her will and construction

finally began in 1892.[35] The school that was eventually built, though large and elaborate, was considerably smaller than Harris's original scheme. Instead of housing two hundred young women, it had accommodations for only forty-two students, the principal, and two teachers. Consequently, the school held on to the two houses it already had until 1901, when the building was enlarged. The final design of the new building owed a great deal to L'Hommedieu. Three stories in height and constructed of brownstone and brick, it was relatively large for its time and attracted many students who went on to notable careers.

As the buildings of Mrs. Stewart's Cathedral City neared completion and the trees and other plantings matured, it took on an impressive appearance. However, as already mentioned, the Stewart fortune was in deep trouble. Judge Hilton had managed the company badly and may have been involved in some illegal machinations. Though Garden City's population slowly crept up to nearly six hundred by 1891, a new view of its future was needed. Still, certain positive elements did persist, as a writer in 1903 commented: "Garden City's cathedral has become the merchant's enduring monument, and still keeps by its healthful agencies part, at least, of his own great fortune engaged in useful and beneficent work."[36]

Sporting and Recreational Utopia, 1893–1907

Though St. Paul's and St. Mary's schools attracted some tenants, A. T. Stewart's insistence on owning all of Garden City's property and renting or leasing houses proved financially unviable. Moreover, Judge Hilton's gross, possibly fraudulent, mismanagement of Stewart's business empire ultimately led

St. Paul's School, 1879–83, Edward H. Harris, architect. Society for the Preservation of Long Island Antiquities

*St. Mary's Cathedral
School for Girls, 1892,
Edward H. Harris and
James L'Hommedieu,
architects.* Village of
Garden City, NY,
Archives Collection

to John Wanamaker's takeover of the A. T. Stewart & Co. department store in 1896.[37] Compounding the problem for Garden City was Hilton's refusal to follow Mrs. Stewart's mandates regarding funds for the cathedral, the schools, and the diocese after her death. And the manager he appointed to run Garden City, one L. H. Cunliff, was apparently irascible and disliked by nearly everybody. His manner tended to alienate potential residents, and he angered the surrounding Hempstead communities by keeping Garden City's tax evaluation far lower than it had been in Stewart's time.

The salvation of Garden City came through a lawsuit filed by Mrs. Stewart's heirs shortly after her death in 1886. Descendants of Mrs. Stewart's brother and a half-brother, the heirs were for the most part full-time or summer residents of the Smithtown-St. James area on the North Shore of Long Island; many had the surname Smith. Led by Prescott Hall Butler, a prominent New York attorney who was married to Mrs. Stewart's niece Cornelia Smith Butler, the complicated, protracted suit was finally settled out of court in 1890. Essentially, Hilton retained control of portions of Stewart's department store and commercial property, but the heirs were granted the huge swath of land on Long Island. This land was divided up: the 5,000 acres to the east of Garden City were incorporated as two independent companies, and in January 1893 the remaining 2,600 acres were incorporated as the Garden City Company.[38] The board of directors included family members and their spouses, one of whom was Stanford White (1853–1906) of

the renowned architecture firm McKim, Mead & White.

With the establishment of the Garden City Company, a new direction for Stewart's utopia became very apparent. As its press release stated: "It will be the aim of the company to make Garden City as complete and attractive a country resort as there is anywhere." The press release noted the wonderful waterworks, the gas plant, and the many "handsome" houses. It also announced a significant departure from Stewart's business model, "The new company will build houses for sale or rent" and "sell land." Though Garden City retained its identification as a "cathedral town," a shift had occurred. As the "Summer Resort News" section of the *Brooklyn Daily Eagle* reported in 1898, it "attracted a host of summer residents" who wanted to participate in the new activities the town had to offer.[39] Instead of Stewart's original view of it as a bucolic place to live or his wife's vision of it as a religious center, it was now seen as a resort, and new types of activities, from horseback riding to tennis and golf began to dominate the scene.

Assisting in the revitalization of Garden City was George Loring Hubbell (1865–1959), who, as the purchasing agent for the Long Island Railroad, had been instrumental in reorienting the West Hempstead Branch, which made transportation to and from Manhattan easier. Hubbell and his wife moved to Garden City in 1891 and were active in the cathedral and local affairs. He described Garden City as "long on land and short on residents."[40] They were the first to purchase land from

17. *The remodeled Casino, ca. 1905, McKim, Mead & White, architects.* Village of Garden City, NY, Archives Collection

the new Garden City Company and build a house in the Shingle Style on the corner of 1st Street and Cathedral Avenue. He became involved in the company, and in 1897, when the unpopular Cunliff retired, Hubbell took over as general manager. He remained in charge of the Garden City Company until 1919, when a village government was established.

Garden City began to change immediately after the establishment of the Garden City Company. One of the first signs of change was the revamping of the Stewart Arms Inn, adjacent to the cathedral. Originally intended as a place to stay for visitors to the cathedral, it had become by default the town's club and had acquired two grass tennis courts and a small stage for theatricals. The company gave the club money for an extensive remodeling and when it opened in April 1895, renamed the Casino, it contained smoking and billiard rooms, large porches for lounging, a huge dining room, new tennis and croquet courts, bowling alleys, an assembly hall, and a theater. A sprawling affair covered in shingles, it resembled in many ways some of the casinos that McKim, Mead & White had designed and were famous for in Newport and Narragansett Pier, Rhode Island, and elsewhere. Although Stanford White has been associated with the remodeling, there is no direct evidence of his hand.[41] All residents of Garden City could belong and at the opening in April 1895 a newspaper reported: "The spacious ball room was handsomely decorated and an orchestra of ten pieces furnished the music. Dancing began at half-past ten, and at midnight supper was served."[42] A new type of Garden City had come into being.

In 1893 McKim, Mead & White began remodeling the old and by then outdated mansard-roofed hotel. Quite simply the preeminent architecture firm in the United States at the time, their major projects included Boston's public library, several buildings at the World's Columbian Exposition in Chicago of 1893, office buildings in New York, Kansas City, Missouri, Omaha, and many large resort and country houses on Long Island, Newport, the Berkshires, and elsewhere. White, who was the lead architect, transformed the old hotel into a large, 210-foot-long structure with two large wings that enclosed the entry courtyard. Red brick with white trim and classical details, including a cupola, it was a charming Colonial Revival building resembling an eighteenth-century church or a town hall. Consisting of a hundred guest rooms and ten baths, along with all the usual billiard, smoking, reading, card, dining, and children's play rooms, as well as a buffet bar for gentlemen in the basement, it was an instant success. The opening night party in November 1895 started with tea, followed by a vaudeville group of Japanese acrobats, Hindu jugglers, music, dinner, and dancing.

Unfortunately, the hotel caught fire on September 7, 1899, and was destroyed; luckily, no one was injured and insurance paid the Garden City Company for a partial rebuilding. The new hotel, also designed by White and his firm, was completed in 1901 and was "twice as big as the old," with more stories and wings, and a giant tower at the entrance modeled on Independence Hall in Philadelphia.[43] An immediate hit, the hotel became tremendously popular as an event site and as a required destination for people with names such as Vanderbilt, Havemeyer, Belmont, and others. Garden City suddenly found itself at the top of the social ladder. Unfortunately, the hotel was razed in 1973 to make way for a new structure.

Adding to Garden City's attraction as a place to live and/or visit were a variety of other activities,

Garden City Hotel, 1907, McKim, Mead & White, architects. Village of Garden City, NY, Archives Collection

such as a gun club for men, established in 1894. A small clubhouse was built but it proved too modest, so the club joined the Carteret Gun Club of New Jersey and moved into a new location with a pigeon-shooting stand. The new clubhouse was designed by Richard Howland Hunt, a son of the famous Beaux-Arts architect Richard Morris Hunt. The old Mineola Fair Grounds, located on the northeast side of Garden City, had hosted livestock and agricultural exhibits and had been sneered at by the Stewarts. In 1893 the Garden City Company sold some adjacent land with restrictions; the site was graded and a new racetrack, sheds, and a large grandstand were erected. A year later the company sold a large tract of land east of the village to the

Meadowbrook Hunt Club, which had been leasing nearby land for years. The club became one of the first in the United States to establish a polo club and team.

Golf came next; in 1896 a committee led by Hubbell was formed, and renowned gofer Devereux Emmet, a Stewart heir (and brother-in-law of Stanford White), laid out a nine-hole course northwest of the town. The Garden City Company put up $2,500 for it. The game of golf was quite new in the United States in the 1890s, and though there is some evidence that it was played in the later eighteenth century, it was not until the late 1880s that wealthy Americans began to discover St Andrews and other Scottish courses. One of the earliest

Garden City Hotel cab service, 1907. Note the entrance tower, modeled on Independence Hall in Philadelphia. Village of Garden City, NY, Archives Collection

Spectators observe a game of golf at the Garden City Golf Links. Village of Garden City, NY, Archives Collection

courses in the United States was Shinnecock Hills at the extreme eastern end of Long Island, which was finished in June 1891; its clubhouse, designed by Stanford White and completed in 1892, was the first in the nation. A few others followed, and Emmet's Garden City course, the Island Golf Links, which opened in late May 1897, was among the earliest. It succeeded beyond everyone's wildest dreams, and the next year Emmet added nine more holes. In 1899 the name was changed to the Garden City Golf Links. One of its most important and charter members was Walter J. Travis, who won a series of U.S. Amateur Championships and in 1904 became the first American to win the British Amateur. Tournaments were held with great frequency, the modest clubhouse designed by Richard Howland Hunt was vastly enlarged, and Garden City was off to the races as an American sporting center.[44]

As more golf clubs were created both in and around the town, a newspaper proclaimed: "Garden City and golf are synonymous words."[45] The Meadowbrook Hunt Club added a nine-hole course and opened a full eighteen-hole course in 1916. On the southern edge of Garden City a small course known as the Midland Golf Club that admitted women was popular for a number of years beginning in 1899. "Women Barred from Links" read a newspaper headline in 1899 about the Garden City Golf Links' policy, so the Garden City Company decided to build another course, the Salisbury Links, which was open to all.[46] Its designer, Walter Travis, described it as for "the very

top-notcher to the veriest duffer."[47] Located to the south of the Garden City Golf Links and behind the cathedral, it boasted a large clubhouse and operated as a community course until 1916, when it became a members-only facility and was renamed the Cherry Valley Club. The closing of the public course led the Garden City Hotel's management company to open another public course just east of town on the Hempstead Plains that became known as Nassau County's Salisbury Golf Club. Golf links were even laid out on the cathedral's grounds, and a local paper reported: "Rev. and Mrs. W. P. Bird and friends find much enjoyment in the contests almost daily. . . . It is not improbable that the Bishop will soon follow suit."[48]

Another sporting activity that became popular was bicycling. In the mid-1890s a club was established and races were held in Garden City. Automobile racing also caught on as Garden City emerged as the center for wealthy, car-obsessed Americans who had country estates scattered across Long Island. William K. (Willie K.) Vanderbilt, Jr., who had a house in nearby Islip and rented in Garden City, instituted the Vanderbilt Cup Race in 1904.[49] The race's course encircled Garden City and ran ten laps, or 284.4 miles, over public turnpikes, roads, and streets. The headquarters were at the Garden City Hotel. Gigantic events widely covered in the press, the first four races—1904–7—were won by foreign cars, but in 1908 a reporter could finally announce: "The Cup is America's at last; the supremacy of the foreign car has ended; an American built car has won 'The Classic.'"[50]

The risks of using public roads for racing, dramatized by the death of a spectator during the 1906 race, led Vanderbilt to form the Long Island Motor Parkway, Inc., to construct a private speedway that avoided public roads through a network of overpasses and bridges. One end of the speedway ran through the northeast corner of Garden City. It operated both as a toll road that provided easier access to Garden City and as the race course for three years, but in 1910 the New York State Legislature banned road racing on any road, public or private, and the Vanderbilt Cup changed locations. The toll road eventually stretched forty-four miles and became the Long Island Motor Parkway, which lasted until 1938, when it closed.

The development of sports and recreation dominated Garden City from 1893 to 1907, but some important civic developments also took place. To increase year-round residency, the small, mansard-roofed railroad station dating back to the 1870s was removed and a larger station with a "suitable covered driveway" to shield passengers from rain and snow was built. The new station's baggage room could handle large trunks and sporting gear, and the grounds surrounding it were carefully planted and a fountain was added.

In a show of civic spirit, Hubbell convinced the Garden City Company to give the newly created county of Nassau (which split off from Queens) a four-acre site for the construction of the new Nassau County Courthouse.[51] Governor Theodore Roosevelt (whose country residence was in Oyster Bay) laid the cornerstone of the impressive two-story structure in June 1900. Designed by William Tubby in the Palladian manner, with a giant two-story portico of Ionic columns and a dome, it helped symbolize Garden City's coming of age.

Another means of enticing families to move to Garden City was the construction of a low-lying Colonial Revival brick public school for kindergarten through the sixth grade near downtown. Hubbell, who also was president of the school board, proclaimed it "a model school in every respect."[52] By 1907 the school had more than a hundred students. Though the Episcopal cathedral dominated the landscape, other faiths began to hold services in small buildings around town, and in 1903 the Garden City Company sold land at the corner of 5th Street and Franklin Avenue to the Catholic Church for the token amount of $1,000. Soon St. Joseph's Church, an impressive red brick structure with a bell tower and a parsonage in the Italian Renaissance style, went up.

By 1907, Garden City had evolved from a restricted and controlled Garden of Eden and then a Cathedral City into a sporting and recreational mecca, but these activities were limited to certain months of the year. Could it become a year-round garden city?

Suburban Utopia 1907–1929

Major changes in the early twentieth century enabled Garden City to become a more fully realized version of Stewart's ideal of family houses located in a garden—now thought of as suburbia. The automobile was one factor that made suburban living possible, at first only for those who could afford to buy one and also pay the parkway tolls. But over the first twenty or so years of the new century, roads were laid out and paved, and more and more people could reach Garden City not just in Packard limousines but also in Model T Fords. And in 1901 a trolley line began to be built through Garden City, providing another, much more economical method of transportation.

Until the early twentieth century, the only means of transportation for those who worked in Manhattan was a ferry across the East River. But in December 1903 the Williamsburg Bridge opened, followed in December 1909 by the Manhattan Bridge. A promotional brochure from 1907 extolling the pleasures of Garden City announced: "ONLY 30 MINUTES from Broadway when transportation facilities are completed, and 30 minutes from Long Island City now."[53] The reference is to the East River Tunnels, which opened in May 1910 and made commuting much faster. As the day approached, an advertisement appeared: "60 DAYS FROM NOW" the Pennsylvania Railroad would provide "The Largest, Fastest, Best Equipped and Most Comfortable RAPID TRANSIT IN THE WORLD."[54] The train tunnels and the bridges made it possible to live in Garden City and commute to Manhattan by rail and car.

This period in Garden City's history was dominated by continuing real estate development, which was handled by two separate parties, the Garden City Company and Garden City Estates, until 1919, when the town was incorporated as a public entity known as the Village of Garden City with its own elected officers. Equally important was the appearance of large businesses in the town such as Doubleday Page and a branch of the Curtiss Aeroplane and Motor Company.

In late 1906 the Garden City Company sold a large tract of land—about one square mile—west of the town for $1,500,000 to a real estate development firm that took the name Garden City Estates. The president of the firm was Gage E. Tarbell (1856–1936); one of the vice presidents was Timothy L. Woodruff (1858–1913), a former lieutenant governor under Roosevelt; the other vice president was Ernestus Gulick (1865–1913). Tarbell had been

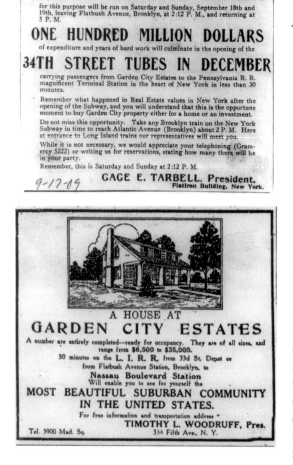

Advertisement for Garden City Estates, 1909.
Garden City Library

Advertisement for Garden City Estates, 1911.
Garden City Library

a vice president of the Equitable Life Assurance Society and was involved in the so-called Hyde Scandal, which triggered a financial crisis on Wall Street and dominated American news in 1905.[55] As a result of the economic downturn, Tarbell, along with other members of the board, turned to real estate and established a number of companies to develop other Long Island communities such as Jamaica Estates.[56] The Garden City Estates' offices were located in the Flatiron Building in New York City, with a branch in Brooklyn. A newspaper article claimed that Tarbell was "a great lover of nature" and intended to build a fine home in Garden City Estates.[57] In 1910 Tarbell left the Estates and joined the Garden City Company; Woodruff and Gulick continued to run the Garden City Estates company.

Kellum's original 1871–73 plan showed a grid layout for the area that Garden City Estates acquired, but nothing had been laid out; it was just flat, prairie-like farmland, with a few dirt roads and the railroad running through it. The Estates company hired engineer Cyril E. Marshall and

prominent landscape architect Charles Leavitt Jr. (1871–1928), who basically followed Kellum's original scheme with a few changes, such as some curving roads on the north side. They also laid out a big north–south street, Nassau Boulevard, which connected the two sides of the development separated by the Long Island Railroad. (Leavitt worked on other planned communities at the time such as Jamaica Estates, Long Beach, and Belle Terre.) The Estates company got right to work clearing, grading, and laying out. At the Nassau Boulevard crossing, a new railroad station and plaza, the Garden City Estates Station (now the Nassau station) was built following the design of Kirby, Petit & Green. The station was low with broad, sheltering roofs, and the plaza was ornate with a pergola and many plantings. John J. Petit (1870–1923) also worked on the landscaping, which followed Stewart's original lavish scheme of many trees and much vegetation.

The Garden City Estates company aggressively promoted the development, publishing brochures with the subtitle: "A Plea for a Sane Life." Shown were the cathedral and St. Paul's and St. Mary's schools and a variety of house designs, accompanied by the commentary, "Our life is too complex and artificial, and our country life has been too simple. A happy medium between the two would constitute a sane life." The economic advantages of suburban real estate investment were stressed, along with the "Perfect sanitation," "Water so pure," and ease of commute.[58] Advertisements in magazines extolled "The joy of gardens, and surroundings that make you welcome your own home-coming at night and send you to business refreshed and glad hearted every morning."[59]

To further increase the appeal of the Estates, Gage Tarbell built a clubhouse for the homeowners. Golf of course played a role, and in 1916 individuals living in the Estates founded yet another golf club, the Garden City Country Club. Walter Travis laid out the course and a large clubhouse was erected. The course took up a large swath of land largely south of the railroad, though a few holes were on the north side. Over time the Estates company sold a portion of its land to other developers and auctioned off the remaining four hundred house sites in September 1921.

Initially, Garden City Estates offered plots and houses of varying sizes with prices ranging from $8,000 to $50,000. When these prices proved too high, however, lower-priced houses were introduced. Kirby, Petit & Green provided the first designs, but Oswald C. Hering (1874–1941) appears to have taken over by 1911. At the smaller end were two-bedroom cottages, some with a Dutch Colonial Revival–style gambrel roof, located on plots measuring 60 x 100 feet.

Up the scale a little were larger houses with Colonial details or in the bungalow mode with large, low-lying pitched roofs. A few houses had some Midwestern Prairie School characteristics. At the larger end were imitation Mount Vernons or large, half-timbered English-style houses. Grandest of all was the house Oswald Hering designed for Tarbell. Occupying a full block on Nassau Boulevard, it was a large, semi–Colonial Revival structure of stucco-clad concrete and tapestry tiles on the roof.[60] In 1918 Glenn H. Curtiss, the pioneering aviator and head of Curtiss Aeroplane and Motoring Company, purchased Tarbell's house. Not to be outdone, Garden City Company vice president Timothy Woodruff built an equally large, three-story, Dutch gambrel-roofed clapboard bungalow-style house two blocks east.

Not all of the houses were designed and erected by the Estates company. Gustav Stickley's Craftsman Home Building Company built a foursquare house covered with half timbering on the second floor for Dr. Mary Richards in 1909. The house had four bedrooms and two baths, and an office for her on the first floor.[61]

The apparent success of Garden City Estates prompted the directors of the Garden City Company, which still controlled the relatively older section, to reimagine their town and expand on undeveloped land to the east, which was diagonally bisected by an old road, Clinton Road. Investing more than $1 million in the expansion, the company increased Garden City's size by a third. This area is sometimes called Garden City East, in contrast to the older section, which was now called Central (or Old) Garden City.[62]

To implement this expansion, the Garden City Company hired Gage Tarbell away from the Estates in 1910 and put him in charge under George L. Hubbell. Tarbell again engaged Marshall and Leavitt to design the layout.

South of the new Stewart Avenue and the Long Island Railroad, which ran through the site, Garden City East was laid out in a grid, but the blocks were smaller and Marshall and Leavitt created a series of short, curved roads. North of Stewart Avenue they laid out curvilinear roads through the site and provided very different house sites. The major element of the whole development was Stewart Avenue Mall, a 180-foot-wide boulevard with extensive plantings and six rows of trees that began at the Garden City Hotel and ran east to Clinton Road, which was then the entrance to the Long Island Motor Parkway.

The Garden City Company continued to employ Charles W. Leavitt, who split from Marshall and created his own landscape and engineering firm. He followed the original Stewart aim, importing trees of all types and lining the newly laid out roads with them. Houses, some of them very expensive, began to appear in the years after 1910. Aymar Embury designed a large house for Ralph Peters, president of the Long Island Railroad, on Carteret Place overlooking the Garden City Golf Club. One of the leading country-house architects of the early twentieth century, Embury (1880–1966) embraced the Arts & Crafts philosophy, maintaining that "a house ought to look as if the people lived in it." Consequently, though a large structure, it was low lying and spread out in a semi-Dutch style. Embury designed at least one more house in Garden City a large, shingled, gambrel-roofed house for Henry S. Orr that contained a hall approved of by Gustav Stickley.[63]

Downtown on Franklin Street and Stewart Avenue near the hotel, the Garden City Company put up a large, residential-cum-commercial three-story building that heralded the changes coming to Garden City. A Georgian Revival–style structure in red brick with the first story clad in white stone, it indicated that Garden City was open to a new type of resident.

Both architecturally and socially, the most interesting development of the Garden City Company involved the move of Country Life Press, owned by Doubleday, Page & Company (later Doubleday, Doran), from New York City to Garden City in 1910. The Garden City Company had decided to promote an area on Franklin Avenue just south of the shopping area of the village as a center for commerce. Serviced by two railroad lines, it promised to be an ideal venue. Very little existed in the area, but seemingly overnight a huge complex of factories, offices, gardens, and housing sprang up.

In a sense, the relocation of Country Life Press to Garden City reflects the English Arts & Crafts

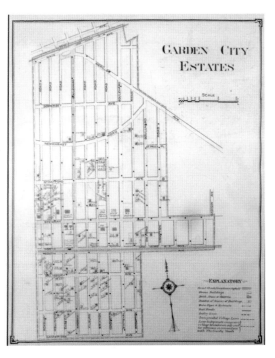

Garden City Estates map. Atlas of Nassau County, Long Island, N.Y. (New York: E. Belcher Hyde, 1914)

movement's concepts of planning the garden city, as expounded by Ebenezer Howard. As noted, Howard derived some of his ideas during his stay in the United States in the 1870s. Central to his notion of a garden city was the small town with a population of about 30,000 that would contain one or, at most, two manufactories, plenty of parks, decent housing for the workers, a huge farm belt, and a shopping area in the center. This town would be linked to others by rail and roads, and there would be no cities with more than 50,000 inhabitants.

Also important was the term *country life*, which was embraced by Arts & Crafts ideology on both sides of the Atlantic and signified a return to a way of living free from the turmoil of the city. Ideally, one would grow one's own food and work with one's hands. In Britain, *Country Life* magazine, an Arts & Crafts–oriented publication that also ran articles on historic English country houses and gardens, began its weekly publication in 1897 and became very popular. In the United States, Doubleday, Page & Company began publishing *Country Life in America* magazine in 1901, edited by Henry H. Saylor, a major writer on American Arts & Crafts houses. A Country Life movement sprang into being, led by Liberty Hyde Bailey (1858–1954), a renowned horticulturalist and landscape designer, and a co-founder of *Country Life in America*. Similar to its English counterpart, the American cousin extolled the country, or the next best thing, garden suburbs.

In March 1910 Gage Tarbell, who had just joined the Garden City Company, announced that forty acres along Franklin Avenue had been sold to Doubleday, Page & Company and then immediately began building the Country Life Press office and printing press there. By late September 1910, the main building was ready to be occupied, and ex-president Theodore Roosevelt laid the cornerstone. In his speech Roosevelt argued: "I feel that everything that tends to spread the population as it becomes congested in the great cities, everything that gives more chance for fresh air to the men, the women, and above all, to the children, counts . . . in the development of our civic life." He went on to praise the magazine for dealing "with country life" and practicing "what it preaches . . . living on the land."[64] In various publications the company explained its move from New York as a business decision: it made economic sense to bring all of its services together in one place where there was "good light" for employees; the community had wonderful services, including water, gas, electricity, sewers, trees, shaded roads and streets, schools, a cathedral, clubs; and there was a "progressive company [Garden City Company] in charge of its affairs." Doubleday, Page also stressed the efficiency of production that would result from the "attractive surroundings."[65]

The main building, which was added to over the years, sat upon a site of about thirty acres, six of which were occupied by the building itself. A steel-

Garden City Estates Station and Plaza, 1908, Kirby, Petit & Green, architects.
Village of Garden City, NY, Archives Collection

frame structure covered in brick with limestone trim, it took only four months to construct. It contained the power plant, the printing and binding facilities, the administrative and executive offices, storage, and shipping. The railroad running along the rear facilitated shipping, and by October 1910 the company was producing 6,500 books a day. In 1930 they were producing 40,000 books a day and 150,000 magazines.

Kirby and Petit designed the building "to resemble Hampton Court in England."[66] The major façade to the west was a large U that recalled the Tudor palace on the Thames, though of course the windows were much larger to allow in light. The forecourt, which was about seven-eighths of an acre, provided some parking and was luxuriously laid out, as was the rest of the site. Designed by Charles W. Leavitt, the court boasted several fountains and pools, as well as manicured bushes. Old-time Garden City residents were used to flatcars rolling through the village loaded with thousands of mature trees, which now landed on the Country Life Press site. Leavitt and his firm laid out extensive gardens on more than sixteen acres on either side of the building, including more than two miles of walks and places for sitting, eating, and contemplation, tennis courts, and a playground. Substantial acreage was also put aside for a vegetable garden.[67] Country Life Press published photos of the gardens, annotated with an enumeration of the plantings and the

historical sources of the design; the Italian Pool, for example, surrounded by tall cedar trees, was inspired by the cypress basin at the Villa Frascati near Rome. Fountains were scattered through the grounds; there was a rose garden and a peony collection, a rock garden and an evergreen garden. The entire ensemble attracted much attention both locally and beyond. One newspaper gushed over the grounds: "the masses of bloom surround the plant, so that from any window one can get a glimpse of lovely greenery."[68]

The new workers moving to Garden City needed housing, and both the Garden City Company and Doubleday, Page stepped up to the task in several ways. Across Franklin Street the Garden City Company erected twenty-five seven-room wood-framed houses intended as rental units for the workers.

But perhaps the most extraordinary development took place behind and somewhat to the south of the Country Life Press building in an awkward V-shaped site created by a split in the rail lines. Walk-through underpasses were constructed and some small houses displaced from the press's Franklin Avenue site were relocated. Beginning in 1912, a group of twenty-two semi-detached, stucco-covered, slate-roofed houses were erected around a small, park-like space. In time more were added to the rear and on surrounding streets. Each had its own brick-walled garden and bow windows. The architects, from the firm Ford, Butler and Oliver of New York, which was designing an addition to the Garden City Hotel,

apparently had been looking at English models, particularly some of the housing courts in Letchworth Garden City and the work of English Arts & Crafts architects such as Parker & Unwin. For several years the English Garden City movement had sponsored "Cheap Cottage" competitions and exhibitions, and the idea made its way across the Atlantic. Garden City's Franklin Avenue cottages could have fit seamlessly into any English Arts & Crafts enclave.[69]

The other major development in the 1910s involved the airplane. Flying first appeared as a sporting and entertainment event in 1911, when the Nassau Boulevard Aerodrome opened northwest of the town. The initial event, the International Aviation Meet, attracted tens of thousands of spectators, and the first airmail flight from Garden City took place on September 23.[70] However, the field stood in the way of Garden City Estates' suburban growth, so it was moved to the east side of town on land leased from the Garden City Company and renamed the Hempstead Plains Aerodrome. Garden City became one of the centers of American aviation activity, presenting annual shows and establishing a flight school. When the United States entered World War I in April 1917, the airfield was used as a training field for the Army's Air Service and was renamed Hazelhurst Field. Part of it was named Roosevelt Field in 1919, in honor of President Roosevelt's son Quentin, who was killed in air action during the war. Another part of it later became Curtiss Field, which was incorporated into Roosevelt Field in 1929.

World War I brought major changes to Garden City besides the use of the airfield as a military training field. Camp Mills, a mobilization center for soldiers shipping out to France, was established, and, most significantly, the Curtiss Engineering Plant was erected to the northeast of the airfield, seemingly overnight. Founded by Glenn H. Curtiss, it was Long Island's first experimental airplane factory and the world's first facility completely dedicated to aviation research and development. It continued to make airplanes in Garden City after the war.

In 1919, the Garden City Company, including Garden City East and Garden City Estates, decided to give up control of the town. Garden City had no elected officials, and municipal matters such as water supply, sewage, lighting, and policing had been handled by the separate companies. They announced that they would no longer handle such issues, and in May 1919, after weeks of negotiation, the Village of Garden City was formed. Although the companies still owed significant acreage and house lots, the Village was an independent entity in charge of its own layout. George L. Hubbell, who had served as general manager of the Garden City Company since 1893, was elected as the first president (the title was later changed to mayor).

In the 1920s, the population of the Village of Garden City grew from 2,420 to 7,180. Municipal buildings and new schools were erected and the business center of town, "Old" and/or "Central" Garden City, expanded. In 1927 Adelphi College, a small women's school in Brooklyn, purchased a site near the Cherry Valley Golf Club and moved to Garden City in 1929. The McKim, Mead & White firm (all the original partners were dead) planned the campus, designing several buildings in a red brick Neo-Georgian style. Landscape designer Helen Swift Jones (1887–1982) lined the campus's central mall with rows of trees.[70] In the course of the decade there were disputes about taxes and other issues, but Garden City retained

its character as a bucolic, tree-lined village with a special emphasis on sports and entertainment. The hotel prospered and people flocked to the town to play golf or watch airplane shows. In 1927 a young Charles Lindbergh spent several days at the Garden City Hotel prior to his pioneering flight across the Atlantic from Roosevelt Field.

Postscript and Conclusion

Since the late 1920s Garden City has maintained its identity as a unique place. The population has grown, of course; as of the 2010 census, it exceeded 22,000. The farming fields that A. T. Stewart originally owned on both sides of Garden City are filled with other suburban developments and shopping centers. Levittown, one of the most famous (or infamous) post–World War II developments is located just a few miles away. Highways and turnpikes surround the city. Roosevelt Field, the old airport from which Lindbergh took off, is now a giant shopping center, one of the first large ones on Long Island, initially designed in 1953 by renowned architect I. M. Pei. It has since been substantially modified. St. Mary's School for girls closed and in 2001was demolished. St. Paul's School for boys closed in 1991 and has sat empty since, slowly deteriorating. Various plans to convert and save it lie fallow. Business fell off at the famous Garden City Hotel; it was sold to a developer and closed in 1971. Two years later it was demolished, ten years after the razing of one of McKim, Mead & White's other great buildings, Pennsylvania Station in New York. The Cathedral of the Incarnation, however, remains in good condition and sits in its park, a dominant element in the landscape. Churches and buildings serv-

ing other denominations have been built around town. New houses of all types, from ranches and split levels to McMansions, have appeared. A bust of A. T. Stewart was installed in front of the railroad station in 1969, and in 1975 the Garden City Historical Society was founded by nine women in reaction to the demolition of the hotel. They rescued one of the original "Apostle" houses, which had been slated to be destroyed, and had it moved and restored; it now serves as the historical society's headquarters. In 1978 a large group of Stewart-era buildings were placed on the National Register of Historic Places.

The history of Garden City from in its inception in 1869 through the 1920s provides unique insights into differing visions of the ideal American way of life. Stewart's vision was an odd mix of a garden spot and a totally controlled, profit-making enterprise. In spite of the beautiful landscaping and the fine houses, it did not appeal. Another vision is of the organization of life around religion, and Garden City exemplifies that trend with its transformation into a cathedral and religious education center beginning in 1876. In the 1890s yet another vision, that of a sports and recreation utopia, took hold, as golf and other sporting activities began to flourish and the hotel was upgraded. Finally, in the early 1900s Garden City began to emerge somewhat along the lines of Stewart's original vision as an ideal place to live year round. Assisting in this change was the new transportation system, which allowed easier and faster access to jobs in the city. Also, and in a sense ironically, some of the ideas of the English Garden City movement, certain aspects of which can be traced back to Stewart's original Garden City, helped create the "modern" town.

3
A MODERN VENICE

H. O. HAVEMEYER'S BAYBERRY POINT

ANNE WALKER

On May 23, 1897, the *New York Times* announced the development of a "modern Venice" along the Great South Bay—a summer community called Bayberry Point that promised to have "every prospect . . . of becoming a Tuxedo of the Seaside and a place well worth a visit."[1] And with Henry Osborne Havemeyer (1847–1907)—the so-called Sugar King—as the driving force behind the new enclave, its beginnings were certainly auspicious. At the age of twenty-two, Havemeyer had been named a partner in Havemeyer and Elder, his family's sugar-refining company in Brooklyn, and went on to become the period's foremost sugar merchandiser as the president of the American Sugar Refining Company. His financial success enabled Havemeyer, his wife, Louisine Elder (1855–1929), and their three children to enjoy a lifestyle commensurate with that of other men of his wealth and standing, a world that included sporting activities, country houses, and art collecting—the arena in which the Havemeyers have become best known.

According to one newspaper account, Havemeyer was "an ardent admirer of Venice" and upon returning from a trip to Italy decided to create a Venice of his own in America.[2] Around 1896, Havemeyer and his brother-in-law Samuel Twyford Peters (1854–1921) embarked on a real estate venture, purchasing 125 barren acres on the Great South Bay near West Islip—then an undesirable stretch of land that became half-submerged at high tide—as well as 45 acres of land that was under water. Although Havemeyer's involvement was later publicized, Peters signed the papers to mask his brother-in-law's association. The area around the Great South Bay became increasingly popular after the South Side Sportsmen's Club, an exclusive hunting and fishing concern, was established in 1866. The undeveloped waterfront region around Oakdale, Islip, and Bay Shore began drawing members of New York society as early as the 1870s, and in the 1900s it offered—in most cases—a low-key alternative to the North Shore. Havemeyer turned to Grosvenor Atterbury (1869–1956), a fledgling Beaux-Arts-trained architect who had only a number of Shingle Style houses on Long Island under his belt, to design a colony of inexpensive and stylish concrete cottages. Though Atterbury went on to great renown with such celebrated projects as Forest Hills Gardens in Queens, at the time he was a curious and unlikely choice. Havemeyer—a man of strong opinions—and his wife had already worked with Charles C. Haight (1841–1917) on the design of their Manhattan mansion at 1 East 66th Street in 1891 and Robert S. Peabody (1845–1917) and John G. Stearns (1843–1917) of Peabody & Stearns on their Greenwich country house, Hilltop, in 1890. However, the couple also greatly admired the work of Louis Comfort Tiffany (1848–1933), the interior designer of their city home. They asked Tiffany to collaborate on the design of Bay-

46

berry Point. At this point, Tiffany and Atterbury likely knew each other, as Atterbury was working on Robert and Emily de Forest's house in Cold Spring Harbor and the de Forests and Tiffany were great friends and neighbors.

Both Tiffany and Atterbury were acquainted with the architecture of northern Africa—Tiffany often drew stylistic inspiration from the area, which he loved and visited frequently, and Atterbury had recently traveled there. It appears that Havemeyer's plan was initially more ambitious than what was actually built. As described by one source in 1897, "By the beginning of 1898 the 35 building plots will be crowned with stately villas owned by Mr. Havemeyer and his many millionaire friends."[3] However, as revealed in Bayberry Point's promotional brochure, "Moorish Houses at Bayberry Point, Islip, L.I., Built for Mr. H. O. Havemeyer," from 1897, Atterbury and Tiffany's plan featured ten stark stucco cottages on a windswept plain bisected by a hundred-foot-wide man-made canal on the western portion of Havemeyer's property.[4] Likely Tiffany, whose opinion the Havemeyers trusted, made suggestions to the still impressionable twenty-eight-year-old architect, who then carried out the scheme. It is unknown exactly for which aspects each designer was responsible, but the houses bore a striking resemblance to the farm buildings on Tiffany's Cold Spring Harbor estate, Laurelton Hall, built several years later, designed by Alfred Hopkins.

Construction, carried out by Sturges & Hill, began early in 1899 and was completed by the spring of 1901. In developing the site, contractor Henry A. Vivian dug two canals—the central canal and another to the east for boats. The point's marshy land was raised four feet with dredged sand and then divided into modest one-and-a-half-acre lots, each with two hundred feet of water frontage. This tendency to carve out the shoreline to create canals, transforming unlivable sites into desirable tracts of land, was relatively new—later developments also made use of such water features as the practice became more commonplace. Atterbury located five houses to the east of the canal and five to the west, enabling all of the houses to look across at one another. A low, sweeping footbridge, reminiscent of Venice, connected the two sides of the development to the south, closer to the mouth of the bay. Atterbury developed four well-organized, compact plans for the ten houses. Although at least two of each type of house were built, Atterbury oriented them differently to create a pleasing sense of variety. And though the houses were well planned, they were not large. They consisted of a living room, dining room, kitchen, five or six small bedrooms, and servants' quarters either in the attic or in a wing. As opposed to the architecture of more established summer resorts along the eastern seaboard, the low-lying cottages with flat red and green Spanish-tiled roofs were not only small but shockingly stark and architecturally dif-

ferent from anything anyone might have expected. For those used to large estates with copious acreage, the small lots were restrictive and lacking in privacy. Nonetheless, Atterbury worked hard to integrate the expanses of rough, sandy-colored concrete into the seaside setting, making up for the lack of interior space with an abundance of porches, piazzas, and outdoor stairs that benefited from the southwesterly breezes.

Havemeyer commissioned Nathan F. Barrett (1846–1919), a Westchester-based landscape architect, to work on the grounds of Bayberry Point. Having played a role in the design of the 1893 World's Columbian Exposition in Chicago, Barrett was also credited with the design of the town of Pullman, Illinois, a development in Deal, New Jersey, and gardens for financier P. A. B. Widener

and lawyer Joseph H. Choate. However, once completed, Bayberry Point had little landscaping, its "ample grounds [of] entirely sand and gravel as a beach."[5] As the promotional material proclaimed, "Trees and vegetation are conspicuous by absence. Not only would they detract from the harmony of the design, but more utilitarian purposes are subserved; they draw mosquitoes and other pests."[6] Although trellises and verandas provided some shade, Havemeyer's development was thoroughly exposed with little means of escape from the sun. In time, ivy on the cottage facades and a number of well-planned flower beds grew up, toning down the stark, exposed quality of the colony and giving it an element of romantic luster.

As Havemeyer intended, "Membership [in the enclave was to] be very select and all elements . . .

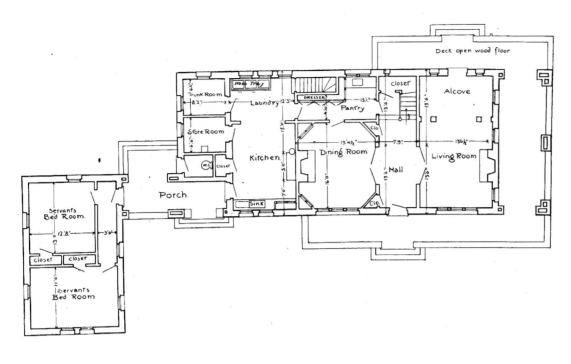

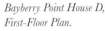

Bayberry Point House D, First-Floor Plan.

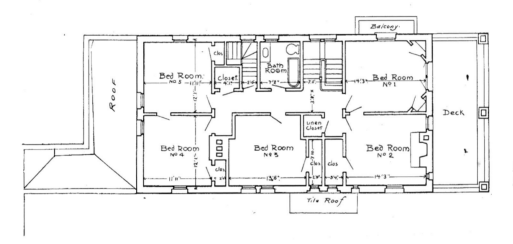

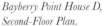

Bayberry Point House D, Second-Floor Plan.

congenial."[7] Given the size of the developed portion of Bayberry Point—a half-mile long and a quarter-mile wide—congeniality was at a premium. Though the development was made thoroughly modern with advanced drainage and sewage systems, the small lots and shared amenities gave it a decidedly communal feeling. A gate marking the entrance to the north opened into a mews with five to ten stables and a windmill. From there the road, arcing to the southeast and southwest, connected to the houses with their accompanying boathouses and bathhouses. Grounds were administered cooperatively, a custodian on site oversaw the entire enclave, and residents could treat their houses individually, with the approval of the other villa inhabitants. To make the houses more attractive in the eyes of buyers, Havemeyer specified that they come furnished and include such features as built-in sideboards and Venetian blinds. Havemeyer moved into the southwesternmost cottage (a House D) for the summer season of 1901; finding it difficult to sell the other homes, he quickly rented them out to family and friends, including tea importer George H. Macy and financiers Edward F. and Franklyn L. Hutton, for $1,000–1,500 a season. By 1907, Havemeyer had rented all of the houses but still remained the primary owner.

Perhaps Havemeyer's vision for Bayberry Point was too progressive—especially for an upper-class summer resort. Advertised as "creations of the fancy," the colony was described as an "advanced social experiment" of collective living.[8] Indeed, Havemeyer's picture of Bayberry Point differed from

other summer communities to which men in his social class were accustomed. However, with the successful Havemeyer as a resident, the *New York Times* proclaimed that Bayberry Point's modest cottages and acreage were bound to become a "Tuxedo of the Seaside"—or, in other words, extremely fashionable.[9] But not only was the community much smaller and very different in character, it also failed as a business venture and never reached the same heights of popularity as Tuxedo Park. It did, however, represent an important early effort in the realm of community planning. The development—a "creation of the fancy" indeed—was a unique place shaped by a distinct vision. In realizing Havemeyer's plan, Atterbury successfully forged a dialogue between the cottages' broad, low massing and light stucco walls and the landscape's flat contours and sandy terrain. At the same time, he gave the concrete an appealing sculptural quality with rounded corners, arched windows, brackets, exterior stairs, and rooftop verandas, which brought out Bayberry Point's Moorish character, also described in *Moorish Houses* as "adobe, familiar to all who have visited California, Arizona or Mexico."[10] Through modest means and materials and limited plan templates, Atterbury was presented the opportunity to contemplate relationships between dwellings and to generate picturesque variety. In that capacity, the architect succeeded, and Havemeyer, who later asked Atterbury to design a scheme for a shooting lodge in Tomotley, South Carolina, must have been happy with his work.[11]

Havemeyer died in 1907 and did not see his houses sell as originally intended. His son, Horace Havemeyer (1886–1956), opted to build his own house, Olympic Point, designed by Harrie T. Lindeberg in 1918, nearby. In 1930 he organized the Bayberry Point Corporation to sell the houses and an additional 117 lots that comprised the property. At that time, the *New York Times* reported that the houses were being offered at $25,000 and that desirable building sites—located on an additional third canal that was expressly dug—were available.[12] Some of the houses continued to rent for $1,500–1,800 a season while being available for sale at $25,000–30,000 throughout the 1930s and 1940s. By 1950, all of the original houses and lots had been sold.[13] Today, all ten of Bayberry Point's original homes exist; though still recognizable, most have been heavily altered. Many of the flat roofs, having been found impractical, have been raised, and various additions and renovations have diminished their Moorish essence. New development hemming in the original cluster has changed the communal atmosphere that existed when the ten stucco homes stood as an artistic ensemble, open and exposed to the Great South Bay.

4
FOR TEACHERS ONLY

PLANDOME AND ITS COMPANIONS

ROBERT B. MacKAY

Plandome

"For teachers only" proclaimed Plandome's earliest promotional material, and its founders' vision certainly set the North Hempstead community apart from those that soon rose around it.[1] In 1905, a group of young New York City neighbors in their early thirties—Walter Barnwell, Roy C. Gasser, Roy Austin, E. L. Ferris, and Milton L'Ecluse—formed the Plandome Land Company and purchased ninety acres with seven hundred feet of frontage on Manhasset Bay from Singleton L. Mitchell. Barnwell, head of the math department at Flushing High School and the first president of the company, was among the earliest to build in Plandome,[2] along with Alfred F. Parrott, a French teacher at Stuyvesant High School, and Almeron Smith, the principal of Public School 89 in Elmhurst. Sales brochures circulated among New York City schoolteachers offered free transportation for anyone who wished to inspect the community, located approximately twenty-one miles east of Manhattan. Plot prices ranged from $500 to $1,800 for waterfront property, offered on reasonable terms with no interest or taxes for two years, after which the buyer could take title with a mortgage for the remaining 60 percent.[3]

Business acumen for the venture was provided by the incorporators, who were not educators. Roy C. Gasser (1874–1961), a corporate attorney who represented the Vanderbilts and had been on the board of the *Harvard Law Review*, and Milton L'Ecluse (1871–1938), a real estate executive at S.

Osgood Pell Company, the Fifth Avenue firm that served as marketing agents for the project, were also among the first residents. Particularly important was the presence of L'Ecluse, a rising star who succeeded Pell as president of the realty concern, which acquired R. L. Burton's residential park in Woodmere in 1908 in one of the era's largest suburban real estate transactions. L'Ecluse, who soon formed his own firm, L'Ecluse, Washburn & Company (H. J. Washburn and L'Ecluse's brother, Ernest, would also reside at Plandome), served as first vice president of the Real Estate Exchange of Long Island and was a crusader for temperance and better business practices. At Plandome, he apparently acted as the general manager, promoting, selling, building, and even defending the community in 1910 against inclusion in a water district they opposed.[4]

In 1909, the *New York Times* reported that more than half of the plots comprising the initial ninety acres had been sold and that the Country Development Company, backed by many of the same investors, had been formed. L'Ecluse and Washburn served as president and vice president, respectively, of the new concern, which acquired an additional 130 acres known as Plandome South.[5] But despite Plandome's progress, the project was undercapitalized from the outset, and half a dozen years after its creation it still lacked paved roads, street lighting, police and fire protection, and adequate water mains. These challenges, along with the concern about the municipal water district,

TYPE OF HOUSES AT PLANDOME

PLANDOME
ON MANHASSET BAY

An all year round section as well as summer resort

BOATING, BATHING AND FISHING AND SHORE RIGHTS FOR ALL

Send for list of houses for rent as well as those for sale

L'Ecluce, Washburn & Co.
18 E. 34th St., N. Y. City—Tel. 4030 Murray Hill

Milton L'Ecluse, a founding member of the Plandome Land Company and a rising star on Long Island's real estate scene, was involved in managing and marketing the new community. Long Island and Real Life (New York: The Long Island Railroad Company, 1914)

fanned home-rule sentiments leading to incorporation as a village in 1911. For L'Ecluse, Plandome must have been a great learning experience, particularly in comparison to his new involvement, posh Woodmere, where the amenities ranged from a pharmacy to a golf course. The days of "cabbage patch business" and "misrepresentation" were over, he acknowledged in 1908.[6] Noting that more investment money was available than ever before, L'Ecluse reasoned that a good deal would go into real estate, if there was confidence that property was being offered honestly and there was at least the prospect of a moderate rate of return on the investment. "People will not pioneer any longer," L'Ecluse concluded; the market would now favor properties with all the "conveniences of a modern colony" and not just concrete curbs and macadam roads but local markets, medical facilities, and telephone service.[7] Soon to become the region's leading realtor, L'Ecluse had his hand in myriad projects. After his country house at East Neck in Huntington was completed in 1907, press accounts indicate that he was more involved with that community. His brother, Ernest, who organized Plandome's Boy Scout Troop, became a junior member of L'Ecluse, Washburn & Company in 1910 and was put in charge of sales at Plandome.[8]

A new village hall, which opened in 1912, addressed a number of Plandome's failings and was immediately hailed by the *Brooklyn Daily Eagle*

as "one of the finest of its kind on Long Island."[9] Accommodating municipal offices, a school, an assembly hall, and even space for a fire engine to be used by the newly organized volunteer department, the building remains the community's civic center a century later. The Tudor Revival edifice, completed for less than $20,000 and financed by the sale of bonds at a cost per resident of 48 cents a year per $100 of assessed valuation, was designed by Fred H. Briggs, another important member of the "founding families." He served as supervising architect for the Plandome Land Company, and all building plans were subject to his approval. He is believed to have designed many of the first houses, such as the handsome shingle-clad Colonial Revival and Dutch Colonial residences, which shared some stylistic features.[10] Briggs was a versatile practitioner, however. By 1914, the community included more than a dozen brick, stone, and concrete houses in a variety of historic styles and set in a most pleasing landscape designed by Gustav A. Roullier (1849–1910). Although described as a landscape architect in the community's 1964 history, Roullier, who had been recruited by L'Ecluse, Barnwell, and Gasser, was a Flushing engineer with a facility for roadwork. At Plandome, his curvilinear street pattern took advantage of the rolling topography to create a variety of plot sizes and house placements.[11]

A 1911 panoramic photograph looking north toward South Drive and framed on either side

by West and Park drives depicts a good portion of the original community and indicates that the landscaping was well under way. Amenities were quickly established. The Plandome Land Company financed the construction of the community's railroad station (1909), which became a flag stop on the L.I.R.R.'s Port Washington line. The Plandome Yacht Club (later the Plandome Field and Marine Club) was organized in 1908, and the following year the Plandome Women's Club was formed, both designed to promote "sociability."[12] The Yacht Club, which soon possessed a dock, bathhouses, tennis courts, and bowling alleys built in the basement of the village hall, could offer membership only to property owners (or renters) in Plandome or Plandome South, as their deeds

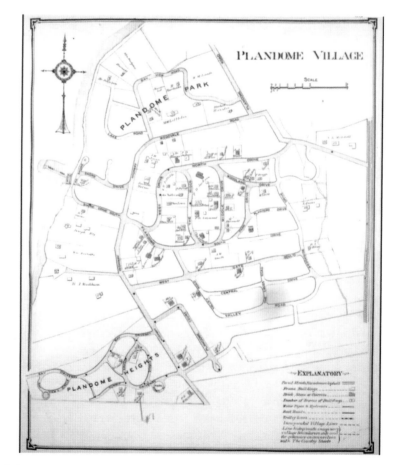

held the beach and mooring rights. With these advantages and the rising tide that was lifting Long Island real estate in anticipation of the completion of the L.I.R.R.'s East River tunnels, Plandome's popularity soared. The community's demographic profile also began to change, and by 1920, census data indicate, only two residents identified themselves as teachers; they had been joined by salesmen, manufacturers, corporate executives, and a range of professionals. The census also recorded a surprising number of domestics, including cooks, maids, gardeners, and even a few chauffeurs and butlers. The suburban experiment launched by a handful of young families had come of age as a balanced suburban enclave with a strong sense of community. Its upscale nature was also reflected in its evolving architecture. Construction of a handsome new brick Colonial for Francis D. Jackson, president of Brooklyn's Hecla Iron Works, received

mention in the press, as did Harry B. James's purchase of Shore Gables, one of the "show places" of Plandome that had been designed by Briggs and to which he had the architect add a conservatory and polo stables.[13] "The best investment," Plandome's later ads proclaimed, "is satisfaction with environment," as found in "a home around cultured surroundings."[14]

Plandome Park

As the first successful residential park in North Hempstead, Plandome encouraged emulation. Two years after the Plandome Land Company purchased the Mitchell farm, Andrew J. Cobe's Manhasset Development Company acquired a fifty-six-acre tract north of the village line and created Plandome Park, a restricted community

The curving drives designed by Gustav A. Roullier and some of the first houses are visible in this 1911 panorama of Plandome. Society for the Preservation of Long Island Antiquities

The Plandome Land Company financed the construction of the community's railroad station in 1909. Frederick Ruther, *Long Island Today* (New York: Essex Press, 1909), p. 59

of about thirty plots of one to three and a half acres overlooking Manhasset Bay.[15] A colorful promoter, Cobe's previous ventures had ranged from striking a coin marketed to raise money for the Cuban independence movement to Wonderland in northern Manhattan. Site of today's Baker Athletics Complex at Columbia University, Wonderland was to have been a thirty-one-acre amusement park designed by the firm responsible for Dreamland at Coney Island and for so many of the residential parks in this study—Kirby, Petit & Green. A wonderful rendering prepared by the architects of the European village–themed Wonderland appeared in the *New-York Tribune* in 1904, but a year later Cobe had sold the property. It is not known if Kirby, Petit & Green played a role at Plandome Park, but Cobe's other career

as a theatrical broker and film producer probably explains why J. Stuart Blackton, founder of Vitagraph Studios, and Frances Hodgson Burnett, author of *Little Lord Fauntleroy*, were among the first to buy plots.[16] Among the park's other residents were Herbert S. Houston, a Doubleday, Page vice president, Thomas Nast Fairbanks, godson of the cartoonist Thomas Nast, and Martin W. Littlejohn, the criminal lawyer who defended Stanford White's murderer, Harry K. Thaw. The planning of the garden at Burnett's Fairseat, an Italian Renaissance villa overlooking Manhasset Bay, may have inspired her 1910 children's classic *The Secret Garden*.[17]

Plandome Heights

Antitrust action against the "Tobacco Trust," the American Tobacco Company, leading to its breakup by a Supreme Court order, was the catalyst for the third residential park to be built in the Plandomes during the Progressive Era. Benjamin N. Duke (1855–1929), son of the founder of the family business and brother of James B. Duke, whose use of cigarette manufacturing machines had revolutionized the tobacco industry, was apparently seeking to diversify his assets in 1909, when his Plandome Heights Company acquired the Bloodgood Cutter farm, adjacent to and south of Plandome, from the American Bible Society, to whom it had been willed. Although legend has it that Duke planned to live at 64 Plandome Court, he never resided in Plandome Heights, and it may not have been his intention, as the Manhattan resident was leasing an estate in Great Neck in 1915.[18]

Laid out by the Great Neck engineering firm J. W. Jacobus, the Heights was to be a textbook example of residential park design, with curvilinear drives and landscaped triangles and circles.[19] As had been the case with Plandome, the street names reflected the topography. Summit Place was on the high ground near Plandome Road, Bay Driveway ran toward the water, and the view of Manhasset

Bay from Grandview Circle was all that the name implied. Cornell-trained Clement B. Brun, who worked in Prospect Park South, designed the first ten houses in the Heights.[20] Affectionately known as the "tobacco houses" by later residents, they were Spanish-style residences constructed of stucco-covered, hollow-tile walls and red tile roofs, building materials that were then popular for suburban homes. In the spring of 1910, the *New York Times* reported that the Plandome Heights Company had 250 men at work on nine houses, the nucleus of "a fireproof village," expected to cost from $10,000 to $15,000 each, and that a clubhouse and private docks were planned. Restrictions prohibited stores, places of business, two-family houses, and other nuisances. By the spring of 1901, company ads were claiming that half the property had been sold, echoing L'Ecluse's concerns about assuring the public that its reputation (or rather Mr. Duke's) was beyond "a shadow of a doubt," that transactions were safe and honest and would net 30–40 percent on the investment. Four years later, the E. Belcher Hyde *Atlas of Nassau County* indicated that the ten houses scattered east and west of Plandome Road had found owners, but progress was gradual and in 1929, the year Duke died, the Heights had approximately forty houses and fewer than three hundred residents. With restrictions due to expire on January 1, 1930, and plans afoot for a Manhasset sewer district that was deemed an unnecessary expense and might have paved the way for garden apartments, the newly formed Plandome Heights Association pushed for incorporation, which was accomplished by election on June 11, 1929. One of the incorporated village's first acts was to pass a building restriction ordinance specifying that only single-family detached houses conforming to strict frontage, setback, lot, and dwelling size requirements would be permitted. Collectively, Plandome, Plandome Heights, and Plandome Park (which became part

Ad for Plandome Heights. New York Times, September 11, 1910

of the Incorporated Village of Plandome Manor in 1931) formed a community that helped popularize residential parks east of the city just at the outset of the Progressive Era. Leading this vanguard of middle-class professionals who would reside there was a group of educators seeking to create an appropriate setting for a new lifestyle. Through trial and adjustment, they succeeded in creating a sanctuary that was widely emulated over successive decades.

5

FROM FLATBUSH TO THE SHINNECOCK HILLS

DEAN ALVORD'S IDEA

ROBERT B. MacKAY

By 1913, when the New York press reported that the Dean Alvord companies, mired in $3 million of unsecured bonded indebtedness, had collapsed, their creator was already half a world away studying flora in the Far East. The real estate impresario, overcome by stress, had unraveled at age fifty-five. Pressure, he later recalled, had become a mortgage "on my vitality."[1] The press speculated that Alvord had never really recovered from the financial panic of 1907, although the two-year recession starting in January 1910, coupled with overspeculation in Long Island real estate in anticipation of the completion of the Long Island Railroad's East River tunnels, could not have helped. For the visionary who had set out to reform the industry and establish real estate development as a science and a safe investment, these events must have been devastating. He would never again be a player on Long Island.[2] His accomplishments, however—handsome residential parks extending from the city deep into Suffolk County—presaged the phenomenon that was to reconfigure the region and the way Long Islanders were to live in the twentieth century.

Born in Syracuse, Dean Alvord (1856–1941) [fig. 1] was the third of nine children of James D. Alvord, a cattle and sheep broker, and Caroline L. Edwards, a descendant of the Puritan fire-and-brimstone preacher Rev. Jonathan Edwards. Caroline was described as "an earnest church worker, a gifted speaker and a poetess of merit."[3] She must

also have been an important influence on her outgoing and devout son Dean, who was later to teach a bible class for the YMCA. While attending Syracuse University for three years with the class of 1882, Alvord joined the campus's oldest fraternity, Delta Kappa Epsilon, whose credo stressed intellectual excellence, tolerance, and morality.[4] Social culture was another "object" of the fraternity, and the popular Alvord no doubt had opportunity to hone his considerable social skills, which this great mixer was to demonstrate throughout his career.

By the mid-1880s, Alvord had moved on to rapidly industrializing Rochester and experiences that would shape his career over the next fifteen years. In 1885, the year he married Nellie Barnum of Syracuse, he was appointed general secretary of the Rochester YMCA. Evidencing a strong interest in education that was shared by the Y's president, Professor George M. Forbes of the University of Rochester, Alvord instituted classes in political science, English, and German, along with instruction in trade skills such as mechanical drawing and stenography. As he later recalled, "I thought I ought to reform the world of young men realizing how much I needed it myself."[5] However, the area in which Alvord really excelled and served as the catalyst for was the creation of a new home for the institution. The five-story building, completed in 1890, which included a pool, a gymnasium, and an auditorium that could seat a thousand, doubled the Y's membership in just two years, while the fund-raising

1. Dean Alvord, ca. 1907. Courtesy Brooklyn Historical Society

effort that made it possible introduced the young man from Syracuse to the city's elite.

Joseph T. Alling (1855–1937), an executive of his family's paper company, Alling and Cory, teacher of a popular bible class and a progressive who led a movement to reform the Rochester school board, was one of the contributors. Alling succeeded Forbes as president of the YMCA and soon became involved with Alvord in an even greater undertaking—the creation of a major cemetery.

Known as the "Flower City" in the second half of the nineteenth century, Rochester was a center of horticulture and home to about thirty nurseries, including the nation's largest, Ellwanger and Barry.[6] Among the city's horticultural attractions were Highland Park, one of the earliest municipal arboretums, and Oxford Street, a handsome residential avenue known for its glorious magnolia trees and planted median. Hence, it was not surprising that the new profession of landscape architecture at the century's close flourished here and influenced Alvord. In 1888, the city's Park Commission retained Frederick Law Olmsted to begin planning Rochester's extraordinary "Emerald Necklace" of parks, and at about this time, W. W. Parce (1861–1940), perhaps the city's first homegrown professional, began his landscape practice.[7] Parce was the son of an engineer and nursery owner from nearby Fairport, New York.

Resigning from the Y in 1891, Alvord brought together his Rochester connections and a growing appreciation of what he was to call landscape art in a bold new enterprise—the formation of the Riverside Cemetery Association (1892). The creation of cemeteries had become financially attractive in the closing decades of the nineteenth century, and although New York State law prevented investors from pocketing more than 50 percent of lot sales, the remainder to be used for maintenance and development, the profit margin was still significant. Alvord served as secretary and treasurer of Riverside, a private venture headquartered in Rochester's Chamber of Commerce building, with Joseph T. Alling as vice president and Edmund Lyon, an astute businessman and one of the largest Eastman Kodak stockholders, as president. Retained to lay out the cemetery on a novel plan was W. W. Parce.

The park lawn concept emphasized pastoral landscape over the picturesque, monument-cluttered rural cemeteries that had been in vogue since the 1830s. Introduced by Adolph Strauch at Cincinnati's Spring Grove Cemetery (1855) in concert with English landscape practices, park lawn planning favored open spaces broadly interspersed with trees and fountains and an absence of enclosures. Grave markers were carefully restricted, rising just a few inches above the ground around the family monuments, which provided the sole statement of artistry, heightening their visibility while greatly simplifying the cemetery's viewsheds.

Riverside's developers assured the public that they had "wisely retained the natural features"

and that landscape architects "trained in modern methods and skillful in the practice of their profession" were in charge of the plan."[8] The *Rochester Union Advertiser* observed in 1893 that considerable progress had been made, with thousands of trees planted and almost a complete absence of headstones preserving the park-like appearance of the cemetery. "Under no circumstances will vulgar and ostentatious display be permitted," the paper went on to note, and though "marble devices" were allowed, there could be no more than one per lot.[9] By hiring J. H. Shepard as superintendent, Riverside's management also signaled that the design principles would be strictly enforced. As a landscape gardener, Shepard had previously been employed by Chicago's Oak Woods Cemetery, also a park lawn design, located just a mile from the city on a beautiful boulevard, reachable by "electric [trolley] cars," and replete with curving drives and landscape lakes, Riverside attracted attention, but the cemetery's 1897 annual report suggests that lot sales were gradual or at least not brisk enough to hold the interest of its entrepreneurial secretary/treasurer for long. For Alvord, Riverside was an exercise in how engineering, horticulture, and landscape design could combine to achieve a desired result—a lesson that he would soon apply to residential suburbs.

As he recalled years later, "I hopped into the real estate business as being the most disreputable field in which I might exercise my questionable talents." Judging the suburban field at that time to be a "little short of a swindler's game,"[10] and seeing an opportunity to reform not just men but an entire industry, Alvord began with "a single lot" in Rochester in 1893. He soon graduated to "a short street,

then to a small tract, which instead of a real estate 'devilment' was a real development."[11] By 1895, he was able to note in his ads that "my experience in building will enable the purchaser to secure a better house for less money" on a number of different plans.[12] However, the former bible school teacher added a caveat that was to be repeated in his later projects. The prospective purchasers must be of "unquestionable moral and social standing," ensuring that "the neighborhood will, therefore, be the most desirable as a home."[13]

While pursuing his own efforts on Rochester's east side, Alvord also participated in a much larger project as a director of the Vanderbilt Improvement Company,[14] whose bold objective was to form "Rochester's Great Industrial Suburb," Despatch, N.Y.[15] Commenced in 1897 by Walter A. Parce on plans prepared by his brother, W. W. Parce, Despatch was to comprise "schools, shops, stores and factories," as well as "suburban homes with city conveniences."[16] Renamed East Rochester in 1907, Despatch was partially realized but never to the extent hoped for by its investors, among them Edmund Lyon. As everything had to be built from scratch, Vanderbilt Improvement struggled to meet demands, and several companies that had located there withdrew, finding the new community too remote from Rochester proper.

Prospect Park South

In 1899, at age forty-two, Dean Alvord left Rochester in search of new horizons. Rochester was "no mean city," he later recalled, but "large enough only for a proving ground."[17] With his wife, Nellie, two small children, and just $2,500 in his pocket, the young entrepreneur arrived in New York City to try out his idea on "the big 'uns."[18] "That idea in a nutshell was the application of landscape art to the development of land for residential purposes," and the rapidly expanding boroughs of Brooklyn and Queens were to be the venue for the trial.[19] Even before relocating, Alvord had made a profit on the sale of property being consolidated to form the Olmsted-designed Forest Park on the Brooklyn/Queens border and was also involved in developing, perhaps with the assistance of Rochester investors, modestly priced houses in the $4,000–6,000 range on Forest Parkway near the entrance to the new park.[20]

Just after his arrival, on approximately fifty acres acquired from the Dutch Reform Church and the Bergen family, Alvord began to fashion a community of great spatial and aesthetic coherence. "Beautiful, beautiful," exclaimed Mayor Seth Low on seeing the eleven blocks of Prospect Park South for the first time.[21] By installing utilities underground, establishing setbacks, prohibiting fences, and stipulating that planting could not extend beyond building lines, Alvord ensured that each detached house would be in harmony with the whole. Lawns were uninterrupted and sidewalks were pushed to the property lines to showcase eight feet of greenery between curb and sidewalk. Planted medians on the principal boulevards, reminiscent of Rochester's Oxford Street, added to the park-like quality. Residents paid fees to maintain the common areas planned by Scottish landscape gardener John Aitkin.[22] The houses were presented in an eclectic sampler of styles, including a Swiss chalet and an attention-getting Japanese house (1902). Streetscapes were enlivened by towers, dormers, and porticos, juxtaposed harmoniously. Stock plan houses were prohibited and the residences were the work of some of the borough's most promising suburban architects, including the talented John J. Petit of

At Prospect Park South, lawns were uninterrupted and sidewalks were pushed to the property lines to allow eight feet of greenery between the sidewalk and the curb, as seen in this photo of Marlborough Road. Society for the Preservation of Long Island Antiquities

Planted medians such as those seen here on Albermarle Road contributed to the park-like feeling at Prospect Park South. Society for the Preservation of Long Island Antiquities

A sampler of architectural styles, including a Swiss chalet and a Japanese house, enlivened the residential park's streetscapes. Society for the Preservation of Long Island Antiquities

Petit & Green. Petit himself was responsible for fifteen houses. Alvord's "artistic houses and grounds" brought something of the ambience of a small town to the big city and appealed to the anti-urban sentiment that is forever part of the American psyche.[23]

While restrictions controlled appearances and led as early as 1905 to the establishment of a neighborhood association dedicated to their enforcement, "character and cash in about equal proportions and in the order named" were the sine qua non for ownership.[24] Plots in the early years were in the $4,000–10,000 range with a premium for those on the principal streets with planted medians, and houses built by the developer ranged from $8,000 to $20,000.[25]

Rus in urbe, or the creation of "a rural park within the limitations of the conventional city block," as Alvord described his project, was an immediate success.[26] "The Gothamites," he later recalled, who could easily reach Prospect Park South by either the Flatbush Electric El or several trolley lines, "just 'ate up' my simple idea."[27] Property values appreciated rapidly, and by the spring of 1905, Alvord was able to announce that he had sold all the vacant lots.[28] There were still houses in various stages of completion to be marketed, and it was two years before he sold his own Petit-designed Tudor on Beverly Road, the community's grandest avenue, for the astounding price of $50,000. However, by then the originator of Prospect Park South was immersed in one of the remarkable projects of the age, well to the east, the creation of the Long Island Motor Parkway.

"And now the day of the automobile has come," A. R. Pardington, the parkway's engineer, remarked at the road's groundbreaking.[29] Alvord witnessed, firsthand, the birth of the phenomenon that was to have such a significant role in creating and defining suburbia in future decades. Recruited for his real estate acumen, he joined the parkway's board in 1905. Awash in captains of finance and industry interested in the region, the board provided him with invaluable contacts for later projects. Alvord's role on the parkway's Plan and Scope Committee, however, which was chaired by Vanderbilt and included Pardington, Automobile Club

of America president David Hennen Morris, and L.I.R.R. president Ralph Peters, among others, may have been of greater consequence. Charged with acquiring the right-of-way with Peters, whose engineers surveyed the probable route, Alvord told the *New York Times* in October 1906 that he had voluntary offers of almost ten miles of property.[30] For the young man only recently arrived from Rochester, the parkway project was not only a valuable lesson in Long Island geography but also led to a role as a real estate advisor to the L.I.R.R. Even as the right-of-way was being assembled, Alvord was acquiring property all over Long Island, including the parcel that later became Garden City Estates, which he purchased from the Garden City Company.[31] And his firm, now located on Broadway in Manhattan, began presenting itself as a specialist in Long Island real estate. Its focus was reported to be on investment and development acreage, summer homes and gentlemen's estates, and particularly shore fronts.[32] J. C. Farnsworth, formerly with the Ackerson Company, a Flatbush rival, was brought in as the manager of the Country Department, allowing Alvord to devote "his personal attention to the selection of investment properties."[33] A syndicate Alvord organized in 1905 bought several hundred acres in Queens on the Merrick Road with the intention of building a second Prospect Park South. He named the tract Laurelton, but within months he flipped it to a bigger figure on the Brooklyn real estate scene, Senator William "Billy" Reynolds, whose Laurelton Land Company was soon building Spanish- and Mission-style villas on the tract. The community's name was spelled out in flowers on the embankment of its elegant new railroad station, which opened in 1907.

Cedarcroft and Shinnecock Hills

Two other Alvord projects from this period, Cedarcroft at Greenlawn (1905) and Shinnecock Hills in Southampton (1905) may have been ahead of their time. "Dedicated to people of moderate means and refined tastes," Cedarcroft was to comprise five-to-ten-acre lots priced at $2,500 or less and given the same "expert landscape treatment" as at Prospect Park South.[34] The site, perched high atop the North Shore's glacial moraine with distant views of Northport and Huntington harbors, was wildly beautiful. However, at more than an hour from the city, half a decade before the East River railroad tunnels were completed, and with the financial panic of 1907 on the horizon, Cedarcroft had limited appeal.[35] Some of the same factors partially explain why the other project, the syndicated Shinnecock Hills & Peconic Bay Realty Company (SHPBRC), didn't fare any better, though the East

End project seems to have been ill starred from the beginning. In 1908, a grass fire destroyed the company's large new hotel, the Shinnecock Inn, designed to introduce prospective purchasers to the magnificent tract of 2,700 acres of rolling grassland depicted in William Merritt Chase's paintings. By 1906, eighteen country houses had already been built on the narrow isthmus between Peconic and Shinnecock bays,[36] which they shared with the iconic links of the Shinnecock Hills Golf Club. Pretty much everything else east of the Shinnecock Canal toward Southampton was the property of the SHPBRC, which retained John Charles Olmsted of the Olmsted Brothers and Downing Vaux, son of the architect Calvert Vaux, Frederick Law Olmsted Sr.'s collaborator on the design of New York's Central Park, as landscape architects. Completed in 1907, their plan called for "villa" sites set amid a curving tracery of roads conforming to the contour lines. "On land and yet at sea" appeared to be an appropriate slogan for the company, as much of the "carefully restricted" property had water views.[37] That year, at the for-mal opening, a large delegation traveling by train out to the inn heard A. R. Pardington speak of the probability of extending the Long Island Motor Parkway through the company's property. Alas, it did not come to pass. The syndicate sold some of the land to the National Golf Links of America, which opened its course in 1911, but most of the property remained undeveloped and was even-tually sold at auctions in the 1920s. Long Island at the outset of the twentieth century, as *House & Garden* commented in 1913, was considered inac-cessible wasteland by the public.[38]

Roslyn Estates

Alvord was not going to take any chances again; he simply decided not to reveal to the public the loca-tion of his next project in the region. In an extraor-dinary series of ads placed in the *Brooklyn Daily Eagle* in the spring of 1908, he promoted a new property suitable for year-round residences, relying entirely on his Prospect Park South reputation and giving his friends the opportunity to buy at a confidential

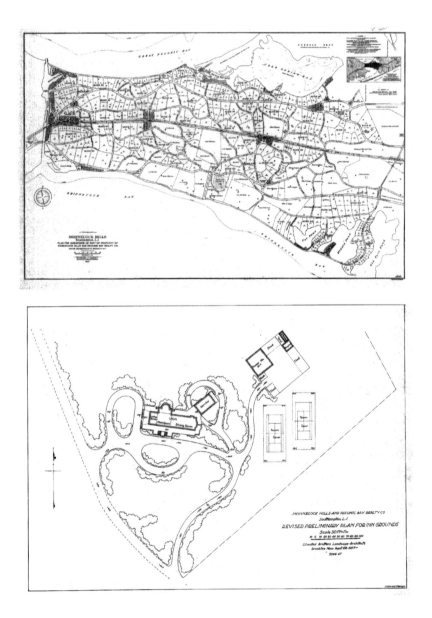

The Shinnecock Hills Subdivision plan by John Charles Olmsted of the Olmsted Brothers and Downing Vaux. Courtesy National Park Service, Frederick Law Olmsted National Historic Site

63

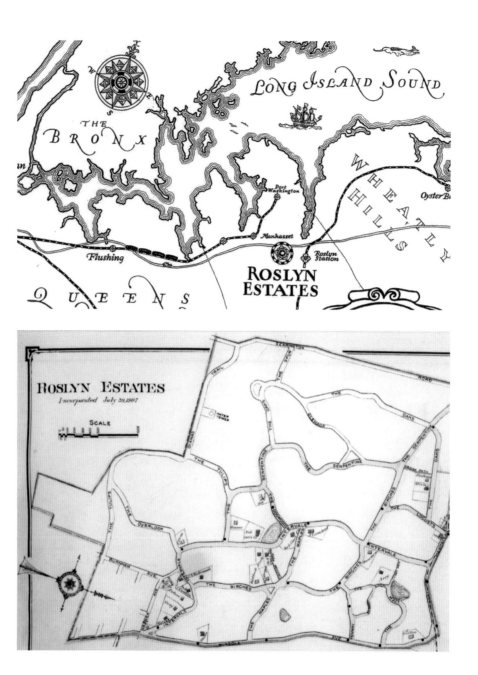

price. The names of those who did appeared in subsequent ads and suspense built in anticipation of the announcement. On May 23, the appointed day, the *Eagle's* readers learned that a 277-acre tract twenty-two miles from Manhattan, just west of the Village of Roslyn, on the L.I.R.R.'s Oyster Bay branch, was the site. Roslyn Estates was a park, Alvord claimed. Streets did not run at right angles or crisscross the landscape with "checkerboard regularity."[39] "Here the landscape architect lays his roadways to secure the most picturesque relation to the building sites," the developer declared, situating the houses at the best locations.[40]

Nor, on the winding drives named largely for trees, were any two plots alike. They ranged in size from half an acre to five. Alvord had left behind the urban street pattern that had constrained him in Brooklyn. On rolling hills he had fashioned "The Eden of Long Island,"[41] a residential park

of "unusual charm and quiet seclusion," set amid "a panorama of ever-changing natural beauty,"[42] as Christopher Morley, who was to reside there, described it. Roslyn Estates was to be different in other ways, too. Alvord commissioned English-born architect Frederick J. Sterner (1862–1931), known to have a particular facility with country houses constructed in concrete, to design four "artistic fireproof structures."[43] Grouped on the terraces around Lotus Pond (later renamed Black Ink Pond), one of several spring-fed lakes within the Estates, the imposing houses were all in different styles, setting a standard for development to come. *Cement and Engineering News* reported that the houses, built by the Fireproof Dwelling Company of New Haven, Connecticut, were constructed entirely of concrete, using English and German methods new to this country.[44] Deed restrictions assured that until 1930, trees and shrubs within the bounds of the

At Roslyn Estates, Alvord broke away from the street pattern that had constrained him in Brooklyn. Laid out on a rolling landscape with winding drives, no two plots were alike. Courtesy John and Michelle Santos collection, Roslyn

roads could not be cut without approval. Alvord's houses and those that followed were detached, single-family, pitched-roof dwellings set back from the street and cost no less than $5,000. Sales at Roslyn Estates were not brisk but were certainly an improvement over sales at Alvord's previous Long Island ventures. Two dozen houses appear in the 1914 atlas, the extent of the community at the time of the developer's bankruptcy.[45]

Activity picked up in the 1920s, and by the time of Roslyn Estates' seventy-fifth anniversary, more than a hundred residences had been added. Twenty-six are said to have been designed by August L. Viemeister, whose first commission in 1914, while he was still a student at the University of Pennsylvania, was his mother's house at 39 Intervale.[46]

The Roslyn Estates experience informed Alvord's philosophy and much of his teaching and writing. He served as a director of the Brooklyn Y.M.C.A. and lectured to the real estate class of the Y's Bedford Branch and Brooklyn's Municipal Club. He wrote a chapter, "How to Develop Acreage," for a popular real estate guide published by Doubleday, Page & Company in 1909.[47] Declaring that he had "the same objection to the real estate speculator" as he had "to a flea—I don't like the way he gets his living," Alvord told his Bedford class that development, if done well, could solve the living problem of the middle class. He thought every architectural student should take a course in landscape architecture.[48] During this period, Alvord's ads began to diverge from those of his competitors. Instead of enumerating the advantages of his residential parks, Alvord encouraged prospective purchasers to study both the properties on offer and the developers who offered them.

A house at Lotus Pond (later renamed Black Ink pond). Roslyn Estates (New York: Union Mortgage Company, 1926)

Belle Terre Estates

Developing apace with Roslyn Estates, and often advertised along with it, was Belle Terre Estates at Port Jefferson. Located sixty-two miles from Manhattan, Belle Terre was not designed "as a home for those whose business demands their daily presence in the city."[49] Rather, it was to be "an ideal spot for a summer house be it a palatial estate or modest bungalow."[50] Reporting on Alvord's 1906 purchase of the 1,300-acre peninsula, the *New York Times* commented that the property, comprising five miles of waterfront, would be improved by adding "an inn of the old English type," cottages, a golf course, and all sorts of recreational facilities.[51] The story of the vast residential park had begun four years earlier. A syndicate of Brooklyn investors, incorporated as the Port Jefferson Company, had bought the old Strong family estate, Oakwood.[52] Early tasks

To ensure a more
fashionable portal to Belle
Terre Estates, Alvord's
new community at Port
Jefferson, his syndicate
purchased and donated a
new site for the depot to
the Long Island Railroad,
which erected the handsome
new station seen here in
1903. Kenneth Brady,
Village of Port Jefferson
historian

Belle Terre Estates'
entrance lodge, a mile
from the station, was
also designed by John J.
Petit of Kirby, Petit &
Green. Kenneth Brady,
Village of Port Jefferson
historian

Belle Terre Estates' main
thoroughfare, Cliff Road,
leading from the entrance
lodge to a pair of pergolas
on bluffs overlooking Long
Island Sound. Society for
the Preservation of Long
Island Antiquities

A carpentry crew, almost all holding their tools of the trade, at Belle Terre.
Kenneth Brady, Village of Port Jefferson historian

included acquiring full ownership of the shoreline from the Town of Brookhaven, a hot political issue until settled by Alvord with a generous now-or-never offer; and the reimaging of the shipbuilding community's lackluster depot. In what became Port Jefferson's exercise in the City Beautiful, Alvord's syndicate purchased and donated to the railroad a site for a fashionable new train station, which was built in 1903 and paid for by the L.I.R.R.[53] It was, of course, fortuitous that Alvord and his good friend Ralph Peters, the railroad's president, were both planning to build houses at Belle Terre.

Resembling a classical pergola, the new station was designed by John J. Petit, now of Kirby, Petit & Green, and was the first in an ensemble of buildings that lent the new community much of its appearance and character. A road led directly from the depot to the châteauesque entrance lodge a mile away, whence the community's main thoroughfare, Cliff Road, wended its way to a pair of pergolas on the bluffs overlooking Long Island Sound. Petit was also responsible for Alvord's Craftsman-style residence, Nevalde, and the Belle Terre Club; he is believed to have designed other buildings in the community as well.[54] Talent was also brought to bear on laying out more than forty miles of roads and bridle paths.

While plans for the development of the residential park, which necessitated the construction of a pier and a water system, were carried out "under the personal supervision of Mr. Dean Alvord," a company brochure stated that the "landscape work is in the hands of Mr. Charles W. Leavitt, Jr."[55] A distinguished landscape engineer, as he preferred to be called, Leavitt had worked for the New York Suburban Land Company before starting his own diverse practice in 1897 and was well versed in city

planning and large-scale projects. On Long Island, his commissions were to include Long Beach, Jamaica Estates, and Garden City, not to mention country houses, cemeteries, racetracks, and myriad other projects. At Belle Terre, where he was assisted by E. Post Tooker, mountain laurel abounded, and at an elevation of about two hundred feet above the water with many picturesque vantage points, Leavitt had a lot with which to work.[56] He fashioned plans that were not only characterized by winding drives and bridle paths but also peppered with topographical points of interest with such names as Sentinel Rock, Giants' Cradle, The Lost Meadow, Nature's Garden, and The Anchorage.

Perhaps the most spectacular landscape feature was a massive, rustic bridge connecting the club grounds with the English section, where eight houses designed by Frederick J. Sterner were the community's tastemakers. On roads bearing such names as Upper and Lower Devon, Sterner exhibited his fluency with half-timbered Elizabethan and Tudor designs. A Belle Terre brochure noted:

> The English Houses are constructed chiefly of brick, stone and concrete and contain from ten to fifteen rooms each. A brick enclosed service yard and massive gateway entrance are a distinctive feature. They bear such appropriate names as "Torquay House," "Teignmouth Hall," "Boylton Grange," "Seaton Hall" and "Dawlish House."[57]

Sterner's houses, including the much-published Teignmouth Hall, were featured in *The Brickbuilder* in 1910, while a Tudor house by Tooker and Marsh, who also worked there, appeared in *Architectural Forum* in 1919.[58] The Druid Hill section north of the club grounds, noted for its architectural variety, was also fashionable. Alvord's own house was situ-

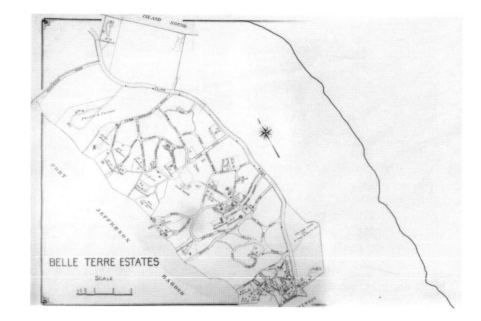

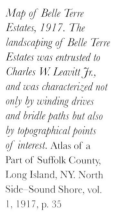

Map of Belle Terre Estates, 1917. The landscaping of Belle Terre Estates was entrusted to Charles W. Leavitt Jr., and was characterized not only by winding drives and bridle paths but also by topographical points of interest. Atlas of a Part of Suffolk County, Long Island, NY. North Side–Sound Shore, vol. 1, 1917, p. 35

ated there, along with the community's largest residence, a Renaissance Revival manse designed by Joseph A. McCarroll for Jacob Meurer, a Brooklyn manufacturer. However, Meurer and N. Leslie Carpenter, a cotton broker who acquired Teignmouth Hall, were not the only audience Alvord was targeting. His ads also focused on those of "moderate" means. In the Bungalow Section, situated near the entrance lodge, one could find "pretty little homes" of six to eight rooms, and "a Japanese landscape gardener" who would "reproduce all the features of a large estate in a plot ten feet square."[59] Among the designers of Belle Terre's bungalows was F. Ernst Lien, a young German émigré draftsman/architect, and Aymar Embury II, the Beaux-Arts-era architect who had developed a national reputation for his small residential commissions.[60] Four of Embury's Belle Terre plans were published in *Architecture* in 1909.[61]

At the center of all this activity stood the superbly appointed Belle Terre Club, the Kirby, Petit & Green–designed Old English Inn, which, given its hooded dormers and gables, was more French in inspiration.[62] With accommodations for a hundred, a commodious dining room large enough for all the residents of Belle Terre to take their meals, if so inclined, and the requisite verandas, billiard room, and barbershop, the clubhouse was exceptional. The inn also featured tennis courts, croquet grounds, a livery, a garage, and golf links designed by Scottish-born Alexander H. Findlay.[63] Whereas at Roslyn Estates a clubhouse had been discussed as a future possibility, at Belle Terre Alvord placed it at the community's heart. With his experience at Greenlawn and Shinnecock Hills in mind, he clearly envisioned a club colony. "No one who is not eligible to membership in the club," *Brooklyn Life* reported in 1909, "can buy land on

this great peninsula reservation as a consequence of the commendable make-haste-slowly policy of the promoter of it all, Dean Alvord."[64] Both the press and the developer were quick to compare the great undertaking at Port Jefferson to Tuxedo Park, and accounts abounded. The *New York Times* commented on opening day at the clubhouse the following year:

> It was a large and jolly crowd that strolled over the lawns, rambled along the forest paths glorious with mountain laurel, rode horseback to view points of the sea, played golf and tennis, or just sat on the big porch overlooking the harbor and renewed the friendships of former years. There was music, luncheon, and dancing to properly launch the season for this popular country club, many of whose members are residents of the Belle Terre Summer colony.[65]

The club's nonresident members included many of Alvord's parkway acquaintances and other prominent New Yorkers, among them John Jacob Astor, O. H. P. Belmont, Howard Gould, August Heckscher, William K. Vanderbilt Jr., Harry Payne Whitney, and Ralph Peters of the L.I.R.R. Only Peters was to build at Belle Terre. It would never have the panache of Tuxedo Park, and the early residents were largely Brooklyn physicians and businessmen. Nevertheless, Belle Terre was regarded as a success, and the Belcher Hyde Atlas recorded almost four dozen residences by 1917. A reporter for a national publication visiting in January 1912 was duly impressed. He came away convinced that "the manufacturing of charming houses set among the most delightful surroundings would win out," and that anyone who wished to verify this had only to see Alvord's most important creations, Belle Terre and Roslyn Estates.[66]

Managing, financing, and hedging the risk involved with multiple projects led to the creation of a holding company. Roslyn Estates, Inc., Belle Terre Estates, Dean Alvord Securities Company, and the Suburban Construction Company of New York were all subsidiaries of the Dean Alvord Company. The money trail behind the projects often ran all the way back to Rochester, where Edmund Lyon was still among Alvord's backers. A 1908 ad in a Rochester paper for 6 percent bonds in the Suburban Construction Company promised:

These bonds offer an opportunity for a safe investment secured by real estate assets, Long Island, where Mr. Alvord has made in the past eighteen years very large profits for his clients. Rochester investors number upwards of 200 of its best citizens—bankers, manufacturers and business men. A bonus of stock in accordance with Mr. Alvord's usual plan accompanies each bond. Issue limited to 100,000 for Rochester, subject to prior sale. Preference given to former and present holders of Dean Alvord securities. [67]

Alvord's ads during this period stressed "the assurance of salability of his properties" and confidence in the appreciation of Long Island real estate values.[68] After all, early buyers at Prospect Park South had "seen their property double, triple and quadruple in value."[69] What more could prospec-

Equestrians in front of the Belle Terre Club, the Kirby, Petit & Green–designed Old English Inn. Kenneth Brady, Village of Port Jefferson historian

tive purchasers of Alvord Securities require? They were assured: "Your principal is safe . . . interest sure" and "profits certain."[70]

Writing in *Munsey's Magazine* in 1912, John Grant Dater, editor of the popular mass-circulation weekly magazine's financial department, took issue. "There is nothing more perilous in the way of speculation than un-improved or partially developed suburban property," he argued.[71] The failure of the New York Central Realty Company that year and the indictment of its principals had brought national attention to the problem.

Then, in January 1913, news of the failure of the Alvord companies hit the New York press and the public learned that their operations had been so extensive that the unsecured bonds amounted to more than $3 million. The difficulty, the attorneys reported, "in meeting recurring interest payments amounting to $200,000 a year" was the result of their inability to market their properties.[72] In the next issue of *Munsey's*, Dater noted that things can go "swimmingly" for suburban land companies as long as properties sell, but when they don't, the bonds of these companies

22. Harbor Oaks, Clearwater, Florida. Clearwater Library

were no better than promissory notes. It was not Dater's intention, however, to suggest that the Alvord projects were comparable to those of the New York Central Realty Company, which had misrepresented their assets. In fact, the Alvord concerns were "regarded as among the strongest companies specializing in the development of New York suburban property."[73] "Suburban schemes look very pretty on paper and read well in alluring literature," he noted, but "expected developments may not, and frequently do not, materialize."[74]

A State Supreme Court justice appointed Brooklyn realty expert Edward Lyons temporary receiver of the Alvord companies under court protection. In July 1913, Lyons succeeded in a re-organization that was backed by the bondholders. The dissolution of Alvord's companies, however, played out for years, and for Belle Terre Estates, in which Rochester businessmen had "invested heavily," it was to be a game changer.[75] Alvord's restricted club colony concept was the first casualty. The *Brooklyn Daily Eagle* reported that the club was to be "popularized," dues abolished, and no effort "made to restrict the club to an exclusive handful."[76] In 1919, for the first time, the club failed to open at all, the press noting it had been a losing venture for several years.[77] In 1934, the community's signature pergolas at the end of Cliff Drive, now in precarious condition, were demolished, and the club was burned down. Belle Terre, fending off threats from sand mining operations, incorporated in 1930, weathered the Depression, and continues to be regarded, a century after its creation, as a prized residential enclave.

At the end of his thirty-thousand-mile journey around the globe in 1912–13,[78] Alvord returned, not to New York but to the then-remote west coast of Florida. He said he had "retired" but was soon at it again, developing Harbor Oaks, Clearwater's first planned residential community.[79] Hailed during the period as the finest project of its type on that coast, Harbor Oaks bore an uncanny resemblance to Prospect Park South with its city conveniences, rich mix of architectural styles, and, of course, deed restrictions. Palm trees replaced evergreens on the planted medians. Now listed on the National Register of Historic Places, the community exudes atmosphere to this day. In a 1935 letter and chronological record sent to Syracuse University in preparation for a volume of its Alumni Record, Alvord made no mention of the collapse of his companies other than to express gratitude for a New York dinner at which he was honored for what he had done to improve the standard of suburban development. Indeed, his work ethic "to do whatever I undertook better than that thing had ever been done before" and lifelong interest in "the application of landscape art to the development of land" had an immediate influence and resonated through the decades that followed. Dean Alvord did perhaps more than anyone to establish the standards and appearance of suburban development on Long Island at the outset of the twentieth century.

6

MRS. MARSH'S BELLEROSE

VIRGINIA L. BARTOS

In his 1912 book, *The Book of New York: Forty Years' Recollections of the American Metropolis*, author Julius Chambers included a chapter on how real estate development had transformed the city and the outlying suburbs. He called the chapter "Selling Real Estate Is a Fine Art," and in it he stated:

> With the improvement of the city came the development of its suburbs. There have been "conveyancers" and real estate agents since the beginning of time, but only within the last twenty-five years has the selling of city and suburban property been reduced to an art. Many of the finest city improvements have owed their inception to the brilliant and suggestive minds of the men of this new profession.[1]

Chambers painted glowing portraits of those he saw as the most talented and accomplished in the real estate field as they changed the face of the city and created new suburbs. His chapter mentioned several successful developments on Long Island, made possible through the efforts of the founders of such real estate enterprises as the Windsor Land Company, which was responsible for developing large sections of Floral Park, Rockville Centre, and Lynbrook, and the Queens Land and Title Company, which was so successful in marketing lands in Massapequa along the Great South Bay that "a city has risen in four years upon what was scarcely occupied farm property."[2] He praised H. Stewart McKnight for starting the McKnight Realty Company in 1905 with very little capital, acquiring land in Bayside, Queens, for attractive lots and villas, and channeling his success into a new endeavor called Great Neck Estates. He mentioned the new developments of Brightwaters near Bayside and Ocean Beach on Fire Island, but overlooked the achievements of the United Holding Company, which was actively carving out a new village just over the Nassau County line in an area known as Bellerose. Like the McKnight Company, the United Holding Company began with limited capital in 1906, acquired seventy-seven acres of farmland, and was building and selling houses by 1910. Perhaps the acreage was too small for Chambers to have considered it or the residential construction too new to be included in his chapter. Another possibility was that, unlike the other companies he wrote about, the general manager of the United Holding Company was a woman.

When it was founded in 1906, the United Holding Company had five directors, two of whom were Mr. and Mrs. Frank A. E. Marsh of Lynn, Massachusetts. Mrs. Helen Marsh (1868–1954) served first as treasurer, but advanced to become the general manager, as it was largely through her vision and efforts that the company was a success in the Long Island real estate market. It was Helen Marsh's idea to transform a large gladiola farm alongside the Long Island Railroad near Floral

Park into a community of affordable homes within easy commuting distance of New York City. It was Helen Marsh who made Bellerose a true community, partly by showing her confidence in Bellerose's success by becoming one of its residents, but more importantly by motivating her neighbors into taking active roles in the community through civic and social groups and continuing in these roles after Bellerose incorporated as a village.

Few if any of the real estate companies would have existed without a convergence of national trends that occurred around the turn of the twentieth century. The foremost trend was the shift of the population from rural to predominantly urban areas, made possible by a growing, wage-earning middle class.[3] As cities became more crowded, the middle class became a ready market for suburban homes, interest in which accelerated as improvements in transportation linked the suburbs to the cities. Another factor was a series of economic depressions that disproportionately affected agriculture, causing steep declines in commodity prices and in the value of farmland.[4] Farms in close proximity to cities found themselves in competition with factories, offices, and shops that offered better wages for workers. Farmers watched as their children left for steady wage jobs in the cities and saw little recourse but to take the best available offer for their lands.[5] Census records for Queens and Nassau counties showed steady declines in the number of farms between 1880 and 1910, dropping from 2,966 to 1,737.[6]

On Long Island, improvements in the railroad already linked summer resorts with New York City, enabling city dwellers seeking temporary relief from the heat to escape to the country or the seashore. These part-time Long Island residents were ready to become permanent residents as soon as the commute to and from the city could be done within a day. As the Long Island Railroad made additional improvements, real estate developers scooped up available farmlands and carved out new, year-round settlements geared toward wage earners desiring more space and an affordable house in a healthy climate where they could raise a family.

According to one account, it was the Long Island Railroad that gave Helen Marsh her first glimpse in 1899 of what became the Village of Bellerose.[7] Mrs. Marsh was a veteran of the real estate field, employed by attorney Calvin Tuttle in her hometown of Lynn, Massachusetts, to manage his property holdings. After reading about plans to connect Manhattan with Long Island via new bridges and tunnels, she saw an opportunity to strike out on her own as a real estate developer

Helen Marsh, ca. 1900. Courtesy Historical Commission, Village of Bellerose.

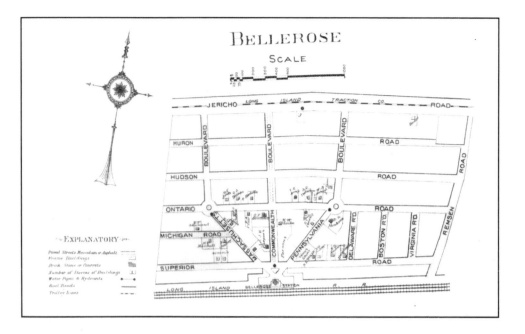

Map of Bellerose, ca. 1920. Atlas of Nassau County, Long Island, NY (New York: E. Belcher Hyde, 1914)

and embarked on an exploratory tour of Long Island. As she crossed from Queens into Nassau County, she saw the large farm of Joseph Rose and returned to it after looking at other possible properties. The Rose Farm was ideal; being at the edge of the Nassau County line, it was far enough away from the city to be picturesque but close enough to travel to the city within an hour. After creating the United Holding Company in 1906 and raising $155,000, Mrs. Marsh acquired seventy-seven acres between the Jericho Turnpike and the Long Island Railroad just east of the Nassau County boundary with Queens.

Before any planning or work could be done on the company's new suburb, the Panic of 1907 hit Wall Street. The crisis was triggered by the failure of the Knickerbocker Trust Bank, one of the largest banks in the country, and it caused the stock market to decline, brought investments to a halt, and put the entire Bellerose project in jeopardy. Added to this were rising prices and increased unemployment. Undaunted, Mrs. Marsh was determined to see the Bellerose project through and brought in an engineer to begin laying out streets and plots. She pledged her own securities for the project and obtained additional financing from farmers in Floral Park who were also eager see the development become a reality. Their lands created the village, and the last thing they wanted was for the United Holding Company to go into foreclosure.

By 1910, Bellerose was starting to take shape. Recognizing that the railroad was a focal point of the community, Mrs. Marsh's engineer laid out the streets in a pattern similar to that of some large cities where boulevards converged at public spaces, rather than in the standard grid pattern. The streets of Bellerose fanned out from the newly named Superior Road, which ran parallel to the railroad tracks. Three wide boulevards converged at Superior. In the center was Commonwealth Boulevard, which had center islands for trees and flowers. Halfway between Superior and Jericho Turnpike, a cross street connected the boulevards with roundabouts at the intersections. The village was oriented toward the railroad and away from Jericho Turnpike, which became the commercial district. The street pattern effectively shielded the residents from the busy turnpike but ensured that they were within walking distance of shops and stores. As the houses were built, Mrs. Marsh had them landscaped to enhance the suburban experience and hired a caretaker to do additional gardening as well as keep the sidewalks clean and clear of snow in the winter.[8]

Like the developers of other planned communities on Long Island, Mrs. Marsh insisted on complete architectural control and approval of all house designs, with the intention that no two houses would be alike.[9] Whereas some real estate developers employed an architect to design houses, Mrs. Marsh's control effectively eliminated the need for architects at Bellerose, and none was required as house plans were readily available through newspapers and magazines. One of these publications was Edward Bok's *Ladies' Home Journal*, the most widely circulated magazine in the country. By 1903, it had a circulation of more than a million readers. The house patterns featured in the magazine were geared toward purchasers with an average annual income of $1,200–2,500, putting homeownership well within the reach of the middle class.[10] Houses were also modest, lacking the ornate embellishments that inflated costs and were often statements more about the builder's skill and the tastes of the homeowner. Magazines like *Ladies' Home Journal, House Beautiful, Collier's,* and *Munsey's* set about reshaping the way Americans thought about their homes and neighborhoods. Plans were heavily weighted toward the Arts and Crafts and Colonial Revival styles, although some innovative designs from a Chicago architect named Frank Lloyd Wright also appeared in the publications. The purpose of the designs was to popularize the idea of owning a tasteful, efficient, affordable home that could be a refuge from the cares of work in the city.[11]

Mrs. Marsh was certainly aware of the house styles popularized by the magazines. The United Holding Company began by building model homes, but as lots were sold, homeowners could supply their own house plans as long as they received Mrs. Marsh's approval. Between 1910 and 1922, 117 residences were built in Bellerose, many of them reflecting the tasteful, popular styles seen in the magazines. Several of the homes featured the Tudor Revival half-timbering or the sweeping, asymmetrical Arts and Crafts façade with its steeply pitched roofline and projecting entrance. Many more were gambrel-roofed Dutch Colonials. All houses were two stories, of wood-frame construction, and with either clapboard or stucco exteriors. Despite the similarities of styles, Mrs. Marsh was true to her word, and each house was different from the next. A row of Dutch Colonials had variations in porch widths, entrance locations, projecting entrances, and window placements. Some were sited with the gambrel end facing the street and some had hipped roofs. Variations were also seen in the Tudor Revival and Arts and Crafts homes, though all had the characteristic peaked gables and high-pitched roofs. Over the years, garages were added that mimicked the style of the house, also with official approval.

From the outset, Mrs. Marsh kept a close watch on her enterprise, moving into a house that already existed on the property when construction began on the first of the homes. As new homes were built, she moved from one house to another, presumably selling the houses as she left them. No reason was ever stated for this interesting fact, but it could be assumed that Mrs. Marsh used the buildings as model homes to show to prospective buyers. A tastefully furnished home was much more appealing than an empty shell and provided visual suggestions on how one could decorate beautifully. Furthermore, an occupied house created the impression that people were moving into the community. To increase the appeal of the house, she added flowers and shrubs and continued to supply plantings for all houses built in Bellerose. She also chose the building paint schemes, further guaranteeing that each house would be different from the next.

Suburban homes were designed with family living in mind. When it came to marketing, Mrs. Marsh clearly targeted women; that is, she promoted the domestic aspect of Bellerose and went beyond the traditional sale approaches with personal appeals. Like its competitors, the United Holding Company placed notices of land for sale in the classified sections of newspapers. In addition to ads, Mrs. Marsh maintained an apartment in Manhattan where she invited prospective couples for tea and to learn about Bellerose in a more relaxed setting. For those unwilling or reluctant to take the train ride to the new development, it was a way to bring Bellerose to the potential customer and sell them on the charms of suburban living. She also held receptions in Bellerose for new brides at whichever house she was living in at the time.

Women were also encouraged to take an active role in the community through two organizations: the Bellerose Association and the Bellerose Women's Club. The Bellerose Association was established in 1908 to give property owners a voice in determining how to use their collective resources for the improvement of the community. These improvements included maintaining roads and building parks. Each member had a vote in which projects to promote, and membership was open to both men and women. In 1917, it was renamed the Bellerose Civic Association, and membership was limited to male property owners, with the exception of Helen Marsh, who retained final approval on construction projects and building plans. The purpose of the reorganized association was to establish bylaws for the fledgling community, conduct business with utilities and private companies for improvements, and set construction standards. The association even established a range for construction costs from $2,500 to $6,000, well within the reach of the middle class.[12] The 1920 federal census listed a number of white-collar workers, ranging from clerks and sales personnel to shopkeepers and managers, living in Bellerose. Mrs. Marsh's efforts on behalf of Bellerose resulted in its designation as an official stop on the Long Island Railroad and the construction of a new station building. She also added important services, including the volunteer fire department and firehouse, as well as water, telephone, and eventually electric service. The association continued adding amenities such as gas service, a

police station, a church (St. Thomas Episcopal Church), a grocery delivery service, and an
omnibus for travel to the train station. When
Bellerose incorporated as a village in 1924, the
civic improvement tasks, which included continuing bylaws and restrictions initiated by Mrs.
Marsh and the association, were taken over by
the village government.

With women restricted from joining the reorganized association, the Bellerose Women's Club
became their outlet for community participation.
Founded in 1911 by Mrs. Marsh, it originally had
a membership of three but quickly grew, with
Mrs. Marsh serving as its first president and hon-
orary president thereafter. The club was part of
the national Woman's Club movement, which was
an outgrowth of the literary study clubs found
all across the country. By the turn of the twentieth century, the clubs expanded their role from
socialization and self-improvement to "committee"
work, which created subgroups to improve schools,
build libraries, establish parks, beautify communities, promote health and sanitation, and establish
scholarships.[13] The Bellerose Women's Club met at

first in the train station but raised money to purchase land and construct its own building in 1922.
In 1933, a Junior Women's Club was organized to
take over the majority of the "committee work,"
specifically charity work geared toward children
and education. In 1962, the club reorganized and
officially associated with the General Federation of
Women's Clubs, a national organization that was
founded in 1890.

All of the organizations founded by Mrs. Marsh
survived in one form or another. Duties handled by
the Bellerose Civic Association were taken over by
the village and building approvals formally passed
to an Architectural Review Board when it was created in 1970. Both women's clubs continued to be
very active and the Junior Women's Club created an
annual scholarship named in Mrs. Marsh's honor
for a deserving high school senior. The village itself
has survived remarkably intact. A description from
1929 could be applied to Bellerose today: "prettily
laid out gardens of the home owners, the trees and
shrubs which line the streets, and the fact that no
two houses are alike from outward appearances,
have greatly enhanced the beauty of the surround-

ings and thereby added another contributing factor to Bellerose's likeability."[14] The street plan is still evident and although the old railroad station was replaced, Bellerose is still a stop on the Long Island Railroad.

Success allowed Mrs. Marsh to have a winter home in Sarasota, Florida, where she died in 1954. Her husband, Frank, kept his residence in Lynn, Massachusetts, where he died in 1948. Helen and Frank Marsh are buried next to each other in Pine Grove Cemetery in Lynn, but neither grave has a marker. It seems ironic that the "final residence" of such an innovative and creative woman would be relatively obscure. The success of Bellerose and its adherence to her vision serves as a living monument to her remarkable life and achievements, and she deserves to be counted among Julius Chambers's roster of "the brilliant and suggestive minds . . . of this new profession."

7

KENSINGTON AND DOUGLAS MANOR

THE RICKERT-FINLAY REALTY COMPANY

KEVIN WOLFE

In 1904, just two years after its founding, the Rickert-Finlay Realty Company advertised itself as "the largest developer of real estate in Queens Borough—over 10,000 lots within the limits of New York City."[1] Beginning in 1902, the fledgling firm purchased more than a thousand acres of prime land for developments they planned at Long Island City (Norwood, 1904) and Astoria (East River Heights, 1904), Bayside (Bellcourt, 1904), Flushing (Broadway-Flushing, 1906) Douglaston (Douglas Manor, 1906), Little Neck (Wesmoreland, 1907), all in Queens, and at Great Neck (Kensington, 1909) in Nassau County.

The firm's modus operandi was always the same: to buy farmland, typically a waterfront site or one with water views, and market it to the ever-increasing middle class as an upscale community. Rickert-Finlay continually refined their plan, taking what they learned from one development and applying it to the next, and with each new one they strove for a more prosperous clientele.

Their first two developments, East River Heights in Astoria, a 160-acre site with a mile of waterfront facing the East 80s, and Norwood, several blocks in Long Island City facing East 96th Street, consisted of multifamily, low-rise apartment buildings that sought to compete with the increasingly crowded apartment blocks and tenements on the East Side of Manhattan. At Norwood, four-story-high, freestanding masonry apartment buildings were built out of Indiana limestone and brick with two units per floor and courtyards separating the sides and rear of the buildings. The buildings were advertised for their lightness and airiness, as well as for their proximity to the newly built Queensboro Bridge ("six minutes") and the soon-to-be-opened tunnels to midtown Manhattan under the East River. Each of the buildings also included a playground on the roof and a roof garden, and lot coverage was 50 percent instead of the usual 70 percent, ensuring "ample opportunities for light and air around the building." Norwood was intended to appeal to "residents who want all of the available benefits of suburban homes."[2] Rickert-Finlay built some of the apartment houses at Norwood but also sold lots to other apartment developers. The firm aimed its advertising campaign squarely at the Manhattan apartment dweller who was tired of the city's congestion and cramped apartments with few amenities. This urban apartment dweller, fed up with the city but dependent on working there for his livelihood, was the slice of the market that Rickert-Finlay continued to mine for all of their developments, even the most exclusive ones, over the next two decades.

They soon branched out from apartment developments—though they continued to develop Norwood into the 1920s—to communities of single-family houses, culminating in their most luxurious of all, Kensington, just over the New York City line in Nassau County and just "29 minutes from Broadway" by rail.[3]

The Rickert-Finlay firm had three partners: Charles E. Finlay and the brothers Edward J.

Rickert-Finlay's sales office at the Broadway-Flushing railroad stop. The Douglaston and Little Neck Historical Society (DLNHS)

(E. J.) and Charles H. Rickert. Midwesterners by birth, the Rickerts and Finlay were well educated and socially prominent in the small cities in which they lived and worked. Finlay was born in 1861 in Quincy, Illinois, and graduated from the University of Notre Dame in 1885 with a law degree. He immediately moved to Kansas City to start his career. E. J. Rickert was also born in 1861, in Dubuque, Iowa, and he, too, graduated from Notre Dame with a law degree. Charles Rickert, five years older than his brother, had attended the University of Minnesota. All three were already familiar with single-family house development by the time they moved to New York. Both E. J. Rickert and Finlay had worked in Kansas City real estate for nearly two decades independently of each other. E. J. had had his own general real estate and loan company, which specialized in subdivisions.[4] Charles Rickert had lived in Galveston, St. Louis, and Denver before moving to Kansas City.[5]

Finlay gained a reputation as a successful developer of single-family subdivisions in Kansas City, which was burgeoning in the late nineteenth century. In 1902, at age forty, he was profiled in a book entitled *Men Who Are Making Kansas City* (the Rickerts were not). The authors state that as the organizer and president of the Charles E. Finlay Real Estate Company, "one of the largest real estate companies in the city,"[6] Finlay had platted 40 subdivisions and built 350 houses since his arrival in Kansas City in 1885. His developments were considered desirable (today, a century later, realtors still advertise these

houses as being in "the Finlay subdivision"), and he and his wife, Ann Redfield Finlay, were active socially, hosting parties and participating in philanthropic community efforts.

In addition to Finlay's accomplishments as a real estate developer, he was the secretary and general manager of the Apex Oil Company—"one of the largest oil companies in Texas"—and the secretary and treasurer of the Southwestern Oil and Steamship Company, a "transport company to carry refined and crude oil from Texas to the North Atlantic and Gulf ports." The book also mentions that he was a resident of Kansas City, with offices in New York.[7] But in fact, Finlay had already moved to Englewood, New Jersey, in 1898, and become a mortgage broker. It is likely that he left his Kansas City endeavors in the hands of the Rickert brothers while he laid the groundwork for a new company in New York. Soon after moving east, he founded Aetna National Bank, naming himself president. It was later absorbed by the Broadway Trust Company. By 1902, he and E. J. had founded the Rickert-Finlay Realty Company in New York; they opened an office at 45 West 34th Street, two blocks from Pennsylvania Terminal, already under construction, and started buying land in Queens.

When the Rickerts and Finlay made the move to New York, each was in his forties at the height of a prosperous career and, in Finlay's case, a well-established social life. Over the next thirty years they used their education, social connections, and experience to create multiple real estate enterprises that

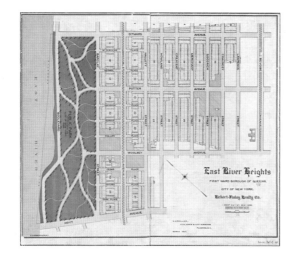

Map of East River Heights showing the park land facing the East River and Manhattan set aside as part of the Rickert-Finlay development.

covered everything from banking and mortgage brokering to subdivisions and house construction.

Upon their arrival in the city, the three men were poised to participate in one of the biggest land booms in the country's history, the result of a nexus of transportation development by multiple private entrepreneurs that was aimed at connecting Manhattan with its newly annexed suburban territories following the consolidation of New York City in 1898. No other American city was building a transportation system on such a scale; the construction of trolley lines, subways, the East River tunnels, and roads for automobiles, as well as the electrification of the North Shore rail line running from the new Pennsylvania Terminal through Queens and

into Nassau County, were all taking place in one frenetic decade between 1900 and 1910.

The Rickerts and Finlay saw the North Shore of Long Island, from Astoria to Great Neck, a stretch of less than twenty miles, as among the most profitable places to develop new, mostly suburban neighborhoods, and they had the experience and know-how to do it. While other developers of their time faltered or were ruined by the panic of 1907 and the other economic ups and downs that followed, Rickert-Finlay Realty thrived.

The partners concentrated all of their development energies along the north shore of Queens, never venturing farther east than their Kensington development in Great Neck, just over the city line, and they did this in a span of just seven years. The North Shore Railroad, later the Long Island Railroad, had built the rail line to Great Neck way back in 1866. In the first decade of the twentieth century, the forty-year-old infrastructure was undergoing major improvements: construction of the East River tunnels for a direct connection to Manhattan; electrification; and double-tracking of the rail line to increase service.[8]

In advertisements for their first two developments, East River Heights and Norwood, Rickert-Finlay boasted that the land cost a tenth of land in Manhattan and that the new subway lines, the East River tunnels, and the Queensboro Bridge would connect these two sites to Manhattan with a short commute. In an ad in the Queens Cham-

The nearly mile-long allée of trees planted thirty years earlier was a strong selling point for the Kensington development, giving the place a sense of being "established." Village of Kensington Archive (VKA)

Entrance to Douglas Manor

Douglas Manor

A BEAUTIFUL
REJIDENTIAL PARK
With over a mile of Jhore Front
DOUGLAJTON L.I.

TWENTY MINUTEJ FROM
HERALD JQUARE
When the tunnelJ are completed

Rickert-Finlay Realty Co
45 WEJT 34th JT.

A Rickert-Finlay advertisement extolling the virtues of its new development at Douglas Manor. DLNHS

ber of Commerce, designed to attract developers to buy parcels at Norwood, Rickert-Finlay made no small claims, stating:

IF YOU WANT TO PROFIT from the construction of **THE GREATEST RAPID TRANSIT SYSTEM IN THE WORLD**, investigate **NORWOOD** which will have a five-cent fare over every foot of the **dual subway system** in Greater New York, **with four hundred and eighty-six miles** of track costing **three hundred and fourteen million dollars.** This will give Norwood **better rapid transit facilities** than any other part of the Bronx, Brooklyn, or Manhattan north of 59th Street.[10]

By the time Rickert-Finlay started developing luxurious single-family houses at Kensington in Great Neck in 1909, they were light-years away from their earliest projects in terms of the level of development and the affluence of the buyer they pursued. If Norwood was intended as a greener version of the urban East Side of Manhattan—four-story apartment buildings separated by trees and courtyards—Kensington was only a step down from the vast North Shore estates of millionaires nearby.

The 130-acre former farm tract that Rickert-Finlay bought at Great Neck was the most "improved" of their developments, and the most ambitious. Thirty years earlier, the previous owner of the property had had the foresight to plant a nearly mile-long allée of linden and maple trees along what would become the main thoroughfare, Beverly Road, giving Kensington the air of an "established place" by the time Rickert-Finlay bought it.[11]

The site was in an ideal location for getting to Manhattan quickly and easily. The Great Neck

railroad station was four blocks away, and when the East River rail tunnels opened in 1910, the commute from Kensington to Pennsylvania Station on the Port Washington line was clocked at twenty-six-minutes, and there were forty-four trains daily.[12]

In an age before zoning, Rickert-Finlay essentially created their own zoning code, using deed restrictions to limit and define the character of all their developments and focusing the later ones exclusively on single-family houses. Deed restrictions prohibited commercial development, mandated setbacks, prohibited front yard fences, dictated the location of stables and outbuildings, and required a minimum construction cost for the houses. At Kensington they even established an architectural review board to ensure that any houses built would be "tasteful."

Rickert-Finlay established a property owners' association for each development, and once a critical mass of residents lived there, the firm relinquished control of the association to the homeowners. The restrictions were incorporated into each homeowner's deed and had no expiration date. It was up to the property owners' association to carry out enforcement. The deed restrictions required each homeowner to contribute a yearly fee to the association, which maintained common property and the streets, plowed roads and sidewalks, cut the hedges and grass strip between the roadway and the public sidewalk, and removed trash. No one could not belong to the homeowners' association.

Both Kensington and Douglas Manor included park and recreation facilities that the homeowners owned in common. Douglas Manor was touted as the most improved development on Long Island. When the property opened for sales in March 1906 during a severe snowstorm, 1,200 people showed

81

William P. Douglas.
DLNHS

up at the former Douglas estate to buy lots. In two weeks Rickert-Finlay sold more than $1 million worth of lots, more than any development before it, proving there was a market for more sophisticated planning and improvements.[13]

Three years later, Rickert-Finlay upped the ante at Kensington, increasing their investment significantly with bigger lots, buried utilities, and an extensive recreation complex on Manhasset Bay. Aimed at a savvy buyer with lots of money to spend, Kensington was designed to impress. Unlike Douglas Manor, it had no modest, middle-class "starter" houses —Kensington was intended to be the be all and end all for most people.

Douglas Manor proved an ideal site—geographically, the 188-acre peninsula was the best site Rickert-Finlay ever had—in which to try a premium development of freestanding single-family houses. In naming the development, Rickert-Finlay was banking on the cachet of the estate's fame and the glamour of its Gilded Age owners. William P. Douglas was a media darling of the late nineteenth century, known for being a playboy sportsman. He successfully defended the America's Cup with his yacht, *Sappho*, in 1871 and promoted polo in the United States along with his best friend, James Gordon Bennett Jr., owner of the *New York Herald*. When Douglas married socialite Adelaide Townsend, the peninsula became the scene of glittering galas and social events, and the Douglases hosted many celebrities of the day.

Rickert-Finlay saw a great marketing opportunity for the Manor, promoting its luster as one of the country's great estates, graced with ancient trees and a scenic waterfront, and at the same time touting its new technological amenities such as electric lights, gas service, and easy access to some of the best-paved automobile roads in the U.S., as well as a relatively quick commute to the city by rail on the Port Washington line. In a promotional brochure for Douglas Manor, Rickert-Finlay extolled the transportation improvements that would link their property to Manhattan, including the new East River tunnels and Pennsylvania Terminal: "It is the greatest transportation development the world has ever seen, and will turn into Long Island the enormous flow of population that has heretofore poured into the Bronx and the northern suburbs."[14]

As with their earlier developments, Rickert-Finlay established deed restrictions for Douglas Manor that were remarkably simple but, in the era before zoning (the first New York City zoning code wasn't established until 1916), contained language assuring buyers that their property would be protected from the industrial incursions that were negatively transforming Manhattan's toniest neighborhoods. Prominent among the restrictions was that private, single-family houses on individual lots would surround any lot buyer. No industry or commercial development was allowed; nor were two-family houses or apartment houses. In addition, houses could not have flat roofs, and fences were prohibited in front yards, ensuring a uniform green space along the street. There were no restrictions on architectural styles or building materials; as a result the houses were eclectic, reflecting the many revival styles of the time. Most houses were custom designed by architects, but there were also speculative houses by builders who bought individual parcels.

The peninsula was divided into 57 blocks with 2,473 lots and 14 streets running east–west, following Manhattan's rectilinear grid plan, in place since 1811, when the city fathers decided to lay out the city's streets in a north–south, east–west grid. Each lot had a frontage of 20 feet and was approximately 100 feet deep, also in accordance with typical New York City lot subdivision.

Deed restrictions dictated lot size, and Rickert-Finlay "zoned" the peninsula from east to west, specifying minimum lot purchases depending on location. The minimum size for a parcel facing Udalls Cove on the east side was two lots, or 40 x 100 feet, whereas the minimum size for a parcel facing the open waters of Little Neck Bay on the west was five lots, or 100 x 100 feet, thereby ensuring a mix of middle- to upper-middle-class homeowners.

Purchasing a lot in the Manor meant buying into two basic ideas: first, all residents would get to know their neighbors because they would be in close proximity to one another; second, everyone would share the use and maintenance of the jointly owned landscape—the mile-long waterfront, with its boat dock and beach. The relatively small lots and the shape of the peninsula, which is only three blocks wide at its base near the railroad station, and the narrow streets designed for horse-drawn carriages rather than cars, reinforce the village-like quality of the Manor to this day.

Early residents ranged from schoolteachers and civil servants of modest means to CEOs of corporations, lawyers, and other professionals. The Manor's relative isolation—despite its accessibility—attracted a good number of silent screen and theater stars who worked at the nearby Astoria Studios and on Broadway. They would flock to Kensington as well.

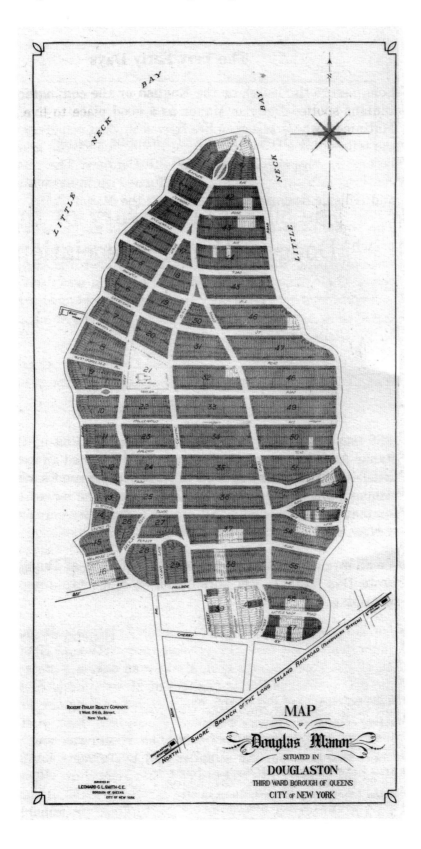

A Rickert-Finlay map of Douglas Manor. DLNHS

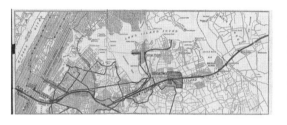

Map of rail lines through Northern Queens highlighting the location of Rickert-Finlay's Broadway Flushing development.

A hundred years ago, the majority of lots in the Manor had a view of Little Neck Bay because of the Douglas estate's open meadows and predominantly hilly topography. Some of the most desirable lots were not on the waterfront at all, but on the hilliest terrain close to the railroad station, and that is where a number of the Manor's largest and most impressive houses were built. From these hills one had a panoramic view of Little Neck Bay to Fort Totten in Bayside and beyond, an unobstructed view of Lower Manhattan, where skyscrapers like the Singer Building, Liberty Tower, and the Woolworth Building were clustered, each of which held for a moment—sometimes for only a few weeks—the title of "Tallest Building in the World."

Despite its seeming rigidity, the Manor's grid plan proved to be quite flexible, and the layout of the roads was adjusted to accommodate the hilly topography, resulting in some lots with a depth greater or shallower than the normal 100 feet, which added quirkiness and visual variety to the plan. The subtle curve of the roads created enticing glimpses of the woods along the east side, facing the tidal estuary of Udalls Cove and Gabler's Creek, and of Little Neck Bay to the west. None of Rickert-Finlay's developments followed the then-fashionable curvilinear layouts employed by Olmsted and Vaux at developments in the Midwest like Riverside, near Chicago, or closer to home, by the Olmsted Brothers at Forest Hills Gardens and by Robert Anderson Pope at nearby Great Neck Estates, just across the bay from the Manor.

The Manor's streets were given appropriately English-sounding names—Kenmore, Beverly, and Arleigh Roads, for example (also used at Kensington)—meant to evoke the stability of Old England; the north–south street names—East, Centre, and West Drives—were directional.

More sophisticated planning went into creating Douglas Manor than Broadway-Flushing, Westmoreland, or Bellcourt, including the preservation of some of the features that made it special, such as its ancient trees. Unlike the other Rickert-Finlay sites, which were all originally farms, the peninsula, owned by the Douglas family for nearly seventy years, was a pleasure ground. Both William P. Douglas, who sold the estate to Rickert-Finlay, and his father, George, planted the property with trees from all over the world, acquired by their friend Samuel Parsons, of the famous Parsons Nursery in Flushing. By the time the estate was sold, the peninsula contained a mature collection of carefully sited specimen trees, including Long Island's oldest white oak—then five hundred years old—a stand of native oaks and beech trees more than 150 years old, and a pinetum. Rickert-Finlay saved as many of these trees as possible. In some spots, the roads were made to jog gracefully around a large tree to preserve it; at horse-and-carriage speed, the presence of a majestic tree in the middle of a road only added to the picturesque effect.

The Manor's trees were heavily promoted and were often favorably compared with those of Central Park, which had come into its own as one of New York City's great attractions. According to Rickert-Finlay's promotional materials, ". . . Central Park does not possess a greater variety of rare trees."[15] The trees of the Douglas era and their exotic provenance proved highly marketable, as did the idea of living in a private park. The company produced a separate pamphlet—"The Trees of Douglas Manor by W. R. Griffith." Handed out to

A bird's-eye view of the Douglas Manor peninsula for a promotional brochure showing the subdivision's proximity to two railroad stations at Little Neck and Douglaston, both within walking distance. DLNHS

View of the east side of the Douglas Manor peninsula, facing Great Neck Estates. Its roads are still unpaved and its quasi-rural character is still intact.
DLNHS

Rickert-Finlay made an effort to preserve trees at the Douglas estate, even if it meant that a tree would be in the middle of a roadway, as seen here at the intersection of West Drive and Knollwood Avenue.
DLNHS

prospective buyers, it described the trees in the most romantic possible way:

Sunlit groups of White and European Beeches greet the eye, including the penciled outline of the Fern Leaved; Great Elms, Sweet Gums with their pretty tassel balls and most varied of rich coloring in the fall; the rare sweet blossomed Yellowwood; splendid great Sugar Maples and Scarlet Maples, glories of autumnal color; Horse Chestnuts, flowering Tulip Trees and native and exotic Limes; great satin barked Oriental Sycamores, so popular in France, sturdy Black Oaks, columnar Lombardy Poplars, grand spreading Chestnuts, and the virile Ash; while among the many evergreens are found the Great White and Austrian Pines, the Canadian White Fir, Blue Spruces, contrasting with the cheerful constant greens of their congeners, the Oriental and the bristling Tiger-tail, also layered Hemlocks, and the neat compact Swiss Stone Pine.

Rickert-Finlay also planted trees, thousands of them, and fifteen miles of California privet hedge to separate front yard property lines from the public sidewalk. The maintenance of the hedges was borne by the association. The street trees the firm

planted were silver maples, a financial choice, as maple saplings cost 3 cents apiece, whereas oak saplings cost 5 cents. Silver maples have a rapid growth pattern, and their form is similar to that of the vase-shaped American elm. The maples were planted both on the green strip between the public sidewalk and the curb and on the property owners' side of the sidewalk in a staggered pattern roughly twenty-five feet apart. The intent was to create a cathedral-like arching of branches over the narrow streets, and when the trees planted on both sides of the four-foot-wide concrete sidewalk reached maturity, they formed a narrow pedestrian allée delineated by the their strong, muscular form and shaggy silvery bark.

Remarkably, the layout of roads of the Douglas era was incorporated into the subdivision. It is thought that these roads may have been beaten into the earth by the Matinecoc Indians, the first inhabitants of the peninsula, and then used by Colonial settlers as roads separating the fields and meadows of their farms. The roads are described in various ancient deeds and maps.[16]

Later additions, like the nineteenth-century carriage turnaround near the tip of the peninsula, the culmination of one of the pleasure drives that Douglas built, were also incorporated into the design. Curved concrete sidewalks now outline what had once been the circumference of the turning circle for horse and carriage.

By 1911, the old pier and boathouse of the Douglas estate were reconstructed in concrete and steel, and a roofed dancing pavilion was added at the end of the pier. DLNHS

The Van Wyck house, built in 1735, became the headquarters of the Douglaston Country Club when the Douglas Manor subdivision opened in 1906, but was later sold for use as a private house. DLNHS

Rickert-Finlay also saw fit to save and reuse most of the Douglas estate's existing buildings, including the 1819 Federal-style mansion with twenty-two bedrooms that had served as the Douglas residence for eight decades. Located at the center of the peninsula on a three-acre site, it was converted into the Douglas Manor Inn and operated as a hotel. A stable and a windmill were converted into a house and guesthouse, respectively. The Greek Revival–style 1848 Allen mansion, which the Douglases had used as a guesthouse, and an 1870s tenant farmhouse were sold for use as private homes. The Douglases' rustic, wooden, 200-hundred-foot-long pier and boathouse at the foot of Beverly Road were retained for the use of all homeowners. They were soon reconstructed in concrete and steel, and a roofed dancing pavilion was built at the end of the pier.

The 1735 Van Wyck farmhouse—one of the oldest Dutch houses in New York City—was converted into the Douglaston Country Club, and a nine-hole golf course overlooking the bay was built. Initially, membership in the club was obligatory, to promote "social intercourse" among the residents.[17] By 1921, however, the Van Wyck house was sold for private use and the golf course for building lots. The club was reorganized as the Douglaston Club, and membership for Douglas Manor residents was no longer required. The club bought the Douglas mansion and its three-acre site from the hotel operators and remains there to this day.

Shore Road at the original Douglas dock, where the mast of the Douglas yacht, Sappho, was used as a flagpole. DLNHS

Perhaps Rickert-Finlay's most radical notion was to give ownership of the mile-long waterfront to the residents, providing them all with access to Little Neck Bay. To own land in common with your neighbors was an unusual idea in 1906. Other developments of the time, like those that began in the 1870s at nearby Bayside, typically placed private lots along the most desirable waterfront, denying visual or physical access to Little Neck Bay to anyone other than the lot owners.

The common ownership of the shorefront at the Manor was not only a brilliant planning device but also an incredibly smart marketing ploy. Providing all lot owners with access to the entire waterfront meant that every lot in the Manor—no matter what the location—could command a higher price and that Rickert-Finlay would get a higher return from

their development in general. As a result, there were no "bad" lots, even though the eastern third of the peninsula faced a tidal creek and wetlands at Udalls Cove that became mud flats at low tide.

Shore Road, which separates the houses from the waterfront on the western side of the peninsula— where there were no mud flats at low tide, only rocky beach—remains a beloved amenity today. This lightly traveled, one-lane roadway is still used as a pedestrian promenade and bikeway, though walkers and cyclists do share it with an occasional car.

Rickert-Finlay's deed restrictions made no provision for an architecture committee to review proposed house designs and make aesthetic judgments. The company later decided that this omission was a flaw and sought to correct it at Kensington. As E. J. Rickert commented:

One of the largest houses built at Douglas Manor on Shore Road, designed by Lionel Moses, an architect from the office of McKim, Mead & White, 1907. DLNHS

This early Douglas Manor house displays all the amenities of houses typical of the era—open "piazza," covered porch, canvas awnings, and shutters to cool the house in the hot summer months. DLNHS

In the development of previous properties, the Company found that it was not safe to leave the architectural character of the houses to the discretion of the purchasers, for whereas a majority of the homebuilders would employ good architects, others would not do so, and the beauty of the property would be marred by architectural failures.[18]

The Manor's new residents hired mostly Brooklyn and Queens architects, some of whom lived in the Manor, as well as better-known Manhattan architectural firms, from Buchman & Fox, designers of department stores on Ladies' Mile, to Lionel Moses from the office of McKim, Mead & White. Other well-known architects included Diego de Suarez, designer of the gardens at Villa Vizcaya, the Deering estate outside of Miami, and gardens at Villa La Pietra near Florence, Italy; Frank For-

ster, who designed many estate houses on Long Island and was part of the team that designed the Harlem River Houses, the first public housing project in New York City; George Keister, designer of Manhattan theaters and hotels; and Gustav Stickley, the leader of the American Arts and Crafts movement, whose magazine, *The Craftsman*, promoted the Arts and Crafts style by publishing house plans.[19] Three Stickley houses were built. The Manor includes what may be the largest collection of Arts and Crafts–style houses in New York City, and many of the other revival-style houses feature Arts and Crafts touches and detailing.

The architecture of the Manor reflects its time—eclectic, reserved, and for the most part, sharing a commonly held middle-class notion of "good taste." Materials included wood shingle, clapboard, or

The white concrete entry
gate to Rickert-Finlay's
Kensington development,
modeled on the gate of one
of the palazzos at Frascati
outside of Rome. VKA

E. J. Rickert's "Italianate-
style" mansion, designed
by C. P. H. Gilbert, at
the north side of the entry
to Kensington. By 1919
he had sold this house
and bought an estate in
Connecticut. VKA

stucco siding, and wood, slate, or tile roofs. Exterior detailing was simple, with doors, trim, and windows limited to basic shapes, the windows sometimes elaborated with leaded glass. The more exuberant styles and multicolored exteriors of the Victorian age were no longer fashionable; Manor residents built houses in the Tudor Revival, Colonial Revival, and Mediterranean Revival styles, in addition to the Arts and Crafts style, which emphasized earthy colors and architecture that connected the building to its site and indoors to outdoors. Many houses had open porches, or "piazzas," with canvas awnings for shade, screened porches, or vine-covered arbors to retreat to in a time before air conditioning lured people indoors during the summer.

When Rickert-Finlay started to develop Kensington in 1909, they decided to pursue an even more

affluent buyer. At the entrance to the development on Middle Neck Road, the main north–south road on the Great Neck peninsula, the firm built an impressive white marbleized concrete gateway modeled after the gateway of one of the great Renaissance palazzos at Frascati outside Rome, and echoing those of the estates being built nearby.[20]

The scale of the early houses at Kensington— including E. J. Rickert's and Charles Finlay's own mansions, which flanked the development's main gateway—rivaled in size and opulence some of the grandest North Shore mansions. Advertising materials mentioned the close proximity to Kensington of the estates of some of the richest families in America, including the Vanderbilts, Whitneys, and Morgans, to name a few.[21] Although the "typical" Kensington houses were not as impressive as

Rickert's and Finlay's, they cost from $12,000 to $60,000, which was a small fortune relative to what most Americans could afford, considering that the average salary was $750 per year. Kensington residents were among the economic elite.

The well-known architects C. P. H. Gilbert and Aymar Embury II designed many of Kensington's early houses.[22] Like other established architects working in Kensington in the early years, Gilbert and Embury were simultaneously designing extravagant country houses nearby for industrialists until the establishment of a national income tax in 1913 began curtailing the lifestyles of America's very wealthy. Rickert-Finlay seemed to anticipate this diminution of grandeur, or at least the desire among the very well-to-do for a lower-maintenance lifestyle, while still enjoying a large house with luxurious amenities nearby. At Kensington, Rickert-Finlay created a setting for small estate-like parcels on lots of a half acre or more. The typical lot had 300 feet of street frontage and was 100 feet deep, to ensure that there would be no crowding of houses, a criticism of their earlier developments.

The posh Great Neck Golf Club, just outside of Kensington, was within walking distance. Kensington also had its own police force with watchmen's boxes at key entry points. And though the site was on the waterfront, Rickert-Finlay's brochures assured prospective buyers that Kensington was safe from disease: ". . . possessing an elevation of 150 feet, practically eliminating mosquitoes, malaria and other objections to water-level locations."[23]

Unlike Rickert-Finlay's other developments, Kensington was not within New York City but in Nassau County, so its only organized local government was the Town of North Hempstead. And though Kensington had the typical amenities for developments at the time—macadam roads, cement sidewalks, street tree plantings, and gas service—these amenities and the level of service exceeded anything developers had ever done before. Through an easement, electric and telephone lines were located at the center of the blocks out of sight, and decorative poles with buried electric lines brought light to the privately owned streets. The development included two complete drainage systems, one for sewage that was state approved and cost more than $100,000 to build and another for surface water (Douglas Manor to this day still relies on cesspools and septic systems).[24] They even built a sprinkler system for "dry spells."[25]

E. J. Rickert's mansion just to the north of the entry gateway was a massive stucco villa designed by C. P. H. Gilbert in what was described as the "Italianate style," and Finlay's equally elaborate Southern Colonial–style mansion, directly opposite to the south, was designed by Little & Brown with a two-story-high colonnaded entry portico and extensive and fantastic gardens. Both houses were made of the latest fireproof terra-cotta tile—another feature the company heavily advertised for new construction at Kensington—which was then coated with stucco and finished with white marble dust that reflected the light, to match the finish of the entrance gate to the development. The entry with the two flanking mansions became a great theatrical pièce de résistance, attesting to Rickert and Finlay's skills and their personal commitment.

The Charles Finlay mansion at Kensington was designed by Little & Brown and included elaborate formal gardens. Starrett, "A Beauty Spot," *Architecture and Building* 46 (May 1914), p. 189

Doctor Friedrich Franz Friedmann arrives in New York at the behest of Charles Finlay, with a promised cure for tuberculosis. Left to right, C. A. H. Friedmann, brother of Dr. Friedmann; C. de Vidal Hundt, Friedmann's secretary; C. E. Finlay; Dr. F. F. Friedmann; an unidentified man. Flickr Commons Project 2009 and the *New York Times*, May 30, 1913

With this grand gesture, the two men announced to anyone who passed by—or read about Kensington in the press—the importance of this development in their lives. Not only were they willing to make a huge financial investment in the place, but they also wanted to live there. And they did so as lavishly as their wealthy neighbors building estates north and east of them on the Great Neck and Sands Point peninsulas. (Charles Rickert lived in a luxurious rental apartment in Flushing until his death in 1939.)

For the first time in their New York real estate careers, Rickert-Finlay built both custom and speculative houses for buyers at Kensington, having held a competition to garner twenty of the most impressive architects of the time for buyers to choose from. In addition to Gilbert and Embury, the roster included Walter L. Hopkins, Alfred Busselle, Forman & Light, Frederick Wallick & D. W. Terwilliger, Barnard & Wilder, and Shape & Bready, all accomplished and well known.

Of the three Rickert-Finlay partners, the younger Rickert, or E. J., as he was always identified in the press, became the company spokesman. He was the most outspoken, always at the ready with a pithy quote for news reporters, brimming with data to back up claims about their developments, and endlessly promoting the firm. He repeated the same theme over and over again: Rickert-Finlay developments provided a beautiful, healthy, alternative to the industrialized, despoiled city, yet from each of their developments, one could get to the "City" easily and quickly.

For someone who had arrived in the city so recently, E. J. Rickert rose quickly in New York society. In 1911, with a townhouse on West 72nd Street and his newly completed Kensington mansion, E. J. and his wife presented their daughter Helen to New York society with a party in the newly opened Plaza Hotel's Grand Ballroom, which was decorated with "palms and smilax." Some two hundred guests attended.[26]

Charles Finlay's wife, Ann Redfield Finlay, belonged to the WASP Old Guard. A member of the Daughters of the American Revolution, the Founders and Patriots of New York City, and the North Shore Riding Club,[27] she had honed her hostess and entertaining skills in Kansas City, her entertainments regularly featured in the social pages of the *Kansas City Star*.

Except for discreet references in the social pages, Charles Finlay never appeared in the newspapers. He made headlines in 1913, however, when he announced that he would award $1 million to anyone who would provide a provable cure for tuberculosis. One of the provisions of the award was that the serum had to cure his daughter Neva's husband, who had recently contracted the disease. Finlay interviewed hundreds who showed up at his door, including many cranks, and courted doctors from as far afield as Germany, notably Dr. Friedrich Franz Friedmann. Each was convinced that he was on the verge of a discovery. But eventually the idea was dropped, and Finlay vanished from news accounts.[28] His son-in-law took the cure at a sanitarium at Saranac Lake, and his health improved.[29] Neva later divorced him.

E. J. continued to maintain a high profile, plugging Kensington and Rickert-Finlay tirelessly in the newspapers. He was a man of great imagination, with a will to match. For all of Kensington's ready-built charms, including its centerpiece, the lush and mature allée of trees lining Beverly Road, its convenience to the city, and recreational assets like the nearby Great Neck Golf Club, the site initially lacked a waterfront, a key amenity for Rickert-Finlay's most spectacular development yet. But E. J. was not to be thwarted in his desire for Kensington to be on the water. In an extensive article in *Architecture and Building* magazine in 1914, which included many pages of photos and floor plans of houses already built at Kensington, he explained: "Kensington was at that time nearly half a mile from the head of Manhasset Bay, and it was decided that, as Kensington could not be moved to the water, the water would have to be brought to Kensington."[30]

Rickert-Finlay negotiated with neighboring landowners and the Town of North Hempstead for three years, finally reaching an agreement to allow construction of a 2,000-foot-long canal to reach Manhasset Bay and create a waterfront park at Kensington. The company dredged and filled wetlands to accomplish this: "The canal is two hundred feet wide and has ten feet of water, permitting yachts and motor boats to go right to the dock at Kensington," Rickert said in the article. "It is of generous size, being approximately of the same width as the Panama Canal."[31] The dredging operation also yielded a man-made, 500-foot-long crescent of sandy beach for saltwater swimming. By 1912, the canal was finished, and construction of the other amenities for the waterfront park that all of Kensington's residents would share, had begun.

Created out of landfill, the private waterfront park had a dock that accommodated large yachts, a 5,000-square-foot outdoor swimming pool fed by artesian wells, changing rooms, a "casino" with a restaurant intended to rival the best in Manhattan, a swimming beach on the bay, decorative ponds, and tennis courts, all within a ten-acre site, landscaped in the Japanese style. E. J. Rickert promised that the Japanese-style garden would be the largest in the United States and "an attraction sufficient to bring people from all parts of the country to see."[32] As he told a reporter:

> When it is remembered that Great Neck may be reached by motor car in forty minutes, you can realize the probable popularity which this beautiful garden will have. The general environment, added to by the lights of many Japanese lanterns and of boats on the canal, will serve to complete the illusion of complete isolation from the western world and will undoubtedly attract many motoring parties from busy Broadway for dinner in this unusually beautiful spot.[33]

When questioned, E. J. said he planned to prevent "an undesirable class" of people from visiting the garden by issuing admission cards to Kensington residents and their friends and "desirable New Yorkers known to the owners of the garden." He

Rickert-Finlay created a 500-foot-long sandy beach for saltwater swimming in Manhasset Bay from the dredging operation for the canal, and a dock where the water was ten feet deep at low tide, deep enough to accommodate large yachts.
VKA

E. J. Rickert promised that the ten-acre Kensington park would have the largest Japanese-style garden in the country, with naturalistic ponds and Japanese-style teahouses to serve as private dining rooms. VKA

Tables, benches, and umbrellas surrounded Kensington's hedge-lined, artesian well–fed swimming pool, advertised as one of the largest in the United States, with a constant temperature of 69–75 degrees, summer and winter. VKA

promised that the restaurant would be run by "a well-known New York hotel man, who will have a cuisine satisfying to the critical metropolitan taste." The garden would include "a number of small Japanese tea houses, with thatched roofs, which will be used as out-of-door private dining rooms, and from which Japanese lanterns and lights on the water may be seen to best advantage."[34]

The commission for the park and its structures was given to Embury, who had designed so many of the early houses at Kensington. Despite the press reports in 1912, it is not clear how much of the Japanese-style garden and some of the other features Rickert promised were actually built.

What was built at the waterfront park, however, was spectacular, and unlike that of any other devel-

The classically styled recreation building at Kensington was described as being modeled on Hadrian's Villa outside of Rome. The train trestle is visible in the background.
VKA

The pool complex offered many amenities geared toward families, including a large sandbox at one end.
VKA

opment of the era. Photos of the newly completed Kensington recreation facility from 1914 show an elaborate swimming pool advertised as one of the largest in the United States, a recreation pavilion (said to be modeled on Hadrian's Villa), tennis courts, a yachting dock, and a swimming beach, all hatched out of the incredible imagination of a man who saw the possibility of converting "swampland" and a creek into this lavish community amenity. [fig. 25] Not to mention the expensive feat of creating a navigable shoreline where none had existed for the neighboring properties north of the site and on both sides of the new canal, making it possible to get to Kensington from Manhasset Bay. Or E. J.'s none-too-modest boast comparing Kensington's canal to one of the greatest engineering marvels of

Kensington's promotional material was designed to attract young, well-to-do families interested in engaging in a healthful, sporting lifestyle. VKA

A colorized postcard of the swimming pool at Kensington. Society for the Preservation of Long Island Antiquities

the twentieth century, the Panama Canal. This was a man with no small dreams.

Kensington was the pinnacle of Rickert-Finlay's achievement, the end of the learning curve: "The first property developed was Bellcourt, in Bayside, which was improved along the same lines as had heretofore prevailed on Long Island—that is gravel sidewalks were laid, streets were graded and shade trees were set out, no other improvements being made," E. J. commented in the *Architecture and Building* article. He continued:

In the sale of Bellcourt, however, it was found that there was a demand for better improvements,

and consequently, when Douglas Manor was developed, cement sidewalks were laid, macadam roads were built and trees and hedges were set out. Broadway-Flushing and Westmoreland, which came next, were developed to about the same extent as Douglas Manor, all then being considered the best-improved properties on Long Island.

In the sale of these properties, however, it was found that a certain class of people were not satisfied with the improvements and wanted something better, and it was therefore decided, largely as an experiment, to give purchasers in Kensington every improvement that had been demanded on the other properties.[35]

The tennis courts in Kensington's park were a popular attraction in the development's early days. VKA

Kensington emerged as a thoughtfully designed, highly exclusive enclave of privilege—gated and guarded—that rivaled nearby estates but without burdening the residents with maintaining large acreage or expensive amenities like outdoor swimming pools.

In contrast to the firm's earlier developments, where small lots necessitated neighborliness, the generous lots at Kensington ensured a degree of privacy and separation from one's neighbors, except at the waterfront park, where residents were expected to mingle. And the property itself, a narrow, rectangular, essentially landlocked slice of a site that runs east–west and is only three blocks wide—left little room for casual or accidental socializing at easily accessible open spaces, which were so characteristic of the earlier developments.

Nothing the Rickerts or Finlay worked on in the ensuing thirty years matched the ambitions of Kensington. But the concept of Kensington envisioned in their promotional brochures as a place with lavish facilities and a tight, socially focused community was short lived. Though Kensington endures as a high-quality, extremely desirable residential neighborhood to this day, the waterfront park that was meant to set it apart bears no resemblance to the highly planned recreational core of the community that Rickert-Finlay created. Kensington residents still share this parcel on Manhasset Bay. But the waterfront park is now separated from the development by a busy four-lane highway with traffic lights, so it feels completely disassociated from the place it

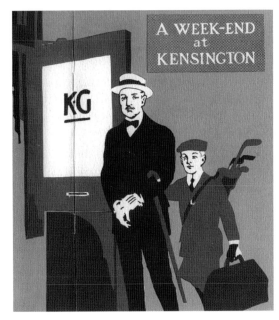

The cover of a Kensington promotional brochure that described an imaginary weekend spent enjoying all of Kensington's many activities and amenities, including dinner, dancing, card games, and golf. VKA

was supposed to be the center of. The magnificently landscaped pool and casino are long gone, replaced during the 1980s by the most banal pool and cabanas. Today, the shoreline is such a weedy tangle that there is no view of the water, and no trace of the sandy, crescent-shaped beach remains. The dock has vanished, too, and the view today is of a partly industrialized landscape of adjacent gas tanks and commercial operations to the north and south.

At the main entry, the gateway survives, but the two mansions Rickert and Finlay built were demolished long ago, the grand lifestyle they represented no longer viable or desirable. The only vestige of

Finlay's Bonnie Manse estate is the carriage house, now covered in aluminum siding and serving as the Kensington Village Hall; the balance of the site is a park of trees and grass, the elaborate formal gardens also bulldozed. Rickert's mansion, Kenwood, was demolished and replaced by an apartment house half a century ago.

Of all the forces of the twentieth century that sabotaged Rickert-Finlay's vision, it was perhaps Kensington's early transition from oversight by a private, self-governing property owners' association with deed restrictions to its incorporation as a village in 1921 that was most responsible. Residents in the early years paid taxes to the Town of North Hempstead but received few services in return, and they paid dues to the property owners' association to maintain roads, lights, the sewage system, a police force, and the private park. Incorporation as a village ensured that these services would be paid for by village-levied taxes, and the association was disbanded. But the village could not or would not sustain Rickert-Finlay's maintenance-heavy vision of a community anchored by the elaborate park and canal. By the mid- to late twentieth century, most of the waterfront park's amenities—casino building, gardens, and tennis courts—had disappeared, replaced by more utilitarian structures or, like the shorefront and dock, abandoned.

Some of Rickert-Finlay's more modest early developments have fared better, albeit with varying degrees of success, ceding their private roads to New York City and taking advantage of city services when private funds failed during the Great Depression. Because of the small lot sizes and natural geographic boundaries, some

of these developments had a built-in sense of community, a factor that seems key to their survival, especially when coupled with an active property owners' association. Broadway-Flushing and Bellcourt, for example, were developed by Rickert-Finlay in a similar way, but have differing fates. Both are based on the New York City street grid and its typical 20-x-100-foot lot subdivisions. The minimum building plot required was 40 x 100 feet, with larger houses typically built on 60- or 80-foot-wide lots. The relatively small lot sizes ensured that most neighbors would know each other. Both developments were within walking distance of a train stop with a commercial development, where residents might meet while shopping or commuting. One edge of Broadway-Flushing is bounded by Bowne Park, a city park with a pond that provided a picturesque focal point for the development; Bellcourt had no such focal point. To this day, Broadway-Flushing has an active homeowners' association, which has battled successfully to enforce deed restrictions.

At Bellcourt, in contrast, visual vestiges remain—a stone entry column here, a grand house there—but the spirit of the place has vanished. Subsumed by ordinary subdivisions and garden apartments built around it, the initial core of the neighborhood that Rickert-Finlay left behind has been unable to buffer itself and maintain a strong sense of place. No neighborhood association has enforced the Rickert-Finlay deed restrictions there for decades.

Douglas Manor, though less extravagantly planned than Kensington and with far more modest houses, has miraculously survived within the

Swimming at the dock at Douglas Manor on hot summer days and sailing on Little Neck Bay were among the development's many attractive features.
DLNHS

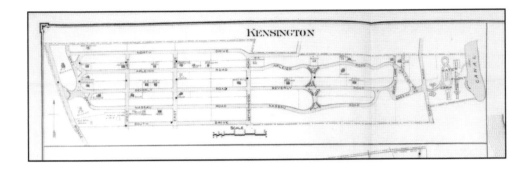

confines of New York City. Here, more than in any of their other developments, Rickert-Finlay's planning ideas remain largely and visibly intact. It was not the ultimate expression of their planning ideas, but Douglas Manor may actually be the most successful of their developments, thanks to factors other than planning.

The geography of Douglas Manor—a mile-long peninsula surrounded on three sides by water and separated from the rest of Queens at its southern end by the L.I.R.R. tracks—initially served to physically buffer the Manor from many of the negative forces that chipped away at other, less isolated neighborhoods throughout the twentieth century. Geography clearly reinforced the sense of community that Rickert-Finlay's design laid the groundwork for—there are no other subdivisions pressing against it except for two blocks just south of the railroad tracks, where the houses are virtually indistinguishable from those built at the Manor. The Douglas Manor Association has remained active and involved for more than a century, ensuring the survival of the basic concepts—in particular the common ownership of the mile-long waterfront.

Though E. J. Rickert had misgivings about the lack of architectural review at Douglas Manor, it seems to us today that there were relatively few "architectural failures" until the latter part of the twentieth century. In the 1950s, open garden lots started being sold off as development sites and typical tract houses sprang up in these spaces, eroding the architectural character of the Manor. During the 1980s, the teardown phenomenon began and several beloved old houses were replaced. The Douglas Manor Association found that deed restrictions and an active association were no match for the forces actively reshaping the neighborhood with developer-driven "McMansions."

Residents eventually banded together and began lobbying New York City for landmark district status. Their nine-year effort culminated in the creation of the Douglaston Historic District in 1997. The district includes all 593 of Douglas Manor's houses, six undeveloped lots, and its landscaped waterfront. Alterations to the houses and any new construction are now subject to Landmarks Preservation Commission review and approval, and the deed restrictions that Rickert-Finlay created are cited and reinforced by the designation. No doubt, E. J. Rickert, Charles Rickert, and Charles Finlay would have been surprised and gratified by such an outcome—their vision of a new way of life protected to some degree by New York City government, their Douglas Manor development built out but still evolving, and a century later considered to be one of the most desirable neighborhoods in New York City.

8
LONG BEACH

SENATOR WILLIAM H. REYNOLDS'S
CITY BY THE SEA

ANTHONY W. ROBINS

Long Beach—the New Atlantic City, America's New Ocean City, the World's Greatest All-Year Shore Resort, the City by the Sea—was the brainchild of one of New York's most imaginative developers, Senator William H. Reynolds (1868–1931).

Senator William H. Reynolds

Reynolds had a strong record as a developer of residential neighborhoods, constructing thousands of houses and apartment buildings in Brooklyn and Queens, but he also built and operated theaters, created the Jamaica Racetrack, took a stab at building the world's tallest skyscraper, and laid out Dreamland, a vast seaside entertainment complex on Coney Island rivaling Luna Park. He brought to his projects business savvy, a legal background, political know-how, a high tolerance for risk, unbounded ambition, a genius for advertising, and an unmatched flair for showmanship. He employed all of those talents and abilities on his greatest success, the project with which his name will always be most closely associated: Long Beach.

Born in 1868, Reynolds was the son of a Brooklyn builder who, as Reynolds himself liked to recount, inadvertently got the boy started on an early path to riches:

When I was going to the high school . . . I received my first lessons in building. My father was putting up a good many houses, and after school he sent me around to sweep the plaster out of them and clean

them up. As I grew older I used to do his collecting for him. He was a good business man, but he was sometimes a little slow in paying his bills. . . . I told the tradesmen that if they would give 2 per cent discount to me I would pay their money to them on the first of the month. I then asked my father to let me pay his bills and relieve him of that bother and he consented. In this way I had obtained $200 when I was 18 years old.[1]

With that capital, Reynolds went out on his own as a builder, and before long had taken on his father as an employee. In press interviews he claimed to have built "between 1000 and 1500 houses in Borough Park." In 1898, the *New York Times* reported a deal in which Reynolds purchased a large portion of Bensonhurst real estate, noting that "this entire section of Brooklyn is now in Mr. Reynolds's hands."[2] And Reynolds helped build up other Brooklyn neighborhoods as well, among them Bedford-Stuyvesant, Westminster Heights, and Vanderveer Crossing.

Early in his career, Reynolds involved himself in local Brooklyn politics as a Republican candidate for the State Assembly. As reported in an 1892 press account:

Mr. Reynolds is known in common parlance as a hustler. He is a man of means, a member of the Union League Club, and a hail-fellow-well-met. Nobody thinks of calling him anything but "Billy!" and Reynolds would be just as sure to say, "Hello, old man, how have you been?" The mere fact that Reynolds never saw the man before

wouldn't alter the case in the least. [Reynolds] likes that sort of familiarity . . . [which] makes him one of the people, as it were, and it has elected more than one man in Brooklyn before now. . . . To be sure, Reynolds is inclined to be somewhat of a sport and takes an interest in prize fights, but it is doubtful if that bent of mind will cause him to lose many votes.[3]

The following year, at the age of twenty-four, Reynolds won election to the New York State Senate. Though he held that title for just a single two-year term, he remained known as "Senator Reynolds" for the rest of his career.

As one of Reynolds's associates, Frank Bailey, recalled, "There was nothing small-scale about Reynolds." He remembered Reynolds as:

a politician, a gambler, a man about town, a great salesman, an athlete, a ladies' man, a practical joker with a flair for the gargantuan, altogether a fabulous character. He was what was known as a "business producer," an arranger of deals, with an engaging, lively personality that made people do things they had never had any intention of doing. . . . Who has ever spent an hour under [his] magic influence . . . without a quickening flood of friendship toward him, the reduction of the price of brick or the purchase of two lots restricted to the erection of one dwelling?[4]

Bailey also admired Reynolds' physical strength:

Reynolds had trained a frail constitution to great athletic prowess. . . . [H]e used to keep himself in

condition by constant exercise during one month so that he could "go on the bum" for the next month. Some of the greatest pugilists of the time were his friends, and he once boxed Bob Fitzsimmons for four rounds, at the end of which the mighty heavyweight said he had had enough.[5]

Laurelton in Queens

By 1901, Reynolds was looking beyond the urban precincts of Brooklyn to more suburban areas. Asked by the *Brooklyn Daily Eagle* about the prospects for new real estate development, he explained:

I don't think there has ever been a time . . . when the outlook for the sale of real estate has been better in Brooklyn or its suburbs than it is at the present time. I want to say a word here about the suburbs in particular. The tendency of people who are now living in flats and apartments seems to be to get a home of their own and more light and air. . . . There have been thousands of houses sold within the last two or three years to this class of people. . . . I advise everybody that has any idea of purchasing real estate in the suburbs of Brooklyn to do so at once.[6]

By 1906, Reynolds had turned his attention to Queens, where he planned an entire suburban community in Laurelton. He moved on before the neighborhood could be fully developed, but ads he placed in the press that year suggest his thinking:

Laurelton, Long Island
The Garden Suburb in New York City
Unexcelled Transit—All Public Utilities
A well developed community on the south side
   of Queens Borough
Wonderful shade trees and beautiful flowers
Highly restricted but moderately priced
Twenty-five minutes from Manhattan[7]

Reynolds paid the Long Island Railroad to construct a handsome train station for Laurelton, and according to a press account of 1910, many Manhattanites discovered Laurelton:

as a result of having seen it from the window of the Long Island Railroad trains on their way to visit places further out on the Island. The majority of the houses at Laurelton are of white stucco, with red or green tiled roofs and as everyone riding on the Montauk Division of the railroad has to pass through the Laurelton property, or stop at Laurelton station, the attractiveness and growth of the suburb is called to the attention of thousands of railroad passengers every day.[8]

The reporter noted:

One of the features of the development which ex-senator William H. Reynolds has made at Laurelton is the broad streets, with parking through the center. There are present over three miles of these boulevards laid out with the parkings planted with the finest shrubbery and flowers.[9]

The Montauk Theatre

Even while pursuing such large projects, Reynolds found time to indulge his taste for the theatrical. The extension of Flatbush Avenue to the Manhattan Bridge, announced in 1903, led to the demolition of many local landmarks. Among them:

the Montauk Theatre, the leading playhouse in Brooklyn, will have to give way to the march of progress, after an existence of less than eight years. . . . The Montauk Theatre is owned by a syndicate, of which William H. Reynolds is the leader. . . .

The theatre was opened in 1896, and since then has been the leading one in Brooklyn, and for the last few years has been the only one to give high class legitimate productions exclusively.[10]

The following year Reynolds announced plans to build a new Montauk Theatre:

As the Montauk is the only playhouse in the borough that is devoted exclusively to high class legitimate drama, it became almost a public necessity to provide another house to take its place. With that end in view the Hanover Theatre Company was organized several weeks ago by ex-Senator William H. Reynolds. . . . It is planned to call [the new theater] the New Montauk. . . . J. J. Petit, of Kirby, Petit & Green, Manhattan architects, is now busy completing the plans. No expense will be spared to make the new playhouse as modern and complete in every detail as any theatre in America. . . . The building will be constructed in the French Renaissance architecture of brick and terra cotta . . . . William H. Reynolds . . . will have charge of the construction.[11]

Architects Kirby, Petit & Green worked on various Reynolds projects, from altering commercial buildings in midtown Manhattan[12] to designing larger projects at Coney Island (see below) and, eventually, Long Beach.[13]

Dreamland-by-the-Sea

Even as Reynolds worked with Kirby, Petit & Green on the Montauk Theatre, the builder and his architects were hatching plans for entertainment on a far grander scale:

Another big amusement enterprise which, it is said, will be a rival to Luna Park, is being planned for Coney Island. . . . Ex-Senator William H. Reynolds will probably head the company which is to run the enterprise. According to the present plans, it is to be one of the biggest things of the kind in the country. The new amusement garden is to be built after the fashion of the famous London Hippodrome, and will contain many of the features of that enterprise. . . . The promoters of the scheme say that fully $1,000,000 will be spent in carrying out the plans.[14]

Dreamland opened the following year to rhapsodic praise in the press:

Dreamland-by-the-Sea: A New and Unique City of Pleasure Throws Open Its Doors to the Public

What is Dreamland as an amusement attraction? It would be easier to say what it is not, for it includes within its ample borders about every form of entertainment that has of late proved its right to public esteem, and has added many more attractions that none but a bold and original genius would have invented in moments of inspiration. That it has a theatre, a circus, an animal show, a "shoot the chute," and a dozen other features of the sort goes without saying. It also has many novelties that call for a somewhat extended description. . . . The construction work, all of artificial stone, was started last December by ex-Senator William H. Reynolds, the president of the Dreamland company, and all through the winter months, up to the time of the opening, more than two thousand carpenters, ironworkers, masons and other employes have worked in shifts night and day to push Dreamland through to completion. The result is a bewildering array of attractions, unsurpassedly situated.[15]

The attractions included a "Grecian"-style animal arena; a medieval-style building presenting "Our Boys in Blue"; an Illusion Building in "the Eastern style of architecture" featuring "a hypnotized girl moving over the heads of the audience"; a Funny Room and Haunted House "after the old mission style of Southern California and old Mexico"; a fishing pond "conducted by the popular Irish comedian, Andrew Mack"; a simulation of "the mountains of Switzerland"; a reproduction of a Japanese temple serving "Japanese refreshments"; an "exact reproduction of the Doge's Palace at Venice" in which the visitor "steps into a gondola, and is poled . . . through the canals and lagoons of that picturesque city"; an airship building, a "French Renaissance-style ballroom," an Electricity Building, a Submarine Boat Building, and "Fighting the Flames," which "represents an actual fire, in a way that will stir the heart of every man, woman or child that witnesses the thrilling representation."[16]

As remarkable as all these attractions must have seemed to the New Yorkers of 1904, Dreamland owed much of its fascination to its location and layout:

To thousands of New-Yorkers one of the most irresistible magnets of Dreamland will be its unrivalled situation, right on the water's edge. Broad and deep as its landed property is, the buildings are so laid out and planned that whenever there is an ocean breeze Dreamland visitors will get the benefit of it. . . . The grounds are laid out on the plan of a wide central plaza, with a spacious lagoon in the centre, the plaza being flanked by the various buildings that contain the features and attractions.[17]

That layout was possible because:

the architects had in planning and laying out Dreamland . . . a "clean slate" to write upon. . . . They had a blank tract of land, so many acres of bare sand, with so many hundred feet waterfront, and carte blanche, with ample funds, to make these seashore acres as fascinating, as imposing and as tasteful as the latest state of their art would enable them to do. . . . The avenues are broad, the vistas superb and the cooling breeze blows freely to every corner. This new city by the sea has only sprung up within the last six months.[18]

The Lure of Long Island

Just two years later, in 1906, Reynolds and his architects took many of the ideas worked out at Dreamland farther out on Long Island, where they found "a blank tract of land" with "so many hundred feet waterfront" and "carte blanche" to erect there a "new city by the sea."

Various writers of the time saw Long Island as New York's ideal suburb, with articles bearing such titles as "Long Island to Solve City Toilers' Problem—Country Life, Plus Modern Improvements, Gaining in Popularity";[19] "Residential Parks Feature of Realty—Beauty Spots Being Wisely Developed by Men of Large Ideas."[20] In an interview in the Eagle in 1907, while he was still involved with Laurelton and beginning his work at Long Beach, Reynolds laid out his own expansive view for Long Island:

Am I optimistic as to Long Island's future? Perhaps the best answer to the question is the evidence of my present large interests there. . . . The great movement which Long Island is now experiencing is only the beginning; her expansion is yet in its infancy. . . . In fact, I doubt if the most enthusiastic of us had any adequate realization of what the next ten, yes, even five years, has in store for Long Island's up-building.

With Greater New York's permanent population of nearly five millions of people increasing at the rate of three to four hundred thousand annually; with the great majority of congested Manhattan's overflow, already sweeping out over Brooklyn and Queens; and with the trebling and quadrupling, at least, of this overflow, the moment the great transportation improvements become operative, it takes no prophet to foresee what will become of Long Island's accessible territory.[21]

Reynolds had learned the lesson of Laurelton, and the value of its new train station serviced by the Long Island Railroad:

The extension of Long Island Railroad's third rail system, the great network of steam and trolley lines, the rapid transit connection with New York by the Pennsylvania, Belmont and Interborough tunnels, new bridges and subways—these are the factors which are at last bringing Long Island into its own. When even the outer circle of the city limits, and points for some distance beyond that, can be reached from Herald Square and Wall Street in from thirty to forty minutes, it is no wonder that the great tide of population has already set forth so strongly in this direction, and that the demand is so keen for realty here, in anticipation of these tremendous improvements.[22]

He also foresaw the impact of the new automobile on Long Island's development. In the same way as the train that passed through Laurelton gave passengers the opportunity to admire its houses and layout:

Advertisement for Long Beach. New York Sun, *May 5, 1907, p. 8*

The touring car has done much to advertise Long island's beauties to the world—for all the world comes to New York at one time or another, and a

large part of it takes a spin out over the island, to say nothing of the race meets.[23]

And he expressed his preference "for the south shore":

I believe the Montauk division is to be more and more the great highway for the entire length of the island. . . . With Montauk Point as a great port of entry, which it is destined to be, the importance of the main line to New York is instantly seen. The many thriving towns along this line are already feeling the stimulus, and will eventually become cities in themselves and grow together. Certainly every acre of ground from Lynbrook and Long Beach to the East River will become solidly built up within a very few years[24]

Casting his eye along the South Shore, Reynolds found the perfect location for his new development: Long Beach.

The Birth of Long Beach

Reynolds planned Long Beach as New York's answer to Atlantic City, only better sited, more attractive, and much closer to the nation's metropolis. He envisioned it as a combination resort and residential community, making it significantly different in character from other planned communities on Long Island. And he specifically targeted it to what he unabashedly called "the wealthy classes." In an early advertisement of 1907 placed in *Success* magazine, he declared:

As a nation we are lovers of the sea and delight in its many pleasures. During the last generation individual wealth has increased at a tremendous rate, producing a class which can afford to pay handsomely to gratify its desires. This created a demand for seashore property, which resulted in placing all the best of our Atlantic Coast in the hands of permanent owners, with the exception of one long stretch known as "Long Beach," which, owing to legal causes, now overcome, could not be placed upon the market until this spring.[25]

He pitched Long Beach as a "monopoly"—likely because he thought that would appeal to those wealthy classes:

The ownership of Long Beach constitutes a monopoly because IT IS THE ONLY COAST PROPERTY POSSESSING ALL THE QUALIFICATIONS WHICH MAKE IT DESIRABLE.

Then he laid out the advantages of his development:

These qualifications are, that the beach is long and sloping, the sand is white and clean, the climate is invigorating, the prevailing wind is from the ocean,

A bird's-eye view of Long Beach from a 1907 Estates of Long Beach brochure. Society for the Preservation of Long Island Antiquities

the surf bathing is glorious, and there is still-water available for boating and bathing, as well as surf-water; there is excellent railroad service, and it lies within a shorter distance of a dense population and of our most important business center than any other ocean-front property. In addition it is the only ocean-front property where the development comprises everything for the comfort and delight of the wealthy classes, including a five-mile board-walk 50 feet in width, costing $90,000 per mile, macadamized streets, cementine sidewalks, curbs and gutters, a splendid club house, a first class garage, fine running water from an artesian well, gas, electricity and a sewage-disposal plant assuring surf purity, and it is the only property of the kind controlled by one man, and a man (Senator William H. Reynolds) whose name is a synonym for complete comprehensiveness and high quality.[27]

When Reynolds first saw Long Beach, it was largely uninhabited, occupied for the most part by one hotel and a handful of cottages—an out-of-the-way fisherman's retreat, with few amenities, According to a 1909 description:

Long Beach has for many years been a great resort for surf and deep sea fishermen, most of them putting up over night at Billy Rightmeyer's and other summer resorts on the channel.[28]

The *Brooklyn Eagle* explained why the land had lain fallow for so long. In March 1880, the Town of Hempstead leased the waterfront:

for fifty years to a corporation formed by the late Austin Corbin, to develop the island on the leasehold plan. Bonds to the amount of $1,000,000 were issued, and this money was used in improvements and buildings, including the great hotel, one of the largest on the Atlantic coast, having accommodations for over a thou-

sand guests and a spacious covered veranda hundreds of feet long.[29]

Unfortunately, the project died, leaving the land tied up in litigation. Until Reynolds's involvement, one of the most likely plans for the future of Long Beach involved a New York State initiative, promoted by the newspaper *The World*, to create a "seaside park" to provide "free bathing for the poor" as well as:

hospitals for convalescents. . . . The seaside park will also be equipped with recreation pavilions and playgrounds, and should be of incalculable benefit to the public health of the city.[30]

Reynolds saw enormous possibilities for the property as a "seaside park," though not for "the poor." As with his development at Dreamland, he could start from scratch. Also, as at Dreamland, he could reshape the actual landscape to his liking. As he recalled in 1910, looking back on the beginnings of the project:

I had never been to Long Beach until a little more than two and a half years ago. My first visit there was sufficient to convince me of the merits of the property and I immediately bought it. Work began at once and my dream of this all-year-round seaside resort became a thing of reality.[31]

Reynolds envisioned Long Beach as something of a cross between a beach and entertainment complex like Dreamland and a planned community like Laurelton. He regularly compared Long Beach to Atlantic City, assuring all who would listen that Long Beach would far surpass the resort on the New Jersey shore.

He couldn't acquire the entire property all at once. As explained in the *Brooklyn Eagle* in 1907:

As is well known to Eagle readers, this property was acquired in two different parcels of over a thousand acres each. The first, comprising the entire beach frontage and practically all the available building land upon the island, together with the mammoth hotel, cottages, etc., was purchased last year after long and difficult negotiations. . . . The second section, which was purchased from the Town of Hempstead about a month ago, consists of 1,084 acres, partly marsh and partly under water, which were needed to complete the comprehensive plan for laying out and developing the resort in a manner commensurate with its possibilities as a great future watering place. This whole northern or inland section will be filled in and leveled to the established grade, and the bay shore line bulkheaded upon a 1,000 foot channel 10 feet deep, which is to be dredged the entire length of the island.[32]

The second sale caused some controversy:

At every place where meetings have been held, the attendance has been large and the interest intense. Not only has the opposition been manifest at the Reynolds meetings, but the men who are opposed to selling the town lands for what they term "a mess of pottage" have held meetings to denounce the proposition, and have succeeded in working up a strong sentiment against the sale. It is conceded that a big vote on the question will be polled on Tuesday, and the result is by no means easy to forecast.[34]

But Reynolds won the vote and set to work, soon boasting of his operation's speed and extent:

In the brief time which has elapsed since we took charge, two and a half miles of fifty-foot boardwalk has been completed and facing on it is a million dollar hotel, a bathing pavilion, casino and numerous stores. The largest dredges in the world are pumping for the channel night and day, sand for the fill, while the inlet is being widened and deepened so that it will be able to accommodate all shipping, even the largest vessels in the navies of the world . . . while active work has been started on the big amusement pier.

The dredging operation was enormous in scale. Charles Prelini, author of a 1911 book on dredging, noted that the practice of "dredging for the sole purpose of filling up valuable lands" had been growing in many places, but especially in New York, where property values in the suburbs were rapidly rising, and attracting speculative development:

The boldest of all these speculations is the construction of an entire new city . . . located on Long Beach, Long Island. The lowlands which surround Long Beach have been filled up with sand removed from the shallow bottom of the

ocean by two hydraulic dredges, and the material conveyed through a long line of pipes. The dredges have dug also a navigable channel between the ocean and the large body of water existing between the mainland and Long Beach, thus permitting large vessels to enter and approach the surrounding lands, which will be improved for industrial purposes. Considering the selling prices of the building lots the dredging is certainly remunerative.[35]

Estates of Long Beach Opens Its Doors

"Estates of Long Beach" formally opened on May 15, 1907, with the project already well under way.[36] Ten days later, the Eagle described the project's almost instant success:

The Long Beach inn is already opened and large crowds were present at the beach last Sunday. The Wednesday previous a special train of ten cars carried nearly a thousand people to the opening sale of villa and hotel sites, and it is said that over $700,000 worth of land has already been sold. The interest which the Pennsylvania-Long Island Railroad is manifesting in the Long Beach development is evidenced by its plans for through service between New York and Long Beach . . . and the building of one of its finest depots to replace the present Long Beach terminal station. . . . Direct runs to upper and lower Manhattan will be made in from 30 to 40 minutes.[37]

By 1908, Long Beach was generating stories about its new developments. In March 1908, *Brooklyn Life* commented on the great change to the area:

Time was when Long Beach seemed destined never to progress beyond the stage of being a little summer settlement of one hotel and a group of cottages. That was before the days of rapid transit. Today Long Beach is on the eve of being brought within easy reach of town. Already, the old Long Beach is a thing of the past. In its stead is rising a great watering place along the lines of Atlantic City.

The article went on to describe progress on a "fire-proof steel and concrete hotel which will cost $1,500,000" and a "boardwalk reinforced with concrete, fifty feet wide and five miles long.[38]

In June of the same year, in an article entitled "Long Beach Busy: Two Miles of the Boardwalk Are Already Built," the *New York Times* reported:

A new $1,500,000 hotel is to take the place of the Long Beach Hotel, which was burned, and the promoters expect to have the structure ready for occupancy by this time next year. Plans for Montgomery & Stone's theatre, which will be located two blocks

Long Island Railroad Station at Long Beach. Society for the Preservation of Long Island Antiquities

below the Casino on the Boardwalk, have been filed. The new playhouse will be modeled after the Empire Music Hall, London. Work on the Pennsylvania Railroad station will begin soon. . . . Bathing facilities will be better than ever this year. The new pavilion, which has 1,000 bathhouses, and which can accommodate 5,000 bathers with comfort, opened yesterday. . . . The Inn on the Boardwalk has opened for the season. . . . The work of reclaiming the meadows and low grounds is going on at the rate of 900,000 cubic yards a month.[39]

A month later, the same paper ran an article entitled "Long Beach a City Built As If by Magic":

Long Beach . . . last year a dream, a mere vision seen only by ex-Senator William H. Reynolds . . . but to-day a city complete in every particular is proving one of the most attractive places within reach of this city.[40]

In particular, the *Times* admired a recently completed venue:

One of the most attractive buildings in this magic city is the Casino. . . . Flagpoles jut upward from the roof and balconies of this inviting structure and most of the exterior seems to be made up of glass-covered balconies. Private dining rooms swarm all over the second floor . . . and the remainder is given over to a ballroom of generous size. . . . Over the glass roof of the balcony tables a steady sheet of water is kept flowing, so that the sun beating on the glass during the day does not make things uncomfortable for diners. . . . There's an oaken grill and a bar adjoining, and . . . a rathskeller of pretension.[41]

And in August 1909, *Field & Stream* could describe a largely completed city:

Where twenty months ago there was to be seen only a narrow stretch of barren sand dunes some ten miles in length, may now be found a growing city by the sea. . . . Along the surf-washed beach has been constructed perhaps the finest ocean board-walk in existence . . . ten feet broader than the walk at Atlantic City. . . . Within another year it will have been extended . . . affording five miles of seashore promenade unexcelled anywhere in the world for the marine view afforded. Facing this walk will be found one of the finest hotels on the coast, The Nassau, with a capacity of 350 rooms . . . a bathing pavilion of 800 rooms; a picturesque and admirably equipped casino with banquet halls, private dining-rooms, restaurant and other attractive features for the entertainment of guests; novelty stores, bazaars and other like conveniences of the modern city by the sea. Forming the northern boundary of the city limits is a magnificent channel, 1,000 feet in width and five miles in length, which . . . must ultimately become the finest motor boat course in the vicinity of New York.[42]

The *Eagle* gushed over the potential of the new city:

Situated at the very threshold of the greatest city on the continent, with nearly five millions of people and constantly growing at the rate of three or four hundred thousand annually, [Long Beach] will hardly lack for local support. Yet its popularity will presumably become world-wide, once it is thoroughly established. For besides its advantage of location, it has, in the opinion of many, all the natural attractions of Atlantic City, its island location and climactic conditions, superb beach, surf bathing and ocean outlook

and every essential save the physical development. And since this latter is now provided for and under way, with unlimited capital and indomitable energy behind it, there would seem little doubt but that New York will at last have an all-year resort that shall outrival the world's most famous watering places.[43]

Planning and Architecture

The scale of the development, its tabula rasa character, the rearranging of the landscape, and the trappings of a great resort, all suggest the lessons of Dreamland—even the plan to maximize the comforts of ocean breezes. Dreamland was "laid out and planned that whenever there is an ocean breeze Dreamland visitors will get the benefit of it."[44] In an advertisement that Reynolds placed in *Success* magazine in 1907, he recounted a conversation between A. J. Cassatt, the president of the Pennsylvania Railroad, and "a friend," in which Cassatt asked the friend about the advantages of Long Beach as a potential investment:

> The friend replied, "It has many, but one of the greatest is that it lies due East and West, facing the South, and as the winds of the Atlantic Coast . . . blow from the South-West with almost the steadiness of trade winds, as is proved by tendency of all exposed trees, shrubs and plants to lean toward the North-East, Long Beach has steady ocean breezes, while almost all the resorts—Atlantic City in particular—lie so that most of the winds that reach them are land breezes.[45]

Though the overall plan reflected Reynolds's work at Dreamland, the physical layout of the Estates of Long Beach—the residential portion of the development—including its architectural character and its landscaping, resembled Reynolds's plans for Laurelton.

In 1908, *Brooklyn Life* explained that Long Beach would be "constructed in accordance with a homogeneous idea and [be] in many respects quite unique." The article noted the careful control of architectural styles planned for the development:

> All buildings, on the boardwalk, as elsewhere at Long Beach, will be restricted to certain types of architecture, according to the use they are put. This has been decided upon to avoid having architectural freaks or eyesores so that eventually, the resort will present a beautiful and harmonious appearance from the viewpoint of both architect and landscape gardener.[46]

Those restrictions were encapsulated in the new city's zoning law and building codes.[47]

The houses of the Estates of Long Beach, built of concrete, faced with white stucco and capped with tiled roofs, would be reminiscent of Laurelton's houses. Reynolds rhapsodized about his development:

> Long stretches of sand have been changed into brick-paved boulevards and streets and dotted with beautiful houses of concrete and with red tile roofs. And, still more, a hundred of these homes are now in construction.[48]

The *New-York Tribune* described the careful restrictions determining the appearance of the houses, noting:

> A popular restriction has been adopted, in imitation of one which prevails on the Riviera in Italy. Every roof must be of red vitrified tile. This style of roof will make a picturesque appearance, and besides will serve as a protection against fire.[49]

Though Reynolds built many of the houses, some were designed by outside architects. Mr. S. Lorsch commissioned a typical Long Beach house from New York architect Emery Roth, described in the *Real Estate Record and Guide*:

> A stucco residence . . . now nearing completion . . . . will be a welcome addition to a section of the Beach that is destined to be a fine cottage colony. . . . Situated on Penn av, the Lorsch residence is two blocks from the ocean. . . . The house harmonizes well with the general architecture at Long Beach, although it has an individuality distinctly its own. It is a square stuccoed frame building, massive, but simple in design; is trimmed with stained cypress on the exterior and is covered by a Spanish tile roof. The flashings, gutters and cornices are of copper; the porch and balcony floors are tiled. All the bathrooms have, besides the ordinary supply, salt water connections. It is private investments of this character that are rapidly enhancing fee values at Long Beach.[50]

Though some of these houses have since been refaced or replaced, many still stand on red brick–paved avenues, with their white stucco fronts and red tile roofs intact.

The general street plan of the Estates of Long Beach, laid out by landscape architect Charles Wellford Leavitt,[51] included avenues of standard width, but also a number of landscaped "wide boulevards and parkways,"[52] similar to Laurelton's "broad streets, with parking through them . . . planted with the finest shrubbery and flowers."[53] The *New-York Tribune* described the Long Beach street plan:

Another striking feature which will distinguish Long Beach from other cities in the country is the disposition of the streets. . . . All the avenues leading from the ocean to the channel are boulevards, one hundred feet wide, with seventy-five feet between curbs, and are of the boulevard type. Besides, they are virtually made forty feet wider by the restriction on buildings which reserves twenty feet on lots bordering on the boulevards, or twenty feet from lots facing on boulevards, thus giving a wide vista looking toward the ocean and the channel.[54] In addition:

> The east and west streets are not less than sixty feet wide between property lines, with sidewalks twelve and a half feet wide. Two streets, Broadway and Hudson street, are 110 feet wide, and are intended for a trolley line which will belt the island. In addition a parkway running through the centre of the island will be 185 feet wide between property lines. This is intended to accommodate the depressed tracks of the Long Island Railroad's electric lines.[55]

Similar care would be taken on all aspects of the physical plant of the new city:

> Business enterprises of all kinds will be restricted to certain streets—street pavement of macadam or asphalt—sidewalks and curbing of concrete—will be much ornamental shrubbery and flower beds, hedges, shade trees and lawns—complete sewerage, gas, electric lights and fresh and salt water systems—no unsightly poles of wires in the air—lighting, telephone and telegraph in underground conduits . . .[56]

The 1909 street plan of the Estates of Long Beach included a proposed "Sandringham Colony," a subsection on the bay, some six blocks long and eight blocks wide. Within the Colony, the Long Beach grid disappeared, replaced by a series of winding drives. As Long Beach historian Roberta Fiore surmises:

> This resort area was probably conceived with and for August Belmont, Jr. as an Edwardian

Kirby, Petit & Green, the architectural firm so closely associated with the residential park phenomenon on Long Island, designed some of the earliest houses. Brooklyn Life, March 1919, vol. 39

park estate. It was to be completed with formal lanes of trees shading closely clipped turf, with circular drives laid out for horses and carriages leading to mansions of stucco and cobblestone. Still in existence at 657 Laurelton Boulevard . . . is the Senator's model building for this venture—"Cobble Villa"—with covered carriage archway.[57]

The plan bears some similarity to that of Fieldston, in the Bronx, developed at about the same time by an individual developer as a picturesque suburb of Manhattan. The Sandringham Colony, however, apparently came to naught, and the planned picturesque horse-and-carriage drives succumbed to the grid and the automobile.

Long Beach Success, and Mayor Reynolds

Long Beach the resort met with immediate success, as the *Eagle* attested in a June 1909 article entitled "Long Beach Thronged: June Sunday Crowd One of Largest in Resort's History":

> Another crowd, even larger than the one which was at this place last Sunday, visited here yesterday. . . . At the Hotel Nassau there were hundreds of persons, and in the afternoon in front of this hotel the crowd was so large that walking was difficult. The boardwalk for its entire length of two and one-half miles was filled with promenaders and when the electric lights were turned on in the evening there were still on the walk long lines of persons. Both afternoon and evening roller chairs were used by many on the walk. The chairs were introduced here last summer

by former Senator William H. Reynolds. . . . At the bathing pavilion yesterday Manager Loritz had as many patrons as he could well attend to. . . . The air was warm and the temperature of the water was 65 degrees, which made bathing pleasant for the greater number of swimmers. . . . The managers at the Nassau will . . . provide prizes for the winners at cards on regular evenings when whist and other games are played. The card parlors in the hotel are roomy and elaborately finished.[58]

And by 1910, the *New-York Tribune* was calling Long Beach "the new national ocean resort," which was "destined to be the greatest and most attractive ocean city on the Atlantic coast."[59]

Part of the success of Long Beach could be ascribed to Reynolds's aptitude for promotion. In 1912, a study of advertising principals singled out Reynolds, his property manager H. R. Talbot, and his agent Harry T. Meany for their Long Beach advertisements:

> The Long Beach Estates, which are the pride of Mr. Talbot's heart, have been described in advertisements in such a fetching manner that it is no surprise how well the parcels are selling. Readers of *The Evening Mail* are familiar with these advertisements. They are certainly most attractive. They compel attention. . . . Mr. Talbot strikes you with a pretty picture, then good copy; and when you meet him his enthusiasm makes you wish to buy, and you do buy if you have the price. He tells you about a fine property on the ocean front, forty minutes from Wall street, and impresses you with the belief that before very long Atlantic City's

Planted medians, red tile roofs, and red brick streets set the tone in Long Beach. Society for the Preservation of Long Island Antiquities

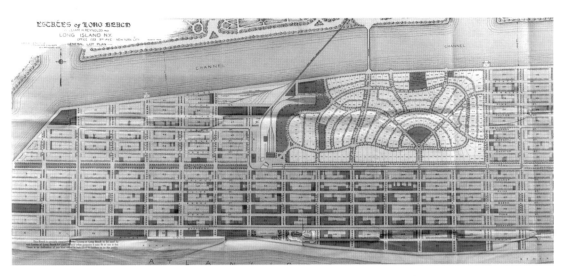

twin sister will have decided to break away from Atlantic City and settle down at the Long Beach Estates.[60]

Long Beach remained a popular resort in the years leading up to World War I. In May 1915, the *Eagle* announced:

> The season at Long Beach is now formally open and preparations are being made to entertain a large crowd over Memorial Day. One of the notable events of the week was the opening by Thomas Healy of his restaurant last night. The opening night of the season was the occasion for the gathering of a number of persons of social prominence and the handsome restaurant was crowded with gay parties of diners all the evening. There was dancing, of course, with two orchestras to furnish music, and there was keen rivalry among the graceful dancers on the floor. . . . Mr. Healy was on hand to greet all his guests on the opening night. Among some of the more prominent who entertained parties were ex-Senator William H. Reynolds, "Diamond Jim" Brady . . . and many others.[61]

Around this time, Reynolds ran into some legal difficulties. In 1917, he was indicted on perjury charges and "charges of misusing municipal funds. He was convicted, and sentenced to six months of prison, but the Appellate Division of the Supreme Court set aside the verdict [in 1920]."[62]

Despite his legal problems, Reynolds carried on with his Long Beach operations. In 1920, he helped form the new Chamber of Commerce for Long Beach, "for the purpose of creating plans and improvements for the benefit of the summer visitors, as well as the for the property holders."[63]

Reynolds had many such plans, but decided he needed more autonomy to pursue them. He had been "Village President" since 1910, but now arranged for Long Beach to incorporate as an inde-

pendent city, and in May 1922 was elected the city's first mayor.[64] That position gave him a level of control impossible to achieve in a Brooklyn or Queens neighborhood:

> On April 13 last [1922] Long Beach became a city. At an election held on May 16 Senator William H. Reynolds, "Father of Long Beach," was elected the first Mayor of the city. The first act of Mayor Reynolds was the letting of a franchise to operate a car line in Park Street the entire length of Long Beach.[65] [fig. 12]

Within days, the press was touting grand new plans:

> The many new improvements announced for Long Beach, among them a new million dollar automobile bridge and a new boardwalk hotel, have created much interest. These and the release of time-worn restrictions have paved the way for one of the greatest real estate movements in the history of Long Beach. With plans for two new hotels on the Boardwalk, many new business buildings, with more than 300 recently completed new homes, Long Beach is well on the way to the "boom" that has long been expected.[66]

111

The same article noted that Long Beach was also becoming more of a year-round city:

> Long Beach is rapidly becoming an all-year-round residential place. More private houses were occupied during last winter than during any previous winter season. The Nassau Hotel, Lido Golf Club and Long Beach Yacht Club also kept open all through the year.[67]

The article also reported:

> In the newer and more easterly residential section, southeast of the yacht clubhouse and the new bridge, the building activity of last year has focused on the construction of bungalows, nearly one thousand of which have been erected.[68]

Lido Beach

Reynolds continued to plan developments in and around Long Beach, including one last major project, an enormous resort hotel on the eastern end of Long Beach, adjacent to one of the country's finest golf courses. Long Beach had been compared to Venice, and this long stretch was named for the great Venetian beach resort, the Lido.

In 1914, a group of wealthy New Yorkers, including Robert Goelet and Cornelius Vanderbilt, acquired what appeared to be a most improbable site for a golf course and brought in the country's preeminent links designer, Charles Blair Macdonald, to turn it into a golfers' paradise. A Wall Street financier and amateur golfer, Macdonald had developed an unlikely parallel career designing some of the most famous golf courses in the country, earning a reputation as "the Father of American Golf Architecture."[69] As recounted in a profile in *The New Yorker* in 1928:

> Anyone who gets about golf courses in the East has played over one or more of the links designed by Charles Blair Macdonald. . . . In 1907 Macdonald, then a stock broker in New York, conceived the idea of reproducing in a classic American course the best eighteen holes to be found in Great Britain. It was a colossal job. He spent months abroad measuring and mapping the best holes. He returned here and got seventy of his golfing friends to finance the project. This resulted in the National Links at Southampton. . . . He thus became the pioneer golf-course architect in this country. With him it has always remained an art, since he has never taken a penny from the game—his career is still on the Stock Exchange.[70]

Macdonald transformed the unpromising setting of Lido Beach into a golf links by adopting Reynolds's approach: reshaping the landscape to suit his purposes. His feat was described in the *New York Times* in 1915:

> Lido golf links at Long Beach will occupy a unique place among the courses of this country and those of England and Scotland. . . . Heretofore the laying out of a course has always forced the designer to consider the limitations put upon him by nature, but in the present instance conditions have been changed. The designer, Charles Blair Macdonald, has really reconstructed nature, and that is why the Lido course will stand as a

wonderful adaptation to the popular pastime. A flat beach, inundated in places by water, has been transformed into a scientific combination of hills and dales. . . . The artificial is present on every hand, but its disguise is so compelling that one would never think that there was anything except the slightest modification of actual conditions. . . . [T]o have looked at the east end of Long Beach a year ago and thought of a golf course would have been most unnatural. Since then powerful dredges have wrought a transformation. Sand sucked from the channel has been spread in places forty feet deep and deposited in hummocks and sand dunes ready for the top dressing that should change it from a barren waste into a green playing ground. The fill is measured at 2,000,000 cubic yards, and on top of that 20,000 cubic yards of top soil will be scattered to a depth of six or seven inches.[71]

Macdonald later wrote in his autobiography, "To me it seemed a dream. The more I thought it over the more it fascinated me. It really made me feel like a creator."[72]

In the Lido course, as in Macdonald's earlier work, the *Times* noted the similarities with renowned courses:

> The Lido course is in every essential his own work, but several of the holes resemble some of those of famous European and home courses. For instance, the first resembles, but does not copy, the Narrows on the National course. The third patterns somewhat the tenth at the Eden of St. Andrews.[73]

The work took several years. According to the magazine *The Golf Course* in 1916:

> The building of the Lido Links at Long Beach is perhaps the most ambitious and most difficult work yet undertaken. Imagine one hundred and thirty acres or so of marsh land, and the greater part of the same an inlet of the sea where good fishing, etc., could always be had, turned into a stretch of hills and valleys, over which there is today a fine, close carpet of turf! It seems like a fairy-tale, to say the least; but nevertheless, it is true. Where two years ago the fisherman, the wild duck and flower held sway,

there is today a fine carpet of close turf on which it will be possible to play in a few weeks' time.[74]

Once it opened, the Lido links quickly earned a stellar reputation as, in the words of the *New York Times* in 1922, "the famous ocean course" and "one of the finest golfing layouts in the country":

> Some have even gone so far as to proclaim it as the best on this side of the water. . . . [I]n 1920, Ted Ray, the British golfer, who then held the national American open titles by virtue of a victory won at Toledo during the Summer, after playing a match against George McLean on the Long Island course, pronounced it one of the finest in the world.[75]

The course was already well established by the time Reynolds turned his attention in its direction. Since the late nineteenth century, many suburban developments had grown up around golf courses and country clubs. The Lido links was one of the best, and from the beginning its promoters had imagined surrounding it with a hotel and a residential development, as noted in 1915:

> Of course, a comfortable clubhouse was part of the scheme, but it was then suggested that many members would doubtless like to live in the vicinity, and a subsidiary corporation was formed which purchased and took under option several hundred acres additional. The plan now involves the erection of a large hotel and the creation of other club features besides golf, which will eventually make Long Beach one of the finest country club centres in the States.[76]

But it was not until 1926 that Reynolds undertook a massive development project to capitalize on the golf course's success. That year the *Times* quoted realtor Edward Mayer, who described it as:

> the new $15,000,000 development begun by former State Senator William H. Reynolds, in the easterly section, to be known as Lido Beach. This operation includes the $4,000,000 Lido Hotel, now being constructed, the eight-story Esplanade Apartment House adjoining the Lido golf course, and the erection of 2,400 dwelling houses.[77]

Plan for Lido Beach, in an ad placed by Senator Reynolds. New York Times, August 5, 1926, p. 36

14. *Lido Beach Hotel after it had been acquired by the United States Navy for use as a receiving station during World War II.* Society for the Preservation of Long Island Antiquities

Reynolds harbored great hopes for Lido Beach. According to the *Times*:

> With 600 of the 2,000 plots at Lido Beach already sold, there is prospect, in the opinion of former Senator William H. Reynolds, who is at the head of the $15,000,000 development on the east end of the island of Long Beach, that the entire area will be taken up and buildings erected on many of the sites before the first snow falls.
>
> Many changes have taken place at Lido Beach since the 10,000-foot stretch on the Atlantic Ocean, the last bit of ocean-front property in the metropolitan area, was thrown open for public sale. Lido Boulevard, the eight-foot-wide thoroughfare bisecting the island at Lido Beach, is gradually being extended, and soon will be opened to motorists who want to travel to the extreme tip of Long Beach. . . . Before the development has been entirely sold to the public, according to Senator Reynolds, all the improvements will be in, without assessment or charge of any kind to the land holders.[78]

Reynolds commissioned W. Albert Swasey (architect of the Winter Garden Theater in New York) and Hughson Hawley to produce a gigantic rendering of his imagined final product. Lido Beach never lived up to Reynolds's grandest expectations, but he did complete the Canals of Lido nearby (with streets named for winners of the U.S. Open), and the Lido Hotel opened on June 15, 1928:

> The hotel, of which William H. Reynolds is the owner, contains 440 rooms with baths, representing an investment of $4,000,000. It is in the form of a giant "X"; the main lobby with two large fireplaces and a great organ occupying space in the center, allowing the maximum in light and air to the rooms occupying the extended wings.[80]

To design the hotel, Reynolds brought in the prestigious architectural firm of Schultze & Weaver, which was known for luxurious hostelries. In Manhattan they built the Sherry-Netherland around the same time, and soon thereafter added the Pierre and the Waldorf-Astoria to their portfolio of more than a dozen grand hotels around the country and abroad. For Reynolds they designed a sprawling, five-story complex in the fashionable Spanish manner—with a red tile roof to conform with Reynolds's architectural preference for Long Beach.

The Lido golf course was demolished in the 1950s, and much else has changed, but the Lido Hotel survives today as a condominium.

The Notorious Senator Reynolds

Reynolds's 1917 indictment was not his only brush with the law. In 1924, he was found "guilty of misusing funds of the municipality" of which he was mayor. *The New York Times*, in reporting the finding, opined:

> It seems probable that Reynolds, like many much more famous railroad builders and empire builders, found the normal legalities sometimes standing in the way of his big plans. Also, it may have been difficult for him to rid himself of a proprietary attitude toward Long Beach—and its public funds.[81]

That conviction, too, was overturned on appeal, though not until 1927.[82]

Reynolds cut a grand, sometimes quirky, figure. Even before arriving in Long Beach, he generated interesting press notices:

In Dreamland, which also had huge crowds, a train of the miniature railroad, in charge of Peter Norfolk, ran off the track and dashed into Bostock's main entrance without hurting any one. It frightened Queen Sheba, the lioness, whose cub Dreamland was recently presented to ex-Senator William H. Reynolds, of the Dreamland Company.[83]

He could be vindictive. In 1908, he pursued actor Arnold Daly to Chicago over a relatively small debt:

Chicago, April 1 - A deputy sheriff, armed with an attachment calling for the seizure of all effects save the clothes he might have on, caught Actor Arnold Daly in the bathtub yesterday. The deputy sheriff took Mr. Daly's trunk and the suit he was going to wear, his bathrobe and even his pajamas, and then walked away with a happy smile, leaving the denuded thespian in the tub without even enough apparel to take him decently back to his suite next door. . . . The deputy sheriff who marooned the hero of "Regeneration" was acting for ex-Senator William Reynolds of Brooklyn, who had brought suit to recover $769 of the actor.[84]

Reynolds's close friendship with Mayor Mitchel led to an accident that made the front page of the *New York Times*:

Mayor Mitchel's pistol accidentally shot ex-Senator William H. Reynolds in front of the Mitchel home at 258 Riverside Drive on Saturday afternoon. . . . The automatic pistol dropped from a holster carried by Mr. Mitchel when he was alighting from his automobile. It struck the sidewalk, breaking the safety clutch set against the trigger and forced the hammer down, exploding a cartridge. The bullet hit ex-Senator Reynolds. . . . His early recovery was expected without serious results.[85]

Reynolds generated headlines for the care he lavished on his dog, Tiger:

The life of "Tige," a great dane, owned by Mayor William H. Reynolds, has been insured for $10,000. The mayor recently employed two of the best physicians in town to care for the animal when he was ill, and an offer of $5,000 for him was refused. "Tige" is a familiar figure to boardwalk strollers, having, during his illness, been wheeled up and down the promenade in a roller chair.[86]

"Tige" even appeared in advertisements for Long Beach auctions:

A Man and his dog on the sand, by the sea. The dog, a tawny-coated Great Dane "pup," glorying in the feel of the soft, yielding sand, the tang of the sea-cooled air and his 16-months of vibrant life in Belgium and at Long Beach. The man, purposeful and resourceful, a builder of Cities, the discoverer and first Mayor of Long Beach. A man of vision who dreamed boardwalks, bridges, miles of streets, houses and hotels *and then made his dream come true.* The man is Mayor William H. Reynolds; the Great Dane is his dog, Tiger, or "Tige" as he is called. . . . "Tige" had a hard hour or two last week when he overheard his master tell a group of friends that a part of his happy romping ground was to be sold at auction—*that means houses to go up on his (Tige's) playground—BUT what's a dog's convenience compared with the fact that this sale means more population and more buildings for Long Beach. . . .*[87]

Long Beach into the Late 1920s

Long Beach continued to grow during the 1920s. In January 1927, the Long Island Railroad expanded its trackage between East Rockaway and the Reynolds Channel, significantly increasing rail traffic into and out of the city. The population expanded accordingly, and taller buildings found their way into Long Beach. Among the most notable was Granada Towers, built in 1928 by the firm of Lang and Rosenberg in a design that picked up on the Spanish Colonial detailing of the earlier houses.[88]

Reynolds continued to dabble in real estate elsewhere, though ultimately he focused all his energies on Long Beach. In 1928, he proposed to build a sixty-four-story "Reynolds Building" on East 42nd Street in Manhattan, billed as the world's tallest "commercial structure." But he decided against it, and sold the project to Walter Chrysler, who built the Chrysler Building on the site.[89] Three years later, Reynolds died, at the age of sixty-three.

An obituary in the *Boston Globe* wrote that Reynolds "devoted his career to the real estate business after brief dabbles in politics and the theatre."[90] But it might be more accurate to say that Reynolds brought politics and theater to his real estate dealings, and that Long Beach, his wonderful city by the sea and his greatest creation, successfully melded all three.

Postscript

Long Beach continues to be an oceanfront destination, but in the decades following World War II it began to decline. Most recently, the community was devastated by "Superstorm" Sandy, which flooded almost the entire island, causing enormous damage. Though its future is uncertain, its basic underpinnings remain intact and can serve as a strong foundation for building the Long Beach of the twenty-first century.

9

THE THOUSAND-ACRE CITY BY THE SEA

T. B. ACKERSON'S BRIGHTWATERS

RICHARD F. WELCH

In the last week of July 1914, just before the cataclysm of the Great War convulsed the world, T. B. Ackerson could often be found standing by the window of his real estate office, looking out on the growing community of Brightwaters, which he had taken from dream to reality. He could have easily turned his gaze from development maps and architectural plans to the potential buyers entering his office. Exiting the building, nodding to the construction crews and visitors, he could climb the steps of the observation tower he had erected to dazzle prospective purchasers and savor the scope, scale, and beauty of his thousand-plus-acre community, which stretched from the shore of the Great South Bay northward into the Pine Barrens.

The sheer ambition of the project was breathtaking, even to its founder. The boat canal, slicing inland from the bay, led to a series of small lakes surrounded by a tracery of winding roads that led in turn to the gracefully designed, arching bridges spanning the water bodies. These gave way to a more conventional grid plan before the entire community melted into the pitch pines and scrub oak. And of course there were the houses—attractively designed, well-built structures that both developers and purchasers preferred to call "cottages," or the more modest bungalows, as well as houses in a variety of styles that fit no particular pattern. All of this was Ackerson's creation, a unique masterpiece of design and execution wrought from a typical South Shore mix of salt-marsh streams, muddy feeder

ponds, and pine forest. Ackerson had every reason to feel the swell of pride and a rush of optimism as he surveyed his master project, unaware that within four years he would have to surrender control and direction of the community he had given so much of his fortune and energy to create.

Thomas Benton ("T. B.") Ackerson (1856–1924) was born in Rockland Lake, New York, and moved to New York City, where he married Carrie E. Ambler in 1888. Ackerson's business acumen was honed through his employment at the Knickerbocker Ice Company, which he joined in 1874. Though the company had no direct connection with real estate, his thirty-year tenure there apparently netted him both the experience and start-up money to begin his building career.[1] Ackerson launched his real estate development operations in 1898, when he incorporated the New York Land and Warehouse Company, which owned and operated warehouses in Hunter's Point, Queens County.[2]

That same year, Ackerson and his brothers, Charles F., Henry Ward, and Pierre T., established a construction and real estate firm dedicated to residential development. Possessing the combined talents of visionary, organizer, and promoter, T. B.'s preeminent position among the siblings was acknowledged in the new firm's name, the T. B. Ackerson Company. The family concern was soon engaged in constructing freestanding houses in the middle-class areas of Flatbush. The brothers erected a number of speculative houses around

Beverly Road between 17th and 18th streets. Some, built in clusters, were dubbed Beverly Square East and Beverly Square West. The Beverly Square projects convinced Ackerson that building custom single, detached houses reduced profits, at least in Brooklyn, and the firm increasingly relied on a number of basic designs, easily individualized with minor modifications.[3] In 1906, they purchased the Cornelius Roosevelt estate in Maplewood, New Jersey, and began work there on another development aimed at the same market demographic.[4]

Though the Beverly Square projects included several features of planned communities, Ackerson's first real foray into community design was Fiske Terrace in Brooklyn. The new project featured several elements that came to characterize Ackerson operations. One was the practice of offering homeowners the option of paying for the houses in monthly installments; another was the fact that the land for the development was originally an estate, as was true of the Maplewood project and, later, Brightwaters.[5] Fiske Terrace took its name from George P. and Elizabeth Fiske, the owners of the property, which was situated in Flatbush adjacent to the Midwood Park development. In 1905 Ackerson paid $285,000 for the land and the Fiskes' house, which occupied the highest elevations between Prospect Park and the ocean. Ackerson's first step was to demolish the residence, an early example of a "teardown."[6] For reasons that remain unclear, but were possibly intended to shield

his investments from risk, Ackerson used his sister-in-law Hattie Ambler to buy and sell some of the Fiske Terrace properties, a role she played in subsequent ventures as well.[7]

Yet another element that seems to have figured in Ackerson's calculations was proximity to mass transportation, in the case of Fiske Terrace the Brooklyn–Manhattan Rapid Transit line (BMT). In the late nineteenth century, New York City's rapid transit lines, originally individually owned, were consolidated into a metropolitan network, allowing middle- and upper-class professionals to move to the less congested areas of the city and enjoy a quick commute to their downtown Brooklyn or Manhattan offices. The *New York Times*, which followed the fast-rising developments in the still semirural sections of the outer boroughs, mused that the BMT line, which served Fiske Terrace, "will probably be used in conjunction with the new subways and bridges in affording quick transit to Manhattan."[8] Indeed, Ackerson's promotional material for the nascent development, the illustrations of which often featured trolley and rail lines, emphasized the ready access to rapid transit awaiting Fiske Terrace homeowners. As events proved, Ackerson was ever astute in grasping the advantages of the region's radically evolving transportation system.[9]

An Ackerson Company standard, already in place by the time of the Fiske Terrace project, was the insistence on quality construction, community amenities, and service. Ackerson boasted that the

Glenwood Road, Fiske Terrace, showing a typical Flatbush-style median, ca. 1905.

company was above the usual run of "land boomers or lot exploiters."[10] How much they differed from other reputable firms is arguable, but the layout, engineering, and landscaping of the development were thoughtfully designed and executed. The streets were wide, sidewalks were installed, and medians and streets were planted with trees. Ackerson's medians, whose greenery bestowed a park-like character on the grid-patterned streets, were based on those that landscape architect John Aitkin had designed for Dean Alvord's 1898 Prospect Park South development (see pages 62–62).[11] Utility lines, including water, gas, and electric, as well as telephone conduits ran from the streets to the lots, awaiting connection to the homes.[12]

The houses were described as custom built, suggesting that Ackerson modified his design catalog to suit individual tastes without losing the cost advantages of working from a set number of basic models. More distinctive structures could be designed and built for those willing to pay for them. Fiske Terrace homes were detached, three-story, "suburban style" structures. Interiors featured heavy oak ornamental mantels, stairways, beamed ceilings, and built-in bookcases. Hardwood trim, parquet floors, steam heat, and electric lighting were standard features as well.[13] The cost of the Fiske Terrace residences ranged from $6,500 to $15,000.[14]

Ackerson's "suburban style," like that of most of the nearby Brooklyn developments, drew inspiration from the Arts and Crafts movement, popularized in America by Gustav Stickley, who emphasized "rustic domesticity" in his work. Another strong influence was the Colonial Revival, which had grown in popularity after the Centennial and continued to exert a powerful influence on architecture and design well into the twentieth century. Ackerson's architects borrowed freely from both styles, often producing homes with an eclectic mixture of the prevailing fashions.[15] The developer enlisted the services of several Brooklyn architects who worked extensively in the newly suburbanizing sections of Kings County. A. White Price was deeply involved in the Fiske Terrace Projects, as was the partnership of John Slee and Robert Bryson, whose fluency in a range of architectural styles made them the most prominent local firm in the new developments at Fiske Terrace and adjacent Midwood Park.[16] The prolific suburban home designer Benjamin Driesler also lent his talents to Fiske Terrace, as he did to many of the other Brooklyn projects.

It should be noted that although all of these architects drew up the plans for many, if not most, of the Fiske Terrace homes, evidence suggests that they sometimes simply filed plans taken from pattern books or other readily available models.[17] Whatever the source, the architectural harmony of Fiske Terrace derived from a general reliance on designs that were similar or compatible, though not identical. The late twentieth-century fad for "making a statement" by imposing the most jarring design on a neighborhood or landscape was foreign to Ackerson and his fellow developers in Brooklyn and farther east on Long Island.

The Ackerson Company functioned as both a real estate firm and a building contractor, and, as he had done for the Beverly Square operation, Ackerson erected a real estate office for Fiske Terrace.[18] Strategically located alongside the BMT lines, the real estate office was sold in 1907 to the BMT, which promptly converted it into a subway station house.[19] The entire Flatbush area suburbanized rapidly and

Fiske Terrace sold out quickly. Of the 150 houses in the development, "all but one sold before completion."[20] In a 1907 brochure, the Ackerson Company claimed that Fiske Terrace was developed so quickly that the area went "from a wooded hilltop to a high class developed suburban home site" with such speed that the project would "go down in history as being the most rapidly developed of its kind on record."[21] Beverly Square, Maplewood, New Jersey, and Fiske Terrace gave Ackerson extensive experience in creating a "planned suburban development." Even before the Fiske Terrace and Maplewood projects were completed, Ackerson, hailed in *Brooklyn Life* as "among the foremost in the development of real estate in Queens and Brooklyn boroughs and New Jersey,"[22] had already launched a much more ambitious endeavor about sixty miles to the east.

Ackerson's attentions were drawn to an area located a little west of the village of Bay Shore. The first inhabitants were the Secatogue Indians, who may have called the spot Wohseepee, which was interpreted as "Brightwaters."[23] This stretch of the South Shore was dotted with small villages inhabited by many baymen, who plied their trade along the Great South Bay, which lies between Long Island and Fire Island—a large barrier island that shields Long Island from the Atlantic Ocean. By the early twentieth century, parts of Suffolk County's South Shore were already colonized by wealthy families from the city and elsewhere who established large estates in the manner of their contemporaries on the North Shore "Gold Coast." Hotels and boarding houses soon cropped up in the coastal villages, providing accommodations for summer visitors seeking water-oriented recreation.

The core of the new development came from the estate of Charles E. Phelps, who had a home in the area that he called Brightwaters, possibly after the presumed Indian name. In 1907, T. B. Ackerson

purchased 525 acres from Phelps for "a little under $500,000."[24] The initial acreage was augmented by another 500 acres, acquired from Charles L. Lawrence in 1910, quickly followed by another 300 acres, for a total of 1,300 acres.[25] The aggregate lent itself to one of Ackerson's real estate blandishments, "The Thousand-Acre City by the Sea." The entire development lay between Windsor and Bayview avenues and stretched from the Great South Bay to just north of the Long Island Railroad tracks. The 400 acres north of the tracks were reserved for experimental farms.[26] Ground was broken at the Brightwaters development on July 8, 1907, with T. B. tossing the first, symbolic, shovel of soil.

From the start, Ackerson conceived of Brightwaters as a suburban planned community, or "colony," as such seaside developments were often called. Indeed, in his earliest publicity, released even before the groundbreaking took place, he explained that the "Ackerson Lakeside and Bayshore Colony"— the name suggests that he had not yet settled on Brightwaters—was based on "the development of the land on the colony scheme, but with the view of making it an all-year home colony instead of a summer stopping place."[27] The colony's street plans, housing plots, architectural styles, and communal amenities and services were apparently well formed in Ackerson's mind—and committed to paper— before construction began, as the new development took shape with the same speed and dispatch as his more modest Fiske Terrace project.

As was the case in Kings County, T. B. was aware of the importance of transportation in the marketing of his new project, and he envisioned Brightwaters—which quickly replaced the mundane "Lakeside and Bayshore Colony"—as a planned community of resident commuters who could take advantage of the newly opened East River railroad tunnels to work in the city. Speaking to the press

Groundbreaking day at Brightwaters, July 8, 1907. T. B. Ackerson, right, tosses the first ceremonial shovelful. Bay Shore Historical Society

after touring the newly opened Pennsylvania Station in 1910, Ackerson stated that few recognized the "significance of [the upgraded Long Island Railroad facilities] in the development of all parts of Long Island within commuting distance."[28] Ease of commuting to Manhattan became a mainstay of Ackerson Company advertisements and promotional material. For example, an advertisement from the same year described Brightwaters as "A community of contented homes an hour from Herald Square," which gave the Long Island Railroad a lot more credit than it merited.[29] The banner "Commuters Paradise" was featured in a 1912 display ad, alongside small sketches of sailboats representing Ackerson's other main advertising lure.[30]

Conceptually, Ackerson's grand design combined elements of the "romantic suburb" with aspects of South Shore water-oriented recreation. But the key concept can be expressed in one word: Venice. The Brightwaters site originally extended northward to about the location of Pilgrim State Hospital— just south of today's Long Island Expressway—an area of scrub pine forest, upland woods, and salt marshes. Five small ponds in the uplands fed a small stream that meandered out into the Great South Bay. Working from this modest natural endowment, Ackerson sculpted five attractive lakes out of the upland ponds and converted the salt marsh stream into a 175-foot-wide, 20-foot-deep canal that extended about a mile, from the Great South Bay to the South Country Road. These improvements were intended to "to make Brightwaters as near like Venice as possible."[31] Work on the canal, which cost Ackerson $250,000, commenced in 1908 and was completed in 1910.[32] Like most of the work at Brightwaters, the project was carried out with manual labor and horse-drawn equipment. Dubbed

the Venetian Canal and Yacht Harbor, it provided every Brightwaters resident with mooring space. Two piers, extending approximately 800 feet into the bay, capped the canal's recreational possibilities. At the inland end of the canal, the Grand Plaza, a remarkable Renaissance Revival–inspired boat landing, including balustrades and flanking pavilions, served as both a focal point and a ceremonial entrance to the community. Situated on the southern edge of the Montauk Highway and illuminated at night, the Grand Plaza beckoned passing motorists to investigate the growing new community. The Italianate architectural theme was continued in the Venetian-style bridges that spanned the freshwater lakes Ackerson had created out of the swampy feeder ponds.

Though the Canal was the centerpiece of the community, the Ackersons endowed their project with many other amenities designed to enhance the aesthetic and social qualities that would also promote sales. They remodeled the former Alexander residence and donated it to the Brightwaters Association for use as a social center. Despite its name, the Casino, gambling was prohibited; the building was used as a site for parties, commemorations, theatrical performances, fund-raising, and dining. It housed a hostelry and clubroom on the main floor and a bowling alley, pool, and billiard rooms in the basement. The social center was suitably decked out for Decoration Day (Memorial Day), 1910, and opened the "entertainment season" on July 2 with a minstrel show.[33] A bathing pavilion erected on the east side of the canal, on the shore of the Great South Bay, was presented to the community on June 25, 1910. It quickly became a focal point for swimming and water games, as well as a prime spot for viewing

The focal point of Brightwaters: the boat basin, pagodas, and plaza. This scene is virtually unchanged since its development, ca. 1910. Bay Shore Historical Society

Brightwaters Casino,
ca. 1910. Society for the
Preservation of
Long Island Antiquities

Boat basin at Brightwaters,
ca. 1910. Bay Shore
Historical Society

Bathing pavilion at the
entrance to the Venetian
Canal, ca. 1910. Bay
Shore Historical Society

regattas held in the area. Other community assets created by the Ackersons included Wohseepee Park, which opened in 1912. The park featured a cabin that provided an additional indoor venue for social functions. Baseball diamonds and tennis courts were laid out, enhancing the sporting life of the nascent community. The lakes were stocked with trout, swans, and geese to augment their aesthetic appeal and recreational possibilities.[4]

The canal, sculpted lakes, and connecting waterways were intended to stamp Brightwaters with a distinctive upscale character, though Ackerson always used the terms *middle-class* and *moderate* to describe his market. In addition, he emphasized the community's salubrious, sports-and-recreation-oriented lifestyle, which was a major feature of the romantic suburb/planned-development phenomenon. An illustrated flyer issued by the Ackerson Company around 1910 touts Brightwaters as a "beautiful Arcadia of Springs, Lakes, Pine Woods and Sea Shore."[35] The word *Recreation* in boldface type tops the flyer, which boasts that Brightwaters had it all except mountain climbing. Indeed, "Nowhere on Earth is there Opportunity for a greater Variety of Outdoor Sports and Pleasures..." The vignettes bordering the single-sheet handout depict happy Brightwaters residents at play. Not surprisingly, most illustrate water sports—sailboating, fishing, beach play, swimming, canoeing on the lakes, and duck hunting, as well as ice skating and curling in winter. Land-oriented activities were not neglected, with horseback riding, golf, and motoring also making an appearance. All in all, the flyer, whose message was repeated in other promotional materials, was intended to entice Ackerson's primary market—prosperous, young, urban profes-

sionals who worked in the city but sought respite from the crowded, hectic, metropolitan scene in a healthy, rejuvenating suburb.

Work on the development began in 1907, and some homes were finished and sold by 1909. However, it was not until February 1910 that Ackerson held a banquet in his Fiske Terrace home to formally announce Brightwaters' "opening."[35] By that time fifty-five of the approximately one hundred houses available had been sold. The Ackerson Company had also completed forty miles of streets and boulevards and installed water and gas mains, as well as an electric-light system.[37] The Ackersons' total investment between 1907 and 1911 was reckoned at "upward of $1,250,000."[38]

Newspaper advertisements from 1909 to the onset of World War I reiterated the "good life" theme. "The 'Venice of America' is attracting the most desirable class of people," was the way Ackerson publicity couched it in a 1909 ad.[39] In 1910 Ackerson explained which "desirable class of people" he foresaw as Brightwaters residents:

> We are building homes for a progressive, ambitious class of people of moderate means who have been unable to fulfill their ideals of home within the City. By reason of our wholesale purchases of materials and facilities for large building operations we are able to meet the home seeker more than halfway by giving him a home practically at cost price, and on easy monthly payments. We are instituting a second mortgage installment plan that is an innovation in suburban development. Our desire is to attract the responsible home owner rather than the speculator. My theory is that the home owner himself should receive the benefit from the enhanced value of property which is bound to be realized in the increased building operations and permanent establishment of our community, for it is a well-

Title page from a Brightwaters promotional booklet, ca. 1908. Bay Shore Historical Society

Birds-eye artist's rendering of the Brightwaters development, ca. 1910. Bay Shore Historical Society

known fact that where a community is established their values must increase.[40]

Though the canal, lakes, pavilions, and cascades were intended to endow Brightwaters with a distinctive character, it was the housing that drew the residents. The T. B. Ackerson Company had always boasted of its construction and described itself "as one of the most extensive 'Builders of Houses of Merit.'"[41] Taking advantage of the different types of terrain in the development, the Ackersons divided Brightwaters into sections: Bay, which included the land alongside the canal; Lakes, the plots in the feeder-lake sections; Oaks and Pines, in the scrub oak zone; and yet later, Pine Terrace, Bungalow Gardens, and in 1915, Pine-Aire. Farther north, Brightwaters Farms, which extended through the scrub oak forest to Pilgrim State Hospital, was not developed residentially.[42]

For the housing plots, Ackerson announced his intention "not to cut the land into Carmel lots and expect to develop them into gingerbread sales. Such a cheap small lot development is a curse to Long Island."[43] Consequently, though housing plots in Brightwaters varied in size to some degree, most were approximately 100 x 150 feet, noticeably larger than previous lots in the area. The construction of Ackerson houses was generally overseen by Charles F. Ackerson, described as the de facto "general manager in charge of construction."[44] The labor force was heavily Italian, and in April 1910 about two hundred workers attempted a strike when they heard that workers on a nearby project were earning twenty-five cents a day more than they were.[45] The Ackersons had two of the leaders "hauled into court for intimidation," but they were quickly released on their promise to leave Brightwaters and not return. The laborers, cowed by the Ackersons' use of the law against them, returned to work. The company decided to sweeten the blow by voluntarily raising the workers' wages.[46]

The Ackerson Company offered homes in styles described as "cottage," "bungalow," "semi-bungalow," and simply "artistic." The designs themselves were produced by a number of architects whom Ackerson had previously employed in Brooklyn. Slee & Bryson and A. White Pierce, veterans of the Fiske Terrace project, contributed designs to the new development. Half a dozen Brightwaters bungalows designed by James L. Burley were illustrated in a popular guide to this building type published in 1911 by *House & Garden* editor Henry H. Saylor.[47] There were likely other architectural contributors whose names have become lost.[48] Whether the company also utilized pattern books as they probably did in Brooklyn is unclear.[49]

Though most of the homes at Brightwaters, especially in the first years, were built by the contracting branch of the company, T. B. Ackerson was content simply to sell plots as well. "[P]urchasers of plots at 'Brightwaters' are under no obligation to employ their [Ackerson construction] services," an advertisement explained. "On the contrary, every encouragement is given purchasers to build homes upon their plots, and no restriction is placed upon them as to their selection of architect, builder or materials."[50]

Though most of the houses that the Ackerson Company built were basic models, they also constructed dwellings "under special contract," that is, according to the wishes or designs of their clients. For example, a Dutch Colonial was built for Edward D. Fisher, deputy controller of New York City, while others requested, and got, Queen Anne cottages, "Elizabethans," and Italianate villas.[51] Not surprisingly, Henry Hornbostel, partner in

Substantial "cottages" in the "Bay" section along the canal. Henry Hornbostel was the designer of the Queensboro Bridge. Bay Shore Historical Society

Modest bungalow house commonly found in the inland "Pines" section. Brooklyn Historical Society

Henry B. Ackerson Arts and Crafts–influenced home on Lakeview Avenue. Brooklyn Historical Society

Palmer & Hornbostel, the architects of the Queensboro Bridge, designed his own home at 98 South Windsor Avenue.

Prices varied according to style, and the different sections tended to feature one or the other. The more expensive, and larger, homes were concentrated in the Bay and Lakes sections, with the costs dropping proportionately as one moved farther from the water. According to the *New York Times*, "Each section has a different class improvement, ranging in cost from cottages in the Lake and Bay sections at $8000 to $40,000, in the Oaks at $4500 to $6000, to the Bungalows in the Pines and Bungalow Gardens from $1950 to $6000."[52] Pine-Aire,

the last section to be developed, offered plots beginning at $75 and six-room, stucco bungalows for $1,230.[53]

The average price of the firm's bungalows in 1909–12 was about $3,225.[54] The somewhat larger cottages were more costly, kicking in at a little under $4,000. Typical Ackerson bungalows were built on concrete foundations with cellars, boasted "big" brick fireplaces, kitchen ranges, bathrooms, hot and cold water, laundry tubs, electric lighting, shades, screens, and verandas. The grounds came with walks and seeded lawns. The firm claimed there was "plenty of room for stable or garage, poultry yard, garden and flowers," not to mention "congenial neighbors."[55] The generally larger prewar cottages had "spacious living rooms with wide open fireplace set in an artistic mantel frame." The dining room was likewise "commodious," and the kitchen was complete with modern appliances, including a range. The laundry room contained soapstone tubs, and a butler's pantry was situated nearby. The large back porch had adequate space for an "ice box," which the purchaser evidently bought for himself. Like the bungalows, the cottages came with electric light fixtures. Hardwood floors, shades, and screens were standard. The second floor held three bedrooms, closets, a modern bathroom, and "separate toilet." The third floor, or attic, contained two finished rooms and storage space. As was true of the bungalow, the grounds were graded and seeded, and had laid-down walkways.[56]

Ackerson did not aim his development at those who fall into today's "sub-prime market," but he was nevertheless quite happy to arrange financing for those who could not come up with the total price of his land and/or homes. "All courtesy is extended to those who desire outside aid," one of his 1909 ads announced. Another, in 1912, beckoned buyers with the assurance that "You can own one of these comfortable year-'round homes by making a small cash payment, with the balance in amounts about the same as rent."[57] Who could resist such blandishments and decline to live the happy and healthy lifestyle enjoyed by those residing in the "Land of Sunshine"?

To protect and perpetuate the upscale environment and social cohesion of its new enterprise, the Ackerson Company inserted a number of restrictive covenant clauses in their deeds. As was common in residential parks, plot purchases were prohibited by "sensible restrictions" from erecting anything other than "one family detached dwellings," with a minimum of fifty-foot frontage on a street and a value not less than $2,500.[58] Ancillary structures were confined to those "appropriate to a Gentlemen's County Residence." Restrictions were also placed on proximity to adjoining plots. Regarding residential borders, purchasers were forbidden to plant a

Ackerson Company advertisement featuring water recreation. From a Long Island Railroad booklet, ca. 1917

T. B. Ackerson Company real estate office and observation tower, from which prospective buyers could select their building lot. Bay Shore Historical Society

hedge or build a fence over four feet tall. "Tight board or close built fences" and advertising signs were also banished from Brightwaters. Purchasers also undertook to prevent overflow or discharge from "any cesspool or stable . . . to be discharged, or drained, into any of the Waterways or tributaries" in the development. The covenants, which could be amended by mutual agreement between the Ackerson Company and the seller, were to run until January 1, 1920.[59]

As an additional draw to prospective buyers from the city, the T. B. Ackerson Company provided bus service from the Bay Shore train station to Brightwaters. When interested parties arrived at the Ackerson real estate office, they could look over various maps and architectural renderings of the project to see what was available and where. However, Ackerson had a more dramatic method of convincing people to buy at Brightwaters. He constructed an observation tower alongside the office that allowed buyers to look out over the entire site in order to choose their land. Such a vista also took in the Atlantic, the Great South Bay, the Venetian

Canal, and the system of lakes with connecting streams, falls, and cascades. This astute and dramatic marketing stratagem reflected T. B.'s many years of experience and calculation, and it is easy to imagine him climbing to the top of his tower and surveying his creation with pride.

As Brightwaters developed, so did the amenities, services, and necessities. Whereas the plan of the Bay section was largely a grid, determined by the straight line of the canal, streets in Lakes and Pines tended to be more curvilinear. Ackerson originally intended to include sidewalks, as he had in Brooklyn, but discovered that the residents preferred their neighborhoods without them, opting for a more rural atmosphere. Water mains, fire hydrants, and telephone service all appeared in short order. The streetlights were electrified in 1910. Costs for the communal benefits and improvements were borne by the residents, who were assessed for the development's common roads, parks, and waterways.[60] Such fees went to the Brightwaters Association, essentially the development's government, which was established by T. B. Ackerson.

The association, which was in operation by 1910, provided for three classes of membership: active, resident, and nonresident. Samuel K. Kellock was the first president, with T. B. Ackerson serving as vice president.[61] Kellock's relationship to the Ackersons is unclear, though he was probably a business associate. In any event, the vice presidency was enough for T. B. to maintain supervision of the community. His determination of the overall scale, housing styles, plots, costs, demographics, and atmosphere remained constant from the development's inception to 1918, when events forced him to relinquish his control. But his vision and standards were positive and, as he boasted in advertisements, he offered "a home-site made picturesque and wholesome surroundings on sensibly restricted 'Land Worth Owning.'"[62]

The residents, largely of the same socio-economic class with similar interests, enjoyed a wide range of community events. Swimming, boating—including the new sport of motorboating—regattas, dances, and events at the Casino were all part of life at Brightwaters. One idiosyncratic feature of Brightwaters' social life was the practice of pitting teams from the different sections against one another, with the losers being tossed into the canal. Gentler activities such as rowing or slowly drifting along the lakes are depicted in period photographs.

Heavily advertised, aesthetically pleasing, and benefiting from the South Shore's natural recreational potential, Brightwaters drew not only young, upwardly mobile professionals, but its share of the era's celebrities as well. The pioneering Vitagraph Film Company established a branch studio at 94 Fourth Avenue in nearby Bay Shore in 1915. T. B. himself is credited with convincing the Vitagraph principals, whom he had known in Brooklyn, to make the move to the Brightwaters area. He provided bungalows for the company's staff when they first arrived, and later built homes for the studio heads.[63] Ralph Ince, whose acting and directing career lasted into the 1930s, became head of the Bay Shore operation in 1916. He had bought property in Brightwaters as early as 1913, and Ackerson built a house for him and his actress wife, Lucille Stewart, on Lakeview Avenue West. Three years later Ince's sister-in-law and a major Vitagraph star, Anita Stewart—"the Sweetheart of the Silent Movies"—constructed her home, Wood Violet, on Windsor Avenue.[64] The "Marvelous Millers," a popular vaudeville troupe of the time, built a retreat for themselves and fellow performers in Brightwaters. On August 27, 1913, they organized an "all-star" vaudeville show, the proceeds of which went to purchase equipment for the Brightwaters Fire Company.[65]

Like Fiske Terrace, Brightwaters filled up quickly; between 1907 and 1917 the T. B. Ackerson Company built about two hundred homes, not to mention community structures, bridges, roads, and the like, making Brightwaters one of the most successful of the planned suburban developments of the period. Indeed, in 1915, the year the Pine-Aire section opened, the company announced a new record, with sales increasing more than 130 percent over the previous year. This occurred in what the

Canoeing in the "Lakes" section of Brightwaters, ca. 1910. Bay Shore Historical Society

seven hundred lots. Easy-to-meet installment payments were arranged to guarantee the plots, and the Bay and Lakes sections were disposed of in the August 11, 1917, auction. Buyers needed to put only 10 percent down, pay another 10 percent before September 11, 1917, with the remainder spread out over thirty equal monthly payments.[70] The auctioneer observed that though there were many "attractions to stimulate values at Brightwaters . . . to offset these we have a real estate market in the doldrums with many more people seeking to sell than buy."[71] Nevertheless, he thought the incorporation of the village would help, as it would "assure future upkeep of the property."[72]

The 1917 auctions did not generate enough capital to keep the Ackersons going, and another auction was scheduled for the summer of 1918. Seeking an explanation as to why Ackerson was selling in a down market and thereby losing a "sure, worthwhile profit," the *New York Times* real estate reporter concluded that the company had reached a point "where the cost of managing and selling the property . . . would be greater during the two or three years it would take than the amount of money that could be obtained from it."[73] Nevertheless, speculation continued regarding the Ackersons' sudden abandonment of their project. The *New York Times* repeatedly expressed surprise that the Ackersons would sell in a sluggish market, ensuring a loss. Other developers, they maintained, were waiting for better conditions, and characterized the Ackerson move as "a mystery." Speaking for the firm, T. B. Ackerson stated, "The [auction] advertisements tell the story. We are through as developers at Brightwaters, and if our property brings only 25 cents on the dollar, we are going to sell it. The die is cast."[74] Though the causes of the apparent reversal of fortune are unclear, the events suggest that the Ackersons were overleveraged and, despite recent sales figures, faced cash-flow problems.

Not only were all remaining parcels of land put on the block, but the farm plots in the demonstration farm and virtually all of the company's other property—stables, railroad siding, public garage, contractors' yard—were offered as well. The 1918 sale was more successful than that of the previous year and all plots were reported sold, including the recently opened Pine-Aire section and the farm plots. At the conclusion of the auction, T. B. addressed the attendees, claiming that the auction "would mean the reconstruction of Brightwaters in a broader and more extensive scope and with the assistance of the present residents there and the greater demand that will result from the purchase activities, more than 200 homes should be erected in the near future."[75] Considering the circumstances, exactly what T. B. meant by this

New York Times described as a generally "inactive" suburban market.[66] T. B. Ackerson attributed the increase in sales to Brightwaters' "diversified topography, which led to [a] correspondingly wide latitude in prices."[67] He also cited the fact that he had kept his prices steady for three years, despite growing evaluations resulting from "the large amounts of money extended by us in improvements."[68]

The following years, however, witnessed a major change in Brightwaters' governmental organization. In 1916, a core area of 620 acres in Brightwaters, from the bay to a mile or so north of the railroad tracks, became the incorporated village of the same name. The incorporation suggested a weakening of Ackerson's hold, as he had earlier gone on record against incorporation, arguing that such a measure would "increase political and governmental expenses and raise taxes."[69] T. B. Ackerson transferred the canal and yacht harbor, chain of lakes, parks, and streets to the new village. The Brightwaters Association was dissolved, though Ackerson continued his leadership role as "president" of the new incorporated village.

World War I put a damper on suburban development on Long Island and elsewhere. In 1917 and 1918, Ackerson held public auctions to sell some

somewhat vague prediction is difficult to fathom. But one thing was certain. T. B. Ackerson and his company were no longer the lords of Brightwaters.

In 1920, Ackerson declared bankruptcy. Unlike many who were forced to fold at the time, he repaid all of his creditors and retained enough capital for one last venture in Long Island real estate. In 1924, Ackerson began developing a section in Roslyn named Flower Hill. While overseeing operations there he contracted a cold that quickly worsened. He died a week later.[76] Though his last enterprise took him to the North Shore, Ackerson's crowning achievement lies thirty miles to the southeast in the "Thousand-Acre City by the Sea"—Brightwaters—which still bears his imprint a century later.

Indeed, in 2007 the Village of Brightwaters celebrated its centennial. The commemoration featured the appropriate festivities and events, but the real star was the village itself. Despite being surrounded on all sides by the type of patchwork development that characterized Long Island after the World War II, Brightwaters remains a virtual time capsule of Ackerson's original design. Over two-thirds of the village's pre-1918 structures survive and the landscape features remain largely as Ackerson conceived them. Indeed, if T. B. could return to Brightwaters today, he would be pleased to find his vision largely intact in both physical appearance and ambience. A community that takes pride in its distinctive identity and remains committed to its preservation, Brightwaters flourishes as a testament to T. B. Ackerson's creativity and perseverance.

10
GREAT NECK ESTATES

HARVEY STEWART McKNIGHT AND
THE McKNIGHT REALTY COMPANY, 1907–1916

ELLEN FLETCHER RUSSELL AND SARGENT RUSSELL

G reat Neck Estates captured the interest of the Long Island real estate world from the moment its developer, the McKnight Realty Company, announced its first land purchase east of the New York City border early in 1909. Brokers and developers alike avidly followed the rise of The Estates at Great Neck because of the boldness of its concept and timing. It was begun at a time of financial uncertainty, during a severe recession that had decimated the mortgage market. At more than four hundred acres, Great Neck Estates was the largest Long Island development of its time. Its high, wooded location overlooking Little Neck Bay was spectacular. The competition among landscape professionals for its design, announced simultaneously with the principal land purchase, was novel. And the five McKnight brothers were known and respected for the many high-quality projects they had already completed in the borough of Queens.

H. Stewart McKnight, the founder and president of McKnight Realty, emerges from this story as a heroic character. During his long career he practiced law, published newspapers, headed his family's real estate company, acted as his own contractor, and masterminded about a dozen residential developments. During the entire period of the Great Neck project, McKnight was on the brink of bankruptcy, but he carried on with persistence and verve. At one point he supported himself clearing lots and digging foundations for builders in his own development, and he raised animals and cut hay on the part of the property that he still owned.

At his finances' lowest ebb, McKnight was rescued: he was offered the post of Nassau County attorney, which he accepted, and embarked on the final and most influential period of his life.

Before their real estate business began, Stewart McKnight had been a lawyer; his four younger brothers, stenographers.[1] Born near Chambersburg, Pennsylvania, the five boys grew up in West Virginia; they all moved to Bayside, Queens, between 1890 and 1892. Stewart found the practice of law not to his liking, and in 1895 he bought a foot-powered printing press and started publishing several local newspapers, doing every task himself, from writing articles and selling advertisements to running the press. Involving himself in Queens County politics, McKnight was elected justice of the peace for Flushing, then deputy attorney general, and he spoke at Republican meetings statewide. He remained active in Republican politics and played a key role in Nassau County government for the rest of his life.

In 1903, Stewart McKnight made his first real estate investment, a seventeen-acre tract on Bell Boulevard in Bayside.[2] Through his relationship with the Bell family, McKnight met Charles E. Finlay, of the Rickert-Finlay Realty Company, and advised him on the purchase of a Bell-owned tract near McKnight's own land. To McKnight's surprise, Finlay was willing to pay considerably more for his chosen tract than Queens farmland was worth at the time. McKnight, who helped Finlay close the deal, then watched with awe. Within

130

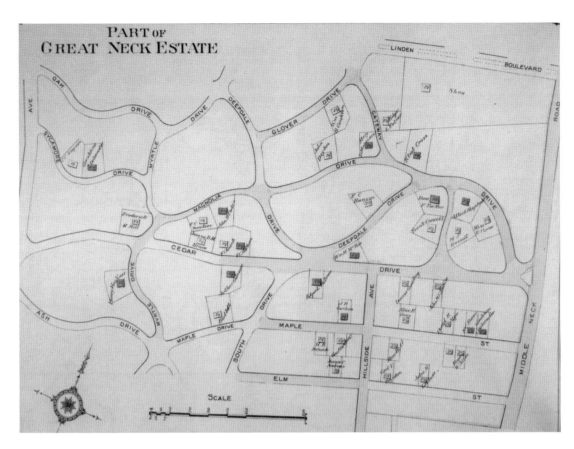

PART OF
GREAT NECK ESTATE

*The E. Belcher Hyde
Atlas of Nassau
County, 1914, shows the
new 450-acre Great Neck
Estates between Little Neck
Bay and Middle Neck
Road.* Courtesy Society
for the Preservation of
Long Island Antiquities

a week, Finlay had surveyors laying out building lots, followed by a contractor grading streets and lots. In no time at all the newspaper advertisements began: "Bellcourt, Bayside, Long Island," with prices higher than the McKnights could have imagined. To their astonishment, buyers turned up daily, and the lots sold fast. "This was the beginning of the boom in real estate on Long Island," Stewart McKnight wrote later, "which lasted from 1902 to 1907 when it collapsed in the panic of that year."[3]

Finlay's company had undertaken successful developments in St. Louis, Missouri, and before that in Indianapolis and Galveston. Charles Finlay predicted a boom in metropolitan New York real estate, particularly in Nassau County close to the Queens border—and the McKnight brothers wanted to be part of it. Emulating Rickert-Finlay, Stewart McKnight decided to develop his own Bayside tract, which was all wooded and full of stones. Unlike Finlay, however, McKnight did the rough contracting work himself. "I purchased a team of horses and a wagon," he later recalled, "employed a couple of husky Polacks and began . . . clearing the tract."[4] He sold the best trees to the telephone company for poles and cut the rest as firewood. He borrowed a stump puller from Fort Totten and dug up stones and boulders. It took three months, but finally McKnight called in a surveyor to lay out streets and lots. Then he placed newspaper advertisements, cagily noting that the lots on offer were adjacent to "Bellcourt." Not surprisingly, the buyers came. Stewart and his brothers handled the sales as

a team, each responsible for certain blocks of lots. They offered these blocks to subdevelopers—and sold them all in a single weekend.[5]

Elated by the success of this first venture, the five McKnight brothers decided to give up all other business "and make New York suburban real estate their life's occupation."[6] Rickert-Finlay had transferred their base of operations from the Midwest to the North Shore of Long Island about 1902, and the McKnights considered that a good sign. They incorporated the McKnight Realty Company as a real estate developer; the brothers held much of the stock and each one was an officer and a director. Other stockholders were former employers and professional colleagues, including a former governor, investment bankers, and a publisher. The McKnight company took an office in the Corn Building, 347 Fifth Avenue, opposite the Waldorf Hotel and not far from Rickert-Finlay's Manhattan headquarters.[7] For each project it undertook, McKnight Realty incorporated a subsidiary company to hold the title and maintain an on-site office. The parent company acted as manager and sales agent, and loaned the money for the development. Over the next five years, McKnight Realty spun off ten subsidiaries. The developments were in Bayside, Steinway Park, Murray Heights, Lawrence Manor, Flushing, Whitestone, and several other Queens sites.[8] A 1907 newspaper article about the brothers described their approach to development: "It has always been the policy of the McKnight brothers to keep their properties active. They use every legit-

2. *The force behind Great Neck Estates was Harvey Stewart McKnight, whose real estate company included his four younger brothers.*
Courtesy Nassau County Department of Parks, Recreation & Museums, Photo Archives Center

imate means to get improvements on their properties, both public and private, sewers, city water, gas and electric lights they persistently pursue until they get them, and if they cannot get them from existing corporations . . . they put their own money into them, but get them they will." The article also noted that the McKnights built parks and parkways on their properties and "some of the handsomest [houses] to be found anywhere near New York." And the article claimed that "the McKnight brothers build their [own] homes and live where their properties are being developed, and they confine their energies to the single purpose of development of above-average properties."[9]

By 1907, H. Stewart McKnight was president of the Real Estate Exchange of Long Island, which had been incorporated that spring to promote the developments of its members (and to discourage the "unworthy" projects of certain others).[10] The exchange vigorously lobbied for improvements in commuter transportation, particularly the opening of the East River railroad tunnels and the electrification of the Long Island Railroad's Port Washington line. "It may be easily imagined," Stewart McKnight wrote in a *New York Times* article, "what the effect on values and on population will be in [the North Shore region] upon the completion of the Pennsylvania Railroad improvements . . . [a commuter may then enjoy the] advantage of a home in the suburbs, among beautiful surroundings, where one may have his own little grass plot and his own little garden . . . a man who is fond of outdoor sports and outdoor exercise will also appreciate" the newly accessible North Shore.[11]

In the fall of 1907, the stock market crashed.

During a severe recession caused in part by the 1906 San Francisco earthquake, an investor failed in a spectacular attempt to corner the market in copper stock. As he went under, he dragged a tail of banks and trust companies down with him. Fear ran wild and people pulled their money out of banks, first in New York and then all over the country. Bankruptcies burgeoned, especially in New York, and the depleted banks slowed down on loans and—disastrously for the developers—on real estate mortgages. In the wake of the crash, late in 1907, McKnight Realty Company sales came nearly to a standstill. At the same time, H. Stewart wrote, overhead continued. Mortgages and taxes still had to be paid. In fact, to counter the recessionary market, the company doubled its advertising and made advances to sales agents to keep them working. But "our cash was soon exhausted and we began to borrow to meet deficiencies."[12]

Writing of the 1907 meltdown, when things went bad for him, Stewart McKnight said of his models Rickert and the Finlays: "Their vision was all right. Our following their lead was all right. They, with their experience, however, did not seem to know when to stop expanding and liquidate and, of course, we with no experience could not know." And what happened to the McKnights was dire: "They from their experience saved something from the deflation; we lost everything."[13]

When the McKnight brothers opened their New York office in 1902, their father, John, had given them some financial advice. "Boys," he said, "you are going to expand your purchases of property and will borrow money for that purpose. Never put a note in the bank unless [you are] prepared to pay it off when due—even if you borrow again the next day."[14] The brothers followed this advice and were never refused credit, and were never asked to put up collateral. When they needed money to buy a property, they just called the cashier at one of "their" banks and asked him to put the money in their account. Spendthrifts might have ruined themselves on such confidence, but not the McKnights. "We declared no dividends," Stewart wrote. We "took out of the business only our necessary simple living expenses. . . . All McKnight Realty Company net income went back into additional properties."[15]

The next year brought improvements in the stock market, and the McKnights hoped that all would soon be back to normal. In a spirit of optimism, they assembled four hundred acres of Great Neck farmland in seven parcels that would become Great Neck Estates, closing the deal in April 1909. Two ancient farms, formerly owned by the Thorne and Duryea families, comprised much of the land; these had been purchased in the boom year of 1905 by a Brooklyn realtor named Desmond Dunne.[16] Except for a few additional parcels later added to the development, this was the last property the company purchased.[17] The McKnight subsidiary created to develop Great Neck Estates was named the Villa Park Association.[18]

"Some very novel development ideas will be worked out at Great Neck within the next three months," said Arthur Maxwell McKnight, the company's treasurer, in April 1909, when the brothers purchased an additional thirty-six acres with frontage on the bay.[19] Over the next year, the McKnights continued adding parcels to the site they now called Great Neck Estates, and they challenged several American landscape[20] designers to compete for a plan that would enhance the property's hilly topography and bay views. A young planner named Robert Anderson Pope received a prize of $1,000 for "the best layout . . . following his own adaptation of certain famous old English country estates, [and] incorporating in his final scheme the best ideas [of] the five other architects who had competed for the prize."[21] It is likely that the competition took place in 1909, because by May 1910, the *New York Times* reported that the development already had "winding drives," and that "handsome residences" were under construction there.

Pope, a landscape planner working in New York City and a student of Frederick Law Olmsted Jr.,[23] spoke against the highly classicizing City Beautiful movement at a 1909 conference in Washington, D.C. Two years later, the Boston Dwelling House Company called on him to fix a plan for a model suburb that the Olmsted firm had designed in Jamaica Plain, Massachusetts. Pope reduced the lot sizes to make the houses affordable for workingmen, and he aligned the building envelopes so that each house would have a clear view. That same year he laid out a community ("with a distinctive old European flair") at Smith's Point on Fire Island for developer F. J. Quinby.[24] These professional experiences shortly after the McKnight competition suggest the style and skills Robert Anderson Pope brought to bear on the challenges posed by the hills and valleys and views of the nascent Great Neck Estates.

By early 1910, the McKnights had formalized the Pope landscape plan, which guided them in laying out and building a sinuous system of some twenty-six miles of drives that followed the sloping contours of the land. Pope laid out house lots as well and may also have suggested building envelopes that would protect each property owner's view.[25] Most of the development followed the sinuous plan, but a section known as Thornewood[26] in the Maple–Elm streets area is rectilinear, with lots varying in size from 20 x 100 feet to 110 x 100 feet. Lots were sold and houses built in this section early; in fact, at least one lot had a house on it when it was sold in July 1910.[27] Elsewhere in the development, "villa lots" were larger, and many were irregularly shaped. Several historic farmhouses were left standing when the parcels were assembled. Only a few houses went up in the Estates in 1909, but in the next year ten were under construction, with six built in the year after that (minimum cost $10,000).[28]

"The work of development will be started at once," the *New York Times* announced in mid-

In the spring of 1911, ten or eleven families lived in Great Neck Estates. Within four years, the number of families had quintupled. This handsome, two-and-a-half-story gambrel-roofed Dutch Colonial was photographed with its trim yard and spindly young trees in 1913. It is now the site of the Village of Great Neck Estates village hall. Courtesy Village of Great Neck Estates

1910.[29] About the same time, the McKnight company issued a free booklet aimed at investors interested in purchasing blocks of lots and building houses on them.[30] Another booklet contained eighteen "modern house plans."[31] These plans probably showed picturesque Tudors and elegant Georgian Revivals, Mediterranean villas and Dutch Colonial gambrels—the styles of the earliest houses that still grace the winding streets today. The McKnights wanted to ensure that any investor who looked at Great Neck Estates could not miss its distinctive character and quality. The houses they promoted were a key factor in that perception. "Folks are more and more showing preference for houses built to order rather than those that come 'ready for sale' in most so-called developments," one of the brothers told a reporter in 1914. "At Great Neck Estates we have anticipated this demand, and have built no houses ourselves. We are selling the vacant land, however, with certain basic restrictions, and financing the building of . . . homes wherever occasion requires. We also act as agents for the various builders now erecting houses on the Estates."[32]

"The services of a well-trained architect are invariably employed in the better suburban sections," reported an article about Great Neck and the McKnights. "It is just as cheap to live in an artistic house as it is to reside in . . . some monstrous effort." The article reported that moderate suburban houses cost between $8,000 and $25,000, and the preferred styles were "the old Colonial or Georgian type, the early Tudor, or the half-timbered English version [which] invariably harmonize with the rural surroundings.[33] The names of only a few of Great Neck Estates' architects are known.[34] They include Frank J. Forster,[35] George Hardway, Oswald C. Hering,[36] E. R. Tuchs,[37] and Irving B. Ells.[38] Later, in 1925, LeRoy Ward designed the Kenwood apartment building on Middle Neck Road; and in 1938 Frank Lloyd Wright built his first house east of Buffalo, on Magnolia and Myrtle drives, for publisher Ben Rebhuhn.

By May 1910, Great Neck Estates was attracting a lot of attention in the press, due to its great size— it was the largest development near Manhattan at that time. It was praised for its elegance—the hills, trees, winding drives, and water views were universally admired—and for its proximity to several great estates.[39] The newspapers were impressed by the McKnights' ambitious plan to build a "central utility plant" that would supply gas for cooking and for "running dynamos," and a central refrigerating and heating plant that would supply all the houses in the park, "giving them the same advantages as apartment dwellers."[40] Although the central plant was never built, at least sixteen houses had gone up by 1911, and according to the papers, five of them

had been sold "from the plans."[41]

In April 1911, Great Neck Estates had ten or eleven resident families. H. Stewart McKnight had reserved for himself a one-acre lot containing the seventeenth-century Allen house overlooking Little Neck Bay. It had been standing on the Duryea tract when the McKnights assembled their property. Another brother kept the Thorne mansion, another of the early farmhouses, although he probably never lived there.[42] Each of the other three McKnights had reserved one acre for himself. Although according to his autobiography, Stewart McKnight did not move from Bayside to Great Neck until 1914, the Allen house was important to him. His wife, whom he had married in 1901, was Brooklynite Frances Oakey, whose mother had been an Allen.

The McKnights called the resident families to the Thorne house for an important meeting in late March or early April 1911. The purpose of the meeting was to discuss incorporation as a village in order to protect the character of the development and the quality of its residents' lives. The McKnights' promotional literature had called the Estates a "great private park" and suggested that the residents would have some common amenities: an "artistic wall" with gate and lodge would separate them from the rest of Great Neck; the "great dynamo" was still spoken of;[43] and the residents were to share a private dock, yacht club, and casino. They had miles of drives and lanes, and a sea wall. The literature indicates that the McKnights had an exclusive approach to lot sales: "a careful selection among intending purchasers" was cited, favoring those "who will co-operate along the broad lines of the general project." The advertising explicitly targets the "higher salaried and professional classes . . . [whose incomes average] from $2,500 a year upwards."[44] Every single resident had come to Great Neck from New York City, and the men commuted to work there. Every single resident had come to enjoy the pleasures of country living, surrounded by compatible neighbors. The development "would be hedged about with restrictions," the sales brochure promised, "which will confer upon each property owner every convenience and pleasure of country life, yet keep him restricted from becoming an annoyance to his neighbors by reason of anything unsightly or unpleasant."[45]

With the support of most of the residents, Great Neck Estates was incorporated on April 16, 1911. Incorporation put the community beyond the reach of the Town of North Hempstead with its schedule for public improvements and its property taxes to pay for the improvements it saw fit to install. As a village, Great Neck Estates (and its developer) was responsible for its own infrastructure, policed

itself, and ran its own affairs. Property owners paid taxes to their own village, and nominal amounts to the county and the state. The McKnights thought that the incorporation "conserved the rights of residents against possible encroachments," as well as against "unforeseen assessment."[46] McKnight had another reason for incorporating his development: he had seen the high taxes and overbuilding that had resulted from the annexation of Brooklyn and Queens into Greater New York City, and he feared Nassau County would be absorbed next. He believed that every settlement should incorporate, no matter how small. "I never knew a village that would disincorporate," he wrote, "or would consolidate. . . . The safety of the Town and County units lies in incorporated villages that will never vote to become . . . part of a city."[47]

In the early spring of 1912, the Great Neck Golf Club, with "one of the sportiest nine-hole courses on Long Island," was opened in the southwest quadrant of Great Neck Estates, and the Thorne mansion was remodeled as its clubhouse. The McKnight subsidiary, the Villa Park Association, leased the club its property.[48] The club's officers included McKnight's role model Charles Rickert as treasurer, and H. Stewart McKnight himself as secretary. Great Neck Golf Club, which opened in the heyday of the golf-and-country-club boom on Long Island, was considered an important attraction for the new development, as it was believed that "the completeness of a neighborhood seems to hinge on its possession of a well-managed country club."[49] By 1915 the club had been renamed the Soundview Golf Course, and it was prominent in Great Neck life until a fire destroyed the clubhouse and the Depression ended its life altogether. In

1939 the land it stood on was sold to a developer who marketed it in plots to builders.[50]

As much of an asset as it was to the brand-new village, the golf course was supposed to be little more than an ornament to a far greater project that was announced early in 1911.[51] A three hundred-room "million-dollar hotel" (the small print admitted that the actual cost with furnishings would have been half a million) was to rise on ten acres of the southwest quadrant, the project backed by a syndicate of New York capitalists. Designed by Frank M. Andrews, the architect of the newly built Hotel McAlpin on Broadway in Manhattan, it would have been a luxurious, year-round, fireproof hostelry. According to the *New York Times* in April 1911, the land had been leased from the McKnights and construction was about to begin.[52] Something happened to the deal, however, and nothing was built but the golf course. The hotel was never mentioned in the press again.

In 1910, the opening of railroad tunnels under the East River did away with the need for Long Island commuters to transfer from train to ferry en route to Penn Station. In October 1913 the Port Washington branch of the Long Island Railroad was improved by the addition of a double track beyond Great Neck, and electrified, further streamlining the commute. The McKnights and the other suburban developers had been working for and anticipating these improvements for years. As they had predicted, better transportation fueled a new burst of North Shore house building.

While these great improvements were gestating and the construction of houses in Great Neck Estates was booming, the McKnight Realty Company was experiencing continuing—and devastat-

ing—hard times. When sales improved somewhat in 1908 after having decreased to virtually nothing in 1907, the McKnights were led to believe that the market was on an upswing. It was in that spirit that they had purchased the Great Neck tracts. But in 1910, sales in their Queens projects fell to 1907 levels, and the brothers found themselves spending everything they had to prevent foreclosures. By the end of 1914, according to Stewart McKnight's recollections, no assets were left and the subsidiary companies whose property was mortgaged were wiped out. When bad times came, the banks that had been so friendly to the McKnights on the way up turned hostile. They demanded bonuses for renewing loans, then refused to renew at all. When the McKnights ran out of assets to put up against their loans, they lost everything they had invested in the effort to save their business.[53]

At the end of his rope, Stewart McKnight, made a daring move. In 1913,[54] he went to London with an associate, Herbert Fell, who was trying to raise money for utility companies. The two took an office in the financial district and McKnight began trying to sell preferred stock in the realty company. Part of his plan was to get a few English investors to buy up the company's 6 percent mortgages as they came due (these investments were not available in England then and the interest rate was very attractive). If it succeeded, this intervention would get the McKnights "out of the clutches of mortgagers" who were bleeding the life out of them.

Herbert Fell, meanwhile, was looking around for someone who had recently come into a lot of money. He found Sir Frederick Mirrielees, whose wife had just sold her share of the Union Castle Steamship Line and had received "the largest check that ever went through the Bank of England in a private transaction."[55] Fell persuaded Sir Frederick to invest in his utilities, and then, after a weekend at the Mirrieleeses' country estate, Fell and McKnight presented the real estate proposal to him. After brief reflection, Mirrielees agreed to invest. "This [transaction] seemed to solve our financial problem," McKnight wrote.[56]

McKnight arrived home in the early spring of 1914, accompanied by Sir Frederick's son, Douglas, who took a position in the McKnight office at Great Neck. While McKnight was straightening things out with his creditors and paying taxes and other debts on the development, young Douglas busied himself on the land.[57] Mirrielees had acquired property in several sections of the Estates, one of which lay to the west of Bayview Avenue and to the south and east of the golf course. A printed prospectus at the village hall includes a plan titled "Mirrielees Park," featuring a trio of east–west streets terminating at Mirrielees Circle, and a drawing of a large, English-style house.[58] Douglas Mirrielees recruited students from Amherst College and the Massachusetts Institute of Technology, who spent the summer of 1914 felling trees, clearing underbrush, and grading roads. The Mirrielees investment also included a section of smaller lots east of Bayview near Mirrielees Park, and some fifty villa lots in the Estates proper.

That August, Sir Frederick Mirrielees came to Great Neck to see his investment. "He was enthusiastic," wrote Stewart McKnight, and he urged the brothers to continue to develop Great Neck Estates.[59] If they needed more money, Mirrielees told McKnight, he would arrange to loan it to them. So, optimistic again at long last, the McKnight brothers gambled one more time. Instead of paying off a large bank loan with the Mirrielees money, they used it to continue developing Great Neck Estates and meet their overhead. Their land sales, even in 1914, had not improved enough to cover their operating expenses. But the McKnights knew they could rely on their new investor to cover the bank loan when it came due.

But disaster struck yet again. Soon after Sir Frederick Mirrielees arrived home, he died.[60] The estate had to be settled. Young Douglas returned to England, and the Mirrielees representatives on the McKnight Realty board began trying to force a liquidation to protect the estate. In the midst of all this, war broke out, tangling the situation further. "We were in a worse position than before Sir Frederick came into the company," wrote Stewart McKnight.[61] His brother Arthur Maxwell, the company's treasurer, managed to get himself to England. He went to see Mrs. Mirrielees, her husband's executrix, hoping to persuade her to honor his commitments. She told him that her husband's investments were of little interest to her, and she could not be bothered with them. She had turned the matter over to attorneys with instructions to squeeze out what they could.

So, "after three years of struggle to hold on to all [our] properties," Stewart McKnight wrote, "sacrificing every asset we had to meet obligations and avoid receivership, we were closed out by mortgagers foreclosing mortgages and lenders taking . . . collateral on the loan."[62] By the end of 1914, McKnight Realty was finished.

The brothers scattered. Ira Thomas took the records of the original company, along with the furniture, and opened an office in Manhattan. John Calvin took a partner and carried on the company's Bayside business. Scott went to Miami Beach. H. Stewart and Arthur Maxwell stayed on in Great Neck, in reduced circumstances, and worked tirelessly to pay off the company's obligations.[63]

For a few years after 1914, H. Stewart McKnight lived off the land in Great Neck Estates. He still held the title to much of the property, and much of it was still undeveloped, so he was able to pasture livestock, cut wood, make hay, sell topsoil, and grow vegetables for sale. While his wife ran a shoestring fire insurance business in the Bayside office, Stewart worked as a contractor, probably in Great Neck Estates, building foundations, grading sites, and hauling debris. Paying off his debts took virtually all of his contracting income. He wrote that they would have been destitute if not for his wife's insurance business, and they would have starved without the produce they raised themselves.[64]

One day in the fall of 1915, Stewart McKnight "was on a concrete mixer putting in a foundation . . . in the Estates," when a relative involved in county politics came and asked him if he would like to serve as Nassau County attorney.[65] Elated at the opportunity, McKnight assumed office in April 1916. A Republican dating back to his time as a justice of the peace in Queens County in the early 1900s, McKnight served as county attorney until 1934. McKnight's fortunes gradually improved, and he lived in Great Neck Estates until his death sometime after 1947. He never went back to real estate development; in fact, he considered his later public service career the most constructive work of his life.[66]

Lot sales and house building in Great Neck Estates and the other Great Neck developments were strong in 1912–1914, spurred by the electrification of the Port Washington line late in 1913—the new twenty-minute commute made western Nassau County more attractive to Manhattan businessmen.[67] As the McKnight literature reminded them, the professional and business classes could no longer afford an urban life nearly as good as the life awaiting them in the suburbs. By the spring of 1914, fifty houses in the Estates were occupied, and several more were under construction.[68] According to the *Brooklyn Daily Eagle*, which was inclined to exaggerate a little, in May 1914 an open house and sales event drew some two hundred people in automobiles to Great Neck Estates for a look around.[69]

Construction activity in the Estates in 1915 exceeded that of every prior year.[70] By the following summer there were sixty houses in the development, ranging in cost from $6,000 to $30,000, on lots from a quarter of an acre to one acre in size. Seven years after its opening, Great Neck Estates was still growing, still attracting residents, and still adding fine houses, built singly and in groups. Its developer was out of the picture, but the village structure H. Stewart McKnight had imposed on the development was in place to ensure the comfort and security of the community far into the future. The real estate development had become a municipality.

Great Neck Estates continued to grow and thrive as a village with a distinct character. In 1921, a building-zone ordinance went into force, establishing a residential district and two business districts on Middle Neck Road. In the residential district, property owners were limited to a single house and a garage or other accessory structure per lot, and in the business districts many uses were prohibited.[71] By 1922, there were around 150 houses in the village.

During the 1920s, the village attracted luminaries from the literary and entertainment world. F. Scott and Zelda Fitzgerald lived on Gateway Drive for a couple of years while he wrote part of *The Great Gatsby*.[72] He based West Egg on Great Neck Estates and East Egg on the more rarified Sands Point. Ring Lardner lived near Great Neck and was the Fitzgeralds' frequent cocktail partner. Actress Paulette Goddard spent time with relatives on Aspen Place, songwriter Victor Young lived on Myrtle Drive, and Fanny Brice and Ed Wynn spent time in the Estates. Babe Ruth and W. C. Fields both played golf at Soundview Golf Course. In 1922, the impresario Morris Baron built the Great Neck Playhouse on Middle Neck Road at Maple Avenue, a 1,650-seat palace for vaudeville performances and movies, with three floors of apartments above. The business thrived only moderately until 1925, when the lessees thought of bringing Broadway tryouts to the Great Neck Playhouse.[73] In 1925, work on the magnificent Kenwood Apartments on Middle Neck Road at Linden Boulevard was begun, to be completed two years later. Its developer was Rickert-Finlay, and its architect LeRoy Ward.[74]

By 1924, the Estates had its own private bathing beach, with bathhouses and docks.[75] The next year saw the creation of a park with a pool and a baseball diamond, thanks to the efforts of H. Stewart McKnight, who, still a resident, arranged for the village to acquire wetlands on Little Neck Bay in return for the promise to fill them in.[76] The park was modernized in 1949 and continues to provide recreation today.

Great Neck Estates had by 1927 become "a center of wealth and social influence, one of the wealthiest towns in the state of New York."[77] A great influx of newcomers from New York City during the 1920s due to improvements in road and rail had swelled the population of the village and of surrounding Great Neck.[78]

Great Neck Estates still recalls the story of Frank Lloyd Wright's appearance in the village one day in the Depression year of 1936. He showed up, unrecognized and tatterdemalion, at the office of realtor Bob Freedman, looking for a lot on which to build a house. The selected site was at the place where Myrtle and Magnolia drives diverge. This was Wright's first commission east of Buffalo, a house for publisher Ben Rebhuhn and his wife, Anne, a sculptor. "The neighbors were aghast," recalled a man who had watched the construction as a child. "It was a humble yet grand house," he said.[79] Building a Wright house was tricky during the 1930s. An older generation of tradesmen, accustomed to the Tudor, Colonial, and Mediterranean styles then popular, did not understand Wright's ideas about walls, windows, or trim. They did not understand skylights or heated floors. Further, the Rebhuhn

Scott Fitzgerald may have written part of The Great Gatsby *in Great Neck Estates. Great Neck was his model for the novel's West Egg. Whether or not Fitzgerald was writing while he was here, he and Zelda were certainly socializing, as they were in this photograph of a party at their house. Zelda faces right in the back row while Scott sits on the floor third from the left.*

With the permission of the Princeton University Library and the Fitzgerald Literary Trust

House was designed around a standing tree, which rose through the dining room ceiling. Because the house was heated, the tree put out leaves through the winter—it was dead before the first year was out. The seven-room house was furnished with a combination of Wright-designed pieces and the Rebhuhns' own furniture. Ben Rebhuhn died in 1966, and Anne lived in the house until it was damaged by fire in 1970. It has since been restored.

The Soundview Golf Course did not survive the Depression. Socially important in the 1920s, the club slid downhill after 1929. A fire destroyed the old Thorne mansion, which served as its clubhouse, and in 1939 it went out of business. The land was sold to a developer, and after World War II Paul Jeffries filed a map and sold lots to builders, who constructed the houses that stand in the southwest quadrant of the village today.

House by house, developers and homeowners continued to build out the original Pope plan for Great Neck Estates. After World War II, the village retained many undeveloped lots, which were filled in successively with Colonial Revivals smaller than those built in the early part of the century, then with ranches and bi-levels and even a few International Style structures. By 1958, Great Neck Estates hit its peak population of 3,200; as of the 2010 census, 2,761 people lived in the village. New houses are still being built today, some of them on lots where the original houses have been demolished.

After his retirement from real estate, H. Stewart McKnight and his wife, Frances, continued to live in Great Neck Estates, in the old Allen house on McKnight Drive.[80] For decades the local paper recorded their comings and goings—to Ithaca, to Albany, to visit a brother in Florida, entertaining friends at a club—as it did other local notables.[81] The McKnights' fortunes more than recovered during the time Stewart was Nassau County attorney. In 1935, when Stewart McKnight was seventy years old, he was struck by a cab on Park Avenue in Manhattan. Although injured, he lived on for at least twelve more years, some of which he spent writing an autobiography that details his rich personal and professional life. His story highlights the strong relationship that bound the five McKnight brothers and the fearless, inventive attitude that made him such a creative and resilient developer.

11
PAUL V. SHIELDS AT GREAT NECK

GREAT NECK VILLA AND GRENWOLDE

ELLEN FLETCHER RUSSELL AND SARGENT RUSSELL

In the early spring of 1909, two years after a collapse of the stock market crushed Long Island's burgeoning growth in residential development, two ambitious young men from the upper Midwest arrived in New York hungry to break into the world of North Shore real estate and make their fortunes. For them, real estate development was the first step toward greater accomplishments; they went on to found a Wall Street brokerage firm, and one became a governor of the New York Stock Exchange.[1] The Shields brothers, nineteen-year-old Paul (1890–1962) and twenty-two-year-old Louis (1887–1931),[2] sons of a businessman and manager for Northern Pacific Railroad, acquired a twenty-six-acre parcel on the west side of Great Neck and began subdividing it into plots.[3] The land was on the south side of the new Shoreward Drive, on the flanks of a rise that clambered steeply up from Manhasset Bay. Great Neck Villa Estates got under way at around the same time as the McKnight Realty Company's much larger Great Neck Estates, and it had a similar picturesque quality, enhanced by a system of gracefully curving roads. It is possible that the Shields brothers were influenced by the work of Stewart McKnight, much as McKnight had been influenced by the more experienced Charles E. Finlay, of the Kensington development firm Rickert-Finlay.[4]

The Shields brothers developed their land under the name Great Neck Villa Company, and their first action was to create "villa plots" sized from one-eighth of an acre to two acres.[5] The Villa property was bounded by Shoreward Avenue to the north, Highland Avenue to the west, Schenck Avenue (then called Manhasset Boulevard) to the south, and York Drive to the east. To the west of the Villa, Great Neck Hills and Avalon were already under way on the old George Schenck farm, promoted by Walter W. Davis of the Great Neck Improvement Company. The Shields's Villa development featured the kind of street layout favored by the Frederick Law Olmsted landscape firm and its followers: a sinuous tracery of roadways delineating ovals and teardrops and naturalistic sweeps instead of neat, rectilinear blocks.[6] At several "gateway" intersections, the Shields placed pairs of handsome cobblestone posts with bronze plaques inscribed "1909," which remain today.

Brief notices of Great Neck Villa Estates appeared in newspapers in the spring of 1909, one of which mentions two houses—a Dutch Colonial and a "California bungalow"—under construction, and another about to be started.[7] The Shields brothers placed their first advertisement for the Villa in June. "A restricted residence park," Great Neck Villa represented the "country estate idea" for "the family man in fairly comfortable circumstances who desires a large enough plot of ground to enable him to emulate the country life of a rich man on a moderate scale."[8] This lifestyle might include, according to the advertisement, such features as gardens and stables. Lest one dismiss the

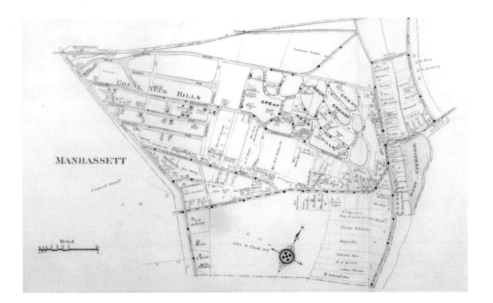

Streets are curved at Great Neck Villa, and lot sizes are in general larger than in the rest of the town. Society for the Preservation of Long Island Antiquities

Villa Estates as a "visionary prospect" that existed in the mind's eye alone, the Shields assured potential purchasers that the site was not only beautiful and convenient to the city but also *under construction*, with "fine semi-bungalow . . . homes being built regularly on the property."[9] Whereas some of the other early Great Neck real estate developers—the McKnight brothers at Great Neck Estates, for example—subdivided lots and sold them to speculators or potential residents, who then built their own houses, at Great Neck Villa the Shields brothers had some of the first houses built to show how the development could look. Though their reasons for doing so are not known, it may have been that they wanted to create a look and a style for the Villa by building key properties, or, as the *Brooklyn Daily Eagle* suggests, they wanted prospective purchasers to see that the development was a real place.[10]

The Shields brothers deliberately used snobbery to market Great Neck Villa Estates. Though some of the plots were considerably smaller than an acre and the houses were worth less than $10,000, the development was nevertheless targeted to "refined, educated people who desire to . . . meet their own kind" and socialize as well as reside together.[11]

The following spring, Paul Shields advertised for a "man of selling ability" to work for commission in his real estate business. The salesman could expect to earn around $3,000 per year.[12] Great Neck Villa Estates grew apace during the spring and summer of 1910; nine houses were being built to join the three

already standing. Among them was a ten-room residence that architect E. W. Hazzard was building for himself.[13] It is not known whether Hazzard designed other Great Neck Villa houses. The Shields brothers themselves were at work on infrastructure projects, including "the Ashley sewerage system" to serve the "artistic dwellings" then in the works.[14]

In 1911, the Shields brothers took an option on an eighty-three-acre parcel of land a little to the south of Great Neck Villa and announced plans to create small-acreage plots in the near future.[15] Nothing seems to have come of the plan, however, because no mention of it appeared in the newspapers. At this time, the real estate pages of New York and suburban newspapers were crammed with news of the tiniest events in the suburban developments on Long Island's western North Shore. They printed advertisements, puff pieces, photographs, notices of house sales, mentions of individual houses going up, tree and garden tips, and even income-producing schemes for the new suburban homeowner.

That same year, Paul Shields began using picture postcards as a marketing tool for the Villa Estates.[16] The property had by then become photogenic—the *Brooklyn Daily Eagle* called it "the Berkshires of Long Island"[17]—with appealing, widely spaced, two-and-a-half-story houses on rolling, landscaped terrain overlooking Manhasset Bay.

Though 1910 and 1911 were lackluster years for Long Island real estate sales, due largely to

In 1911, Shields & Company began using postcards to promote Great Neck Villa. This photograph, taken around 1914, looks north from Schenck Avenue at Lincoln Road. In the foreground is one of the original stone posts that were placed at several of the development's key entries. The concrete sidewalk delineates the street, which is still unpaved. Courtesy Great Neck Library

These brand-new houses on Windsor Road were photographed for Shields & Company ca. 1912–13. Both have long shed dormers to accommodate full-height second floors. The photograph emphasizes Great Neck Villa's sinuous curved roads, cobblestone curbs, and the many little trees and shrubs that had been planted to soften the development's harsh new lines. Courtesy Great Neck Library

The first houses in Great Neck Villa were under construction in the spring of 1909; one of them was described as a "California Bungalow." This advertising postcard may show that very house, set in a grove of spindly young trees, ca. 1911. Courtesy Great Neck Library

lingering effects of the stock market crash in the fall of 1907, development had continued apace in Queens, and the momentum was pushing eastward. According to the *New York Times*, 1912 would be Long Island's year.[18] The opening of the Long Island Railroad's East River tunnels had reduced commuter travel time by thirty minutes, and electrification of the Port Washington line was eagerly anticipated. The time had passed, another article in the *Times* stated, when a speculator could buy a run-down farm, print a map, and call it a development. No, the writer noted, using Great Neck Villa as his good example, the modern suburban developer had to install macadamized roads and concrete sidewalks, gutters, a water-supply system, and above all, he had to build model houses. Great Neck Villa Estates, he wrote, had around fifteen houses in the works at that moment, which, when added to the ones already built, would make a community of some fifty houses—most built in the past eighteen

months.[19] Three months later, all was still bustling at the Villa Estates, with houses being built and sold,[20] and the successful Paul Shields was ready for his next venture.

Great Neck Villa survives with considerable integrity to this day. The trees that were small in the second decade of the twentieth century have grown, and many sites that looked barren then are lush today. Views that once swept across Manhasset Bay are now obscured by the Villa's own greenery. The development's cobblestone gateposts, streets, gutters, lots, and many of its early houses—called "Old English," "Colonial," and "Mediterranean" —retain their original appearance, although many have had alterations and replacement windows and doors. Great Neck Villa was not completely built out in its first few years and now contains houses that date from the 1930s through the early twenty-first century. Some of the early houses have been replaced by newer ones, but they are the exceptions.

Grenwolde's waterfront casino can be seen on the 1914 Belcher Hyde Atlas of Nassau County. No houses appear, although four had been built by March 1913. Originally, a few lots stretched down to Little Neck Bay, but the casino and deeded rights-of-way gave all the Grenwolde property owners waterfront access. Society for the Preservation of Long Island Antiquities

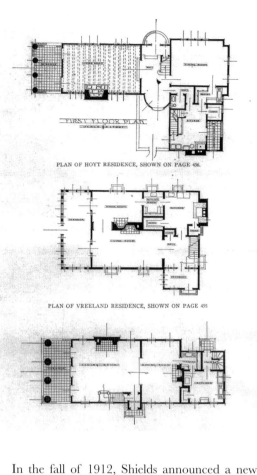

FIRST FLOOR PLAN

PLAN OF HOYT RESIDENCE, SHOWN ON PAGE 456.

PLAN OF VREELAND RESIDENCE, SHOWN ON PAGE 458

The Grenwolde houses are substantial, comfortable residences. Each property had guaranteed waterfront access, and the use of the community casino. The houses were originally marketed for around $15,000, or advertised for rent for $1,500 a month. Architectural Record 36, no. 4 (October 1914), p. 460

In the fall of 1912, Shields announced a new Great Neck project, one with a twist that made it unique. He had assembled a syndicate of New York businessmen[21] and bought a waterfront parcel of about forty acres, carved out of the vast Skidmore Estate, which stretched along Long Island Sound for more than a mile.[22] The Skidmore Estate owned property in and around New York City, including buildings in Manhattan. in addition to this desirable Great Neck shorefront, It had been tantalizing Great Neck developers for a decade, and one parcel after another was bought, subdivided, and sold for development.[23]

Paul Shields's dealings with the Skidmore Estate may have led to his acquaintance with attorney Walter F. Vreeland, who became a Grenwolde neighbor and eventually shared Shields's responsibilities for sales and rentals of the houses. Like Shields, Vreeland had an office in the financial district in lower Manhattan.[24] He specialized in real estate matters, including mortgages and foreclosures, and he often represented the Skidmore Estate.[25]

Grenwolde

For Grenwolde, Shields chose one of the last waterfront parcels that remained on the market in Great Neck.[26] Whereas at the Villa Estates, he had been in partnership with his brother Louis, at Grenwolde he formed a syndicate to buy the property but retained sole responsibility for development and

sales.[27] Shields stated that Grenwolde was the last large tract left for development on the west side of the Neck (the better side, in his opinion).[28] It lay on a bluff at the northern end of Bayview Avenue, a major thoroughfare that bisected Great Neck Estates, and had a thousand feet of water frontage on Little Neck Bay near Elm Point, previously known as Steamboat Landing. One of Shields's first acts at Grenwolde was the construction of a waterfront casino for the community. It had a club, locker rooms, and retiring rooms, a dining room equipped with a dumbwaiter that connected it to a kitchen, bathing apartments, and quarters for a keeper.[29] Shields also designed a sewerage system with an on-site sewer treatment plant,[30] buried electrical and telephone wires, and laid out lots and roads.[31] Only a few of the lots included waterfront, but each property owner had a right-of-way to the water and use of the pier and casino.[32]

For Grenwolde, Paul Shields's last and most important development, he hired the young landscape designer Robert Anderson Pope for the critically important layout of lots and roads.[33] Pope, a former student of Frederick Law Olmsted Jr., had laid out the much-admired Great Neck Estates a few years earlier.[34] He had also redesigned an Olmsted suburb near Boston, reducing lot sizes to make them more affordable for workingmen and to ensure that each house had a clear view. At Fire Island, Pope had designed a development "with a distinctive old European flair."[35] Paul Shields must have found this latter work of Pope's of particular interest because he wanted to give Grenwolde the ambience of "a typical English cottage settlement of the better class."[36] Grenwolde's street plan is simple, featuring a drive off Bayview Avenue that leads to an oval road surrounded by lots, and a lane leading down the bluff to the casino on the shore. Grenwolde was designed for fourteen or fifteen houses.[37]

Paul Shields's express purpose for Grenwolde was to provide a kind of housing as yet unavailable on the North Shore. "I worked out this project and interested the present owners," he said in March 1913, "after I had found in selling other properties... that there exists a certain class of New York residents who [have] not yet found a place in the country suited to their requirements. It was with absolute knowledge of this class of prospective buyers that Grenwolde was purchased. This is one of the principal reasons to my mind why our project met with practically instant success."[38] A look at the Shields projects of Great Neck Villa and Grenwolde as they are today illuminates the contrasts between the two developments. The Villa houses are comfortable yet modest Tudor, Colonial, and Mediterranean types, whereas the Grenwolde houses are larger, several

New York architect Frank J. Forster, then part of the firm Caretto & Forster, designed this Norman-style house (1913) at Grenwolde for John R. Hoyt. Said to be Forster's first commission, the L-shaped Hoyt House centers on a round, two-story, engaged turret with conical roof. This house still stands on Grenwolde Drive today. Architecture, September 1914

of them rather careful copies of historic English houses, adapted for comfort and convenience. Grenwolde offered larger lot sizes and waterfront access for all property owners.

Indeed, Grenwolde was imagined as a corner of the English countryside, quaint and exclusive, with each large house modeled on a specific historic building.[39] One was "adapted from a rambling old house at Carhampton"; another was "inspired by a charming little thatched roof cottage nestling by the roadside near Evesham in Worcester."[40] However, the houses were not exactly what they appeared to be. Picturesque on the outside, the interior of the Grenwolde houses provided every comfort and convenience that modern design and technology could offer. "Quaint houses," Shields said, "should not be ruined by impractical interior arrangement."[41] So, a rambling, half-timbered house at Grenwolde might boast a "thatched" roof, but it would be faux. Shields acknowledged that thatch was impractical for Great Neck's climate (not to speak of its builders), and he didn't consider using it. The roofs at Grenwolde that resembled thatch were in fact shingles "turned over the eaves and stained to match the color." Another sprawling, half-timbered, cottage-inspired Grenwolde house had a brick-bordered cement terrace, a large hallway with closets for coats and storage, a living room copied from a house in Gloucestershire, a modern kitchen, and cross-ventilated servants' rooms.[42]

By March 1913, four houses had been built at Grenwolde, "three after the English pattern and one designed after the Dutch Colonial type."[43] According to a March 1913 article in the *New York Herald* entitled "Cottage Colony at Great Neck from Ideas Obtained in England," the houses had been designed by an architect named Edward King, about whom nothing has been found. However, a year and a half later, in October 1914, the *Architectural Record* published photographs and floor plans of what must be three of those four houses. These are the John R. Hoyt house (at 34 Grenwolde Drive today), an L-shaped, half-timbered, Norman-style stucco house with a round engaged tower at the entry; the Walter J. Vreeland house (at 11 Grenwolde Drive today), a half-timbered stucco house with sweeping eaves turned to resemble thatch; and the Charles W. Brazier house (street number not

This sturdy Dutch Colonial built for Charles W. Brazier is the only original Grenwolde house that was not designed in the style Shields called "Old English." Like the other original houses, Brazier's was designed by Frank J. Forster. Architectural Record 36, no. 4 (October 1914), p. 459

Real estate attorney Walter J. Vreeland helped Paul Shields with sales and marketing for Grenwolde, and one of the four original houses was built for him in 1913. Frank J. Forster designed this brick-and-stucco, half-timbered house with a gabled roof, eyelid dormers, and sweeping eaves turned under at the soffit. The roof was originally "thatched," but in keeping with Shields's concept that quaintness should not exclude modern conveniences, the roofing material was actually wood shingles, turned over the eaves and stained. Architectural Record 36, no. 4 (October 1914), p. 458

In 1920, architect Chester A. Patterson designed Paul Shields's own Grenwolde house. Sleek and streamlined, its strong horizontal lines and single-story height gave the Shields house, which is on Grenwolde Drive, a more modern look than its older neighbors. Architectural Forum 35 (September 1921), pl. 44

known), a large, gambrel-roofed Dutch Colonial. They are attributed to the firm of Caretto & Forster. Frank Joseph Forster (1886–1948) was a New York architect educated at the Cooper Union and in Europe. Upon his return to the United States in 1908, Forster worked with other architects for a few years before establishing his own practice.[44] There are several other extant Forster-designed houses in Great Neck Estates. No matter whose pen inked the plans for the early Grenwolde houses, it must be remembered that the detailed concept for these large, quaint, English-inspired buildings with every modern convenience under their sweeping roofs came from the developer, Paul Shields.

Throughout the spring and early summer of 1913, and again in the spring of 1914, Paul Shields advertised Grenwolde, and individual Grenwolde houses, for sale. An advertisement in April 1913 mentioned "property restrictions and conditions of sale" intended to "insure a community of refined and congenial people."[45] An advertisement the next week was aimed at attracting yachtsmen and motorboat sportsmen to the Grenwolde development.[46] Still other advertisements in the spring of 1913 targeted golf, tennis, and polo players, automobile drivers, Manhattan commuters, and new brides. Each advertisement used the phrase "Old English" to describe all but one of Grenwolde's houses.[47] The exception was the Dutch Colonial owned by Charles W. Brazier. Apparently newly completed in the early spring of 1913, this house was advertised on its own a year later. The Dutch Colonial stood on a wooded acre and a half, with a right-of-way to the beach. It had hardwood floors, "every modern convenience,"

large open fireplaces in the living and dining rooms, a tiled pergola, four large bedrooms, two baths, a large attic, and a service wing with its own baths and stairway.[48] One advertisement indirectly suggested an asking price of $15,000—a moderate price for a good development house, neither at the bottom nor at the top of the range offered at the time.[49] In the early summer of 1914, W. J. Vreeland advertised a "new thatched roof cottage" at Grenwolde for rent. For $1,500 a month, the tenant would have ten rooms, three baths, and a large lot.[50] The advertised house matches the description of Vreeland's own house. Vreeland advertised his rental several more times that summer and fall, describing the property as "a new Old English stucco house and garage . . . with right of way to the water."[51]

Eventually, Paul Shields built a house in Grenwolde for himself and his family. Though he already had residences on Sutton Place in Manhattan, in Southampton, Long Island, and in Palm Beach, Florida,[52] the look and the life of Grenwolde must have appealed to him, and by the middle of 1921, he had his own Tudor-modern house, which stands today at 2 Grenwolde Drive, outside the oval at the intersection of Kings Point Road.[53] Compared to the Grenwolde houses built a decade earlier, the Shields house was of a simple design. Sleek, slate-covered, lengthy hipped roofs capped the low, stucco-clad ground floor, the whole pinned to the ground by a pair of heavy brick chimneys. The strong horizontals were relieved—and a hint of Tudor styling revealed—only by the off-center entry vestibule, comprising an engaged pair of steep gables in which the half-timbered inner gable peeps out from behind the staunch, stuccoed outer gable. The architect was Chester A. Patterson, who worked on estates and in suburban communities in the New York area, including some Long Island locales, during the 1920s.[54] The Shields house has been modernized and altered during its history, and in 1984 it was raised to a full two-story height.[55]

Most of Grenwolde's original (1913–14) houses survive today, and there are now fourteen properties on the drive.[56] The original gateway still offers a reserved welcome for motorists passing between its tall brick piers with their patinated bronze plaques. In spite of later development pressing in on its boundaries, in spite of elaborate modern houses within the oval, in spite of the Merchant Marine Academy looming nearby, Grenwolde is still an arresting place. The half-timbered houses are not period standards, but unique, distinctive structures whose character has not been diminished by modernizations. Yet, whereas early photographs indicate the proximity of the water, this is not evident today. Trees that were twiggy in 1914 are now dense with foliage; they enclose the oval in green and obscure long-range views. Grenwolde is as elegant today as it was a century ago, its ambience just as rarified.

Paul V. Shields's career as a real estate developer appears to have ended around 1914, when he was twenty-four years old. In 1923, he founded Shields & Company, a Wall Street brokerage house active in underwriting industrial securities, especially those of chain stores. In 1924, his brother and former real estate partner Louis G. joined the firm, as did their brother, yachtsman Cornelius Shields. Louis Shields had previously been associated with Merrill, Lynch & Company. In 1929, Shields & Company was reorganized as an investment firm on the New York Stock Exchange. Among Paul Shields's own investments was a company called National Automotive Fibers, which he acquired in 1956. In 1960 the firm's name was changed to Chris-Craft.[57]

Paul Shields was married to Veronica Gibbons Balfe, whose daughter by a previous marriage, Veronica, married actor Gary Cooper and lived in Los Angeles.[58] After his wife's death, Shields, by then senior partner of his investment firm, was an eligible bachelor. During the 1960s he was often observed socializing with celebrities, including actress and model Suzy Parker.[59] Shields died on December 24, 1962, and was buried at the Sacred Hearts of Jesus and Mary Roman Catholic Church cemetery in Southampton. He is remembered today primarily for his distinguished Wall Street career. He is also remembered as a brother of Cornelius Shields, who dominated the American yacht-racing scene from the 1920s through the 1960s and is credited with creating the International One-Design class of sailboat.

In July 1961, many years after his career as a Progressive Era developer ended, Paul Shields (seated) was photographed enjoying an afternoon of sailing off Newport with his brother Cornelius. Paul's boat, the Columbia, was a 12-meter sloop built for the America's Cup defense in 1958. Courtesy Mystic Seaport, Rosenfeld Collection, Box 1.10.9

12
CARL GRAHAM FISHER AND MONTAUK BEACH

"I JUST HAVE TO SEE THE DIRT FLY!"[1]

ELLEN FLETCHER RUSSELL AND SARGENT RUSSELL

Late in April 1924, Carl Graham Fisher wrote to a friend that he had "looked over the Montauk property on Saturday."[2] A realtor had taken him to see ten thousand acres for sale at the extreme eastern end of Long Island. He saw a vast sweep of dunes, beaches, and rolling meadows, barren and windy, at the end of the South Fork. Little but grass grew on the meadows. For centuries the land had been used to graze cattle and sheep, and some pasture still remained.[3] Later, Fisher said that with its rolling hills and towering chalk cliffs, Montauk reminded him of the English Downs and the White Cliffs of Dover.[4] It is characteristic of Carl Fisher to have likened Montauk to a place he had never seen, but his fertile imagination had no trouble concocting so suitably detailed an image. In fact, Montauk does resemble parts of the English seacoast, but the downs Fisher envisioned and created on Long Island was a "Hollywood" version, glamorized with manor houses, sleek equestrians, and jaunty golfers.

Montauk had been of interest to far-seeing investors for decades. Railroad developers saw it as a possible deepwater port connected by rail to New York and beyond, and by sea to transatlantic and coastal trade. In 1885, Austin Corbin, president of the Long Island Railroad, had announced a plan to create an international entry port at Montauk for steamships to and from Europe. Passengers would disembark at Montauk's Fort Pond Bay and take fast trains to New York, cutting their transatlantic

voyages by about a day. A bill to this effect failed in Congress in 1886, but the L.I.R.R. extended its line to Montauk anyway, and the trains were used mostly to carry fish back to New York. Corbin never gave up the Montauk port idea and was preparing to push another bill through Congress in 1895 when he was killed by a runaway carriage.[5]

All the land Fisher was shown had once been part of the Benson property, which comprised most of the eastern end of the South Fork. The Benson land had been divided before Fisher's time. Part of it had been developed by Arthur W. Benson himself, who had formed the Montauk Association in the early 1880s and built seven Stanford White–designed summer houses on the eastern ocean bluffs. The colony's landscaping had been designed by Frederick Law Olmsted.[6] By the time Carl Fisher arrived, the colony was virtually abandoned. The rest of the Benson land belonged to the Montauk Company, controlled by Long Island Railroad and Pennsylvania Railroad interests invested in the idea of developing it as a port. The railroad men had incidentally used wild Montauk for hunting and fishing expeditions for themselves and their friends.[7]

Around the time Carl Fisher was taking his first look at Montauk, young Robert Moses, the new president of the Long Island State Park Commission, was making an offer of his own. He saw Montauk as the crown jewel in the system of Long Island parks he envisioned, close enough to the crowded city for people to get to on his projected parkways.

Carl Fisher (1874–1935) was a sixth-grade dropout from Indiana with a showman's flair that propelled him into the fledgling automobile industry. In this undated photo, he is seen resting during a game of croquet, a bit disheveled, with a rose in his lapel. Montauk Library

Moses planned to pay for the land with the proceeds of a November 1924 bond issue. Carl Fisher's plan for a luxury resort at Montauk could not have been more different from Moses's idea for public parks. But Carl Fisher had cash in hand, outbid Moses, and got the land.[8] A few years later, despite Fisher's opposition to public parks anywhere near his development, Moses won back land for two parks, one at Hither Hills and the other around the Montauk Point Lighthouse.[9]

In a syndicate with General Motors man Howard Coffin and bankers Charles Hayden and Richard Hoyt, Fisher announced the Montauk purchase for $2.5 million in September 1925.[10] The size and scope of Carl Fisher's projected development were unprecedented, but he was credible, given his standing among professionals and his own personal wealth. Many affluent friends and associates had seen his energy, determination, daring, and imagination. They did not doubt his prowess and they trusted his integrity.

Carl Graham Fisher was born in 1874 in Greensburg, Indiana, and dropped out of school after the sixth grade to work in a grocery store. By the time he launched his career as a resort developer in 1912, he was a thirty-eight-year-old multimillionaire. When he was young, he scrambled from one high-energy job to another, saving his money until he had $600 to open a bicycle repair shop in Indianapolis.[11] Bike racing and daredevil stunts spiced Carl's life and brought him into con-

tact with men who transitioned with him from bicycles to automobiles as the nineteenth century rolled into the twentieth. Many of these friends of his Indiana youth stayed with him throughout his life as he catapulted from selling cars to manufacturing carbide headlights to building tracks and roads to developing two of America's most important resort communities, Miami Beach and Montauk Point.[12]

The turn of the century was an age of technological breakthroughs; new fields opened up and were quickly flooded with competing enterprises. Advertising that grabbed attention gave competitors the edge in the battle for growing markets. A born promoter, Carl Fisher had a genius for showmanship. He once threw a bicycle off the roof of Indianapolis's tallest building. A few years later, to tout his Reo, Packard, and Stoddard-Dayton dealership, he pushed a car from another rooftop and drove it away.[13] Another caper, in the fall of 1908, netted him millions of lines of free publicity— and won the heart of fifteen-year-old Jane Watts, whom he married the next year.[14] Fisher ordered a giant hot-air balloon with "Stoddard-Dayton" emblazoned on the side and suspended a brand-new white convertible from it. In the driver's seat, Carl floated high over the city for nearly two hours as onlookers gaped from below. After the balloon came down, Fisher *appeared* to drive the car back to his dealership. In fact, the whole stunt was highly orchestrated. The car had been stripped of its motor and other heavy parts, and the tires had been

inflated with helium. When the flight was over, Carl abandoned the stripped vehicle and climbed into an identical car he had hidden at the landing site.[15] The furor after this exhibition made Carl Fisher a household name, and customers flocked to his showroom to buy his cars.[16]

In 1904, a few years before the balloon escapade, Fisher and his friend Jim Allison borrowed money and organized the Prest-O-Lite Corporation of America to manufacture canisters of carbide gas for automobile headlights. The challenge they faced was figuring out how to compress the gas to produce a flow that would remain lit for several days. The danger was that the gas was highly explosive under pressure—so volatile, in fact, that fifteen Prest-O-Lite factories blew up before Fisher and Allison worked out a safer technology for filling the tanks.[17] It was the sale of Prest-O-Lite in 1911 for $9 million that capitalized Carl Fisher's first real estate venture in Miami Beach.

Fisher sold automobiles for a living, but they were a passion as well. Like many in that business, he raced cars and sponsored racing, not only to publicize his brands but also to test and improve the performance and safety of American cars. In 1905, he went to France with the American driving team to compete in the James Gordon Bennett cup races, where he and his compatriots made a poor showing due to the inferiority of American cars. Fisher wanted to improve them and he believed that the key was to test them at high speeds. But there were few good roads on which a driver could put a car through its paces. Indeed, early races had to be held at state fairgrounds. Carl dreamed of something better: a dedicated racetrack where cars could be accurately timed and observed on a uniform course. After several years of promoting the idea, seeking investors, and locating a site, in 1909 Fisher, his partner Jim Allison, and a few other automobile men incorporated the Indianapolis

Motor Speedway Company and built a two-and-a-half-mile track.[18]

In October 1909 Carl Fisher and Jane Watts were married. A month or so later, they went on a long honeymoon cruise on their new yacht, the *Eph*. Several of Carl's friends went along, roistering all the way. When they reached Mobile Bay, they ran into stormy weather. Because Carl didn't have the patience to wait out the storm, marine engineer John Levi, Fisher's yacht broker, offered to sail the yacht around the Florida peninsula to Jacksonville, where the Fishers agreed to meet him. But when Levi reached the southern tip, he telegraphed: "Miami pretty little town. Why not meet me here?"[19] That is when Carl Fisher saw Miami for the first time, and from that moment the city's future was determined.

Almost immediately, Fisher began acquiring property in Miami, and in 1910 he bought (by mail) a large, tree-shaded house at the edge of Biscayne Bay, which he called The Shadows. From its front porch the Fishers could see a strip of swampy, uninhabited jungle, known to locals simply as "the Beach," across the bay. While living at The Shadows, Carl Fisher got the idea to buy and improve the mangrove-strangled peninsula. Exploring the intriguing place, Fisher saw that the ocean side of the swampy strip was a beautiful beach, partially lined with coconut palms. "Look honey," he said to his disgruntled young wife, "I'm going to build a city here! A city . . . like romantic places you read about and dream about but never see. It's going to be a place where the old can grow young . . . the sort of place Ponce de Leon dreamed about."[20]

Looking across the bay, Fisher could see an unfinished bridge, an attempt by an avocado farmer, John S. Collins, to link the beach (where his crop languished) to the mainland market. But Collins had run out of money.[21] In return for Fisher's help finishing the bridge, Collins gave him 200 acres of land on the beach. In exchange for loaning some money to another family developing Miami Beach property, Carl received another 105 acres. These landholders, the Lum brothers, and John Collins's relatives, were planning their own seaside resort project, already under way before Carl Fisher got involved in the creation of Miami Beach.[22]

What set Carl Fisher apart was the completeness of his concept, which entailed enhancing residential development with social and recreational amenities. And Fisher succeeded in transforming the peninsula and the bay from a mangrove swamp into a landscaped paradise fringed with artificial islands linked to the mainland by causeways. From late 1912 through the end of 1913, Fisher had men and machines ripping up palmettos and mangroves and dredging sand to make dry land where the swamps had been.

Carl Fisher's new land did not look like a tropical paradise. A jungle no longer, it was now a flat, dun-colored moonscape where nothing grew. While still paying scores of workers to plant grass blade by blade and set out palms and pines, Fisher opened the Alton Beach Realty Company and began selling lots.[23] He was not the first developer to offer Miami Beach land for sale, but he was the first to reveal an integrated master plan for the place.[24] In December 1913 he described it to the *Miami Herald*. More than a hundred acres already sported velvety grass and young trees, and streets and boulevards coursed across the peninsula. Houses were under construction, and a 325-acre golf course had been laid out. Tennis courts, a clubhouse, and an ocean pier were under construction, and an office building was in the works. Fisher also had the plans for the first of several hotels.[25] Designed by August Geiger,[25] his modest, unsplashy Lincoln Hotel with thirty-two rooms was just big enough to handle the overflow of Fisher's own guests, whom he invited to Miami Beach as friends and potential buyers of lots. This hotel, along with the golf course, yacht club, polo field, swimming pools, tennis courts, casino, and everything else that adorned Fisher's Florida development, had only one purpose: to help sell real estate. Carl Fisher's big idea, the notion behind all of the extras, was to generate profits through the enhancement of land values. Every other form of revenue was of secondary importance to him. By building the most desirable amenities, Fisher was increasing the value of his winter playland.[27]

Fisher's ideas about promotion had matured from the days of pushing cars off the tops of tall buildings. While the other Miami Beach developers were giving away prizes of china and glassware as they auctioned off building lots, Carl came up with a better idea. In 1919, when lot sales were slow, he didn't hire an auctioneer. He didn't lower prices. Rather, he *raised* prices by 10 percent, and promised to do so every year thereafter. Sales took off. "We try to give our customers an investment that substantially and steadily grows in value," Fisher explained.[28] That same year, he embarked on his first big publicity campaign, writing many of the advertisements himself. Miami Beach was "America's Greatest Winter Playground," he wrote, and up in lights over Times Square, "It's Always June in Miami Beach," "Where Summer Spends the Winter."[29]

Carl Fisher used popular sports and activities to lure friends, acquaintances, and other potential buyers to Miami Beach. He held regattas and winter festivals, and invited celebrities—including President Warren G. Harding—to stay in his hotel. He founded a fishing club and invited Midwestern sports enthusiasts down for holidays on the water. To glamorize the beach, Carl and Jane made heroic efforts to import flamingos from the Bahamas. There was a baby elephant named Rosie who gave rides and caddied at the golf course, to generate glowing newspaper coverage for the Fisher enterprise.[30] And girls in bathing suits. Everywhere.

Even though Miami Beach claimed a good deal of Carl Fisher's time, another major project occupied him almost as much. In Europe he had discovered that not only were American cars inferior to their European counterparts, but so were the roads. He loved to drive, but the frustration of floundering in the mud or getting lost in a signless wilderness all too often ruined the experience for him. Better roads were needed—all over the country. But at a time when driving was considered a sport for rich men, there was little likelihood that the government would do anything about it. It made sense to Carl that the automobile industry should finance a highway that crossed the country. After all, automakers could sell more cars if people had somewhere to drive them.[31] So in the late summer of 1912 he gathered his friends at his Indianapolis home and persuaded them to support his new project. "See America first" was the most long lasting of the slogans for Fisher's campaign to build a good concrete highway from San Francisco to New York. Eventually named the Lincoln Highway, the 3,150-mile road was funded by contributions and in-kind donations from automakers, road contractors, Chambers of Commerce, and progressive businessmen across the nation. Fisher's winning personality and his dogged perspicacity attracted friends and funding, and by 1915 the highway was essentially complete.[32]

No sooner was the Lincoln Highway finished than Fisher embarked on a second long-distance road, the Dixie Highway, to bring drivers from the North and Midwest to the coastal South, and in particular, across the Collins Bridge to Miami Beach. This highway was important to Fisher personally, because many of his friends and potential Miami Beach property buyers were car men, and they wanted to drive south. But southern roads were notorious; some of them were among the worst in the country. The Dixie Highway, which made driving to Florida a pleasure, was finally completed in the late 1920s.[33]

In Miami Beach Carl Fisher demonstrated a management style that would serve him well throughout his real estate career. He sought advice—and investment—from old automobile industry friends and from bankers he had known for years. He put these men on the boards of his companies and kept in touch through voluminous correspondence, much of which survives.[34] He also invited them to visit him at the beach, where he entertained them lavishly. Life was fun around Carl Fisher, and scores of his friends—and their friends—bought winter homes in Miami Beach.

Even more important, Carl assembled a group of competent and intensely loyal managers and engineers to oversee day-to-day operations, and many of them moved from Miami to Port Washington to Montauk with him. Some of those he recruited for the development of Miami Beach—such as the young landscaper Fred Hoerger, engineers John Levi and Thomas Ringwood, and mechanical genius Albert Webb—stayed with him and helped to execute his projects for the rest of his life.[35] Joining the managers as they followed the seasons up and down the coast were crews of experienced workers.[36]

In contrast to Fisher's managers and engineers, who had permanent status, the architects and contractors who provided design and construction services for his developments varied. In Miami Beach, Fisher commissioned New Haven architect August Geiger to design not only his first hotel but also his Lincoln Road house,[37] another Shadows. The Philadelphia firm Price & McLanahan laid out the residential Star Island and provided plans for some of its houses.[38] A "De Garmo," referred to in some Fisher correspondence,[39] was Walter C. De Garmo, an Illinois architect who came to Miami in 1904. There are also references to Harry S. Bastian, a Miami architect Fisher occasionally employed, who provided him with plans for houses he could build where he chose.[40] In a letter to his colleague James H. Snowden, president of the Fisher company that owned Star Island, Carl wrote that he wanted several distinct styles of houses for Miami Beach, as some buyers preferred Bastian's "Colonial style" houses over the flat-roofed, stucco-clad Spanish type. Other Star Island houses were designed by different architects[41] for the property owners.[42]

Fisher's first hotel, the Lincoln, had been modest; his second, the Flamingo, built in 1920, was grander, and exotic. It was designed by an Indianapolis architect (after Price & McLanahan's plan was rejected for being too expensive),[43] but the gondolas were pure Hollywood. Jane Fisher had sent Carl a gondola while she was in Venice that year, and Fisher had rushed his boat builders to make copies. He planned to hire handsome Bahamians to pilot them. "They are all going to be stripped to the waist," Carl boasted, "and wear big brass earrings.

Miniature golf at the Nautilus Hotel, Miami Beach, 1924. Although Carl Fisher built the first, and later the most opulent, Miami Beach hotels, he was not in the hospitality business. His hotels were meant to attract the kinds of people that would buy his real estate. Photograph by Claude Matlack, HistoryMiami

And possibly necklaces of live crab or crawfish."[44] In 1923, Fisher commissioned the New York firm of Leonard Schultze and S. Fullerton Weaver (Schultze & Weaver) to design his third hotel, the Nautilus. The Flamingo was definitely flamboyant, but the gorgeously ornate Spanish Baroque–style Nautilus was a pleasure palace. Intended for wealthy guests, it featured luxurious rooms, highly decorated public areas with beautiful stairways and chandeliers, a swimming pool with cabanas, and an adjoining polo field. The La Gorce Golf Course was nearby.[45] There was nothing understated about the Nautilus. Carl Fisher would have known of Schultze & Weaver as the architects of the Biltmore in Coral Gables and the Breakers in Palm Beach, both Florida resort towns that attracted the wealthy residents and visitors Fisher wanted to lure to Miami Beach. Schultze & Weaver also designed Fisher's Lincoln Road office building and important buildings in Montauk.[46]

However grand some of Fisher's Miami Beach hotels were, he was not in the hotel business; he dealt in land. The hotels were built on cheap land that would not otherwise have been developed, and they raised the real estate values around them. In fact, the hotels were come-ons, intended to draw the kinds of customers Fisher wanted, ensure that they had a good time at the beach, and hold them long enough for his salesmen to sell them house lots.[47]

As Fisher began selling lots, he drew up a series of restrictions, one set for each subdivision. Buyers in most of the neighborhoods were required to spend a certain minimum on the construction of the residence, and they could build only certain kinds of outbuildings. Commercial and industrial uses were prohibited in the residential neighborhoods, and liquor sales were not allowed. All residential neighborhoods had a Caucasians-only policy, although there was a provision for live-in servants. A few horses and other animals were permitted in subdivisions with larger lots, but not in others.[48]

By 1922, the Florida land boom was on, and for Carl Fisher it came just in time. He had nearly exhausted his funds after years of dredging, clearing, filling, and building, but finally his big gamble was paying off. Several factors came together around this time that propelled him to search for something new to do. First, he was recouping his money at last. Second, his marriage to Jane was deteriorating. They had lost an infant son that year and were not handling it well. Third, the Lincoln Highway had opened, leaving a void in Fisher's active life. Finally, the previous summer, he and Jim Allison had begun thinking about getting a place on Long Island to spend the hot season.[49]

In June 1922, Fisher sold his Indianapolis house, rented a place in Sands Point on the North Shore, and took an office in Manhattan to be "near the seat of war," as he worked to raise money to build more Miami Beach hotels.[50] A couple of years later, he rented a large house on Manhasset Bay in Port Washington and then bought the house next door on a large tract of land. Port Washington was a maritime town, with three established yacht clubs.[51] Fisher liked it, so he quickly remodeled the house to provide himself with a home, an office, and a project. He amused himself over the next few years with the twenty-three-acre real estate development he called the Bayview Colony, where he planned to house some of his executives.[52] In 1925, Fisher brought his Indiana and Miami boat builders, Ned and Gil Purdy, to Port Washington and built a shipyard for them next to the colony. There they built racing boats for Fisher and his friends. Eventually, Fisher established a station for the Montauk Yacht Club there as well. Another reason he had set himself up on Long Island was to look for a site for a new resort—a summertime complement to Miami Beach.

In the mid-1920s, Carl Fisher's wealth peaked. His net worth was estimated at anywhere between $50 and $100 million, and he sold off several million dollars' worth of Miami Beach assets to kick off the work at Montauk.[53] Some of his friends and Miami investors questioned the wisdom of the new project, chief among them John Collins's son Irving, who had reluctantly invested in Montauk. There were obstacles at Montauk that Miami didn't present, Collins said. For one thing, Montauk was three times the size of Miami Beach. For another, its weather was unpredictable and often nasty, unsuitable for leisurely, pleasant vacations. Collins wrote to Fisher: "I hope it is not too late for you to retire gracefully from the proposition." Collins wondered why Fisher went ahead with it, when he certainly didn't need the money.[54] "Damn your soul," Carl exploded, according to ex-wife Jane. "Who said I'm building Montauk for the money? Miami Beach is finished, and there's nothing left for me to do there but sit around in white pants looking pretty!"[55] And about Montauk's drawbacks? "At least I don't have to make the land," he retorted.[56]

The ink had hardly dried on the Montauk deeds before Carl Fisher got to work. He told Jane that he was going to bring the whole Miami Beach organization north with him, and there he was going to "duplicate everything" he had built in Miami, including a Star Island with a yacht club on it.[57] Before the end of September, Fisher's engineers and surveyors, under the direction of Thomas Ringwood, were at Montauk, mapping the area and laying out roads.[58] Many of Fisher's Montauk managers and professionals had come with him from Miami Beach; they were intensely loyal to the flamboyant developer. "Carl Fisher's men," reported the East Hampton newspaper, "whether they be at Miami Beach, New York, Port Washington or Montauk, are for him to a man. Everyone speaks well of him as an employer."[59]

On October 27, 1925, Fisher incorporated the Montauk Beach Development Corporation to execute the project, which he called Montauk Beach.[60] However, he said, "No attempt whatsoever will be made at this time to sell property or invite investors."[61]

Reading the breathless newspaper reports and promotional pieces about Montauk Beach encouraged some people to think that it had sprung into being as Carl Fisher waved a magic wand and intoned a secret spell. To some extent, he encouraged this notion. For example, after Thomas Ringwood and his engineers had charted every feature of the place and Fisher had made decisions about where things would go, the developer took a

Visualization of Montauk Beach, 1934. On a sunny day in 1926, Carl Fisher took staff members and a reporter out on the yacht to show them how Montauk Beach was shaping up. Montauk Beach lived in all its glory in Carl Fisher's mind before the first shovel touched the ground. Gibbon Catlett Studios, Society for the Preservation of Long Island Antiquities

reporter out on the *Shadow K* and waved his arms around. As they chugged along, Fisher described his vision from notes he had scrawled on a site map. His young chief executive, Walter Kohlhepp, appeared to take dictation. Fisher "saw" a "high-grade summer resort" and sports center. The first hotel would be "on this high point overlooking the ocean." The second hotel would be on the lake-front. He would name *that* Lake Montauk (it had been Lake Wyandannee) and cut a channel through to it from the Sound for a yacht harbor. The yacht club and pier would be on the lake island. The first golf course would go *there*, with the clubhouse and first tee on *that* high point.[62]

"Lay out the business district here," Fisher continued. "Locate a village of 100 comfortable homes over here, save this area for residential estates and build at least 20 high grade houses here. There on the ocean front, build a bathing pavilion . . . a series of tennis courts *here* and the polo fields will fit this flat valley. . . . Oh, yes, there used to be sheep on this land. Put a thousand head of sheep out to graze in the spring."[63]

Carl told Jane that the resort would have Old World charm. It would be a place of medieval cottages with thatched roofs, windmills, and sheep. Roads and streets, business buildings and hotels would be hidden behind low hills and grassy moors.[64] There would also be a bathing pavilion, three golf courses, a polo field, a gentlemen's driving track, and enclosed tennis courts capable of seating many thousands of spectators.[65]

Things calmed down at Montauk as the winter

of 1925 set in, but the early spring of 1926 brought a whirlwind of activity. Fisher announced that he was bringing a thousand workers from Miami Beach to Montauk,[66] and he began making provisions for the first two hundred of them right away. About half were housed in a bunkhouse that had been thrown up near the site designated for the first hotel. Engineer Tom Ringwood and thirty-five of his assistants in khaki and puttees lived and worked at the Montauk Inn, a sturdy, Shingle Style hostelry built by the Montauk Company in 1901 and run by the long-time innkeeper, Mrs. Theodore Conklin.[67] Locally prominent and well connected, Mrs. Conklin was someone to be taken seriously. She was invited to stay on to serve Fisher's engineers, but she declined because she disliked the alterations the company made to her inn and the disruptions caused by the development. Ringwood recommended that Fisher engage her as the hostess of the new hotel (its designated site was right in front of the old inn), but she did not take the job. The engineers ended up fending for themselves that spring, living simply and eating plain food served by a commissary contractor.[68] On April 29, the old inn burned to the ground, and the engineers moved to a temporary office in Montauk Village.[69]

Among their first projects was the employees' village at Shepherd's Neck, a point that extended along the west side of Fort Pond. Thirty wood-and-stucco houses went up with astonishing speed—one reportedly finished in a single day. These were earmarked for the families of men in charge of Fisher's construction work.[70] One hundred houses were

planned for the employees' community, which was intended to be "as picturesque as an ancient English hamlet."[71] It was to have single-family and multi-family houses, bachelor apartments, stores, a playground, a school, a hospital, and churches. Nearly everything built was in a "modified Tudor style," the "type of architecture [Carl Fisher thought] best adapted to Montauk."[72] By the end of that first spring, Montauk was already a good-sized community, "though populated only by the workers."[73]

Carl valued the fishing village, and making peace with it was one of his first priorities. However, he apparently put his foot in his mouth right away, offering to move it, lock, stock, and barrel, to some other part of Montauk. He probably had good reasons for wanting it moved—Austin Corbin's idea for an international port right where the village sat was still much on Fisher's mind; also, the village squatted right in the middle of the view from his planned luxury hotel. The outraged reaction of the villagers made him backpedal. "I consider the fishermen . . . one of our most valuable assets," he telegraphed to his vice president Hugh Davis. "Get word to them immediately that we have no idea of moving them . . . [be sure to tell them that] we want them to remain there and furnish good supplies to our hotels and home buyers."[74] In a letter to Robert Bacon, he was more forthcoming: "[T]hey supply sea food and one or two cases of first-class scotch that has not been doctored."[75] The fishermen were useful in yet another way: "They are also a Vigilance Committee and we want to do all we can to help them . . ." (Fisher counted on their familiarity with local law enforcement to help him avoid trouble in his clubs and hotels, and he wanted very much to

keep them sweet.)[76] "I will figure out a plan to put them up a community house, theatre or something that will hold them with us."[77]

However, according to Jane, "The old residents of the historic Montauk region did not look with too much favor on the proposed new development."[78] It is not hard to imagine why. For centuries Montauk had been nearly isolated. Most of the existing population, some three–four hundred people, lived in what was called, simply, the fishing village, or Montauk Village, which straggled along a bridge of land between Fort Pond and Fort Pond Bay, and northward toward Culloden Point. Settlement of the village had begun in third quarter of the nineteenth century, as French-Canadian, Scandinavian, and Long Island fishermen arrived with their families. Most of the younger people worked seasonally for members of the Montauk Company and the Montauk Association, either tending their houses and land or taking them out to hunt and fish. In the Prohibition-era 1920s, most of the fishermen did a bit of bootlegging on the side, picking up shipments of Canadian liquor and sending it off to speakeasies in the Hamptons.[79] This self-contained community was leery of Carl Fisher. They were anxious about the development and what it would mean for the quiet, specialized life they had created for themselves there at the end of the world. The promised influx of thousands of workers, to be followed by even greater numbers of summer residents and casual visitors, was threatening, but who knew what other changes might be in store. It seemed to portend the end of their way of life.

To be conciliatory to the village and gain its cooperation, Fisher built a public school in the hills halfway between his employees' community at Shepherd's Neck and the fishing village on the bay. Completed in 1928, the school was designed by architect and engineer Richard Webb and built by Albin Pearson, whose construction company built many of Fisher's Montauk buildings.[80] The fishing village children did go to the school, and so did the MBDC children. Inevitably, the two groups did not mix well. The fishing villagers thought the Midwesterners and Miamians of Shepherd's Neck looked down on them, and that might have been the case. So Carl Fisher came up with some special concessions. He donated land for churches and built a theater for vaudeville and movies. He also built an ice-skating rink just for the year-rounders, and he kept some of the recreational facilities open in the wintertime.[81]

Even before the winter ice melted, Montauk began to roar with construction work. In February, Fisher announced that he had contracted the New York firm of Robbins & Ripley to build a bridge to Star Island in Lake Montauk, and piers for the Montauk Yacht Club there.[82] This firm, he said, would be responsible for nearly all of that kind of work at Montauk. In March, Fred Hoerger arrived from Miami to become general superintendent, in charge of "all the work done by the Montauk Beach Development Corporation outside of the work [done under] contract."[83] In addition to his supervisory activities, Hoerger set up a huge nursery for trees and shrubs to beautify the barren dunes.[84] Speed and more speed," wrote Jane about this early time. "An anthill could not have been busier."[85] Men and machines arrived on nearly every train. Infrastructure was going in, Jane said, and houses were rising. Ground was broken for Carl Fisher's own house, a Mount Vernon–like mansion designed by Arthur W. B. Wood to stand on fifteen hilltop acres, overlooking the future golf course, ocean, and sound.[86]

Also in March, the company received Schultze & Weaver's plans for "Hotel No. 1," the magnificent gabled and turreted Tudor-style hostelry that would anchor the development.[87] It was to sit atop one of Montauk's highest hills, near the place where the old Montauk Inn had stood. "I cannot impress upon you too strongly," Hugh Davis wrote to Fisher in Port Washington, "the importance of getting under way with Hotel No. 1. With a bad market [and] a skeptical community . . . I should very much like to see a tangible start on our building program." But, he went on, we "should reduce building costs," and get right to work on it. "We all know," he cautioned, "that speed is not one of the points of Schultze & Weaver."[88]

In Montauk, Carl Fisher followed his Miami practice of using many different architects rather than depending on a single firm.[89] Schultze & Weaver designed Montauk Manor and its accessory buildings, a second hotel—never built—for the west-

Bird's-eye view of the fishing village. When work started at Montauk Beach, most local residents lived in the fishing village straggling along the narrow shore between Fort Pond and the bay. Houses were ramshackle and comforts were few; railroad men were known to help out by deliberately dumping coal along the tracks for people's stoves. Fishing was the main occupation, although younger residents worked as groundskeepers and guides for Montauk Association members.
The 1938 hurricane destroyed most of the village and its boats, and the site was marginally occupied until the Navy chose it as a torpedo-testing range during World War II. Montauk Library

157

ern shore of Lake Montauk, and the development corporation's seven-story office building off Montauk Highway, downtown.[90] The Montauk Struck Company did "practically all the building on the development,"[91] including the Manor and the Fisher office building. They also built some fifty employee houses, as well as bunkhouses and mess halls for the laborers.[92] The Montauk Struck Company's office was in a building facing the circular park near Fisher's headquarters, and their materials yard was in the industrial area west of the fishing village. At least one of Fisher's investors cautioned him to keep a careful eye on the architecture at Montauk. "If you can kill off the construction of any yellow brick building," wrote Roy Chapin, "be sure to do so."[93]

Engineer Richard Webb, son of Fisher's old friend Al Webb, designed many of the project's other important buildings, including the Montauk Public School, the Montauk Arms Apartments (for single employees) on Fort Pond, the Supper Club on Star Island (1928), the seaside Bathing Casino (1928), and the clubhouse for the Montauk Downs Golf Course. Webb also designed several of the large private houses: for Long Island Railroad vice president and Fisher colleague George LeBoutillier (1927), for engineer Tom Ringwood (1928), "House No. 3" for W. Stewart Gayness, the Spanish-style Raymond house (1928), a Fairview Avenue house named Windy Hill (1926), and quite a few others. Webb is also credited with developing the drawings for the Community Church after consultation with architect A. G. Lamont from the Board of National Missions of the United Presbyterian Church in the United States. Many of the buildings Webb designed were built by Albin Pearson's construction company.[94] The Pearson Construction Company

was often mentioned in newspaper notices from the 1920s, as was "the Posposil firm," a contractor who came to Montauk from Mineola.[95]

Other architects who designed buildings for the Fisher development included the New York firm of Walker & Gillette, which was responsible for the Montauk Yacht Club and sportsman Caleb Bragg's unusual seven-building compound, both on Star Island. The contractor for both Walker & Gillette projects was Young & French of New York.[96] Other architects working at Montauk were A. J. Thomas, who designed the 1926 Windmill House on Fairview Avenue; McKenna & Irving, who were responsible for St. Therese of Lisieux Roman Catholic Church; and Robert Tappan of Forest Hills, who designed the half-timbered Montauk Theatre (financed and built by the Pearson Construction Company) and submitted many sketches for houses resembling the Shepherd's Neck dwellings, some of which were published in the MBDC's first promotional booklet.[97] This booklet, an unusual but charming sales tool, features many photographs of buildings under construction and gives nearly as much attention to construction information and descriptions of the accommodations for the Fisher employees as to the great houses to come.

Early in June, excitement flared as a huge floating dredge lumbered into Fort Pond Bay. It announced the Packard Dredging Company's arrival to begin digging a channel to link Lake Montauk with Block Island Sound and deepen part of the lake to create a safe harbor for the largest yachts.[98] Jane Fisher thought this was the first time a freshwater lake was ever joined to a body of salt water.[99]

By this time, the logistics of housing and feeding the army of construction workers were daunting even to the ever-resourceful development corporation. Between eight hundred and a thousand men were toiling daily on scores of projects, a few of which involved hospitality for the workers. Shepherd's Neck provided good housing for upper-level employees, some of whom had their families with them, but the vast majority of laborers lived in bunkhouses and ate in canteens that had been thrown together virtually overnight.

At some point during the summer of 1926, Carl sat down and drafted a schedule of restrictions for the Montauk project that resembled the ones drawn up for Miami. "Carl thought of every possible restriction," Jane recalled.[100] Just as in Miami, minimums were established for the construction cost of buildings, depending on location, and all designs were to be approved by the corporation. Setbacks and uses were described. No alcohol was to be sold. As in Miami, no lots were to be sold to non-Caucasians (or even to a firm with any non-Caucasian member or stockholder). The restrictions were to be in effect until January 1, 1950, and were renewable after that.[101] One of the restrictions, however, came back to bite the developer himself. It prohibited lot owners from keeping livestock on their properties. Any livestock. The first thing Fisher did on his own acreage was to build a stable and put four horses in it. When he was reminded that he was violating his own restrictions, he groused: "It's up to you fellows to straighten this thing out. I'm not going way down to the polo barns every time I want to ride a pony." According to Jane Fisher, Tom Ringwood

had to get waivers from every property owner in the vicinity to permit Carl to keep his stable full of horses.[102]

All in all, Montauk's 1926 summer construction season was a tour de force. It was "the busiest spot in the United States," crowed the local newspaper.[103] The hotel and office were well under way; roads had been built; water and electricity were installed nearly everywhere. There was a bathing casino with cabanas, swimming pool, and boardwalk; a golf course had materialized; Shepherd's Neck was a hamlet with dozens of houses; and brand-new mansions studded the hills. There was a supper club on Star Island next to Caleb Bragg's unusual compound. A downtown street boasted a theater and several stores with apartments above. There were two churches, a new school, a lumberyard, steam laundries.[104] Finally, Fisher was ready to start selling real estate; in late July, his old Indiana friend Al Webb organized the Montauk Point Realty Corporation and set up a small office for himself in a "pretty little shingled house" on the Montauk Highway.[105] And if that wasn't enough, living quarters were going up to house even more workmen.[106] "Our greatest trouble now," Carl Fisher assured the still-reluctant Irving Collins in early September, "is to get some place for the people to eat and sleep."[107]

Then disaster struck. A Category 4 hurricane slammed Miami Beach on Saturday, September 18. Bursts of 128-mile-an-hour wind raised the water in Biscayne Bay and drove it into the new islands and causeways, whose narrow channels couldn't

One of the most ambitious projects at Montauk Beach was the dredging of a channel to link Lake Montauk (the former Wyandannee) with Block Island Sound. Dredge spoil was used to enlarge the thirty-five-acre Star Island to hold a yacht club, a casino, and a cluster of summer houses. Detroit automobile magnate Howard Coffin, an original Montauk investor, received land in return for undertaking the monumental dredging project. Here, Montauk Beach Development Corporation executives join the laborers in digging the last few shovelfuls of the "cut." Montauk Library

handle it. All the dredging and filling had blocked the natural escape valves, and torrential rains and towering waves sucked beaches, roads, and walls right out to sea. In the darkness and confusion as the hurricane roared, things seemed to be worse than they were..[108] According to Jane, Carl Fisher was on the *Shadow K*, en route to Montauk, when he got the radio message from a salesman: "Miami Beach total loss. Entirely swept away by hurricane. Untold damage."[109] Without stopping to check the report's accuracy, Fisher put in to shore, telephoned his men at Montauk, and ordered them to stop all work. Jane thought that that decision was one of the worst errors of Carl's life and marked the beginning of the end for the Montauk development.[110] Jane's account was somewhat overdramatic: the *East Hampton Star* reported that Fisher had been in Montauk when he got the news, that he had taken it "calmly and philosophically and refused to be hurried into a special train." Fisher told the reporter he was going south to aid the homeless and to get his people working on reconstruction: "Miami Beach was built from a mangrove swamp," he said, and "what was once done can be done again."[111]

Fisher did order work stopped at Montauk after the Miami hurricane, but not for long. He downplayed the destruction to Miami Beach, and in fact, his solidly built structures had not sustained irreparable damage. Rebuilding was an expensive proposition—partially covered by insurance—but the Fisher developments were soon restored and Miami Beach was lovely again.

Fisher had faced the disaster with aplomb, but in its wake something began to shift in his world.

According to biographer Mark Foster, Fisher seemed to lose his magic overnight, making a series of decisions and commitments that turned out badly and from which he could not recover. Even as he threw nearly $1 million into the Miami Beach cleanup, he sank another $5 million of his own into Montauk.[112] Carl was spreading himself too thin. As Jane Fisher wrote, "Montauk Point was slipping from his grasp."[113]

Even so, Fisher seemed optimistic in press releases and correspondence. In a December 1926 letter to his Montauk vice president Hugh Davis, Fisher bubbled over with an idea for a "Montauk Club." He wanted "the Booklet" revised to showcase what a member of this full-service country club could expect. Let it "show a polo scene in action," he ordered, "a driving track, hunt club and dogs, picture of sheep, picture of speed boats and sailboats, golf course, people on the beach, riding club . . . toboggan slides, casino layout . . . indoor tennis courts, yacht club [with] more facilities than any in the world . . ." The object was to raise money to build it all through the sale of memberships. Further on, Fisher's tone went from optimistic to manic; the proof is the escalation in price and membership goals in the same letter. We will build it, he wrote, with $1,000 memberships, say, 1,000 of them. Then he revised upward: the memberships will be $1,500, and there will be 2,000 of them. Let's see, that's 2,000 memberships at $2,000 per . . .[114] Cautiously, Davis responded that he would ask Fisher's friend and investor Jack LaGorce, vice president of the National Geographic Society and a renowned travel writer, to assess the booklet and the club idea.[115]

Montauk quieted down over the 1926–27 winter, but promotion escalated. Carl Fisher strategized about how to reach various groups: for the family of means, he wrote, he would advertise in *Town & Country*, *House Beautiful*, *Vogue*, and *Country Life*. Fishermen would be lured by *Field & Stream* and the hunting and fishing section of the *Herald Tribune*. He also planned how to reach golfers and those who would buy property for investment purposes.[116] Advertising copy was written and vetted, and puff pieces were prepared for selected publications. The Long Island Railroad's late 1926 Information Bulletin featured a lengthy piece extracted from Fisher's promotional literature. It described houses that the development corporation was building on the "exclusive residential estates": The houses were stucco and brick, with half-timbering and slate roofs. Each had three bedrooms and two servants' rooms over two-car garages.

Vice president and general manager Walter Kohlhepp, probably energized by his boss, arranged an ill-advised, mid-December promotional visit by

Carl Fisher believed in promotional materials like this poster (produced around 1929). On it, happy residents enjoy every popular summer sport. Pride of place belongs to opulent Montauk Manor, its lozenge flanked by game fish leaping for the angler's line. Society for the Preservation of Long Island Antiquities

train for a dozen or so bankers, lawyers, and businessmen. There seems to have been a hint of desperation in it. In a long memo to Fisher, after the fact, Kohlhepp explained what happened. Before setting out, he said, he had telephoned out to Montauk and learned that the weather was clear. At some point during the two-hour-and-forty-minute trip, however, a winter storm had blown in, and the special guests had detrained into a scrim of snow and ice. Apparently game, the group had slipped and stumbled over the dunes to inspect the resort. Kohlhepp declared the trip a success. "Of course, if we had had a good, clear day," he admitted, "their enthusiasm would have been much greater."[117]

As the spring of 1927 approached, Carl Fisher needed money. He wanted to—felt he ought to—buy out Irving Collins, who had never really wanted to be part of Montauk. Fisher approached bankers for short-term loans. Richard Hoyt, a partner in Hayden, Stone & Co. and a Montauk property owner, analyzed the shortcomings of the Montauk Beach Development Corporation and urged Fisher not to buy Collins out. In fact, he said Fisher should spread the risk by expanding his partnership base. But following this recommendation, he explained that he had reservations about recommending such an investment to his own clients.[118]

Montauk Manor had a gala opening on June 1, with the orchestra from Fisher's Flamingo Hotel shipped north to provide the music. The hotel was thronged with politicians, bankers, Miami personages, sportsmen, realtors, and millionaires. Some of Fisher's Miami residents were building, now, in Montauk. Yet through the general celebration ran a thread of melancholy. "To the lovers of the . . .

picturesque and rugged atmosphere of Montauk, the opening of this hotel means the passing of an age." The reference was to the loss of the old Montauk Inn, and the quiet, rustic era of which it was a part.[119] Many of Fisher's other Montauk attractions were up and running for the 1927 summer season as well. Infrastructure—roads, water, electricity—was complete. There were clubhouses for the golf course and polo fields. The great yacht harbor in Lake Montauk was still being dredged, though, and the yacht club was still in the offing.[120]

During the summer of 1927, Carl's health deteriorated considerably. He ignored everything his doctors recommended; he drank, smoked big cigars, and ate bushels of salted peanuts, joking that he was "trying to get [his] liver copper plated so that [he could] continue to enjoy life."[121] The Montauk of the 1920s, the resort Fisher created, was a kind of mirror image of the man himself—raffish, hard-partying, teetering precariously on the edge. In June, Carl married Margaret Collier, his former secretary, a domestic arrangement that may have pleased his friends but did nothing to rein in his extravagant habits or improve his worsening health.[122]

Around this time, Jane Fisher said she asked Carl when he expected to stop building. "Will there ever be an end to all of this?" He didn't stop to think. "Not until we get our ocean port," he answered.[123]

George LeBoutillier, vice president of the Long Island Railroad and an investor in and board member of the Montauk Beach Development Corporation, had always been positive about the Austin Corbin scheme for a transatlantic port at Fort Pond Bay. Fisher had never publicly counted on it. "They have talked about Montauk for a port for the last twenty years," he wrote, "but nothing is done. . . . We can do without it easily."[124] But in 1927, the port scheme came back to life, with a new twist. President Coolidge was interested. A fleet of swift new superships was to be built under the auspices of the United States government, and the American docks for them would be built either on eastern Long Island or in New England. Montauk was being considered. One of Fisher's stockholders and property owners, Illinois State Representative Fred Britten, was chairman of the House Naval Affairs Committee, and he pushed the idea hard. A flurry of activity came the next spring, as the Army Corps of Engineers investigated Fort Pond Bay, and the Long Island Railroad announced it would build four great piers there. Some international shipping lines sent people out to look around. Then the idea sank, quickly and without a ripple. Carl Fisher knew why. "It is a very expensive proposition," he wrote, "and it is up to somebody to raise the cash to complete the piers, the laundries, the blacksmith shop, etc, that go with a port of this kind. I feel certain that some day it will be a port, but probably not for the next several years."[125]

In August 1927, Fisher and Jim Allison sold the Indianapolis Speedway to their old friend Captain Edward (Eddie) Rickenbacker, flying ace and Montauk resident. Carl plowed his $5 million share straight into Montauk. His Lincoln Highway associate Henry B. Joy had reservations about investing more money with Fisher "because it just goes into Montauk Company's maw."[126] He was not accusing Fisher of dishonesty—no one, ever, did that—just of imprudent decisions.

The first rumblings of trouble for Montauk and Carl Fisher began after the 1927 season ended. In November, Fisher told employees he was closing the New York office and moving everyone out to Montauk to save money. The seven-story office building was not yet ready for occupancy, and Carl had hoped to use the yacht club, but it wasn't finished either. They ended up working in one of the old Montauk Association Stanford White houses on the bluff, which Fisher had bought and remodeled for them.[127] Throughout the winter, Carl fired off memos to various department heads, trying to reduce expenses wherever he could. Manager Parke Haynes and chief engineer Thomas Ringwood fought back, though, stressing the importance of each job Fisher tried to cut.[128] "Never before had I seen Carl harried by anxiety," Jane recalled. "I realized that . . . men who once had believed in him were beginning to doubt . . ."[129]

In May 1928, the Montauk Beach Development Corporation announced new officers. Carl Fisher was no longer president. Detroit automobile man Howard E. Coffin had replaced him in the top executive spot, although Fisher retained 51 percent of the stock and remained chairman of the board.[130] The shift was represented as a move to relieve him of some of the details of construction and operations, but it was also a move that brought in some $2.5 million in new capital from railroad interests. Later that month, $3 million in bonds were secured by a 6 percent mortgage. By this time, Carl had no income from Montauk and was living entirely on sales of assets in Miami Beach.[131] In August, the district attorney announced that he had instructed the sheriff to watch Carl's Island Club for evidence of illegal gambling.[132] That same month, Carl's oldest friend and first partner, Jim Allison, died.[133] In spite of good property sales figures and full occupancy at the hotel, one thing after another went wrong for Carl Fisher that summer.

As his financial problems worsened, Carl Fisher began to involve himself in management minutiae as he had never done before. Usually patient and tactful with his staff, he began lashing out: when guests complained that company salesmen were

Designed by engineer Richard Webb and built in 1927 by the Pearson Construction Company, this long, low, stone-and-shingle house hugs the top of Montauk's highest point. It was the home of Long Island Railroad vice president George LeBoutillier. A later owner, the Prohibition-era operator of the casino on Star Island, used his home as a lookout for police raiders. If he saw any, he had the booze brought here and locked away in the hall closets. An addition was built by Dave Webb, son of the original engineer.
Montauk Library

chasing them into the hotel and drinking on the job, Fisher turned on manager J. G. McCaffrey: "I hold you responsible," he wrote, "and you have muffed the job."[134] A month later he ordered the new replacement, Parke G. Haynes, to fire all the stenographers, who had been dancing in the hotel and mixing with the guests. He demanded that all staff members stay out of the hotel and away from the guests. "This means you," he emphasized, "and all people under you."[135]

Fisher also began to distract himself by dabbling in odd projects unrelated to his business. In the spring of 1928 he started promoting a streamlined trailer called the Aerocar, invented by his friend the airplane designer Glenn Curtiss. Fisher claimed to be thrilled with the Aerocar, and imagined scores of uses for it, from tourist camping to hauling VIPs in comfort from Miami to Montauk. He fantasized about selling millions of them, and actually did sell a few, keeping one for himself.[136] He also tried to promote a solar-operated air-conditioning system and a skid-proof material for rubber shoe soles.[137] Then there was the prefabricated steel-and-transite house he worked on for a year as an affordable alternative for Montauk—he built a sample, but his own requirements for construction cost minimums stymied its further use.[138]

Many facilities were completed during the fall and winter of 1927–28, including the Yacht Club on Star Island, the bathing casino and boardwalk on the oceanfront, the office building, and some fifteen large estates. The second golf course, at Hither Hills, and a huge, enclosed tennis auditorium near Montauk Manor were under construction. Carl Fisher's own house was almost finished, a showplace on the highest point between Lake Montauk and Fort Pond Bay.[139] Fisher also wanted to build an airplane landing and reasonably priced houses for his salesmen.[140] Once again, the latter effort was stymied because of his construction cost requirements.

The 1929 summer season, like the previous one, had very good press. Articles extolled the progress of the development and enthused over celebrities buying property or staying at the hotel. On the surface, things seemed rosy. But in midsummer there was a gambling raid at the Montauk Island Club, complete with property seizures and arrests.[141] More ominous for Montauk's future, though, were the layoffs of construction workers that the corporation announced in July, and the cessation of dredging in Lake Montauk.[142] The layoffs that came in October were even worse, virtually curtailing winter activity and leaving many without the employment they had counted on.[143]

Late in the summer, someone, possibly the investors, ordered an audit of the Montauk Beach Development Corporation. The auditors were appalled by what they found. Bookkeeping had been very casual, and records were incomplete. But the lack of information could not conceal the awful fact that expenditures exceeded income by more than $4 million.[144]

On October 3, Fisher told LeBoutillier he had reached the limits of his financial capacity;[145] four days later, manager Parke Haynes informed the railroad man that the development corporation was "in no position to continue any form of activity or organization." Clarifying, he added that the company didn't have "sufficient funds at this time to meet . . . payrolls after next week." He recommended that all but five or six key men be let go immediately.[146]

"Don't think for a minute I have changed my mind on Montauk," Carl Fisher asserted to LeBoutillier the day the big layoff was announced, eleven days before the stock market crashed. "I am [not] going to quit on the job if there is any way of avoiding same."[147] But for Fisher, this time there was no avoiding failure, at least of the financial kind. On October 29, Wall Street devastated the nation. Right after that, $3 million worth of

Montauk bonds came due. Carl Fisher had guaranteed the bonds, many of them held by friends, with his Miami Beach holdings. Jane remarked that Carl might have told the bondholders, "Take your bonds. You bought them, and you're as responsible as I am." But he did not. He made good on them the first year out of what was left of his personal fortune, but by the next year he could not meet them.[148] He lost his Miami Beach properties one by one—the hotels, the polo fields, the golf course. His castle-like home on Biscayne Bay was sold and turned into a gambling casino.[149] He sold his brand-new, colonnaded house at Montauk and moved into the old Montauk Association house he had remodeled for his staff.[150]

Fisher realized that his investors, most of them staggering after the crash, could not help him. "The financing of the company is entirely on my shoulders now," he wrote to an associate.[151] And he didn't hold back, then or later, even when he might have. In fact, a bankruptcy trustee's report on the Montauk bonds contains, among pages of accounting minutiae, a very unusual tribute to Carl Fisher's integrity. "In forming the new corporation," the committee wrote, "[we feel it due to Mr. Fisher] to state that . . . [he] has sincerely demonstrated his . . . intentions of . . . [promoting] any plan or reorganization whereby you and all others who have invested in Montauk securities shall receive proportionable [*sic*] and equitable treatment."[152]

Fisher tried everything he could think of to raise money to keep Montauk afloat. He appealed for lower property assessments, but was denied.[153] He was turned down for loans at bank after bank. He engaged the prominent New York realtors L'Ecluse,

Washburn & Co. to make any deal they could to sell his Montauk properties—all of them.[154] Ernest L'Ecluse claimed he was being careful not to make it look like "a fire sale,"[155] but by then Fisher just wanted to unload property, and he didn't really care how it looked. He even offered his property at a loss to his old adversary Robert Moses and the Long Island State Park Commission.[156] Carl Fisher would never be a wealthy man again. For the rest of his life, he lived on a modest salary paid by the Collins and Pancoast families, who set him up in a small office at Miami Beach.[157]

The summer seasons of 1930 and 1931 went surprisingly well at Montauk, with the Manor fully booked and a whirl of social and sporting events. Yachts crowded one another in the landlocked harbor, and the clubhouses sparkled with parties and fun. The newspapers reported big-time gambling at Montauk, not just at the Island Club but at the hotel itself[158]—a dark underside to that strange time. The privileged world for which Montauk had been built was either undaunted by the financial crisis or putting a good face on things.

In May 1932, the Montauk Beach Development Corporation went into temporary receivership, with $9 million in assets and $6 million in liabilities. The company was solvent, but unable to meet its obligations. Carl Fisher remained on the board of directors, and his former chief engineer, Thomas Ringwood, was appointed permanent receiver.[159] That summer, the corporation defaulted on mortgages and property taxes, and Suffolk County began auctioning parcel after parcel.[160] In 1933, the Bankers Trust Company foreclosed on the $3 million mortgage, and the next year it sued the corporation for defaulting on its bonds.[161] In 1934, the MBDC filed bankruptcy proceedings.[162] Montauk limped along, diminished, for part of the summer of 1936, under Ringwood's capable supervision. Only the hotel was open that year, floated by advances from the Carl G. Fisher Corporation of Miami (a holding company comprising some twenty-one of Fisher's business entities). Other facilities were allowed to languish.

In 1935, the Carl G. Fisher Corporation declared bankruptcy.[163] Although Fisher's health had gotten worse, he spent the summer in his Montauk cottage, enjoying the season and puttering around the house and garden. But "I won't live here next year," he said. "It's dull and gloomy."[164] And it was. A reporter from Queens went to take a look at Montauk that November, and found an eerie, abandoned-looking place. It was "overgrown with weeds," he wrote. Most of the home sites had never been developed. The empty seven-story office building rose "so absurdly out of the sand dunes" that motorists stopped to stare at it with their mouths open.[165]

In mid-June 1938, the Montauk Beach Development Corporation was reorganized for the last time, its name changed to the Montauk Beach Company, Inc. Investment banker and aviation official C. M. Keys took the helm. Although Carl Fisher remained on the board, he lost control of the real estate. The new company inherited some $8 million in debts, which were covered by a new bond issue. The chief executives of the new company were Lindsey Hopkins of Atlanta, who hired Alfred I. Barton as operating manager, and two of Fisher's most loyal and long-standing employees, engineer Thomas Ringwood and manager Fred Humpage, who had shouldered much of the legal and financial paperwork for years.[166]

The new company sputtered into gear mid-season, pushing to open the hotel, clubs, and other facilities so they could get busy selling real estate. An intensive promotional campaign, together with a full calendar of special events, carried Montauk through yet another season,[167] but on September 21, a Category 3 hurricane made a direct hit on Long Island and New England. Seventeen-foot storm surges and 120-mile-an-hour winds swept away beaches and boardwalk, and the fishing village and its boats were tossed to pieces. The more fortunate residents sheltered in Montauk Manor, although several were lost, presumed drowned, in the storm. Downtown Montauk suffered some damage, but most of the other resort buildings survived intact.[168]

Separated now from his second wife, Carl Fisher lived in a small house in Miami Beach. He spent time in his office, which was next door to Irving Collins's Bay Shore Company. There he kept up with Montauk, visited with people, and dictated chatty letters to old friends. On July 15, 1939, he was rushed to the hospital with a gastric hemorrhage (the consequence of the disastrous eating and drinking habits he would never give up), where he

Carl Fisher's estate, aerial view, 1930s. Fisher began planning his own Montauk home in the fall of 1927, reminding designer Arthur W. B. Wood that he admired Mount Vernon and the American Colonial style. The compound included a garage with guest quarters above it, a caretaker's cottage, and a stable (proscribed by his own property restrictions). The house was finished in early 1929. Montauk Library

The foundation for the Montauk Beach Development Corporation's seven-story office tower, designed by Schultze & Weaver, was laid in May 1926. The landmark of the business section, the building's main purpose was to sell real estate; potential buyers could survey all of Montauk while they listened to the master salesman. The development corporation occupied the tower until its bankruptcy in 1934; the next year the structure was vacant. During World War II, the Navy used it as a barracks and a hospital. In the 1980s the tower was remodeled as condominium apartments. Montauk Library

died that afternoon.[169] He was sixty-five years old. When Fisher's estate was settled, it was discovered that the ebullient resort developer, once magnificently wealthy, had left around $50,000.[170]

After Carl Fisher's death, detractors wrote the occasional letter and editorial deploring the developer's supposed shady practices. One such indictment was published in a New York paper on July 25, 1939. Loyal Thomas Ringwood fired off an immediate response. Fisher *did not* die broke, Ringwood wrote. "He had an independent income . . . in the neighborhood of $20,000 a year, and if you don't think that's something, you go out and try to dig up that [much] these days." And Mr. Fisher *did not* operate . . . on "other people's money," he controlled all of his companies with his own money, Ringwood declared. Ringwood also pointed out that Fisher *had not* made his money at Miami Beach, but had gone there with $5 or $6 million, and spent it making Miami Beach. Also, Ringwood corrected a misapprehension that very likely originated with Carl Fisher himself: "Mr. Fisher *did not* merely mark on maps the sites of the various resort facilities . . . *I* marked the maps, and Mr. Fisher went over the property . . . and proceeded to build them." It was especially important to Ringwood to set one last count straight: "Mr. Fisher *did not* flop at Montauk." He could have taken a loss and gotten out in 1929, leaving the investors (who were his friends) to shift for themselves. Instead, he pledged his Florida holdings for new financing, and threw in nearly $2 million of his own money with no obligation to do it, and no security. "How many . . . captains of industry do you know . . . who would do that?" Ringwood closed the letter with a tribute all the more powerful because of

the many years he had served his former boss. "Mr. Fisher was without exception the finest man I ever knew," Ringwood wrote. "He was one of a group of men who are dying off much too rapidly for the good of this country and they are going to be missed."[171]

After the Fisher era ended, Montauk languished for decades until some new development began in the 1950s and early '60s. The Montauk Beach Company continued to sell real estate until 1958; thereafter, other firms sold the former development company's property.[172]

Before and during World War II, several branches of the military took over much of Montauk, considering the eastern tip of Long Island vulnerable to enemy invasion. The Army established Camp Hero on the site of the old fishing village, disguising the military presence behind faux-quaint facades. Dirigibles occupied giant hangars at the Montauk Naval Station. The yacht club on Star Island became a naval base, and private yachts patrolled the waters. The Army considered demolishing Montauk Manor, but finding it too solidly constructed to blow up, used it—and the office building—as barracks instead. The Army closed Camp Hero in 1957, when it was taken over by the Air Force to watch for incoming Soviet bombers. In 1982, the military began selling its installations as surplus property.[173]

Many of Long Island's early twentieth-century developments were suburban enclaves where New York commuters could live in comfort and style among like-minded people. Montauk Beach was not like that. It was not a suburb but a seasonal resort, a place built specifically to provide an exciting life. Montauk offered sports and social life, new people

Thomas E. Ringwood was one of Carl Fisher's longest-serving and most loyal executives. Hired in Miami, the young engineer was one of the corporation's first professionals to go to Montauk Beach, where he supervised an intensive survey in the fall of 1925. After the 1935 bankruptcy, Ringwood was named permanent trustee. He was responsible for running the hotel, the clubs, and the other resort facilities as, one by one, they were sold off. Ringwood tried to retain some of Fisher's own assets for him as things went from bad to worse.
Montauk Library

and invigorating experiences. It was racy, too, flirting at the portals of vice with its Prohibition-flouting casinos and its storied love nests. Its isolated location at the extreme end of Long Island made the resort dependent on modern forms of transportation; visitors arrived on trains, in cars, or even aboard powerful diesel-engine yachts. In fact, getting there was half the fun, and once there, one had privacy. Although Montauk's deliberately quaint, English-themed architecture gave the place the semblance of antiquity, Fisher's resort was deliberately progressive in its use of modern technology, materials, and machines; his wealthy clientele expected the latest in comfort and convenience. Montauk was promoted in a modern way as well. Not only were there advertisements in every form of print media, there were also rotogravure-like sales booklets studded with photographs. And Fisher ensured that Montauk made the news, too—whenever anything happened there, from the arrival of a giant dredge to a celebrity visit, the newspapers covered it.

Today, Montauk is a haunting seaside hybrid of Carl Fisher's 1920s formality and the comfortable rusticity of later years. One of the most striking changes is that trees and grass and flowers grow at Montauk. Before Carl Fisher and Fred Hoerger, the place was barren sand, with a spray of tough grass here and there that the cattle had ignored. The Fisher landmarks give the place distinction; they are not what's expected in a beach town. Montauk Manor, closed down in the 1960s, was converted into condominium residences with a few hotel rooms in the late 1980s. The exterior and the lobby have been restored to something close to their original appearance, though the rooms and auxiliary areas have been

completely changed. Just downhill from the hotel, Fisher's tennis auditorium has been converted into a playhouse. The seven-story office building, after languishing for a long time, was remodeled as condominiums in the 1980s. The downtown district, bisected by the Montauk Highway, looks much as Fisher might have known it, with most of the original buildings in use. The office built for the Montauk Struck Company still stands across the circle from Fisher's office building. On Star Island, the yacht club still operates. Remodeling has changed its look, but the original tower gives its secret away. Up in the hills, Shepherd's Neck village still clusters on its Fort Pond point; the little stucco Tudor houses, now tucked behind pretty gardens, are desirable properties. On the bluffs, the Montauk Association houses stand, protected. And on the highest heights, on both sides of Lake Montauk and around the golf course, the elegant mansions built for Fisher and his friends and investors are still treasured homes.

Some people claim that Carl Fisher failed at Montauk, but that assessment undervalues what he accomplished there. Thomas Ringwood challenged such opinions with a financial argument, saying that Fisher could have walked away when the bonds came due. But Montauk makes its own argument for Fisher's success. If it had not been for Fisher, with his extravagant vision and his investment of money and labor, Montauk might have been a linear beach town like hundreds along the East Coast, with a boardwalk and T-shirts and ice cream shops. Instead, it is a much more complex place, with neighborhoods both stately and charming, with private, curving lanes, and with sensory delights for tastes both rustic and refined.

13
ROBERT L. BURTON'S WOODMERE

MILLICENT D. VOLLONO

The turn of the twentieth century encompassed all that was right and wrong with the
American capitalist system. While progressives and social reformers advocated for improvements in the lives of working Americans, the power
and fortune of a single man could create or destroy
a community. Robert Burton's purchase of the entire
village of Woodsburgh in 1901 and its subsequent
sale in 1909 was an exercise in personal wealth. He
probably did not realize that he was a pioneer in a
movement that would determine much of the future
development of suburban Long Island.

Before the Civil War, the rural Rockaways were
connected to the main population centers by a
stagecoach route that followed old Indian trails.
The expansion of the South Side and Long Island
railroads, coupled with the establishment of service
to the beach resorts in the Rockaways, were the catalysts for the development of communities along
the railroads' Rockaway Branch. Samuel Wood
(1795–1878), an entrepreneur at the end of a life
worthy of a Horatio Alger story, joined other major
landowners such as the Hewlett family, the Marsh
brothers (Samuel and Thomas), and the Lawrence
brothers (Newbold, Alfred, and George) in donat-
ing land to the South Side Railroad. Between
1868 and 1869, the wooden stations erected on
that land ensured that their communities would be
stops on the new route. Those locales today comprise the area known as Long Island's Five Towns:
the municipalities of Hewlett, Woodmere, Cedarhurst, Lawrence, and Inwood. Wood's station was

known as Woodsburgh until the establishment of
a post office in 1890, when the name Woodmere
was adopted to avoid confusion with another Long
Island village.

Samuel and his three brothers had grown up
on a Rockaway farm before departing in 1814 to
make their fortune as liquor merchants in Manhattan. The brothers pledged to never marry and, as
each died, to bequeath his property to the remaining brothers. Samuel inherited the fortune in 1868
and began to acquire Rockaway farmland in the
area known as Brower's Point to fulfill his dream
of improving the community of his childhood. The
Brooklyn Daily Eagle chronicled the hiring of work
crews for the project, which engaged Wood for the
rest of his life, beginning with laying out the Boulevard, which stretched from the main thoroughfare
(Broadway) to the bay.[1] One hundred fifty men
worked steadily through the winter of 1869–70 so
the resort could be opened the following summer.
The first structure to be built was a board-and-bat-
ten railroad depot, followed by the Grand Hotel, or
Pavilion, a smaller hotel (later called the Neptune),
and five cottages.

The Pavilion, a handsome, well-appointed hostelry in the fashionable French Second Empire style
with encompassing piazzas, could accommodate
four hundred guests, while the Neptune across
Broadway lodged a hundred. Cottages measuring
at least twenty 25 x 40 feet were built on either
side of the grand Boulevard. A half-mile long and
eighty feet wide, with sidewalks and shade trees on

both sides, the graded road was the first of many that would link the Rockaway villages and bring visitors to Mr. Wood's new paradise.

Far Rockaway's fashionable Marine Pavilion (1833–64) had set the standard for the area's luxury seaside resorts and for thirty years attracted the rich and famous to the area. Within a few years, neighboring Lawrence Beach boasted resort hotels such as the Osborne House (1884–1900) and the Isle of Wight Hotel, which eventually eclipsed the aging Woodsburgh Pavilion.

As more of New York's business community summered in the area, the Rockaway Hunting Club (founded in 1878 as the Rockaway Hunt Club) became the center of social activity. Originally formed around equestrian pursuits, the club's elite membership included prominent figures in finance and industry. As many resided in New York City, they stayed in the club's facilities when visiting in the Rockaways. The original clubhouse, built in 1884, was destroyed by fire less than a decade later. The building that replaced it was designed by architect and club member James Monroe Hewlett. Considered to be the largest, best-appointed clubhouse on Long Island, it overlooked a polo field, four-mile steeplechase course, and Reynolds Channel. By the turn of the century, as the surrounding countryside became more inhabited, the nature of the club changed. Polo, golf, and tennis replaced fox hunting when it was discontinued and, as the club's membership increased, more city dwellers discovered the beauty of Long Island's South Shore. Summer rentals abounded as the elaborate "cottages" and accompanying amenities were marketed to affluent vacationers, quickly establishing the area as a viable alternative to Long Branch, New Jersey, and Newport, Rhode Island. In what Cromwell Childe refers to as the "third stage" of post–Civil War rural development,[2] many club members invested in real estate and built their own country houses on the land surrounding the Hunting Club and the exclusive Isle of Wight in Lawrence.

Although Samuel Wood had made provisions for the posthumous establishment of a hospital and a music conservatory, his will was successfully challenged in the decades following his death. By the time Abraham Hewlett, Wood's nephew and heir, died in 1899, most of the estate had been consumed in legal fees. According to Alfred H. Bellot's *History of the Rockaways,* the Woodmere Land Improvement Company was formed at this time to manage the interests of the various landowners. Local residents Divine Hewlett, Thomas W. Martin, Joseph S. Wright, George M. Hewlett, Edward Schenck, and Julian T. Davies were active in the endeavor. Within a year, Robert L. Burton, a Manhattan industrialist and Rockaway Hunting Club member, offered to buy the entire town from the company, ostensibly for his personal use,[3] and negotiations began in earnest. Events threatened to derail the deal, as some residents held out for better terms, but in the end, the transaction was completed at a cost of $130,000 and Burton

expanded his initial purchase by procuring the adjacent George Hewlett farm.

Robert Lewis Burton was born in New York City on February 28, 1861, the second son of Josiah Howes and Lucia (Clark) Burton. After a public school education, he embarked on a business career and, until his retirement in 1909, was a partner in Burton Brothers, a textile firm founded by his elder brother, Frank V. Burton. While elaborate country houses had been built in the neighboring hamlets of Cedarhurst and Lawrence, the area formerly known as Woodsburgh had, by 1901, lost its panache as a resort. Burton decided to reinvent it by razing the hotel and demolishing or relocating the remaining buildings. The Pavilion, which had been closed for about four years, was torn down in July of that year and by August, any homes that had not been demolished were moved to other sites in the village.

> Eight frame cottages, surrounding the pavilion [*sic*] have been moved back to sites near the railroad track and in their former sites five handsome modern brick and stone cottages, plans for which are already made, are soon to be built. This however, is but a beginning of the work to be done. Over a hundred men are at work laying out winding roads built of Peekskill gravel and serpentine walks. The whole tract will be seeded down into a velvety lawn, and trees and shrubs will be set out in all parts of the grounds.[4]

Burton built his own home, Albro House, adjacent to the Rockaway Hunting Club, around 1900. He lived there with his wife, the former Florence Southwood Crawford, and their three children, Florence, Louisa, and Crawford, for at least ten years. John Howes Burton, Robert's younger brother, was an interesting character in his own right. After attending Harvard for only one year (1886–87), John entered the family business, often collaborating with the eldest brother, Frank, on Manhattan real estate ventures. After 1915, John was instrumental in the Save New York Committee, the principal purpose of which was the establishment of a factory district west of Seventh Avenue (today's Garment District) and the preservation of the midtown area from 32nd to 59th streets as a site for theaters, department stores, and office buildings. John Burton, as chairman of the Save New York Committee, effectively designed the blueprint for Manhattan as it exists today.[5]

At the same time as Robert Burton was purchasing the Wood properties, a syndicate led by attorney Joseph Auerbach and his partner, Richard W. Stevenson, was investing in the square mile of farms southeast of Woodmere that would soon be known as Hewlett Bay Park.[6] Between the two purchases, the parties controlled a "strip of nearly 1,500 acres of land, extending from Cedarhurst to East Rockaway, with a shore front four or five miles in length and with two stations of the Long Island Railroad adjoining, or nearly adjoining the same,"[7] and twenty miles of winding paved roads, which they had created. Both sets of investors also employed dredging companies to create a deep-water channel that would allow the existing waterways to accommodate yachts and a proposed ferry to Freeport and Long Beach. The material retrieved from the dredging was used for paving the new roads, which became so popular with automobilists that the *Brooklyn Daily Eagle* reported the presence of prominent signs on the Burton properties prohibiting automobiles from entering, offering protection against

> the outrages perpetrated by automobilists, who run their machines at a high rate of speed and endanger the lives of drivers and pedestrians. . . . Occupants of the cottages all have fine blooded stock [horses], and as the animals become frightened at the puffing machines Mr. Burton has wisely made the ruling prohibiting their entering his grounds.[8]

Burton envisioned the creation of an affluent residential community on the scale of Tuxedo Park,

New York, or Germantown, Pennsylvania, which provided residents with stores, schools, recreational facilities, and transportation links. Yet only a handful of intimate friends were allowed to purchase houses, most properties being available only as seasonal rentals, as Burton retained complete control over the process. Electrical and telephone services utilized underground conduits at Woodmere, and sewers and water mains were also below grade. The well-maintained macadam roads planned by Major Clarence T. Barrett, a respected sanitation engineer and landscape architect, conformed to the topography, and the landscape features were designed to complement the architecture of the individual houses.[9]

In 1902, a tract of about 550 acres with nearly a mile of bay frontage was slated for development by another real estate consortium, the Cedarhurst Land Association, in collaboration with Burton.

Lake at Woodmere. Collection of Millicent Vollono

Houses at Woodmere, ca. 1910. Collection of Millicent Vollono

Charles Barton Keen.
Courtesy Sara Pilling

The developers created a causeway to connect Woodmere and Cedarhurst, cutting the traveling distance by a mile.[10] Designed by several leading architects, the houses were mainly in the Dutch Colonial and Shingle styles that were then popular on Long Island's South Shore. New construction techniques, such as the use of hollow-tile blocks finished with tinted concrete, were employed in an effort to emphasize aesthetics, climate control, and fire resistance. Hollow-tile construction was adaptable to a variety of styles and had the ability to create a harmony of design between house and outbuildings.[11]

Architect Charles Barton Keen of Philadelphia (1868–1931) was given a number of commissions for the Woodmere project, including the design of the railroad station, built jointly by the Cedarhurst Land Improvement Company and the Long Island Railroad in a style compatible with the homes. Gneiss and mica schist—stone from the excavation of the New York City subway system—was transported by rail for the foundations, walls, and chimneys of many of the houses. It was also used for the new Woodmere station and the Fireman's Hall in nearby Lawrence. Built on a three-hundred-foot-long brick platform, the station was promoted as being within a ten-minute walk from any portion of Woodmere. Its multiple rooms included a women's parlor and dressing room, stylish tile bathrooms, a ticket office, and a baggage room. At a cost of about $10,000, it provided an elegant welcome to the arriving visitor or commuter. Burton, as sole owner of Woodmere, made every effort to ensure the highest standards for his residential park, underwriting the entire cost of maintenance—at an

annual loss of several thousand dollars.[12] A *New York Times* article from 1909 recounts:

> The story is told of the difficulty that was encountered in finding any butcher willing to open a shop in Woodmere on account of the prospective lack of patronage throughout several months of the year. This did not daunt Mr. Burton. He picked out a butcher and told him to run the right kind of shop in Woodmere and send him the bill. The butcher did as he was told and according to a trustworthy report the bill has been about $5,000 a year.[13]

Though some of the Woodmere houses rivaled the scale of country houses being built in Long Island's other aristocratic communities, most of the Keen homes were designed to offer the highest-quality features available at a modest cost. A 1906 article in *Country Life in America* describes the trade-off:

> "[T]he chief efforts were made to secure a unique and artistic design, convenience of plan, beauty and consistency of finish and the highest possible excellence of construction. Therefore, a small house, only forty-two feet four inches by thirty-two feet six inches, exclusive of porches, has cost over $10,000 to build. A house of the same size and similar in appearance might have been built for $7,000, but at every point some sacrifice would have been made for the sake of economy. . . . Possibly the plumbing was more costly than necessary, but there is extravagance nowhere else—only the determination to have the best. In many respects this little house in Woodmere approaches perfection."[14]

One of Woodmere's most photographed houses was designed by Lewis Colt Albro (1876–1924) and Harrie T. Lindeberg (1879–1959) for Carleton Macy, the president of the Hewlett Bay Company. Featured in several prominent magazines of the era, it was a marvel of traditional English cottage style combined with modern construction techniques. The shingled roof had the appearance of thatch, created by the application of shingles in a wavy line over a "cushioned" foundation of lead. Aymar Embury describes the home in *One Hundred Country Houses*:

> The residence of Carleton Macy, at Woodmere, Long Island, has been one of the most admired of the past few years. In it the shingle treatment has been carried further than has ever before been attempted, with unique and satisfactory results. The house is thoroughly modern in every respect, for the columns, while Greek in detail, are so unusual in their handling that they may fairly be called modern design. The roof-lines are symmetrical, and the chimneys are placed at either end of the main ridge,

where the need for some emphasis is always felt. The windows are quite simply handled in a manner suggestive of Colonial, and the shutters are solid below with louvers above. The setting is such as to show the house to its best advantage, and was very carefully thought out by the architects. The house is one which has brought much and well-deserved reputation to its authors, for its brilliancy is the result of virile and thoughtful design.[15]

Ehrick Kensett Rossiter (1854–1941) and Frank Ayres Wright (1855–1949) created several brick-and-stucco houses in the Dutch Colonial style for Robert Burton. Rossiter and Wright homes featured simple lines with attention to both exterior and interior details such as sunrooms, Dutch tile floors, a paneled inglenook area, and a separate porch for the servants. Louis Boynton's houses,

which sold for between $12,000 and $15,000, were designed to be attractive and fire-resistant. Hollow terra-cotta blocks supported by concrete beams were utilized in the weight-bearing walls.[16] Earth tones such as sienna, yellow ochre, and Indian red were mixed with a white cement and applied to the blocks within ten days of the walls' construction. The colorizing process for the concrete could be used on exterior as well as interior walls and was celebrated for its weather-resistant properties. Spanish tile roofs mounted on wooden rafters completed the effect. The Woodmere houses designed by Arthur Redfern Cornwell and Alfred Hopkins also featured innovations in brickwork and the use of decorative concrete. Other notable Woodmere houses were those designed by William Beers for George deForest Lord (1914) and the shingled home of

House designed by Charles Barton Keen. Collection of Millicent Vollono

Carleton Macy Residence, designed by Lewis Colt Albro and Harrie T. Lindeberg. Collection of Millicent Vollono

WOODMERE L.I.

The Finest Residential District of New York.
45 Minutes from Wall Street or Herald Square.

Arthur Nelson Peck (1910), designed by William Adams, the architect of nearby Lawrence High School and the Woodmere Academy.

Architect Henry Otis Chapman (1862–1929) designed his own home (ca. 1900) at 120 Ocean Avenue in Woodmere in collaboration with his partner, John Stewart Barney. The façade gables, clustered brick chimneys, and half-timbered second story gave the edifice the classic appearance of an English Tudor country home.

James Alexander McCrea, who held the positions of vice president of the Pennsylvania Railroad and general superintendent of the Long Island Railroad, was a member of both the Rockaway Hunting Club and the Cedarhurst Yacht Club. Charles A. Platt designed his home, which was located at the termination of South End Avenue, on Hempstead Bay Drive, and had a beautiful view of Woodmere Bay. After the incorporation of a residential portion of Woodmere as Woodsburgh, McCrea served as its mayor from 1914 to 1918. The house was impressive in both size and setting:

> A seven-bay, two-and-a-half story central section was flanked by two-story wings of three or four bays in width, one devoted to service, the other designed for a drawing room with bedrooms above. The interior plan . . . emphasized a dominant short axis from entrance hall to rear loggia, crossed by perpendicular corridors to connect major rooms on the first and second floors. The relation of the house to its surroundings was zoned with an entrance on the north, a vista across open lawns to

the water on the south, a formal flower garden to the west, and a service court to the east.[17]

By 1906, the stage was set to attract year-round inhabitants. The commuter, wrote C. E. Whittlesey in his 1911 article "The Commuter's Long Island,"[18] was once the subject of jokes. It was considered folly to attempt to live in the country and work in the city. Following Burton's purchase, however, advances in technology reversed this opinion. The Rockaway Branch was electrified in 1905 and by 1910 the Long Island Railroad reported that twenty-eight million passengers used its services. Suburban commutation was a viable alternative to urban living. The average commuter traveled a route of about twenty-five miles each way in about forty-five minutes at a cost of approximately eight dollars a month. This sea change reversed the aforementioned seasonal "lack of patronage" and substantially increased the value of Burton's property.

As early as 1904, Burton employed Milton L'Ecluse, a rising star in the Long Island real estate business, to manage the Woodmere properties, and in 1908 Burton began the process of divesting himself of sole ownership, selling his holdings to the Woodmere Land Association, while retaining a controlling interest in the company.[19] The following year, newspapers from New York to Oregon proclaimed the sale of the hamlet of Woodmere to a syndicate headed by Maximilian Morgenthau, President of the Hudson Realty Company of New York. A front-page story in the *New York Times* called the $3 million sale, in which Burton was represented by the firm of L'Ecluse, Washburn & Company, as "probably the largest real estate deal in the history of the New York suburban district."[20] Burton had spent over \$2 million on forty cottages at a cost of between \$8,000 and \$50,000 each, \$20,000 on the Woodmere station, and over \$500,000 on the landscaping of forty-seven acres of roads[21] and the installation of electric lights, gas, water, and telephone services. Morgenthau's consortium was incorporated in 1909 under the name of the Woodmere Realty Company.

Morgenthau had as directors Samuel H. Jacobs, Samuel Weil, Emil S. Levi, Max Katz, John Howes Burton, Clarence G. Galston, Julius C. Morgenthau, James Frank, Leon S. Mendel, and bankers Henry S. Herman and Joseph Fox. With the exception of John Howes Burton, these men were not Rockaway Hunting Club members and represented a new ethnicity—German-Jewish immigrants who had previously summered in Far Rockaway. In an era when "restricted development" often resulted in the exclusion of certain ethnic or religious groups, Robert Burton apparently put no such restrictions on his sales. Burton's deeds and covenants primarily established commercial zoning restrictions and clearly showed efforts to keep the properties residential and of a uniform quality and aesthetic.

The oldest of fourteen children, Maximilian Morgenthau was born in Mannheim, Germany, in 1847 and emigrated with his family to the United States in 1865. After obtaining a law degree from New York University, he pursued other interests and locations before returning to New York in 1898 to enter a real estate syndicate formed by his brother Henry, an influential figure in Woodrow Wilson's administration who eventually served as ambassador to Turkey. Active in philanthropic movements and civic affairs, the brothers formed an early friendship with Felix Adler, founder of the Ethical Culture Society. Their association with Adler led Henry Morgenthau to donate a house in Woodmere as the home of the Woodmere Academy, a school founded on the principles of Ethical Culture. Maximilian, who had made his fortune in New York real estate, resided in Woodmere and served as a director on the boards of at least nine realty concerns and financial institutions, in addition to the Woodmere Realty Company.

In interviews following the transaction, Morgenthau stated that the construction of a club-

The Brooklyn Daily Eagle, *November 10, 1909.*

THE BROOKLYN DAILY EAGLE

PICTURE AND SPORTING SECTION ★ NEW YORK CITY, WEDNESDAY, NOVEMBER 10, 1909. PICTURE AND SPORTING SECTION

TOWN OF WOODMERE, L. I., BOUGHT FOR \$3,000,000.

Unique Woodmere Villa of Carleton Macy.

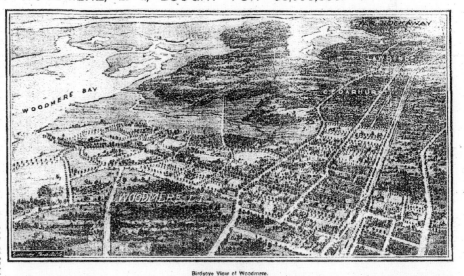

Birdseye View of Woodmere.

Woodmere Station.

New Clubhouse to Be Built at Woodmere, L. I.

175

house and tennis courts was imminent and that the establishment of a private golf club was also in the works. The Woodmere Club, with its nine clay tennis courts, was erected near the station and opened in May 1910. Plans to acquire frontage and build a waterside casino and boathouse began almost immediately.[22] The new clubhouse, an imposing adaptation of the Dutch Colonial style by Ralph C. Lynch in keeping with the designs by Keen and others, was dedicated in 1912. Built at a cost of $18,000, the clubhouse featured a first floor clad in stucco, a wide veranda with massive pillars extending its full width, and a second story of white-painted shingles..[23]

With the establishment of the Woodmere Realty Company, the marketing of Woodmere began in earnest, as did land speculation. At the end of 1910, the *New York Times* reported that a plot at the intersection of Burton Avenue and Crawford Road was resold by F. W. Avery and Company for the third time that year.[24] Woodmere Realty Company's exhibit at the 1911 Real Estate Show in Madison Square Garden was designed to attract attention:

> The display is a panoramic view of Woodmere, Long Island, showing the houses in miniature, overlooking a wide sweep of forest and ocean, with sailboats cruising on Woodmere Bay. This display is only a small part of the exhibition of the Woodmere Realty Company, the greater part of which is in the concert hall, where there is a large drop depicting a forest scene upon which pictures of artistic and attractive homes are also displayed. These portray the advantages, conveniences and attractions of living in an ideal suburb such as Woodmere. It further demonstrates

how to construct ideal homes from a building standpoint, landscaping its various phases and, in fact, it deals with everything pertaining to an ideal home. Around the sides of the concert hall the alcoves are artistically hung with colored views of Woodmere's ideal homes and bungalows. Of special interest are the pictures from the Henry Morgenthau collection, showing the New York of fifty and one hundred years ago.[25]

In its 1911 brochure, the Woodmere Realty Company made its appeal directly to the commuting businessman. While stressing the bucolic vistas and moderate temperatures of Long Island's South Shore,[26] the advertising educates prospective buyers about the excellent and modern facilities, the quality of future neighbors, and the ease of travel to Manhattan from Woodmere.

In 1911 and 1912, Burton became the subject of litigation that accused him of collusive business dealings in the original purchase of the Wood property. Benjamin E. Valentine of Woodmere, a disbarred lawyer and convicted felon who was involved as early as 1897 in a similar lawsuit against Burton, was by this time the principal shareholder in the Hewlett Land and Improvement Company. He and Burton had had an incendiary relationship over the years and the courts had already decided in Burton's favor. The later suits renewed the original charges and added to the complaints. In 1912, however, Valentine was convicted of forging a deed in another case and sentenced to a year in Sing Sing, and it appears that the charges against Burton were dismissed. By 1914, Burton had relocated to Dutchess County, New York, where he ran a successful dairy farm and assumed the duties of county food administrator. He died at Crawford Farms, his Millbrook, New York, residence, in 1927.

Over the next decade, the Woodmere Realty Company sold the remaining plots to developers. Gas and electricity were provided by the Queensboro Gas and Electric Company; telephone service, by the New York Telephone Company. In a precedent set in 1912, the Far Rockaway telephone exchange in Queens (including Cedarhurst, Lawrence, and Inwood) was charged five cents per call, whereas the adjacent Woodmere exchange was charged fifteen cents per call. As the result of a lawsuit brought by a Woodmere resident, the Public Service Commission decided in favor of the Woodmere residents and the fees were equalized in 1920.[27]

The Queens County Water Company, which supplied water to the area, derived its water from driven wells located on a nearby woodland watershed.[28] Burton's Woodmere Land Association had seen to it that water mains were laid in all developed streets. In his proposal for sewage disposal

in Woodmere, Theodore Horton, chief engineer of the project, had written in 1908 that the forty houses in Woodmere would soon grow to a proposed six hundred and projected a flow of 450,000 gallons of sewage a day, which was to empty into Brosewere Bay. By 1910, Morgenthau's Woodmere Realty Company was planning $350,000 to $400,000 worth of dredging in Woodmere Bay and Mill Creek. The intention was to enlarge and deepen 200 feet of the waterway to a depth of 15 feet, straighten and extend the channel, and reclaim about 120 acres of meadowland. The Atlantic Gulf and Pacific Company was engaged for the job, which Maximilian Morgenthau said in 1910 would allow the "Woodmere or Cedarhurst yachtsman . . . [to] moor a 200-foot yacht in their back yard, so to speak."[29] The dredging was never completed, however, and resulted in a series of legal battles.

Morgenthau's own home, a large fieldstone structure at the intersection of Willow Lane, Keene

Page from Woodmere Realty Company brochure, 1911. Hewlett-Woodmere Public Library Collection

Lane, and Woodmere Boulevard,[30] was designed by Ernest Flagg (1857–1947), who had also designed several houses for Burton in Woodmere. Another celebrated architect of the Morgenthau era was Olive Frances Tjaden (1904–1997), who was at one time the only female member of the American Institute of Architects. Among her 2,000 buildings are houses in Woodmere, which she designed in the 1930s for Harold Jacobi Sr. and his brother, Sanford,[31] founders of Schenley Distillers, and the homes of Arthur Marks[32] and William Recht. B. E. Stern, an architect of the Nassau Hotel in Long Beach, New York, designed a Georgian Colonial house in Woodmere for attorney Lester Hofheimer (d.1936). Stern's use of Italianate details capitalized on the location's natural light and breezes; latticework and a portico complement the exterior elements.[33]

For Woodmere, as for many of the neighboring villages, the process of incorporation was considered a necessary step to implement improvements, independent of the Town of Hempstead. If Woodmere embraced incorporation, then Woodmere Boulevard, neglected in spite of its status as a town road, had a better chance of receiving the renovations that residents felt were sorely needed. [fig. 12] Police and fire protection were also part of the plan of incorporation. In a meeting at the Woodmere Club on May 6, 1910, a committee was formed to begin the incorporation of its affluent residential portion, with James McCrea, superintendent of the Long Island Railroad, as its chairman. The business district and the more

modest residential areas were not included in the area to be incorporated and were to retain the name of Woodmere, while the new village would be incorporated under the name of Woodsburgh. A population of four hundred and the consent of one-third of the property owners and twenty-five freeholders were requirements for incorporation. The *New-York Tribune* reported that the proposal had the active support of the Woodmere Realty Company.

The Woodmere Improvement Society, comprising about a hundred property owners, met for its first meeting at the Woodmere Club on October 28, 1910. The society was created to organize police and fire protection, maintain roads, improve street lighting, and establish rules for sanitation and public safety. By November 1910, representatives from Woodmere and Cedarhurst were joining colleagues in Lawrence to collaborate on efforts to build a sewer system and disposal plant that would serve the three communities.[34]

A vote was held on October 29 at the Keene Lane home of attorney Arthur F. Cosby, resulting in a decision of 28–0 in favor of incorporation. Among the participants in this event were Edward H. Pershing, physician; financiers Arthur Nelson Peck, Frederic H. Hatch, James L. Timpson, and Robert Sloan; railroad executive James A. McCrea; and Henry Ziegler, president of Steinway Piano Company. Other residents of the newly incorporated village included Maximilian Morgenthau and his brother Julius C. Morgenthau; Carleton Macy, president of the Hewlett Bay Company; William

Fox, founder of Fox Film Corporation; brothers Harold and Sanford Jacobi, founders of Schenley Distillers; attorney George deForest Lord; real estate developer George L. Stebbins; and financiers George W. Van Siclen and Louden S. Wainwright Sr. Woodsburgh officially became an incorporated village on November 8, 1912, reviving the original name of the community.

Twenty-first-century Woodsburgh is an active and thriving community. Seventy-five percent of its homes were built after 1939 and, though a number of stately homes still stand, builders have subdivided many of the Burton-era estates or demolished older homes entirely in favor of more modern edifices. Winding roads and magnificent trees remain—a testament to the gracious lifestyle of the early residents as the area introduces new generations to the charms of one of the South Shore's most historic and congenial communities.

14

THE GRAND SCHEME

FELIX ISMAN, ERNESTUS GULICK,
AND THE CREATION OF JAMAICA ESTATES

CARL BALLENAS AND THE AQUINAS HONOR SOCIETY

Jamaica Estates, hailed by the press as a grand scheme, was launched in 1907. The key players in its creation were the well-connected and politically astute real estate developers and speculators Ernestus Gulick (1865–1913) and Felix Isman (1874–1943).

"Major" Ernestus Schenck Gulick, a native of Illinois, came to New York City in 1883 and opened a real estate office in Brooklyn. From modest beginnings he built a thriving business, and by the time of his death in 1913, he was president of the Ernestus Gulick Company, Hempstead South Company, and Long Island Estates and vice president of Garden City Estates. In addition to his Long Island real estate projects, Gulick amassed some of the biggest parcels of the era in downtown Brooklyn to build the Frederick Loeser and Co. and Abraham & Straus department stores. He is credited with introducing the term *estates* in reference to suburban development projects, a thought that occurred to him while in London, where he observed that real estate agents were called estate agents.[1] His military rank derived from serving in the Twenty-third Regiment of the National Guard, where he rubbed shoulders with some of Brooklyn's leading citizens. His partner, Felix Isman, born in Philadelphia in 1874, amassed a fortune estimated at $30 million by the age of thirty-three. A real estate impresario and theatrical manager, Isman stunned New Yorkers in 1902, when he spent $1.55 million for property on the southeast corner of Fifth Avenue and 42nd Street. His famous doctrine was: "You can be 75 percent wrong and still make money in Manhattan real estate."[2]

"The physical joining of Manhattan Island with Long Island by tunnels and bridges," Gulick proclaimed in 1908, "must cause a rise in values which no financial depression can possibly stop."[3] He was referring to the transportation improvements that took place in the first decade of the twentieth century, including the erection of the Queensboro and Manhattan bridges (1909) and the construction of the East River railroad tunnels (1910), which prompted the boom in Long Island real estate.

In June 1907, the Ernestus Gulick Company leased the first floor of the Cambridge Building at 334 Fifth Avenue at 33rd Street, not far from the most important new gateway to Long Island, Pennsylvania Station, and set about to purchase the site for Jamaica Estates, which had been under consideration as a city park during the administration of Mayor George B. McClellan. Title to the eight thousand lots that had originally been assembled by Edward C. M. Fitzgerald was acquired from the Matawok Land Company, whose investors were reportedly Philadelphia capitalists and L.I.R.R. president Ralph Peters, in 1906.[4] The newly formed Jamaica Estates Corporation had a strong board, with Gulick as president and Isman, who would soon succeed Gulick, as first vice president. Directors included several bank presidents

and influential politicians, among them former New York State lieutenant governor Timothy L. Woodruff and former New York City comptroller Edward M. Grout.[5]

Jamaica Estates "promises to be an important realty development," reported the *Long Island Farmer* in 1907. "It is the intention of the promoters of the project to make it a Long Island Tuxedo."[6] Developed in 1885 as a resort for the social elite, where New York's "Four Hundred" came to play, Tuxedo Park was the creation of Pierre Lorillard IV, the tobacco millionaire and sportsman. Comprising more than thirty miles of roads, a village center, a clubhouse, and handsome country houses referred to as cottages, this Orange County luxury enclave was certainly a model to emulate, but in reality, Gulick and Isman were aiming at an entirely different demographic: those dependent on public transportation to get to work. The developers took some unusual steps to ensure that their community was only "eighteen minutes from Herald Square."[7] They commissioned a number of gasoline-powered, double-decker omnibuses, then popular in London and Paris, which could seat forty-eight, and made arrangements with the Long Island Railroad for the construction of an express passenger station located three blocks to the south of the community. The company purchased the property along Homer Lee Avenue (now Edgerton Boulevard) leading to the new depot. The new station, called Hillside, opened in 1911.

"On the wooded heights north of Jamaica," the *New York Times* reported on May 31, 1908, "the Jamaica Estates Company is making a beautiful residential park . . . about 500 acres."[8] Laid out in sections under the direction of noted landscape architect Charles W. Leavitt (1871–1928), the community soon boasted a wide main boulevard (today's Midland Parkway) that connected with Hillside Avenue, where an "attractive lodge [was] to be built."[9] The boulevard was to be both paved and "parked" with planted medians. "The land has high elevation," the *Long Island Farmer* observed, creating an advantage for the landscape architect, whose street plan bore a closer resemblance to "park drives than the average residence street of city folk."[10] Leavitt, described as "a rare combination of engineer, artist, and diplomat,"[11] designed a number of residential parks on Long Island, as well as the Belmont Park racetrack, hotel grounds in Puerto Rico, and federal parks in Cuba.

The company commissioned another professional well versed in residential park design, John J. Petit of Kirby, Petit & Green, to design the stone lodge. Petit established a practice in Brooklyn in the early 1890s and his firm was active during the first decade of the twentieth century designing everything from the American Bank Note Company in New York City to Dreamland, the Coney Island amusement park. But Petit was primarily known for his residential

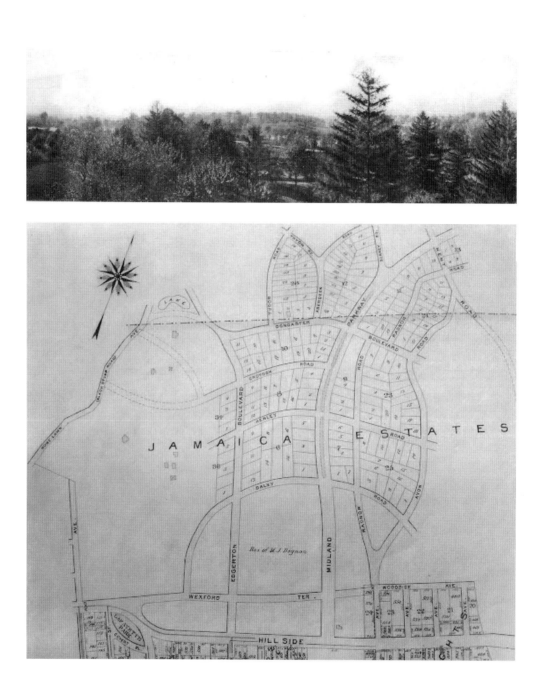

*A photograph from an
advertisement in the June
1908 issue of* Country
Life in America *shows
a panoramic view of
Jamaica Estates.* Aquinas
Honor Society Archives

*The earliest map of
Jamaica Estates, dated
1907; the city plan was
designed by landscape
architect Charles W.
Leavitt.* Aquinas Honor
Society Archives

work in Brooklyn's Prospect Park South (see pages 61–62). According to local papers, the cost of the entrance lodge, designed in the picturesque style favored by English country estates, was an astonishing $50,000. "In keeping with the generally high character of improvement planned by the Jamaica Estates Corporation," the *New York Times* observed in May 1908, "is the new Elizabethan Lodge with imposing pillars and gateway, just completed at the entrance to the property."[12] The adjacent gatehouse, situated on the median at the entrance of the parkway, still stands today

and now houses the community's War Memorial. The lodge was sadly razed years ago.

In keeping with the style of the entrance, a number of Jamaica Estates' early houses were built in the Tudor style, many on streets with English names such as Aberdeen, Kent, Avon, Wexford, and Tudor. Though Tudor was the prevalent style, others such as Italian Renaissance, Spanish Colonial, and Dutch Colonial made an early appearance.[13]

In 1908, the Gulick Company contracted the Degnon Company to make improvements to the Jamaica Estates property. Builders of five sections

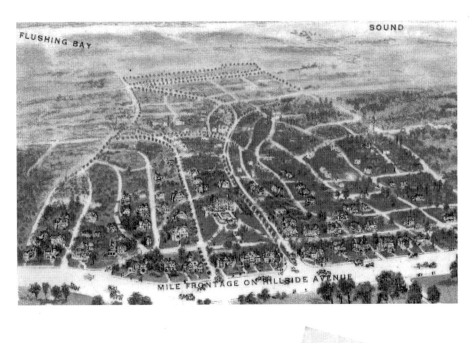

FLUSHING BAY   SOUND

MILE FRONTAGE ON HILLSIDE AVENUE

of the New York subway, Degnon had also been responsible for the East River railroad tunnels and was one of the largest construction companies in the country.

"Present plans call for the expenditure of about $1,000,000 in development work," the *New York Times* reported in May of that year: "The general scheme of improvement includes the building of macadamized roads, which will follow the natural contour of the land, as well as the installation of sewers, water supply, gas, electricity, and telephone conduits."[14]

Michael Degnon, who was also a director of the Jamaica Estates Corporation, was an engineer, contractor, and philanthropist. One of the first to purchase land in Jamaica Estates—a sixteen-acre block—he retained the architectural firm of Thompson & Frohling to design his residence, valued at $50,000 when completed in 1910. Built of hollow terra-cotta blocks, with a limestone and brick exterior, the Degnon residence was later sold to the Passionist order of the Catholic Church.[15]

The idea of creating an affluent resort with all the usual amenities was actively pursued during this

An early postcard of the Jamaica Estates entrance, labeled with one of the older names of the area. The sign on the lodge reads Jamaica Estates Office. Aquinas Honor Society Archives

early phase. Engineers laid out a hundred-acre golf course on the northwest side of Jamaica Estates.[16] It became known as the Hillcrest Golf Course; by 1924, it had been redesigned by Devereux Emmett, who expanded it to eighteen holes and added a clubhouse. Closed in 1936, it was sold to the Vincentian order of the Catholic Church, which established St. John's University on the site. The Jamaica Estates Corporation also built three clay tennis courts near the lodge in 1910. Showers, lockers, and dining facilities were installed in a new addition to the lodge, as management hoped to attract some of the most prominent players in the country to a tournament that fall.

Advertisements extolling the advantages of living in Jamaica Estates soon appeared. A promotion in *Brooklyn Life* claimed:

> When New Yorkers fully realize the uniqueness of this undertaking, we predict such a rush for lots as has never been equaled in the real estate annals of New York City. To those who have been cramped and crippled in the crowded city, it is difficult to realize that right here, in their own city, is a residential park dowered by nature with all that goes to make a park beautiful, to be improved by Art under the superintendence of the very best talent in the country.[17]

Homebuyers could "select a house from plans already drawn up or . . . submit their own ideas, which will be arranged in a practical manner."[18] By 1912, in response to "many requests from plot holders," the company installed a building exhibit in the lodge featuring "Corbin Homes" by the prolific Brooklyn builder John R. Corbin, designed by "New York's most prominent architects."[19] A 1910 Jamaica Estates booklet entitled "An Established Development of Distinction" listed building restrictions typical of residential parks:

Nothing but one family, private, detached dwellings within Jamaica Estates—no business of any kind. House must be of not less than two stories and attic in height, with cellar, and no houses with flat roofs. No house costing less than $6,000 exclusive of cost of land; in some sections $8,000 and in others $10,000 is the minimum. No house nearer the sidewalk line than 25 feet; in some cases 35 feet and in others 45 feet is the minimum. No dwelling nearer either side line than 10 feet. No fences; but hedges may be used if desired. Only one dwelling on any plot. Garages and stables are permitted, but must be at least 80 feet back from the sidewalk line, and not nearer either side line or rear line than 10 feet, and must have sewer connections. All restrictions run to January 1, 1930.[20]

Timothy Woodruff, who succeeded Felix Isman in 1910 as president of Jamaica Estates, aggressively promoted the community, often engaging in joint promotions with Garden City Estates, in which he and Gulick were also involved. A March 1910 ad in the *New York Daily Tribune* offered no-deposit, ten-day residence plot reservations to the public in anticipation of the fact that "60 days from now the Pennsylvania Railroad will open between Manhattan and Long Island the largest, fastest, best equipped and most comfortable rapid transit in the world."[21]

A number of prominent people invested or built homes in Jamaica Estates in the early years. Clarence H. Mackay, heir to a mining and communications fortune, purchased eight plots on the east side of Radnor Road in 1914. Businessman and avid equestrian Harry Payne Whitney, whose wife, Gertrude Vanderbilt Whitney, founded the Whitney Museum of American Art, and William K. Vanderbilt, the railroad magnate and grandson of the Commodore, were also investors. Among those who built residences was Chauncey Depew (1834–1928), a two-term United States senator and

One of the original half-timbered Tudor-style houses built at Jamaica Estates. Brooklyn Historical Society

The Michael J. Degnon residence, 1910, located on the sixteen acres of land he purchased, was designed by Thompson & Frohling. Aquinas Honor Society Archives

attorney for Vanderbilt railroad interests.[22] A great admirer of President Lincoln, Depew had met the president on a number of occasions and had the distinction of escorting Lincoln's body through New York State as it traveled to Springfield, Illinois, for burial. His Jamaica Estates residence on Midland Parkway was a tribute to the president, a brick replica of Lincoln's house in Springfield.[23] Actor Edmund Breese bought a plot at the corner of Avon Road and Lancaster Boulevard and built a home there in 1908.[24] Evangelist William "Billy" Sunday and Michael J. Cullen, founder of King Kullen, America's first supermarket, also lived in Jamaica Estates.

For all its early success, however, Jamaica Estates was not immune to the overspeculation in Long Island real estate that became apparent after the opening of the East River tunnels. In 1915, the Matawok Land Company, whose principals included L.I.R.R. president Ralph Peters and Philadelphia financiers connected with the Pennsylvania Railroad, sued Jamaica Estates over unpaid mortgage interest on part of the property.[25] Foreclosure followed, with Matawok selling two thousand lots at auction in 1929.[26] Shortly before the expiration of restrictions that year, Jamaica Estates Association was formed. By the time the association reached its fortieth anniversary,[27] many of the original houses had been razed to make way for the Grand Central Parkway (1933), which cut through the community. However, the association had been successful over the years in ensuring that the Estates remained a community of single-family homes. A zoning classification obtained in 1930 and extended in 1935 effectively barred apartment buildings in most of the community.[28]

More than a century since its founding, Jamaica Estates is still a community of largely single-family homes. It is a vibrant neighborhood that is both diverse and inviting. Its early history has been rediscovered and carefully documented through a special research project conducted by the Aquinas Honor Society students of the Immaculate Conception School located in the community.[29]

15

ROBERT WEEKS DE FOREST

FOREST HILLS GARDENS
AND MUNSEY PARK

VIRGINIA L. BARTOS

In 1910, the new suburban community of Forest Hills Gardens was heralded in the newspapers as a model of planning, offering affordable homes that could help to alleviate housing problems in crowded, unhealthy urban areas. According to the *New York Times*, Forest Hills Gardens was "to have separate houses for families and also apartment houses. There are to be beautifully laid out streets and small parks, with playgrounds for the children, and the homes will have the best of modern sanitary improvements."[1] Nearly twenty years later, similar comments appeared in the newspapers about the new Manhasset suburb of Munsey Park, which was also to have well-laid-out streets with affordable Colonial-style homes nestled in the rolling hills of a former private estate. Planned during the early years of the Great Depression, Munsey Park was to include shops and an office building "with the object of stimulating employment."[2]

Though credit for the new "model" communities went to two different organizations, the Russell Sage Foundation for Forest Hills Gardens and the Metropolitan Museum of Art for Munsey Park, one person was largely responsible for the existence of the two suburbs. Robert Weeks de Forest (1848–1931) held leadership roles in both organizations and used his position to bring together the financing and talent that created Forest Hills Gardens and Munsey Park. For de Forest, these suburbs were models of cooperation and aesthetics, as well

as examples of how proper planning could result in better housing that benefited both developers and residents.

In addition to his roles in both organizations, Robert Weeks de Forest was involved in a wide range of civic and welfare efforts. He fit the profile of the turn-of-the twentieth-century progressive, a reformer who, for the most part, was well off financially and well educated, had social connections, lived in the one of the major urban centers (generally in the Northeast), and was committed to one or more social causes. Born in New York City in 1848, de Forest grew up in Greenwich Village and lived there throughout his adult life, except for seasonal sojourns at Wawapek Farm, his country estate in Cold Spring Harbor on Long Island. After private school, he attended Yale, where he earned his bachelor's degree in 1870 and a master's degree in 1873. In between these two degrees, he briefly studied abroad at the University of Bonn and obtained a law degree from Columbia University in 1872. A lawyer by profession, de Forest initially worked in his father's firm, but in 1893 he and his younger brother Henry established their own firm. Specializing in corporate law, de Forest served the needs of important clients such as the Central Railroad of New Jersey (his father-in-law's company), where he organized the legal department. Another client was the financier Russell Sage and later his widow, Olivia Slocum Sage, who figured prominently in de Forest's career.

The firm benefited from the de Forests' social standing. One of the city's oldest and finest families, the de Forest lineage traced back to the early seventeenth century and the earliest days of New York City's Dutch settlement, when Jesse de Forest and several other Walloons (French-speaking Protestant exiles from Belgium) were recruited to help settle the New Netherland Colony. Others who burnished the illustrious pedigree were the brothers' maternal grandfather, Robert D. Weeks, who served as the first president of the New York Stock Exchange, and their paternal grandfather, who established a thriving shipping business in the early nineteenth century. The de Forest brothers also had their father's stellar reputation as a lawyer behind them.

Housing reform and art were two of Robert de Forest's passions. His reform career included terms as tenement housing commissioner for both New York City and the State of New York, working with the American Red Cross to organize relief after the 1906 San Francisco earthquake, service with the Wartime Housing Committee during World War I, and membership on the Committee on a Regional Plan of New York and Its Environs (now the Regional Plan Association), formed in 1922 to review infrastructure planning for New York City and the surrounding suburbs. While serving in these various capacities, de Forest became a trustee of the Metropolitan Museum of Art and its president in 1913. He was also a founder of the American Federation of the Arts, which he headed from 1913 to 1930. His brother Lockwood de Forest was a well-known artist, friend of Frederic Church, and an early business partner of Louis Comfort Tiffany, whom the brothers had known since childhood.

Most of Robert de Forest's reform work was done through the New York City Charity Organization Society, part of the larger Charity Organization movement, which had chapters in all major cities in the United States in the late nineteenth and early twentieth centuries. Based on a British model, the American movement began in Buffalo, New York, in 1877 with the goal of coordinating various private charitable agencies to better assist the deserving poor. Each Charity Organization Society chapter had the goal of guiding the less fortunate toward self-improvement, in other words, to provide a hand up rather than a handout, with the purpose of making the poor less dependent on assistance. The hallmark of the organization was investigation; caseworkers, often referred to as "friendly visitors," were sent out to gain an understanding of the plight of the poor by seeing firsthand the circumstances that resulted in poverty. The New York City chapter was founded in 1882 by Josephine Shaw Lowell, the widow of Civil War general Charles Russell Lowell. Her personal interests in charity work focused on issues related to women and children, which led to her appointment to the New York State Board of Charities in 1876.

De Forest joined the New York Charity Organization Society in 1883, becoming its president in 1888, a position he held until he retired from it in 1928. He also joined the society's Tenement House Committee, becoming its chair in 1898. As president, he saw the workings of the entire organization and soon determined that there was a need for proper training of the "visitors," or caseworkers, as they came to be called. In 1898, de Forest organized a six-week summer training course, which was the first social-work training program in the United States. This led to the founding seven years later of the New York School of Social Work, a permanent, year-round school that eventually became part of Columbia University. His involvement in the Tenement House Committee brought him firsthand knowledge of a number of issues facing the working poor, among them the lack of financial services. Under his direction, the society created the Penny Provident Fund to accept small deposits and hold the funds until the depositor had accrued enough to open an account in a bank. In 1894, he created the Provident Loan Association, which provided low-interest loans to those who were in a position to start a personal business or were in dire straits due to some unforeseen catastrophe.[3] The fund was based on a government-sponsored program in Belgium, and de Forest bemoaned the fact that such government plans were lacking in the United States. "If we really understood the workingman's needs and were trying to serve him," he stated in a 1902 interview, "we would evolve some such plan . . . which has all the features of a building and loan association."[4] This concept was too radical and too much of a financial risk for established banks, forcing de Forest to create the fund with his own money and donations from friends and associates.

Interest in housing for reformers like de Forest came at a time when the country was shifting from a nation of farmers to one of city dwellers. In the decades following the Civil War, rural areas lost population as repeated cycles of agricultural depressions and the attraction of better economic opportunities in the urban centers drove large numbers of job seekers to the cities, especially in the Northeast In addition to this shift in population, newly arrived foreign immigrants sought the same opportunities in the same places. Villages became cities and large cities became metropolises, resulting in a number of problems such as overcrowding, poor sanitation, inadequate housing, and rising crime rates. Many reformers considered housing to be the problem most in need of attention. They believed that improvements in living conditions would have a far-reaching impact by solving a whole host of related problems. Lawrence Veiller, a housing-reform advocate in New York City, stated, "As one house thus changes in a neighborhood, before long the whole neighborhood becomes similar, and we have a large population living in houses not adapted to the uses to which they are put, with the inevitable results of bad sanitation, overcrowding, and the numerous other physical and social evils which soon follow."[5]

De Forest's work with tenement housing issues through the Charity Organization Society led to his appointment as the head of the New York State Tenement Housing Commission by Governor Theodore Roosevelt in 1900. The commission worked diligently to get New York State to adopt legislation regulating tenements, and in 1901 the legislation was enacted. It required new standards for tenement housing that took into consideration the size and arrangement of interior spaces, adequate ventilation, and proper sanitation. As a result, de Forest was named head of New York City's Tenement House Department by Mayor Seth Low, and in 1910 he became president of the National Housing Association.

De Forest's work with the Charity Organization Society also provided him with a solution to a client's problem. After Russell Sage died in January 1906, Olivia Slocum Sage inherited the bulk of his substantial estate, estimated at between $7 and $10 million. Russell Sage had had a reputation for being miserly when it came to charitable giving, whereas his wife was known for being more generous and often donated separately to the same charities, thereby offsetting her husband's lack of generosity. Throughout their marriage, Mrs. Sage had advised her husband on gifts to worthy charities. She had her own favorite projects, particularly those that focused on education, including donations to her alma mater, the Troy Female Seminary (now known as Emma Willard School).[6] Receiving begging letters was a common occurrence among the wealthier members of society, and in the past, Mrs. Sage had been able to manage the requests personally. Sensing that the floodgates had opened after the death of her husband, however, letter writers besieged Mrs. Sage with requests for money, ranging from heartrending tales of woe to veiled attempts at extortion. With a library literally overflowing with requests, she turned to Robert de Forest for advice. He suggested that letters with a personal connection or from an organization be directed to her and that all individual requests be investigated by the Charity Organization Society. With her consent, de Forest organized the Sage Fund and contracted with the society to review the individual requests and respond accordingly. Any grants of financial assistance were to come out of a fund in the amount of $10,000 that would be replenished by Mrs. Sage as needed.

In addition to this fund, de Forest suggested that Mrs. Sage devote her philanthropy to a single purpose, underwritten by what he described as a benevolent trust. Knowing that she shared his interests in reform, he recommended that the focus be on investigating the causes of adverse social conditions, specifically poverty, and on developing effective solutions for these conditions. With such a general mission statement, he pointed out, the projects could range from setting up convalescent homes to improving the living conditions of the working poor. His role would be to use his legal skills to organize the trust, while Mrs. Sage's would be to select the recipients.[7] The result of this collaboration was the Russell Sage Foundation, incorporated in 1907 and administered by a board of trustees, including de Forest.

When Mrs. Sage expressed an interest in investing in real estate in New York City, de Forest saw an opportunity to put the latest principles of urban planning and housing reform into practice. He suggested that the Sage Foundation consider the possibility of developing working-class housing in the borough of Queens. At the turn of the twentieth century, Long Island was a land of promise for reformers, developers, and real estate companies. Reformers had been dealing with overcrowding and inadequate housing for the working poor in New York City for more than half a century, and Long Island offered new opportunities, especially in places like Astoria, where new factories offered steady employment. And the newly created Nassau County offered the potential for new communities surrounded by open spaces, trees, and clean air, all accessible by recent improvements in transportation. De Forest and others involved in housing reform envisioned an exodus from the crowded city to Long Island by those who were willing to abandon the cheap tenements for their own small house in the suburbs. The problem for reformers was that they had the desire to provide the opportunities but lacked the means to act. All they could do was leave the job of enticing the buying public to Long Island to the real estate developers and hope for the best.

Presented with this rare opportunity, de Forest had to act quickly. His first task was to convince Mrs. Sage that her interests in real estate were compatible with the purpose of the Sage Foundation. Without her support and the resources of the foundation, creating affordable housing on Long Island would remain an unfulfilled dream for de Forest, seriously hampering his efforts to expand his reform work beyond his involvement with the Charity Organization Society. When Mrs. Sage expressed concern over diminished returns on investments that were viewed as risky experiments in working-class housing, de Forest reminded her that the object was to sell houses at affordable prices, not give them away, and that such housing was part of the foundation's role in alleviating the causes of poverty. Apparently persuaded by de Forest's arguments, she reluctantly agreed to have the foundation support such projects, as long as it received a return of at least 3 percent.[8] With Mrs. Sage's approval, as well as that of the trustees of the foundation, de Forest could forge ahead with his vision for a model working-class suburb on Long Island.

When word of the project leaked out and newspapers began reporting that the foundation was interested in a property in Queens, de Forest encountered his next hurdle: soaring property prices. In 1909, the foundation made a deal with developer Cord Meyer to purchase 142 acres of land that had originally been intended for his 536-acre Forest Hills subdivision north of Richmond Hill. Meyer had named it after a large park at its western end and laid out streets following the standard grid pattern, which he planned to subdivide into 6,000 rectangular lots. The purchase price was much higher than de Forest had anticipated, averaging roughly $6,000 per acre. Keeping in mind the promise he had made to Mrs. Sage, de Forest was forced to make a subtle shift in describing the purpose of the project to the press, changing it from working-class housing to a model of a "garden city" or, in other words, attractive suburban planning following the most modern "scientific" trends. The *New York Times* reported that the Sage Foundation trustees realized that the land was too valuable for anything but a "fairly high-class development. Houses are to cost from $7,000 to $15,000 and over, a large hotel is to be built, and many other attractive features included. There will also be two-family houses."[9]

De Forest had no intention of abandoning his goal of affordable housing for a wide range of prospective buyers, even though the necessity of a 3 percent return made the goal less likely to become a reality for the average factory worker. His new emphasis on the "garden city" was based on the ideas of another reformer, London-born Chicagoan Ebenezer Howard, who introduced his garden city concept in *To-Morrow: A Peaceful Path to Real Reform*, published in 1898. Howard envisioned a self-sufficient city with a limited population, ringed by farms that afforded inhabitants access to the country, clean air, and fresh food. An important part of the plan was the elimination of private property by putting land ownership under the control of a limited company. This control, combined with the outlying farms, created a physical buffer that kept the garden city from being absorbed by larger, nearby cities.[10] De Forest also had the example of Garden City, Long Island, a suburban community established in 1869 by A. T. Stewart to provide housing for managers and workers of his Manhattan department store, among others. Although paternalistic in nature, Garden City demonstrated that success came from offering a good variety of affordable housing on well-laid-out, beautifully landscaped streets, with lots of parks and within walking distance of rail transportation to Manhattan.

While the foundation was still negotiating with Cord Meyer, de Forest was putting together a team that shared the vision of a garden city and could bring the required talents to oversee all aspects of the project. One of the first he reached out to was architect Grosvenor Atterbury (1869–1956), whom he knew well. Atterbury had studied architecture at Columbia University and got his professional start working for the firm of McKim, Mead & White, where he designed a number of large homes for wealthy clients on Long Island, including de Forest's estate in Cold Spring Harbor on the North Shore. Atterbury was also active in early housing-reform efforts in New York City, having designed model tenements for the city's Tenement House Department, which he continued to do after de Forest's departure from the department in 1903. De Forest later called on Atterbury to design the Sage Foun-

dation's Manhattan headquarters, a nine-story office building located on East 22nd Street (1912). They teamed up again in 1917, becoming two of the founding members of the National Housing Association, which dealt with housing shortages during World War I. As part of his efforts in housing reform, Atterbury pioneered new cost-saving construction techniques that made apartments and private homes more affordable for a wider market. Beginning in 1907, the Sage Foundation funded his research and development of new building materials and construction methods, which carried over into his work in the Forest Hills Gardens project and continued through the 1920s.[11] In bringing Atterbury, a fellow reformer, on board, de Forest provided him with a large-scale project that would demonstrate the practicality of his new construction methods and his dedication to affordable housing. Atterbury described the Forest Hills Gardens project as a rare chance to demonstrate that "[w]hile any town, whatever its birth and family history, may aspire to set such a high standard of living that it may be called in a general sense 'model,' the word is now taking a new and special meaning, following the beginning of organized attempts to apply scientific, aesthetic, and economic principles and methods to the problem of housing civilized humanity."[12]

In 1908, de Forest reached out to Frederick Law Olmsted Jr. (1870–1957), inviting him to be part of the Forest Hills Gardens project. Olmsted and his stepbrother John (1852–1920) continued the work of their illustrious father, Frederick Law Olmsted Sr., in landscape design and park planning. Like his father, Rick Olmsted (as he was known) believed that cities needed proper planning and provisions for free, open spaces for community gatherings, parks, and playgrounds. He also believed that planning should be left to trained professionals rather than profit-driven real estate speculators. Educated at Harvard, Olmsted traveled to Europe to see firsthand how planners there were putting the new theories into practice in crowded industrial centers. He had begun a three-month study tour in December 1908, when a letter from de Forest reached him in Berlin, asking him if he would be willing to take on the role of advising landscape gardener for "housing on a fairly large scale, in the suburban district of New York." De Forest explained:

> Our plan is not merely to give houses but to lay out these tracts in some way different from the abhorrent rectangular city block, and to make our garden city somewhat attractive by the treatment and planting of our streets, the possibility of little gardens, and possibly some public places. It will be an equation between the cost of attractiveness and cheap rents. Nor are we simply considering

Atterbury-designed street lamp, Forest Hills Gardens. Field Services Bureau Photo Collection, New York State Office of Parks, Recreation and Historic Preservation

Ascan Avenue, ca. 1920.
Courtesy Church-in-the-
Gardens Library and
Archives, Forest Hills
Gardens

the housing of so many people. We would like to set an example to the growing suburban districts of New York and other cities of how the things can be done tastefully and at the same time with due regard for profit. I believe there is money in taste.[13]

De Forest added that his friend Grosvenor Atterbury was joining as consulting architect and the project also had a real estate expert (unnamed at the time). Olmsted responded from Berlin, stating that he was interested in the offer and that his meetings with planners in various cities in Europe could be beneficial to the project. He intended to visit England, where a garden city was being planned, and to see other model villages. He asked if de Forest was willing to wait for him to return the following March. De Forest quickly replied that "we will hold things up until you get back. . . . The English garden cities, though in embryo, are well worth seeing and suggestive."[14]

Once Olmsted returned to America, de Forest held regular meetings with his designers and the Sage Foundation to begin the practical matter of selecting street layouts, building designs, and a name for the settlement. They eventually settled on calling the development Forest Hills Gardens. In the end, Atterbury provided designs for public and private buildings, including a train station, an inn, a church, a public school, a plaza with shops and an apartment building, row houses, semi-detached houses for two families, and single-family homes of various sizes and prices. Though each building type varied in size, form, and function, all the buildings were unified by an Arts and Crafts aesthetic, featuring tiled roofs, masonry exteriors (some with intricately patterned brickwork), and stucco that simulated half-timbering. Most windows were double-hung sashes, but the use of multiple small panes gave the illusion of casement windows. Rooflines varied but followed patterns of narrow, peaked gables punctuated with dormers and tall chimneys. Covered walks connected the train station to the shops and the inn, creating an enclosed plaza and clearly separating a large, open, very public space from the more private neighborhoods of houses and smaller, more intimate gathering places of parks and gardens. Atterbury even designed street lamps and building and streets signs that left the visitor and resident in little doubt that they were in Forest Hills Gardens.

While Atterbury was busy designing the architecture, Olmsted turned his attention to street patterns and landscaping. His initial plan for uninterrupted curved roads was thwarted by the terms of sale with Cord Meyer, which required that two existing through roads (Ascan and Continental) be retained. Meyer had sold a small portion of his Forest Hills lands to the Sage Foundation, and his own suburban development needed the through roads for direct access to Queens Boulevard and the Long Island Railroad. After several committee meetings, a street plan was finally agreed upon that established the intersection of Continental Avenue and the train station plaza, known as Station Square, as the point from which streets would fan out to connect with Greenway North and Greenway South, Olmsted's core curved roadway. In addition, a labyrinth of smaller, narrower streets wending their way to Greenway North and South or to small commons and parks was to be created. Olmsted gave the much wider Ascan Avenue thoroughfare the illusion of being closer in size to the surrounding streets by lining it with trees. According to Olmsted, his street plan illustrated three important principles of city planning. The first was the limited use of thoroughfares that were "direct, ample, and convenient" and spaced widely apart from one another. The second was that the "streets not needed as thoroughfares should be planned and constructed to meet the purposes" of quiet residential areas and "while not fantastically crooked, they are never perfectly straight for long stretches." The final principle incorporated into Olmsted's plans was "the deliberate setting apart of certain areas for the common use and enjoyment of the residents."[15]

With the land acquired and plans by Olmsted and Atterbury approved, construction began in August 1910 and the first public sales were held in June 1911. Once the building of Forest Hills Gardens was well under way, de Forest left the business aspects of the project to another team member, real estate developer William Harmon. Also selected for his work in housing reform, Harmon shared de Forest's progressive ideology that providing housing opportunities for working-and middle-class wage earners formed the foundation of larger, more socially stable communities.[16] Harmon's real estate firm was already known for developing more than a hundred suburbs in twenty-six cities in the United States and for introducing the payment installment plan in 1880 with a project in Cincinnati. The plan was designed for those who desired a home but lacked the capital to make an outright purchase. The contract between buyer and seller stipulated a low down payment and low monthly payments, with the deed held by the developer until payment had been made in full. De Forest thought that the installment plan might prove useful in the Forest Hills Gardens project, especially as the high cost of the land had necessitated higher house prices. When sales began in 1911, a 2 percent down payment was required; it was raised to 5 percent in 1912.

Harmon was also known for instituting restrictive covenants in his suburbs, and de Forest saw the need for some kind of oversight at Forest Hills Gardens as well. Atterbury, Olmsted, and de Forest knew that city planning in Europe involved considerable government control of properties and that houses were generally rented, rather than sold to individuals. They had little hope of the same happening in the United States. De Forest wrote to Olmsted, "Methods of land tenure are very different, social habits are very different, and to run counter to ordinary methods of land tenure and social habits, even under the stimulus of continental or English success, would be a very doubtful experiment."[17] The Jeffersonian concept of individual land ownership was so ingrained in American thinking that government controls were unthinkable.

Harmon introduced a series of covenants in 1911 and suggested that someone experienced in dealing with prospective residents and implementing the restrictions be hired as general manager of the Forest Hills Gardens project. He recommended Edward Bouton, the general manager of the Roland Park suburb in Baltimore, for the position. Bouton had long experience with covenants and was one of the first to include restrictions in property deeds.[18] To reassure prospective homeowners, the Sage Foundation Homes Company stated that individual property owners would have a voice in managing their own property and that restrictions were issued to keep harmony and avoid unsightly nuisances, all for the common good.

De Forest's role in the project was to oversee legal matters; he formed the Sage Foundation Homes Company and named Russell Sage Foundation board member John Glenn to head it. Once de Forest finally had his managers and designers in place, he had one more important issue to resolve. A key to the success of the suburb was a railroad station, but the Long Island Railroad balked at the cost of building a new station for Forest Hills. As in other suburban developments on Long Island, the intended market was the rising middle class, many of whom had jobs in the city, and it was essential for the new communities to be connected by rail with relatively short commute times. Beginning in the 1880s, the Long Island Railroad focused on becoming a commuter rail line, first by consolidating smaller local lines into three main lines and then by branching out with smaller connectors.[19] Commute times became a regular selling point in real estate advertising, and it clearly worked, as the population of Queens County dramatically increased from 152,999 to 469,042 between 1900 and 1920. In the same time period, the population of Nassau County increased from 55,448 to 126,120.[20] A Queens Chamber of Commerce publication boasted: "To everyone who loved the soil and grass, or who cherishes the trees and pure air, a new life is opened. Within ten or fifteen minutes after boarding a modern electric train at Pennsylvania Station, or rapid transit trains of the city's subway system, one finds himself looking out upon neat suburban homes and gardens, refreshing the eyes wearied by the city with its scenes of

FOREST HILLS INN · FOREST HILLS LONG ISLAND

SOME people do not realize that such a charming hotel as Forest Hills Inn is located in the City of New York, within fifteen minutes of the Pennsylvania Station at Seventh Avenue and 33d Street. A family hotel that has established an enviable reputation by its excellent table, good service, and competent management.

74 Electric Trains Per Day
REFERENCES
TEL. 6290 FOREST HILLS

Advertisement for the Forest Hills Inn, 1917, in a Long Island travel guide published by the Long Island Railroad. Private collection

rush and bustle and its monotonous stretches of brick and stone."[21] Forest Hills Gardens finally got a railroad station after the Sage Foundation Homes Company, the Long Island Railroad, and developer Cord Meyer agreed to split the cost of construction equally.

Building construction and residential sales in Forest Hills Gardens remained steady until World War I brought a slowdown and a shortage of materials that continued into the early 1920s. Mrs. Sage died in November 1918 without ever seeing a 3 percent return on her investment and would have been appalled if she had lived to see that her foundation actually lost $360,000 on the project. In 1922, most of Forest Hills Gardens was developed and the trustees of the Sage Foundation decided that it was time to end their association with the project. They sold the Sage Foundation Homes Company to the newly organized Forest Hills Gardens Homes Company for nearly $2 million, finally realizing a profit and replenishing the foundation's funds.[22] This could have been an end to de Forest's model garden suburb, but the company consisted of residents of Forest Hills who decided to retain the covenants and "keep up the standards set forth by the Sage Foundation as to [the] architecture of the homes to be built and the kind of people to whom they will be sold." They even retained Grosvenor Atterbury as supervising architect.[23] As to the types of people buying homes, the company published a map in 1930 that included the names and professions of many of the residents, ranging from several professionals (doctors, lawyers, architects) to a few bank presidents, small business owners (photographers, a funeral director, pharmacy owners), artists, inventors, playwrights and laborers (carpenters, printers).[24]

De Forest's experience with the Forest Hills Gardens project provided him with a solution for dealing with a large parcel of land in Long Island

that had been given to the Metropolitan Museum of Art. During his tenure as president, the museum received a bequest from the estate of publisher and newspaper owner Frank A. Munsey, who died in December 1925. Newspapers estimated Munsey's fortune at between $20 and $40 million; it was a well-timed gift, as the museum was facing a deficit due to increased operating costs and decreasing city support.[25] Back in 1920, de Forest had warned that the partnership between the city and the museum seemed to be in jeopardy:

> Our new south wing, begun by the City six years ago, has never been completed. Work on it has been at a standstill since 1917. There is no city appropriation to continue it. Ten years ago (1909) the City contributed 68 percent of our cost of maintenance. Five years ago (1914) this was 43 percent. Last year (1919) it was 28 percent. . . . Our future development, the extent of our future service to the people of New York, depends upon the degree to which the city will provide buildings and contribute to the cost of operation. In Europe Government supplies to art museums not only all the buildings, but all the cost of operation and almost all the purchase funds. In New York Government is now supplying less than half of the cost of operation and none of the purchase funds."[26]

Furthermore, the museum's collections, programs, and building were constantly growing, but the endowment failed to grow in proportion. The Munsey gift was viewed in the press as a new endowment, and one writer suggested that the money could be channeled either into purchasing new works of art or into expanding the educational activities.[27] De Forest cautioned that the speculation about the monetary value of the gift and the suggestions about how to spend the money were premature, as the museum was to receive the balance after outstanding debts, other gifts, and executors' expenses were paid. When the estate was finally settled in 1929, the amount the museum actually received was $17,305,594.[28]

Before the final settlement, de Forest knew that as a portion of the bequest the museum was to receive 671 acres of land, appraised at just over $3 million. The immediate intent was to sell the property as part of settling the estate and a debate ensued about how best to dispose of the property. The trustees of the estate wanted the land divided into twenty-foot lots and sold off at auction, but de Forest saw another opportunity to bring suburban development based on the latest principles of urban planning to the region, while benefiting the Metropolitan Museum of Art. He contended that a wholesale auction would result in a devaluation of the surrounding land and that this driving down of values would negatively reflect on the museum. He also argued that any new development should honor Frank Munsey's legacy and that "Mr. Munsey undoubtedly would have chosen that this land be devoted to a development of the highest class."[29] Eventually, a compromise was reached: the land north of the Flushing & North Hempstead Turnpike (now Northern Boulevard) would be developed by the museum and the land south of the turnpike would be left for the estate trustees to turn over to a broker for auctioning.

With the disposal of the lands settled, the museum now had eighty-seven acres of land on which to create its tribute to Frank Munsey, to be called Munsey Park. De Forest looked to his experience with Forest Hills Gardens and returned to the formula of dividing the tasks of planning the community, designing the landscape, building the homes, and selling them. Instead of creating a new organization like the Sage Foundation Homes Company, the museum selected Alexander Bing and his Hasset Realty Company to work with a select committee of museum directors on the project. Bing and his brother previously operated the Bing & Bing real estate company, one of the best known in New York City in the early twentieth century. Alexander Bing left the company in 1921 to work on affordable-housing projects, the best known of which, Sunnyside Gardens in Queens, begun in 1924, consisted of low-scale brick row houses and apartment buildings with landscaped courtyards. Bing's architect for the project was Frederick Ackerman, who came along with Bing to serve as supervising architect for Munsey Park. Ackerman had received his degree from Cornell University and partnered with Alexander Trowbridge, an architect and the former dean of the College of Fine Arts at Cornell, from 1906 to

1920. Ackerman developed an early interest in housing reform, having done a study of housing and planning movements in England before 1917. During World War I, he served as the chief of the Department of Housing and Planning for the U.S. Shipping Board, and he became known for proposing a peacetime housing plan that was rejected by Congress for being too radical.[30] He later designed the buildings for New York City's first public housing project, known as First Houses, which opened in 1935 on the Lower East Side.

Ackerman was an interesting choice as supervising architect for Munsey Park because he had little confidence in such planning projects, especially those based on the garden city model. His observations had led him to conclude that municipal governments were reluctant to enact strong enough controls and were more inclined to protect private property rights, defeating the purpose of good planning. After his 1917 study trip to Britain, he remarked:

> We must deal with the land question with respect to both rural and urban areas. The increment of value created by collective occupancy and use must be wrested from the speculators and so organized that it may be used for the benefit of all. This is the "first" step which must be taken before the national physical plan can be realized in terms of collective provision.[31]

Perhaps he consented to the project after learning that deed restrictions would be put in place to prevent property owners from subdividing lots and that all house designs were to be approved by Bing's associates and the museum trustees. The New York Times reported that "restrictions to safeguard the growth of the future Munsey Park community have been worked out and the general architectural design to be followed has been approved by the officers of the Metropolitan Museum."[32] The restrictions required that all plots would be no smaller than sixty-five feet by one hundred feet and that no house built would be valued below $6,000 or taller than two and a half stories. As the community grew, Ackerman contributed two buildings to the project, designing a combination store and office building to serve as a local shopping center and a clubhouse for the local golf course following designs compatible with the rest of Munsey Park.

One of the museum trustees active in the Munsey Park project was William Sloane Coffin, who was part of the de Forest team that brokered the land compromise with the Munsey estate trustees. Coffin was a merchant and was also associated with the Hasset Realty Corporation. Like de For-

est, Coffin was a progressive, involved in various reform movements, including the New York City Mission Society, which worked with immigrant populations to assist them as they made their transition into American society. He was also active in housing issues and explored ways to alleviate the problem of overcrowded, substandard apartment buildings in the city. As president of the Hearth and Home real estate corporation, he went against the standard practice of demolishing old buildings and replacing them with much larger structures. Coffin recognized that the old buildings had a certain charm, especially those that were sound, and renovated a number of them for a middle-class clientele. His 1920 renovation of the buildings on McDougal and Sullivan streets transformed groups of run-down, early nineteenth-century Greek Revival–style rowhouses into a neighborhood of Colonial Revival buildings with many of the early nineteenth-century features restored to their former glory.

Coffin's appreciation for historic architecture dovetailed with de Forest's love of Early American art and architecture. Both de Forest and his wife, Emily Johnston, were longtime collectors of Early American decorative arts and funded an entire wing at the Metropolitan Museum of Art to house the growing collection of American paintings, sculpture, and furnishings, much of it donated by the de Forests, their friends, and associates. The American Wing (completed in 1924) was designed by Grosvenor Atterbury,

who reused the façade of the 1824 Branch Bank of the United States, which was salvaged when the building was demolished in 1915. Not only was the façade of the new wing an important architectural artifact, but historical architectural objects were displayed throughout the interior galleries and period rooms. For de Forest, the Colonial era represented a time when America was truly democratic and its art displayed a "simplicity of form, an appropriateness to use, a lightness and alertness of line which was typical of the American character of pioneer days."[33]

By the time of the Munsey Park project, the general public shared de Forest's view that Colonial-era buildings expressed what was truly American. The modest proportions and restrained decoration of Colonial architecture were often described in the general literature as "simple" and "honest," the same terms used to describe the values of the early Americans, making this legacy a source of national pride.[34] The general public further embraced all that was Colonial when newspapers and magazines reported on the progress of the restoration of Colonial Williamsburg, a project initiated in 1926 and funded in large part by the Rockefeller family. The accounts gave a wide audience a look at America's prerevolutionary past and emphasized the fact that this important piece of American history had nearly been lost. Though drawings and plans of historic buildings had been available for several decades, Colonial Williamsburg captured the interest of the general

public, increased the popularity of the Colonial style, and created a market for living in the past, but with modern amenities.[35]

When it came to choosing an architectural style for Munsey Park, there was little surprise that the museum trustees selected Colonial American. Bing and the trustees encouraged architects to copy suitable historic examples, and two model homes were built, one a copy of a seventeenth-century house in Wenham, Massachusetts, and the other featuring a staircase copied from one on display in the American Wing. The streets were laid out following the contours of the topography and mature trees were planted to give the illusion that Munsey Park was an old, established Long Island settlement. On February 19, 1928, the model homes were formally introduced by de Forest and Coffin to a crowd that was estimated at 1,500. In the weeks following the event, a large number of potential buyers visited the model homes. Initially, the plan was to limit home construction to twenty-five houses in the first year, but the demand for houses was so great that by November 1928 thirty-eight new houses were built and sold, at prices ranging from $13,500 to $18,500.

Interest in the development continued at a steady pace, even after the 1929 stock market crash. Toward the end of 1930, it was reported that sales had passed the $1 million mark and that two hundred new homes had been constructed since the project's beginning. The rapid growth resulted in clashes with the Town of North Hempstead and Nassau County over a range of issues, including utilities and protective services. To deal with issues affecting the whole community, the residents of Munsey Park met on January 27, 1930, and voted to incorporate as a village. The incorporation became official on March 1, 1930. In taking control of their own community, they also adopted the position of continuing the restrictive covenants, which would be renewed automatically every twenty years. They also approved the sale of ten acres of land in 1930 to the Manhasset School Board for a school.

For de Forest, Munsey Park was more than a housing development; it was also a way for the museum to expand its program beyond the confines of the building by turning the development into a living exhibit of American art and architecture. Streets were named after prominent American artists, including Bellows, Ryder, Inness, and Eakins, and a park was named for eighteenth-century artist John Singleton Copley. The Colonial-style architecture provided lessons in Colonial history for residents and visitors alike. Pieces from the museum's collections were even transported outside of its walls and incorporated into the houses as decorative features (doors, fireplaces, staircases, and the like). Just as de Forest saw Colonial architecture as representative of American values, he considered the museum and its work a democratizing force, available to all. In his address on the occasion of the museum's fiftieth anniversary, he noted that one of the museum's crowning achievements was its active role in community life through its growing program of traveling exhibits, guided tours, off-site programs, lectures, and publications:

> Such activities demonstrate to the people of our city that our Museum is a real, living, human organism, with heart as well as mind; that it is ready not only to open its doors to invited guests, but go out "into the by-ways and hedges" and to bid all to come in and all that who do come in will be equally welcome. . . . This is our contribution toward making art free for democracy.[36]

Sales of land and houses temporarily put the museum back on sound financial footing, but within a few years, de Forest reported even higher deficits as costs rose and revenues decreased. After his death in 1931, the museum received his bequest of $100,000 to endow free concerts for the public. William S. Coffin was elected as its new president. Upon his acceptance of the position, Coffin announced that he was committed to continuing the education and exhibit programs that de Forest had expanded but that he would also explore new ways to continue moving it toward being one the premier art museums in the world.[37] It was a fitting tribute to de Forest that the growth of the museum would continue, even in the face of economic uncertainty.

It was also a fitting tribute that Forest Hills Gardens and Munsey Park carried on in the spirit that de Forest had envisioned when both suburbs were taking shape. Both communities recognized that their architecture, landscaping, and community parks set them apart from other residential developments, and they made a conscious effort to uphold the policies established by de Forest and his planning colleagues. When covenant violations began creeping into Forest Hills Gardens, the residents formed the Gardens' Community Council to voice their concerns, which led to the founding of the Forest Hills Gardens Corporation, an organization that continues to play an active role to this day. When Munsey Park went through large expansions in 1938, 1940, and 1941, new streets were named after artists and the Colonial style remained the predominant house type, although French Provincial was gaining in popularity. In 1933, a committee was organized to collect donations from residents for a fund that would be used to make confidential loans to those in the community who faced foreclosure due to the Depression. General knowledge of the fund was kept secret by the committee until 1951, when the small amount that remained was donated to the local Civil Defense Community. If de Forest had been alive at the time the fund was created, it certainly would have reminded him of the Penny Provident Fund, and he well might have been willing to make a contribution. Architects and planners may still argue over whether de Forest's experiments with Forest Hills Gardens and Munsey Park were successes as model communities, but what they do show is that de Forest was extremely adept at finding the right people to combine their talents and accomplish a common goal. Otherwise, Forest Hills Gardens and Munsey Park would be indistinguishable from much of the rest of Queens and Manhasset.

16

HAPGOOD'S SHOREHAM

ARTS AND CRAFTS BY THE SEA

MARY ANN OBERDORF AND JOSEPH FALCO

Early one morning in the fall of 1923, Herbert Hapgood, developer of Shoreham, Long Island, and Mountain Lakes, New Jersey, bid farewell to a trusted employee, hastily departed his Mountain Lakes office, and boarded a steamer for South America "in quest of health." He was never to return to the communities he created or regain his health, dying six years later, at age fifty-nine, in Sydney, Australia, of "sclerosis of the liver [*sic*] and complications of the kidneys."[1] He'd left behind a pile of debt, numerous legal actions by creditors, a wife and two teenage children, and two splendid residential parks, one of which, Mountain Lakes, was sadly unfinished at his departure.

For the wildly ambitious Hapgood (1870–1929), Mountain Lakes was both his crowning achievement and his ultimate downfall. Shoreham, one-tenth the size of Mountain Lakes and begun two decades earlier, was, in a way, a dress rehearsal for its younger, grander cousin to the west. Yet the successful Shoreham development represented beginner's luck for the entrepreneur, who had had no prior experience as a residential developer.

In fact, the story of Shoreham, located on the North Shore ten miles east of Port Jefferson, begins not with Hapgood, but with another man of vision and ambition, the banker and businessman James S. Warden (1849–1906), who arrived on the scene in 1894, just ahead of the railroad.

When Warden first saw it, Shoreham—then called Woodville Landing for the boat landing on Long Island Sound where woodcutters hauled cordwood to waiting ships—was a sparsely settled collection of orchards and abandoned farms. But Woodville Landing had attributes that made it attractive as a summer colony. Though lacking a harbor, it possessed one of the finest beaches on the North Shore—wide and sandy by North Shore standards. There was a break in the bluffs that afforded easy beach access, and the surrounding hills formed a kind of northward-facing amphitheater, so configured that virtually every building lot would have a water view, especially as the land had already been cleared of trees through logging and farming activities. In addition, a natural spring on the beach at the landing assured an abundant supply of fresh water. Woodville [Landing] Road, once used for logging, ran south one mile from the shore to North Country Road, which linked Woodville Landing to the world at large. Woodville Road also bisected the valley it traversed, forming the boundary between two distinct yet friendly neighborhoods that later took shape on the slopes flanking the road and comprising the two halves—one more modest, the other more opulent—of what would eventually become Shoreham.

Recognizing the isolation and development potential of the North Shore east of Port Jefferson, in 1892 the Long Island Railroad (L.I.R.R.) organized a subsidiary, the North Shore Branch,

for the purposes of extending the Port Jefferson line eastward through Woodville Landing to its terminus at nearby Wading River. The imminent arrival of the railroad prompted land speculation at Woodville Landing, starting in 1892–94, when Herbert H. Walker, a former L.I.R.R. employee, endeavored to purchase the properties of local farmers John R. Dickerson, John J. Woodhull, and Sylvester M. Woodhull. But he exhausted his line of credit and the land purchases defaulted to his loan guarantors, business associates Jabez B. Upham, James S. Warden, Charles L. Flint Jr., and Curtis L. Perkins, who succeeded in purchasing a total of four farms, comprising about 2,000 acres.[2] Upham (1820–1902), a Harvard-trained surgeon who had served in the Civil War, had moved to New York around 1880 and had entered the business world, co-founding the Corbin Banking Company with Austin Corbin, who was also president of the L.I.R.R.[3] Upham's business associate James S. Warden was married to Upham's niece Frances Walker. Warden, whose family was originally from upstate New York, had been engaged in banking, investing, and land speculation in Kansas before moving back east. He became enthusiastic about the project after his visit to Woodville Landing in spring 1894 and decided to become the active partner in its development. That summer he moved there with his family and began construction of his seaside resort, dubbed Wardenclyffe, which opened for business six years later, on June

1, 1900.[4] Wardenclyffe originally consisted of the Shoreham Inn (an expansion of the 1840 Elbert Woodhull farmhouse, where the Warden family lived), about six cottages for rental, and a few resort amenities, including tennis courts, a bathing beach, and a bathing pavilion precariously built right into the face of the bluff. A nine-hole golf course was soon added. By 1903, there was a total of ten cottages and three substantial homes.

The second phase of Warden's development plans involved laying a grid of roads and constructing summer residences. It is not certain exactly what kind of community Warden envisioned, given his untimely death on a 1906 business trip to Scotland, but his plans apparently extended beyond the creation of a summer resort. He was in the process of building a community that he hoped would be largely self-sustaining, including farms and an orchard to supply residents with fresh produce and a communal icehouse with a cellar for storing fruits and vegetables. This structure would also serve as the utility building that supplied the community with water and be equipped with a laundry for the adjacent inn.

To help ensure the economic viability and further growth of his new community, another facet of Warden's grand plan was to attract and develop industry on its outskirts, taking full advantage of the new rail service..With this goal in mind, he founded the North Shore Industrial Company to establish and operate various commercial enter-

The Shoreham Inn (1900), photographed by Arthur S. Greene, ca. 1910, served as the cornerstone and sales office for Warden's resort and Hapgood's development. Louise Bellport Collection

The Pavilion, photographed by Arthur S. Greene, ca. 1910. It served the Wardenclyffe resort as a gazebo, observation platform, and dance floor. The lower level had changing rooms for bathers. Kenneth Brady Collection

prises. Among these was a brick works in Sills Gully, just east of Woodville Landing, which had a large deposit of clay. The company manufactured bricks from 1900 to 1903, when its manual operation was rendered obsolete by mechanized factories elsewhere.

In 1901, New York businessman and real estate mogul Charles R. Flint (1861–1904) assisted in the transfer of two hundred acres of the North Shore Industrial Company's holdings near the Wardenclyffe train station to famed inventor and radio pioneer Nikola Tesla.[5] Tesla had outgrown his Manhattan laboratory and was in need of a large site for experiments on the long-distance transmission of radio waves. Financed by J. P. Morgan, Tesla constructed a 187-foot transmitting tower on the Wardenclyffe property and a stately brick laboratory designed by New York architect Stanford White. (At the time of this writing, the laboratory is the subject of restoration efforts as the Tesla Science Center at Wardenclyffe). Warden promptly filed two separate plats of street plans with Suffolk County, one for the seaside resort community of Wardenclyffe, the other for a company town that he anticipated would spring up adjacent to Tesla's laboratory, which he hoped would be the seed for a prominent radio-transmitting and manufacturing center that would support a work force in the hundreds. But this workers' community went largely unbuilt because J. P. Morgan pulled the plug on his support of Tesla a few years later, when Marconi beat Tesla in establishing transatlantic radio transmission. In fact, Tesla had misrepresented the true purpose of the tower to his financier. Although ostensibly to be used to transmit radio signals, Tesla actually had in mind free, wireless transmission of electricity and thus had not put much effort into the transatlantic radio venture. This frustrated Morgan's expectation of a return on his investment.

Nikola Tesla's Experiment Station, photographed by Arthur S. Greene, ca. 1905. The 187-foot transmission tower was demolished in 1917. Kenneth Brady Collection

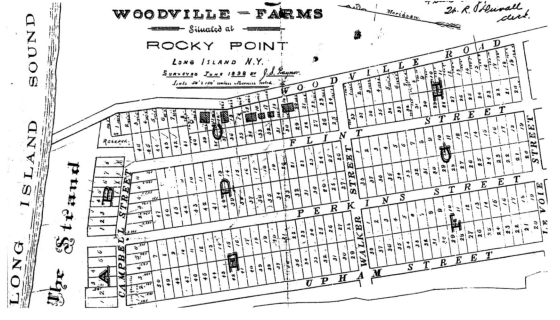

"Map of Woodville Farms at Rocky Point, Long Island," 1899. This was the original proposed street plan for the Wardenclyffe development, a rectilinear grid that ignored the steep slopes on the west side of Woodville Road. Mary Ann Oberdorf Collection

In addition to Flint and Upham, Warden ultimately involved entrepreneur Herbert J. Hapgood in the Wardenclyffe project. Hapgood, an 1897 Dartmouth graduate from Peru, Vermont (where the Hapgood family still owns a general store), had come to New York and founded Hapgood's National Association of Brain Brokers,[6] one of the first placement firms for college graduates—professionals and men with technical skills. Hapgood also marketed products and inventions, notably the safety razor. By 1905, Hapgood and Warden were officers in each other's corporations, both located on the fifth floor of 309 Broadway.[7] Because Warden had named Hapgood and Hapgood's father-in-law, Charles J. Tagliabue (1852–1922), as co-executors of his estate, Hapgood was well positioned to take over the Wardenclyffe development after Warden's death in 1906. Tagliabue, a successful Brooklyn manufacturer of precision scientific and industrial measuring instruments, had the financial means to back his son-in-law's subsequent development efforts at Wardenclyffe, and he was also an early booster of the community, having built his own summer home there in 1905.

In 1906, Hapgood first set his sights on the large, oak-covered hillside west of Woodville Road and founded the Oak Ridge Company to develop it. Lacking experience as a developer or builder, Hapgood nonetheless possessed overarching ambition and self-confidence, an ability to attract investors, and considerable skill as an impresario in hiring talent in areas that he lacked. As a first step, he engaged the architect and landscape architect Arthur T. "Pinky" Holton (1876–1928), who had previously worked in Yonkers, Brooklyn, and New York City and went on to help in the layout of Miami Beach in the 1920s.[8] Holton modified the original rectilinear grid pattern into graceful, intersecting curvilinear streets that followed

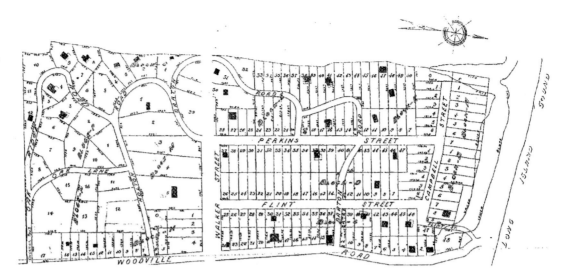

the topography of the hills west of Woodville Road and their sea views. An early photograph of Sturgis Road, originally called Holton Road after Arthur Holton, shows the result of his redesign. For the design of the houses to be built on these streets, Hapgood employed no well-known architects, and the source of his house plans is a matter of conjecture. They likely came from common sources of the time, notably the designs and floor plans available for a modest fee from magazines, including *Ladies' Home Journal* and Gustav Stickley's *The Craftsman* magazine.[9] Hapgood was clearly an acolyte of the Arts and Crafts movement championed by Stickley, and a number of Hapgood's homes were, and still are, decorated with Stickley furniture. The homes, about sixty of which were built on the western slope, had the simple, clean lines and boxlike shape of the American Foursquare house form[10] that became popular in the early twentieth century in reaction to the architectural excesses of the preceding Victorian era, with their turrets, gables, and ornate trim. Houses ranged from modest one-story cottages to substantial three- or four-bedroom two-story residences. Many had screened-in porches to catch the cooling sea breezes. Lot sizes varied considerably but averaged about two-thirds of an acre. A feature of the Shoreham homes (and later of their Mountain Lakes counterparts) was the use of local materials, including stone for hearths and chimneys and dried seaweed for insulation. Typical sales prices for the houses in 1906–8 ranged from $3,500 to $4,500. As a measure of the success of the community and the real estate market at the time, some of the same houses resold in 1912–13 for $6,000–7,350. It appears that Holton and the builders whom Hapgood employed, including Edwin S. Child, embellished and customized a few basic designs by varying the scale and exterior appearance, including a number of different

rooflines—some houses had hipped roofs, others had gambrel roofs, and one had a distinctive cross-gable design that Hapgood referred to as "Swiss Chalet." In keeping with its Alpine name, Hapgood situated this Swiss Chalet on the top of a wooded hill. An early view of the new village from one of its promontories shows the variety of house types. A hallmark of Hapgood's Shoreham homes is the Shoreham Overhang,[11] a long, overhanging eave without a soffit, leaving the ends of the roof beams exposed. This overhang serves to shade the windows from the hot summer sun and divert rainwater from the house and its foundation, an especially useful function in the absence of gutters. A charming feature of the larger homes is their accompanying detached garages or guest cottages, each designed as a miniature version of the main house, mimicking its roofline, shape, and color scheme. Hapgood placed his first advertisements for Wardenclyffe in the *New York Times* and the *Brooklyn Daily Eagle* in May and June 1906. The ads featured a view of Woodville Landing showing the original clubhouse and early houses.

In 1910, mindful of the needs of his residents, Hapgood built a combined store and post office in the heart of the burgeoning development, a gambrel-roofed structure similar in design to a number of the newly constructed houses in the community and featuring an upstairs residence for the shopkeeper's family. The relocation of the post office from near the train station to Woodville Road coincided with the change in the name of the community from Wardenclyffe to Shoreham. Reputedly, the new name had been suggested by his partner Richard D. Upham's wife, Elizabeth, after England's Shoreham-by-Sea.[12] Indeed, though many of Shoreham's original settlers were Irish American and its first church was Roman Catholic, early Shorehamites were clearly Anglophiles. In emulation of Edwardian England, they

An early Shoreham postcard shows the graceful curve of its tree-lined, concrete streets (paved in 1914). This view has changed little in a century. Louise Bellport Collection

A hilltop Swiss Chalet cottage in a sylvan setting, photographed by Arthur S. Greene, ca. 1910. Note the use of native locust logs as porch posts. Louise Bellport Collection

This early postcard shows the variety of house types at Shoreham shortly after their construction, 1906–10. Mary Ann Oberdorf Collection

A New York Times *ad placed by Hapgood on May 20, 1906, p. 20, titled "Log Cabin": "Log Cabins, bungalows, or Colonial Houses will be erected and furnished according to individual taste, with estates ranging from one to ten acres according to the wish of the purchaser. Cottages will be rented to those who desire to build. H. J. Hapgood, Wardenclyffe, Long Island, or 307 Broadway, New York City."*

Brooklyn Daily Eagle *ad placed by Hapgood on June 11, 1906, p. 15, titled "Log Cabin" and "Estates": "A tract of several hundred acres . . . is cut up into estates ranging from five to fifty acres, overlooking the Sound. Log Cabins, Bungalows or Colonial Houses will be erected according to the owner's taste. Cottages will be rented to those who desire to superintend the construction of their own houses. Excellent investment. Rapidly increasing in value; exclusive. References required. H. J. Hapgood, Wardenclyffe, L. I., or 307 Broadway, N.Y."*

embraced cocktail culture, yachting and equestrian traditions, a proper garden club with juried shows and formal teas, and Anglican-style Sunday evening song.

This is not to say that the early residents enjoyed all the creature comforts that they had left behind in the city. Until 1914, their evening entertainment was held by the light of candles and kerosene lanterns, and they were unperturbed by the annoying ring of telephones. But that year, after five years of attempting to arrange electric service, the community finally let a franchise to the Port Jefferson Electric Light Company. At first, there was considerable trouble with the wires due to falling trees and branches, including, the very next year, the accidental electrocution of William H. Blatch, husband of famed suffragist Harriot Stanton Blatch; he had been trying to move a wire felled by a storm.[13]

Telephone service followed soon thereafter. The little community had its own exchange. Its switchboard was located in a tiny native-stone house on Woodville Road, staffed by a Miss Overton, who could place calls requested by name because she had memorized the names and numbers of all of Shoreham's telephone subscribers.[14]

By 1909, Hapgood had largely completed work on the western section of Shoreham, first called Hapgood's Bungalow Colony and in recent years referred to as the Old Village. (The original official name of the development, Oak Ridge, never caught on with the residents.) He next turned his attention to the hills on the east side of Woodville Road, along Briarcliff and Tower Hill roads. But just at that turning point in Shoreham's development, the ever-ambitious Hapgood was lured away to northern New Jersey by the promise of a far grander project. Through advertisements and articles, Hapgood's successful Shoreham development was becoming known throughout the region and apparently caught the attention of New Jersey surveyor and land developer Lewis van Duyne, who was in need of a building partner to realize an audacious plan to transform a forlorn, hilly landscape of brush and swamp twenty-five miles west of New York City into a high-class commuter town. The plan hinged on the new Hudson train tunnels that would link an existing railroad line directly with Manhattan. Van Duyne was damming local streams to create a series of lakes—an ideal canvas for Hapgood's brush: wooded hills sloping down to scenic shorelines with a rail link to the city. Aptly called Mountain Lakes, the new community was to have five hundred stately homes—Shoreham times ten. Over the next decade, Mountain Lakes, Hapgood's masterpiece, would be his ultimate undoing. Before taking on the Mountain Lakes project, Hapgood had entered into a contract to purchase 338 hilly, water-view acres in the East Neck section of Huntington along the same North Shore L.I.R.R. line as Shoreham, but thirty miles to the west, where he planned to develop another seaside community modeled after Shoreham. But in June 1909, after committing to the Mountain Lakes project, he sold these purchase rights to the Huntington Bay View Association.[15]

In 1911, Hapgood moved his young family one hundred miles due west from Shoreham to Mountain Lakes to commence construction of the lakeside community. He also took along his landscape architect and right-hand man, Holton, as well as his Shoreham foremen, stonemasons, and carpenters, which accounts for the overall resemblance between the two communities: the same sweeping curves of the streets as they ascend the hills (even some of the same street names), and the similar layout, rooflines, and architectural details of many of the houses. As in Shoreham, Hapgood used local building materials for the houses and even built a sawmill to make use of the native hardwood trees cleared in constructing Mountain Lakes.[16]

Occupied with Mountain Lakes, Hapgood had little direct involvement in phase two of the Shoreham project—development of the east side. The major part of that task fell to his partners Richard D. Upham (son of Warden partner Jabez Upham, who had died in 1902) and Henry B. Johnson. Richard Upham had purchased the east-side tract, comprising 1,194 acres, for $61,000 at a 1905 public auction resulting from a bankruptcy proceeding against the estate of Charles L. Flint, one of the original partners of James Warden and the late Jabez Upham. That property had been held in Flint's name prior to his death.[17] Richard Upham then immediately transferred ownership of the property to the Suffolk County Land Company, which had been created by the Hapgood partners for the development of the parcel. However, this complicated transaction was dogged by allegations of financial irregularities, including claims that the property had been undervalued and that Flint's estate and the second mortgage holder had been defrauded. As a result, the transaction was held up briefly. But this maneuver was only the first in a series of creative financing schemes and multiple changes of ownership of the east-side property between the principals and their corresponding land companies, as well as a 1910

View of Shoreham, photographed by Arthur S. Greene, ca. 1919, showing the beach pavilion, second clubhouse (low structure at center of photo), which stood until 1987, when it was destroyed by fire, and early houses. Note the footbridge spanning the gulley through which Woodville Road descended to the beach. Louise Bellport Collection

The Shoreham store, which also housed a post office until 1961, was constructed in 1910 and served the community until its conversion to a private residence in the 1980s. Its gambrel roof is a feature of a number of Shoreham houses. Mary Ann Oberdorf Collection

The stucco-clad William Ashley residence, 1911, John P. Benson, architect, is the grandest of the estate homes built on large, five-to-ten-acre plots east of Woodville Road. Shoreham Village Archives

lawsuit against Hapgood, Upham, and Johnson by an outside group of Port Jefferson investors in the project, who felt that the three had defrauded them by awarding themselves generous salaries and real estate from the company's landholdings.[18] With these complications and without Hapgood's direct involvement, the east side of Shoreham developed more slowly, and in a less organized fashion, than the west side had. The on-site effort was led by Richard Upham, who corresponded frequently with partner Johnson, based in Manhattan. Contemporary advertisements for this "Estates" section east of Woodville Road—along the recently constructed Tower Hill and Briarcliff roads—offered prospective buyers five- to ten-acre lots for the construction of large estate homes, as an upscale alternative to the more modest bungalows on smaller lots on the west side. With their large lot sizes, only about a dozen homes were built. Estates section deed restrictions stipulated minimum prices of between $5,000 and $15,000 (two typical Estates section homes sold in 1909 for $12,500 and $14,250, respectively). Whereas Hapgood had offered specific house models for the bungalow section to the west, most buyers in the Estates section engaged their own architects, resulting in a broader array of styles. Though most of the homes on the west side were of wood-frame construction, many of the estates on the east side were of masonry and stucco.

New York architect John P. Benson designed at least four houses in this section, the grandest being the Ashley Estate, purchased in 1911 for $29,000 by attorney William Ashley. It was featured in the March 30, 1912, issue of *Town & Country* magazine. The elegant, understated, wood-shingle cottage Cliff House, owned by Hapgood partner Henry B. Johnson, featured spectacular water views and a distinctive L shape. Benson worked in reinforced concrete to create Hapgood partner Richard D. Upham's hilltop house overlooking the Sound. A photo and floor plan of the house appeared in a book published by the Atlas Portland Cement Company[19] extolling the virtues of concrete for summer—cool and fireproof. This estate's next incarnation was distinctly Gallic; Richard Upham's son, Donald, redesigned it in grand fashion as a Norman château for his French bride. Fittingly, it was converted into the French summer boarding school of Manhattan's Lycée Français after Donald Upham's death in 1947.

A more modest "semi-bungalow" on Tower Hill Road was designed by Nora Stanton Blatch, the first female civil engineer to graduate at Cornell, and built for her mother, the New York suffrage leader Harriot Stanton Blatch, whose own mother, national women's suffrage leader Elizabeth Cady Stanton, had been an early summer resident of Wardenclyffe until her death in 1902.

In keeping with the quasi-utopian community Warden envisioned, many of Shoreham's earliest residents were progressives and intellectuals. They included the aforementioned suffragists; scientists (radio pioneers Tesla and Lee De Forest); a number of male and female physicians, among them "electrical psychiatrists" William J. Herdman and Margaret Cleaves; actors Tully Marshall and his wife, Marion Fairfax; and the noted playwright and theater critic Channing Pollock, who became

Architect John P. Benson designed the waterfront wood-shingled Cliff House, ca. 1912, for Hapgood partner Henry B. Johnson. Shoreham Village Archives

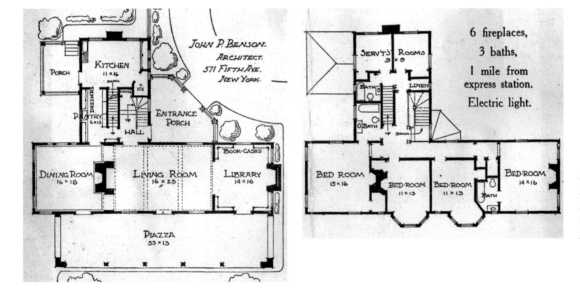

Floor plan of the Johnson Estate, Shoreham, Long Island, ca. 1912. Shoreham Village Archives

a devoted lifelong resident and served as the new village's constable. Pollock waxed lyrical about his newfound home, writing in 1943 about the moment in 1908 when he first laid eyes on Shoreham, "About three in the afternoon, almost a whole day after leaving New York, we reached Shoreham. I thought then and still think it is the most beautiful spot in the world. The only possible rival I ever saw is on the Bay of Tunis in North Africa. Scores of visitors have remarked the likeness of our coast to that of the Riviera. . . . Five minutes after I first laid eyes on the place I knew we were going to live and die there—if it didn't cost too much. 'Too much,' I decided meant more than we could beg, borrow or steal."[20]

With the coming of Hapgood and the growth of the community, there was a cultural shift,

marked by the arrival of prosperous professionals and business leaders. They were a sociable crowd that enjoyed their parties, their cocktails, and their sport. Many came from Brooklyn, and for a time Shoreham was referred to as "Little Brooklyn," with the comings and goings of prominent Shorehamites recorded in the society column of the *Brooklyn Daily Eagle*.[21]

Hapgood helped encourage the establishment of institutions that promoted the cohesiveness of the community, notably the Shoreham Country Club, founded in 1916, and its subsidiary Garden Club and Boat Club, which, along with the tennis courts and the beach, became centers for recreation and socializing in the new community. (Corresponding clubs and organizations also took root in Mountain Lakes.) Shorehamites took (and

still take) play very seriously: there were juried flower shows, Sunday boat races, an annual tennis tournament, children's swimming races, and every Labor Day weekend—uninterrupted from 1924 to the present—a lively intercommunity tennis competition with neighboring Wading River. Although only in residence seasonally, Shorehamites took great pride in the appearance of their community, and, with the help and encouragement of the Shoreham Garden Club, they improved the sandy soil and replaced the open, clear-cut landscape with lush gardens and ornamental trees and shrubs. As a result, of course, water views became scarcer. Locust trees were initially cultivated for their quick growth and for the durability of the wood when fashioned into fence posts and railings, until residents discovered—the hard way—that these tall, straight trees with shallow roots were especially prone to toppling over onto houses, streets, and power lines during hurricanes and windstorms.

The "amphitheater" topography that guaranteed almost universal water views also proved to be Shoreham's curse—all of the storm water from the south, west, and east funneled down into Woodville Road, creating mud, washouts, and flooding (still a source of consternation a hundred years later). To address the problem, the village incorporated in 1913 so that the community could raise an $18,000 bond to pave its steep, muddy roads and install its first storm drains. When the work was done, Shoreham became the first municipality in New York State with 100 percent paved roads. The new village's zoning ordinance

folded in many of the restrictions found in individual deeds, especially those granted to home buyers by James Warden and his successors. The restrictions excluded any industry, with the exception of professional offices, from residential areas and banned any agricultural pursuits considered distasteful, such as harboring swine or operating slaughterhouses. The upscale Estates section was not annexed to the village until 1951, but its residents were welcome to take advantage of the social amenities of the village, including the country club and tennis courts.

In the wake of the stock market crash of 1929, the village experienced a decline. Rail service was scaled back that year, and the Wading River line was permanently abandoned in 1938 because of a decline in ridership as a result of the Depression and because of a shift toward automobile travel. As improved state highways (Rtes. 25 and 25A) reached the area in the 1910s and 1920s, the car trip from the city became relatively fast and easy.[22]

Nineteen twenty-nine was also the year that Herbert Hapgood died in far off Sydney, Australia, having fled the United States. in 1923 to avoid imminent bankruptcy and legal actions against him. He had become severely overextended in the construction of Mountain Lakes and at the same time had lost the backing of his chief financier, Charles Tagliabue, who died in 1922. He also faced criminal charges and civil suits stemming from financial irregularities, including allegations that he had sought mortgages for houses that did not exist and had forged his late father-in-law's

Residence of Harriot Stanton Blatch, designed by her daughter Nora Stanton Blatch. Coline Jenkins/Elizabeth Cady Stanton Trust

The elegant, Craftsman-style interior of the Harriot Stanton Blatch House, featuring extensive chestnut woodworking. Coline Jenkins/ Elizabeth Cady Stanton Trust

signature on loan guarantees.[23] Hapgood's business partners and Tagliabue's estate were largely held harmless in the legal and financial maneuvers that followed his departure, so the banks, subcontractors, workers, and property owners involved in the Mountain Lakes development shouldered the ensuing losses. Owing to the shame associated with these accusations and Hapgood's subsequent flight, his widow, Ethel, and their children, who returned to Shoreham after Hapgood's departure, never spoke of him, even though Ethel lived in the community and in the house constructed by her husband for many decades, until her death in 1969. As a result, Shoreham residents and Hapgood's own descendants had no idea of the central role he had played in creating their beloved community. It was only on the occasion of Shoreham's Centennial in 2013 and the rediscovery of the Shoreham–Mountain Lakes connection that Shorehamites began to understand the extent to which their community was indebted to Hapgood's vision.

A preservation movement began in Mountain Lakes in the 1990s, and residents started proudly

displaying shiny brass "Hapgood Home" plaques on their houses. In Shoreham, where local architects in the 1960s and 1970s had updated some Hapgood homes with modern exterior colors, materials, and windows, glass walls (in a few cases), and open-plan interiors, and a few original Hapgoods were lost to fire or were torn down, many Hapgood homes nevertheless remain largely intact. A renewed appreciation for them has spurred preservation and restoration efforts. And so Hapgood's vision of elegant, understated homes in a beautiful natural setting, of a little village with a strong sense of community, continues and thrives as Shoreham enters its second century.

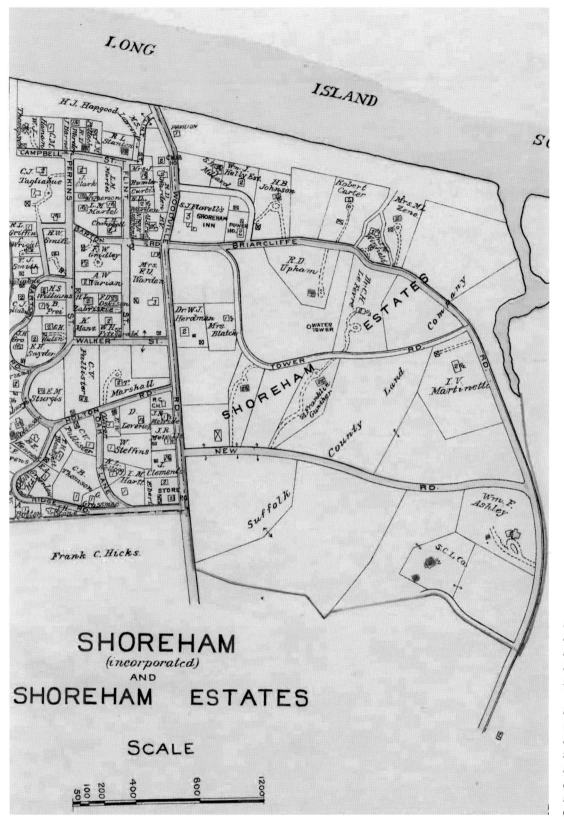

LONG

ISLAND

SHOREHAM
(incorporated)
AND
SHOREHAM ESTATES

SCALE

Frank C. Hicks.

E. Belcher Hyde map of Shoreham, 1917, showing the contrast between the large lots of the Shoreham Estates section east of Woodville Road and the smaller lots of the Oak Ridge section of the original incorporated village west of Woodville. Shoreham Estates was annexed to the village in 1951. Mary Ann Oberdorf Collection

17
BEACON HILL

A GEM IN THE DIADEM

LYNN STOWELL PEARSON

In 1911, Charles Edward Tuxill (1877–1967), a thirty-four-year-old real estate entrepreneur from upstate New York, decided to test his talents on a bigger stage. Acquiring 160 acres of farmland in Port Washington known as Beacon Hill, with breathtaking views and 1,600 feet of beach frontage on Hempstead Harbor, Tuxill jumped into one of New York's hottest suburban real estate markets with a bold vision of an upscale community for city dwellers seeking a better lifestyle within commuting distance of Manhattan.[1]

Tuxill's career began in 1900 in his hometown of Auburn, New York, where his first project, Tuxill Square (1904), was immediately praised as a "beautiful residential street and a credit to the city."[2] Woodlawn Avenue, almost twice the size of his first project at thirty-four lots, followed in 1905.[3] During this period of rapid development, Tuxill Realty and Improvement Company expanded to Rochester, and Charles's older brother Wilfred moved there to supervise.[4] By 1906, sixty brick houses had been built, yet Charles continued to search for even better opportunities.[5] "The handsomest real estate dealer in Auburn, Charles E. Tuxill, was a caller in our village Monday," a Syracuse paper reported; the local press also recorded his frequent trips to New York City.[6] Before long, Charles persuaded his younger brother Frank to join him in opening Tuxill Realty Company in Manhattan at 337–39 Fifth Avenue, opposite the original Waldorf-Astoria, a neighborhood full of real estate offices.[7] By 1912,

both brothers had moved to Port Washington to oversee the development of Beacon Hill.[8]

Charles Tuxill's entrance into New York's metropolitan real estate arena garnered immediate attention. In *The Book of New York*, 1912, author Julius Chambers describes him as a "hustler."[9] Backed by investors from Auburn and Syracuse, who had already realized handsome profits from his upstate enterprises, Tuxill was able to raise money for his Long Island project by offering bonds at a 6 percent return.[10] The investors followed Beacon Hill's progress with enthusiasm, including Dr. Frank Kenyon, who, upon his return from Port Washington in October 1913, praised Tuxill's hands-on management style, applauded the number of lots sold and houses built, and touted the abundant clean water supply from the newly built storage facility.[11]

Unlike Tuxill's much smaller upstate developments with their tightly packed grid plans, Beacon Hill's abundant rolling acreage presented Tuxill with unlimited possibilities. Here, applying what he had learned upstate, he could unleash his imagination on a blank canvas. And his choice of Port Washington could not have been better timed.

After the Long Island Railroad extended its branch to Port Washington in 1898, this North Shore community, a mere forty-five-minute trip from Penn Station, became ripe for development as a commuter suburb. Already popular with city dwellers during the summer months because of its seaside hotels and noted lack of mosquitoes, Port

Charles E. Tuxill, the developer of Beacon Hill, ca. 1906. Auburn Daily Advertiser, December 1906. Courtesy Seymour Library, Auburn

Washington offered a host of requisite support services: four fire companies, artesian wells, electric streetlights, phone lines, fine schools, and several churches.[12] The *Brooklyn Daily Eagle* praised its macadamized roads, noting that "there are not better ones anywhere on the Island."[13] And yet, rural life abounded: grazing cows and "farmers [who] still mow the grass with their old-fashioned scythe and the sound of the whetstone as the sharpening is done, blends strangely with the honk of the flying automobile."[14] The *Brooklyn Daily Eagle's* Charles Shepard noted:

> Few sections of the United States are richer in natural attractions than the north shore of Long Island from Little Neck to Wading River. Such a

succession of harbors and bays of high sand bluffs crowned with forests along its waterfront and its lofty ridges, comprising what is known as the backbone of Long Island, offer a panorama of grandeur and variety of scenery to delight the eye of every beholder.

> The village of Port Washington . . . [is] one of the central gems of the diadem, with a variety of hill and valley and waterfront scenery hard to match. . . .[15]

Another *Eagle* article proclaimed Port to be a yachtsman's paradise:

> Perhaps the greatest single factor [contributing to the growth of Port Washington] has been its unsurpassed water privileges. . . . It would be difficult

Tuxill's real estate office in Auburn, New York, ca. 1906. The board in the background shows his real estate listings. Auburn Daily Advertiser, December 1906, p. 28. Courtesy Seymour Library, Auburn

to describe the scene presented on the waters in and about Port Washington when the yachting season opens. The bay is white with sails. Steam and sailing craft navigated by pleasure seekers are everywhere. . . . No more delightful way to spend a summer afternoon can be found than at one of these meetings on the verandas of a Long Island yacht club.[16]

Yachting enthusiasts could choose from three clubs: The Port Washington Yacht Club (known then as the Port Washington Club) held its first race in 1905; the Manhasset Bay Yacht Club, well established by 1907; and the Knickerbocker Yacht Club (1907).

By 1913, the train line was electrified all the way to Port Washington, reducing the trip to Manhattan from forty-five to thirty-six minutes, and developers were quick to predict "a new epoch in North Shore real estate."[17] The impact that the train line had on this burgeoning commuter suburb was borne out by a dramatic rise in population figures: within just twenty-five years, this sleepy town grew from eight hundred, when the first train arrived in 1898, to a staggering twelve thousand.[18] In addition, a trolley, operating from 1908 to 1920, connected Port Washington with Mineola and Roslyn.

Beacon Hill was just one of several planned communities cropping up all over Port Washington during the boom years of the early 1900s.[19] Across town, Baxter Estates (1910) was developed by two local boys, Charles E. "Buck" Hyde (1870–1945) and A. Percy Baxter, who became big real estate agents in the area. Because of their local connections, Hyde and Baxter, unlike Charles Tuxill, did not find it necessary to have an office in New York City or buy much ad space in city papers. Their

seventy-acre property, once part of the Baxter homestead (the ca. 1795 house is extant), provided the perfect hillside setting, partially excavated by sand mining, for their meandering roads, which culminated at a pond. Hyde & Baxter began offering plots for $1,500–5,000 and residences for $8,000–25,000, with beach rights for all owners.[20] They also assured a certain class of neighbor: "[E]very restriction which will keep the tract an exclusive home colony has been enforced."[21]

The entire North Shore of Long Island had great appeal, but some of the most promising aspects of an ideal community came together in Port Washington: wonderful scenery, convenient transportation, support services, and ample leisure pursuits. Recognizing a golden opportunity, Charles Tuxill set out to create the ideal residential park, capitalizing on Beacon Hill's own set of advantages: walking distance from the train station, beach rights, and sweeping views from the top of the hill.

Throughout 1912 Tuxill targeted city dwellers with display ads in the *New York Times*: "Living in this suburban residential park . . . brings all the conveniences and improvements you could obtain in the city—electricity, pure water, sanitary drainage, clean, smooth drives and shady walks. Stores, churches and schools convenient. All you miss is the noise, dust, and stifling heat of the city."[22] During the July 4 weekend, another ad teased readers: "Now if you were only living at Beacon Hill you could enjoy your half holiday today at home—boating, fishing, tennis, bathing; a quarter mile of white sandy beach—acres of cool shade. . . ."[23]

News reports in Port Washington's bi-weekly paper, *Plain Talk*, championed the developer's vision, "This will be a high class development with reasonable restrictions. . . . It is a park development,

A postcard of Baxter Estates and Baxter Pond. Courtesy Port Washington Public Library, Local History Center

the roads winding in curves through it, flanked by trees and shrubbery without sidewalks, but surfaced by a dustless macadam."[24] "Villa" plots, one-third to three acres, were being laid out so that each lot would have an unobstructed view of Hempstead Harbor.[25]

For the infrastructure, Charles Tuxill selected the best materials and the latest innovations; its progress was chronicled in *Plain Talk* from 1912 to 1914.[26] As in many other early planned communities, the entrance was announced by two ornamental pavilions and five acres were set aside at the top of the hill for a hotel, which never materialized.[27] "[Tuxill Reality Company's] new entrance from the end of Main Street curves into their main boulevard [Beacon Hill Road] in an attractive manner and anyone desiring to take a pleasant walk will be repaid by taking this road to the top of Beacon Hill where the view is the finest we have."[28]

In 1912, to help realize his vision for a residential park, Tuxill turned to Philadelphia's celebrated landscape architect Oglesby Paul (1877–1915), a nephew of Mrs. William Waldorf Astor. Paul, who had made the first topographic survey of Beacon Hill for the previous owner,[29] is best known for his work on Philadelphia's renowned Fairmount Park. He graduated from Harvard's Department of Landscape Architecture in 1901, having studied there under Frederick Law Olmsted Jr.[30] In 1905, Paul designed the garden and grounds of Woodcrest (today Cabrini College, Radnor, Pennsylvania), where he worked in concert with Horace Trumbauer, a Main Line architect, and where Olmsted's influence has been recognized in the recently restored garden pergola.[31]

Oglesby Paul almost certainly played a major role in designing Beacon Hill's curvilinear roads, which follow the site's dramatic topography to best scenic advantage, much in the manner of Frederick Law Olmsted's classic layout of Riverside, Illinois. However, Paul's sudden, early death in 1915 at the age of thirty-eight marked the end of a promising career.[32] Although the full extent of his contribution is not known, he undoubtedly designed the landscaped islands, as well as the ninety-foot-wide central "parkway," which runs the length of Beacon Hill Road. Appearing on the earliest surveyed maps, this parkway, with turning circles at the intersections and a paved median at the center, was to be planted with trees, ornamental shrubs, and flowers.[33]

In keeping with the planned communities of its day, Beacon Hill's restrictions stipulated single-family houses that could not be built for less than $3,500–5,000 (by 1923, $8,000 was the threshold), and all building plans had to be submitted to Tuxill Realty Company for approval.[34] By the 1920s,

YES, WE'RE MOVING OUT TO PORT WASHINGTON—COME AND VISIT US.

Front cover of Port Washington's local paper. The illustration originally appeared in the Telephone Review, a publication for telephone employees, and it refers to the switchboard girls, whose average length of employment was about three years. The artist has chosen a common scene—a switchboard girl leaving her employ to live in Port Washington with her new husband. Plain Talk, April 26, 1913. Courtesy Port Washington Public Library, Local History Center

Cover of Charles Tuxill's Beacon Hill brochure, ca. 1911. Courtesy Sue Sturman

*A postcard showing
the entrance pavilions
on Beacon Hill Road,
ca, 1912.* Courtesy
Cow Neck Peninsula
Historical Society,
www.cowneck.org

the job of policing the deed restrictions fell to the Beacon Hill Residents Association, established in 1919.[35] The *Brooklyn Daily Eagle* found this relationship to be especially noteworthy, suggesting that the Residents Association was "practically partners in the development."[36]

Tuxill Realty Company began offering lots in 1912, and the earliest residences date from 1914 to 1918.[37] Sales were brisk, with lots selling for $1,500–5,200, and in 1913, Charles Tuxill boasted that sales had totaled $92,000 in seven months.[38] His success can be credited to his aggressive approach: "Beacon Hill is about the only development around here that is doing any business. While others are waiting for something to happen they [Tuxill Realty] are hustling."[39] Tuxill frequently advertised "easy terms," offering lots for 10 percent down with the balance in "easy monthly payments," or a 10 percent discount for cash.[40] Tuxill Realty Company built several houses on speculation, though buyers could hire their own architects with plans subject to approval, and by May 1914, five new Tuxill Realty Company houses had been completed.[41] Charles's brother Frank also built houses, though on a more limited scale. Immediately after selling the house at 23 Crescent Road for $12,000 in 1914, Frank set out to build another.[42]

One of the earliest residences on the "Hill," 32 Summit Road, belonged to Frederick C. Franke, sales manager for Tuxill Realty Company. His wife, Helen, bought the property in July 1913 for $3,576.75, and announced that she would build a $10,000 house with an uninterrupted view all the way to Manhattan.[43] In August 1914, this house appeared in a full-page ad promoting the Beacon Hill development.[44] That same year, Port Washing-

ton resident Arthur Keevil, a vice president of U.S. Mortgage & Trust in Manhattan, purchased a plot of land at 50 Crescent Road. Eleven years later, he hired the New York City architectural firm of Tillion & Tillion to design his Tudor Revival house, which still retains its original English steel casement windows.[45]

In addition to sales of individual lots, Charles Tuxill sold blocks of property to other developers, including a fellow resident from upstate, Charles E. Wethey, who in 1914 bought seventeen plots for $50,615.00.[46] Wethey planned to build a house for himself and "modern and artistic houses" on the remaining lots.[47] However, a year later, he was in financial trouble: "I am forced to dispose of 20 [*sic*] villa plots within 10 days; it means an unusual opportunity and cannot be duplicated at double the price . . ."[48] Wethey held on to at least one lot, where he built an Arts and Crafts–style house in about 1918, at 9 Summit Road, and lived there until the mid-1920s.[49] A newcomer to the real estate field, Wethey had sold his successful hardware business, located near Tuxill's hometown of Auburn, a year before buying the Beacon Hill property.[50] It is tempting to surmise that Wethey followed Tuxill to Port Washington to capitalize on the booming real estate market but lacked the experience and possibly the bravado of a Charles Tuxill to make a success of it.

One of the largest and most dramatically positioned houses on the Hill is a Mediterranean Colonial Revival at 3 Hampton Road, commanding the attention of anyone traveling up Beacon Hill Road (it is seen under construction above). In 1917, Tuxill Realty offered this stately home for $18,500, with $500 down and $130 per month.[51]

I. Jones Cobin (1859–1934) and his family lived there from 1920 to the early 1930s. Cobin, who retired from the silk industry in New York City before the move, quickly became caught up in Port's booming real estate market and formed a partnership with Arthur Cocks, an established local builder. Together they constructed several houses on the Hill.[52]

By 1923, thirty-five houses had been built on Beacon Hill; two years later the total rose to sixty-four, nearly 24 percent of the development.[53] Today there are 269 houses on the Hill. Those built between the wars are in a range of styles, including Colonial Revival, Georgian Revival, Tudor Revival, Dutch Colonial Revival, and Arts and Crafts. Houses built immediately after World War II were also Colonial Revival in style and blended in well with existing residences. It was not until the 1950s, long after the original restrictions had been relaxed, that ranches, modern, and Cape Cod–style houses were constructed, some as fill-ins, but the majority along roads that were laid later.

In April 1923, Charles Tuxill sold a large portion of his Beacon Hill interests to a syndicate, with Edgeworth Smith acting as broker.[54] Smith, who managed other Long Island developments, including Kew Gardens and Island Park in Long Beach, said he planned to develop Beacon Hill like Port Washington Estates, "[his] other high class development [in Port]."[55] Tuxill did, however, retain some Beacon Hill property, and in 1934, at the height of the Depression, Vincent Howells, holder of the original 1911 mortgage, placed liens on Tuxill Realty Company (they were canceled in 1939).[56]

Class of residences now built.

BEACON HILL

Reasons Why a Homeseeker Should Locate There.

AIR the purest in the vicinity of New York.
VIEW includes western L. I. Sound, the sky scrapers of New York and the Palisades of the Hudson.
ELEVATION of summit above tide is 280 feet.
RAILROAD station but 300 yards from western entrance.
BATHING beach and clean water along eastern boundary.
PARK-LIKE drives and landscaping.
COMMUTERS live here the year round in comfort.
THE 162 ACRES are all good building sites; no swamps.
RESTRICTIONS are reasonable, insuring an attractive neighborhood.
ALL CONVENIENCES, gas, electricity, water, telephone, etc.
PRICES moderate; write for views from photographs made on the property. The first purchasers get the best selection. Write now.

TUXILL REALTY CO., Telephone Murray Hill 1238 **339 Fifth Ave., New York**

32 Summit Road, the home of Frederick C. Franke, sales agent for Tuxill Realty Company, Beacon Hill, 1914. Plain Talk, August 1, 1914. Courtesy Port Washington Public Library, Local History Center

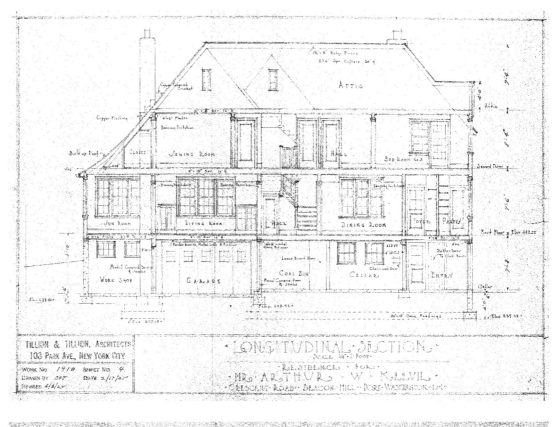

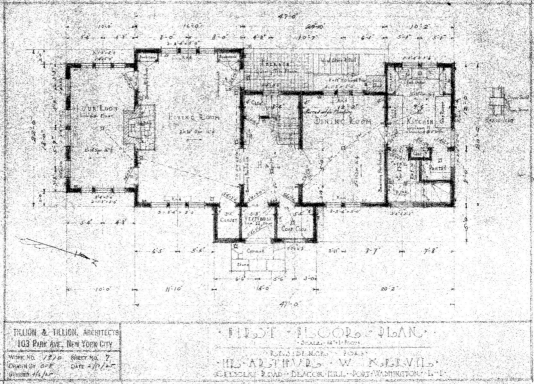

The original architectural plans for 50 Crescent Road, Beacon Hill, by the New York City architectural firm of Tillion & Tillion, dated February 17, 1925. Courtesy Margaret Dildilian

Tuxill appears to have left Port Washington in 1923, and by 1927 he was living on West End Avenue in Manhattan.[57] He maintained his Manhattan real estate office through the 1930s, although he seems to have floundered during the Depression, which may explain why, in the early 1940s, he was managing a convalescent home for torpedoed seamen at Kermit Roosevelt's former residence in Oyster Bay, Long Island.[58] By the mid-1940s, with the economy on the rise again, Tuxill embarked upon his last real estate venture, located in the Catskills, in Wurtsboro, New York.[59] Carl Tuxill, a nephew of Charles and son of Frank, spent his honeymoon there in 1950.[60] Recalling the mountain retreat of Wurtsboro Hills, Carl described his uncle's residence as the largest in the development, with commanding views from the top of the mountain.[61]

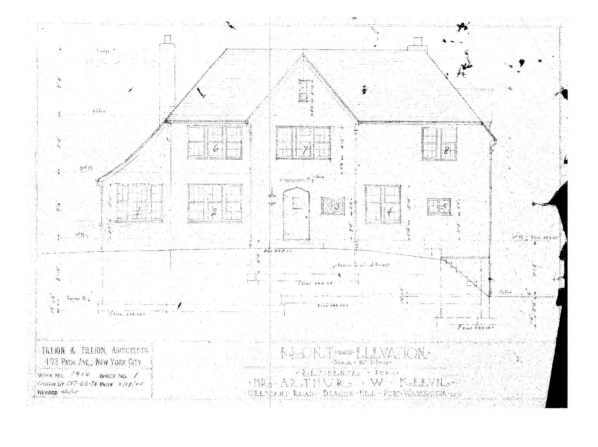

An early photograph of 50 Crescent Road, Beacon Hill, ca. 1925, taken prior to completion of the installation of the steel casement windows. Courtesy Margaret Dildilian

Although Charles Tuxill had left Beacon Hill in the early 1920s, adherence to his deed restrictions and the cohesive appearance of this residential park owes as much to his vision as it does to the early residents, who, through the Plans Committee of the Beacon Hill Residents Association, assured the integrity of the development through the 1940s by overseeing all building plans and, if necessary, going to court to uphold the original restrictions.[62]

The Residents Association was also dedicated to preserving the overall appeal of the community. To that end, when the Works Progress Administration announced plans for laying sidewalks on nearly all of Beacon Hill's roads in 1935, residents were opposed. Mindful of the need to support the WPA program yet preserve the park-like aspect of their community, the association suggested that the WPA focus on road grading, paving, and drainage gutters, instead of sidewalks.[63]

Not only did Beacon Hill succeed in becoming a "high-class" community but it also attracted a number of prominent artists, writers, successful businessmen, and architects. Port Washington in general had become a magnet for creative and notable residents, including Sinclair Lewis (1885–1951), the first American to receive the Nobel Prize in Literature, who lived near Beacon Hill on Vanderventer Avenue in 1914–15.

Colonel LeRoy Barton (1887–1959), an architect and resident who designed several houses on the Hill, became the driving force behind the Beacon Hill Residents Association's efforts to follow Tuxill's original restrictions. In 1926, Barton was praised for his unfailing efforts on behalf of the

Plans Committee.[64] He probably designed his own 1920s Colonial Revival house at 39 Crescent Road, and his wife, Anna, was founder of the Port Washington Garden Club.

Before moving to Beacon Hill, John Floyd Yewell (1885–1963), another prominent architect and resident who helped to enforce the original restrictions, had achieved great success for his small, well-planned, practical, and affordable houses. In 1919, Yewell's award-winning small brick house, located in Atlanta, Georgia, was heralded as "America's Most Popular Small House Plan."[65] The working drawings for this house, widely sold through design books, were said to have been used "more times throughout the country than any other designed."[66] Yewell, who bought his Beacon Hill property in 1923 from the

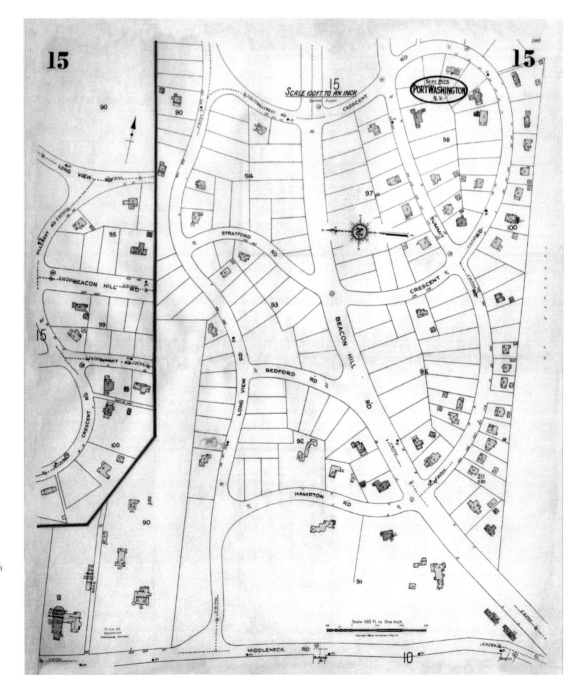

A layout of Beacon Hill's roads and lots, showing houses that had already been built. Sanborn Map, 1925. Courtesy Cow Neck Peninsula Historical Society, www.cowneck.org

newly installed Bi-Harbor Realty Group, designed his own English Tudor Revival at 50 Beacon Hill Road and lived there with his family through the late 1940s.[67] [fig. 14] For the landscaping, he turned to his close friend Loutrell Briggs, best known for his landscape design work in Charleston, South Carolina.[68] Yewell also designed other houses on the Hill, including a "National Competition Winner," an English cottage at 12 Crescent Road, about 1928.[69]

Other prominent early residents included Fontaine Fox (1884–1964), whose popular cartoon, the Toonerville Folks, also known as the Toonerville Trolley, was syndicated by newspapers across the country from 1913 to 1955; Impressionist painter Peter Bela Mayer (1887–1992), who lived at 27 Summit Road for more than sixty years; and Clarence Budington Kelland (1881–1964), a novelist, short story writer, and contributor to the *Saturday Evening Post*, whose house was designed by Wesley Sherwood Bessell, another Beacon Hill architect and resident, who also designed a number of local schools.[70]

Beacon Hill remains remarkably intact, with attractive houses in the Arts and Crafts, Tudor Revival, and Colonial Revival styles—very few have been compromised by later additions—and it is an outstanding example of a cohesive early twentieth-century residential park located on Long Island's North Shore, a true gem of survival.

18
SURF AND CONTROVERSY

REALTY ASSOCIATES & NEPONSIT

ROBERT B. MACKAY

Developed as a textbook residential park by one of the region's most experienced realty concerns, Neponsit on the Rockaway peninsula was billed as "the last ocean beach property in New York City."[1] Private and public visions for the western Rockaway shore front, however, were on a collision course from the outset.

Incorporated in December 1908, the Neponsit Realty Company was a subsidiary of Realty Associates, the hugely successful New York concern that became one of the country's largest producers of moderately priced homes.[2] Its principals were Frank Bailey, who ran the Brooklyn office of the Title Guarantee and Trust Company, ex-state senator William H. Reynolds, the borough's colorful developer, and some of Bailey's associates at Title Guarantee.

Son of a country doctor from Chatham, New York, Bailey attended Union College on scholarship, joining the Title Guarantee and Trust Company as a clerk in 1885. Dispatched two years later to manage the firm's Brooklyn office, a sleepy outpost on Montague Street nestled among the dozen or so trust companies that comprised the borough's real estate finance world, Bailey's new assignment appeared to be anything but a promotion, but it proved serendipitous. He had arrived at a time of great opportunity, and his position gave him the perfect vantage point to witness to the dramatic expansion of the nation's third-largest city, whose population came close to doubling between 1880

and 1900. Though the title company was not allowed to invest in second mortgages, nothing prevented Bailey from doing so as an individual. Not long after taking up his Brooklyn post, the astute investor met Senator Reynolds. In 1898, they incorporated a company to develop Borough Park and three years later formed Realty Associates with capitalization of $3 million and Bailey as chair. "Reynolds did the building and I tried to sit on the lid," Bailey recalled half a century later.[3] Soon they were building in the other boroughs and in Nassau County, completing as many as 925 houses in a year, and were widening their focus to include upscale projects. Acquired from the West Rockaway Land Company, the four hundred–acre Neponsit tract lay west of Belle Harbor on the remote peninsula, which stretched between the ocean and Jamaica Bay. Transportation was the developers' immediate concern. Rockaway Beach Boulevard was extended through the property, as was the Ocean Electric Company's trolley line, which was up and running by 1912, with Neponsit Realty paying half the cost of the improvement. By "swift electric trains," Neponsit was now just forty minutes from Manhattan.[4] The following year, the company's ads were heralding an additional advantage for commuters, an hour-and-fifteen-minute steamboat connection between the Battery and Neponsit's landing on Jamaica Bay.

The company hoped that the lure of their new community, "where summers are five Septembers

long," would be anchored in property-owner rights to its private ocean beach.[5] Extending a hundred feet back from the high-water mark, the beach without a boardwalk would be noticeably free of the attractions found not far to the west on the Coney Island peninsula.

Soon a large force of men was at work installing a model sanitation plant based on the French septic sedimentation plan, five miles of water mains, six miles of macadam streets, and other city conveniences. More than 1,700 lots were offered on reasonable terms with a small down payment and monthly payments at 1½ percent. An annual maintenance fee of $4 per lot covered the upkeep of the community's infrastructure, and a premium was attached to ocean frontage, which was sold for $10,250 in plots of five lots, only one of which faced the water. Approximately half as much secured a five-lot plot on a principal street, and three- and two-lot plots at $150 to $800 per lot were offered elsewhere throughout the property. For those who purchased before July 1, 1911, the company offered either to build a house at cost or to sell already built dwellings for $5,000–20,000. Train tickets were sent on request to those wishing to attend the Neponsit Home Show in October of that year to see "single-family residences of the finest modern construction featuring stucco on hollow tile, with six rooms and a bath or twelve rooms and three baths," which the company maintained could be occupied year round.[6] A Neponsit brochure trumpeted the community's many advantages, which were safeguarded by restrictions governing the appearance of dwellings and prohibiting commercial activity. Protecting the community's interest was a property owners' association, which served as custodian of the maintenance fund.[7]

"One approaches the property through an ornamental monolithic gateway of pure white after an original design by Kirby & Petit architects for many of the houses on the property," the *Brooklyn Times* observed.[8] Specialists in suburban architecture, the firm had established a near hegemony on residential park design. Principal John J. Petit had been associated with the development of Prospect Park South (see pages 61–62) and was involved in half a dozen of the other residential parks discussed in this study. Petit was probably also responsible for the Neponsit Realty Company's handsome, on-site office, which the *New-York Tribune* reported was so appealing that several customers had requested its design for their own houses.[9] The Neponsit Reality Company considered the community's architecture a "particularly attractive feature," describing it as consisting of "English cottages and picturesque bungalows" and also as "dainty stucco, tile roofed homes."[10] In reality, a range of styles was employed. Mediterranean themes compatible with the stucco-on-hollow-tile construction were utilized by the company's subsidiary, the Neponsit Building Com-

Neponsit's neoclassical entrance gates and many of its residences were designed by Kirby & Petit. Brooklyn Public Library, Brooklyn Collection

Neponsit Realty Company's handsome office on site could be reached by 1912 by trolley, steamboat, motor, or carriage. Courtesy Museum of the City of New York, the Byron Company Collection, 93.1.1.2920

pany, whereas the bungalows reflected Craftsman and other influences. Standard plans prepared by the architects could be used only four times within Neponsit, although purchasers could furnish their own designs.[11] Planted or "parked" medians similar to those employed a decade earlier at Prospect Park South graced Rockaway Beach Boulevard and other streets.

In addition to the ocean beach, amenities included the Neponsit Club, built in 1912 on Jamaica Bay, which was rapidly emerging as a center for yachting following the establishment of the fashionable Belle Harbor Yacht Club (1905) just to the east. Designed in the Colonial Revival style, the Neponsit Club had a billiard room, a bowling

alley, tennis courts, and a pier where pleasure craft could be moored. It soon became the center of community events sponsored by the company and an important promotional tool. In the spring of 1913, Frank Bailey hosted a well-attended outing and dinner there for the Brooklyn Board of Real Estate Brokers.

Neponsit was a popular community from the outset. Fifty houses either built on spec by the company or made to order for plot owners were in various stages of completion by the fall of 1911. *Brooklyn Life* reported that twenty families had been in residence at Neponsit that summer, the majority of whom intended to live there year round. Two years later, seventy residences had been completed,

despite the malaise in Long Island real estate following the opening of the L.I.R.R.'s East River railroad tunnels. By 1914, the year the *Brooklyn Daily Eagle* reported that Rockaway operations were leading the suburban market, the company was ready to stage the first in a series of auctions of the less desirable plots, a typical phenomenon of the residential park development process.[12] Two hundred eighty-five lots, including fifty-nine on Jamaica Bay and three completed cottages, went on the block on Decoration Day. A final sale of the unsold lots took place in August 1919.[13] The Neponsit Realty Company, which had also sold 248 acres in 1912 at the west end of its property for the tidy sum of $1,250,000 to the city, which had long considered

establishing a public beach there, was now ready to wrap up its affairs.

In 1917, however, a grand jury investigating the sale to the city of the property known as Seaside Park (later Jacob Riis Park) and Dreamland, the Coney Island amusement park Reynolds had built, indicted the ex-senator for perjury. The alleged offense had been committed five years earlier, in June 1912, when Reynolds appeared at the condemnation hearings for the Rockaway park as a realty expert for Neponsit Realty, testifying that he didn't have an interest in the property. The district attorney maintained, however, that he held at least a 20 percent interest in the company at that time.[14] By October 1917, the Neponsit sale indictments

had widened to include Bailey, his trusted lieutenant William H. Greve, vice president of Neponsit Realty, and Charles O'Malley, a real estate expert for the city, all of whom were arraigned on charges of conspiracy to defraud the city. "Tammany lie," claimed John Purroy Mitchel, the reform mayor and a friend of Reynolds, who was running for reelection that fall against a Tammany candidate, noting that his comptroller had taken "the extraordinary precaution of having an auction to protect the city's interest."[15] The indictments were never brought to trial and were dismissed in 1920, a Supreme Court justice citing the "reasonable presumption that there was no evidence . . . upon which a conviction could be had."[16] The prospect of a lucrative sale to the city, however, may explain Reynolds's early departure from Neponsit Realty. "Wherever Reyn-

olds is, there is trouble,"[17] Bailey once commented about his turbulent partner, and Neponsit may have been a classic example of his sitting on the lid. It was also illustrative of the way politics and real estate became intertwined as the city expanded and the intense competition for desirable tracts became a high rollers' game.[18]

Neponsit's streets continued to fill in during the 1920s as the remaining plots were built up, but as was the case with a number of residential parks, the clubhouse did not survive the departure of the developers for long. Closing in 1925, it was torn down in 1935.[19]

The Neponsit Property Owners' Association incorporated in 1919 and was soon playing an important role in defending the community's interests, winning, in the 1930s, a landmark case concerning the right of a homeowners' association to foreclose on a lien for unpaid annual maintenance fees and damages when the city condemned the ocean frontage. As the association nears its centennial, it continues its defense of the eleven-block community's interests and character, maintaining the "parked" medians (or island malls, as they are now called) on the boulevard and 142nd and 147th streets. Though time has wrought some changes, including the removal of Kirby & Petit's classical gateway, which decades ago proved to be a traffic hazard, and unsympathetic alterations to some original houses, much of the original building fabric is surprisingly intact. "The Riviera of the Rockaways," as Neponsit is sometimes called, continues to be the upscale summer and year-round community conceived by its creators. It has been home to two mayors of the City of New York—Abraham Beame, who rented there, and William O'Dwyer—and remains one of its borough's most desirable residential areas.

19
GONDOLAS IN COPIAGUE

VICTOR PISANI, ISAAC MEISTER, AND THE CREATION OF AMERICAN VENICE, 1925–1929

MARY CASCONE

Venice on Long Island—a residential development modeled after the celebrated "City of Canals"—promised a unique lifestyle, incorporating traditional architectural and cultural elements of the romantic Adriatic city into a modern American suburb. Before the close of the 1920s, the American Venice Corporation transformed marshland into a community for New York City residents and real estate investors looking to escape the crowded metropolis. Touting "Your 'Little Castle' in American Venice," the company courted potential home buyers:

> Now you can have a little castle all your own on the sun-lit shores of the Great South Bay of Long Island. A cozy Venetian Villa in American Venice—an hour's ride from New York City. A place where your children, healthy and happy, may continue to thrive in their growth, enjoying every outdoor sport summer and winter. Just think of such a home in a real Venetian setting—away from the maelstrom of the city! Broad winding canals, a beautiful lagoon, imported gondolas, graceful arched bridges, charming Italian gardens, wide-paved boulevards and a wonderful bathing beach on the Bay. Everything making for beauty, culture and the joy of living—all within the reach of the man with a moderate income.[1]

The project was bold and drew curiosity seekers at its debut. Although the stock market crash of 1929 curtailed the growth of the community, the originators of American Venice succeeded in producing many of the features they promised. Today, the neighborhood is a mix of architectural styles, a few dating back to its inception, and interest in the community's celebrated history remains strong.

The very name *American Venice* evoked sentiments of "Old World" Europe amid "New World" America. Advertisements proclaimed: "Old Venice modernized in America!" This fusion of old and new also applied to the creators of American Venice, immigrants Victor Pisani and Isaac Meister. Born in Rome, Victor Pisani (ca. 1879–1941) came to the United States as a young man. His mother, the Marchese Leoni, came from an old noble family,[2] and Victor was the namesake of his paternal ancestor Vettore Pisani, the venerated fourteenth-century admiral who commanded the Venetian fleet during the war with the Genoese and was credited with saving the Adriatic city.

Looking back on his arrival at Ellis Island on June 12, 1893, Isaac Meister (ca. 1879–1936) described himself as a fourteen-year-old Russian Jew with thirty kopeks in his pocket (enough money to feed himself for about two days). He quickly found work at a French steam laundry and adopted the language spoken by his co-workers. He thought that he had been learning English, but soon discovered that he had been absorbing Italian![3] His ability to speak several languages, however, turned out to be an asset in his real estate career.

How Pisani and Meister met is unknown.

Though they came from differing backgrounds, they both spoke both Italian and English, were the same age, and, apparently, shared an acumen for the burgeoning field of New York City real estate. By 1905, both men were among the directors of the Prince Realty Co., based in Manhattan[4] and became principals of other realty companies, including Enrico V. Pescia & Co.,[5] Arrochar Park Realty Co.,[6] Meister & Bache Realty Company,[7] and Pisani Brothers & Co. However, the entity with which they were primarily associated was Meister Builders, formed in 1914, with Isaac Meister as president and Victor Pisani as vice president. The new company also included Max Bache and Eugene M. Kramaroff as officers.[8] Meister Builders' vast holdings and real estate transactions spanned all five boroughs of New York City and parts of New Jersey. Operating as property owners/sales brokers, the company purchased hundreds of acres of undeveloped land and bought, sold, and built all types of dwellings, from seaside bungalows and one- to three-family homes to "bachelor apartment houses,"[9] six-story tenements, and high-rise apartment buildings. It was not until 1925 that Meister Builders ventured east of New York City. Along the Great South Bay in the Town of Babylon, at Copiague, they purchased 364 acres of land with plans for their largest and most innovative enterprise, a Venice for America.[10]

The property chosen for their novel community was a peninsula known as Copiague Neck, which is framed by Strong's Creek on the east and

Great Neck Creek on the west, both flowing into the bay. The northern border, Montauk Highway, was reportedly built along Native American trails; the settlement of the neck by Europeans was documented in the 1658 "Indian Deed of Three Necks, Southside," between Grand Sachem Wyandance and Henry Whitney.[11]

From colonial times to the nineteenth century, the lands along Long Island's South Shore were used for gathering salt hay grass for livestock. By the late 1800s, the South Shore bustled with new residents, and Copiague Neck was partitioned among a handful of new owners. By 1910, Copiague Neck was acquired and consolidated into one parcel by the Copiag Land Company, which sold the prop-

An advertisement for "Your 'Little Castle' in American Venice," which debuted in the New York Times *on March 14, 1926.*

Victor Pisani. Courtesy
Teresa Pisani

*An aerial view of
American Venice, ca.
1926, showing its stretch
from the bustling Montauk
Highway to the Great
South Bay.* Courtesy
Calandrino and Natalie
Families

erty to the newly formed American Venice Corp. on September 16, 1925.[12] Just a few years prior to the sale, the unpopulated bay front property had supposedly been used as a United States Army Air Corps aviation training field.[13]

Immediately after the American Venice Corp. purchased the property, news of their project began to appear in local newspapers, with headlines such as "Big Project Is Little Venice"[14] and "Rival of Venice to Be Built on Long Island."[15] Details of their grand plans began to emerge; they boasted that they would spend $10 million on the project, complete with imported gondolas, a 240-foot-wide

lagoon, and "2,000 houses of Venetian type from plans of an architect who is now in Italy completing his sketches with local 'color.'"[16] Appealing to the modest buyer, they initially stated that each house would sell for no more than $5,000. Underscoring the development's architectural theme, they asserted that all structures would be required to reflect Italian architecture.

The official start of construction took place on September 29, 1925, and "was heralded far and wide" by the Manhattan dailies "as one of the biggest developments Long Island has ever witnessed."[17] A "large gathering of prominent New

One of the Venetian-style bridges spanning the Santa Barbara Canal, amid construction, ca. 1926. Courtesy Marie and Louis Steinbrecher

York and Brooklyn citizens," the press reported, was present "when the first shovelful of earth was removed from the site of the Venetian Lagoon."[18]

Venice's Piazza San Marco features a single column crowned by a winged lion, the traditional emblem of the city and symbol of St. Mark, its patron saint. On an ornate plaza at the head of the American Venice's Grand Canal, a pair of columns topped by winged lions was installed, flanking two real estate administration buildings.

Original designs indicate that at least five Venetian-style bridges were planned for the development, "each one of which [was] patterned after Venetian architecture and represent[ed] some well-known bridge in Venice."[19] Under the direction of Alfred C. Janni,[20] portrayed as a "noted architect and authority on Venetian architecture," the first one planned was described as a steel-and-concrete replica of Venice's famed Ponte della Paglia, or Straw Bridge, which spans the Rio di Palazzo near the Ducal Palace.[21] However, there is evidence that only two bridges were completed: those constructed along East Riviera and West Riviera drives, which flank American Venice's Grand Canal and join the north and south sections across the east–west Santa Barbara Canal. Though Janni has been credited with the design, construction of the Riviera Drives' Venetian-style bridges and the winged-lion columns is attributed to Donald McPherson of Lindenhurst, described as "a master plasterer who had learned his craft in Scotland."[22]

The first set of filed development plans reveals that the designers intended to build fourteen "finger" canals around the perimeter of the neck and two principal canals that would intersect in the center of the community, creating four residential quadrants.[23] Within a few months, however,

those plans were abandoned; the revised plan called for just three canals, carving the land into five sectors. The design change decreased the amount of dredging required while adding to the number of building lots. East Riviera and West Riviera drives flank the administration plaza and run north–south along the Grand Canal. Each drive has a single Venetian-style bridge, and the two drives provide the only access to the southern residential "isles" of the community. The two northern sections have direct access to Montauk Highway. Most east–west streets run on both sides of the Grand Canal, as indicated by their names, such as Alhambra Avenue East and Alhambra Avenue West.

The first canal to be excavated at American Venice was the "Canal Grande," or Grand Canal, stretching from Merrick Road in the north to the Great South Bay. At the canal's north end is the Laguna San Marco (St. Mark's Lagoon), in the center of which was an island with a domed gazebo, where bands performed for residents and visitors. Mirroring it at the south end was another island and gazebo, the Rialto, named for the famous Ponte di Rialto (Rialto Bridge), which spans Venice's Grand Canal. The Santa Barbara Canal, connecting the Copiague and Great Neck creeks, runs east and west, and the Canal Lugano extends from the Santa Barbara Canal to the Great South Bay.

The first of many gondolas arrived in April 1926, a month before the grand opening: "Four of the fleet of 20 gondolas which have been ordered for the American Venice development," the Amityville Record reported, "arrived from Italy, where they were built, on the S.S. 'Lucia.'"[24] Prospective home buyers were whisked from the administration plaza by gondola for a survey of the development,

and gondola rides for residents continued through the 1930s.

Some of the street names were of Italian origin (Doges, Lido, Piave, Riviera, and Venetian); others were of Spanish or Mediterranean origin (Alhambra, Buena Vista, Granada, and Miramar); but the majority reference the seaside (Clearwater, Halcyon, Saltaire, and Seacrest).

Early photographs indicate that the first homes built in American Venice were five two-story Mediterranean-style residences, with tile roofs and arches punctuating the façade, on the south side of Alhambra Avenue West. Located just to the west of the administration plaza, they were most likely model homes and, being somewhat larger than other houses of that period, they may have been examples of the more expensive styles available.

Announcements of home construction began to appear in April 1926, when it was reported that Palermo Construction Corp. would build "approximately 100 dwelling houses [following] the Venetian style of architecture set . . . for all buildings in the development."[25] Building lots of 20 x 100 feet were offered for between $600 and $700, and a minimum of two lots was necessary for home construction. Newspaper reports indicated that Palermo's Venetian-style houses would contain "six rooms and bath, attractive porch, tile roof, wrought iron balcony on [a] lot of 40 x 100 feet." In addition, property ownership included "waterfront rights as well as gondola and bathing privileges."[26]

Deeds from the American Venice Corp. and its subsidiaries contained ten paragraphs of building and property restrictions for individual property owners, including "the right to use in common with other owners of property . . . the water ways,

seashore and streets" in the community. Buildings could not be placed on lots less than 40 feet wide, or closer than 20 feet from the street. Garages, boathouses, and other outbuildings were required to be set back at least 50 feet from the street, and "outside toilets" were prohibited. Houses built on "lots in Blocks lettered A, B, J and K and all lots in Blocks numbered 1 to 8 inclusive" were required to be valued at no less than $5,000; all other houses were to be valued at no less than $3,500. Flat roofs were specifically restricted. All buildings, including outbuildings, were required to have "what is generally known as 'cottage roofs,'" and furthermore it was decreed that "no building or other structure, shall be erected or maintained . . . until the plans, specifications and color" were approved by the American Venice Corp. The covenants and restrictions were binding on both the American Venice Corp. and property owners until January 1, 1940, at which time it was stated that "they shall cease and terminate."[27]

In the two northern quadrants, business buildings were permitted only on Montauk Highway, Miramar Boulevard, and Buena Vista Boulevard. In the southern portion, businesses were permitted along the Great South Bay and Marine Avenue East and West. Original plans included the construction of a bridge over the Canal Lugano along Marine Avenue East, but it was never built, and there is no evidence that any commercial buildings were erected there among the residential properties.[28]

In preparation for the May 1926 grand opening, construction updates specified the completion of "875,000 cubic yards of dirt for landscaping and fill; 800,000 square feet of sidewalks; 100,000 lineal feet of streets; 26,000 lineal feet of bulkheading;

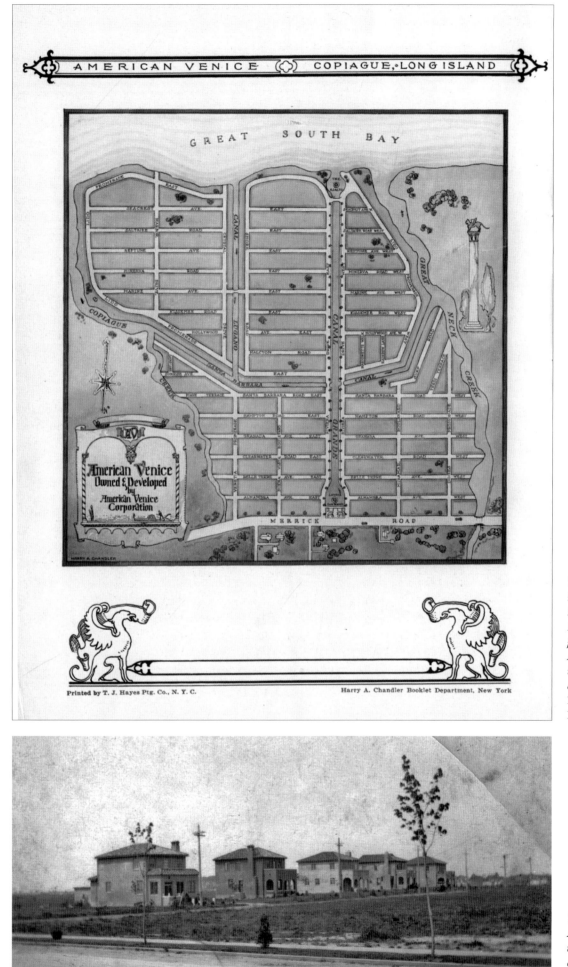

This map, which appeared in a brochure designed by the Harry A. Chandler Booklet Dept, ca. 1925, presents the layout of American Venice, with its three intersecting canals. Courtesy Queens Borough Public Library, Long Island Division

These five houses on Alhambra Avenue West were likely the first houses constructed in American Venice. Courtesy Marie and Louis Steinbrecher

13,000 lineal feet of broad canals; 8,000 lineal feet of beach frontage; Highways, Electricity, Water, etc."[29] In a full-page advertisement two months before the official opening, the company declared the first section of the development completely sold.[30]

In the summer of 1926, American Venice advertised the affordability of its residences as "Ideal villa homes containing every modern convenience and improvement [for] $8500, payable in monthly installments averaging $60 per month, reducing principal and interest, and a small initial amount."[31] The following year, home-building reports cited plans for fifty dwellings "of the five-room-and-bath type, to sell for $6,750," emphasizing that "[s]trict adherences will be required to building restrictions in all coming construction. All buildings must be built of stucco, stone or brick, and size restrictions have been made to assure ample lawns."[32] Later that same year, accompanying a charming sketch of an American Venice home, was this proposal: "$250 Cash Gives You Immediate Possession of this Venetian Home. Balance $65 per month. Includes interest and principal until paid. Five rooms and tiled bath. All improvements, steam heat, Spanish tile roof. Large plot. Few feet from waterfront. Price $6,950." It carried the new tag line "American Venice, L.I.—The Homeland Charmingly Different."[33]

Amid the optimism of the Roaring Twenties, the American Venice Corp. was keenly aware of how to attract an urban population seeking culture and recreation, for health and pleasure, as reflected in their advertising. Shortly before the community's grand opening, Henry Tudor Mason, president of

the All National Association, a consortium "composed of the highest type of artists, musicians, singers, authors and persons of wealth who are attracted to art," proposed creating "'Masonia,' a home colony for artists" at American Venice.[34] The renowned Italian operatic tenor Giovanni Martinelli made headlines with his purchase at American Venice. The *New York Times* announced, "Mr. Martinelli has purchased a plot 100 by 100 feet on Riviera Drive East and Belle Terre Avenue, overlooking Laguna San Marco, for improvement with a villa for his own occupancy."[35]

While American Venice Corp. was transforming swampland into a residential idyll, its greatest promotional tool was pictorial advertising. Advertising images were circulated long before the completion of buildings, streets, and canals, promulgating the mystique of an American Venice. Just a few weeks after the first bulldozer appeared on the site, the marketing campaign began, encouraging prospective buyers to examine the unique summer enclave suitable for year-round living. The first pictorial advertisement appeared in the *New York Times* on October 18, 1925, shortly after construction began, offering this vision: "A turquoise lagoon under aquamarine sky! Lazy gondolas! Beautiful Italian Gardens! Is it Venice on the Adriatic? No—Venice in America! Soon this will be a reality."[36] The sketch revealed an administration building with an ornate arched window and a lagoon with a small gazebo. Stylish people strolled along the plaza as a gondolier paddled in the moonlight. The following month, four more unique advertisements were published, featuring sketches of large Venetian vil-

Artist's depiction of a "typical Italian Villa at American Venice." The sketch was featured in an advertising booklet designed by Frank Kiernan & Co., New York, 1927. Courtesy Agnes Scheuermann

A 1920s home located on Venetian Promenade, owned by Edward and Lena Ligouri. The house is similar to the artist's rendering of a "typical Italian Villa at American Venice," as featured in the advertising booklet. Courtesy Hugo Mascari

las and a rendering of the planned administration plaza. The last of these ads invited prospective buyers to "Come Out and Inspect American Venice on Thanksgiving Day."[37]

For city dwellers concerned about traveling to the South Shore of Long Island, transport via the Long Island Railroad was promoted by offering free railroad tickets and special trains to the Lindenhurst station, where buses would shuttle visitors to American Venice.[38] Bus rides from Broadway and 42nd Street in Manhattan directly to American Venice were also offered, and prospective buyers were invited to write away for a "beautifully illustrated, free book describing the American Venice

development [including railroad] tickets without charge or obligation."[39] Its location on the well-traveled Merrick Road (now Montauk Highway) was also an advantage to city dwellers motoring out to the countryside. By the time of American Venice's inception, Sunrise Highway had been extended to the western border of Suffolk County and Robert Moses had established plans to create the Southern State Parkway, both only a few miles from American Venice.

Advertisements listed M. Michaels Realty & Construction Corp. as the sole selling agents. In a November 1925 newspaper article extolling the bright future of the Long Island real estate market, Michaels wrote, "As one of the highest spots on the Great South Bay, some two years ago we recognized that this land represented extremely valuable waterfront property, and just the place for a Venice in America."[40]

The marketing campaign appears to have been effective. The unique development attracted investors before a single building was completed or the first canal dug. Decades later, waterfront property became universally accepted as precious real estate, but before American Venice, uninhabited marshland was not prized for residential dwelling. One local newspaper marveled at the development's initial success, contrasting it with the property's former status: "American Venice on Montauk Highway has become a mecca of homeseekers during the last few weeks. People who would not pay $1200 an acre for property five years ago are now eagerly purchasing plots for this amount. Twelve real estate salesmen worked throughout Sunday in the heavy rain signing up purchasers in that development."[41]

Just a few months into the project, American Venice was so renowned that neighboring developers sought to capitalize on their proximity to it. Announcing the sale of the Schuler estate, "one of the last available parcels in Copiague," the property was described as "immediately adjacent [to] the Meister Builders' development, known as the American Venice,"[42] and a full-page advertisement for the Hawkins Estate development described it as "opposite and adjoining American Venice."[43]

From the fall of 1925 through the summer of 1926, twenty-six advertisements appeared in the *New York Times*, including seventeen unique illustrated ads, most of which ran in the Sunday real estate section. Though other new communities sprang up along Long Island's South Shore in the mid-1920s, few came close to matching American

The first newspaper advertisement for the new American Venice development appeared in the New York Times *on October 18, 1925.*

Visitors at the American Venice administration plaza. Courtesy Teresa Pisani

The picturesque cover of the American Venice advertising brochure designed by the Harry A. Chandler Booklet Dept., ca. 1925. Courtesy Queens Borough Public Library, Long Island Division

Venice in sheer quantity of enticing advertisements.[44]

The advertisements were clearly aimed at attracting New York City buyers. A few articles about the progress of the real estate development appeared in local papers. But, with the exception of a single advertisement published the week before the official grand opening on May 23, 1926, none of the pictorial advertisements were published locally.[45] Rather, all advertising appeared in New York City periodicals: the *New York Times*, the *New-York Tribune*, and the *Brooklyn Daily Eagle*. A typical ad read:

> A perfect home community, combined with a marvelous all-year-round playground. A garden spot where the whole family can grow up in the healthiest and happiest atmosphere to be found near Manhattan. Comfortably removed from the disadvantages of the city's turmoil and congestion. Convenient to all commercial, educational, social and recreational facilities.[46]

American Venice flourished through the end of the 1920s. But on July 16, 1930, less than ten months after the 1929 stock market crash, the principals of the American Venice Corp., Isaac Meister and Victor Pisani, filed bankruptcy petitions.[47] By this time, both Meister and Pisani were involved in various New York City hotels. In 1927, operating as Meister Builders, and sometimes as Meitani Realty, they purchased the Hotel Raleigh[48] and leased the Hotel President.[49] The following year, they opened the largest of their hotels, the twenty-two-story

Hotel Victoria.[50] and in 1929 the hotels Plymouth[51] and Emerson.[52]

The economics of the 1930s led to a variety of new home designs in American Venice. In 1930, Venetian Home Builder[53] announced plans for new steel-framed cottages,[54] with a ten-year home financing plan.[55] By the next year, Venetian American Properties, Inc., was formed and assumed management of the development and ownership of all unsold properties; neither Meister nor Pisani was mentioned in association with the new managing company.

Victor Pisani passed away on April 17, 1941. His obituary described his association with Isaac Meister and their hotel operations, and stated, "Mr. Pisani also was a developer of the American Venice tract in Long Island."[56] Isaac Meister had died five years earlier, on October 3, 1936. His obituary highlighted his developments in Brooklyn and Staten Island, his hotels, and his philanthropy benefiting Zionist and Jewish causes, but made no mention of his American Venice connection.[57]

The American Venice Civic Association was incorporated on July 21, 1942, and soon thereafter acquired the community clubhouse and bathing beach from Venetian American Property, Inc.[58] The *Lindenhurst Star* reported that the clubhouse would be renamed the Venice Community House and Yacht Club and that the Civic Association had "elaborate plans for entertainment of various kinds," and entitled owners to "exclusive use of the property."[59] Around this time, as old-time residents

A postcard features a photograph of an American Venice beach along the Great South Bay. Courtesy Town of Babylon, Office of Historic Services

The twin buildings in the administration plaza were used as sales offices for the burgeoning community. Courtesy Teresa Pisani

often recall, actors Steve Allen and Jayne Meadows lived in the community, and Guy Lombardo and his orchestra played in the gazebos on the islands in the Grand Canal.

Venetian American Property, Inc. sold the administration plaza and Laguna San Marco in 1953 to a private owner.[60] The site was converted into a retail boat business and private marina. In 1961, the two former administration buildings were joined by an extension to create one larger building.[61] Early in 1964, Suffolk County acquired from Venetian American Property, Inc. the eighty-seven-acre man-made southeast island of the community, which it designated as a bird sanctuar.[62] The island remains the largest undeveloped parcel along the Great South Bay in western Suffolk County.[63]

In the 1980s, there was mounting concern that the two Venetian-style bridges along East Riviera and West Riviera drives were no longer suitable for vehicular traffic. When the former town superintendent of highways proposed replacing them with flat-steel bridges, the American Venice Civic Association, joined by citizens and other community groups, fought to save the original spans, which were successfully restored by the Town of Babylon in 1989.[64] Historic district status was given to American Venice by the Town of Babylon in 2007, citing the street and canal layouts, the Riviera Drive bridges, and the administration plaza as its distinctive historic features. In 2011, the Society for the Preservation of Long Island Antiquities placed the administration plaza and Laguna San Marco on its List of Endangered Historic Places.[65]

Today, few original stucco houses can be found amid the hundreds of homes erected since the development's inception. The Rivera Drive bridges remain, as do the two age-worn winged-lion columns. The frames of the twin administration buildings still stand, but their once elaborate details are hidden under a contemporary façade. Despite these changes, American Venice endures, as envisioned by its founders, as "a place where [our families,] healthy and happy, continue to thrive in their growth, . . . summer and winter, . . . in a real Venetian setting— away from the maelstrom of the city."

20
OLD FIELD SOUTH

RICHARD F. WELCH

Of the many developers active on Long Island from the 1920s to the 1950s, none had as much combined experience in residential building, historical reconstruction, community improvement, and philanthropy as Frank Melville Jr. (1860–1935) and his son, Ward Melville (1887–1977). Ward Melville's most famous project was the restoration of Stony Brook Village, an undertaking that included not only the rehabilitation of original eighteenth- and nineteenth-century structures but also the building of Stony Brook Crescent, a shopping center in Colonial style. Late in life, he was instrumental in establishing the State University of New York at Stony Brook. Less well remembered are his planned-community developments.

The Melville presence in the North Shore community known as the Three Villages (Old Field, Stony Brook, and Setauket) began in 1901, when Frank Melville Jr. bought property in Old Field, joining a summer colony of wealthy city dwellers.[1] Frank Melville's country house, Sunwood, was completed in 1919; his son, Ward, purchased and renovated a property that was dubbed Widewater a few years later.

Both father and son were enamored of the landscape, architecture, and traditions of the Three Villages and were determined to nurture, preserve, and restore the community and its colonial past. In their restorations they were driven more by aesthetics and social interests than by profits. The senior Melville embraced the aesthetics and principles of the Colonial Revival movement, which waxed strongly in the United States in the wake of the 1876 Centennial. He passed on his passion to his son, who in many ways fulfilled his vision. Their love of the Three Villages propelled their activities, many of them philanthropic, but they were also determined to carry out their development and restoration projects on their own terms and according to their own standards. Indeed, the Melvilles and their affluent neighbors quickly assumed control of the area, creating the Old Field Improvement Association in 1902 to construct or improve roads leading to Setauket and the Stony Brook Railroad depot.[2]

Frank Melville Jr., whose wealth derived from shoe manufacturing, founded the Nassakeag Land Company in 1925 as the corporate entity to purchase, design, and market his real estate holdings. In 1940, Ward Melville set up the Suffolk Improvement Company, which apparently absorbed Nassakeag's operations.[3] As the holding company and owner of the 250 acres south of the original village of Old Field, Suffolk Improvement functioned as the legal entity through which the Melvilles created Old Field South, their upscale planned community."[4]

According to Suffolk Improvement Company pamphlets, residents of the affluent Village of Old Field, led by Frank and Ward Melville, acquired the Old Field South property over a period of thirty years.[5] Though profit was clearly one of their objec-

tives, their avowed goal was "protecting their own shore estates in Old Field" by controlling the extent and nature of development, and selling homes "to desirable residents only"[6] "Desirable" translated into "discriminating people that would have been acceptable to [Frank Melville] and his neighbors."[7] Frank and Ward Melville may have seen suburbanization as inevitable, but they intended to shape and dictate its nature in their own bailiwick.

The projected community was to retain the rustic, low-density feel of the nearby estate areas through a master plan that was drawn up by the Olmsted Brothers, the highly regarded landscape architectural firm from Boston. The Olmsted Brothers' plan laid out roads, parks, and open spaces, as well as grounds for a club—Old Field Club—which was intended to become the focal point of the nascent community's social life.

The Suffolk Improvement Company contended that "careful study has been given to the legal means of thoroughly safeguarding purchasers in their common exclusive rights to the use of the Sound beach, the pool, and waterways, the tennis courts, the clubhouse, the parks and roads, and against the danger of injury to their homes from future building as well as uncongenial neighbors."[8] In other words, the zoning, the selection of potential buyers, and access to amenities were all carefully monitored and screened.

A board of governors, effectively Suffolk Improvement's zoning/architecture committee, was in charge of approving the design, location, and color of every house in Old Field South. According to Old Field South publicity, the committee consisted of officers of Suffolk Improvement and its engineering subsidiary, the Spaulding Construction Company. Walter T. Spaulding, president of the eponymous firm, was also a Suffolk Improvement vice president. The Olmsted Brothers had a representative on the board, and Richard H. Smythe lent his talents as the "Consulting Architect." Smythe (1889–1965), had been Ward Melville's Columbia University roommate and later became Melville's corporate architect, working closely with him throughout his career. Frank Melville, Suffolk Improvement's president at its inception, or Ward, who was the organization's treasurer until he took full control after his father's death in 1935, probably represented the company on the board. Harry E. Robinson, a member of E.C. Benedict & Co., a stock brokerage, was another possible representative of the owners. The board's intertwined professional and personal relationships ensured that the new community would protect and promote Melville interests.

As landowners of Old Field South, the partners controlled all aspects of the prospective community—landscape and housing design, sales, community demographics, and much of the internal social dynamic as well. Ward Melville, who oversaw the development during its major years of growth, was careful to assign the sales operations to trusted friends and area residents. Initially, the L.C. Clarke Agency handled sales for Old Field South, but by the mid-1930s the real estate agency of Carl J. Heyser Jr., Melville's personal lawyer, became Suffolk Improvement's marketing arm. Another important player was Bayles Minuse, member of an old Setauket clan, who was an investor in several of Melville's projects and was sometimes described as Melville's "right-hand man." Even plumbers and house inspectors were drawn from those close to the principals.

Although the Olmsted Brothers' master plan was not completed until 1929, scattered references suggest that Melville and his partners were involved in preliminary work on the development as early as 1924, when Smythe submitted designs for some of the houses. Home building, originally the domain of Spaulding Construction, was well under way in 1929, with a number of homes and the clubhouse in progress, and the first promotional brochures available for distribution.

The timing of the Old Field South development was less than fortuitous, as it coincided with the stock market crash and onset of the Great Depression. Nevertheless, the project went forward, and fourteen were homes ready for buyers by May 1934.[10] The following April, Carl Heyser announced that the first group of houses had sold and five more were in the works. Heyser optimistically declared that the "long awaited break in the suburban real estate market had arrived," and predicted, "We are destined for a period of home construction unrivalled in its intensity and breadth."[11] Heyser attributed the new "boom" to a shortage of housing, especially single-family units.[12]

How quickly new homes went up, and how successfully Melville and Suffolk Improvement were able to buck the dismal economics of the 1930s, is unclear. What is certain, however, is that the

project, well funded and ably managed, did not falter, continuing to grow throughout the 1930s and 1940s and into the great suburban boom of the 1950s.

Though marketed as exclusive, Old Field South was intended to be affordable for the middle and professional classes. The Melvilles and their partners attempted to project a sense of tradition and venerability by limiting house types to those "built thoughtfully on Colonial lines"[13] and extolled the community's "English country atmosphere."[14] And though plot sizes as small as a quarter acre were available, Suffolk Improvement's agents were careful to explain that nearly all the plots were wooded, creating "the impression of larger sites than the actual acreage—more like the impressive large estates that surround the property."[15]

Like the promotional material of many, if not most, of the Long Island developments of the time, Old Field South's lured prospective buyers with visions of an active, healthy, and secure lifestyle. In addition to the various sports available at the Old Field Club and the Stony Brook Yacht Club, nearby golfing, swimming, and sailing facilities were touted. Advertising also featured equestrian activities, and photographs of the Smithtown Hunt often appeared in brochures, along with whimsical drawings of unhorsed riders and frolicking foxes. The North Shore Horse Show, a three-day event marking "the peak of summer," was held on Old Field Club grounds, drawing a large number of the socially prominent from across Long Island.[16]

The clubhouse, clearly seen as a major drawing card, was also designed by Smythe and was erected on eight acres next to a tidal pool. Smythe's architectural style, which dominated the new community's appearance, was clearly displayed in the structure. According to architectural historian Nicholas Langhart, the clubhouse reveals:

Olmsted Brothers' master plan for Old Field South. Collection of the Three Village Historical Society, L.I., NY

Old Field Club, designed by Richard Haviland Smythe, ca. 1930. Collection of the Three Village Historical Society, L.I., NY

Students of the Old Field South Country Day School, seen here outside the Old Field Club. Florenz Mahoney, Old Field police chief, is on the right and Ward Melville is at center. Collection of the Three Village Historical Society, L.I., NY

Smythe's interest in reducing the apparent size of the structure by avoiding continuous rooflines, fronting entrances with small porches, and employing plans of several wings, often set at angles to create a picturesque, "added-on" effect. He used these devices until the end of his career. The horse-show stable (1931), a low, simple U-shaped enclosure of about twenty-four horse stalls, prefigures the Stony Brook Crescent in its plan, and places emphasis on the center, which is topped by a cupola.[17]

Tennis courts adjoined the clubhouse, and cabanas were available on a section of Sound beach owned by the club. The Suffolk Improvement Company assured prospective residents that "no one not in every respect satisfactory to the membership of the Old Field Club will have the privilege of either joining the Club or buying property."[18]

The partners also pledged to cover any possible club deficits for at least five years. Organized as a not-for-profit membership association, the club held a twenty-five year lease at a "nominal rental" for three years, with fees rising thereafter. The membership could buy the entire property from the corporation at book value at any time. By appointing representatives to the club's board of governors, House and Grounds Committee, and Membership Committee, Suffolk Improvement exercised control over the club during its early years. It also reserved the right to make a limited number of regular mem-

berships available without the initiation fee. These were given to property buyers—subject, of course, to the individuals' election to the club.[19]

Suffolk Improvement explicitly and implicitly tailored its pitch for Old Field South to what might be called the "snob factor," that is, an appeal to those who aspired to join the ranks of the socio-economic elite and sought to demonstrate their status by acquiring the semblance of the affluent lifestyle, including an exclusive address. Promotional material released by Carl Heyser's real estate company commonly referred to Old Field South houses as "cottages"—conjuring up images of rustic English villages. Other releases described the development as "A fragment of New England on PEACEFUL Long Island."[20] The more overtly class-conscious terms *estates*, *small estate*, *pocket estate*, and *miniature estate* were used as well. Indeed, the entire community was touted as offering "Small Estates for Country Gentlemen."[21]

Exclusivity permeated Old Field South's brochures and pamphlets, making it clear that plots, homes, and club membership were all intertwined and reserved for "the right people," or "discriminating people that would be acceptable to [Melville] and his neighbors who had made their homes in Old Field many years before."[22] While somewhat apologetic about the hour-and-forty-minute commute from Pennsylvania Station to Stony Brook, Suffolk Improvement pointed out that the travel

time "is compensated for in part by the pleasant trip in club cars and by the fact that it aids in keeping away certain undesired elements."[23]

Additional guarantees of exclusivity were contained in restrictive covenants that were intended to govern Old Field South until 1950. After that date, the covenants were renewable for twenty-year terms, with the possibility of amendment or alteration by majority vote of the property owners. The covenants prohibited all but single-family homes and outlawed any commercial activity. All housing designs or alterations were subject to approval by the "grantors"—Suffolk Improvement. Moreover, the covenants forbade the use or occupation of residences "in whole or in part by any person of African or Asiatic descent or by any person not of the White or Caucasian race except that domestic servants, chauffeurs and gardeners of other than the White or Caucasian race may live on or occupy the premises when their employer resides at or occupies said premises."[24] In the parlance of the times, "Asiatic" may have been intended to bar Jews as well. In any event, Melville and his colleagues imposed a standard of homogeneity in terms of both class and race/ethnicity, a not uncommon practice at the time.[25]

The look and ambience of Old Field south owed much to the talents of Melville's favorite architect,

Richard Haviland Smythe, who earned a degree in architecture from Columbia in 1909. In addition to his work on Old Field South, which lasted from 1924 to 1956,[26] Smythe, whose offices were located in Manhattan, was directly involved in several other Melville enterprises, including the neo-colonial Stony Brook Crescent, the restored Three Village Inn (1939), and the reinterpreted—or reimagined—bridge, mill house, and post office in Setauket, which were incorporated into the Frank Melville Memorial Park, which Ward Melville donated to Setauket in 1937.

Although prospective buyers of property in Old Field South had the option of designing their own house, approval had to be obtained from the board of governors. Further conformity with the Melville-Smythe architectural vision was assured through "our architects and construction engineers [who] will carry out your own ideas without extra cost."[27]

Plots in the projected "estates" ranged from one-quarter to three-quarters of an acre. Most seem to have been built on a half acre.[28] Smythe's designs, generally derived from eighteenth-century models, included Cape Cods, generic two-story saltboxes, and hybrids that might have a two-story section with a Cape Cod–style addition. [fig. 5] He even designed one model as a "Substantial Bar Harbor Cottage." Costs varied depending on size. Prices listed in one selection of four houses from the 1930s ranged from $6,496 to 16,000.[29] Suffolk Improvement offered homes for a cash down payment, with the remainder to be paid off in monthly installments, or simply on a "terms arranged" basis.[30] One brochure stated that the houses described therein "cost on the average more than $23,000, without the land, and are offered much below cost, at $16,500, subject to change or withdrawal without notice."[31] It is hard to see how sales at such a loss could have been sustainable for any length of time, though in the midst of the Depression such measures might have been necessary to retrieve some capital.[32]

During the 1930s, at least, the names of new buyers were published in the papers. These included the then well-known radio commentator H. V. Kaltenborn, who purchased a house on Mt. Grey Road in 1938.

Old Field South was never Melville's only enterprise. Though he remained active overseeing the progress of the community, the focus of his attention shifted elsewhere.[33]

In 1940, Ward Melville announced his plans for the restoration/recreation of Stony Brook Village, a project his father had considered but not pursued.[34] Fittingly, he unveiled his proposal in the Three Village Inn, which opened in August 1939, following another Smythe restoration job. Melville was probably influenced by the Rockefellers' preservation/restoration of Colonial Williamsburg, which, from its inception in 1926, established the model for outdoor museums throughout the United States.[35] Indeed, he sometimes spoke of Stony Brook as his "living Williamsburg," referring to the fact that the village was an organic community inhabited by working- and middle-class people pursuing modern interests and professions, as opposed to Williamsburg's position as a frozen-in-time, tourist-dependent enclave.[36]

The restoration/reconfiguring of Stony Brook began in 1941 with the clearing of a block of buildings for a village center.[37] The Colonial Revival Stony Brook Crescent was erected in an arc on the high ground overlooking what became the village's major thoroughfare.[38] His publicly stated rationale for the village facelift was to create an aesthetically pleasing commercial hub that would enhance Stony Brook's prestige and foster "an increase in business."[39]

A January 1943 Suffolk Improvement balance sheet shows revenues from several projects, including a development at Rocky Point, the Three Village Inn, the Old Field Club, and, of course, Old Field South. The contracts receivable from the latter totaled $106,825.47, a healthy amount in 1940s dollars.[40] Old Field South also benefited from the great postwar suburban boom. A 1950 tabulation lists capital expenditures of $8,300, with eleven houses built and five sold.[41] Work on the development fell off as the fifties progressed, as most of the land had already been built on.[42]

Though Old Field South was designed and developed as a discrete community under the overall control of the Suffolk Improvement Company, it never achieved the status of an autonomous entity, as had the Incorporated Village of Old Field, and there is no evidence that Melville ever sought to have it operate as such.[43] The original covenants, drawn up in the 1930s, were intended to run for twenty-year periods and were extendable.[44] By the 1950s, the ethno-racial restrictions had vanished, and the documents carried standard restrictions mandating non-commercial, single-family structures and required approval for extensions, renovations, or alterations to the landscape.[45] On May 17, 1977, Melville transferred his remaining interests, titles, and rights in the community to the Old Field South Property Owners Association, which was then to enforce the remaining structural and landscape regulations independently.[46] Three weeks later he was dead.

In the last two decades of his life, Melville had busied himself with other enterprises.[47] His last major initiative was to provide the land that became the State University of New York at Stony Brook, now called the Stony Brook University. The deal for the 450-acre tract, estimated at $2,400,000 in 1960 dollars,[48] was concluded with a handshake with Governor Averell Harriman. Melville, whose commitment to his conception of the colonial rural character of the area was undiminished, envisioned an institution in an architectural style modeled after that of William and Mary in Williamsburg, Virginia. However, Harriman's successor, Nelson Rockefeller, favored contemporary designs, and Melville could only watch in dismay, if not disgust, as the university took on a radically different appearance.[49] Indeed, after his death, Melville's widow stated that it was the university, whose design and architecture ran so counter to his vision, that killed him.[50]

Perhaps. But north of Route 25A, in the Three Villages, his vision prevailed. Indeed, later developments undertaken by different companies were heavily influenced by Old Field South. The Nassakeag Ridge community, built by Paavo Elio's Quaker Ridge Corporation, followed the older community's pattern so consciously that they submitted their own architect's designs to Richard Haviland Smythe, "who must pass on all new construction and alterations contemplated by property owners there."[51]

In their concern for aesthetics and tradition, Ward Melville and his father had succeeded in preserving, and sometimes creating, the ambience and patina of the past that still characterizes so much of the Three Village area, sparing it from obliteration by tract housing and strip malls. This remains the Melvilles', especially Ward Melville's, enduring achievement. To paraphrase the epitaph above Sir Christopher Wren's tomb at St. Paul's Cathedral in London: if you seek their monument—just look around.

Ward Melville, ca. 1977, at his Stony Brook Crescent Colonial Revival Shopping Center. Collection of the Three Village Historical Society, L.I., NY

21
WHAT IF?

PLANNED COMMUNITIES
THAT MIGHT HAVE BEEN

ROBERT B. MacKAY

For all of the projects that reached fruition on Long Island during the Progressive Era, there were an equal number that failed. Three planned on a prodigious scale during the era and one in the late 1920s that would have received wide acclaim, had they been fully realized, were Beaux-Arts Park on Huntington Bay, Tangiers Manors in Mastic, New Versailles at Port Washington, and Midhamptons at Wainscott between Southampton and East Hampton. Beaux-Arts bears the closest resemblance to the residential parks that are the focus of this study. Tangiers would have been an American version of a European new town; New Versailles, a precursor of the garden-apartment phenomenon just then being introduced to the region by the Queensboro Corporation at Jackson Heights; and Midhamptons, a recreational mecca.

Beaux-Arts Park

The colorful Bustanoby brothers,[1] Basque restaurateurs and proprietors of Manhattan's celebrated Café des Beaux-Arts, came the closest to achieving their vision. André Bustanoby, who had studied architecture at the École des Beaux-Arts in Paris before immigrating to America and immersing himself in the hospitality industry, was well prepared to take on at least the first phase of their project on the shores of Huntington Bay. Aiming to create a "fashionable Elysium," he opened a restaurant worthy

of Monaco, where music could be heard every day and Neapolitan singers serenaded the guests from a launch on the bay in the evening. The Château des Beaux-Arts consisted of a casino (1905–7), bathing pavilions, lawn tennis courts, and a polo field. The Bustanobys also envisioned constructing a hotel to replace the old Locust Lodge, which served as the temporary hostelry. The grand scheme must have resonated with the architects of the casino, Delano & Aldrich, who worked in association with a French colleague, Maurice Prévot. The three architects, who had also studied at the École, were reported to have drawn inspiration from the Pré Catalan, the fashionable Parisian restaurant in the Bois de Boulogne.[2] The Bustanobys also sought to position their project as "an ideal rendezvous for automobiles and yachtsmen,"[3] complete with a large pier for yachts and a state-of-the-art garage that could accommodate fifty "motors," and thousands did come. In 1907, the *Brooklyn Daily Eagle* reported the remarkable sight of more than 250 automobiles parked there on a given Sunday,[4] and period photographs of the international motorboat races for the Harmsworth Trophy held on Huntington Bay in front of the casino depict a huge fleet of private yachts.

To the rear was Beaux-Arts Park, originally conceived as a 34-lot project when laid out by C. P. Darling, C.E., in 1908 and increased to 113 lots two years later, replete with curvilinear streets. By August 1911, the Bustanobys were able to

announce the sale of a number of lots in Beaux-Arts Park. The *Long-Islander* reported that roads named for famous French artists and writers were being opened up on a "rather unique and attractive plan" and that a contract had been signed with the Property Holders Realty Company to build a "number of stucco on hollow tile, French villas on one-third-of-an-acre plots combining in their construction the graceful beauty of La Belle France with all of the comfort and convenience of practical America."[5] Among the first buyers was Antoine "Tony" Martzolf, a Bustanoby protégé who would soon launch his own restaurant, the elegant Château des Tourelles at Long Beach. Yet a year later, the Commercial Trust Company of New York foreclosed on the entire Beaux-Arts property. The Bustanobys had gotten ahead of themselves, and Milton L'Ecluse, the well-known realtor whose country house was just to the east of the casino, had stepped in to acquire the sixty-five-acre property.[6] In 1915, L'Ecluse, whose firm often advertised itself during this period as club specialists, announced the formation of the Huntington Bay and Country Club, which would seek to take over the Beaux-Arts facilities, adding a nine-hole golf course by summer.[7] Half a decade after the foreclosure, however, the E. Belcher Hyde *Atlas of Suffolk County* (1917) indicated that little progress had been made on the residential park, now known as Huntington Bay Estates, with the streets renamed.[8] Five houses in a variety of styles had been built, three on a speculative basis by L'Ecluse, Washburn & Company or Wanser & Lewis, Huntington builders. Martzolf, whose Long Beach restaurant failed in 1913, does not appear as a landowner, and the only occupied residences were those of Stefano Berizzi, a principal in Ambrosio American, the silent film company, and a Dr. Coe.

Tangiers Manors

In August 1910, the *New York Times* reported on a project that was contemporary with the Bustanobys'. The purchase of a final parcel of land on the Great South Bay, sixty miles east of the city, brought to ten thousand acres the property owned by the Tangiers Manors Corporation. The vast tract assembled by the corporation had been acquired from heirs of William "Tangier" Smith, the holder of the seventeenth-century patent to the property known as the Manor of St. George, and was said to comprise more than thirty miles of waterfront on the ocean, bays, and rivers between Bellport and Mastic.[9]

The enormous sum of $4 million was to be spent on Tangiers, based on a plan reflecting "the latest ideas and experience of the German and English in town planning design."[10] Robert Anderson Pope, designer of the Jamestown Exposition—the 1907 Tercentennial—and a student of Frederick Law Olmsted Jr., was to be the land-

scape architect for the project, working in cooperation with a noted authority, Professor Stanley D. Adshead, director of the University of Liverpool's Department of Civic Design.[11] Tangiers' amenities were to include those commonly found at other Long Island residential parks of the era such as a clubhouse, eighteen-hole golf course, and bathing pavilions, but the scale of the endeavor, which also called for a steel and reinforced-concrete drawbridge across the Great South Bay that was to rise seventy-five feet over the water, a high-rise administration building, and a grand concourse extending five miles along the Great South Beach, was unprecedented east of Forest Hills. Tangiers was also being planned by a team that had a very different vision. Pope was a social progressive, an advocate of new towns on the European model to relieve urban congestion. The City Beautiful movement's narrow focus on aesthetics was anathema to Pope and his fellow progressives, such as Benjamin C. Marsh of the Committee on Congestion of Population in New York City. In comments to a U.S. Senate committee in 1909, Pope stated, "We have assumed without question that the first duty of city planning is to beautify," noting that contemporary park planning mainly benefited "the wealthy and leisure classes."[12] Period news accounts and advertisements suggest a centrally controlled project reflective of German

planning. Sites reserved for public buildings and land-use controls were to determine the location of commercial structures. An elaborate transportation system was to feature both boulevards and an electric trolley system, and houses were to be built at cost for those acquiring lots. How different Tangiers might have been from other planned communities will never be known, however. In 1915, the *New York Sun* observed that "little or no headway" had been made, and the following year the *Brooklyn Daily Eagle* reported that development planned on a "cyclopean" scale had been sold to a Bridgeport syndicate.[13]

New Versailles

Billed as a New World version of Versailles, to enable Americans to live like kings, a 1916 luxury development planned for the shores of Manhasset Bay [promised residents all the amenities of royal life. Designed by the distinguished architectural firm of Carrère & Hastings, New Versailles was the $30 million vision of a group of prominent artists, including J. Alden Weir, Frederick Mac-Monnies, Maxfield Parrish, Penrhyn Stanlaws, and Walter Russell, as a center for artistic creation and patronage that would make New York the art mecca of the world. Stanlaws and Russell, developers of Manhattan's Hotel des Artistes, a coopera-

tive apartment building for artists, gave the project credibility and were the principal catalysts. Hastings, whose recent commissions had included the New York Public Library and House and Senate office buildings in Washington, D.C., told the press it would be the greatest commission of his career and prepared plans that were placed on exhibit at the National Academy of Design. A marble palace of cooperative apartments, set amid extensive gardens with fountains by the sculptors Robert Aiken, Paul Bartlett, and Frederick MacMonnies, was to rise sixteen stories and extend nearly five city blocks. Amenities were to include everything imaginable, including forty-seven tennis courts, a pool for aquatic sports, a running track, a skating rink, equestrian facilities, indoor and outdoor theaters, and, for children, a Peter Pan house and Montessori school. Eligibility for ownership of the cooperative units, which were expected to sell for $10,000, and for membership in New Versailles' club was to be determined by a committee. Emphasis was also placed on transportation advantages. Though the apartment complex was only a stone's throw from the new Plandome railroad station, where club cars would be available, residents would also be able to opt for passage on commuting yachts from the community's dock or keep a "motor" in New Versailles' thousand-car garage. Significant press coverage accompanied

the announcement of the plans for New Versailles in May 1916. The *New York Sun*, *New York Times*, and *Brooklyn Daily Eagle* were among the papers following the story.[14] The *Eagle* reported that the syndicate had acquired, in nine transactions, more than 180 acres for the project, and in December of that year, that J. Stuart Blackton, co-founder of the silent film studio American Vitagraph, had become president of Dominion of Versailles, as the project was also known.[15] Although New Versailles was clearly a production fit for Hollywood, Blackton was an unusual choice. He probably traveled in the same circles as fellow U.K. émigré Penrhyn Stanlaws, who would soon embark on his own Hollywood career, but Blackton's involvement was rooted in events occurring three thou-

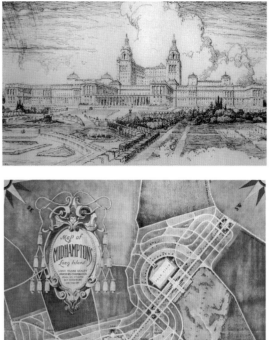

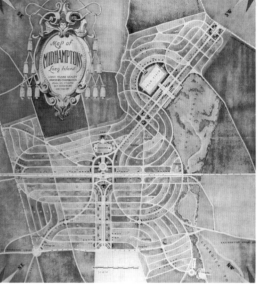

sand miles away. War had broken out two years earlier in Europe, an important market for Vitagraph, and the resulting loss of distributors led to the decline of the company, which Blackton left in 1917. Looking for new opportunities, he must have been intrigued with New Versailles' potential, but on April 6, 1917, the United States entered the war and any chance of financing such a colossal project must have expired with the hostilities. The artists' community was to remain an "air castle," as one news account termed it.[16] The area, which was only to be known on paper as New Versailles, is the location today of Manhasset Bay Estates at Port Washington.

Midhamptons

Designed in 1927 by Mann & MacNeille for the Manhattan-based Long Island Realty Investors Corporation, the huge Wainscott project [fig. 12] would have extended for thousands of acres from a central mall north of the Montauk Highway. Well versed in community planning, Horace B. Mann had studied architecture at Columbia University, winning a scholarship to continue his education in France and Italy. During World War I, he was a consulting architect in industrial housing for both

the Army and the United States Shipping Board. His partner, Perry R. MacNeille, was a founder and president of the City Planning Commission of Summit, New Jersey. Understanding the need for recreational amenities in community planning, which by the late 1920s was being espoused by groups such as the National Recreational Society, Mann & MacNeille envisioned playgrounds, athletic fields, pools, a golf course, beach facilities, and even a polo field. The plan, as Alastair Gordon has suggested, was a garden city concept reminiscent of the work of the great British planner Ebenezer Howard. Streets were laid out (today's East Gate and West Gate roads flanked the central mall), but the Depression ensued and Midhamptons, which might have transformed a good stretch of the South Fork, is known today only by the survival of the architects' wonderful plan.

The failure of these projects presents an interesting window into the boom-and-bust cycles of Long Island real estate during, and after, the Progressive Era, a distant mirror of our own times. In the first two decades of the twentieth century, developers had to contend with financial panics, overspeculation based on transportation improvements such as the L.I.R.R.'s East River tunnels, and the outbreak of war.

NOTES

Preface and Acknowledgments

1 Isaac Hicks to Mary E. Thompson, Ogontz, PA, March 7, 1900. Hicks Nursery Archives, Westbury, N.Y.

2 The Hamlet of Copiague: A Historical Snapshot, copiaguechamber.org/local-history/neighborhoods.htm#amityharbor

3 Richard Longstreth, "The Levitts, Mass-Produced Houses, and Community Planning in the Mid-Twentieth Century," in *Second Suburb: Levittown, Pennsylvania*, ed. Dianne Harris (Pittsburgh: University of Pittsburgh Press, 2010), pp. 123–74.

4 The Aquinas Honor Society, established in 1905 as a program for academically gifted sixth-, seventh-, and eighth-grade students at the Immaculate Conception School of Jamaica Estates, began with a challenge by their moderator to learn about the history of their school and has blossomed into an exploration of the origins of their parish and community. Over the past half decade, they have discovered, catalogued, preserved, and celebrated the remarkable history of Jamaica Estates.

The Residential Park Phenomenon on Long Island

1 As quoted in Susan L. Klaus, *A Modern Arcadia: Frederick Law Olmsted Jr. and the Plan for Forest Hills Gardens* (Amherst, MA: University of Massachusetts Press, 2004), p. 3.

2 Lewis lived at 20 Vanderventer Avenue in 1914 and 1915 while writing *The Trail of the Hawk*.

3 Burnett considered even the best hotels in Europe, but "strict economy in comparison." Christopher Morley, a Roslyn Estates resident for close to four decades, wrote many of his essays and novels in his studio, the "Knothole," behind his house at 38 The Birches.

4 Fitzgerald resided at 6 Gateway Drive in Great Neck Estates while writing *The Great Gatsby*, and Ginger Rogers rented a house at 27 Richmond Road in the 1930s and later at 369 Beverly.

5 "Residential Parks Feature of Realty." *New York Times*, May 31, 1908.

Garden City

1 "Garden City, The Eden of Long Island," *Brooklyn Daily Argus*, May 17, 1876. For background information I am indebted to the Garden City Historical Society and Brian A. Pinnola, as well as to Robert MacKay and the staff of the Society for the Preservation of Long Island Antiquities. Important published sources I have used include Mildred Hess Smith, *History of Garden City*, rev. ed. (Garden City: Garden City Historical Society, 1980); hereafter, Smith, *History*; M. H. Smith, *Garden City: Long Island in Early Photographs, 1869–1919* (Mineola, NY: Dover Publications, 1987); hereafter Smith, *Garden City*; and Vincent F. Seyfried, *The Founding of Garden City 1869–1993* (privately published, 1969); hereafter Seyfried, *Founding*.

2 "The Hempstead Plains," *Harper's Weekly*, August 7, 1869. Quoted in Smith, *History*, book jacket.

3 William S. Pelletreau, *A History of Long Island*, vol. 2 (New York: Lewis Publishing Co., 1903), p. 96.

4 Thomas More, *Utopia*, ed. J. C. Collins (Oxford: Clarendon Press, 1904).

5 Psalm 48.

6 Governor John Winthrop, "A Model of Christian Charity," in *The Journal of John Winthrop, 1630–1649*, ed. Richard S. Dunn, James Savage, and Laetitia Yeandle (Cambridge, MA: Belknap Press of Harvard University Press, 1996).

7 Ellen Weiss, *City in the Woods: The Life and Design of an American Camp Meeting on Martha's Vineyard* (New York: Oxford University Press, 1987); Chris Stoddard, *A Centennial History of Cottage City* (Oak Bluffs, MA: Oak Bluffs Historical Commission, 1980).

8 For background, see Clifford Edward Clark, Jr., *The American Family Home, 1800–1960* (Chapel Hill, NC: University of North Carolina Press, 1986); John Archer, *Architecture and Suburbia: From English Villa to American Dream House 1690–2000* (Minneapolis: University of Minnesota Press, 2005).

9 Richard Guy Wilson, "Idealism and the Origin of the First American Suburb: Llewellyn Park, New Jersey," *American Art Journal* 11 (Autumn 1979), pp. 79–90.

10 Kenneth T. Jackson, *Crabgrass Frontier: The Suburbanization of the United States* (New York: Oxford University Press, 1985); Dolores Hayden, *Building Suburbia: Green Fields and Urban Growth* (New York: Pantheon, 2003), pp. 61–65.

11 Lewis Mumford, *The Highway and the City* (New York: Harcourt, Brace & World, 1963), p. 63.

12 Smith, *History*, p. 15, notes the conflicts on Stewart's birth date.

13 Smith, *Garden City*, p. 2.

14 Seyfried, *Founding*, p. 33.

15 *Artistic Houses* (New York: D. Appleton & Co., 1883–84).

16 Seyfried, *Founding*, p. 4.

17 "The Hempstead Plains," *Harper's Weekly*, August 7, 1869. Quoted in Smith, *History*, book jacket.

18 Smith, *History*, p. 18.

19 Advertisement on cover of Seyfried, *Founding*.

20 Details on the various houses and types are confusing and I have relied upon Seyfried, *Founding*; Smith, *History*; and *Brooklyn Daily Argus*, May 17, 1876.

21 "Garden City." *New York Trade Reporter*, September 2, 1876.

22 Seyfried, *Founding*, pp. 30–31.

23 *Flushing Journal*, August 23, 1873. Quoted in Seyfried, *Founding*, p. 22.

24 Seyfried, *Founding*, p. 22.

25 Pelletreau, *A History of Long Island*, vol. 2, p. 96.

26 *New York World*. Quoted in Jackson, Crabgrass Frontier, pp. 83–84.

27 "The Stewart Gift," *Harper's Weekly*, June 6, 1885.

28 Pelletreau, *A History of Long Island*, vol. 2, p. 97.

29 Phoebe B. Stanton, *The Gothic Revival and American Church Architecture: An Episode in Taste 1840–1856* (Baltimore and London: The Johns Hopkins University Press, 1968).

30 *New York Sun*, Nov. 7, 1878. Quoted in Smith, *History*, p. 35.

31 There are many accounts; the fullest is in Seyfried, Founding, pp. 37–40.

ERRATA

The following references were omitted in error from the notes to chapter 1.

NOTES

The Residential Park Phenomenon on Long Island

6 P. G. Wodehouse and Jerome Kern, "Bungalow in Quogue," from *The Riviera Girl*, produced by Klaw & Erlanger (New York: T. B. Harms Co., 1917).

7 *Brooklyn Daily Eagle*, October 12, 1902.

8 Robert W. Gibson diary, "Annals of North Point." Society For The Preservation of Long Island Antiquities.

9 Kenneth T. Jackson, *Crabgrass Frontier: The Suburbanization of the United States* (New York: Oxford University Press, 1985), p. 99.

10 *Brooklyn Daily Eagle*, June 30, 1915.

11 Paul D. Cravath, "Preserving the Country Lanes," *Country Life in America* (January 1913), p. 27. The Rockaway Hunt Club (1878), whose equestrian events were to receive national press coverage, and the Meadow Brook Club (1881) had reestablished the eighteenth-century pastime of fox hunting, dividing present-day Nassau County on a line between Rocky Point Beach and Mineola in 1893. Meadow Brook was also soon recognized as the "Heart of American Polo." Horse shows became summer fixtures at Bay Shore, Huntington, and Locust Valley.

12 W. P. Stephens, *The Seawanhaka Corinthian Yacht Club: Origins and Early History 1871–1896* (New York: privately published, 1963), p. 27.

13 *Brooklyn Daily Eagle*, August 17, 1907.

14 Of particular significance for the planned communities were those appearing in Queens and Nassau, including Oakland at Bayside (1896); Queens County at Glen Cove (1895), which became the Nassau Country Club in 1899; Meadow Brook (1894), the club that has been called the "hub of golf" in New York; Garden City, opened as the Island Golf Links in 1897, and those created under the auspices of the Garden City Company, Midland (1899–1907) and Salisbury Links (1907).

15 *Brooklyn Daily Eagle*, August 10, 1907.

16 "Financial Crisis to Aid Suburban Development," *New York Times*, January 5, 1908.

17 Sean Kass, "The L.I.R.R. and Its Promotion of Long Island, 1900–1930," *The Long Island Historical Journal* 17 (Fall 2004/Spring 2005), p. 92. Kass notes that the establishment in 1899 of the "El Connection," the first rail route to Manhattan from Brooklyn's Flatbush Avenue, served a limited audience, involved time-consuming transfers, and was "not conveniently accessible to most L.I.R.R. trains."

18 A. R. Pardington, "The Modern Appian Way for the Motorist," *Harper's Weekly* 51 (March 16, 1907), p. 390.

19 Frank Bailey, as told to Hannah Geffen, *It Can't Happen Here Again* (New York: Alfred A. Knopf, 1944), p. 118.

20 John J. Petit, "The Builders of Flatbush," in Herbert F. Gunnison, ed., *Flatbush of Today*, vol. 2, no. 1 (Brooklyn, 1908), p.103.

21 Dean Alvord (Prospect Park South, Cedarcroft, Roslyn Estates, and Belle Terre), Gage E. Tarbell (Garden City Estates), Charles Edward Tuxill (Beacon Hill), and Frank Bailey (Neponsit) were from upstate New York. Harvey Murdock (North Country Colony) and Timothy L. Woodruff (Garden City Estates) were natives of Connecticut. Carl G. Fisher (Bay View Colony and Montauk) and the partners Charles H. Rickert and Charles E.

Finlay (Westmoreland, Douglas Manor, and Kensington) hailed from the Midwest. The McKnight brothers (Great Neck Estates) were from West Virginia. Only Robert de Forest, the New York attorney (Forest Hills Gardens) and William H. Reynolds, (Laurelton, Long Beach Estates), son of a Brooklyn builder who had emigrated from England, had any connection to the region.

22 Originally known as the Long Island Real Estate Exchange, it became the Real Estate Exchange of Long Island, Inc., in 1907. Its offices were in Manhattan. Stockholders included Milton L'Ecluse, M. Stewart McKnight, C. H. Rickert, Ernestus Gulick, Gage E. Tarbell, T. B. Ackerson, A. R. Pardington, and many more involved in Long Island real estate ventures. *Brooklyn Daily Eagle*, March 23, 1901; January 16, 1908.

23 The *New York Times* reported in 1903, the year Bailey was also arraigned for speeding on Ocean Parkway, that ex-State Senator W. J. La Roche would never travel downtown again in Bailey's "devil wagon" after the automobilist lost control, jumping a curb and plowing into a house at the corner of Remsen and Clinton streets. New York Times, May 13, 1903.

24 *New York Times*, May 16, 1915. Automobiling also cost one planned-community figure his life. S. Osgood Pell, the real estate agent for Plandome and developer of Wampage Shores in Manhasset, was struck by an electric train as his auto was crossing the tracks near Long Beach in 1913, just behind W. K. Vanderbilt Jr.'s car, in which his wife was riding.

25 Tarbell and Woodruff, creators of Garden City Estates, were important early boosters of aviation; the latter chaired the second International Aviation Tournament held at the Nassau Boulevard Aerodrome in that community in 1911, during which the first airmail flight took place. Finlay and McKnight were golfers. Bailey, Reynolds, and Woodruff, accomplished equestrians, rode at the posh McKim, Mead & White–designed Brooklyn Riding and Driving Club; Fisher had a string of polo ponies. Bailey and Reynolds stumbled on their first big project, Borough Hall, while on a horseback excursion from this club, which was located at Prospect Park Plaza.

26 Bailey, involved in everything from the building of Brooklyn's Academy of Music to the Botanic Garden, which he chaired, was one of ten appointed by the mayor to the City Beautiful Commission in 1904. He served with Whitney Warren and Daniel Chester French and again with Warren and de Forest on the mayor's committee to explore a New York World's Fair in 1913. See "Mayor Names Men to Make City Beautiful," *New York Times*, March 13, 1904, and "City Beautiful Committees," New York Times, April 3, 1904. The committee was later renamed the New York City Improvement Commission. Bailey served on both the executive and highway and parks committees. See "Committee to Pass on 1913 Exposition," *New York Times*, June 14, 1910.

27 *Brooklyn Daily Eagle*. February 25, 1908, and December 22, 1900.

28 Jon A. Peterson, *The Birth of City Planning in the United States 1840–1917* (Baltimore and London: The Johns Hopkins University Press, 2003): 109–10.

29 *Brooklyn Daily Eagle*, June 3, 1908.

30 John M. Carrère, "Better Taste in Small Houses," *Country Life in America* 20, no. 2 (May 15, 1911), p. 20.

31 The Brighton Beach elevated (today's BMT) and various trolley lines.

32 *Brooklyn Life*, September 26, 1891.

33 John J. Petit, "The Builders of Flatbush, p. 103.

34 Dean Alvord, "Prospect Park South," in Gunnison, *Flatbush of Today*, p. 86.

35 Marc A. Weiss, *The Rise of the Community Builders: The American Real Estate Industry and Urban Land Planning* (New York: Columbia University Press, 1987), p. 3.

36 Klaus, *A Modern Arcadia*, pp. 114–16; Charles Zehren, "The Dream Builder," www.akrempl.com/geohome/labellesimone/Levitt.doc.

37 Dolores Hayden, *Building Suburbia: Green Fields and Urban Growth, 1820–2000* (New York: Pantheon, 2003), p. 69.

38 David L. Ames and Linda F. McClelland, "Historic Residential Suburbs: Guidelines for Evaluation and Documentation for the National Register of Historic Places," in *National Register Bulletin* (Washington, DC: U.S. Department of the Interior, National Park Service, 2002), p. 32.

39 When trouble ensued, Title Guarantee also took care of foreclosures such as Senator Reynolds's Lido hotel complex after his death in 1931.

40 Wayne Somers, "Bailey, Frank," in *The Encyclopedia of Union College History* (Schenectady, NY, 2003), p. 76.

41 Ibid., p. 128. Reynolds and Bailey formed the Long Beach Estates syndicate. Henry Morgenthau Sr., Patrick McCarran, the Republican politician, and a number of bankers purchased Long Beach in 1906.

42 "Munsey Park at Manhasset, Long Island," Hasset Realty Corporation, 1928.

43 "Active Lot Market in Near-by Suburbs," *New York Times*, October 8, 1922.

44 *Brooklyn Daily Eagle*, June 12, 1913.

45 *Brooklyn Daily Eagle*, June 12, 1915.

46 Ray Stubblebine, *Stickley's Craftsman Homes* (Layton, UT: Gibbs Smith, 2006), p. 343.

47 Ibid., p. 32. Stickley, Ray Stubblebine notes, "embraced almost every new development and product in the construction industry," recommending Ludowici-Celadon clay tiles, Ruberoid roofing rolls, and Johns-Manville asbestos shingles for roofs, while Natco Hollow Tile block, Tapestry brick, and the Van Guilder concrete method were among his choices for walls.

48 Atterbury was the principal architect of Forest Hills Gardens. Embury did a lot of work in Garden City, Belle Terre, and Harbor Acres. Wilson Eyre was responsible for a project at Belle Terre. C. P. H. Gilbert designed much of Glen Cove's North Country Colony and developer Rickert's own residence at Kensington. Robert W. Gibson designed A. H. Langjahr's house at Jamaica Estates, and F. L. Wright's house for Ben Rebhuhn is at 9a Myrtle Avenue in Great Neck Estates. Delehanty, the Craftsman architects, and McKim, Mead & White were responsible for the residences at 5 Grosvenor Street, 11 Hollywood Avenue, and 4 Ardsley Road in Douglas Manor, respectively. Peabody, Wilson & Brown were among the approved architects working at Forest Hills Gardens. F. J. Sterner's work can be seen in the Tudor section of Belle Terre and he designed at least four of the early houses at Roslyn Estates ("New Houses at Roslyn," *Brooklyn Daily Eagle*, December 26, 1908).

49 Others with multiple commissions include F. Ernst Lein, a young German émigré at Belle Terre, and Frederick J. Sterner (see note 48). August L. Viemeister is said to have designed twenty-six at Roslyn Estates, Oswald C. Hering was responsible for at least eight at Garden City Estates; Grosvenor Atterbury, for more than fifty freestanding houses at Forest Hills Gardens, in addition to all his other projects there.

50 Among the firm's clients were Alvord, Woodruff, Gulick, Reynolds, and Tarbell.

51 Gunnison, Flatbush of *To-day*, p. 88.

52 "To Develop 8,000 Lots," *New York Times*, August 11, 1907.

53 "Developers Hard at Work," *New York Times*, January 6, 1907. They would soon design Doubleday, Page & Company's Country Life Press (1910) in the manner of a Tudor palace at Garden City.

54 "Three of the Favorite Types of Seashores Bungalows," *Brooklyn Times*, March 28, 1914.

55 Petit was an usher at the wedding of Richard M. Upjohn's son Dudley and was present at a boisterous banquet of the Brooklyn chapter of the American Institute of Architects in the Delano-designed Beaux-Arts Casino on Huntington Bay. *New York Times*, October 5, 1907, and August 1, 1909.

56 Effendi Hill (1914–16) at Mill Neck, Long Island, was the firm's second country house commission for Frank Nelson Doubleday.

57 Petit's restaurant clients included Sherry's, and he is credited with the restoration of Washington, D.C.'s New Willard after a fire destroyed its interior, as well as with undertaking decorative work at the Waldorf Astoria in New York and the Bellevue-Stratford in Philadelphia. See "The Late John J. Petit," *Brooklyn Daily Eagle*, August 15, 1923.

58 Research for SPLIA's 1997 study, *Long Island Country Houses and Their Architects, 1860–1940*.

59 *The Flushing Daily Times*, quoted in Barbara Kreisler, "Brightwaters: Keeping Memories Alive," *Newsday*, March 28, 1987, pp. 32–33.

60 Ellis Parker Butler, "The Adventures of a Suburbanite," *Country Life in America* 18, no. 1 (May 1910), p. 53.

61 Henry James, *The American Scene* (Las Vegas, NV: IAP, 2010), p. 153.

62 Nicholas Bloom, "Suburbanization of Leisure," in *Encyclopedia of Recreation and Leisure in America*, vol. 2 (Woodbridge, CT: Charles Scribner's Sons, An Imprint of the Gale Group, 2004), p. 318.

63 "Garden City Estates," 1908.

64 *Brooklyn Daily Eagle*, June 15, 1915.

65 The McKnights Great Neck Golf Club was later renamed Soundview Golf Course and is no longer extant.

66 H. Stewart McKnight, "The Biography of Harvey Stewart McKnight, Ancestry and Recollections," unpublished typescript, p. 71. Village of Great Neck Estates.

67 Kevin Wolfe, *This Salubrious Spot: The First 100 Years at Douglas Manor 1906–2006* (Douglas Manor, NY: Douglas Manor Association, 2006), p. 29.

68 Following Great Neck Estates and Plandome were Shoreham (1913), Brightwaters (1916), Kensington (1917), Garden City (1919), Bellerose (1924), Belle Terre (1930), and Roslyn Estates and Plandome Heights (1931).

69 Paul L. Bentel, "The Regional Plan of New York," in *Long Island Architecture*, ed. Joann P. Krieg (Interlaken, NY: Heart of the Lakes Publishing, 1991), p. 13.

70 Peter Blake, *God's Own Junkyard: The Planned Deterioration of America's Landscape* (New York: Holt, Rinehart and Winston, 1968), p. 17.

71 James Howard Kunstler, *The Geography of Nowhere: The Rise and Decline of America's Man-Made Landscape* (New York: Touchstone, 1994), p. 48.

72 Ibid.

73 Richard Moe, "Preservation for a New Century," *Forum Journal*, Spring 2010, p. 5.

32 Smith, *History*, p. 33.

33 "Garden City," in *History of Queens County New York* (New York: W. W. Munsell, 1882), p. 189.

34 *New York Sun*, June 26, 1884. Quoted in Smith, *Garden City*, p. 27.

35 "The New St. Mary's School," *Brooklyn Daily Eagle*, March 29, 1892, p. 6.

36 Pelletreau, *A History of Llong Island*, vol. 2, p. 102.

37 Harry E. Resseguie, "The Decline and Fall of the Commercial Empire of A. T. Stewart," *Business History Review* 36, no. 3, Autumn 1962. See also Seyfried, *Founding*, p. 50; Smith, *History*, p. 158.

38 "The Garden City Company Incorporated," *Brooklyn Daily Eagle*, January 22, 1893, p. 2.

39 "Summer Resort News: Garden City," *Brooklyn Daily Eagle*, July 3, 1898, p. 28.

40 Quoted in Smith, *History*, p. 44.

41 Smith, *Garden City*, p. 37.

42 Quoted in Smith, *History*, p. 50.

43 "New Garden City Hotel," *Brooklyn Daily Eagle*, January 14, 1900, p. 12.

44 William L. Quirin, *America's Linksland: A Century of Long Island Golf* (Chelsea, MI: Sleeping Bear Press, 2002); William L. Quirin, *Golf Clubs of the MGA: A Centennial History of Golf in the New York Metropolitan Area* (Chicago: Triumph Books, 1997).

45 "Out on Hempstead Plans: Garden City," *Brooklyn Daily Eagle*, August 24, 1902, p. 15.

46 "Women Barred from Links," *Brooklyn Daily Eagle*, October 10, 1899, p. 16.

47 Quoted in Smith, *History*, p. 78.

48 Quoted in Smith, *History*, p. 60.

49 "Vanderbilt at Garden City," *Brooklyn Daily Eagle*, October 23, 1901, p. 17.

50 Quoted in Smith, Garden City, p. 49.

51 "Mineola's County Seat Boom," *Brooklyn Daily Eagle*, September 28, 1898, p. 13.

52 Quoted in Smith, History, p. 78.

53 "Garden City Estates: A Plea for a Sane Life" (New York: Garden City Estates Co., [1907]), [p. 3].

54 Advertisement for Garden City Estates, *New-York Daily Tribune*, March 19, 1910, p. 13.

55 Patricia Beard, *After the Ball: Gilded Age Secrets, Boardroom Betrayals, and the Party That Ignited the Great Wall Street Scandal of 1905* (New York: Harper Collins, 2003).

56 "Real Estate," *Brooklyn Life*, March 5, 1910, p. 30; "Financial Crisis to Aid Suburban Development," New York Times, January 5, 1908.

57 "Gage E. Tarbell Works from Sheer Love of It," *Brooklyn Daily Eagle*, July 13, 1907.

58 "Garden City Estates: A Plea for a Sane Life," [pp. 1, 2, 3].

59 "The Life Worth Living," *Country Life in America*, September 1, 1911, p. 3.

60 Illustrated in *Architectural Record*, March 1913, p. 221.

61 Advertisement in *The Craftsman*, May 1909; Ray Stubblebine, *Stickley's Craftsman Homes* (Layton, UT: Gibbs Smith, 2006), p. 290.

62 Smith, *History*, chapters 10, 12.

63 "Country Houses Designed by Aymar Embury Which Express the Modern American Spirit in Home Architecture," *The Craftsman* (November 1909), pp. 164–71. Embury also published *One Hundred Country Houses: Modern American Examples* (New York: Century Co., 1909), which contained his Garden City designs.

64 *Homes of Doubleday, Doran and Company, Inc.: Garden City; London; Kingswood, Surrey; Toronto* (Garden City, NY: privately printed, 1930), [p. 3].

65 *The Country Life Press: Garden City, New York* (Garden City: Doubleday, Page & Company, 1919), pp. 10, 13, 26.

66 Quoted in Smith, *History*, p. 90.

67 Mrs. Irwin [M. H.] Smith,"Country Life Press," *Garden City News*, August 12, 1977.

68 Quoted in Smith, *History*, p. 92.

69 Harriet Sisson Gillespie, "An English Cottage Group," *House Beautiful*, August 1919, pp. 74–76; Architecture 32 (November 1915), pp. 305–6.

70 Robert Schoendorf, *The Pioneer Flights of Garden City Estates, New York: 1911* (New York: Al Zimmerman Publisher, 1982).

71 Cynthia Zaitzevsky, *Long Island Landscapes and the Women Who Designed Them* (New York: W. W. Norton and Society for the Preservation of Long Island Antiquities, 2009), p. 243.

A Modern Venice

1 James Pooton, Jr., "Henry O. Havemeyer's Venice," *New York Times Supplement*, May 23, 1897, p. 14.

2 "A Little Venice of His Own," *The Spokesman-Review* (May 22, 1897), p. 8.

3 Ibid.

4 *Moorish Houses at Bayberry Point, Islip, L.I., Built for Mr. H. O. Havemeyer* (1897). See also *Pittsburgh Architectural Club Exhibition*, Carnegie Galleries (1900), p. 20; *Pittsburgh Architectural Club Exhibition*, Carnegie Galleries (1903), pp. 29, 70; "The Pittsburgh Architectural Club's Exhibition," *American Architect and Building News* 92 (November 30, 1907), pl.; Aymar Embury II, *One Hundred Country Houses: Modern American Examples* (New York: The Century Co., 1909), pp. 96–98; "Some Work at Bayberry Point, L.I., by Grosvenor Atterbury," *The American Architect* 96 (September 8, 1909), pp. 94–96, pls.; Russell F. Whitehead, "American Seaside Homes," *Architectural Record* 28 (August 1910), pp. 79–87; *Pittsburgh Architectural Club Exhibition*, Carnegie Galleries (1910); Oswald C. Hering, *Concrete and Stucco Houses* (New York: McBride, Nast and Company, 1912), pp. 78–79; Grosvenor Atterbury, Stowe Phelps, and John A. Tompkins, Architects, *Architectural Catalog* (April 1918), pls.; "Bayberry Point Homes," *New York Times*, July 7, 1930, p. 39; Robert B. MacKay, Anthony K. Baker, and Carol A. Traynor, eds., *Long Island Country Houses and Their Architects, 1860–1940* (New York: Society for the Preservation of Long Island Antiquities and W. W. Norton 1997), p. 51; Harry W. Havemeyer, *Along the Great South Bay: From Oakdale to Babylon, the Story of a Summer Spa, 1840–1940* (Mattituck, NY: Amereon, 1996), pp. 227–31.

5 *Moorish Houses at Bayberry Point, Islip, L.I., Built for Mr. H. O. Havemeyer* (1897)..

6 Ibid.

7 Ibid.

8 Ibid.

9 James Pooton, Jr., "Henry O. Havemeyer's Venice," p. 14.

10 *Moorish Houses at Bayberry Point, Islip, L.I., Built for Mr. H. O. Havemeyer* (1897).

11 A rendering of Atterbury's scheme can be found in the Pittsburgh Architectural Club's exhibit of 1907: *Pittsburgh Architectural Club Exhibition*, Carnegie Galleries (1907).

12 "Bayberry Point Homes," *New York Times*, July 7,

1930, p. 39. At that time, some of the purchasers and residents included J. C. Bennett, H. C. Sharpe, Alfred F. Ingold, Anthony F. Brown, Frank Gulden, and Francis B. Thorne.

13 Havemeyer, *Along the Great South Bay*, pp. 227–31.

For Teachers Only

1 *New York Times*, May 25, 1906.

2 Plandome is thought to derive from the Latin *planus domus*, which means "plain or peaceful home" and may have been coined by Matthias Nicoll, who bought land there in 1670.

3 The terms for the initial two years were $22.00 down and $2.20 per month per $100 of valuation. For payment within a year, there was an 8 percent discount, 4 percent within two years, and 2 percent within three.

4 "Manhasset Water Supply," *Brooklyn Daily Eagle*, August 7, 1910.

5 See "Building at Plandome," *New York Times*, March 21, 1909. They were also involved at this time with Manhasset Park, a development of modest homes opposite the Manhasset Railroad Station on the Old Haviland farm, which had been acquired by the Plandome Land Company. *Brooklyn Times*, April 22, 1909.

6 *The Long-Islander*, September 9, 1908.

7 Ibid.

8 *Brooklyn Life*, December 10, 1910.

9 "New Village Hall Open at Plandome," *Brooklyn Daily Eagle*, December 28, 1912.

10 Among the houses Briggs probably designed were those of E. E. Adams and Milton L'Ecluse, pictured in the *New York Times* on September 28, 1913.

11 Plandome appears to be Roullier's only planned community design. Despondent over personal problems and lack of work, he took his life in 1910.

12 Clare Sutherland, *The Plandome Story: The Story of the Incorporated Village of Plandome 1911–1965* (Plandome, NY: The Plandome Association, 1965), p. 47.

13 Designed by Briggs and built about 1913. *New York Times*, August 8, 1913. The rendering illustrated here, dated April 1920, is in the author's collection.

14 *New York Times*, March 31, 1907.

15 Cobe's initial purchase was known as the Frederick W. Wright property, which included the historic Plandome Hill. In 1906, an ad and article in the *New York Times* reported that two Manhattan firms, the Property Development Company and Taylor-Storm Realty, had formed the Manhasset Point Company to develop this property as a restricted community of "about 100 villa plots" on an "artistic plan" furnished by landscape architect John Thomas Withers, but this project, perhaps due to the financial panic of 1907, did not reach fruition. *New York Times*, May 5 and 13, 1906. Subsequently, Cobe acquired three adjoining waterfront lots from the Bloodgood Cutter estate. *New York Times*, November 20, 1907, and February 14, 1909; *Brooklyn Daily Eagle*, March 1909.

16 "Buying in New Residential Park" *New York Times*, May 10, 1905.

17 Fairseat burned after Burnett's death in 1921, and the property was later purchased by Mr. and Mrs. Leroy Grumman.

18 "B. N. Duke Leases Dugmore estate," *New York Times*, May 6, 1915.

19 Jacobus appears to have worn many hats. He had been superintendent of Great Neck schools before embarking on a career in real estate. He was involved in selling the Plandome Park property to A. J. Cobe, who later partnered with him on a number of Great Neck real estate transactions.

20 Brun, who designed the George V. Tomper House at 125 Buckingham Road in Prospect Park South, received his B.S. in architecture from Cornell in 1890 and worked in partnership with George H. Pierce (Pierce and Brun) and Leo Hauser (Brun and Hauser) in the 1890s.

From Flatbush to the Shinnecock Hills

1 Dean Alvord to O. C. Kenyon, February 20, 1935. Syracuse University Archives.

2 Alvord left a trusted assistant, Charles E. Baylis, in command. By 1912, Baylis held the title President of Dean Alvord Companies. See *New York Times*, February 16, 1912.

3 Samuel Morgan Alvord, *A Genealogy of the Descendants of Alexander Alvord: An Early Settler of Windsor, Conn. and Northampton, Mass.* (Webster, NY: A. D. Andrews Printer, 1908), p. 521.

4 Though some sources indicate that Alvord graduated from Syracuse and later taught there, records at the Syracuse University Archives indicate he left at the end of his junior year in June 1881. "I got through college by the back door," he later recalled, and he worked as a bookstore clerk in Syracuse (1882–83) and selling subscription books (1884). Dean Alvord to O. C. Kenyon, February 20, 1935. Syracuse University Archives.

5 Ibid.

6 Patrick Barry edited A. J. Downing's nationally known publication, *The Horticulturalist*, after it was purchased by Rochester's mail-order seed king, James Vick, in 1853. Barry and his partner, George Ellwanger, a German émigré and horticulturalist, donated a portion of their nursery to the City of Rochester in 1888, which became Highland Park.

7 Listed as a landscape gardener in the 1893 Rochester Directory, he is identified as a landscape architect four years later. In 1898, he formed a partnership with Alling DeForest (1875–1957), who had worked in the Olmsted office, and the partners designed, among other projects, one of the most celebrated real estate developments in upstate New York, the General Electric Realty Plot in Schenectady.

8 Riverside Cemetery Association, *A Debt and a Duty: Being a Timely Suggestion of an Obligation and the Way for Every One to Meet It (Rochester, NY: The Genesee Press, The Post Express* Printing Company, 1897).

9 *Rochester Union Advertiser*, January 24, 1893.

10 Dean Alvord to O. C. Kenyon, February 20, 1935. Syracuse University Archives.

11 Ibid.

12 *Rochester Democrat and Chronicle*, July 27, 1895.

13 Ibid., July 17, 1895.

14 "New Corporations," *New York Times*, January 5, 1897.

15 Despatch took its name from the Merchants Despatch Company, a railroad car manufacturing concern, which Walter A. Parce persuaded to relocate to the new suburb.

16 "Despatch, N.Y. Rochester's Great Industrial Suburb." Perinton Historical Society, Fairport, N.Y.

17 Dean Alvord to O.C. Kenyon, February 20, 1935. Syracuse University Archives.

18 Ibid.

19 Ibid.

20 "Big Profit in Park Land," *New York Times*, October 14, 1898.

21 *New York Times*, May 24, 1902. Alvord was treasurer of the Union Land Improvement Company, which was building houses on Forest Parkway.

22 Aitkin's previous experience had been at Sir George Napier's Milikin Park, Lord Eggleton's Skillorme, and Lady Hamilton's Chnoa House, as well as a Hudson River estate. "A New Residence Park, " *Brooklyn Daily Eagle*, March 19, 1899.

23 "Prospect Park South, Dean Alvord, Owner," *Brooklyn Daily Eagle*, October 5, 1902.

24 "Prospect Park South," 1900.

25 *New York Times*, September 20, 1901.

26 Herbert F. Gunnison, ed. *Flatbush of To-Day*, vol. 2, no. 1 (Brooklyn, 1908), p. 86.

27 Dean Alvord to O. C. Kenyon, February 20, 1935. Syracuse University Archives.

28 *Brooklyn Daily Eagle*, May 18, 1905.

29 Pardington's remarks were delivered at the groundbreaking for the Long Island Motor Parkway on June 6, 1908. A. R. Pardington, "The Modern Appian Way for the Motorist," *Harpers Weekly* 51 (March 16, 1907), pp. 390–92.

30 "Four Auto Routes Planned for Speedway," *New York Times*, October 29, 1906.

31 Gunnison, *Flatbush of Today*, p. 92.

32 *Brooklyn Daily Eagle*, September 9, 1906.

33 *New York Times*, May 21, 1905.

34 "Cedarcroft," *Brooklyn Daily Eagle*, June 18, 1905. Few lots appear to have sold.

35 The February 1905 map of Cedarcroft by C. P. Darling, C.E., which was filed by Alvord with the Suffolk County Clerk on July 8, 1905, shows a total of twenty-seven lots along Arbutus Avenue. Later maps and atlases indicate there was little activity. Though some lots sold, by the end of 1910 the Long-Islander was referring to the property as the "former Alvord development." *Long-Islander*, December 2, 1910. A portion of the property was later acquired by Herman D. Roosen while assembling property for his estate, Laurel Lodge. See Catha Grace Rambusch, Barbara Snowden Christen, and Robert C. Hughes, *The Landscape and Architecture of Laurel Lodge: A little Known Early 20th-Century Summer Estate on Long Island's North Shore* (privately printed, n.d.).

36 Acquired from an English concern, the purchase of the property boosted Alvord's ownership of Long Island shorefront to over twenty-five miles. *New York Times*, October 29, 1905. The syndicate had spent half its $200,000 budget for improvements on the Inn. *Long Islander*, April 10, 1908. And three roads had been constructed: the North Highway, connecting Good Grand and Southampton, ran by the inn; the South Highway crossed the L.I.R.R. tracks at the Shinnecock Hills Station; and Peconic Road ran north–south, passing the Suffolk Downs Station. *Brooklyn Life*, March 7, 1908.

37 *Brooklyn Daily Eagle*, June 9, 1907.

38 A. W. Dean, "What Long Island Offers the Home Seeker," *House & Garden*, March 1913, p. 159.

39 *Brooklyn Daily Eagle*, June 3, 1908.

40 Ibid.

41 "Roslyn Estates: The Eden of Long Island," Dean Alvord Company, Managers, Roslyn Estates Incorporated, 111 Broadway, New York, n.d.

42 Robert Sargent, "Dean Alvord: The Founding Father of Roslyn Estates," Village of Roslyn Estates, n.d.

43 "New House at Roslyn," *Brooklyn Daily Eagle*, December 26, 1908.

44 "To Build Concrete Homes," *Cement and Engineering News*, June 1910, p. 251.

45 *Atlas of Nassau County* (New York: E. Belcher Hyde, 1914), p. 37.

46 Viemeister developed plans for Union Mortgage Company after it took over as developers of Roslyn Estates and later became chief designer for Emery Roth and Sons. Peter Viemeister, *Start All Over: An American Experience* (Bedford, VA: Hamilton's, 1995), pp. 40–44; Ruth Rohland Hinrichs, "Childhood Memories Revisited," part 3 in a series of historical briefs by village residents in connection with the seventy-fifth anniversary of Roslyn Estates.

47 Dean Alvord, "How to Develop Acreage," in *Practical Real Estate Methods for Broker, Operator and Owner* (New York: Doubleday, Page & Co. for Westside Y.M.C.A., 1909).

48 "Dean Alvord Discusses Acreage Development," *Brooklyn Daily Eagle*, May 16, 1908.

49 "Beautifying Vast Park Overlooking the Sound," *New York Times*, May 31, 1908.

50 "Roslyn Estates—Belle Terre," *New York Times*, September 8, 1910.

51 "Long Island Tract Sold," *New York Times*, October 14, 1906.

52 There were five members of the Port Jefferson Company Syndicate, including Alvord, who served as president. Clinton L. Rossiter, a trust company and transit executive, Col. Timothy Williams, who had succeeded Rossiter as president of the Brooklyn Transit Company, and Martin Joost, president of the Bond and Mortgage Company. Alvord purchased the company's holding in 1906 for a reported $650,000. "Long Island Trust Sold," *New York Times*, October 14, 1906.

53 The builders were the Loper Brothers, who also erected Belle Terre's pergolas and entrance lodge, although some sources indicate that the station was erected earlier and that only the columns were added in 1903.

54 Petit was also likely to have designed a huge but unrealized addition to the club in 1912. *New York Times*, February 25, 1912. The name Nevalde was derived from the initials of Alvord's family's first names.

55 "Belle Terre," Belle Terre Estates Incorporated, 277 Broadway, New York City, n.d.

56 E. Post Tooker (b. 1886), who had grown up in Port Jefferson and had graduated from Lehigh University in 1907, went to work for Alvord at Belle Terre and from 1908 to 1913 served as a landscape engineer in the office of Charles W. Leavitt Jr. before organizing his own firm. Eugene L. Armbruster, *Long Island: Its Early Days and Development with Illustrations and Maps*, History of Long Island, vol. 29, no. 182 (Brooklyn: *Brooklyn Daily Eagle*, 1914), p. 60.

57 "Belle Terre: The Riviera of America," Belle Terre Estates, Inc., n.d.

58 *The Brickbuilder 19* (December 1910), pls. 168–70; *The American Architect* 99, no. 1830 (January 18, 1911), p. 56; *Architectural Forum* 11, no. 3 (September 1919), pls. 47–48.

59 "Belle Terre: The Riviera of America," Belle Terre Estates, Inc.; "Belle Terre Estates," *The Sun*, June 16, 1907.

60 Four of five known Lien commissions, including the annex to the Belle Terre Club, survive. "Wolf Schafer Belle Terre Legends and Facts, Architectural and Otherwise" *Belle Terre News* 8, no. 3 (September 2008), pp. 5–8.

61 "Bungalows and Plans Belle Terre, Long Island," *Architecture* (July 1909), pp. 100–101.

62 Gavin Townsend has observed that similar hoods can be found in sketches Kirby made in Normandy in the 1880s. Similar features were used by the firm at Kononsioni. Robert B. MacKay, Anthony K. Baker, and Carol A. Traynor, eds., *Long Island Country Houses and Their Architects, 1860–1940* (New York: Society for the Preservation of Long Island Antiquities and W. W. Norton, 1997), p. 238.

63 The nine-hole course opened on Memorial Day in 1908. An eighteen-hole course designed by Devereux Emmet was laid out north of the Findlay course in 1924.

64 *Brooklyn Life*, June 12, 1909, p. 21.

65 "Opening Day at Belle Terre," *New York Times*, June 12, 1910.

66 *United States Investor* 23, part 1 (January 18, 1912), p. 825.

67 "Suburban Construction Company of New York," *Rochester Democrat and Chronicle*, June 16, 1909.

68 *Brooklyn Daily Eagle*, May 1909.

69 *Brooklyn Daily Eagle*, May 13, 1908.

70 *Rochester Democrat and Chronicle*, June 16, 1909.

71 John Grant Dater, *Munsey's Magazine*, December 1912.

72 "Alvord Companies Pass to Receivership, " *New York Times*, January 11, 1913.

73 John Grant Dater, "Real Estate Bonds Again," *Munsey's Magazine*, January 1913, p. 1021.

74 Ibid.

75 "Will Reorganize Belle Terre Co.," *Brooklyn Daily Eagle*, June 18, 1913.

76 Ibid.

77 The Navy expressed interest in buying the portion of the property owned by the bondholders early in 1918 with the idea of establishing a naval base at Port Jefferson, but the prospect probably came to an end with the Armistice later that year. William Todd Wilcox to Rear Admiral N. R. Usher, Commandment, Third Naval District, U.S. Navy Yard, New York, February 18, 1918. Port Jefferson Village Historian's office.

78 On his grand journey in 1911–12, Alvord visited Egypt and then the Far East and Europe, studying "flora in public and private gardens, with particular reference to its application to landscape art" in Ceylon, India, Burma, Malay, Java, China, the Philippines, Japan, Siberia, Germany, Switzerland, France, Spain, and England, contributing along the way articles to the *Brooklyn Daily Eagle* under the title "Jottings of a Thirty-Thousand Mile Journey." Dean Alvord to O. C. Kenyon, February 20, 1935. Syracuse University Archives.

79 Alvord had intended to buy only a lot at Clearwater on which to build his house, but the owner of the property in which he was interested, a former citrus grove, was only willing to sell the entire tract. Alvord's Harbor Oaks residence at 313 Magnolia Drive survives.

80 Dean Alvord to O.C. Kenyon, February 20, 1935. Syracuse University Archives.

Mrs. Marsh's Bellerose

1 Julius Chambers, *The Book of New York: Forty Years' Recollections of the American Metropolis* (New York: The Book of New York Company, 1912), p. 405.

2 Ibid., p. 424.

3 Alan Trachtenberg, *The Incorporation of America* (New York: Hill and Wang, 1992), p. 87.

4 Kenneth T. Jackson, *Crabgrass Frontier: The Suburbanization of the United States* (New York: Oxford University Press, 1985), pp. 128–29.

5 David Traxel, *1898: The Birth of the American Century* (New York: Alfred A. Knopf, 1998), pp. 21–23.

6 *Historical Census Browser*. Accessed April 25, 2011, from the University of Virginia, Geospatial and Statistical Data Center: http://fisher.lib.virginia.edu/collections/stats/histcensus/index.htm.

7 Carol Kennedy Mylod, *75th Anniversary History of Bellerose Village* (n.p., 1999), p. 7.

8 Mylod, *75th Anniversary History of Bellerose Village*, p. 8.

9 Ibid., p. 7.

10 Leland M. Roth, "Getting the Houses to the People: Edward Bok, the Ladies' Home Journal, and the Ideal House," *Perspectives in Vernacular Architecture* 4 (1991), pp. 187–91.

11 Ibid., p. 188.

12 Mylod, *75th Anniversary History of Bellerose Village*, p. 8.

13 Sarah Platt Decker, "The Meaning of the Woman's Club Movement," *Annals of the American Academy of Political and Social Science* 28 (September 1906), p. 1.

14 *Long Island: The Sunrise Homeland*, 8th ed. (New York: Committee on Publications, Long Island Chamber of Commerce, 1929), p. 80.

Kensington and Douglas Manor

1 *Real Estate Record & Guide*, March 31, 1906, p. 564.

2 "Comfortable Types of Flats," *New York Times*, July 10, 1910, p. X10.

3 Theodore Starrett, "A Beauty Spot," *Architecture and Building* 46 (May 1914), p. 179.

4 S. Ferdinand Howe, *The Commerce of Kansas City in 1886* (Kansas City: Ramsey, Willett & Hudson, 1902), p. 105.

5 "Charles E. Finlay, a Realty Operator," *New York Times*, July 11, 1940, p. 19.

6 George Creel and John Slavens, *Men Who Are Making Kansas City: A Biographical Directory* (Kansas City: Hudson-Kimberly Publishing Co., 1902), p. 43.

7 Ibid.

8 Display ad, *New York Times*, May 19, 1907, p. S8.

9 "Apartments for L.I. City," *New York Times*, June 13, 1909, p. 14.

10 Advertising brochure, Chamber of Commerce of the Borough of Queens, 1913, unpaginated.

11 Starrett, "A Beauty Spot," p. 180.

12 Rickert-Finlay Realty Company prospectus, January 20, 1912, unpaginated.

13 "Increased Amount of Building in Queens," *New York Times*, April 22, 1906, p. XX4.

14 Rickert-Finlay Realty Company promotional brochure, "Douglas Manor: The Finest Private Park on Long Island," n.d., unpaginated.

15 Ibid.

16 Wendy Joy Darby, "Historic Landscape Report, Douglas Manor, New York," 1994. Prepared for the Douglaston and Little Neck Historical Society.

17 New York City Landmarks Preservation Commis-

sion, "Douglaston Historic District Designation Report," June 24, 1997, p. 10.

18 Starrett, "A Beauty Spot," p. 188

19 New York City Landmarks Preservation Commission, "Douglaston Historic District Designation Report," p. 18.

20 "Fine Kensington Residence," *New York Times*, February 20, 1910, p. X10.

21 Rickert-Finlay Realty Company promotional brochure, "A Weekend at Kensington," 1915, unpaginated.

22 Starrett, "A Beauty Spot," pp. 184, 191, 192, 193, 195, 197, 203.

23 "A Weekend at Kensington."

24 "Wonderful Growth of Long Island Villages," *New York Times*, April 4, 1912.

25 Advertisement, "Kensington, Great Neck," *Brooklyn Daily Eagle*, June 11, 1915.

26 "Miss Rickert Introduced," *New York Times*, December 1, 1911.

27 "Mrs. Charles E. Finlay," *New York Times*, March 8, 1937.

28 "Charles E. Finlay, A Realty Operator," *New York Times*, July 11, 1940, p. 19.

29 "Finley's [*sic*] Son-In-Law Better," *Special to The New York Times*, March 16, 1913, p. 12.

30 Starrett, "A Beauty Spot," pp. 182–83.

31 Ibid., p. 183.

32 "Kensington's Japanese Garden," *Plain Talk* 2 (July 20, 1912), unpaginated.

33 Ibid.

34 Ibid.

35 Starrett, "A Beauty Spot," p. 182.

Long Beach

1 "The Story of William H. Reynolds," *Brooklyn Daily Eagle*, May 5, 1907, p. 3.

2 *New York Times*, July 21, 1878, p. 10.

3 *New York Times*, October 23, 1892, p. 16.

4 Frank Bailey, as told to Hannah Geffen, *It Can't Happen Here Again* (New York: Knopf, 1944), p. 118.

5 Ibid.

6 *Brooklyn Daily Eagle*, August 24, 1901, p. 13.

7 Roberta Kossoff and Annette Henkin Landau, *Laurelton*, Images of America (Mount Pleasant, SC: Arcadia, 2011), p. 13.

8 *Brooklyn Life*, May 7, 1910, pp. 28, 30.

9 Ibid.

10 *New-York Tribune*, June 14, 1903, p. A11.

11 "New Montauk Theatre: Plans for Brooklyn Playhouse Are Elaborate," *New-York Tribune*, May 22, 1904, p. A6.

12 These included altering a set of tenements, offices, and stores on the future site of the Chrysler Building. See *New York Times*, July 12, 1912, p. 14.

13 For more on Kirby, Petit & Green see the Introduction.

14 *New York Times*, July 18, 1903, p. 7.

15 "Dreamland-by-the-Sea: A New and Unique City of Pleasure Throws Open Its Doors to the Public," *New-York Tribune*, May 15, 1904, p. A10.

16 Ibid.

17 Ibid.

18 Ibid.

19 *New York Times*, April 14, 1907, p. R7.

20 *New York Times*, May 31, 1908, p. L2.

21 "Long Island Towns Will Become Cities," *Brooklyn Daily Eagle*, April 13, 1907, p. 9.

22 Ibid.

23 Ibid.

24 Ibid.

25 *Success Magazine* 10 (July 1907), p. 514.

26 Ibid.

27 Ibid.

28 *Field & Stream* 14 (August 1909), p. 357.

29 *Brooklyn Daily Eagle*, May 25, 1907.

30 *The World Almanac and Encyclopedia 1907* (New York: The Press Publishing Co., New York World, 1906), p. 21.

31 "Estates at Long Beach," *Brooklyn Life*, March 5, 1910, p. 29.

32 *Brooklyn Daily Eagle*, May 25, 1907.

33 *Brooklyn Daily Eagle*, October 31, 1909, p. 19.

34 "Estates at Long Beach," *Brooklyn Life*, March 5, 1910, p. 29.

35 Charles Prelini, *Dredges and Dredging* (New York: D. Van Nostrand Co., 1911), pp. 242–43.

36 "Estates of Long Beach Opened," *New-York Tribune*, May 16, 1907, p. 16.

37 *Brooklyn Daily Eagle*, May 25, 1907.

38 *Brooklyn Life*, March 7, 1908, p. 24.

39 *New York Times*, June 14, 1908, p. X4.

40 *New York Times*, July 26, 1908 p. C4.

41 Ibid.

42 *Field & Stream* 14 (August 1909), p. 357.

43 *Brooklyn Daily Eagle*, May 25, 1907.

44 Ibid.

45 *Success Magazine* 10 (July 1907), p. 514.

46 *Brooklyn Life*, March 7, 1908, p. 24.

47 *Zoning Law, Building Codes of the City of Long Beach New York* (Long Beach, NY: City of Long Beach, n.d.).

48 "Estates at Long Beach," *Brooklyn Life*, March 5, 1910, p. 29.

49 "The Story of the New National Ocean Resort," *New-York Tribune*, April 3, 1910, p. B1.

50 "A Good Type of Ocean-side Cottage," *Real Estate Record and Builders Guide* 86, no. 2208 (July 9, 1910), p. 58.

51 See nomination of the Pauline Felix House to the National Register of Historic Places (04NR05378), www.oprhp.state.ny.us/hpimaging/hp_view. asp?GroupView=100938.

52 *Brooklyn Daily Eagle*, May 25, 1907.

53 *Brooklyn Life*, May 7, 1910, pp. 28, 30.

54 "The Story of the New National Ocean Resort," *New-York Tribune*, April 3, 1910, p. B1.

55 Ibid.

56 *Brooklyn Life*, March 7, 1908, p. 24.

57 Roberta Fiore and Elizabeth Coffin Allerhand, "Sandbar to City: William H. Reynolds and the Planned Community of Long Beach, 1906–1922," in *Nassau County: From Rural Hinterland to Suburban Metropolis*, A Long Island Studies Institute Publication from Hofstra University, ed. Joann P. Krieg and Natalie A. Naylor (Interlaken, NY: Empire State Books, 2000), p. 268.

58 *Brooklyn Daily Eagle*, June 21, 1909, p. 6.

59 "The Story of the New National Ocean Resort," *New-York Tribune*, April 3, 1910, p. B1.

60 William Coolbaugh Freeman, *One Hundred Advertising Talks by William C. Freeman: Selected and Arranged by George French* (New York: The Winthrop Press, 1912), pp. 21–22.

61 *Brooklyn Daily Eagle*, May 29, 1915, p. 8.

62 *Boston Globe*, October 14, 1931, p. 19. See also "Court Exonerates Senator Reynolds," *New York*

Times, May 13, 1920, p. 22: "The indictments were obtained by District Attorney Swann in 1917, when the late John Purroy Mitchel was a candidate for re-election as Mayor, and were used as anti-Mitchel literature by Tammany in the campaign. Ex-Senator Reynolds was a close personal friend of Mayor Mitchel, and every effort was made to link the two in the statements which were put forward then."

63 *New-York Tribune*, October 10, 1920, p. A15.

64 *Brooklyn Daily Eagle*, May 17, 1922, p. 1.

65 "Opportunity Now to Buy Lots at Long Beach," *New-York Tribune*, June 18, 1922, p. B2.

66 *New-York Tribune*, May 28, 1922.

67 Ibid.

68 Ibid.

69 Paul Daley, *Golf Architecture: A Worldwide Perspective*, vol. 4 (Gretna, LA: Pelican Publishing Company, 2008), p. 211.

70 "Golf Architect," *The New Yorker*, August 11, 1928, pp. 13–14.

71 *New York Times*, June 27, 1915, p. 19.

72 Charles Blair Macdonald, *Scotland's Gift, Golf: Reminiscences 1872–1927* (New York: Scribner's, 1928), cited in Daley, Golf Architecture, vol. 4, p. 19.

73 *New York Times*, June 27, 1915, p. 19.

74 "The Lido Links at Long Beach," *The Golf Course*, June 1916, pp. 58–59.

75 *New York Times*, March 28, 1922.

76 "Golf at Long Beach All Year Around," *New York Times*, February 14, 1915, p. S2.

77 *New York Times*, August 8, 1926, p. RE2.

78 *New York Times*, August 29, 1926, p. RE21.

79 Roberta Fiore, "The Legendary Lido Golf Course and the Origins of Lido Beach," *The Nassau County Historical Society Journal* 61 (2006), pp. 28ff.; this is an excellent account of the history of Lido Beach.

80 *Long Island Railroad Information Bulletin* 5, no. 6 (1928), p. 6.

81 "A Master Builder in Trouble," *New York Times*, June 21, 1924, p. 12.

82 "Reynolds Cleared of Larceny Charge," *New York Times*, March 6, 1927, p. 6.

83 *New-York Tribune*, May 16, 1904, p. 4.

84 "Daly Loses His Clothes," *Syracuse Herald*, April 10, 1908.

85 "Mayor's Pistol Shot Reynolds," *New York Times*, June 25, 1914, p. 1.

86 "Life of Famous Dog Insured for $10,000," *Washington Post*, August 28, 1923.

87 Advertisement, *New York Times*, May 27, 1923, p. RE3.

88 For more information, see the nomination of Granada Towers to the National Register of Historic Places (90NR01715).

89 *New York Times*, February 2, 1928, p. 17; June 6, 1928, p. 44; October 4, 1928, p. 50.

90 "William H. Reynolds," *Boston Globe*, October 14, 1931, p. 19.

The Thousand-Acre City by the Sea

1 T. B. Ackerson Company Records, 1884–1926, Historical/Biographical Note, Long Island Division, Queens Borough Public Library (QBPL).

2 The warehouse company later evolved into the Long Island City Factory Company, which began acquiring property in the area in 1906, on which they erected commercial structures of various sizes that they sold or leased to different firms. T. B. Ack-

erson Company Records, 1884–1926. Historical/Biographical Note, Long Island Division, QBPL.

3 Ibid. The biographical introduction to these records claims that Ackerson resorted to building two-family houses, but this is contradicted by contemporary news accounts.

4 Ackerson was engaged in the Maplewood project until July 1909, when he sold his remaining building plots in order to concentrate on Brightwaters. *New York Times*, July 27, 1909, p. 10.

5 *Brooklyn Daily Eagle*, April 12 1902, p. 15.

6 New York City Landmarks Preservation Commission, June 24, 2004, http://www.nyc.gov/html/pc/downloads/pdf/reports/avenueh.pdf.

7 Ackerson Company Records, 1884–1926. Historical/Biographical Note, Long Island Division, QBPL.

8 New York City Landmarks Preservation Commission.

9 Ackerson also touted proximity to "multiple forms of public transportation" in his promotional material for Maplewood, New Jersey. Ackerson Company Records, 1884–1926. Historical/Biographical Note, Long Island Division, QBPL.

10 New York City Landmarks Preservation Commission.

11 Adina Back and Francis Morrone, *Flatbush: Neighborhood History Guide* (Brooklyn: Brooklyn Historical Society, 2008), unpaginated.

12 New York City Landmarks Preservation Commission.

13 *Brooklyn Daily Eagle*, February 2 1902, p. 9.

14 The price range includes homes sold by the John Reis Company for the Ackersons. This suggests that Ackerson properties were listed by companies other than T. B. Ackerson itself. It is unclear whether any of these houses were in Fiske Park. See *New York Times*, July 19, 1906. Houses in Beverly Square West ran from $7,000 to $10,000 and those in Beverly Square East from $10,000 to $15,000. See *Brooklyn Daily Eagle*, April 12, 1902, p. 15.

15 New York City Landmarks Preservation Commission, March 18, 2008. Designation Report, Fiske Terrace-Midwood Park, pp. 26, 28.

16 Ibid., p. 30

17 Ibid., p. 28.

18 Ackerson also lived there until he moved to Brightwaters.

19 It was recently designated a New York City Landmark. New York City Landmarks Preservation Commission.

20 Ibid.

21 Ibid.

22 *Brooklyn Life* 33 (March 3, 1906), p. 36.

23 Other sources claim that the Indian name was Manetuck Neck, meaning "pine swamps." Rhonda C. Milligan, "Early History of the Village of Brightwaters," unpublished sheet, ca. 1970.

24 Harry W. Havemeyer, *Along the Great South Bay: From Oakdale to Babylon, the Story of a Summer Spa, 1840–1940* (Mattituck, NY: Amereon), p. 283.

25 Ibid.

26 Ibid., p. 286.

27 Advertisement, *Brooklyn Life* 35, no. 903 (June 22, 1907), p. 24; see also the report on the same page.

28 *New York Times*, August 7, 1910, p. X6.

29 *New York Times*, July 17, 1910, p. 13.

30 *New York Times*, April 7 1912, p. XX5.

31 *The Flushing Daily Times, quoted in Barbara Kreisler,* "Brightwaters: Keeping Memories Alive," *Newsday,* March 28, 1987, pp. 32–33.

32 Havemeyer, *Along the Great South Bay,* p. 285.

33 *New York Times,* May 29, 1910, p. X10.

34 Ibid.

35 Promotional flyer, ca. 1910, Bay Shore Historical Society.

36 *New York Times,* February 17, 1910, p. 14.

37 *New York Times,* June 19, 1910, p. X14.

38 *New York Times,* August 13, 1911, p. XX1. Based on the Consumer Price Index, the 1910 dollar was worth about $23.30 in 2009 money. Consequently, the Ackersons' reported 1911 investment in Brightwaters would be approximately $29,125,000 in 2009 dollars. MeasuringWorth.com.

39 *New York Times,* October 10, 1909, p. 21.

40 *New York Times,* August 14, 1910, p. X7.

41 *New York Times,* October 10, 1909, p. XX1.

42 Apparently, T. B. intended to attract and encourage farmers in an area where agriculture was still dominant. This was not unprecedented at the time, as the Long Island Railroad had established experimental farms at Medford and Wading River. The projects were intended to attract more residents to the area, basically the Pine Barrens, which had been considered poor terrain for farming. Facilities at the 400-acre demonstration farm included a greenhouse, horse and cow barns, a two-story "hennery" and incubators, as well as a dairy, creamery, silos, carpenter shop, and nursery. According to Ackerson's agricultural "expert," the farms were "proposed to demonstrate here the principles in practical and profitable agriculture which has cost the Government an enormous amount of money and many years of experimentation to reach, and we are providing a thorough equipment with this end in mind and also allow the surrounding farm owners to profit by our equipment on a cooperative basis at practically a cost price to us." *New York Times,* April 9, 1911, p. XX2.

43 Ibid.

44 *Bay Shore Sentinel and Journal,* 1957–58, Brightwaters file, Bay Shore Historical Society.

45 *New York Times,* April 3 1910, p. X11.

46 *New York Times,,* April 3, 1910.

47 Henry H. Saylor, *Bungalows* (Philadelphia: The John C. Winston Company, 1911).

48 Ackerson Real Estate Company Archives. Personal communication with Bart Ackerson. October 16, 2010.

49 An exchange in a website devoted to Brooklyn homes contends that Ackerson began with custom designs at Fiske Terrace, but then switched to "pattern book" because he was losing money on the individually designed houses. See www.brownstoner.com/profile/erin%20Joslyn.

50 *New York Times,* October 10, 1909, p. XX1.

52 *New York Times,* August 13, 1911, p. XX1.

53 *New York Times,* August 12, 1915, p. XX3.

54 This is based on prices listed in *New York Times,* advertisements.

55 *New York Times,* September 8, 1912, p. X15.

56 *New York Times,* April 7, 1912, p. XX5.

57 *New York Times,* September 8, 1912, p. X15.

58 Deed, T. B. Ackerson Company and Marie L. Wolley, May 6, 1908, and June 22, 1908. Ackerson Company Records, QBPL.

59 Ibid.

60 Hancock, "Brightwaters Centennial 1907–2007." Bayshore Historical Society-BayShore Brightwaters Public Library pamphlet, 2007.

61 *New York Times,,* May 29, 1910, p. X10.

62 *New York Times,v,* October 10, 1909, p. XX1.

63 Liz Finnegan, "Long Island Film Festival Honors," *Islip Bulletin* 33 (November 19, 2011).

64 Hancock, "Brightwaters Centennial."

65 Ibid.

66 *New York Times,* August 22, 1915, p. 55.

67 Ibid.

68 Ibid.

69 *New York Times,* May 3, 1910, p. 14.

70 *New York Times,* August 5, 1917, p. RE4.

71 Ibid.

72 Ibid.

73 *New York Times,* July 14, 1918, p. 84.

74 *New York Times,* July 28, 1918, http://query.nytimes.com/mem/archive-free/pdf?Res.

75 *New York Times,* July 14, 1918, p. 84.

76 Ackerson Company Records, Historical/Biographical Note, QBPL.

Great Neck Estates

1 The McKnight brothers were: lawyer Harvey Stewart (1865–post-1947) and stenographers John Calvin (1868–1928), Arthur Maxwell, Ira Thomas, and Edgar Scott. There was also a sister, Margaret Grace Schaaf. Most were born in Jackson Hall, near Chambersburg, Pennsylvania. The family soon moved to Charles Town, West Virginia. Then, between 1890 and 1892, all relocated to Bayside, Queens. Dissatisfied with his prospects practicing law, H. Stewart first went into newspaper publishing (he owned, published, reported for, edited, and printed several papers by himself) and became involved in Queens politics. Shortly after 1900, Stewart and Ira T. both bought tracts of land in Bayside and entered the real estate business. There they met "a Mr. [C. E.] Finley . . . from St. Louis, MO," a lawyer who was trying to buy the Bell Farm adjacent to their tracts. (This was the firm of Rickert-Finlay.) See *Brooklyn Daily Eagle,* July 13, 1907; *Brooklyn Daily Eagle,* November 2, 1912; *Who's Who in NY City and State,* 1911, p. 631; obituaries of John (father), *New York Times,* June 27, 1914, and John Calvin McKnight, *Great Neck News,* April 14, 1928; "The Biography of Harvey Stewart McKnight, Ancestry and Recollections," an unpublished, hand-paginated typescript, filed at the Village of Great Neck Estates; hereafter "Autobiography."

2 "Autobiography," p. 63.

3 Ibid., p. 65.

4 Ibid.

5 Ibid.

6 "Five McKnights Form McKnight Realty Co.," *Brooklyn Daily Eagle,* July 13, 1907. In this article McKnight mentions a decision made years earlier.

7 "Autobiography," p. 67. McKnight does not give dates for Rickert-Finlay's move to Long Island, although the context suggests 1902 or 1903, or for the incorporation of the McKnight Realty Company, although he discusses company business beginning in 1902.

8 Ibid.

9 "Five McKnights Form McKnight Realty Co." By the phrase "the McKnight brothers build their

[own] homes," the writer meant that the brothers lived in their developments, some in new houses and others in historic houses. Although the McKnights may have occasionally contracted for a house or two, their strategy was to sell lots without houses.

10 "Real Estate Exchange of Long Island Incorporated," *Brooklyn Daily Eagle*, March 23, 1907.

11 H. S. McKnight, "Attractions of the North Shore Region Which Will Benefit Most by East River Tunnels and Bridges," *New York Times*, April 26, 1908.

12 Ibid.

13 "Autobiography," p. 66.

14 Ibid., p. 68.

15 Ibid.

16 *Brooklyn Daily Eagle*, August 14, 1909; *Atlas of Nassau County* (New York: E. Belcher Hyde, 1906).

17 "Autobiography," p. 68.

18 Ibid., p. 71.

19 "Purchase at Great Neck," *New York Times*, April 11, 1909.

20 In the early years the development was sometimes called The Estates at Great Neck.

21 "Big Development Superbly Planned. Modern Ideas Adopted in Laying Out Great Neck Estates. Welfare of Colony Forever Protected. Accomplished by Incorporating Entire Tract into a Separate Village," *New-York Tribune*, May 24, 1914. It is sometimes said that the competition for the Great Neck Estates plan was won by Harold L. Bartlett, C. E. (a civil engineer). The village owns a set of plans drawn up by Bartlett in 1910, and there is no known copy of a Pope plan. Further complicating the design issue is a statement in "Our Village, Great Neck Estates," undated pamphlet, apparently ca. 1958, distributed by the Great Neck Civic Association: "Russell Pope designed and engineered our village." However, the Robert Anderson Pope attribution is confirmed by the above-cited *New-York Tribune* article, along with additional information about the career of Robert Anderson Pope. [John] Russell Pope, by 1909 a distinguished architect who was involved in little landscape design, is not a likely candidate for the Great Neck Estates plan.

22 "Handsome Residences Under Construction in the Great Neck Section," 14, May 22, 1910. Supporting this date are the Harold L. Bartlett plans, dated November 1910.

23 Frederick Law Olmsted Jr., son of Central Park designer Frederick Law Olmsted, headed a large landscape-planning firm that designed scores of suburban communities, developments, and parks throughout the eastern United States. In 1908 the Olmsted firm, then working on Forest Hills Gardens in Queens, was retained by the Great Neck Improvement Company to design Great Neck Hills. "Thomaston," undated pamphlet, p. 11. Great Neck Public Library. Olmsted may be the link between the McKnight brothers and Robert Anderson Pope.

24 Information on Robert Anderson Pope, the Conference on City Planning at which he spoke, and the planning projects at Jamaica Plain and Smith Point, as well as another community he designed in the Philadelphia suburb of Narberth, was all found through an online search.

25 Pope may have suggested building envelopes at Great Neck Estates as he did at Jamaica Plain.

26 The name Thornewood, applied to this linear section of Great Neck Estates, appears in several newspaper notices, including "R. A. Coe Is Building a 2½-Story Frame House . . . ," *New York Sun*, 1912 (real estate notes, rest of date, and title information cut off microfilmed copy).

27 "McKnight Realty Company Sales," 14 Ibid., July 10, 1910.

28 "New Hotel and North Shore State Highway Great Aids in Long Island Development," *New York Times*, April 2, 1911.

29 "Purchase at Great Neck," *New York Times*, April 11, 1909.

30 "Estates at Great Neck" is an eight-page promotional brochure printed in 1909 or early 1910. A copy is owned by the village. Describing the challenges presented by the site, it says that fifteen landscape architects and engineers competed in the planning contest. The development was conceived as a "great private park, open only to the dwellers therein," and it was to be "hedged about with restrictions."

31 *New York Times*, March 15, April 4, and June 23, 1910.

32 "Building Active at GN, LI," *Brooklyn Daily Eagle*, April 25, 1914. The McKnights claimed that they "never" built houses themselves, although they had houses built for their own residences.

33 "Artistic Homes Add to Attractiveness of Long Island's Residential Centres," *New York Times*, June 18, 1911.

34 The village's building department records were destroyed by fire. Known contractors include R. A. Coe, E. Folsom house, Maple Street west of Hillside Avenue, and Elm Street west of Hillside; H. Stadelman, Vista Drive near Circle; Wilson Dayton, two stucco houses on Deepdale Drive near Gateway; A. G. Dalameter, subdeveloper, concrete stucco house on Sycamore Drive and Spanish Mission house on Ridge Drive East.

35 Frank Joseph Forster (1886–1948), educated at Cooper Union and abroad, set up private practice in 1911, having worked for various firms from 1908 on. He specialized in domestic architecture, designing a stucco and half-timbered house in Great Neck for John R. Hoyt in 1920. Henry F. Withey and Elsie Rathburn Withey, *Biographical Dictionary of American Architects (Deceased)* (Los Angeles: Hennessey & Ingalls, 1970), p. 215; Robert B. MacKay. Anthony K. Baker, and Carol A. Traynor, eds., *Long Island Country Houses and Their Architects, 1860–1940* (New York: Society for the Preservation of Long Island Antiquities and W. W. Norton, 1997), pp. 170–71.

36 Oswald C. Hering (1874–1941), a noted domestic architect, studied at MIT and in Paris. He worked in the suburbs of Boston, Philadelphia, and New York, especially on Long Island. He designed the Fifth Avenue Brentano's bookstore. Withey and Withey, *Biographical Dictionary of American Architects* (Deceased), p. 279. In Great Neck Estates he designed three houses for John R. Corbin, a Dutch Colonial and two Tudors, on Magnolia and Ridge, 1914.

37 E. R. Tuchs, Gateway Drive, 1914.

38 "Many New Homes Built at Great Neck, L. I.," *Brooklyn Daily Eagle*, June 6, 1915. Irving B. Ells, five houses for The Frank Crowell, Inc., 1915.

39 "Handsome Residences under Construction in the Great Neck Section," *New York Times*, May 22, 1910.

40 Ibid. The purpose of the "dynamos" is not known,

and the plant was never built. Perhaps they were generators for individual houses.

41 "To Build Fine Houses at Great Neck Estates," *Brooklyn Daily Eagle*, March 15, 1910. Each house would cost between $15,000 and $20,000 to build.

42 The Thorne mansion became the clubhouse of the Great Neck Golf Club in the southwestern quadrant of the Estates in January 1912.

43 The gated wall and lodge were never built, nor was the "great dynamo."

44 "Estates at Great Neck," a promotional brochure printed in 1910 or 1911. Its few photographs show a great deal of picturesque scenery, one unpaved road, a sidewalk, and no houses.

45 Ibid.

46 "Big Development Superbly Planned. Modern Ideas Adopted in Laying Out . . . Welfare of Colony Forever Protected . . . ," *New-York Tribune*, May 24, 1914.

47 "Autobiography," p. 77.

48 "Home Seekers Looking to the Suburbs for Living Comforts at Moderate Cost," *New York Times*, February 18, 1912.

49 "Suburban Communities on Long Island Jumping into Activity for the Summer," *New York Times*, May 19, 1912.

50 Frieda Kessler, "The History of Great Neck Estates" pamphlet (n.p., n.d.). Great Neck Library. Kessler further noted that the Soundview water hole survives as the village's Pond Park.

51 "Syndicate of New York Capitalists Buy Site for Million-Dollar Hotel at Great Neck, Long Island," *New York Times*, April 1, 1911.

52 Ibid.

53 "Autobiography," p. 69.

54 McKnight gives no dates in this part of his autobiography. The date for the trip is based on the 1914 death date of Sir Frederick Mirrielees.

55 "Autobiography," p. 69.

56 Ibid., p. 70.

57 The information about Douglas Mirrielees's work on developing the Mirrielees Park section of Great Neck Estates is based on primary research done by Ilse Kagan, Great Neck Estates historian.

58 Mirrielees Park prospectus on display at Great Neck Estates village hall.

59 "Autobiography," p. 70.

60 According to Ilse Kagan's research, Mirrielees committed suicide.

61 "Autobiography," p. 70.

62 Ibid.

63 Ibid., p. 71.

64 Ibid.

65 Ibid., p. 73. McKnight was putting in a house foundation at Great Neck Estates for lawyer Bertram Pettigrew when North Hempstead Republican town leader Ed Allen approached him to ask if he was interested in being appointed Nassau County attorney.

66 "Autobiography," p. 71.

67 "Effect of Electrification," *New York Sun*, November 2, 1913.

68 "Building Active at GN, LI," *Brooklyn Daily Eagle*, April 25, 1914.

69 "Great Neck, LI, Home Nearing Completion," *Brooklyn Daily Eagle*, May 15, 1914.

70 "Many New Homes Built at Great Neck, LI . . . ," *Brooklyn Daily Eagle*, June 6, 1915.

71 Great Neck Estates Building-Zone Ordinance, December 19, 1921. On display at Great Neck Estates village hall.

72 "Living in Great Neck Estates: A Wealth of Attractions," *Newsday*, June 12, 1983.

73 Ilse Kagan, personal communication; Frieda Kessler, "The History of Great Neck Estates."

74 Ilse Kagan, personal communication.

75 "Great Neck Estates Has Its Own Private Bathing Beach . . . ," *Brooklyn Daily Eagle*, August 12, 1924.

76 Our Village, Great Neck," pamphlet, ca. 1958, distributed by the Great Neck Civic Association.

77 "Section Known as Great Neck School District . . . ," *Brooklyn Daily Eagle*, March 20, 1927.

78 Ibid.

79 Jill Silverman, "Humble Yet Grand, Wright House Leaves Its Mark on L. I.," *New York Times*, December 5, 1982.

80 The house is no longer standing.

81 Social notes in the *Brooklyn Daily Eagle* during the 1930s include several mentions of the McKnights' activities. One such reference can be found in the February 25, 1933, issue.

Paul V. Shields at Great Neck

1 *New York Evening Post*, July 22, 1941. Paul Shields, senior partner in the Wall Street brokerage firm founded in 1923 that bore his name, had just tendered his resignation as a governor of the New York Stock Exchange. He was preparing to be called to Washington to serve in "some branch of the government." "Louis G. Shields Dies on a Hunting Trip," *New York Times*, December 8, 1931. At the time of his death, L. G. Shields was a partner in Shields & Company and, like Paul and their brother, Cornelius, a prominent yachtsman.

2 Paul V. Shields was born in St. Paul, Minnesota, on October 24, 1890, and died in Manhattan on December 24, 1962. He is buried at Sacred Hearts of Jesus and Mary Roman Catholic Church cemetery in Southampton, Long Island. Findagrave.com, memorial #51304560. Louis G. Shields was born in Grand Forks, North Dakota, on June 6, 1887, and died on a hunting trip in Hampton Bays, Long Island, on December 7, 1931. "L. G. Shields Dies On A Hunting Trip," *New York Times*, December 8, 1931. Their younger brother, Cornelius Shields, was born in 1895. Cover story, "Cornelius Shields," *Time*, September 27, 1959.

3 Nothing is known about the financing of the Shields brothers' first real estate purchase. It is likely to have involved mortgages and construction loans secured by the value of the land and the houses.

4 Though no definite link has been found between Great Neck Estates and Great Neck Villa, the McKnight brothers developed Great Neck Estates under the name Villa Park Association and the Shields brothers used the name Great Neck Villa Company. Both developments feature the naturalistic landscape and infrastructure layout pioneered by Frederick Law Olmsted, and both the McKnights and the Shields worked with the landscape designer Robert Anderson Pope. Given that the McKnight brothers were experienced Long Island developers and the Shields brothers were young and new to the New York area, it is possible that the McKnight development model influenced the Shields's work.

5 "Great Neck's Development . . . ," *Brooklyn Times*,

March 27, 1909. This article mentions lot sizes from one-eighth to two-thirds of an acre, while an ad placed by Paul Shields in the *Brooklyn Daily Eagle*, October 24, 1909, "Great Neck Villa Colony," mentions lot sizes between one-half acre and two acres.

6   It is interesting to note that Great Neck Villa was laid out in the same year as Great Neck Estates, and its plan resembles, on a smaller scale, Robert Anderson Pope's plan for Great Neck Estates. Pope had had a relationship with the Olmsted brothers' firm for several years before winning a competition to design Great Neck Estates. Paul V. Shields chose Pope to be the landscape designer for his next Great Neck development, Grenwolde, in 1912.

7   "Great Neck's Development . . . ," *Brooklyn Times*, March 27, 1909; "Building Activity in Great Neck," *New York Times* May 23, 1909. The New York Times article states that the Dutch Colonial was being built by John M. Clark, and the California bungalow by Charles W. Dillon. The house about to be started was being built for Vincent Parke. A later notice (New York Times, May 22, 1910) implies that these new houses were the residences of the men mentioned; they were probably not the builders or contractors.

8   "Great Neck Villa Estates," an advertisement placed by Louis G. and Paul V. Shields, 1 Wall Street, *Brooklyn Daily Eagle*, June 12, 1909.

9   Ibid.

10 Ibid.

11 "Great Neck Villa Colony," advertisement, *Brooklyn Daily Eagle*, October 24, 1909.

12 "Real Estate Notes," *New York Herald*, May 22, 1910.

13 "Handsome Residences under Construction in the Great Neck Section," *New York Herald*, May 22, 1910.

14 "While 1910 Has Generally [Been] an Off Year . . . ," *New York Herald*, May 28, 1911. What the Ashley sewerage system was is not known. It may have been similar to the system planned for Grenwolde, which featured an on-site sewer treatment plant.

15 "New Hotel and North Shore State Highway Great Aids in Long Island Development," *New York Times*, April 2, 1911.

16 Several of these postcards, labeled "Great Neck Villa. Shields Co. 1 Wall St. N.Y.C.," are in the collection of the Great Neck Public Library. Two of the cards are on display at the Thomaston Village Hall.

17 "In the Berkshires of Long Island," *Brooklyn Daily Eagle*, May 13, 1911; postcards in the Great Neck Public Library.

18 "Home Seekers Looking to the Suburbs for Living Comforts at Moderate Cost," *New York Times*, February 18, 1912.

19 "Long Island's Popular Suburban Resorts Showing Evidences of Building Activity," *New York Times*, March 24, 1912.

20 "Progress the Watchword of Long Island Through All Its Suburban Communities," *New York Times*, June 16, 1912.

21 Besides Paul Shields, the only syndicate member whose name has been confirmed is Walter J. Vreeland. "Cottage Colony at Great Neck from Ideas Obtained in England," *New York Herald*, March 9, 1913, Section 4, p. 3.

22 "New Development at Great Neck, Long Island," *New York Herald*, October 6, 1912. This article states that the parcel developed as Grenwolde was part of the Skidmore Estate.

23 "Exclusive Colony To Be at Great Neck," *New York Herald*, October 25, 1902, p. 11. The realty firm Osgood & Pell announced the sale of 105 acres of the Skidmore Estate to a syndicate of wealthy New Yorkers for a colony of summer homes. It would not deny the rumor that U.S. Steel president Charles M. Schwab was involved in the plan. "Great Neck Favored by Many Men of Millions." *New York Herald*, April 6, 1904, p. 18. Mrs. H. Bramhall Gilbert purchased thirty acres of the Skidmore Estate on West Shore Road where she is building a magnificent summer residence. "Real Estate Notes," *Brooklyn Daily Eagle*, May 4, 1907, p. 4.

24 Shields's office was at 1 Wall Street; Vreeland's, at 129 Front Street.

25 W. J. Vreeland's name appeared in a number of legal and real estate notices in New York papers. "Mortgages," *New York Sun*, July 17, 1912, p. 13. Vreeland was attorney for a mortgage on a twelve-story building at 598 Broadway that was given to the Skidmore Estate by Thomas Howell. Following this notice came other notices of a foreclosure and a land swap involving property near Grenwolde.

26 *Brooklyn Daily Eagle*, May 4, 1907, p. 4. "The only two properties with waterfront on the market are the R. G. Mitchell estate . . . and the Skidmore estate of 100 acres held at $350,000."

27 "New Development at Great Neck, Long Island," *New York Herald*, October 6, 1912. This article mentions the "New York syndicate," and Shields's responsibility for development and sales.

28 "Grenwolde," *New York Sun*, March 2, 1913.

29 Ibid.

30 It is not known whether the Grenwolde sewage treatment facility was ever built, but according to real estate advertisements, the Grenwolde houses today are among the few in Kings Point that have a sewer system rather than septic tanks.

31 "New Development at Great Neck, Long Island," *New York Herald*, October 6, 1912.

32 Ibid. Shields is quoted as saying: "A casino will immediately be erected on the shore front reserved for plot owners not having actual water frontage . . ."; "For rent at Great Neck, LI," *New York Herald*, October 25, 1914, p. 4.

33 "New Development at Great Neck, Long Island," *New York Herald*, October 6, 1912, For more on Pope, see Great Neck Estates, pages xxx and xxx. and this essay page 6

34 Ibid.

35 Information on Robert Anderson Pope and the planning projects at Jamaica Plain and Smith's Point on Fire Island was found through an online search. The Watson Engineering Company was the contractor for the road and general development work at Grenwolde. See "New Development at Great Neck, Long Island," *New York Herald*, October 6, 1912.

36 "Cottage Colony at Great Neck from Ideas Obtained in England," *New York Herald*, March 9, 1913, Section 4, p. 3.

37 "Greater Great Neck," a map for real estate operators, developers, and others by Roger W. Allen, printed by the *Great Neck Record*, January 20, 1933. This map features all the neighborhoods and developments on the Great Neck peninsula and indicates the number of houses in each. Grenwolde appears

to have fifteen houses. The Kings Point assessor's office, however, lists only fourteen lots along Grenwolde Drive. The fifteenth property on the Allen map might have been the casino.

38 "Cottage Colony at Great Neck from Ideas Obtained in England," *New York Herald*, March 9, 1913.

39 "Grenwolde, Long Island's English Colony," *New York Sun*, March 2, 1913. The concept of English cottage–style houses was almost certainly Paul Shields's own.

40 Ibid.

41 Ibid.

42 Ibid.

43 "Cottage Colony at Great Neck from Ideas Obtained in England," *New York Herald*, March 9, 1913, Section 4, p. 3. *Architectural Record* 36, no. 4 (October 1914), pp. 456–61, features photographs and floor plans of three Grenwolde houses.

44 Henry F. Withey and Elsie Rathburn Withey. *Biographical Dictionary of American Architects* (Deceased) (Los Angeles: Hennessey & Ingalls, 1970), p. 215.

45 "Waterfront Property," *New York Herald*, April 6, 1913. This advertisement mentions deed restrictions, cites Edward King as architect, and includes a pretty engraving of a Grenwolde house.

46 "The Yachtsman Will Find . . . ," *New York Herald*, April 13, 1913.

47 "English Cottage at Grenwolde," *New York Times*, February 16, 1913; "An Exclusive Glory," *New York Herald*, March 1, 1913; "Grenwolde, Long Island's English Colony," *New York Sun*, March 2, 1913; "Waterfront Property," *New York Herald*, April 6, 1913; "The Yachtsman Will Find . . . ," *New York Herald*, April 13, 1913; "Grenwolde, Great Neck, LI," *New York Times*, May 30, 1913; "The Bride's Home," *New York Times* June 6, 1913; "Demand for Long Island Real Estate . . . New Bungalow at Grenwolde," *New York Times*, June 8, 1913; "Grenwolde, Great Neck, LI," *New York Herald*, June 15, 1913; "A Dutch Colonial Home," *New York Times*, March 10, 1914.

48 "A Dutch Colonial Home," *New York Times*, March 10, 1914.

49 "Grenwolde, Great Neck, LI," *New York Herald*, June 15, 1913. "If you are looking for value in a country home, $15,000 at Grenwolde has greater purchasing power . . ."

50 "At Grenwolde, Great Neck, LI," *New York Times*, July 26, 1914.

51 "For rent at Great Neck, LI," *New York Herald*, October 25, 1914, p. 4.

52 The Shields residences are listed in the death notice of Paul's wife, Veronica Gibbons Balfe Shields, who died on October 28, 1958, at Southampton, Long Island. Findagrave.com.

53 *Architectural Forum* 35 (September 1921), pl. 44. The house is also pictured in the *Architectural Record* 51 (June, 1922), pl. 500, 501, and 502. The Shields house at 2 Grenwolde Drive was originally one and a half stories tall, a long, low, simple design with hipped roofs and an engaged, double-gabled entry bay.

54 Ellen Fletcher Russell, "Chester A. Patterson," in Robert B. MacKay, Anthony K. Baker, and Carol A. Traynor, eds. *Long Island Country Houses and Their Architects, 1860–1940* (New York: Society for the Preservation of Long Island Antiquities and W. W.

Norton, 1997), pp. 331–32; websites for Soundview Manor, White Plains, New York, and Sutton Manor, New Rochelle, New York.

55 Building Department, Village of Kings Point, Section 1, Block 69, Lot 21.

56 Assessor's Department, Village of Kings Point; website maintained by Trulia, a firm specializing in high-end properties in the Great Neck area.

57 Chris-Craft Industries Company History, ChrisCraft.com., entry for 1956.

58 Findagrave.com/memorial #51304560. This site also states that Gary Cooper (1901–1961) was the step-uncle of actress Brooke Shields.

59 *People*, September 21, 1959. "Actress Model Suzy Parker, 26, was seeing a lot of Wall Street's impeccable, rich 70-year-old widower Paul V. Shields, brother and investment banking partner of champion yachtsman Cornelius Shields, 'the grey fox of Long Island Sound.' . . . Gary Cooper, 58, is the real-life son-in-law of Paul V. Shields."

Carl Graham Fisher and Montauk Beach

1 Carl G. Fisher (CGF) to John "Jack" LaGorce, spring 1925, in Jane Fisher, *Fabulous Hoosier* (New York: Robert M. McBride & Co., 1947), p. 216.

2 CGF to W. A. Kohlhepp, April 28, 1924. HistoryMiami, Archives & Research Center, Carl Fisher Collection (HistoryMiami).

3 Jerry M. Fisher, *The Pacesetter: The Untold Story of Carl G. Fisher* (Fort Bragg, CA: Lost Coast Press, 1998), p. 274.

4 References to the English Downs occur several times in Fisher's correspondence, and in Montauk advertising, specifically in materials prepared in 1926. HistoryMiami.

5 Ralph Hausrath, "Carl G. Fisher and Montauk," *Long Island Forum*, November 1981, p. 225; Fisher, *The Pacesetter*, p. 274; Mark S. Foster, *Castles in the Sand* (Gainesville, FL: University Press of Florida, 2000), p. 248. The use of the early Montauk trains to carry fish is documented in oral histories conducted by the Montauk Library with descendants of fishing village residents.

6 Walking Tour of the McKim, Mead & White Association Houses on the Montauk Bluffs, September 24, 1994, sponsored by the Friends of the Montauk Library; Lucy Lawless, Caroline Loughlin, and Lauren Meier, eds., *The Master List of Design Projects of the Olmsted Firm, 1857–1979*, 2nd ed. (Washington, DC: National Association for Olmsted Parks and National Park Service, Frederick Law Olmsted National Historic Site, 2008).

7 Polly Redford, *Million Dollar Sandbar* (New York: E. P. Dutton & Co., 1970), p. 160; *New York Times*, September 20, 1925, p. 30; Fisher, *The Pacesetter*, p. 274; Fisher, *Fabulous Hoosier*, p. 186.

8 Hausrath, "Carl G. Fisher and Montauk," p. 226.

9 "Montauk Park Title Is Upheld by Court," *New York Times*, September 21, 1928, p. 17.

10 "Buys Big Montauk Tract," *New York Times*, , September 20, 1925; *East Hampton Star*, September 18, 1925. The purchase did not actually close until the following February: *East Hampton Star*, February 19, 1926; "Buys 10,000 Acres at Montauk Point," *New York Times*, February 26, 1926, p. 4.

11 Fisher, *The Pacesetter*, p. 8.

12 Some of Fisher's earliest colleagues who stayed with him through the Montauk project included race

car drivers Barney Oldfield and Thomas Milton, motorboat racer Gar Wood, aviator Eddie Rickenbacker, cyclist A. C. Newby, engine designer Jim Allison, and General Robert Tyndall.

13 Fisher, *The Pacesetter*, pp. 16–18.

14 Fisher, *Fabulous Hoosier*, pp. 50–51.

15 Fisher, *The Pacesetter*, pp. 36–37.

16 Ibid., p. 37.

17 Ibid., p. 28.

18 Ibid., pp. 46–47.

19 Ibid., p. 69.

20 Fisher, *Fabulous Hoosier*, p. 85.

21 Ibid., p. 139.

22 Foster, *Castles in the Sand*, p. 149.

23 According to Jane Fisher in Fisher, *Fabulous Hoosier*, p. 130, Alton Beach was named for a freight car Carl Fisher had seen and he liked the sound of the name. However, there is an Alton Drive in Indianapolis, which Fisher might have known. Google Earth, Indianapolis, Indiana.

24 Foster, *Castles in the Sand*, p. 148.

25 "Alton Beach Today Seems Like a Fairy Land," *Miami Herald*, December 10, 1913.

26 Abraham D. Lavender, *Miami Beach in 1920* (Charleston, SC: Arcadia Publishing, 2002), p. 70. August Geiger was born in 1888 and came to Miami in 1905 from New Haven, Connecticut. He designed schools and other public buildings, as well as clubs and residences. *From Wilderness to Metropolis: The History and Architecture of Dade County 1825–1940*, 2nd ed. (Miami: Metropolitan Dade County Office of Community Development, Historic Preservation Division, 1992), p. 194.

27 Much later, at Montauk, manager J. G. McCaffrey acknowledged this key idea in a letter to Carl Fisher: "We all know . . . that the reason why we have the hotel, the office building, the golf club, the polo field and all the rest of the development . . . [we] have built these attractive features with one purpose in mind, and that is to sell property." McCaffrey to CGF, August 24, 1927. *HistoryMiami*.

28 Foster, *Castles in the Sand*, p. 196.

29 Fisher, *Fabulous Hoosier*, pp. 145–47.

30 Ibid., pp. 150–51. Rosie was given to Jane and Carl Fisher by Ed Ballard, another Hoosier, and former owner of the Ringling Brothers Circus.

31 Ibid., p. 70.

32 For a discussion of the Lincoln Highway, see Fisher, *The Pacesetter*, pp. 74–138. The Lincoln Highway has been subsumed by today's interstates 1, 30, 40, and 50. I-80 most closely follows the Lincoln Highway's original route.

33 "Dixie Highway," Wikipedia. Parts of the Dixie Highway survive today as various numbered highways and local streets.

34 The major repositories of Carl G. Fisher's correspondence are at HistoryMiami, Archives & Research Center (the former Historical Museum of Southern Florida), the Wolfsonian Museum at Florida International University, and the Montauk Library.

35 Jane Fisher thought very highly of Fred Hoerger, the inexperienced "youngster" who had been assistant gardener at their Indianapolis house. Carl gave Hoerger full responsibility for planting at Miami Beach (in the sterile slurry thrown up by the dredging), "and how that faith was justified!" she remarks in Fisher, *Fabulous Hoosier*, p. 132. In fact, Fred Hoerger rose to become general superintendent of the Miami project, then moved to Montauk in March 1926 to do the same job there.

36 "Florida Resorts Boom LI," *New York Times*, January 10, 1926. "Mr. Fisher has stated that he will transfer 1000 of his employees from Miami to Montauk in the summer, thus enabling him to settle a very important economic question of labor." The oral histories of Montauk in the Fisher era recorded by the Montauk Library also confirm that managers and laborers moved from one Fisher project to another. One interviewee noted that Montauk filled up with people from "Miami Beach and Port Washington and Indianapolis" who came up with Fisher from Miami.

37 Architectural drawings dated 1920 and signed by August Geiger for The Shadows are bound into a scrapbook apparently compiled as a sales aid for Fisher's Lincoln Road estate. The house stood on 4 ½ bay front acres near the La Gorce Golf Course, had an observation tower, 6 bathrooms, a garage, boathouse, swimming pool, dock landing, and landscaped grounds. HistoryMiami, Archives & Research Center, acc. no. USFL/xc1993.703/photo album.

38 John Levi to CGF, April 23, 1919, Wolfsonian Museum. William L. Price and M. Hawley McLanahan practiced architecture in Philadelphia. Price began as a draftsman for the Pennsylvania Railroad and designed stores, commercial buildings, and large houses. McLanahan specialized in large resort hotels. Henry F. Withey, and Elsie Rathburn Withey, *Biographical Dictionary of American Architects (Deceased)* (Los Angeles: Hennessey & Ingalls, 1970), pp. 412, 489.

39 John Levi to CGF, April 23, 1919. HistoryMiami. Levi was about to start the grading on Star Island. He told Fisher that a Mr. Hausman of St. Louis was having "DeGarmo" draw up plans for a $30,000 house on his 1 ½ lots. Walter C. DeGarmo is indexed in *From Wilderness to Metropolis*, p. 193.

40 CGF to James H. Snowden, April 26, 1919. HistoryMiami. "I looked over the two houses that Bastian had laid out and they are suitable for Star Island. . . . I am perfectly willing to build these two houses myself or to select two more from Bastian and have him get them all up by December." Harry S. Bastian is described as a busy Miami architect in 1920 in Lavender, *Miami Beach in 1920*, p. 76.

41 CGF to James H. Snowden (president of the Miami Ocean View Company, owners of Star Island), HistoryMiami. "I have found in building houses that we need all kinds, some people don't like the Spanish type with flat roofs. Our Colonial style houses, which Bastian has built for us, are selling very well."

42 Ibid.

43 Fisher, *The Pacesetter*, p. 198; Redford, *Million Dollar Sandbar*, p. 124.

44 Carl Fisher to John LaGorce, no date, quoted in Redford, Million Dollar Sandbar, p. 127.

45 Ibid., p. 250.

46 The Wolfsonian Museum at Florida International University mounted an exhibition on Schultze & Weaver, *In Pursuit of Pleasure, Schultze & Weaver and the American Hotel*, in 2010. The museum owns many of the firm's drawings, including those for the Nautilus Hotel, Montauk Manor, the unbuilt second Montauk hotel, and a Montauk residence for Arthur Brisbane.

47 Redford, *Million Dollar Sandbar*, p. 135; Fisher, *The Pacesetter*, p. 250.

48 Typescript of restrictions for the Fisher subdivisions, undated. HistoryMiami, box 11. The subdivisions named are: Mid-Golf Subdivision, Osborn Tract, Island View Subdivision, Subdivision of Block 80, Pine Ridge Subdivision, Belleview Subdivision, Third Commercial Subdivision, Palm View Subdivision, Nautilus Subdivision, Ocean Front Subdivision, First Pine Tree Subdivision, and Sunset Lake Subdivision.

49 CGF to G. Maurice Heckscher, August 21, 1921. HistoryMiami.

50 Redford, *Million Dollar Sandbar*, p. 159.

51 Fisher, *The Pacesetter*, p. 272.

52 George L. Williams, "Bayview Colony," *Journal of the Cow Neck Peninsula Historical Society*, Fall 1999, pp. 23–33; Fisher, *Fabulous Hoosier*, p. 214, notes that CGF planned to use the home office to meet New Yorkers interested in Montauk, and to house Bob Tyndall, Art Reed, and other employees at Bayview Colony.

53 Fisher, *The Pacesetter*, pp. 251, 278; Fisher, *Fabulous Hoosier*, p. 167; Foster, *Castles in the Sand*, p. 199.

54 Irving Collins to CGF, May 19, 1925. HistoryMiami.

55 Fisher, *Fabulous Hoosier*, p. 216. Another investor who advised against Montauk was Jack LaGorce, vice president of the National Geographic Society. Jane heard Carl say to him, "Hell, Jack, I've got to build something. I just have to see the dirt fly!" This is a variant on the quote cited in note 1.

56 Ibid., p. 214.

57 Fisher, *Fabulous Hoosier*, p. 213.

58 *East Hampton Star*, September 25, 1925, p. 1; Composite Map Showing Property Under Development. The Montauk Beach Development Corporation, Montauk, NY. This very large map, signed by Thomas E. Ringwood, a copy of which is at the Southampton Town Hall (2011.51), shows various water-level readings with dates between October and December 1925.

59 "Carl Fisher Inspects Construction Work . . . This Week," *East Hampton Star*, May 21, 1926.

60 "Organization of the Montauk Beach Development Corporation, October 27, 1925. . . to acquire and develop . . . certain properties on the extreme eastern end of Long Island." HistoryMiami, box 12.

61 *East Hampton Star*, September 25, 1925, p. 1.

62 "Carl Fisher Planned Montauk Transformation in Single Afternoon," information brochure, Long Island Railroad, March 1927. Long Island Division, Queens Borough Public Library.

63 Ibid.

64 Fisher, *Fabulous Hoosier*, pp. 214–15.

65 Hausrath, "Carl G. Fisher and Montauk," p. 231.

66 "Florida Resorts Boom LI," *New York Times*, January 10, 1926.

67 "Montauk Inn a Beehive of Activity," *East Hampton Star*, April 9, 1926.

68 Kohlhepp, October 13, 1925. HistoryMiami.

69 "Construction Work at Montauk Given Impetus by Last Week's Fire," *East Hampton Star*, May 7, 1926.

70 "Montauk Beach on Long Island. The Miami Beach of the North. A Carl Fisher Development," an undated promotional booklet produced by the MBDC in early 1926. It includes many photographs of Montauk under construction and emphasizes the workmen and the development process. This publication was popular with MBDC salesmen and executives, and was referred to as "the Booklet." Copies found at the Montauk Library and at the Wolfsonian Museum.

71 Ibid.

72 Ibid.

73 Ibid.

74 CGF to Hugh W. Davis, telegram, March 13, 1926. HistoryMiami.

75 CGF to Rep. Robert L. Bacon, December 6, 1926. HistoryMiami.

76 The Montauk Library oral history project recorded a resident of the fishing village saying that many of her neighbors were on the payroll of the Star Island Club (Fisher's nightclub, next door the Yacht Club). Their job was to look out for the police. At their signal, staff inside the club would efficiently transform the interior to look like a dining room. The interviewee's brother was a bootlegger who supplied the Fisher enterprise. (Many of the interviewees admitted that their fathers or uncles had been bootleggers.)

77 CGF to Hugh W. Davis, March 1, 1926. HistoryMiami.

78 Fisher, *Fabulous Hoosier*, p. 215.

79 Oral histories of the Carl Fisher era. Montauk Library.

80 Richard Webb, "Builder's Record of Progress," a photographic record of construction during the peak years of 1927 and 1928, with information on designers and contractors, and photographs of most of the buildings under construction. Montauk Library.

81 Oral histories of the Carl Fisher era. Montauk Library.

82 "Let Contract for Piers . . . ," *East Hampton Star*, February 2, 1926.

83 "Work Started on Houses in Employee Village," *East Hampton Star*, March 26, 1926.

84 Fisher, *Fabulous Hoosier*, p. 215.

85 Ibid.

86 Ibid. Jane Fisher is one source for the spring 1926 start date for Fisher's house. A second is Jeannette Edwards Rattray, *Montauk: Three Centuries of Romance, Sport and Adventure* (Montauk, NY: Star Press, 1938). For the architectural attribution to Wood, see *Private Residences and Public Buildings from the Carl Fisher Era* (Montauk, NY: privately printed pamphlet, 1994) at Montauk Library. This source says that the house was designed in 1928.

87 Schultze & Weaver, Job # 140, Hotel No. 1, Montauk Point, Montauk Beach Development Corporation. March 1, 1926. The roll of drawings also includes sets of plans for Job #140-A, the Service Building and Garage, dated June 7, 1926. These buildings, which no longer exist, were stucco-on-lath, half-timber structures with slate roofs. The Wolfsonian Museum at Florida International University, Works on Paper. The Wolfsonian's Schultze & Weaver collection also includes drawings for Hotel No. 2, dated September 17, 1926, and annotated "do not believe this was built as there are no revisions on drawings. A.M.M." There are also drawings for Fisher's Nautilus Hotel, the Gorce [*sic*] Island Club, and Arthur Brisbane's Montauk residence.

88 Hugh H. Davis to CGF, March 30, 1926. HistoryMiami.

89 "Montauk Beach on Long Island."

90 CGF to Roscoe T. Tracy, Patchogue Chamber of Commerce, April 2, 1926. Fisher says he has "ordered a seven-story office building to be erected . . . where we expect to be located in about four months." Attribution to Schultze & Weaver in "To Erect Seven-Story Building at Montauk," *East Hampton Star*, May 7, 1926. *Private Residences and Public Buildings from the Carl Fisher Era* also attributes the building to Schultze & Weaver and says that S & W used the same plans that they developed for Fisher's Lincoln Road office building in Miami. Photographs of the Miami building confirm a general resemblance; both buildings had square footprints, seven stories, and setback penthouses surrounded by terraces.

91 "Rapid Progress Made at Montauk," *Suffolk County News*, September 17, 1926, p. 11.

92 Ibid.

93 Roy D. Chapin to CGF, April 10, 1928. History-Miami. Chapin was concerned about the appearance of the bathing casino and the proposed second hotel, which at that time Fred Britten wanted to build.

94 Most of the information on Richard Webb and the Pearson Construction Company is from Richard Webb, "Builder's Record of Progress." See *Private Residences and Public Buildings from the Carl Fisher Era* for information on the Community Church.

95 A long-time Montauk resident interviewed for the Montauk Library oral history project recalled that the Posposil family came from Mineola and added that quite a few of the people involved in building and construction at Montauk came from the Mineola vicinity.

96 Leon N. Gillette and A. Stewart Walker were highly regarded as residential architects in the 1920s and had worked on Long Island before becoming involved with Montauk. See Withey and Withey, *Biographical Dictionary of American Architects (Deceased)*, pp. 235–36. Caleb Bragg's seven-building compound included two gatehouses with servants' and guests' quarters; a house for kitchen, pantry, and dining; a house used as a living room; a house used as a playroom with a dance floor; and other houses for sleeping and music. See *Private Residences and Public Buildings from the Carl Fisher Era*.

97 Robert Tappan sketches are in Album #1698, Montauk Library. The library also owns a copy of the MBDC promotional booklet. An undated clipping in the *Suffolk County News* from 1927, "Lake Inlet Opened," contains an article based on information provided by Albin Pearson about the theater building.

98 "Huge Dredge Arrives . . . ," *East Hampton Star*, June 8, 1926; "Huge Dredge Arrives at Fort Pond . . . ," *East Hampton Star*, June 11, 1926; "Carl Fisher Works Wonders," *Suffolk County News*, July 1, 1926.

99 Fisher, *Fabulous Hoosier*, p. 217.

100 Ibid., p. 220.

101 "Schedule of Restrictions," n.d., filed with documents from May 1926. HistoryMiami.

102 Fisher, *Fabulous Hoosier*, p. 220.

103 "Montauk," *East Hampton Star*, July 30, 1926.

104 Rattray, *Montauk*, p. 82.

105 "Montauk," *East Hampton Star*, July 30, 1926.

106 "Work Starts on Seven Stores and Eleven Apartments. Rapidity Amazes People. Rushes All Branches of Construction," *East Hampton Star*, July 23, 1926.

107 CGF to Irving Collins, September 10, 1926. History-Miami.

108 Redford, *Million Dollar Sandbar*, pp. 167–75.

109 Fisher, *Fabulous Hoosier*, pp. 232–33.

110 Ibid., p. 233.

111 "Carl Fisher and Guests Rush from Montauk to Miami . . ." *East Hampton Star*, September 24, 1926.

112 Foster, *Castles in the Sand*, p. 277. In Redford, *Million-Dollar Sandbar*, p. 179, Polly Redford analyzes Montauk as it stood at the end of 1926. Fisher, she writes, had by that time spent $6 million on Montauk Manor, the seven-story office building, docks, a yacht club, polo fields, and an unfinished golf course. (She leaves out the expensive infrastructure, the dredging, the downtown buildings, and all the houses and other facilities for MBDC staff, as well as the school and other "perks" for the Montauk villagers. There were also a number of mansions built by Fisher and others.)

113 Fisher, *Fabulous Hoosier*, p. 240.

114 CGF to Hugh Davis, December [date illeg.], 1926. HistoryMiami.

115 Hugh Davis to CGF, December [date illeg.], 1926. HistoryMiami.

116 CGF Memorandum to Montauk executives, December, 1926. HistoryMiami.

117 Walter A. Kohlhepp to CGF, December 13, 1926. HASF. HistoryMiami.

118 Richard Hoyt to CGF, January 10, 1927. History-Miami.

119 Long Island Railroad Information Bulletin, June 1927. Queens Borough Public Library, Long Island Division.

120 A status report on work done in Miami and Montauk in 1926–27 is found in a small printed book, probably for Fisher's salesmen, dated October 31, 1927. HistoryMiami.

121 Fisher, *The Pacesetter*, pp. 392–93.

122 Fisher, *Fabulous Hoosier*, p. 243. Carl Fisher drank heavily, ate poorly, and had cirrhosis of the liver.

123 Ibid., p. 244.

124 CGF to Edwin B. Wilson, City Editor, *Brooklyn Daily Eagle*, August 24, 1927.

125 Ibid.

126 Henry B. Joy to O. D. Treiber, October 19, 1927. HistoryMiami.

127 A Walking Tour of the McKim, Mead & White Association Houses . . . , 1994. Montauk Library. Six years later, after Carl had lost his big house on the hill, he moved into this one, where he spent summers comfortably, if less grandly. CGF to Thomas Milton, April 29, 1933. HistoryMiami.

128 Parke Haynes to Thomas Ringwood, October 24, 1927; Parke Haynes to CGF, October 25, 1927. HistoryMiami.

129 Fisher, *Fabulous Hoosier*, p. 240.

130 Hausrath, "Carl G. Fisher and Montauk," p. 256; L.I.R.R. Information Bulletin, April–May 1928. Queens Borough Public Library, Long Island Division. Howard E. Coffin was vice president of the Hudson Motor Car Company, Detroit, chairman of the National Airways Transport Co., and owner of a Montauk tract.

131 Robert H. Tyndall to CGF, July 18, 1928. History-Miami.

132 "Jury May Probe Montauk Gambling," *New York Evening Post*, August 21, 1928.

133 Fisher, *The Pacesetter*, p. 333. Jim Allison died of pneumonia in Indianapolis on August 3, 1928.

134 CGF to J. G. McCaffrey, August 24, 1927. History-Miami.

135 CGF to Parke G. Haynes, September 27, 1927. HistoryMiami.

136 Foster, *Castles in the Sand*, p. 286; photograph of Glenn Curtiss and Carl Fisher with the Aerocar on July 20, 1928, in Port Washington. Port Washington Public Library, Ernie Simon Collection.

137 Foster, *Castles in the Sand*, p. 291.

138 CGF to Thomas Milton, Detroit (a friend from car racing days), April 29, 1933; for the restriction prohibiting the building of these houses, see Thomas Ringwood to Fred Humpage, March 5, 1938. HistoryMiami.

139 "Latest Developments at Montauk Beach," *Long Island Railroad Magazine*, January–February 1929, pp. 10 ff.

140 CGF to George LeBoutillier, May 9, 1929. History-Miami.

141 Fisher, *The Pacesetter*, p. 346.

142 Ibid., p. 347.

143 *East Hampton Star*, October 18, 1929, quoted in Hausrath, "Carl G. Fisher and Montauk," p. 256.

144 Foster, *Castles in the Sand*, p. 268.

145 CGF to George LeBoutillier, October 3, 1929. HistoryMiami.

146 Parke G. Haynes to George LeBoutillier, October 7, 1929. HistoryMiami.

147 CGF to George LeBoutillier, October 18, 1929. HistoryMiami.

148 Fisher struggled to make good on the investments his friends had made in Montauk. A typical example: Carl sent ex-racing car driver Tommy Milton a deed to a Montauk lot in return for his stock in the dying corporation. Milton did not ask for the deed, but Fisher insisted he take it. Deed to a lot at Montauk, CGF to Thomas Milton, June 30, 1931. Letter, CGF to Thomas Milton, May 1, 1931. HistoryMiami.

149 Fisher, *Fabulous Hoosier*, p. 246.

150 Ibid., p. 195; CGF to Thomas Milton, April 29, 1933. HistoryMiami.

151 CGF to A. J. Jones, November 14, 1929. HistoryMiami.

152 To the Holders of Montauk Beach Development Corporation First Mortgage and Collateral Trust 6% Gold Bonds . . . , May 5, 1937. Wolfsonian Museum.

153 "Reviving a Grandiose Vision for Montauk," *New York Times*, August 14, 1977, p. 2.

154 CGF to Ernest L'Ecluse, January 13, 1930. HistoryMiami.

155 Ernest L'Ecluse to CGF, January 9, 1930. HistoryMiami.

156 CGF to LI State Park Commission, September 29, 1931. HistoryMiami.

157 Foster, *Castles in the Sand*, p. 293, recounting an interview by Polly Redford with "Pete" Chase, October 5, 1966.

158 "Big-time Gambling at Montauk Manor," New York World, July 14, 1930.

159 "Montauk Properties in Receivers Hands," *New York Times*, May 7, 1932, p. 30; "William H. Robbins Discharged . . . ," *Suffolk County News* October 19, 1934, p. 9, announces Ringwood's appointment as permanent receiver.

160 "Suffolk County Tax Sales," *Long-Islander*, November 11, 1932. This piece includes almost a full page

of MBDC properties, as well as properties owned by contractor Albin Pearson and the Montauk Sand & Gravel Corporation. Filed in Montauk Library.

161 "Carl G. Fisher Concern Sued," *New York Times*, July 8, 1934, p. N10.

162 Hausrath, "Carl G. Fisher and Montauk," p. 259; Fisher, *The Pacesetter*, p. 383.

163 Foster, *Castles in the Sand*, p. 291.

164 CGF to Margaret Fisher, Labor Day, 1935. History-Miami.

165 *Long Island Daily Press*, November 27, 1935.

166 "C. M. Keys Heads Montauk Company," *New York Times*, June 14, 1938, p. 36; Foster, *Castles in the Sand*, p. 299.

167 "Six Weeks of Intensive Publicity," September 30, 1938 (a broadsheet accompanying a status report from operations manager Alfred I. Barton). Montauk Library.

168 "Victims of the Storm. Nine More Bodies Found at Beaches," *New York Times*, September 25, 1938, p. 35; oral histories at Montauk Library.

169 "Carl G. Fisher Dead at Beach," *Miami Herald*, July 16, 1939; "Carl G. Fisher Dies," *New York Times*, July 16, 1939, p. 33; Fisher, *The Pacesetter*, p. 396.

170 "Miami Beach Talks Honor for Creator," *New York Times*, July 23, 1939, p. E6; Fisher, *The Pacesetter*, p. 397.

171 Thomas E. Ringwood to Westbrook Pegler of the *New York Telegram*, July 27, 1939. HistoryMiami.

172 "Montauk Beach Company . . . ," *East Hampton Star*, July 18, 1958; "Inexpensive Montauk Units," *East Hampton Star*, July 23, 1958.

173 "Montauk, the 300-Year War Zone," *East Hampton Star*, March 22, 2012.

Robert Burton's Woodmere

1 "Woodsburgh: A New Watering Place at Brooklyn's Door," *Brooklyn Daily Eagle*, May 11, 1870, p. 3.

2 Cromwell Childe, "Long Island Country Seats Are Built around Their Lawns," *Brooklyn Daily Eagle*, October 12, 1902, p. 37.

3 "Samuel Wood Estate sold for $130,000," *Brooklyn Daily Eagle*, May 20, 1901, p. 10.

4 "Work Is Already Under Way," *Brooklyn Daily Eagle*, August 1, 1901, p. 13.

5 "The Save New York Zone Extended to Protect Times Square, Theatre, Hotel and Motor Sections from Manufacturing Invasion," *New York Times*, February 20, 1921, p. RE1.

6 Auerbach would become the attorney for the Hewlett Bay Company, established ca. 1906, with Woodmere resident Carleton J. Macy as its president.

7 "Work Is Already Under Way," *Brooklyn Daily Eagle*, August 1, 1901, p. 13.

8 "Automobiles Are Barred," *Brooklyn Daily Eagle*, July 17, 1902, p. 7.

9 "Forty-three Cottages Being Completed This Year by the Cedarhurst Land Association," *Brooklyn Daily Eagle*, March 29, 1902, p. 18.

10 "Far Rockaway," *New York Times*, August 31, 1902, p. 32.

11 Gardner Teal, "The Cement House and Its Place in Our Architecture," *The Craftsman* 19 (October 1910–March 1911), pp. 571–73.

12 "$3,000 Deal a Feature in Long Island Market," *New York Times*, August 16, 1908, p. C5.

13 "To Hasten Woodmere's Development," *New York Times*, November 14, 1909, p. XX1.

14 Wilfred H. Schoff, "The $10,000 Country Home," *Country Life in America* 10, no. 6 (October 1906), pp. 651–80.

15 Aymar Embury II, *One Hundred Country Houses: Modern American Examples* (New York: The Century Co., 1909), p. 202.

16 "Attractive Concrete Home," *New York Times*, December 26, 1909, p. 12,

17 Robert B. MacKay, Anthony K. Baker, and Carol A. Traynor, eds., *Long Island Country Houses and Their Architects, 1860–1940* (New York: Society for the Preservation of Long Island Antiquities and W. W. Norton, 1997), p. 348.

18 C. E. Whittlesey. "The Commuter's Long Island," *House & Garden*, March 1911, p. 209.

19 The 1909 *Trow's New York Directory* lists the Woodmere Land Association at 432 Fifth Avenue, New York; its officers: Robert L Burton, President; D. Edward McAvoy, Secretary; John H. Burton, Treasurer. It also lists this additional information: "Woodmere Land Assn N Y . . . Capital $10,000 Directors: D. Edward McAvoy, John H and Robert L Burton, Frank Cotter, A. Macdonald Watts 432 5th ave." McAvoy was later the chairman of the Long Island Division of the Home Mortgage Advisory Board. See *Wall Street Journal*, May 5, 1933, p. 3.

20 "Morgenthau Buys a Town," *New York Times*, November 10, 1909, p. 1.

21 "Woodmere Land Ass'n," *Brooklyn Daily Eagle*, March 7, 1909.

22 The Woodmere Club's first Board of Governors included William B. Bryant, John H. Burton, George De Lacy, James Frank, Clarence G. Galston, Frederic Gurney, D. E. McAvoy, Maximilian Morgenthau, and Watson Vredenburgh.

23 Its wide veranda, with massive pillars, opened into the lounge or living room on first floor, a reception hall, secretary's office, ladies' parlor, the dining room, kitchen, locker rooms, and shower/baths. On the second floor was an assembly room and ball-room, three smaller reception or card rooms, a coat room, and steward's apartments. The basement housed two bowling alleys, the boiler room, and storerooms. Large fireplaces provided atmospheric warmth in both the assembly room and the elegant living room. The building is described in Dalton Wylie, "Country Club Architecture," *Country Life in America* 18 (September 1910), p. 557.

24 "Resale at Woodmere," *New York Times*, December 15, 1910, p. 15.

25 "Real Estate Show Drawing Crowds," *New-York Tribune*, April 30, 1911, p. B4.

26 The brochure states: "It has been determined by Government Statistics that this section of Long Island is from 10 to 15 degrees warmer in winter, and relatively cooler during the hot summer months, than most of the coast and inland resorts of the country. Devotees of out-door sports may therefore indulge in their pastimes late into the Fall and early in the Spring at Woodmere."

27 New York State Public Service Commission, *Reports of Decisions of the Public Service Commission, Second District of the State of New York: from January 1, 1920, to December 31, 1920*, vol. 9 (Albany: J. B. Lyon Company, 1921), pp. 113–18.

28 The story of the watershed, known locally as the Woodmere Woods or the Lord's Woods, is chronicled in Robert Arbib, *The Lord's Woods: The Passing of an American Woodland* (New York: W. W. Norton, 1971).

29 "Big Canal Scheme across Long Island," *New York Times*, April 17, 1910, p. XX8.

30 "To Hasten Woodmere's Development," *New York Times*, November 14, 1909, p. XX1.

31 Tjaden's landscaping for the Sanford Jacobi estate included 10,000 tulips as a temporary measure until the final garden was completed. Tjaden also proudly noted that on the Harold Jacobi house, she designed everything—"<u>not</u> decorator." See http://rmc.library.cornell.edu/eguides/manuscripts/15-6-2919.html.

32 Mrs. Marks was the daughter of Harold Jacobi. See *Brooklyn Eagle*, August 29, 1943, p. 19.

33 "A Country House in the Italian Style," *House & Garden*, August 1918, p. 29.

34 "Payor Sewers," *Rockaway Journal*, November 4, 1910, p. 1.

The Grand Scheme

1 First used at Garden City Estates, the expression was soon adopted by other developers such as Dean Alvord at Roslyn Estates. "As to Estates," *Brooklyn Life*, March 5, 1910.

2 "Famous 5th Av. Corner Sold for $1,500,000," *New York Times*, October 27, 1906.

3 "Closed Banks and Realty," *New York Times*, January 5, 1908.

4 "The Real Estate Field," *New York Times*, September 1, 1915.

5 Franklin P. Duryea served as second vice president of Jamaica Estates and Clayton S. Goss as secretary. Directors of the corporation included A. D. Bennett, president of the Night and Day Bank; Samuel N. Jarvis, president of the National Bank of Cuba; Myron T. Herrick, former governor of Ohio; George J. Smith, president of the Bayside Flushing Company; and M. J. Degnon, builder of the Belmont Tunnels.

6 "Jamaica Estates: A Grand Scheme," *Long Island Farmer*, August 13, 1907.

7 Undated Jamaica Estates promotional postcard, ca. 1907.

8 "Residential Parks Feature of Realty," *New York Times*, May 31, 1908.

9 Ibid.

10 "Jamaica Estates: A Grand Scheme," *Long Island Farmer*, August 13, 1907.

11 Julius David Stern, *Memoirs of a Maverick Publisher* (New York: Simon & Schuster, 1962), p. 154.

12 "500-Acre Development on Highlands near Jamaica," *New York Times*, May 3, 1908.

13 Among the architects of the earliest houses were Robert W. Gibson, who designed a Spanish Colonial residence for A. H. Langjahr, Upjohn & Conable, and C. F. Rosberg, who designed several, including a Dutch Colonial for Dr. J. Wilbur Chapman.

14 "500-Acre Development on Highlands near Jamaica," *New York Times*, May 3, 1908.

15 The first mass of the new parish, named Immaculate Conception, was celebrated on July 5, 1924, in the Degnon mansion library. The building, which became a parish office, monastery, and retreat house, was razed in 1952 and replaced by the Bishop Molloy Retreat House.

16 "To Develop 8,000 Lots," *New York Times*, January 19, 1908.

17 *Brooklyn Life*, October 5, 1907.

18 "Jamaica Estates Improvements," *New York Times*, June 30, 1912.

19 "Building Exhibit," *Brooklyn Life*, August 24, 1912.

20 Jamaica Estates Corporation, "An Established Development of Distinction," 1910. The same booklet also listed some of the "facts" about Jamaica Estates for potential buyers: "The property is divided into residence plots with areas from three to ten lots Spacious plots can be purchased as low as $2,025, including all the improvements, and convenient terms can be arranged; liberal discounts will be allowed for cash payments."

21 *New York Daily Tribune*, March 19, 1910.

22 The location of Depew's house had become lost over time. But after an Aquinas student discovered a 1913 engraving of the house, designed by architectural firm Mann & MacNeille, in the *New York Times*, it was found still standing on Midland Parkway and the Grand Central Service Road.

23 Another notable figure who lived in Jamaica Estates was classical composer Bohuslav Martinu; though not a resident, he found refuge there after fleeing war-ravaged Europe in 1942. He composed his Symphony No. 1, a violin concerto, and a cello sonata while staying at the home of the Castagnolia family on Croydon Road. Other musical talents who owned homes in Jamaica Estates include James Kendris, composer of "I'm Forever Blowing Bubbles" and other hit tunes, who lived on Cedarcroft Avenue, and Richard Husch Gerard of Kingston Place, composer of the famous "Sweet Adeline" barbershop quartet ballad.

24 A vaudevillian, monologist, dialectician, and playwright, Breese made his talking picture debut in Al Jolson's *Sonny Boy* (1929) and went on to play Herr Meyer in *All Quiet on the Western Front* (1930) and Prime Minister Zander in the Marx Brothers' classic film *Duck Soup* (1933).

25 "To Foreclose $281,000 Mortgage on Jamaica Estates," *New York Times*, September 1, 1915.

26 "To Sell 2,000 Lots in Jamaica Estates," *Brooklyn Daily Eagle*, May 30, 1929.

27 Thomas J. Lovely, *The History of the Jamaica Estates, 1929–1969* (Jamaica Estates, NY: Jamaica Estates Association, 1969).

28 In 1938, a new zoning regulation again limited property use to single-family houses.

29 In 2010, the Aquinas Honor Society secured funding through the assistance of State Senator Frank Padavan to erect a historical marker behind the gatehouse—the original entrance to Jamaica Estates. The text on it reads: "JAMAICA ESTATES—A RESIDENTIAL PARK In 1907, Real Estates Developers Ernestus Gulick and Felix Isman purchased 500 acres of land north of the colonial village of Jamaica and established the Jamaica Estates Corporation. Their purpose was to erect an affluent resort with an English flavor. Early partners included Lieutenant Governor Timothy L. Woodruff and NYC engineer and contractor Michael J. Degnon. An imposing entrance, with Elizabethan-style lodge and gatehouse, was designed by celebrated architect John Petit. The street system, with Midland Parkway as the centerpiece, was designed by well-known landscape architect Charles Leavitt. Jamaica Estates is distinguished for its Tudor style homes and beautiful landscapes."

Robert Weeks de Forest

1 "A Model City," *New York Times*, September 4, 1910, p. XA4.

2 "Munsey Park Stores," *New York Times*, January 18, 1931, p. RE4.

3 James A. Hilya, "Four Ways of Looking at a Philanthropist: A Study of Robert Weeks de Forest," *Proceedings of the American Philosophical Society* 124, no. 6 (December 1980), p. 412.

4 Jane Addams and Mr. de Forest, "The Housing Problem in Chicago," *Annals of the American Academy of Political and Social Science* 20 (July 1902), p. 106.

5 Lawrence Veiller, "The Housing Problem in American Cities," *Annals of the American Academy of Political and Social Science* 25 (March 1905), p. 251.

6 Ruth Crocker, *Mrs. Russell Sage: Women's Activism and Philanthropy in Gilded Age and Progressive Era America* (Bloomington, IN: Indiana University Press, 2006), pp. 308–9.

7 Ibid., pp. 219–24.

8 Ibid., p. 226.

9 "Artistic Home Community at Forest Hills Gardens," *New York Times*, December 4, 1910, p. X11.

10 Spiro Kostof, *A History of Architecture: Settings and Rituals* (New York: Oxford University Press, 1985), p. 679.

11 Susan L. Klaus, *A Modern Arcadia: Frederick Law Olmsted Jr. and the Plan for Forest Hills Gardens* (Amherst, MA: University of Massachusetts Press, 2002), p. 50.

12 Grosvenor Atterbury, "Model Towns in America," *Scribner's Magazine* 52, no. 1 (July 1912), p. 21.

13 Robert W. de Forest to Frederick Law Olmsted, December 7, 1908, letter reprinted in William E. Colman, ed., "Frederick Law Olmsted, Jr., the Garden City Movement and the Design of Forest Hills Gardens," *Forest Hills Gardens*, no. 2 (1994), p. 15.

14 De Forest to Olmsted, January 4, 1909, in Colman, *Forest Hills Gardens*, p. 17.

15 "Artistic Home Community at Forest Hills Gardens," p. X11.

16 Klaus, *A Modern Arcadia*, pp. 47–48.

17 De Forest to Olmsted, January 4, 1909, in Colman, *Forest Hills Gardens*, p. 17.

18 Klaus, *A Modern Arcadia*, p. 114.

19 Edward J. Smits, *Nassau Suburbia, U.S.A.: The First Seventy-five years of Nassau County, New York 1899 to 1974* (Garden City, NY: Doubleday & Company, 1974), p. 3.

20 Historical Census Browser. Retrieved May 2, 2012, from the University of Virginia, Geospatial and Statistical Data Center: http://mapserver.lib.virginia.edu.

21 Chamber of Commerce of the Borough of Queens, *Queens Borough, New York City, 1910–1920* (New York: L. I. Star Publishing Co., 1920), p. 113.

22 Klaus, *A Modern Arcadia*, p. 145.

23 "To Continue Work of Sage Foundation," *The Daily Star*, July 31, 1922, p. 2.

24 Susan Purcell, "The Maps of Forest Hills Gardens," *Forest Hills Gardens*, no. 2 (1994), 30–37.

25 R. L. Duffus, "Munsey Gift Puts Museum on a New Plane," *New York Times*, January 10, 1926, p. 5.

26 Robert de Forest, "The Fiftieth Anniversary of the Museum: An Address," *The Metropolitan Museum of Art Bulletin* 15, no. 6 (June 1920), p. 127.

27 Duffus, "Munsey Gift Puts Museum on a New Plane."

28 "Art Gets $17,305,594 of Museum Estate," *New York Times*, April 9, 1929, p. 1.

29 "Art Museum Enters the Realty Business," *New York Times*, December 30, 1929, p. 25.

30 Paul Emmons, "Diagrammatic Practices: The Office of Frederick L. Ackerman and Architectural Graphic Standards," *Journal of the Society of Architectural Historians* 64, no. 1 (March 2005), p. 4.

31 Michael H. Lang, "Town Planning and Radicalism in the Progressive Era: The Legacy of F. L. Ackerman," *Planning Perspectives* 16 (2001), p. 151.

32 "Open Munsey Park with Model Home," *New York Times*, February 19, 1928, p. 49.

33 De Forest, quoted in Hilya, "Four Ways of Looking at a Philanthropist," p. 416.

34 David Gebhard, "The American Colonial Revival in the 1930s," *Winterthur Portfolio* 22, no. 2/3 (Summer–Autumn 1987), p. 110.

35 Ibid., pp. 117–18.

36 De Forest, "The Fiftieth Anniversary of the Museum," p. 125.

37 "W. S. Coffin Chosen Art Museum Head," *New York Times*, December 2. 1931, p. 25.

Hapgood's Shoreham

1 National Archives and Records Administration (NARA), Washington, D.C., General Records of the Department of State, Record Group: RG59-Entry 205, Box number: 4148, Box Description: 1910–1929 Australia A to Re.

2 Randall Warden, "The Saga of Woodville Landing," *The Shoreham Scribe* 1, no. 9 (August 24, 1934); *Port Jefferson Echo*, May 19, 1894, p. 3.

3 J. Baxter Upham obituary, *New York Times*, March 19, 1902, p. 9.

4 Warden, "The Saga of Woodville Landing."

5 Marc Seifer, *Wizard: The Life and Times of Nikola Tesla, Biography of a Genius* (New York: Citadel Press, 1996), p. 260.

6 Patricia Herold, *Mountain Lakes 1911–2011: One Hundred Years of Community* (Mountain Lakes, NJ: privately printed, 2010), p. 7.

7 *The Trow (Formerly Wilson's), Copartnership and Corporation Directory of the Boroughs of Manhattan and the Bronx, City of New York* (New York: Trow Directory, Printing, and Bookbinding Co., 1906).

8 "Mountain Lakes Marks 50th Year of Controlled Growth," *New York Times*, Oct 20, 1974, p. NJ12.

9 Herold, *Mountain Lakes 1911–2011*, pp. 54–55.

10 *The Hapgood Houses of Mountain Lakes* (Mountain Lakes, NJ: Landmarks Committee, Borough of Mountain Lakes, 1983).

11 Judy Oliver Salgado, member, Shoreham Village Centennial Committee, personal communication with the author, 2012.

12 "The Glorious Fourth," *Shoreham Scribe*, July 6, 1934.

13 "W. H. Blatch Killed by Loose Live Wire: Suffrage Leader's Husband Steps on Broken End in Channing Pollock's Yard," *New York Times*, August 3, 1915, p. 4.

14 Mervin G. Pallister, *A History of the Incorporated Village of Shoreham in the Town of Brookhaven* (written, 1976; privately printed, 1995).

15 "Big Real Estate Transaction," *Long-Islander*, June 25, 1909, p. 5.

16 Herold, *Mountain Lakes 1911–2011*, p. 6.

17 "Big Tract Under the Hammer," *Brooklyn Daily Eagle*, February 15, 1905, p. 5.

18 "Land Co. Stockholders Make Serious Charges," *Brooklyn Daily Eagle*, December 31, 1910, p. 5.

19 *The Atlas Portland Cement Company, Concrete Houses and Cottages*, vol. 2 (New York: The Atlas Portland Cement Company, 1909), p. 35.

20 Channing Pollock, *Harvest of My Years: An Autobiography* (New York: Bobbs-Merrill Co., 1943), p. 176.

21 "Shoreham Colony Has Gypsy Bazaar: Long Island's 'Little Brooklyn' Raises Funds for Its Club," *Brooklyn Daily Eagle*, September 11, 1921, p. 24.

22 Shoreham, Long Island, photo book. The Shoreham Agency, 11 Wall Street, ca. 1910.

23 Herold, *Mountain Lakes 1911–2011*, p. 41.

Beacon Hill

1 A $275,000 mortgage, dated February 10, 1911, in the name of William Tuxill, father of Charles, was held by Vincent A. Howells of Florence, Italy. Nassau County Clerk, Mortgages, liber 159, folio 279. The 1906 E. Belcher Hyde map shows H. C. Howell as a previous owner of the Beacon Hill property. Tuxill later bought two additional acres for the entrance to Beacon Hill Road off Port Washington Boulevard. *Plain Talk* 1, no. 3 (October 14, 1911), p. 44; "Beacon Hill," *Plain Talk* 2, no. 8 (April 13, 1912), p. 119. Investors from Oswego and Syracuse helped finance the purchase. *Auburn Citizen*, March 29, 1911. Maps filed with the Nassau County Clerk's office show that Charles Tuxill divided the development into four sections, which he had surveyed one at a time by Charles U. Powell (also the surveyor of Douglas Manor). They were filed between April 1912 and April 1915 for Tuxill Realty Company Owners. Nassau County Clerk, Maps nos. 2081, 84, 42, 1702, 1704, and 1755. The final map of the development, with all four sections, was completed by A. U. Whitson and filed on December 31, 1919, with Tuxill Realty listed as owners. Nassau County Clerk, Maps, no. 86. Two months later, another map of the entire development, dated February 28, 1920, was drawn up "under the supervision of G. Horace Krider, Sales Agents." Beacon Hill Residents Association Collection (BHRA; located in the Port Washington Public Library, Local History Center), Maps, Series I, Box 1, Folder 2. According to the BHRA minutes, G. Horace Krider was a sales agent for Edgeworth Smith in the 1920s. It is unclear why Tuxill's name is not associated with this map, as he did not sell the majority of his Beacon Hill interests to a syndicate with Edgeworth Smith acting as broker until April 1923.

2 "Charles F. *[sic]* Tuxill," *Auburn Daily Advertiser*, Holiday Edition, 1906, p. 28. Tuxill Square is actually a T-shaped street with eighteen lots. Charles Tuxill joined other prominent Auburn citizens when he built his own home on the "square."

3 *Auburn Bulletin*, March 24, 1905; *Auburn Democrat-Argus*, May 9, 1905. Boulevard Heights (1907) was his third and final Auburn development. *The Auburn Citizen*, August 8, 1907.

4 *Auburn Daily Advertiser*, Holiday Edition, 1906, p. 28; U.S. Census, 1900 and 1910. Tuxill Realty and Improvement Company was incorporated and capitalized at $100,000 in 1907. *Auburn Semi-Weekly Journal*, January 25, 1907; *The Auburn Citizen*, March 13, 1907, p. 8; *History of Cayuga County New York*, compiled from the Archives of the Cayuga County Historical Society, 1775–1908, vol. 2 (Auburn, NY, 1908), p. 490.

5. *Auburn Semi-Weekly Journal*, January 25, 1907.

6 "This Ought to Bring Advertising," *Auburn Semi-Weekly Journal*, 1907–8, p. 4, quoting a Syracuse paper, the *Weedsport Sentinel*. Tuxill's company purchased property in Syracuse and acted as agents in the sale of sixteen lots for $10,000. Charles Tuxill and some of the directors of Tuxill Realty traveled to Syracuse to look over their new property. *The Auburn Citizen*, April 16, 1909; *Syracuse Daily Journal*, October 11, 1911, p. 12; October 11, 1912, p. 10; and January 10, 1913; and *Syracuse Post-Standard*, October 9, 1912, p. 21. Tuxill drove to New York City in his 20-horsepower Franklin, which clocked 222 miles in one day. *The Auburn Citizen*, August 27, 1908, p. 5; *The Auburn Citizen*, February 16, 1909. It was reported in 1912 and 1913 by two local papers that Tuxill had maintained an office in New York City for "several years." *Auburn Democrat-Argus*, 1912, and the *Auburn Weekly Bulletin*, March 25, 1913.

7 *Auburn Democrat-Argus*, 1909; 1910; 1912; *Auburn Directories*, 1909–11 (Cayuga County Historian's Office, Auburn); New York City Telephone Directories; "Beacon Hill," *New York Times*, June 30, 1912.

8 *Auburn Semi-Weekly Journal*, June 27, 1911; *The Auburn Citizen*, September 30, 1912, p. 8; *Auburn Semi-Weekly Journal*, October 1, 1912, p. 7; *Auburn Directories*, 1912; 1913, p. 372 (Cayuga County Historian's Office, Auburn).

9 Julius Chambers, *The Book of New York: Forty Years' Recollections of the American Metropolis* (New York: The Book of New York Company, 1912), p. 427.

10 Ibid. The $100 bonds were entitled "Beacon Hill Real Estate." *The Auburn Citizen*, November 17, 1911, p. 9.

11 "Auburnians Interested," *The Auburn Citizen*, October 20, 1913, p. 12.

12 Port Washington's topography of rolling hills and sandy soil was not conducive to standing water, the breeding ground for mosquitoes.

13 "Port Washington Rests Secure as to Future," *Brooklyn Daily Eagle*, May 11, 1907.

14 "Port Washington's Part in the New Era of Long Island," *Brooklyn Daily Eagle*, May 28, 1911, p. 3.

15 Charles E. Shepard, "Port Washington on the Nort Shore, One of Nature's Show Places, Has Big Season Ahead; Resort Features Bring Influx of Wealthy Residents, as Larger Estates Give Way to Home Building Programs," *Brooklyn Daily Eagle*, March 13, 1927, p. 1.

16 "Port Washington's Part in the New Era of Long Island," *Brooklyn Daily Eagle*, May 28, 1911, p. 3.

17 "Through Trains on North Shore," *Brooklyn Daily Eagle*, October 25, 1913.

18 *Brooklyn Daily Eagle*, June 22, 1923.

19 Modestly priced, grid-plan developments within a two-to-three-minute walk from the train station were being offered at Port Washington Park (1907), Willowdale Terrace (1910), and Maplecrest (1914). For those seeking slightly larger lots and homes with water views, sited within a ten-minute walk of the train station, buyers could choose from Port Washington Heights (1900), Port Washington Estates (1909), Baxter Estates (1910), Beacon Hill (1911), Bayview Terrace (1922), Overlook (1925), and Carl Fisher's Bayview Colony (1925).

20 Map #10 was filed in November 1910; the original map was drawn July 20, 1910, surveyed and plotted by J. Pender. The Village Hall of Baxter Estates, Port Washington. An early brochure (undated), "Port Washington, Long Island, New York," circulated by Hyde & Baxter for Baxter Estates. Copies are located at the Village Hall of Baxter Estates and at the Port Washington Library, Local History Center.

21 "Manhasset Neck Gradually Being Absorbed by Developers," *New York Herald*, February 16, 1913. In 1925–26, Hyde & Baxter developed another thirty-one plots, called Overlook (also the name of the street), directly adjoining Baxter Estates, with plots selling for $3,000 each and residences for $10,000–15,000 each (today it is part of the Village of Baxter Estates). "Port Washington Will Have Big Development This Spring," *Brooklyn Daily Eagle*, January 24, 1926, p. 2D.

22 "Beacon Hill," display ad, *New York Times*, July 11, 1912, p. 14.

23 "Now If You Were Only Living at Beacon Hill," display ad, *New York Times*, July 6, 1912, p. 13.

24 "Beacon Hill," *Plain Talk* 2, no. 8 (April 13, 1912), p. 119.

25 *Plain Talk* 1, no. 3 (October 14, 1911), p. 44.

26 "The best known system of storm sewers will be installed. . . ." "Beacon Hill," *Plain Talk* 2, no. 8 (April 13, 1912), p. 119. "They are grading streets and will let the contract for water mains soon. The pipe used will be heavy, calculated to stand 130 lb. per square inch pressure." *Plain Talk* 3, no. 9 (April 26, 1913), p. 139. During the summer of 1913, Tuxill Realty Company graded 1½ miles of road, laid 4,000 feet of 6-inch water mains, ¾ miles of concrete sidewalk (on Beacon Hill Road only), and 100 square yards of brick paving at the entrance, erected a pumping station and pressure tank, laid ¾ miles of macadam, and placed two pavilions at the entrance. *Plain Talk* 3, no. 21 (October 11, 1913), p. 55. Beacon Hill has storm sewers throughout, whereas in Baxter Estates, developed at the same time in another area of Port Washington, only a few houses are connected to sewers.

27 *Plain Talk* 2, no. 8 (April 13, 1912), p. 119; *Plain Talk* 3, no. 21 (October 11, 1913), p. 331. Tuxill actively sought an investor for the hotel, but nothing came of it.

28 *Plain Talk* 2, no. 23 (November 9, 1912), p. 363.

29 "Beacon Hill," *Plain Talk* 2, no. 8 (April 13, 1912), p. 119.

30 Susan L. Klaus, *A Modern Acadia: Frederick Law Olmsted Jr. and the Plan for Forest Hills Gardens* (Amherst, MA: University of Massachusetts Press, 2002), p. 26.

31 In 1905, Paul's design for the flower beds that descended in radial lines to a pool of water at Woodcrest were praised in *American Homes and Gardens*. Barr Ferree, "'Woodcrest,' the Estate of James W. Paul, Jr., Esq., Radnor, PA," *American Homes and Gardens* 1, no. 3 (September 1905), pp. 155–63.

32 *New York Times*, October 7, 1915, p. 9.

33 *The Auburn Citizen*, October 20, 1913, p. 12; "Beacon Hill," *Plain Talk* 2, no. 8 (April 13, 1912), p. 119; Nassau County Clerk's Office, Map no. 2081, April 1912, and Map no. 84, June 16, 1914.

34 After Tuxill left, his successor, Bi-Harbor Realty Company, approved the building plans along with the Beacon Hill Residents Association. BHRA Constitution, By Laws, Restrictions, Series I, Box 1, Folder 1. Nassau County Clerk, Deed, no. 15401, liber 792, folio 397, June 22, 1923, the John Floyd Yewell lot.

35 One of the association's first important acts was to acquire land for use as a private beach for residents on Hempstead Harbor. In a copy of the beach property deed, dated January 9, 1923, Charles Tuxill sold this property to the Beacon Hill Residents Association, "Subject also to purchase money mortgage held by Vincent A. Howells in the principal sum of $275,000, dated February 10, 1911," indicating that Howells still held the mortgage for the 1911 sale of Beacon Hill. BHRA Deeds, Series I, Box 1, Folder 3, January 9, 1923.

36 *Brooklyn Daily Eagle*, April 15, 1923 (no page number appears on the fultonhistory.com copy of this article).

37 Charles Tuxill was the first resident of the development. He moved with his family in May 1912 into what was most likely a house that had already been standing on the property when he bought it in 1911. The local paper reported that the first house to be built was begun in June 1913 and completed and occupied by January 1914. The Tuxill house burned to the ground in late September 1912. *Plain Talk* 2, no. 9 (April 27, 1912), p. 134; *The Auburn Citizen*, September 30, 1912, p. 8; "Summer House Burned," *Auburn Semi-Weekly Journal*, October 1, 1912, p. 7; *Plain Talk* 4, no. 3 (January 31, 1914), p. 48.

38 "Buying Home Sites on Beacon Hill," *New York Times*, June 23, 1912, p. XX1; *Plain Talk* 3, no. 9 (April 26, 1913), p. 139.

39 "Consequently they have recently sold [3] plots. . . . Plans for specifications for five houses are completed and their erection will begin soon." "Public Improvements," *Plain Talk* 3, no. 15 (July 19, 1913), p. 229.

40 These terms refer to plot 80, 7,000 square feet, "or 3½ city lots," for $1,762.00. "Beacon Hill," *New York Times*, July 28, 1912, p. XX3.

41 *Port Washington News*, May 2, 1914, p. 4; Port Washington News, May 16, 1914, p. 8. In February 1913, it was reported that Tuxill Realty Company would build five homes on speculation. "Manhasset Neck Gradually Being Absorbed by Developers," New York Herald, February 16, 1913.

42 This home was sold to Mr. & Mrs. William C. Montross of Manhattan. "Local News," Plain Talk 4, no. 13 (June 20, 1914), p. 209. Town of North Hempstead, records for Section 6, Block 33, Lot 155. "Sales Activity at Beacon Hill," Port Washington News 12, no. 27 (July 4, 1914), p. 1.

43. *New York Times*, July 26, 1913, p. 12; *Plain Talk* 3, no. 16 (August 2, 1913), p. 247. Her view overlooked Manhasset and Little Neck Bays, Long Island Sound, and Great Neck Peninsula.

44 *Plain Talk* 4, no. 16 (August 1, 1914), inside front cover, p. 246.

45 The plans, dated February 17, 1925, are with the current owner, who purchased the home from Keevil's two daughters in 1969. In 1928, Tillion & Tillion designed Manhattan Towers, a twenty-five-story [*sic*] "skyscraper" hotel that was incorporated into the Manhattan Congregational Church on Broadway at 76th Street. "Manhattan Church to Build 23 [sic] Stories," *New York Times*, January 8, 1928, p. 34; "Church Hotel Opened," *New York Times*, March 9, 1930, p. 169.

46 "Local News," *Plain Talk* 4, no. 5 (February 28, 1914), pp. 81–82.

47 Ibid.

48 "Long Island—For Sale or To Let," display ad, *New York Times*, July 11, 1915, p. S6. By this date, Wethey had built at least one house that he offered for sale "at cost" for $9,750. "Waterfront Property," display ad, *New York Times*, July 11, 1915, p. S6.

49 BHRA, Membership Lists, Series I, Box 2, Folders 1–2; BHRA, Minutes, Directors Meeting, Series I, Box 1, Folder 4, June 1, 1926. A postcard of the house at 9 Summit Road in the collection of the current owner, Sue Sturman, lists Wethey as the owner on the face of the card. The house is dated ca. 1918 based on information on the back of the postcard and according to family lore.

50 *Auburn Semi-Weekly Journal*, Auburn, February 27, 1906; *Port Byron Chronicle*, August 12, 1954, p. 1 (reporting on the early history of the town from a February 1913 paper); Port Byron newspapers, 1900–1904; 1905–8.

51 Display ads for 3 Hampton Road ran from September to December 1917 in the *New York Times*, including "500 Down, $130 Per Month," September 17, 1917, p. 10; "$500 Secures This Home," *Brooklyn Daily Eagle*, August 19, 1917, p. 16. The home was described in the ads as follows: a stucco house with a red clay-tiled roof, it featured parquet floors throughout, double French windows opening onto a tiled-floor porch, a large hall with pergola, four bedrooms on the second floor and two maids' rooms on the third floor. These features were confirmed in a telephone conversation with the current owner's daughter in February 2011.

52 "I. Jones Cobin, 74, Dies After Long Illness," *Port Washington Post*, March 9, 1934, p. 1; "I. Jones Cobin Dies," *Port Washington News*, March 9, 1934, pp. 1, 8. The pair formed the Cobin & Cocks partnership and built a number of houses on Beacon Hill. In 1927, Cobin and Cocks left the real estate arena to become one of the premier oil burner dealers in the area under the same name. Oleck's Long Island Classified, Telephone Directory, 1924–25; 1925–26; Summer 1926. "Buys Port Washington Residence," *New York Times*, August 24, 1924, p. RE1; "Port Washington on Beacon Hill," *Port Washington News*, June 27, 1924, p. 11; George Williams, *Port Washington in the Twentieth Century: Places and People, Eastern Port Washington* (Port Washington, NY: Cow Neck Peninsula Historical Society, 1995), pp. 12–26. Long Island Library Resources Council Digitization Program, Port Washington Public Library, Local History Center: postcard of Cobin & Cocks, Inc. Ads also appeared as follows: "oil burner salesman," *New York Times*, April 26, 1930, p. 16; display ads in the *New York Times*: March 17, 1931, p. 8; April 17, 1931, p. 16; May 6, 1931, p. 19; and in the *Brooklyn Daily Eagle*, March 23, 1926, p. 8A.

53 "45-Acre Beacon Hill Plot Sold Through Edgeworth Smith," *Port Washington News* 21, no. 16 (April 20, 1923), p. 1. Sanborn Map, 1925. Houses built during the early years ranged in cost from $7,000 to $18,500; by 1923, houses on the Hill were selling for $20,000–75,000. BHRA Constitution, By Laws, Restrictions, Series I, Box 1, Folder 1.*Brooklyn Daily Eagle*, April 15, 1923.

54 The syndicate purchased "the holdings of F. A. Burdett, C. E. Tuxill, the Tuxill Realty Company and the Bayside Homes Company at Beacon Hill, Port Washington, consisting of approximately forty-five

acres." "45-Acre Beacon Hill Plot Sold Through Edgeworth Smith," *Port Washington News* 21, no. 16 (April 20, 1923), p. 1. The syndicate included William Hamlin Childs (president of the Barrett Company), R.A.C. Smith (chairman of the board of Albany & Southern Railroad), and Alrick H. Man (president of the Kew Gardens Corporation). "Syndicate Buys Port Washington Interests," *New York Times*, April 22, 1923, p. RE2. The scope of Tuxill's involvement with Bayside Homes and his association with Burdett are unclear, although in 1916, his Beacon Hill real estate agent, Frederick C. Franke, negotiated the sale of "31 houses, the properties of the Bayside Homes Company, at Bayside, L.I., for investment . . . [and] valued at $252,000." "$252,000 Long Island Trade," *New York Times*, October 6, 1916, p. 19. An engineer, F. A. Burdett is linked to Bayside by the sale of four lots to a developer. "Building Industry Code of Ethics," *New York Times*, December 18, 1921, p. 108; "The Real Estate Field, Long Island," *New York Times*, August 21, 1914, p. 14. Tuxill himself sold homes in Bayside, ranging in price from $6,700 to $9,000, in 1918–1921. *New York Times* articles: "Houses for Sale or To Let, Long Island," July 11, 1918, p. 17; July 22, 1918, p. 16; July 24, 1918, p. 19; July 25, 1918, p. 19; "Broadway—Flushing," November 30, 1919, p. W1; "Bayside—Broadway, Flushing," December 14, 1919, p. W1; "Long Island For Sale or To Let," December 7, 1921, p. 35.

55 "Active Lot Market in Near-By Suburbs," *New York Times*, October 8, 1922, p. 108; "A 700-Acre Development," *New York Times* April 23, 1922, p. 108; "Port Washington Estate[s] Passes into Hands of New Company for Development," *New York Times*, June 25, 1922, p. RE1. In September 1922, before the 1923 sale, Smith was also offering Beacon Hill property for sale with a large display ad: "fully improved villa plots at practically acreage prices" and he assured buyers of "our closest cooperation from the time you select your plot until your home is ready for occupancy." "Beacon Hill," *New York Times*, September 10, 1922, p. RE5. Letters located in the Beacon Hill Residents Association file from 1928 show two different spellings for Smith's realty company, Edgewood and Edgeworth Smith Inc. Smith was also connected with the Bi-Harbor Realty Company. BHRA, correspondence between Beacon Hill Residents Association and Bi-Harbor Realty, Series I, Box 1, Folder 6: July 16, 1928; July 18, 1928; August 4, 1928; and "Report of Roads Committee," 1928. "45-Acre Beacon Hill Plot Sold Through Edgeworth Smith," *Port Washington News* 21, no. 16 (April 20, 1923), p. 1.

56 Nassau County Clerk, Lien Sheet, Section 5, Block 19, August 6 and 7, 1934, *liber* 71, folio 122, with cancelation filed on September 27, 1939.

57 Tuxill had lived at Crescent, Hampton, and Beacon Hill roads, all on Beacon Hill. Telephone Directories, Nassau County, Long Island. A copy of the beach property deed, dated March 20, 1923, indicates that Tuxill was living in Port Washington at the time. BHRA, Deeds, Series I, Box 1, Folder 3. By 1927, Tuxill was living at 505 West End Avenue in Manhattan. Telephone Directory, New York City, Summer 1927–Winter 1928. Tuxill appears on the membership list of the Beacon Hill Residents Association in 1923 as living on Beacon Hill, but from 1924 to 1929, his Manhattan business address at 4 West

34th Street appears next to his name. (There are no lists in the files from 1930 to 1932 and his name does not appear on the 1933 list.) BHRA, Membership Lists, Series I, Box 2, Folder 1. His brother Frank had already left Port Washington by the fall of 1915. Telephone Directory, Nassau County, Long Island, February 11, 1915; June 5, 1915; October 21, 1915. By 1918, Frank was again living in Auburn. Auburn Directory, Cayuga County Historian's Office, Auburn; Auburn Citizen, May 20, 1918.

58 Tuxill maintained an office at 337–39 Fifth Avenue and then later on West 34th Street. "Beacon Hill, It's Everything Its Name Implies," *New York Times*, June 25, 1912, p. 18; "Beacon Hill on Hempstead Harbor, Port Washington, Long Island," *Port Washington News*, April 25, 1914, p. 6; "$500 Down, $130 Per Month," *New York Times*, September 7, 1917, p. 10; New York City Telephone Directories, New York Telephone Company: October 18, 1921–February 1, 1922; October 1924–May 1925; Winter 1928–Summer 1929. In 1930, he was renting an apartment on Powell Avenue in Flushing, Queens, for $130 a month. And yet, in 1931 he was able to afford to hold his daughter's wedding at Manhattan's legendary St. Regis Hotel. During the 1930s, while looking for his next big real estate adventure, Tuxill was involved in real estate transactions throughout the tri-state area. In 1939, he was offering 250 building lots in Lincoln Park, New Jersey, in exchange for a house. U.S. Census, 1930; "Recently Married," [with photo] *Brooklyn Daily Eagle*, Sunday, March 22, 1931, p. 6B; "Builder's Attention," *New York Times*, May 28, 1939, p. W12; "[Wanted] partner with capital to help purchase and develop [a] tract of land . . ." *New York Times*, March 3, 1931, p. 35; "Wanted 300 to 1000 acres tillable land within 75 miles of N.Y.C.," "Farms & Acreage Wanted," *New York Times*, December 11, 1932, p. RE8; "Seamen at Rest Home Prove Adept at Golf," *New York Times*, November 15, 1942, p. F8.

59 Tuxill offered property as well as homes for sale in ads from 1945 to 1957. *New York Times*, June 19, 1946, p. 41; "Homes in Sullivan County," *New York Times*, June 27, 1947, p. 36; *New York Times*, May 22, 1949, p. R15; "Houses in Sullivan County," *New York Times*, June 16, 1949, p. 53; among others.

60 Telephone interview with Carl Tuxill by author on October 1, 2009.

61 Ibid.

62 The Plans Committee reported that they "had met . . . with the Bi-Harbor Realty Co. and [they agreed to] go the limit with us in case of trouble regarding plans. They decided that in the future, a letter would be sent to prospective builders outlining the requirements of the Plans Committee." BHRA Minutes (no copy of this letter appears in the file), Series I, Box 1, Folder 4, August 2, 1926. In 1926, the Plans Committee approved thirteen plans, most of them after negotiations and changes; two sets of plans were rejected. Two years later, the committee investigated a five-foot violation of the setback restriction for a house being built, and members of the association voted to take legal action. The association continued its vigilance well into the early 1940s. BHRA Minutes, Series I, Box 1, Folder 5, January 11, 1927; BHRA Minutes, Series I, Box 1, Folder 6, July 9, 1928, and September 12, 1928. The 1928 Annual Report: "An action was brought by the

Association in the Supreme Court which resulted in the moving back of the house to comply with restrictions." BHRA, 1928 Annual Report, Series I, Box 1, Folder 6. In 1938, the committee rejected two plans on account of garage and setback violations. BHRA Minutes, Series I, Box 1, Folder 16, 1938; BHRA Minutes, Series I, Box 1, Folder 18, December 20, 1940. There is a gap in the minutes of the association between 1944 and 1962 and, in 1964, when a resident questioned why houses being built on Summit Road had not been submitted for approval, he was told that the old covenants and restrictions had been superseded by the Town of North Hempstead's zoning laws. BHRA Minutes, Series I, Box 1, Folder 25, April 17, 1964.

63 BHRA Minutes, Series I, Box 1, Folder 12, December 11, 1935; BHRA Minutes, Series I, Box 1, Folder 13, January 7, 1936.

64 BHRA Minutes, Series I, Box 1, Folder 4, January 14, 1926. In 1938, LeRoy Barton was appointed supervising architect of the public building branch of the U.S. Treasury and the following year he was named as an advisor to the Federal Works Administration. In Port Washington, he designed the town's first library, dedicated in 1926, and the second Flower Hill Firehouse in 1930.

65 Henry Atterbury Smith, *500 Small Houses of the Twenties* (Mineola, NY: Dover Publications, 1990; reprint of *The Books of a Thousand Homes*, vol. 1, published by the Homeowners Service Institute, 1923), pp. 6–7.

66 Ibid. Yewell received first prize for a small house selected by the *New-York Tribune* to be built in Larchmont Gardens, New York, as a model for low construction costs. It was built for $8,842.06. Henry Atterbury Smith, "Novel Home Building Experiment at Larchmont Is Finished," *New-York Tribune*, October 15, 1922, p. B2.

67 Yewell bought the property on June 22, 1923, from the Bi-Harbor Realty Group. Nassau County, *liber* 792, Deed 15401, folio 397. Tuxill's wife, Ethel, released the property to the Bi-Harbor Group on the same date. Nassau County Clerk, *liber* 792, Release 15402, folio 400.

68 "A New Service for Those About to Build," *Country Life* 49, no. 1, November 1925, p. 42. In 1926, Briggs gave a series of lectures on the design of small gardens to the Greenwich Garden Club. "Society in the Suburbs," *New York Evening Post*, April 14, 1926, p. 11. Yewell and Briggs were close personal and professional friends, according to J. David Utterback, who inherited Briggs's office and library collection upon his death in 1977. Email correspondence between the author and J. David Utterback, March 2011.

69 "Home Buying and Building Active Throughout Suburbs," *New York Times*, September 9, 1928, p. 155.

70 Mayer spent fifty years working in the studio at his house, and his impressionistic landscapes of Beacon Hill were featured at the Nassau County Museum of Art in 1984. His earlier work was exhibited at the Corcoran Gallery of Art, Washington, D.C., in 1914; the Art Institute of Chicago in 1923; and the Brooklyn Museum of Art, New York, in 1925 and 1926. Two of Kelland's stories became popular movies: *Speak Easy*, 1932, starring Buster Keaton, and *Mr. Deeds Goes to Town*, 1936, starring Gary Cooper and Jean Arthur, remade as *Mr. Deeds* in 2002 with Adam Sandler and Winona Ryder.

Surf and Controversy

1 *Brooklyn Daily Eagle*, June 2, 1911.

2 For the developers, the Indian word Neponsit meant "place between the waters," but it is also thought to derive from the name of a sachem who signed a seventeenth-century deed.

3 Frank Bailey, as told to Hannah Geffen, *It Can't Happen Here Again* (New York: Alfred A. Knopf, 1944) p. 123.

4 *Brooklyn Daily Eagle*, May 18, 1913.

5 Ibid.

6 *New York Herald*, October 11, 1911.

7 *Brooklyn Life* 64, no. 1129, (October 1911), p. 32.

8 *Brooklyn Times*, March 28, 1914.

9 "Neponsit Transformation in the Last Two Years," *New-York Tribune*, February 22, 1914.

10 *Brooklyn Daily Eagle*, May 12, 1912.

11 "Neponsit an Ideal Settlement on the Rockaway Coast," *New-York Tribune*, February 22, 1914.

12 "Neponsit Property to be Auctioned," *Brooklyn Daily Eagle*, May 17, 1914.

13 Vincent Seyfried and William Asadorian, *Old Rockaway, New York in Early Photographs* (Mineola, NY: Dover Publications, 1999), p. 94.

14 Reynolds had appraised the property at approximately $8,000 an acre, well above the $2,500 to $3,100 that the city's experts thought it was worth. The final price awarded by the Condemnation Commission averaged $5,032 per acre. "Reynolds Indicted in Rockaway Case," *New York Times*, August 25, 1917.

15 "Tammany Lie, Replies Mayor Mitchel; City Not Cheated, Says Controller," *New York Herald*, February 19, 1917.

16 "Court Exonerates Senator Reynolds," *New York Times*, May 13, 1920.

17 Bailey, *It Can't Happen Here Again*, p. 119.

18 Jamaica Estates was also considered a park site by the city.

19 Long-time resident Peter Sammon, whose family has lived in the community since 1909, attributes the demise of the club to a number of factors. It was difficult to maintain, given its expense and the seasonal nature of the community. The Property Owners' Association was saddled with the costs of maintaining the beach and island malls after 1919, and the clubhouse was separated from the bay by the filling in required for the construction of Beach Channel Drive.

Gondolas in Copiague

1 "Your 'Little Castle' in American Venice," *New York Times*, March 14, 1926, p. RE5.

2 "Victor Pisani: Retired Realty Man, 62, Former Co-operator of Hotels Here," *New York Times*, April 18, 1941, p. 21.

3 "Isaac Meister, Brooklyn Jew, Who Came to U.S. With 30 Kopeks, Now the Largest Single Owner of Hotels in New York City," *Brooklyn Daily Eagle*, August 12, 1928, p. B3.

4 "New York Incorporations," *New York Times*, October 22, 1905, p. 24.

5 "This Is Our Bargain Day," *New York Times*, December 21, 1905, p. 14.

6 "New York Incorporations," *New York Times*, May 7, 1907, p. 13.

7 "New York Incorporations," *New York Times*, November 27, 1908, p. 11.

8 "New Incorporations," *New York Times*, February 16, 1914, p. 12.

9 "Real Estate Field," *New York Times*, March 5, 1918, p. 19.

10 "Developers Buy Aviation Field," *New York Times* June 5, 1925, p. 29. The municipal identity of American Venice had been vague from the start. The first news account of this ambitious project described it as lying "between Lyndenhurst [sic] and Amityville." Copiague does indeed lie between Lindenhurst and Amityville, but the fact that American Venice is actually situated in the Hamlet of Copiague, Town of Babylon, has often been overlooked because it was allocated the postal address "Lindenhurst, NY 11757." Rumor has it that postal service for American Venice was given to Lindenhurst because the Copiague branch was considered too small for the expected volume.

11 Charles R. Street, Huntington Town Records, Including Babylon, Long Island, N.Y., 1653–1688, vol. 1 (1887; repr. 1975), pp.16–18. Until 1872, the present Town of Babylon was part of the Town of Huntington. Copiague Neck was negotiated for "twelve coats, . . . twenty pounds of powder, twenty dutch hatchets, twenty dutch howes, twenty dutch knives, ten shirts, two hundred muxes, five pairs of handsome stockens, one good dutch hat, and a great fine looking glass."

12 One Pisani family member has suggested that Meister Builders had considered the former Oakdale estate of Frederick Gilbert Bourne, president of the Singer Manufacturing Company, prior to selecting the Copiague site. The Bourne estate was instead purchased for a Catholic school, La Salle Military Academy, in 1926.

13 *New York Times*, June 5, 1925, p. 29.

14 "Big Project Is Little Venice, Started This Week," *Amityville Record*, October 2, 1925, p. 1.

15 "Rival of Venice to Be Built On Long Island," *Babylon Leader*, October 2, 1925, p. 4.

16 *Amityville Record*, October 2, 1925, p. 1.

17 *Babylon Leader*, October 2, 1925, p. 8.

18 Ibid.

19 "Lay Bridge Cornerstone," *New York Times*, August 1, 1926, p. RE1.

20 Also referred to as Alfredo C. Janni and Count Alfred Janni, a civil and consulting engineer whose patents included a reinforced-concrete ship.

21 *New York Times*, August 1, 1926, p. RE1.

22 "Grandpa's Bridges Falling Down, and a Family Rallies,"*New York Times*, November 20, 1988, p. LI34.

23 "Map of American Venice, Section 1," by Van der Werken & Kuehnle Civil Engineers and Surveyors, Lynbrook and Long Beach, New York, July 1925.

24 "Gondolas at Venice," *Amityville Record*, April 16, 1926, p. 3.

25 "Construction Company to Build 100 Homes in American Venice," *New York Times*, April 7, 1926, p. 39.

26 "Sales at American Venice," *New York Evening Post*, April 3, 1926, p. F15.

27 Deed dated September 20, 1929, filed with the Suffolk County Clerk, Liber 1458, p. 483. In their pursuit to create an aesthetically pleasing, serene suburban experience, the American Venice Corp. also expressly forbid uses of the property "which may be deemed legally as a nuisance or objectionable in any way," including the erection of "any milkman's stable, slaughter house, smith shop, forge, furnace, steam engine, brass foundry, nail, iron or other foundry, or any manufactory for making gunpowder, glue, varnish, vitriol, ink, tobacco, turpentine, or for the boiling of bones, or for tanning, dressing, or preparing of skins, hides or leather, or any building for the carrying of noxious, dangerous or offensive trade or business."

28 Ibid.

29 "See American Venice First!," *New York Times*, March 28, 1926, p. RE5.

30 "First Section of American Venice—Sold Out," *New York Times*, March 7, 1926, p. RE6.

31 "Home Owners Day at American Venice," *New York Times*, August 28, 1926, p. 21.

32 "Construction Started on Fifty South Shore Residences," *New York Times*, March 20, 1927, p. E19.

33 "$250 Cash Gives You Immediate Possession of This Venetian Home," *New York Times*, October 21, 1927, p. 48.

34 "Colony of Artists, 'Masonia,' Planned at American Venice," *Brooklyn Daily Eagle*, November 22, 1925, p. 2D.

35 "Martinelli Buys on Long Island," *New York Times*, March 17, 1927, 40.

36 "Announcing the Opening to the Public of American Venice," *New York Times*, October 18, 1925, p. RE6.

37 "Thanksgiving Greetings!," *New York Times*, November 25, 1925, p. 36.

38 "Come—enjoy a trip on our Gala Gondolas," *New York Times*, June 17, 1926, p. 15.

39 "Now—You Can Visualize Why American Venice . . . Is Long Island's Greatest Achievement," *New York Times*, June 6, 1926, p. RE9.

40 "Michaels Predicts Great Boom in Long Island Realty Coming," *Brooklyn Daily Eagle*, November 29, 1925, p. D15.

41 *Babylon Leader*, November 13, 1925, p. 15.

42 "Acreage Sales Feature Market," *New York Times*, December 20, 1925, p. E21.

43 "Would You Like to Spend the Day on a Millionaire's Estate—Intimate Views of the William E. Hawkins Estate and Vicinity, at Copiague and Lindenhurst, L.I.," ca. 1926.

44 Many of the early advertisements appear to be the work of the Harry A. Chandler Booklet Dept., which designed the first known sales booklet for American Venice in 1925, titled "American Venice on Long Island." Harry A. Chandler was well known for his "Bird's-Eye View Maps." In a 1935 booklet, "How a Pictorial Map Will Help Sell Your Real Estate Development," Chandler detailed their full-service process of creating distinctive real estate sales campaigns.

45 "American Venice at Copiague and Lindenhurst," *Babylon Leader*, May 21, 1926, p. 7.

46 "A Home Paradise in American Venice," *New York Times*, March 21, 1926, p. RE10.

47 "Business Records. Bankruptcy Proceedings," *New York Times*, July 6, 1930, p. 36.

48 "New York Company Buys the Park Central: Hotel Raleigh Sold," *New York Times*, July 29, 1927, p. 32.

49 "New Hotel Leased. Sixteen-Story Structure Taken Over by the Meister Builders," *New York Times* December 31, 1927, p. 30.

50 "Hotel Victoria Opens Tuesday," *New York Evening Post*, July 21, 1928, p. 12.

51 "Leasehold Deals: Meister Builders Take Over New Hotel Near Times Square," *New York Times* June 11, 1929, p. 57.

52 "Leaseholds Listed. Manhattan Properties Recorded Under New Control," *New York Times*, January 14, 1930, 53. Mariam Touba, Reference Librarian at the New-York Historical Society, provided the following information: the Hotel Plymouth (137 W. 49th St.) was torn down in the late 1960s as part of a Rockefeller Center corporation building project; the Hotel President (238 W. 48th St.) currently exists as the Best Western President Hotel; the Hotel Raleigh (119–21 W. 72nd St.) was converted into an apartment house; the Hotel Emerson (164–68 W. 75th St.) was last listed in telephone books around 1977; and the Hotel Victoria (7th Avenue at 51st St.) became the Abbey Victoria Hotel before closing in 1982.

53 The principals of the American Venice Corp. owned and operated at least one construction company besides Meister Builders. A September 20, 1929, deed from Venetian Community Builders Corp. was executed by Meister, as president, and Pisani, as secretary; it may also have been known as Venetian Home Builders or Venetian Builders Corp.

54 Bethlehem Land & Improvement Corp., a subsidiary of Bethlehem Steel Co. of Pennsylvania, purchased several lots from Venetian Holding Corp., in 1933. Examples of the steel-framed cottages are still found along American Venice's Santa Barbara Avenue East, easily identifiable by their concrete-block foundations and angular corrugated-steel roofs.

55 "Building Steel Frame Houses," *New York Times*, June 22, 1930, p. RE6.

56 *New York Times*, April 18, 1941, p. 21.

57 "Isaac Meister, 57, Realty Man, Dead," *New York Times*, October 4, 1936, p. N13.

58 The Venice Community House and Yacht Club later became Cowan's Place restaurant. The building was destroyed by fire in the early 1980s.

59 "American Venice Club Now Owns Clubhouse," *New York Times*, September 4, 1942, p. 3.

60 Deed dated January 2, 1953, filed with the Suffolk County Clerk, under *Liber* 3474, p. 392.

61 Application for Building Permit, Town of Babylon, Suffolk County, N.Y., approved April 17, 1961. Property described as "s/s [south side] Merrick Rd. between Riviera Drive West & Riviera Drive East, Copiague."

62 "County to Take Island for Park: 58 [*sic*] Acre Site Picked Off American Venice," *New York Times*, February 6, 1964, p.7.

63 The Suffolk County Parks Department recognizes the island as "Indian Island County Park (Babylon)." Area maps, however, frequently identify the parcel as "Copiague Neck County Park."

64 "Landmark Bridges To Be Preserved," *New York Times*, March 2, 1989, p. 3.

65 "Grounds for Historical Preservation," *Newsday*, February 22, 2011.

Old Field South

1 Tom Morris, "One Man Leaves Many Footprints," *Newsday*, February 22, 1998, p. H99. Like many Gilded Age manufacturers, the Melvilles retained a residence in Manhattan. See also Ramin S. Jalesh-gari, "Building a Village, Providing for a University," *New York Times*, January 4, 1998. Frank Melville made his fortune through the Melville Shoe Corporation, the parent company of Thom McAn. Ward Melville expanded and diversified the family's interests into what is now CVS Pharmaceuticals.

2 Incorporated Village of Old Field, New York, website, Oldfieldny.org.

3 The Nassakeag Land Company Inc. was incorporated on October 10, 1925, and reincorporated in 1932. Suffolk Improvement Company was incorporated on June 1, 1940. Sometime in the 1930s, the Melvilles and their partners shifted from the Nassakeag title to Suffolk Improvement. Suffolk County Clerk's Office, http://clerk.co.suffolk.ny.us/buscerts/CorpDetails.aspx?ID=42079&.

4 Old Field was incorporated in 1927. At the time it had 271 residents and about sixty homes. As of the 2010 Census, the population of Old Field was 947. See oldfieldny.org.

5 Suffolk Improvement Company, Inc., "Old Field South," ca. 1936, unpaginated. Three Village Historical Society.

6 Ibid.

7 Carl J. Heyser Jr. Agency, "Old Field South," ca. 1941, unpaginated. Three Village Historical Society.

8 Suffolk Improvement Company, "Old Field South."

9 Ibid.

10 *New York Times*, May 20, 1934, p. RE1.

11 News clipping, April 1935. Three Village Historical Society, Housing Folder, Old Field South.

12 Ibid.

13 Carl J. Heyser Jr., "Old Field South," ca. 1935, unpaginated. Three Village Historical Society.

14 Carl J. Heyser Jr. "Old Field South on Long Island's Exclusive North Shore at Stony Brook," ca. 1940, unpaginated. Three Village Historical Society.

15 Ibid.

16 Ibid. Ward Melville and his wife were avid horse-people, and news articles from the 1930s to the 1960s attest to their involvement with the Smithtown Hunt and North Shore Horse Show. Indeed, Melville kept a stable of show horses on his private estate and saved eleven of them from a spreading fire in 1935. *New York Times*, June 24, 1935, p. 19..

17 Nicholas Langhart, "Richard H. Smythe's Design Process in Stony Brook," in Joann P. Krieg, ed., *Long Island Architecture* (Interlaken, NY: Heart of the Lakes, 1991).

18 Suffolk Improvement Company, "Old Field South."

19 Annual dues were set at $50, with summer memberships—available to those who lived within a forty-mile radius—at the same price. Prospective summer members were screened for acceptability. There was also a provision for non-resident members, those residing beyond the forty-mile radius, whose dues were set at $30. Those desiring family membership paid an additional 25 percent. When first organized, the club's membership was limited to four hundred, though that number could be increased if the members voted to raise the limits. Suffolk Improvement Company, "Old Field South."

20 Heyser Jr., "Old Field South," ca. 1941.

21 Heyser Jr., "Old Field South," ca. 1936, unpaginated. Three Village Historical Society.

22 Suffolk Improvement Corporation, "Old Field South."

23 Ibid.

24 Covenant, Suffolk Improvement Company, ca. 1935. Three Village Historical Society.

25 Interestingly, in 1955 Melville became a member of the Fund for the Republic's "Commission on Race and Housing," which studied the housing needs and problems of minority groups, especially blacks. Whether this indicated any change in his de facto segregationist attitudes is unclear. It may have simply been a matter of noblesse oblige.

26 Smythe Papers, Sep. Coll. 134. Three Village Historical Society.

27 Heyser Jr., "Old Field South on Long Island's Exclusive North Shore."

28 These numbers are derived from the three Old Field South pamphlets consulted.

29 Ibid.

30 Ibid.

31 Suffolk Improvement Company, "Three Desirable Residence in Old Field South," ca. 1940. Three Village Historical Society.

32 Indeed, in the mid-1930s Ward Melville tried to ascertain house prices for the entire Three Village area, probably to provide some yardstick for comparison with Old Field South. He was largely unsuccessful because, as he wrote to one of his colleagues, "nearly all the new homes have been built to order—and the owners will not tell what it cost them (for fear of the assessor)," note, Ward Melville to Alan [last name unknown], ca. 1935. Three Village Historical Society.

33 On July 12, 1939, for example, Melville inspected the work of the Hawkins Construction Company in the development. Ward Melville Diaries. Long Island Museum of American Art, History & Carriages.

34 Melville had originally considered Setauket as the site for a reconstructed/reconfigured neocolonial shopping center. He changed his mind after a lengthy discussion with his key factotum, Bayles Minuse. On July 12, 1939, Melville recorded that Minuse thought the project "more feasible in Stony Brook than elsewhere." On September 9, Minuse and Melville began to seriously discuss "the purchase of the Stony Brook village property." Melville reported that "[Minuse] found that there was beginning to be a little gossip about the Stony Brook project and felt that we should take [property] options quickly if we were going to act. I told him to get all the options he could, paying for them any necessary amount which he estimated would not be over $200 total." Ward Melville Diaries. Long Island Museum of American Art, History & Carriages.

35 National Register of Historic Places Registration for Rogers Mansion Museum Complex, October 2011. Society for the Preservation of Long Island Antiquities Archives.

36 Morris, "One Man Leaves Many Footprints."

37 On July 6, 1941, the New York Times reported that five of Stony Brook's "most impressive old houses, each erected over 150 years ago, are being moved to new sites and restored, as far as it is necessary, to their old, colonial appearance." The total number of affected dwellings was greater, and though Melville insisted that residents willingly agreed to see their homes relocated, others remembered that eminent domain was invoked to condemn and destroy or move their property. See Jaleshgari, "Building a

Village, Providing for a University." Melville was candid about his intention, which was not to restore the village to its historic form but "to create a model village, not as it would be planned today, but as our forefathers would have built it around 1750." At least, that is how he and his architect thought they would build it. The Melville-Smythe plan required the rerouting of the existing Main Street (Route 25A), which, in turn, necessitated the relocation or destruction of over thirty houses. See Morris, "One Man Leaves Many Footprints."

38 "1750 Town Is Rebuilt," New York Times, July 6, 1941, p. XX1.

39 New York Times, September 2, 1941, p. 19. Melville put $600,000 into the project and then handed ownership and administration of the shopping center to the non-profit Stony Brook Community Fund (now the Ward Melville Heritage Organization), which he headed. Melville's partner, Bayles Minuse, served as manager of the Stony Brook Community Fund from its inception to 1980. He controlled all maintenance, leases, bookkeeping, and contracts in the shopping center. He was forced out in 1980 in the face of questions about his management.

40 Balance Sheet, Suffolk Improvement Company, January 30, 1943. Melville Family Papers, Three Village Historical Society, Emma S. Clark Memorial Library.

41 Handwritten note, Suffolk Improvement Company, April 15, 1950. Three Village Historical Society.

42 Deed, April 18, 1956. Three Village Historical Society, Folder: Organizations, Old Field Club. Nevertheless, Melville retained some paternalistic interest in the area and its success, and on April 18, 1956, sold a chunk of land on West Meadow Road to the Old Field Club for $10.00.

43 Postcards and promotional material issued by Heyser in the 1940s featured homes labeled as located in "Old Field South, Stony Brook." Legally, however, the development is, and apparently always was, a section of Setauket, though its street contours, landscape, and residential standards were distinct and enforceable through Melville-controlled covenants.

44 Deed, Ward Melville and Suffolk Improvement Company and Old Field South Property Owners Association, Inc., May 17, 1977. Exhibit A, ca. 1950, Covenant. See OldFieldSouth.org.

45 Ibid.

46 Ibid.

47 Melville's business activities are many and beyond the scope of this book. His other community projects included the Frank Melville Memorial Park in Setauket, with its restored mill, bridge, and post office, and the Suffolk County Museum, now the Long Island Museum of History, Art & Carriages, to which he donated his collection of William Sidney Mount drawings and paintings. Melville also contributed heavily to restoring the Caroline Episcopal Church to its original eighteenth-century appearance. He and his father, Frank, and their spouses are buried in its churchyard. This enumeration does not include his purely charitable work.

48 "Campus Is Rising at Stony Brook," New York Times, May 22, 1961, p. 33.

49 Melville was particularly displeased by the first group of dormitories, the design of which many termed "neo-penal." The architecture, and the problems with students in the turbulent late 1960s

and early 1970s, resulted in disenchantment with the university project among many of the older residents of the Three Village area. In 1968, Bud Huber, editor of the *Three Village Herald*, stated that while he and Melville had been early supporters of the university, "both regret what's happened." *New York Times*, March 11, 1968, p. 44.

50 Personal recollections of Noel Gish, March 26, 2010.

51 *New York Times*, May 21, 1961, p. R1.

What If?

1 "The Famous Bustanobys," *Long-Islander*, August 21, 1908.

2 "The Château des Beaux-Arts, Huntington, Long Island, N.Y.," *The American Architect and Building News* 91, no. 1636 (May 4, 1907), p. 188.

3 "Chateau des Beaux Arts," *Brooklyn Daily Eagle*, June 6, 1909. The press also reported plans to extend Huntington's trolley line to the site and establish ferry service to Greenwich, Connecticut.

4 "'Elysium' for the Rich on Huntington Harbor," *Brooklyn Daily Eagle*, July 28, 1907.

5 "The Messrs. Bustanoby Are Opening Up Fine Development," *Long-Islander*, August 18, 1911.

6 The reported price was $300,000, L'Ecluse adding the Beaux-Arts acreage to the adjacent tract of four hundred acres, which he controlled. See "Huntington Beaux Arts Sold," *Long-Islander*, September 20, 1912.

7 The property would not be acquired until 1920, when a Bustanoby investor who purchased the mortgage in 1912 sold the property to the Huntington Golf Marine Club. See *Long-Islander*, May 21, 1920. The club went into foreclosure in 1932. The château and casino were later razed and the property is now the site of the Head of the Bay Club.

8 The E. Belcher Hyde 1917 *Atlas of Suffolk County* indicates that only five houses had been built between Upper and Lower drives.

9 "Plan Manor Sites for Long Island," *New York Times*, August 7, 1910.

10 Ibid.

11 Pope was also working that year on the plan for the McKnights' Great Neck Estates.

12 Robert Anderson Pope, "Some of the Needs of City Planning in America," in *City Planning: Hearing Before the Committee on the District of Columbia, United States Senate, on the Subject of City Planning*. 61st Cong., 2nd sess., S.Doc 422 (Washington, DC: Government Printing Office, 1910), pp.75–79.

13 "Tangier Property, Now in New Hands," *Brooklyn Daily Eagle*, December 17, 1916. A portion of the property was later re-acquired by Smith descendants.

14 *Brooklyn Daily Eagle*, May 14, 1916; *New York Times*, May 14, 1916; and *New York Sun*, May 14, 1916.

15 *Brooklyn Daily Eagle*, May 21, 1916, and December 12, 1916.

16 *New York Times*, April 9, 1916.

SELECTED BIBLIOGRAPHY

Addams, Jane, and Mr. de Forest. "The Housing Problem in Chicago." *Annals of the American Academy of Political and Social Science* 20 (July 1902).

Alvord, Dean. "How to Develop Acreage." In *Practical Real Estate Methods for Broker, Operator and Owner.* New York: Doubleday, Page & Co. for Westside Y.M.C.A., 1909.

Alvord, Samuel Morgan. *A Genealogy of the Descendants of Alexander Alvord: An Early Settler of Windsor, Conn. and Northampton, Mass.* Webster, NY: A. D. Andrews Printer, 1908.

Ames, David L., and Linda F. McClelland. "Historic Residential Suburbs: Guidelines for Evaluation and Documentation for the National Register of Historic Places." In *National Register Bulletin.* Washington, DC: U.S. Department of the Interior, National Park Service, 2002.

Arbib, Robert. *The Lord's Woods: The Passing of an American Woodland.* New York: W. W. Norton, 1971.

Archer, John. *Architecture and Suburbia: From English Villa to American Dream House 1690–2000.* Minneapolis: University of Minnesota Press, 2005.

Armbruster, Eugene L. *Long Island: Its Early Days and Development with Illustrations and Maps.* History of Long Island, vol. 29, no. 182. Brooklyn: Brooklyn Daily Eagle, 1914.

Artistic Houses. New York: D. Appleton & Co., 1883–84.

Atlas of Nassau County. New York: E. Belcher Hyde, 1906.

Atlas of Nassau County. New York: E. Belcher Hyde, 1914.

Atlas of Suffolk County. New York: E. Belcher Hyde, 1917.

The Atlas Portland Cement Company. *Concrete Houses and Cottages.* Vol. 2. New York: The Atlas Portland Cement Company, 1909.

Atterbury, Grosvenor. "Model Towns in America." *Scribner's Magazine* 52, no. 1 (July 1912).

Back, Adina, and Francis Morrone. *Flatbush: Neighborhood History Guide.* Brooklyn: Brooklyn Historical Society, 2008.

Bailey, Frank, as told to Hannah Geffen. *It Can't Happen Here Again.* New York: Alfred A. Knopf, 1944.

Beard, Patricia. *After the Ball: Gilded Age Secrets, Boardroom Betrayals, and the Party That Ignited the Great Wall Street Scandal of 1905.* New York: Harper Collins, 2003.

Bentel, Paul L. "The Regional Plan of New York." In *Long Island Architecture.* Edited by Joann P. Krieg. Interlaken, NY: Heart of the Lakes Publishing, 1991.

Birnbaum, Charles A., and Robin Karson. *Pioneers of American Landscape Design.* New York: McGraw-Hill, 2000.

Blake, Peter. *God's Own Junkyard: The Planned Deterioration of America's Landscape.* New York: Holt, Rinehart and Winston, 1968.

Bloom, Nicholas. "Suburbanization of Leisure." In *Encyclopedia of Recreation and Leisure in America.* Vol. 2. Woodbridge, CT: Charles Scribner's Sons, An Imprint of the Gale Group, 2004.

Buder, Stanley. *Visionaries and Planners: The Garden City Movement and the Modern Community.* New York and Oxford: Oxford University Press, 1990.

Butler, Ellis Parker. "The Adventures of a Suburbanite." *Country Life in America* 18, no. 1 (May 1910).

Carrère, John M. "Better Taste in Small Houses." *Country Life in America* 20, no. 2 (May 15, 1911).

"The Château des Beaux-Arts, Huntington, Long Island,

N.Y." *The American Architect and Building News* 91, no. 1636 (May 4, 1907).

Chamber of Commerce of the Borough of Queens. *Queens Borough,* New York City, 1910–1920. New York: L. I. Star Publishing Co., 1920.

Chambers, Julius. *The Book of New York: Forty Years' Recollections of the American Metropolis.* New York: The Book of New York Company, 1912.

Clark, Clifford Edward, Jr. *The American Family Home, 1800–1960.* Chapel Hill, NC: University of North Carolina Press, 1986.

Colman, William E., ed. "Frederick Law Olmsted, Jr., the Garden City Movement and the Design of Forest Hills Gardens." *Forest Hills Gardens,* no. 2 (1994).

"A Country House in the Italian Style." *House & Garden,* August 1918.

"Country Houses Designed by Aymar Embury Which Express the Modern American Spirit in Home Architecture." *The Craftsman,* November 1909.

The Country Life Press: Garden City, New York. Garden City: Doubleday, Page & Company, 1919.

Cravath, Paul D. "Preserving the Country Lanes." *Country Life in America,* January 1913.

Creel, George, and John Slavens. *Men Who Are Making Kansas City: A Biographical Directory.* Kansas City: Hudson-Kimberly Publishing Co., 1902.

Crocker, Ruth. *Mrs. Russell Sage: Women's Activism and Philanthropy in Gilded Age and Progressive Era America.* Bloomington, IN: Indiana University Press, 2006.

Daley, Paul. *Golf Architecture: A Worldwide Perspective.* Vol. 4. Gretna, LA: Pelican Publishing Company, 2008.

Dean, A. W. "What Long Island Offers the Home Seeker." *House & Garden,* March 1913.

Decker, Sarah Platt. "The Meaning of the Woman's Club Movement." *Annals of the American Academy of Political and Social Science* 28 (September 1906).

de Forest, Robert. "The Fiftieth Anniversary of the Museum: An Address." *The Metropolitan Museum of Art Bulletin* 15, no. 6 (June 1920).

Embury, Aymar, II. *One Hundred Country Houses: Modern American Examples.* New York: The Century Co., 1909.

Emmons, Paul. "Diagrammatic Practices: The Office of Frederick L. Ackerman and Architectural Graphic Standards." *Journal of the Society of Architectural Historians* 64, no. 1 (March 2005).

Ferree, Barr. "'Woodcrest,' the Estate of James W. Paul, Jr., Esq., Radnor, PA." *American Homes and Gardens* 1, no. 3 (September 1905).

Fiore, Roberta. "The Legendary Lido Golf Course and the Origins of Lido Beach." *The Nassau County Historical Society Journal* 61 (2006).

Fiore, Roberta, and Elizabeth Coffin Allerhand. "Sandbar to City: William H. Reynolds and the Planned Community of Long Beach, 1906–1922." In *Nassau County: From Rural Hinterland to Suburban Metropolis.* Edited by Joann P. Krieg and Natalie A. Naylor. A Long Island Studies Institute Publication from Hofstra University. Interlaken, NY: Empire State Books, 2000.

Fisher, Jane. *Fabulous Hoosier.* New York: Robert M. McBride & Co., 1947.

Fisher, Jerry M. *The Pacesetter: The Untold Story of Carl G. Fisher.* Fort Bragg, CA: Lost Coast Press, 1998.

Foster, Mark S. *Castles in the Sand.* Gainesville, FL: University Press of Florida, 2000.

Freeman, William Coolbaugh. *One Hundred Advertising Talks by William C. Freeman: Selected and Arranged by George French*. New York: The Winthrop Press, 1912.

From Wilderness to Metropolis: The History and Architecture of Dade County 1825–1940. 2nd ed. Miami: Metropolitan Dade County Office of Community Development, Historic Preservation Division, 1992.

"Garden City." In *History of Queens County New York*. New York: W. W. Munsell, 1882.

Gause, Jo Allen, ed. *Great Planned Communities*. Washington, DC: The Urban Land Institute, 2002.

Gebhard, David. "The American Colonial Revival in the 1930s." *Winterthur Portfolio* 22, no. 2/3 (Summer–Autumn 1987).

Gillespie, Harriet Sisson. "An English Cottage Group." *House Beautiful*, August 1919, pp. 74–76.

"Golf Architect." *The New Yorker*, August 11, 1928, pp. 13–14.

Gordon, Alastair. *Weekend Utopia: Modern Living in the Hamptons* Princeton Architectural Press, 2001.

Gunnison, Herbert F., ed. *Flatbush of To-Day*. Vol. 2, no. 1. Brooklyn, 1908.

The Hapgood Houses of Mountain Lakes. Mountain Lakes, NJ: Landmarks Committee, Borough of Mountain Lakes, 1983.

Harris, Dianne, ed. *Second Suburb: Levittown, Pennsylvania*. Pittsburgh: University of Pittsburgh Press, 2010.

Hausrath, Ralph. "Carl G. Fisher and Montauk." *Long Island Forum*, November 1981.

Havemeyer, Harry W. *Along the Great South Bay: From Oakdale to Babylon, the Story of a Summer Spa, 1840–1940*. Mattituck, NY: Amereon, 1996.

Hayden, Dolores. *Building Suburbia: Green Fields and Urban Growth, 1820–2000*. New York: Pantheon, 2003.

Hering, Oswald C. *Concrete and Stucco Houses*. New York: McBride, Nast and Company, 1912.

Herold, Patricia. *Mountain Lakes 1911–2011: One Hundred Years of Community*. Mountain Lakes, NJ: privately printed, 2010.

Hilya, James A. "Four Ways of Looking at a Philanthropist: A Study of Robert Weeks de Forest." *Proceedings of the American Philosophical Society* 124, no. 6 (December 1980).

Homes of Doubleday, Doran and Company, Inc.: Garden City; London; Kingswood, Surrey; Toronto. Garden City, NY: privately printed, 1930.

Howe, S. Ferdinand. *The Commerce of Kansas City in 1886*. Kansas City: Ramsey, Willett & Hudson, 1902.

Jackson, Kenneth T. *Crabgrass Frontier: The Suburbanization of the United States*. New York: Oxford University Press, 1985.

Karatzas, Daniel. *Jackson Heights: A Garden in the City; The History of America's First Garden and Cooperative Apartment Community*. Jackson Heights, N.Y.: Jackson Heights Beautification Group, 1998.

Kass, Sean. "The L.I.R.R. and Its Promotion of Long Island, 1900–1930." *The Long Island Historical Journal* 17 (Fall 2004/Spring 2005).

Klaus, Susan L. *A Modern Arcadia: Frederick Law Olmsted Jr. and the Plan for Forest Hills Gardens*. Amherst, MA: University of Massachusetts Press, 2002.

Kossoff, Roberta, and Annette Henkin Landau. *Laurelton*. Images of America. Mount Pleasant, SC: Arcadia, 2011.

Kostof, Spiro. *A History of Architecture: Settings and Rituals*. New York: Oxford University Press, 1985.

Kunstler, James Howard. *The Geography of Nowhere: The Rise and Decline of America's Man-Made Landscape*. New York: Touchstone, 1994.

Lang, Michael H. "Town Planning and Radicalism in the Progressive Era: The Legacy of F. L. Ackerman." *Planning Perspectives* 16 (2001).

Langhart, Nicholas. "Richard H. Smythe's Design Process in Stony Brook." In *Long Island Architecture*. Edited by Joann P. Krieg. Interlaken, NY: Heart of the Lakes, 1991.

Lavender, Abraham D. *Miami Beach in 1920*. Charleston, SC: Arcadia Publishing, 2002.

Lawless, Lucy, Caroline Loughlin, and Lauren Meier, eds. *The Master List of Design Projects of the Olmsted Firm, 1857–1979*. 2nd ed. Washington, DC: National Association for Olmsted Parks and National Park Service, Frederick Law Olmsted National Historic Site, 2008.

"The Life Worth Living." *Country Life in America*, September 1, 1911.

Lingeman, Richard. *Sinclair Lewis: Rebel From Main Street*. New York: Random House, 2002.

Loeb, Carolyn. *Entrepreneurial Vernacular: Developers' Subdivisions in the 1920s*. Baltimore: The Johns Hopkins University Press, 2001.

Long Island: The Sunrise Homeland. 8th ed. New York: Committee on Publications, Long Island Chamber of Commerce, 1929.

Lovely, Thomas J. *The History of the Jamaica Estates, 1929–1969*. Jamaica Estates, NY: Jamaica Estates Association, 1969.

Macdonald, Charles Blair. *Scotland's Gift, Golf: Reminiscences 1872–1927*. New York: Scribner's, 1928.

MacKay, Robert B., Anthony K. Baker, and Carol A. Traynor, eds. *Long Island Country Houses and Their Architects, 1860–1940*. New York: Society for the Preservation of Long Island Antiquities and W. W. Norton 1997.

McKnight, Harvey Stewart. "The Biography of Harvey Stewart McKnight, Ancestry and Recollections." Unpublished typescript. Village of Great Neck Estates.

Moe, Richard. "Preservation for a New Century." *Forum Journal*, Spring 2010.

Moorish Houses at Bayberry Point, Islip, L.I., Built for Mr. H. O. Havemeyer. N.p., 1897.

Mumford, Lewis. *The Highway and the City*. New York: Harcourt, Brace & World, 1963.

Mylod, Carol Kennedy. *75th Anniversary History of Bellerose Village*. N.p., 1999.

Pallister, Mervin G. *A History of the Incorporated Village of Shoreham in the Town of Brookhaven*. Privately printed, 1976.

Pardington, A. R. "The Modern Appian Way for the Motorist." *Harpers Weekly* 51 (March 16, 1907).

Peterson, Jon A. *The Birth of City Planning in the United States 1840–1917*. Baltimore and London: The Johns Hopkins University Press, 2003.

Pelletreau, William S. *A History of Long Island*. Vol. 2. New York: Lewis Publishing Co., 1903.

Pollock, Channing. *Harvest of My Years: An Autobiography*. New York: Bobbs-Merrill Co., 1943.

Practical Real Estate Methods for Broker, Operator & Owner: Thirty Experts on How to Buy, Sell, Lease, Manage, Appraise, Improve and Finance Real Estate. New York: Doubleday, Page & Co. for the West Side. Young Men's Christian Association, 1910.

Prelini, Charles. *Dredges and Dredging*. New York: D. Van Nostrand Co., 1911.

Private Residences and Public Buildings from the Carl Fisher Era. Montauk, NY: privately printed, 1994.

Purcell, Susan, "The Maps of Forest Hills Gardens." *Forest Hills Gardens*, no. 2 (1994).

Quirin, William L. *America's Linksland: A Century of Long Island Golf*. Chelsea, MI: Sleeping Bear Press, 2002.

———. *Golf Clubs of the MGA: A Centennial History of Golf in the New York Metropolitan Area*. Chicago: Triumph Books, 1997.

Rambusch, Catha Grace, Barbara Snowden Christen, and Robert C. Hughes. *The Landscape and Architecture of Laurel Lodge: A little Known Early 20th-Century Summer Estate on Long Island's North Shore.* Privately printed, n.d.

Rattray, Jeannette Edwards. *Montauk: Three Centuries of Romance, Sport and Adventure.* Montauk, NY: Star Press, 1938.

Redford, Polly. *Million Dollar Sandbar.* New York: E. P. Dutton & Co., 1970.

Resseguie, Harry E. "The Decline and Fall of the Commercial Empire of A. T. Stewart." *Business History Review* 36, no. 3, Autumn 1962.

Riverside Cemetery Association. *A Debt and a Duty: Being a Timely Suggestion of an Obligation and the Way for Every One to Meet It.* Rochester, NY: The Genesee Press, The Post Express Printing Company, 1897.

Robinson, Charles Mulford. *The Improvement of Towns and Cities or The Practical Basis of Civic Aesthetics.* New York: G. P. Putnam's Sons and The Knickerbocker Press, 1901.

———. *Modern Civic Art or The City Made Beautiful.* New York: G. P. Putnam's Sons and The Knickerbocker Press, 1903.

Roth, Leland M. "Getting the Houses to the People: Edward Bok, the Ladies' Home Journal, and the Ideal House." *Perspectives in Vernacular Architecture* 4 (1991).

Saylor, Henry H. *Bungalows.* Philadelphia: The John C. Winston Company, 1911.

Schoendorf, Robert. *The Pioneer Flights of Garden City Estates, New York: 1911.* New York: Al Zimmerman Publisher, 1982.

Schoff, Wilfred H. "The $10,000 Country Home." *Country Life in America* 10, no. 6 (October 1906).

Sellers, Christopher C. *Crabgrass Crucible: Suburban Nature & the Rise of Environmentalism in Twentieth-Century America.* Chapel Hill, NC: The University of North Carolina Press, 2012.

Seifer, Marc. *Wizard: The Life and Times of Nikola Tesla, Biography of a Genius.* New York: Citadel Press, 1996.

Seyfried, Vincent F. *The Founding of Garden City 1869–1993.* Privately printed, 1969.

Seyfried, Vincent, and William Asadorian. *Old Rockaway, New York in Early Photographs.* Mineola, NY: Dover Publications, 1999.

Smith, Henry Atterbury. *500 Small Houses of the Twenties.* Mineola, NY: Dover Publications, 1990. Reprint of *The Books of a Thousand Homes,* vol. 1. Homeowners Service Institute, 1923.

Smith, Mildred Hess. *History of Garden City.* Rev. ed. Garden City: Garden City Historical Society, 1980.

———. *Garden City: Long Island in Early Photographs, 1869–1919.* Mineola, NY: Dover Publications, 1987.

Smits, Edward J. *Nassau Suburbia, U.S.A.: The First Seventy-five years of Nassau County, New York 1899 to 1974.* Garden City, NY: Doubleday & Company, 1974.

"Some Work at Bayberry Point, L.I., by Grosvenor Atterbury." *The American Architect* 96 (September 8, 1909).

Stanton, Phoebe B. *The Gothic Revival and American Church Architecture: An Episode in Taste 1840–1856.* Baltimore and London: The Johns Hopkins University Press, 1968.

Starrett, Theodore. "A Beauty Spot." *Architecture and Building* 46 (May 1914).

Stephens, W. P. *The Seawanhaka Corinthian Yacht Club: Origins and Early History 1871–1896.* New York: privately printed, 1963.

Stern, Julius David. *Memoirs of a Maverick Publisher.* New York: Simon & Schuster, 1962.

Stern, Robert A. M, and John Montague Massengale.

The Anglo-American Suburb. Architectural Design Profile Critical Studies Series 37. London: Architectural Design, 1981.

Stoddard, Chris. *A Centennial History of Cottage City.* Oak Bluffs, MA: Oak Bluffs Historical Commission, 1980.

Street, Charles R. *Huntington Town Records, Including Babylon, Long Island, N.Y., 1653–1688.* Vol. 1. 1887. Reprint, 1975.

Stubblebine, Ray. *Stickley's Craftsman Homes.* Layton, UT: Gibbs Smith, 2006.

Sutherland, Clare. *The Plandome Story: The Story of the Incorporated Village of Plandome 1911–1965.* Plandome, NY: The Plandome Association, 1965.

Teal, Gardner. "The Cement House and Its Place in Our Arch- itecture" *The Craftsman* 19 (October 1910–March 1911).

Trachtenberg, Alan. *The Incorporation of America.* New York: Hill and Wang, 1992.

Traxel, David. *1898: The Birth of the American Century.* New York: Alfred A. Knopf, 1998.

The Trow (Formerly Wilson's), Copartnership and Corporation Directory of the Boroughs of Manhattan and the Bronx, City of New York. New York: Trow Directory, Printing, and Bookbinding Co., 1906.

Veiller, Lawrence. "The Housing Problem in American Cities." *Annals of the American Academy of Political and Social Science* 25 (March 1905).

Viemeister, Peter. *Start All Over: An American Experience.* Bedford, VA: Hamilton's, 1995.

Weiss, Ellen. *City in the Woods: The Life and Design of an American Camp Meeting on Martha's Vineyard.* New York: Oxford University Press, 1987.

Weiss, Marc A. *The Rise of the Community Builders: The American Real Estate Industry and Urban Land Planning.* New York: Columbia University Press, 1987.

Whitehead, Russell F. "American Seaside Homes." *Architectural Record* 28 (August 1910).

Whittlesey, C. E. "The Commuter's Long Island." *House & Garden,* March 1911.

Williams, George L. "Bayview Colony." *Journal of the Cow Neck Peninsula Historical Society,* Fall 1999.

———. *Port Washington in the Twentieth Century: Places and People, Eastern Port Washington.* Port Washington, NY: Cow Neck Peninsula Historical Society, 1995.

Wilson, Richard Guy. "Idealism and the Origin of the First American Suburb: Llewellyn Park, New Jersey." *American Art Journal* 11 (Autumn 1979).

Winthrop, Governor John. "A Model of Christian Charity." In *The Journal of John Winthrop, 1630–1649.* Edited by Richard S. Dunn, James Savage, and Laetitia Yeandle. Cambridge, MA: Belknap Press of Harvard University Press, 1996.

Withey, Henry F., and Elsie Rathburn Withey. *Biographical Dictionary of American Architects (Deceased).* Los Angeles: Hennessey & Ingalls, 1970.

Wolfe, Kevin. *This Salubrious Spot: The First 100 Years at Douglas Manor 1906–2006.* Douglas Manor, NY: Douglas Manor Association, 2006.

The World Almanac and Encyclopedia 1907. New York: The Press Publishing Co., New York World, 1906.

Wylie, Dalton. "Country Club Architecture." *Country Life in America* 18 (September 1910).

Zaitzevsky, Cynthia. *Long Island Landscapes and the Women Who Designed Them.* New York: W. W. Norton and Society for the Preservation of Long Island Antiquities, 2009.

Zoning Laws, Building Codes of the City of Long Beach New York. Long Beach, NY: City of Long Beach, n.d.

INDEX

Page numbers in **bold** font indicate photos and illustrations and their captions.

59th Street Bridge, 12, **12**

1910 Real Estate and Ideal Homes Exposition, 17

Abbey Victoria Hotel, New York City, 276*n*52

Abraham & Strauss department store, 180

Ackerman, Frederick, 194, **195**

Ackerson, Charles F., 116, 123

Ackerson, Henry W., 116, **124**

Ackerson, Pierre T., 116

Ackerson, Thomas B., 116–117, **117**, **119**, 127, 129

    See also Brightwaters; T. B. Ackerson Company

Ackerson Company, 62

Adams, E. E., 254*n*10

Adams, Thomas, 21

Adams, William, 174

Adelphi College, 44

Adler, Felix, 175

Adshead, Stanley D., 248

"The Adventures of a Suburbanite" (Butler), 19

advertisements. *See* marketing strategies

Aerocar, 163

Aetna National Bank, 79

affordable housing. *See* housing reform

Aiken, Robert, 249

air travel, 44

Aitkin, John, 61, 118, 255*n*22

Albro, Lewis C., 172, **173**

Albro & Lindberg, 17, **173**

Albro House, 170

Allen, Ed, 261*n*65

Allen, Steve, 239

Allen house, Great Neck Estates, 131, 139, 261*n*80

Allen mansion, Douglas Manor, 87

Alling, Joseph T., 59

Alling and Cory, 59

Allison, Jim, 150, 162, 264*n*12, 266*n*133

All National Association, 234

Alton Beach Realty Company, 151, 264*n*23

Alvord, Dean

    about, 19–20, 58–59, **59**, 71, 254*n*4 (Ch.4), 256*n*78

    bankruptcies, 16

    Brooklyn Life on, 68

    Harbor Oaks and, **70**, 71, 256*n*79

    homes of, **62**, 67, **69**

    Long Island Motor Parkway and, 13, 62

    See also Belle Terre Estates; Cedarcroft; Prospect Park South; Riverside Cemetery, Rochester, New York; Roslyn Estates; Shinnecock Hills

Alvord, James D., 58

Ambler, Carrie E., 116

Ambler, Hattie, 117

Ambrosio American, 247

amenities, 19–20

    See also specific amenities

American Automobile Association, 13

American Bank Note Company, New York City, 181

American Bible Society, 56

American Federation of the Arts, 187

American Foursquare style architecture, 202

    See also Craftsman style architecture; Prairie School style architecture

American Indians, 86, 119

American Institute of Architects, 178

American Red Cross, 187

The American Scene (James), 19

American Sugar Refining Company, 46

American Tobacco Company, 56

American Venice, 228–239, 275*n*10

    administration plaza, **237**, **239**

    advertisements, **236**

    bridges, **231**

    houses, **233**

    houses of, **234**, **235**

    promotional booklets, **235**, **237**

    street layouts, **230**, **233**

American Venice Civic Association, 238, 239

American Venice Corporation

    bankruptcy and, 238

    deed restrictions and, 275*n*27

    marketing strategies of, 228, 230, 231–232, 234, 235

    start of, 230

American Vitagraph, 250

The American Woman's Home (Beecher and Stowe), 23

Ames, David L., 16

Amherst College, 136

Amity Harbor, 8

A Modern Arcadia (Klaus), 252*n*1 (Ch.1)

amusement parks, 14, 17, 18, 56, 102–103, 106

Andrews, Frank, 135

Anglophiles, 202–203

apartment houses, 78

Apex Oil Company, 79

Apostle houses, 30, 45

Aquinas Honor Society, 185, 252*n*4 (preface), 269*n*22, 269*n*29

architects. *See* developers

Architectural Forum, 67

Architectural Record, 145

architectural review boards, 81, 88–89, 99, 241, 244

architectural styles

    control of, 74, 75, 108–109, 224, 241

magazines' influence on, 75
    of residential parks, 16–17
    See also specific style
Architecture, 68
Architecture and Building, 93, 96
Army Corps of Engineers, **160**, 162, 166
Arrochar Park Realty Co., 229
art museums. *See* Metropolitan Museum of Art;
    Whitney Museum of American Art
Arts and Crafts style architecture
    Beacon Hill, 216, 217
    Bellerose, 75
    Belle Terre Estates, **69**
    Brightwaters, **124**
    Douglas Manor, 90
    Fiske Terrace, 118
    Forest Hills Gardens, 191
    Garden City, 41
    Great Britain, 41–42, 44
    Great Neck Estates, 17
    Hapgood and, 202
    magazines' influence on, 75
    See also Craftsman style architecture
Ashley, William, 206, **206**
ash trees, 85
Association of Roslyn Estates, 20
Astor, John J., 68
Astor, William W., Mrs., 215
Atlantic Gulf and Pacific Company, 177
Atlas of Nassau County (Hyde), 57, 68, **131**, **143**, **211**
Atlas of Suffolk County (Hyde), 247, 278*n*8
Atlas Portland Cement Company, 17, 206, **208**
A. T. Stewart & Co. department store, 26, 35
Atterbury, Grosvenor
    about, 14, 190
    Bayberry Point, 46, 47–48, 51
    Forest Hills Gardens, **190**, 191
    Forest Hills Gardens Homes Company and, 193
    Metropolitan Museum of Art designs, 195
Auburn, New York, 212, 270*n*2–270*n*3 (Ch. 17)
auctions
    Brightwaters, 128
    Garden City, 40
    Long Beach, 115
    Montauk Beach, 164
    Munsey bequest, 194
    Neponsit, 225
    Shinnecock Hills, 63
    Shoreham development and, 205
Auerbach, Joseph, 170, 267*n*6
Austin, Roy, 52
auto racing, 13, 38–39, 150
    See also Indianapolis Motor Speedway Company
auto travel
    Burton property restrictions on, 171
    developers' interest in, 13
    early 20th century expansion of, 12–13
    Garden City and, 39
    highway development and, 151
    See also car dealerships
Avalon, 140
aviation, 11
    See also Curtiss Aeroplane and Motor Company;
    Lindbergh, Charles

Babylon. *See* Town of Babylon
Bache, Max, 229
Bacon, Robert, 156
Bailey, Frank
    about, 13, **13**, 14, 16, 222, **223**
    legal difficulties of, 226
    Neponsit Club and, 224
    William Reynolds and, 16, 101
Bailey, Liberty H., 42
Bailey, Vernon H., **195**
Bailey Foundation, 14
Bailey's Arboretum, 16
Baker Athletics Complex, Columbia University, 56,
    147
Balfe, Veronica G., 263*n*52
Ballard, Ed, 264*n*30
Bankers Trust Company, 164–165
bankruptcies
    American Venice Corporation, 238
    Carl Fisher and, 164
    Carl G. Fisher Corporation of Miami, 165
    Charles L. Flint and, 205
    by developers, 16
    H. Stewart McKnight and, 130
    Montauk Beach Development Corporation, 165
    Panic of 1907 and, 132
    Riverside Improvement Company, 24
    Thomas Ackerson and, 129
Barnard & Wilder, 92
Barney, John S., 174
Barnum, Nellie, 58, 60
Barnwell, Walter, 52
Baron, Morris, 138
Barrett, Clarence T., 171
Barrett, Clemens T., 18
Barrett, Nathan F., 18, 48
Barry, Patrick, 254*n*6 (Ch. 5)
Bartlett, Harold L., 260*n*21
Bartlett, Paul, 249
Barton, Alfred I., 165
Barton, Anna, 220
Barton, LeRoy, 220, 273*n*64
Bartos, Virginia, 7
Bastian, Harry S., 152, 264*n*40–264*n*41
bathhouses, 49, 54, 107, 138
Bathing Casino (Montauk Beach), 158
bathing pavilions, 106, 107, 110, 120, **121**
    See also bathhouses; swimming
Baxter, A. Percy, 214, 271*n*21
Baxter Estates, 8, 214, **214**, 271*n*19
Baxter Pond, 214, **214**
Bayberry Point, 46–51
    entry gates, **50**
    houses, **18**
    houses of, **48**, **49**, **50**
Bayberry Point Corporation, 51
Bay Crest, 15
Bayliss, Charles E., 254*n*2 (Ch.5)
Bay Shore Company, 165
Bayside Flushing Company, 268*n*5
Bayside Homes Company, 272*n*45–273*n*54
Bayview Colony, 153–154, 265*n*52, 271*n*19
Bayview Terrace, 271*n*19
beaches. *See* private beaches

Beacon Hill, 214–221
  advertisements, **217–218**
  houses, **219**, **221**
  master plans and maps, **220**
  picture postcards, **214**, **215**
  promotional booklets, **215**
  street layouts, **220**
Beacon Hill Residents Association, 215, 219, 220,
    270*n*1 (Ch. 17), 271*n*34–272*n*35, 273*n*62–
    274*n*62
Beame, Abraham, 227
Beaux-Arts Park, 246–247, 278*n*3, 278*n*7
Beecher, Catharine, 23
beech trees, 85
Beers, William, 173
Bellamy, Edward, 25
Bellcourt, 78, 98, 131
Belle Harbor Yacht Club, 224
Bellerose, 73–77
  master plans and maps, **74**
  street layouts, **76**
Bellerose Association, 75
Bellerose Civic Association, 75, 76
Bellerose Women's Club, 75, 76
Belle Terre Club, 67, 68, **70**, 71, 256*n*63, 256*n*77
Belle Terre Estates, 65–70, 71
  bridges, **69**
  construction crews, **67**
  houses, **66**, **69**
  master plans and maps, **68**
  railroad stations, **66**
  street layouts, **66**
Belmont, O. H. P., 68
Belmont Park, 181
Belmont Tunnels, 268*n*5
Bennett, A. D., 268*n*5
Bennett, James G., Jr., 82
Bennett, J. C., 254*n*12 (Ch. 3)
Benson, Arthur W., 148
Benson, John P., 206, **206**, **207**, **208**
Berizzi, Stefano, 247
Bessel, Wesley S., 221
Best Western President Hotel, New York City,
    276*n*52
Bethlehem Land & Improvement Corp., 276*n*54
Beverly Square projects, 117, 119, 258*n*14
bicycling, 38, 88
Bi-Harbor Realty Group, 221, 271*n*34, 273*n*55,
    273*n*62, 273*n*67
Biltmore Shores, 8, 20
Bing, Alexander, 194, 196
Bing & Bing real estate company, 194
Bird, W. P., 38
bird sanctuaries, 239
Bishop Molly Retreat House, 268*n*15 (Ch. 14)
Bishop's See house, Garden City, 33
Black Inn Pond, Roslyn Estates, 64, **65**
black oak trees, 85
Blackton, J. Stuart, 56, 250–251
Blake, Peter, 21
Blatch, Harriot S., 204, 206, **209**
Blatch, Nora S., 206, **209**
Blatch, William H., 204
Bloodgood Cutter farm, 56, 254*n*15 (Ch. 4)

BMT. *See* Brooklyn–Manhattan Rapid Transit (BMT)
boardwalks, 105, 106–107, **108**, 110
boat basins, **120**, **121**
boathouses, 49, **50**, 87, **87**, 176, 232
boating
  Brightwaters, 19, 120, **121**, 122, 127, **127**
  Long Beach, 105
  Port Washington and, 214
  See also gondolas; yachts and yacht clubs
body snatching, 32–33
Bok, Edward, 74
Bond and Mortgage Company, 16, 255*n*52
The Book of New York (Chambers), 72, 212
bootlegging, 156, 265*n*76
Boston Dwelling House Company, 133
Boston Globe, 115
Bourne, Frederick G., 275*n*12
Bouton, Edward, 15, 192
bowling alleys, 36, 54, 120, 224, 268*n*23
Bowne Park, 98
Boynton, Louis, 173
Boy Scout Troops, 53
Brady, "Diamond Jim," 111
Bragg, Caleb, 158, 266*n*96
Branch Bank of the United States façade, 195
Brazier, Charles W., 145, **145**, 146
Breese, Edmund, 185, 269*n*24
Brice, Fannie, 138
The Brickbuilder, 67
Brick Disciple house, Garden City, **28**, 30
brick works, 200
bridges
  American Venice, 231, **231**, 239
  Belle Terre Estates, 67, **69**
  Brooklyn Bridge, 11, 27
  Manhattan Bridge, 39
  Queensboro Bridge, 12, **12**
  Williamsburg Bridge, 39
bridle paths, 67
Briggs, Fred, 17, 53, 55, 254*n*10 (Ch. 4), 254*n*13
    (Ch.4), 273*n*68
Briggs, Loutrell, 221
Brightwaters, 116–129, 258*n*23
  advertisements, **125**
  canalizing, **19**
  canoeing, **127**
  groundbreaking day, **119**
  houses, **124**
  plaza and pagodas, **120**
  promotional booklets, **2**, **122**
  street layouts, **122**, **123**
Brightwaters Association, 120, 126–127, 128
Brightwaters Casino, 120, **121**, 127
Brightwaters Fire Company, 127
Brisbane, Arthur, 264*n*46
Britten, Fred, 162, 266*n*93
Broadway-Flushing, 78, 98
Broadway Trust Company, 79
Brooklyn Board of Real Estate Brokers, 224
Brooklyn Bridge, 11, 27
Brooklyn Daily Eagle
  American Venice, 238
  auto travel restrictions, 171
  Beacon Hill, 215

Château des Beaux-Arts, 246
club restrictions, 71
Garden City, 35
Great Neck Estates, 137
Great Neck Villa Estates, 141
Herbert Gunnison, 17
homeowners' struggles, 16
H. Stewart McKnight, 261*n*81
Long Beach, 105–106, 107–108, 110, 111
Long Island transformation, 11, **11**
Neponsit, 225
New Versailles, 250
Plandome, 53
Port Washington, 213–214
property viewings, **13**
Roslyn Estates, 63–64
Shields & Company, 141
Shoreham, **204**, 207
sportsman pursuits, 11
Tangiers Manors, 248
Wardenclyffe, 202
William Reynolds, 101
Woodmere, **175**
Woodsburgh, 168
Brooklyn Life
club restrictions, 68
Jamaica Estates, 184
Knickerbocker Field Club, 15
Long Beach, 106, 108
Neponsit, 224
Thomas Ackerson, 119
Brooklyn–Manhattan Rapid Transit (BMT), 117,
118
Brooklyn Times, 17
Brooklyn Transit Company, 255*n*52
Brown, Anthony F., 254*n*12 (Ch. 3)
Brown, George J., 8
Brun, Clement B., 57, 254*n*20
Bryant, William B., 268*n*22
Bryant, William Cullen, 23
Bryson, Robert, 118
See also Slee & Bryson
Buchman & Fox, 89
building restriction ordinances, 57, 137–138
See also deed restrictions
bungalows
Belle Terre Estates, 65, 68
Brightwaters, 123, 124, **124**
Garden City, 41
Great Neck Villa, **142**
Neponsit, 223, 224
Shoreham, 206
S. Lewis,' 10
Burdett, F. A., 273*n*54
buried utilities, 82, 91, 109, 171
Burley, James, 123
Burnett, Frances H., 10, 56, 252*n*3 (Ch.1)
Burnham, Daniel H., 14
Burton, Crawford, 170
Burton, Florence, 170
Burton, Frank V., 170
Burton, John H., 170, 175, 268*n*19, 268*n*22
Burton, Louisa, 170
Burton, Lucia C., 170

Burton, Robert L.
about, 52, 169–170, **170**, 268*n*19
homes of, 170, 176–177
See also Woodmere
Burton Brothers, 170
buses, 181, 235
Busselle, Alfred, 92
Bustanoby, André, 246
Bustanoby brothers, 246–247
Butler, Cornelia, 35
Butler, Ellis P., 19
Butler, Prescott, 35

Cabrini College, Radnor, Pennsylvania, 215
Café des Beaux-Arts, 246
California bungalows, 140, **142**, 262*n*7
California privet hedges, 85
Cambridge Building, New York City, 180
Camp Hero, 166
camp meeting movement, 23
Camp Mills, Garden City, 44
canalizing
about, 18–19
Bayberry Point, 47, **50**, 51
Brightwaters, 120
Kensington, 93, **93**, 95
See also dredging
canalizzazione, 18
canals. *See* American Venice; Grand Venetian Canal
and Yacht Harbor
Canals of Lido, 114
canoeing, **127**
Cape Cod style architecture, 217, 244, **244**
car dealerships, 149–150
Caretto & Forster, **145**, 146
Carl G. Fisher Corporation of Miami, 165
Caroline Episcopal Church, Setauket, New York,
277*n*47
Carpenter, N. Leslie, 68
Carrère, John M., 15
Carrère & Hastings, 248
Carrère & Hastings workshop, **250**
carriages, 32
See also horse-drawn carriages
Carteret Gun Club, 37
caseworkers, 187, 188
Casino des Beaux-Arts, 246, **247**, **248**, **249**
Cassatt, A. J., 108
Castagnolia family, 269*n*23
Cathedral of the Incarnation, Garden City, 32–33,
33, 38, 45
cathedrals, 32–33, **34**
Cedarcroft, 62, 255*n*35
Cedarhurst, 168, 178
Cedarhurst Land Association, 171–172
Cedarhurst Land Improvement Company, 172
Cedarhurst Yacht Club, 174
Cement and Engineering News, 64
cemeteries, 28, 59–60, **60**
See also crypts
Central Park, 24, 84
Central Railroad of Long Island, 27
Central Railroad of New Jersey, 186
cesspools, 30, 91, 126

Chambers, Julius, 72
Chandler, Harry A., 275n44
    See also Harry A. Chandler Booklet Dept.
Chapin, Roy D., 158, 266n93
Chapman, Henry O., 174
Chapman, Josephine W., 17
Chapman, J. Wilbur, 268n13
character. See neighborhood character
Charity Organization Society, 187
    See also New York City Charity Organization
        Society
Charles E. Finlay Real Estate Company, 79
Charles E. Phelps estate, 119
Chase, William M., 63
Château des Beaux-Arts, 246, **248**
Château des Tourelles, Long Beach, 247
Cherry Valley Golf Club, 38, 44
chestnut trees, 85
Child, Edwin S., 202
Childe, Cromwell, 169
Childs, Emery E., 24
Childs, William H., 273n54
Choate, Joseph H., 48
Chris-Craft, 147
Chrysler, Walter, 115
Chrysler Building, 115, 257n12
City Beautiful movement, 13, 14, 133, 248
City Planning Commission of Summit, New Jersey, 251
civic organizations. See specific names
Civil Defense Community, 197
Clark, John M., 262n7
class-conscious terms, 243
Clayton and Bell stained glass windows, 33, 34
Cleaves, Margaret, 206
Cliff House, Shoreham, 206, **207**
club membership restrictions, 68, 71, 87, 127, 243
    See also "desirable" people
Cobe, Andrew J., 55–56, 254n15 (Ch.4), 254n19
Cobin, I. Jones, 217, 272n52
Cobin & Cocks, 272n52
Cocks, Arthur, 217, 272n52
Coe, Dr., 247
Coe, R. A., 260n34
Coffin, Howard E., 149, 162, 266n130
Coffin, William S., 194–195, 196
Cold Spring Harbor, 47, 186, 190
Cole, Thomas, 23
Collier, Margaret, 162, 165
Collier's, 75
Collins, Irving, 154, 159, 161, 165
Collins, John S., 150–151
Colonial Revival style architecture
    Beacon Hill, 217, 220
    Douglas Manor, 90
    Fiske Terrace, 118
    Frank Melville, Jr. and, 240
    Garden City, 36, 41, 139
    magazines' influence on, 75
    Montauk Beach, **158**
    Neponsit, 224
    Plandome, 53
    popularity of, 17
    Stony Brook Village, 240, 245, **245**
    William Coffin and, 195

    See also Dutch Colonial Revival style architecture;
        Mediterranean Colonial Revival style
        architecture
Colonial style architecture
    Garden City, 41
    Great Neck Villa Estates, 144
    Miami Beach, 264n41
    Munsey Park, 186, 196
    Old Field South, 242
    Plandome, 55
    popularity of, 195–196
    Woodmere, 172
Colonial Williamsburg, 195–196, 245
Columbia University, 56
Commercial Trust Company of New York, 247
"Commission on Race and Housing," 277n25
Committee on a Regional Plan of New York and Its
        Environs, 187
Committee on Congestion of Population in New
        York City, 248
common ownership, 88, 99
    See also waterfront rights
community builders. See developers
Community Church (Montauk Beach), 158
community types, 22–24, 25
commutes. See Manhattan commutes
company housing, 43, 155–156, 158, 159
    See also mill villages
Coney Island amusement parks, 15
    See also Dreamland
Coney Island Jockey Club track, 13
Conklin, Theodore, Mrs., 155, **155**
construction crews
    Belle Terre Estates, **67**
    Brightwaters, 123
    Dreamland, 103
    Miami Beach, 152
    Miami Beach and, 264n36
    Montauk Beach, 155–156, 158, 159, 160, 163
    Shoreham and Mountain Lakes, 204
    Woodsburgh, 168
    See also specific building companies
Coolidge, Calvin, 162
Cooper, Gary, 147, 263n58
Copiag Land Company, 229
Copiague and Copiague Neck, 19, 229, 275n10,
        275n11
    See also American Venice
Copiague Neck County Park, 276n63
Copley, John S., 196
Corbin, Austin, 105, 148, 156, 199
Corbin, John R., 184, 260n36
Corbin Banking Company, 199
Cornelius Roosevelt estate, 117
Cornwell, Arthur R., 173
cottage colonies, 15
cottage roofs, 232
cottages
    American Venice, 238, 276n54
    Bayberry Point, 47, 48, 49
    Beacon Hill, 221
    Brightwaters, 123, 124, **124**, 125
    as Grenwolde inspiration, 144, 145
    Long Beach, 105, 106

Neponsit, 223
Old Field South, 243, 244
Shoreham, **203**, **204**, 206
Wardenclyffe, 199
Woodsburgh, 168, 169
Woodsmere, 170
See also English cottage style architecture; Franklin
  Avenue cottages, Garden City
Cotter, Frank, 268*n*19
country clubs, 19
  See also specific country clubs
Country Development Company, 52
Country Life (Great Britain), 42
Country Life in America, 7, 15, 42, 172, **182**, **183**
Country Life Press office, 41–43, **44**
country living enthusiasm, 23
Country Residences (Downing), 23
covenant clauses. *See* deed restrictions
Cowan's Place restaurant, 276*n*58
The Craftsman, 202
Craftsman Home Building Company, 17, 41
Craftsman style architecture, 17, 41, **209**
  See also Arts and Crafts style architecture
Cravath, Paul D., 11
Crawford, Florence S., 170
Crawford Farms, Millbrook, 177
Crosby, Arthur F., 178
crypts, 32, 33
  See also cemeteries
Cullen, Michael J., 185
Cunliff, L., 35
Curtiss, Glenn H., 41, 44, 163
Curtiss Aeroplane and Motor Company, 41
Curtiss Engineering Plant, 44
Curtiss Field, 44
CVS Pharmaceuticals, 276*n*1
cycling. *See* bicycling

Dalameter, A. G., 260*n*34
Daly, Arnold, 115
Darling, C. P., 246
Dater, John G., 70
Davies, Julian T., 169
Davis, Alexander J., 24
Davis, Hugh, 156, 157, 161
Davis, Walter W., 140
Dayton, Wilson, 260*n*34
Dean Alvord Company, 69, 254*n*2 (ch. 5)
Dean Alvord Securities Company, 69
deed restrictions, 15–16
  See also building restriction ordinances
DeForest, Alling, 254*n*7 (Ch. 5)
de Forest, Emily, 47
de Forest, Jesse, 187
de Forest, Lockwood, 187
de Forest, Robert W., 14, 47, 186–190, **187**
  See also Forest Hills Gardens; Munsey Park
De Garmo, Walter C., 152, 264*n*39
Degnon, Michael J., 183, **185**, 268*n*5, 268*n*15 (Ch. 14)
Degnon Company, 182–183
De Lacy, George, 268*n*22
Delano & Aldrich, 246, **248**
Delehanty, Bradley, 17
Delta Kappa Epsilon, 58

Denton, Delameter S., 27
Department of Housing and Planning for the U.S.
  Shipping Board, 194
Depew, Chauncey, 184–185, 269*n*22
"desirable" people, 60, 93, 122, 241, 243
  See also club membership restrictions; snobbery
Despatch, New York, 60, 254*n*15 (Ch. 5)
de Suarez, Diego, 89
developers, 13–15, 20
  See also specific names
de Vidal Hundt, C., **92**
Dickerson, John R., 199
Dillon, Charles W., 262*n*7
discrimination. *See* club membership restrictions;
  "desirable" people; racial discrimination;
  religious restrictions
Ditmas Park, 15
Dixie Highway, 151–152, 264*n*33
dogs, 115
Dominion of Versailles, 250
  See also New Versailles
Doubleday, Frank, 17
Doubleday, Page & Company, 39, 41, 42, 43, 56
Douglas, George, 84
Douglas, William P., 82, **82**, 84
Douglas estate, **86**, **87**
Douglas Manor, 81–89, 96, 98–99
  advertisements, **81**
  houses, **86**, **87**, **89**
  master plans and maps, **83**
  pier and boathouse, **87**
  recreation, **98**
  street layouts, **83**, **84**, **85**, **88**
  trees, **85**
Douglas Manor Association, 20, 99
Douglas Manor Inn, **86**, 87
Douglaston Country Club, 87, **87**
Douglaston Historic District, 99
Downing, Andrew J., 23, 254*n*6 (Ch. 5)
Dreamland, 14, 17, 18, 102–103, 115
dredging
  American Venice, 231
  Long Beach, 106, 113
  Miami Beach, 151, 160
  Montauk Beach, 158, **159**
  Rockaways, 170–171
  Woodmere, 177
  See also canalizing
Driesler, Benjamin, 118
Duke, Benjamin N., 56, **56**
Duke, James B., **56**
Dunne, Desmond, 133
Duryea, Franklin P., 268*n*5
Duryea family farm, 132, 134
Dutch Colonial Revival style architecture, 40, 41, 217
Dutch Colonial style architecture
  Bellerose, 75
  Brightwaters, 123
  Great Neck Estates, **133**, 134, 260*n*36
  Great Neck Villa Estates, 140, 262*n*7
  Grenwolde, 145, **145**, 146
  Jamaica Estates, 182, 268*n*13
  Plandome, 53
  Woodmere, 172, 173, 176

Eastern Parkway, 15
East Hampton Star, 154, 160
East River ferries, 39
East River Heights, 78, 80–81, **80**
East River tunnels
    Cedarcroft and, 62
    Degnon Company and, 183
    intermodal travel opportunities and, 135
    Real Estate Exchange of Long Island and, 13
    real estate market confidence and, 55
    Rickert-Finlay advertising and, 78
    transportation revolution and, 12
East Rochester, New York, 60
E. C. Benedict & Co., 241
economic depressions and recessions
    Bellerose and, 74
    Charles Tuxill and, 218
    Garden City and, 30
    Montauk Beach and, 163–164
    Munsey Park and, 197
    Old Field South and, 242, 244
    real estate development and, 73
    Riverside Improvement Company and, 24
    Shoreham and, 208
    See also Panic of 1907
educational community, Garden City as, 33–34,
    34
Edwards, Caroline L., 58
Edwards, Jonathan, 58
Elder, Louisine, 46
electricity. *See* utilities
Elio, Paavo, 245
Elizabethan style architecture, 123
Ells, Irving B., 134
Ellwanger, George, 254n6 (Ch. 5)
Ellwanger and Barry, 59, 254n6 (Ch. 5)
elm trees, 85
Embury, Aymar, II, 17, 41, 68, 91, 94, 172–173
Emerson, Ralph Waldo, 23
Emmet, Devereux, 37, 184
English cottage style architecture, 172
English Garden City movement, 42, 44
English style architecture
    Belle Terre Estates, 67, **69**, **70**
    Garden City, 41
    Great Neck Estates, 134
    Grenwolde, 145
    Jamaica Estates, 182
    See also Tudor style architecture
Enrico V. Pescia & Co., 229
Episcopal bishops, 32
Episcopal churches, 32–33, **34**
Episcopal Church of America, 32
epitaphs, 245
equestrian activities, 11, 68, **70**, 242, 276n16
    See also bridle paths; hunting clubs
Ernestus Gulick Company, 180, 182
estates, 180
    See also specific estates
Estates at Great Neck, 260n20, 261n44
    See also Great Neck Estates
Estates of Long Beach. *See* Long Beach
Ethical Culture Society, 175
ethnic discrimination, 175, 244, 245, 277n25

The Evening Mail, 110–111
Eyre, Wilson, 17

factory towns, 24
failed communities, 246–251
Fairbanks, Thomas N., 56
Fairfax, Marion, 206
Fairmount Park, Philadelphia, 215
Fairseat, Plandome Park, 56, 254n17 (Ch.4)
farms
    Bellerose, 74
    Brightwaters, 259n42
    Cold Spring Harbor, 186
    economic depressions and recessions and, 73
    Garden City, 27, 31, 45
    Great Neck Estates, 132
    Great Neck Hills, 140
    H. Stewart McKnight and, 137
    LIRR and, 259n42
    Plandome, 56
    Port Washington, 213
    Queens Land and Title Company and, 72
    Rickert-Finlay Realty Company and, 78, 81
    Robert L. Burton and, 176–177
    Rockaways, 168
    United Holding Company and, 72
    Woodmere, 170
    Woodville Landing, 199
Farnsworth, J. C., 62
Far Rockaway, 15, 169, 175, 177
Federal Housing Administration (FHA), 16, 20–21
Federal style architecture, **86**, 87
Fell, Herbert, 136
ferries, 11, 27, 39
Ferris, E. L., 52
FHA. *See* Federal Housing Administration (FHA)
Ficken, Richard, 15
Field & Stream, 107, 161
Fields, W. C., 138
Fieldston, 110
financial difficulties
    Carl Fisher, 161, 162, 163–165, 166, 267n148
    Charles Wethey, 216
    Dean Alvord, 16, 58, 70–71
    Henry Hilton, 34–35
    Herbert Hapgood, 208–209
    H. Stewart McKnight, 137
    McKnight Realty Company, 135–136, 137
    Montauk Beach Company, 165
    Tuxill Realty Company, 217
    village incorporation and, 20
    See also bankruptcies; economic depressions and
        recessions; foreclosures; Hyde Scandal; Panic of
        1907
financing
    Beacon Hill, 216
    Brightwaters, 122, 125, 128
    Great Neck Estates, 134
    Neponsit, 223
    Shoreham development and creativity in, 205–
        206
    William Harmon and, 192
    See also mortgages
Finlay, Alexander H., 68, 79

Finlay, Ann R., 92
Finlay, Charles E.
  about, 78–79, 92, **92**
  homes of, 91, **91**, 98
  H. Stewart McKnight and, 130–131, 132
Fireman's Hall, Lawrence, 172
Fireproof Dwelling Company, 64
fireproof materials, 64, 91, 106, 109
First Houses, 194
fir trees, 85
Fisher, Carl G.
  about, 13, 149–150, **149**, 165–166, 266*n*112
  bankruptcies and, 164
  downfall of, 161, 162–163
  homes of, 150, 153, 157, 162, 163, 164, **165**
  management style of, 152, 154
  marketing strategies of, 149–150, 151, 153, 161, 167
  See also Miami Beach; Montauk Beach
Fisher, Edward D., 123
Fisher, Jane W.
  on Alton Beach, 264*n*23
  on Carl Fisher, 149, 150, 153, 161, 162, 164
  gondola and, 152
  on hurricane, 160
  on Montauk development, 154, 155, 157, 158, 159
  on Montauk Village, 156
fishing clubs, 46, 151
  See also specific clubs
fishing village (Montauk Village), 156–157, **157**
fish shipping, 148, 263*n*5
Fiske, Elizabeth, 117
Fiske, George P., 117
Fiske Terrace, 15, **18**, 117–119, 258*n*14
Fitzgerald, Edward C. M., 180
Fitzgerald, F. Scott, 10, **136**, 138, **138**, 252*n*4 (Ch.1)
Fitzgerald, Zelda, **136**, 138, **138**
Fitzsimmons, Bob, 101
Flagg, Ernest, 178
Flamingo Hotel, Miami Beach, 152
Flatbush, 15
flight schools, 44
Flint, Charles L., Jr., 199, 205
Flint, Charles R., 200, 201, 205
Floral Park, 27, 72, 74
Flower Hill, 129
Flushing Journal, 31
Forbes, George M., 58, 59
Ford, Butler and Oliver firm, 43
Ford, Henry, 13
foreclosures
  Beaux-Arts Park, 247
  FHA and, 16
  Grenwolde, 262*n*25
  Jamaica Estates, 185
  Matawok Land Company, 185
  McKnight Realty Company, 137
  Montauk Beach, 164
  Munsey Park fund, 197
  Neponsit Property Owners' Association and, 226–227
Forest Hills Gardens, 15, 25, 186, 190–193, 196
  street layouts, **191**
Forest Hills Gardens Community Corporation, 197
Forest Hills Gardens Community Council, 196

Forest Hills Gardens Homes Company, 193
Forest Hills Inn, **193**
Forest Park, 61
Forman & Light, 92
Forster, Frank J., 89, 134, **145**, 146, **146**, 260*n*35
Foster, Mark, 161
Fourier, Charles, 23
Fowler, Benjamin, 27
Fox, Fontaine, 221
Fox, Joseph, 175
Fox, William, 8, 178–179
Fox Film Corporation, 179
fox hunting, 169, 242
France, as landscape inspiration. *See* Beaux-Arts Park
Frank, James, 175, 268*n*22
Franke, Frederick C., 216, **217**, 273*n*54
Franke, Helen, 216
Franklin Avenue cottages, Garden City, 43–44
Franklin Court, Bethpage, **45**
Frank Melville Memorial Park, 244
Frederick Loeser and Co. department store, 180
Frederick Wallick & D. W. Terwilliger, 92
Freedman, Bob, 138
French Provincial style architecture, 197
French Renaissance style architecture, 102, 103
French Second Empire style architecture, 168
French septic sedimentation plan, 223
Friedmann, C. A. H., **92**
Friedmann, Friedrich F., 92, **92**
F. W. Avery and Company, 176

Galston, Clarence G., 175, 268n22
gambling, illegal, 162, 163, 164
Garden Cities of To-morrow (Morrow), 25
Garden City, 22, 27–45
  19th century layout, **23**, **24**, **27**
  advertisements, **40**
  casinos, **36**
  churches, **33**
  golf courses, **20**, **38**
  homes, **43**
  hotels, **37**
  houses, **28**, **29**, **43**
  master plans and maps, **27**, **41**
  railroad stations, **30**
  schools, **34**, **35**
  views, **31**
  waterworks, **31**
Garden City Company
  churches and, 39
  Nassau County Courthouse and, 39
  revitalization and, 36, 37, 38, 41, 43–44
  start of, 35
  title guarantee companies and, 16
garden city concept, 189–190, 191
Garden City Country Club, 40
Garden City East, 41
Garden City Estates Company, 39–44, **44**, 62, 180, 184
Garden City Estates Station and Plaza, 40, **42**
Garden City Golf Links, 38, **38**
Garden City Historical Society, 45, 252*n*1 (Ch. 2)
Garden City Hotel, 30, 36, **37**, 38, 43, 45
Garden City movement, 25
Garden of Eden, 22

gardens
    Bellerose, 74, 76
    Belle Terre Estates, 67, 68
    Garden City, 30, 40, 42, 43
    Kensington, **91**, 93–94, **94**
    Plandome Park, 56
garden suburbs, 10, 24
    See also residential parks
Gasser, Roy C., 52
gasworks, 30, 35, 75
    See also utilities
Gayness, W. Stewart, 158
Geiger, August, 151, 152, 264n26
General Electric Realty Plot, 254n7 (Ch. 5)
General Federation of Women's Clubs, 76
The Geography of Nowhere (Kunstler), 21
George Hewlett farm, 170
George Schenck farm, 140
Georgian Colonial style architecture, 178
Georgian Revivals, 134
Georgian Revival style architecture, 217
Gerarg, Richard H., 269n23
German town planning, 247, 248
Gibson, Robert W., 11, 17, 268n13
Gilbert, C. P. H., 17, 91
Gilbert, H. Bramhall, Mrs., 262n23
Gillette, Leon N., 266n96
Glen Cove, 33
Glen Cove's North Country Colony, 15
Glenn, John, 192
God Bless Our Home (Currier & Ives), 23
Goddard, Pauline, 138
God's Own Junkyard (Blake), 21
Goelet, Robert, 112
golf clubs. *See specific clubs*
The Golf Course, 113
golfing. *See specific golf clubs and golf courses*
gondolas
    American Venice, 228, 230, 231–232, **232**, 234
    Miami Beach, 152
Good, Jesse, 14
Gordon, Alastair, 251
Goss, Clayton S., 268n5
Gothic style architecture. *See* Cathedral of the Incarnation, Garden City
Gould, Howard, 68
Granada Towers, Long Beach, 115
Grand Canal, American Venice, 231
Grand Central Parkway, 20, 185
Grand Venetian Canal and Yacht Harbor, 19, **19**, 120, **121**, 127
Grant, U. S., 26
grass mowing, **86**
Great Depression. *See* economic depressions and recessions
The Great Gatsby (Fitzgerald), 10, 138
Great Neck Estates, 10, 20, 130, 132–139
    houses of, **133**, **136**, **139**
    master plans and maps, **131**
    street layouts, **131**, **143**
Great Neck Estates Village Hall, **133**, 136, 261n58
Great Neck Golf Club, 91, 135, **135**
Great Neck Hills, 140, 260n23
Great Neck Improvement Company, 140, 260n23

Great Neck Playhouse, 138
Great Neck Villa Company, 140
Great Neck Villa Estates, 140–143, 262n6
    houses of, **142**
    picture postcards for, **142**
    street layouts, **141**, **142**
Great South Bay. *See* Bayberry Point
Greek Revival style architecture, 87
Greek style architecture, 172
Greenbelt, Maryland, 25
Grenwolde, 144–147, 262n35
    casinos, **143**
    houses of, **144**, **145**
    street layouts, **143**
Greve, William H., 226
Griffith, W. R., 84
Grout, Edward M., 181
Grumman, Leroy, 254n17 (Ch. 4)
Gulden, Frank, 254n12 (Ch. 3)
Gulick, Ernestus, 39, 40, 180, **181**
gun clubs, 37
    See also fox hunting; *specific clubs*
Gunnison, Herbert, 17
Gurney, Frederic, 268n22

Haight, Charles C., 46
Hanover Theatre Company, 102
Hapgood, Ethel, 209
Hapgood, Herbert J.
    about, 16, 198, **199**, 201, 208
    homes of, 201, **210**
    marketing strategies of, **204**
    See also Oak Ridge; Shoreham; Wardenclyffe
"Hapgood Homes" plaques, 210
Hapgood's Bungalow colony, 204
Harbor Oaks, Clearwater, Florida, **70**, 71
Harding, Warren, 151
Hardway, George, 134
Harlem River Houses, 89
Harmon, William, 192
Harmsworth Trophy races, 246
Harper's Weekly, 12, 27, 32
Harriman, Averell, 245
Harris, Edward H., 33, 34
Harrison, Henry G., 33
Harry A. Chandler Booklet Dept., **232**, **237**, 275n44
Haskell, Llewellyn, 24
Hasset Realty Company, 194
Hastings, Thomas, 249, **251**
    See also Carrère & Hastings
Hatch, Frederic H., 178
Hauser, Leo, 254n20
Havemeyer, Henry O., 46, 47, **47**, 49, 51
    See also Bayberry Point
Havemeyer, Horace, 51
Havemeyer and Elder, 46
Hawkins Construction Company, 277n33
Hawkins Estate, American Venice, 236
Hawley, Hughson, 114
Hayden, Charles, 149
Hayden, Stone & Co., 161
Haynes, Parke, 162, 163
Hazelhurst Field, 44
Hazzard, E. W., 141

Head of the Bay Club, 278*n*7

Healy, Thomas, 111

Hearth and Home real estate corporation, 195

Heckscher, August, 68

Hecla Iron Works, 55

hedges, 81, 85

hemlock trees, 85

Hempstead, 19th century layout o, **27**

    See also Town of Hempstead

Hempstead Plains, 27

Hempstead Plains Aerodome, 44

Hempstead South Company, 180

Hendrickson, Samuel, 27

Herald Tribune, 161

Herdman, William J., 206

Hering, Oswald C., 40, 41, 134, 260*n*36

Herman, Henry S., 175

Herrick, Myron T., 268*n*5

Hewlett, 168

Hewlett, Abraham, 169

Hewlett, Divine, 169

Hewlett, George M., 169

Hewlett, James M., 169

Hewlett Bay Company, 178, 267*n*6

Hewlett Bay Park, 170

Hewlett family, 168

Hewlett Land and Improvement Company, 176

Heyser, Carl J., Jr., 242, 243, **244**, 277*n*43

Hicks, Isaac, 7

High Church movement, 32, 33, 34

highways and highway development, 151, 208

    See also specific highways; *specific parkways*

Hillcrest Golf Course, 184

Hilton, Henry, 26, 32, 34

Hinsdale, William R., 31

historical markers, 269*n*29

    See also "Hapgood Homes" plaques

History of the Rockaways (Bellot), 169

Hither Hills, Montauk Beach, 149, 163

Hoerger, Fred, 152, 157, 264*n*35

Hofheimer, Lester, 178

hollow-style construction, 172, 173, 183

Holton, Arthur T., 201–202, **202**, 204

home colonies, 10, 119

    See also residential parks

homeowners' associations, 81, 98

    See also property owners' associations; *specific associations*

home ownership, 16, 74–75, 81

    See also rental costs

homeownership restrictions, 68, 71

    See also deed restrictions

Home Sweet Home (Currier & Ives), 23

Hopkins, Alfred, 47, 173

Hopkins, Lindsey, 165

Hopkins, Walter L., 92

Hornbostel, Henry, 123–124

horse-drawn carriages

    Belle Terre Estates, **66**

    Douglas Manor, 83, 84, 86

    Neponsit Realty Company, **224**

    Sandringham Colony, 110

The Horticulturalist, 254*n*6 (Ch. 5)

horticulture, 59

    See also hedges; landscape architecture; parks; trees

Horton, Theodore, 177

hot-air balloon stunts, 149–150

Hotel des Artistes, Manhattan, 248–249

Hotel Emerson, New York City, 238, 276*n*52

Hotel Nassau, 107, **108**, 110, 112, 178

Hotel Plymouth, New York City, 238, 276*n*52

Hotel President, New York City, 238, 276*n*52

Hotel Raleigh, New York City, 238, 276*n*52

hotels

    Carl Fisher and, 152, **152**

    Douglas Manor Inn, **86**, 87

    Garden City Hotel, 30, 36, **37**, 38, 43, 45

    Great Neck Estates, 135

    Lido Beach Hotel, 113, 114, **114**

    Long Beach, 105, 106, 107, 111

    Montauk Beach, 157, 163, 165

    Montauk Inn, 155, **155**, 162

    Rockaways, 168–169

    Woodsburgh Pavilion, 168, **169**, 170

    See also Montauk Manor

Hotel Victoria, New York City, 238, 276*n*52

House & Garden, 63, 123

House Beautiful, 75, 161

houses. *See specific architectural style*; *specific residential park*

housing reform, 187–189

    See also Ackerman, Frederick; Atterbury, Grosvenor; Coffin, William S.; Harmon, William

Houston, Herbert S., 56

Howard, Ebenezer, 25, 42, 189, 251

Howell, H. C., 270*n*1 (Ch. 17)

Howell, Thomas, 262*n*25

Howells, Vincent A., 217, 270*n*1 (Ch. 17), 272*n*35

Howes, Josiah, 170

"How to Develop Acreage" (Alvord), 65

Hoyt, John R., 145, **145**, 260*n*35

Hoyt, Richard, 149, 161

Hubbell, George L., 35–36, 37, 39, 41, 44

Huber, Bud, 278*n*49

Hudson Realty Company, 174

Humpage, Fred, 165

Hunt, Richard H., 37, 38

hunting clubs, 46

    See also fox hunting; *specific clubs*

Huntington Bay, 15

Huntington Bay and Country Club, 247

Huntington Bay Estates, 247

Huntington Bay View Association, 204

Huntington Golf Marine Club, 278*n*7

hurricanes, 115, **157**, 159–160, 165

Hurricane Sandy, 115

Hutton, Edward F., 49

Hutton, Franklyn L., 49

Hyde, Charles E., 214, 271*n*21

Hyde Scandal, 40

ideal city creations, 22–23

Immaculate Conception School, Jamaica Estates, 185, 252*n*4 (preface)

Ince, Ralph, 127

incorporation. *See* village incorporation

Indianapolis Motor Speedway Company, 150, 162

"Indian Deed of Three Necks, Southside," 229

Indian Island County Park, 276*n*63

Indians. *See* American Indians

Industrial Revolution, 23, 188
infrastructure. *See specific subject*
Ingold, Alfred, 254*n*12 (Ch. 3)
Inn on the Boardwalk, 107
installment plans
    American Venice, 234
    Beacon Hill, 216
    Brightwaters, 122, 128
    Copiague, 234
    Fiske Terrace, 117
    Forest Hills Gardens, 192
    Neponsit, 223
    Old Field South, 244
    Suffolk Improvement Company, 244
    See also mortgages
Interborough Rapid Transit Subway (IRT), 12
intermodal travel opportunities
    as a marketing strategy, 13, 104, 126, 235, 258*n*9
    revolution in, 80, 117
    See also transatlantic ports
International One-design sailboats, 147
International style architecture, 139
Inwood, 168
IRT. *See* Interborough Rapid Transit Subway (IRT)
Island Golf Links, 38
island malls, 227
    See also parked medians
Isle of Wight Hotel, 169
Isman, Felix, 180, **181**
Italianate style architecture, **90**, 91, 120, 123, 178, 230
Italian Renaissance style architecture, 26, 56, 182

Jackson, Francis D., 55
Jackson, Kenneth T., 11
Jacobi, Harold, Sr., 178, 179, 268*n*31–268*n*32
Jacobi, Sanford, 178, 179, 268*n*31
Jacob Riis Park, 225
Jacobs, Samuel H., 175
Jacobus, J. W., 56, 254*n*19
Jamaica Estates, 40, 180–185
    advertisements, **182**, **183**
    houses of, **185**
    master plans and maps, **182**
    picture postcards, **183**, **184**
    street layouts, **182**
Jamaica Estates Association, 20, 185
Jamaica Estates Company, 12, 20
Jamaica Estates Corporation, 180, 182, 183, 184, 268*n*5
Jamaica Racetrack, 100
James, Harry B., 55
James Gordon Bennett cup races, 150
Janni, Alfred C., 275*n*20
Japanese style architecture, 17, 61, **61**, 93, **94**, 103
Jarvis, Samuel N., 268*n*5
Jeffersonian concept of land ownership, 192
Jeffries, Paul, 139
Jenney, William L., 24
Jewish population. *See* religious restrictions
John Reis Company, 258*n*14
Johnson, Henry B., 206, **207**
Johnston, Emily, 195
Jones, Helen S., 44

Joost, Martin, 255*n*52
Joy, Henry, 162
J. P. Morgan, 200

Kaltenborn, H. V., 244
Kansas City Star, 92
Katz, Max, 175
Keen, Charles B., 172, **172**, **173**
Keevil, Arthur, 216
Keister, George, 89
Kelland, Clarence B., 221
Kellock, Samuel K., 127
Kellum, John, 26, 27, 28, **28**, 29–30, **29**
Kendris, James, 269*n*23
Kensington, 81, 82, 83, 88–98
    advertisements, **97**
    houses of, **90**
    master plans and maps, **99**
    street layouts, **80**
Kenyon, Frank, 212
Kern, Jerome, 10
Kew Gardens, 8, 217
Keys, C. M., 165
kickbacks, 27
King, Edward, 145
King, Gamaliel, 27
King Cullen, 185
Kirby, Henry P., 17, 43
Kirby, Petit & Green
    Belle Terre Estates designs, 67, 68, **70**
    Dreamland designs, 17, 102, 103
    Garden City Estates designs, 40
    Jamaica Estates designs, 181
    Long Beach designs, **109**
    New Montauk Theatre, 102
    Plandome Park designs, 56
Kirby & Petit, 223
Knickerbocker Field Club, **14**, 15, 19
Knickerbocker Ice Company, 116
Knickerbocker Trust Bank, 74
Knickerbocker Yacht Club, 214
Kohlhepp, Walter, 155, 161
Kramaroff, Eugene M., 229
Krider, G. Horace, 270*n*1 (Ch. 17)
Kunstler, James H., 21

labor strikes, 123
Ladies' Home Journal, 74, 75, 202
lagoons, 103
    See also American Venice
LaGorce, Jack, 161, 265*n*55
La Gorce Golf Course, 153
Laguna San Marco, 231, **232**, 239
Lake Montauk, 155, 157, 158, **159**, 162, 163
lakes, 29, 120, 122, **171**, 204
Landmarks Preservation Commission, 99
landscape architects, 17–19
    See also specific names
landscape architecture, 59
    See also parks; planted medians; trees
landscape reshaping, 112–113
    See also canalizing; dredging
land sports. *See* recreation
land-use matters. *See* deed restrictions

Lang and Rosenberg, 115
Langhart, Nicholas, 242–243
Langjahr, A. H., 268*n*13
Lardner, Ring, 138
La Salle Military Academy, 275*n*12
Laurelton, 101–102, **102**
Laurelton Land Company, 62
lawn tennis, 15, 246
Lawrence, 168, 169, 178
Lawrence, Alfred, 168
Lawrence, Charles L., 119
Lawrence, George, 168
Lawrence, Newbold, 168
Lawrence Beach, 169
Lawrence High School, 174
Layton, A. G., 158
L. C. Clarke Agency, 242
Leavitt, Charles W., Jr.
    Garden City Estates designs, 40, 41, 43
    Jamaica Estates designs, 181, **182**
    Long Beach designs, 109
    Roslyn Estates designs, 67
LeBoutillier, George, 158, 162, 163, **163**
L'Ecluse, Ernest, 53, 164
L'Ecluse, Milton, 52, 53, 174, 247, 254*n*10 (Ch. 4),
    278*n*6
L'Ecluse, Washburn & Company, 52, 53, 164, 175,
    247, 254*n*5 (Ch. 4)
legal difficulties
    Carl Fisher, 162
    dredging, 177
    Garden City, 35
    Herbert Hapgood, 208–209
    Jamaica Estates, 185
    Neponsit Realty Company, 225–226
    Robert L. Burton, 176
    Shoreham, 205–206
    William Reynolds, 111, 114, 225–226, 257–
        258*n*62
leisure. *See* recreation
Leoni, Marchese, 228
Levi, Emil S., 175
Levi, John, 150, 152, 264*n*39
Levitt, Abraham, 8
Levitt, William J., 15
Levittown, New York, 45
Lewis, Sinclair, 10, 220, 252*n*2 (Ch.1)
L'Hommedieu, James H., 27, 33, 34
Libby, William, 32
Lido Beach, 112–114, **113**
Lido Beach Hotel, 113, 114, **114**
Lido Golf Club, 20, 112–113, 114
Lien, F. Ernst, 68, 256*n*60
Ligouri, Edward, **235**
Ligouri, Lena, **235**
lime trees, 85
Lincoln, Abraham, 185
Lincoln Highway, 151, 153, 264*n*32
Lincoln Hotel, Miami Beach, 151, 152
Lindbergh, Charles, 45
Lindeberg, Harrie T., 51, 172, **173**
Lindenhurst, New York, 275*n*10
Lindenhurst Star, 238
linden trees, 81

LIRR. *See* Long Island Railroad (LIRR)
Little & Brown, 91, **91**
"Little Brooklyn," 207
Littlejohn, A. N., 32, 33, 34
Littlejohn, Martin W., 56
Little Lord Fauntleroy (Burnett), 10, 56
Llewellyn Park, New Jersey, 24
Locust Lodge, Huntington Bay, 246
locust trees, 29, 208
log cabins, **204**
Lombardo, Guy, 239
Long Beach, 104–112, 217, 247
    advertisements, **104**, **105**, **111**
    hotels of, **108**
    houses of, **109**
    master plans and maps, **111**
    railroad stations, **107**
    street layouts, **110**
Long Beach auctions, 115
Long Beach Chamber of Commerce, 111
Long Beach City Hall, **112**
Long Beach Yacht Club, 112
Long Island Automobile Club, 13
Long Island City Factory Company, 258*n*2
Long Island Country Houses and Their Architects 1860–
    1940 (Baker, MacKay, Traynor, and Gill), 7
Long-Islander, 247
Long Island Estates, 178
Long Island Farmer, 181
Long Island Motor Parkway, 12–13, 38, 62, 63,
    255*n*29
Long Island Museum of History, Art & Carriages,
    277*n*47
Long Island Railroad (LIRR)
    Alvord and, 62
    Bellerose and, 75, 76, 77
    Belle Terre Estates and, **66**
    Brightwaters and, 120
    early 20th century expansion of, 12
    electrification of, 132, 137
    farms and, 259*n*42
    Forest Hills Gardens and, 191, 192, 193
    Garden City and, 27, **30**, 39, 40, 45
    Great Neck and, 81
    Hillside and, 181
    Hubbell and, 35
    Jamaica Estates and, 181
    Laurelton and, 102
    Lewis on, 10
    Lindenhurst and, 235
    Long Beach and, 106, **107**, 109, 115
    Montauk Beach and, 148, 162
    Nassau Boulevard and, 40
    North Shore Branch, 80, 198–199
    at Penn Station, **12**
    Peters and, 41
    Plandome and, 54, **55**
    Port Washington and, 212, 214
    Rockaways and, 168, 170, 174
    Roslyn Estates and, 67
    Station Square, 191
    suburban real estate development and, 73, 104
    Tangiers Manor and, **250**
    travel guides, **193**

Long Island Railroad (LIRR) (*continued*)
  Wardenclyffe and, 200
  Woodmere and, 172
  See also Corbin, Austin; LeBoutillier, George;
    Manhattan commutes; McCrea, James; Peters,
    Ralph; railroad stations
Long Island Railroad Information Bulletin, 161
Long Island Realty Investors Corporation, 251, **251**
Long Island State Park Commission, 148, 164
Longstreth, Richard, 8
Looking Backward (Bellamy), 25
Loper Brothers, 255*n*53
Lord, George D., 173, 179
Lorillard, Pierre, IV, 181
Lorsch, S., 109
Lotus Pond, Roslyn Estates, 64, **65**
Low, Seth, 61, 188
Lowell, Charles R., 187
Lowell, Josephine S., 187
Lycée Français, 206
Lynch, Ralph C., 176
Lyon, Edmund, 59, 60, 69, 71

Macdonald, Charles B., 112
Mackay, Clarence H., 184
MacKay, Robert, 252*n*1 (Ch. 2)
MacMonnies, Frederick, 248, 249
MacNeille, Perry R., 251
  See also Mann & MacNeille
Macy, Carlton, 172–173, **173**, 178, 267*n*6
Macy, George H., 49
magnolia trees, 59
Main Street (Lewis), 10
Man, Alrick H., 273*n*54
Manhasset Bay Estates, 250
Manhasset Bay Yacht Club, 214
Manhasset Development Company, 55
Manhasset Park, 254*n*5 (Ch. 4)
Manhasset Point Company, 254*n*15 (Ch. 4)
Manhasset School Board, 196
Manhattan Bridge, 39
Manhattan commutes
  Beacon Hill and, 212
  Brightwaters and, 120
  Douglas Manor and, **81**
  East River Heights and, 80
  Garden City and, 39, **40**
  Great Neck Estates and, 137
  intermodal travel opportunities and, 104
  Jamaica Estates and, 181
  Kensington and, 81, 93
  LIRR improvements and, 135, 192
  Long Beach and, 106
  Neponsit and, 222
  Norwood and, 78
  Port Washington and, 214
  Roslyn Estates and, 64
  Stony Brook and, 243–244
  Woodmere and, 174, 176
Manhattan Congregational Church, 272*n*45
Manhattan views, 84
Mann, Horace B., 251
Mann & MacNeille, 251, 269*n*22
Maplecrest, 271*n*19

maple trees, 29, 81, 85, 86
Maplewood, New Jersey, 117, 258*n*4, 258*n*9
Marine Pavilion, 169
marketing strategies
  American Venice Corporation, 228, 230
  Carl Fisher, 149–150, 151, 153, 161, 167
  Charles Tuxill, 214, 216
  club membership restrictions as, 68, 71, 87, 127, 243
  deed restrictions as, 15
  Herbert Hapgood, **204**
  Jamaica Estates Corporation, 181, 184
  McKnight Realty Company, 134
  M. Michaels Realty & Construction Corp., 236, **236**
  Munsey Park, 196
  Neponsit Realty Company, 223
  Plandome, 52
  Rickert-Finlay Realty Company, 78, 80–81, 82, 84,
    88, 92
  Shields & Company, 141
  Suffolk Improvement Company, 241, 242, 243, 244
  T. B. Ackerson Company, 120, 122–123, 125, 126,
    258*n*9
  to wealthy population, 104–105
  William Reynolds' aptitude for, 110–111
  Woodmere Realty Company, 176
  See also residency enticements
Marks, Arthur, 178, 268*n*32
Marsh, Benjamin C., 248
Marsh, Frank A. E., 72, 77
Marsh, Helen, 72–77, **73**
Marsh, Samuel, 168
Marsh, Thomas, 168
Marshall, Cyril E., 40, 41
Marshall, Tully, 206
marshland, 228, 236
Martin, Thomas W., 169
Martinelli, Giovanni, 234
Martinu, Bohuslav, 269*n*23
Martzolf, Antoine, 247
"Marvelous Millers," 127
Mason, Henry T., 234
"Masonia," 234
Massachusetts Institute of Technology, 136
Matawok Land Company, 180, 185
Matinecoc Indians, 86
Mayer, Edward, 113
Mayer, Peter B., 221, 273*n*70
McAvoy, D. Edward, 268*n*19, 268*n*22
McCaffray, Walter P., **158**
McCaffrey, J. G., 163, 264*n*27
McCarroll, Joseph A., 68
McClellan, George B., 180
McClelland, Linda F., 16
McCrea, James, 178
McCrea, James A., 174
McKenna & Irving, 158
McKim, Mead & White, 36, 44, 89, **89**, 190
McKnight, Arthur M., 133, 137
  See also McKnight brothers
McKnight, Edgar S., 259*n*1
McKnight, Frances, 139
McKnight, H. Stewart
  about, 130, 132, **132**, 137, 139, 261*n*65, 261*n*81
  bankruptcies and, 130

Chambers on, 72
Charles Finlay and, 130–131, 132
on Edward Rickert, 132
Frederick Mirrielees and, 136, 137, 261*n*54
on incorporation, 135
See also Great Neck Estates; McKnight Realty
    Company
McKnight, Ira T., 137, 259*n*1
    See also McKnight brothers
McKnight, John C., 132, 259*n*1
    See also McKnight brothers
McKnight, Scott, 137
McKnight brothers, 16, 131, 132, 134, 259*n*1
    See also specific names
McKnight Realty Company
    Chambers on, 72
    development approach of, 131–132
    landscape competition and, 133
    marketing strategies of, 131, 134, 260*n*32
    Panic of 1907 and, 132
    Shields brothers and, 261*n*4
    start of, 131, 259*n*7
McLanahan, M. Hawley, 264*n*38
    See also Price & McLanahan
McLean, George, 113
McPherson, Donald, 231
Meadowbrook Hunt Club, 37, 38
Meadows, Jayne, 239
Meany, Harry T., 110
medians. *See* planted medians
Mediterranean Colonial Revival style architecture, 216
Mediterranean Revival style architecture, 90
Mediterranean style architecture, 134, **136**, 144, 223,
    232
Meister, Isaac, 18, 228–229, 238
    See also American Venice
Meister & Bache Realty Company, 229
Meister Builders, 229, 238, 275*n*12
Meitani Realty, 238
Melville, Frank, Jr., 240, 241, **241**, 276*n*1
    See also Old Field South
Melville, Ward
    about, 240, 241, **243**, 244–245, **244**, **245**
    business diversifications, 276*n*1
    community projects, 277*n*47
    equestrian activities, 276*n*16
    on home prices, 277*n*32
    Old Field Club and, 277*n*42
    racial and ethnic discrimination and, 277*n*25
    Stony Brook Community Fund and, 277*n*39
    Stony Brook University and, 277*n*49–278*n*49
    Stony Brook Village and, 277*n*34, 277*n*37
    See also Old Field South
Melville Shoe Corporation, 276*n*1
Mendel, Leon S., 175
Men Who Are Making Kansas City (Creel and Slavens),
    79, 256*n*6 (Ch. 7)
Merrick Road. *See* Montauk Highway
Metropolitan Museum of Art, 186, 187, 193–194,
    195, 196
Meurer, Jacob, 68
Meyer, Cord, 189, 191, 193
Miami Beach
    about, 150–153

Arthur Holton and, 201
financial difficulties and, 164
hotels, **152**
hurricanes and, 159–160, 161
Montauk Beach and, 152, 264*n*36
Miami Herald, 151
middle class population
    Bellerose and, 76
    Brightwaters marketing and, 122, 123
    Douglas Manor and, 89
    "Dreamland" and, 14
    Forest Hills and, 192
    Ladies' Home Journal and, 74–75
    Munsey Park, 195
    Old Field South and, 242
    Plandome and, 57
    real estate market trends and, 73
    Rickert-Finlay Realty Company and, 78, 82
    Roslyn Estates and, 65
    Stony Brook Village and, 245
Midhamptons, 251, **251**
Midland Golf Club, 38
military involvement, **164**, 166, 230
    See also World War II preparations
mill villages, 24
Milton, Thomas, 264*n*12, 267*n*148
Mineola Fair Grounds, 37
Minuse, Bayles, 242, 277*n*34, 277*n*39
Mirrielees, Douglas, 136, 137
Mirrielees, Frederick, 136–137, 261*n*60
Mirrielees, Mrs., 137
Mirrielees Park, 261*n*58
Mission style architecture, 62
Mitchel, John P., 115, 226, 257–258*n*62
Mitchell, Singleton L., 52
M. Michaels Realty & Construction Corp., 235–236
Model T, 13
modified Tudor style architecture, 156, **160**
Moe, Richard, 21
Montauk Arms Apartments, 158
Montauk Association, 148, 156
Montauk Beach, 148, 154–165
    advertisements for, **161**
    dredging, **159**
    Fisher's visualization of, **154**
    houses of, **156**, **158**, **163**
    planning of, **153**
Montauk Beach Company, 165, 166
Montauk Beach Development Corporation
    audit of, 163
    bankruptcies, 165
    dredging and, **159**
    incorporation of, 154
    marketing strategies of, 265*n*70
    Montauk Manor and, **160**
    officers of, 162
    offices of, 158, 162, **166**, 167, 266*n*90
    receivership, 164
Montauk Club, 161
Montauk Company, 148, 155, 156
Montauk Downs Golf Course, 158, 162
Montauk Highway
    American Venice, 231, 235
    Brightwaters, 120

Montauk Highway (*continued*)
  Copiague, 229
  Montauk Beach, 167
  Montauk Beach Development Corporation, 158
  Montauk Point Realty Corporation, 159
Montauk Inn, 155, **155**, 162
Montauk Island Club, 162, 163, 164
Montauk Manor
  about, 157, **160**, 161–162, 164, 166, 167
  designer of, 20, 264*n*46, 265*n*87
  hurricane and, 165
Montauk Naval Station, 166
Montauk Point Lighthouse, 149
Montauk Point Realty Corporation, 159
Montauk Public School, 158
Montauk Steamship Terminal, **150**
Montauk Struck Company, 158, 167
Montauk Tennis Auditorium, 20, 163, 167
Montauk Theatre, 102, 158
Montauk Village, 156–157, **157**, 165, 265*n*76
Montauk Yacht Club, 154, 158, 162, 163
Montross, William C., 272*n*42
More, Thomas, 22
Morgenthau, Henry, 175, 176
Morgenthau, Julius C., 175, 178
Morgenthau, Maximilian, 174, 175–176, 177–178, 268*n*22
Morley, Christopher, 10, 64, 252*n*3 (Ch.1)
Morris, David H., 62
Morris, William, 25
Morrisey, Michael, **170**
mortgages
  Beacon Hill and, 270*n*1 (Ch. 17)
  Frank Bailey and, 222
  homeowners' struggles with, 16
  McKnight Realty Company and, 136
  Montauk Beach and, 162, 164
  Panic of 1907 and, 132
  Suffolk County Land Company and, 205
  William Tuxill and, 270*n*1 (Ch. 17)
  See also foreclosures; installment plans
Moses, Lionel, 89, **89**
Moses, Robert, 148–149, 164, 235
Mountain Lakes, New Jersey, 198, 204–205, 207, 209–210
mountain laurel, 67, 68
mowing, **86**
Munnysunk, 16
Munsey, Frank A., 193
Munsey bequest, 193–194
Munsey Park, 186, 194–197
  building of, **195**
  homes of, **196**
Munsey's Magazine, 70–71, 75

Nassakeag Land Company, 240, 276n3
Nassakeag Ridge community, 245
Nassau Boulevard, Garden City, 40, 41
Nassau Boulevard Aerodome, 44
Nassau County, 21, 189, 192
Nassau County Courthouse, 39
Natco, 17
National Academy of Design, 249, **251**
National Association of Brain Brokers, 201

National Automotive Fibers, 147
National Bank of Cuba, 268*n*5
National Conference on City Planning (1916), 16
National Golf Links of America, 63
National Housing Association, 188, 190
National League of Improvement Associations, 14
National Recreational Society, 251
National Register of Historic Places, 8, 45, 71, 257*n*51
National Trust for Historic Preservation, 21
Nautilus Hotel, Miami Beach, **152**, 153, 264*n*46
neighborhood character, 15
  See also deed restrictions; "desirable" people
neighborhood planning, FHA and, 20–21
Neponsit, 222–227, 274*n*2
  houses, **224**, **225**
Neponsit Building Company, 223–224
Neponsit Club, 224, 226, **226**, 274*n*19
Neponsit Property Owners' Association, 226–227, 274*n*19
Neponsit Realty Company, 222, 223, **224**, 225–226
Neptune Hotel, Woodsburgh, 168
Newby, A. C., 264*n*12
New Harmony, Scotland, 23
News from Nowhere (Morris), 25
newspaper coverage
  Carl Fisher, 167
  Miami Beach, 151
  Montauk Beach, 154, 158, 159, 164
  See also specific newspapers
New Versailles, 248–251, **250**, **251**
New York Central Realty Company, 70, 71
New York City Charity Organization Society, 187–188
New York City Mission Society, 195
New York Daily Tribune, 184
The New Yorker, 112
New York Herald, 82, 145
New York Land and Warehouse Company, 116, 258*n*2
New York School of Social Work, 188
New York State Board of Charities, 187
New York State Tenement Housing Commission, 188
New York Stock Exchange, 140, 147, 187
New York Suburban Land Company, 67
New York Sun, 248, 250
New York Telephone Company, 177
New York Times
  American Venice, **229**, 234–235, 236, **236**, 238
  Bayberry Point, 46, 51
  Beacon Hill, 214
  Belle Terre Club, 68
  Brightwaters, 124, 128
  Forest Hills Gardens, 186
  Great Neck, 133, 135, 143
  Jamaica Estates, 181, 182, 183, 269*n*22
  Lido Beach, 112–114
  Long Beach, 106–107
  Long Island Motor Parkway, 62
  Munsey Park, 194
  New Versailles, 250
  Plandome, 52, 57, 254*n*15 (Ch. 4)
  residential parks, 10, 252*n*5 (Ch.1)

Roslyn Estates, 65
Russell Sage Foundation, 189
Shoreham, **204**
Stony Brook Village, 277*n*37
Tangiers Manors, 247
T. B. Ackerson Company, 128
transportation and Long Island development, 132
Wardenclyffe, 202
William Reynolds, 100, 114, 115
Woodmere, 172, 174–175, 176
New-York Tribune, 56, 109, 110, 178, 223, 238
Nichols, J. C., 16
Night and Day Bank, 268*n*5
Nikola Tesla's Experiment Station, **201**
Nolen, John, 16
Norman style architecture, 145, **145**, 206
North Hempstead, 91, 93, 134
North Shore, 11, 12, 15, 18, 80
    See also Douglas Manor; Kensington
North Shore Horse Show, 242, 276*n*16
North Shore Industrial Company, 199–200
North Shore Railroad, 80
Norwood, 78, 80–81
Noyes, John H., 23

Oakey, Frances, 134
Oak Ridge, 201–202, **202**, 204
Oak Ridge Company, 201
oak trees, 84, 85
Oakwood Estate, 65
Oak Woods Cemetery, Chicago, 60
observation towers, 126, **126**
Ocean Beach, 72
ocean breezes, maximization of, 103, 108
Ocean Parkway, 15
O'Dwyer, William, 227
Old English Inn, Belle Terre Estates, 68, **70**, 256*n*62
Oldfield, Barney, 264*n*12
Old Field Club, 241, 242–243, **243**, 276*n*19, 277*n*42
Old Field Improvement Association, 240
Old Field South, 240–245
    houses of, **244**
    master plans and maps, **242**
    picture postcards, **244**
    street layouts, **242**
Old Field South Country Day School students, **243**
Old Field South Property Owners Association, 245
Old Village, Shoreham, 204
Olmsted, Frederick L., Jr.
    about, 14, 190, 260*n*23
    Benson property and, 148
    Forest Hills Gardens and, 190, 191–192
    Rochester, New York, parks and, 59
    See also Olmsted, Vaux, and Withers
Olmsted, John C., 18, 63, **63**, 190
Olmsted, Rick. *See* Olmsted, Frederick L., Jr.
Olmsted, Vaux, and Withers, 15, 24, 260*n*23
Olmsted Brothers, 241, **242**
O'Malley, Charles, 226
One Hundred Country Houses (Embury), 172–173
Oneida, New York, 23
Orr, Henry S., 41
Osborne Hotel, 169
Osgood & Pell, 262*n*23

Overlook, 271*n*19, 271*n*21
Overton, Miss, 204
Owen, Robert, 23

Packard Dredging Company, 158
Padavan, Frank, 269*n*29
Palermo Construction Corp., 232
Palmer & Hornbostel, 124
Panic of 1907, 16, 74, 132, 143
    See also economic depressions and recessions
Parce, Walter A., 60
Parce, W. W., 59, 60, 254*n*7 (Ch. 5)
Pardington, A. R., 12–13, 62, 63, 255*n*29
Parke, Vincent, 262*n*7
parked medians, **18**
    See also planted medians
Parker, Suzy, 147, 263*n*59
parks
    Brightwaters, 122
    Forest Hills Gardens, 191
    Garden City, 22, 25, 28, 43
    Great Neck Estates, 138
    McKnight Realty Company and, 132
    Riverside, Chicago, Illinois, 24
    Rochester, New York, 59
    waterfront, 93–95, **93**, **94**, **95**, **96**, 97, 98
    See also amusement parks; Munsey Park; *specific names*
Parrish, Maxfield, 248
Parrott, Alfred F., 52
Parsons, Samuel, 84
Parsons Nursery, 84
pattern books, 118, 123, 259*n*49
Patterson, Chester A., **146**, 147
Paul, Oglesby, 215, 271*n*31
The Pavilion, Wardenclyffe, **200**
Peabody, Robert S., 46
Peabody, Wilson & Brown, 17
Peabody & Stearns, 46
Pearson, Albin, 157, **160**
Pearson Construction Company, 158, **163**
Peck, Arthur N., 174, 178
Pei, I. M., 45
Pell, S. Osgood, 8, 52
Pender, J., 271*n*20
Pennsylvania Railroad, 16, 39
    See also McCrea, James
Pennsylvania Station, 12, **12**, 45
Penny Provident Fund, 188
perjury charges, 111
Perkins, Curtis L., 199
Pershing, Edward H., 178
Peters, Ralph, 41, 62, 67, 68, 180
Peters, Samuel T., 46
Petit, John J.
    Belle Terre Club, 255*n*54
    on developers, 13
    on Flatbush neighborhoods, 15
    Garden City designs, 40
    Jamaica Estates designs, 181
    Neponsit designs, 223
    New Montauk Theatre, 102
    Prospect Park South designs, 61–62
    Roslyn Estates designs, **66**, 67
    See also Kirby, Petit & Green

Pettigrew, Bertram, 261*n*65
phalanxes, 23
Phelps, Charles E., 119
Philadelphia, 22
piazzas, **89**, 90
Pierce, A. White, 123
Pierce, George H., 254*n*20
pine trees, 85
pinetum trees, 84
Pinnola, Brian A., 252*n*1 (Ch. 2)
Pisani, Vettore, 228
Pisani, Victor, 18, 228–229, **230**, 238
   See also American Venice
Pisani Brothers & Co., 229
Plain Talk, 214–215, **215**
Plandome, 52–56, 254*n*2 (Ch. 4)
   advertisements, **53**
   railroad station, **55**
   Shore Gables, **56**
   students, **54**
Plandome Heights, 56–57, **57**
Plandome Heights Association, 57
Plandome Heights Company, 56
Plandome Land Company, 17, 52, 53, 54, 254*n*5
   (Ch. 4)
Plandome Park, 10, 55–56, 254*n*15 (Ch. 4)
Plandome South, 52, 54
Plandome Women's Club, 54
Plandome Yacht Club, 54, 55
planned communities. *See* residential parks; *specific*
   communities
planted medians, 18
plaques. *See* epitaphs; "Hapgood Homes" plaques
Platt, Charles A., 174
plazas, 40, **42**, **120**, **237**, 239, **239**
Pollock, Channing, 206–207
polo. *See specific clubs*
Pope, Robert A.
   Great Neck Estates designs, 18, 133, 260*n*21–
     260*n*23, 260*n*25, 278*n*11
   Grenwolde designs, 144, 262*n*6
   Tangiers Manors designs, 247
Pope, Russell, 260*n*21
poplar trees, 85
Port Jefferson Company, 65, 255*n*52
Port Jefferson Electric Light Company, 204
Port Washington, 212–214
Port Washington Estates, 271*n*19
Port Washington Garden Club, 220
Port Washington Heights, 271*n*19
Port Washington Park, 271*n*19
Port Washington Yacht Club, 214
Posposil firm, 158, 266*n*95
Powell, Charles U., 270*n*1 (Ch. 17)
Prairie School style architecture, 41, **139**
Prelini, Charles, 106
President's Conference on Home Building and Home
   Ownership (1931), 16, 20
Prest-O-Lite Corporation of America, 150
Prévot, Maurice, 246, **248**
Price, A. White, 118
Price, William L., 264*n*38
Price & McLanahan, 152, 264*n*38
Prince Realty Co., 229

private beaches, 138, 223
Property Development Company, 254*n*15 (Ch. 4)
Property Holders Realty Company, 247
property owners' associations, 81, 85, **86**, 98
   See also specific association
property restrictions, 146, 159, 175
   See also deed restrictions
property titles, 16
Prospect Park South, 15, 60–62
   houses, **15**, **61**, **62**
   lawns, **61**
   planted medians, **61**
   street layouts, **61**
Provident Loan Association, 188
public schools. *See* schools
Public Service Comission, 177
Purdy, Gil, 154
Purdy, Ned, 154

Quaker Ridge Corporation, 245
Queen Anne cottages, 123
Queensboro Bridge, 12, **12**, 78, 80, 124
Queensboro Gas and Electric Company, 177
Queens Chamber of Commerce, 80–81, 192–193
Queens County, 192
Queens County Fairgrounds, 28
Queens County Water Company, 177
Queens Land and Title Company, 72
Quinby, F. J., 133

racetracks, 28, 37, 38, 100, 150
racial discrimination, 15, 153, 159, 244, 245,
   277*n*25
Radburn, New Jersey, 25
radio towers, 200, **201**
rail lines map, **84**
railroads, 16, 27, 39, 80, 168, 186, 240
   See also Long Island Railroad (LIRR)
railroad stations
   Belle Terre Estates, **66**
   Garden City, **30**
   Long Beach, **107**
   Plandome, **55**
   Tangiers Manor, **250**
   See also Long Island Railroad (LIRR); Pennsylvania
     Station
Ray, Ted, 113
Real Estate and Ideal Homes Exposition (1910), 17
real estate development, 65, 72, 73, 129
   See also suburban real estate development
real estate development companies. *See specific names*
Real Estate Exchange of Long Island, 13, 52, 132
Real Estate Record and Guide, 109
real estate transaction enhancement, 16
Rebhuhn, Anne, 138, 139
Rebhuhn, Ben, 138, 139
Rebhuhn house, Great Neck Estates, 138–139
Recht, William, 178
recreation, 11, **11**, 13, 15
   See also specific sport or venue
Reed, Art, 265*n*52
refinancing, 16
   See also financing; mortgages
Regional Plan Association, 187

Regional Plan for New York, 20
religious community, Garden City as, 32–33, **33**
religious enthusiasm. *See* camp meeting movement
religious restrictions, 15, 175
Renaissance Revival style architecture, 68, 120
rental costs, 30, 146
    See also summer rental costs
residency enticements, 36, 39, 49, 75
    See also marketing strategies; recreation
residential parks, 10–21
    See also specific developments
residents' associations. *See* homeowners' associations
restrictions. *See* building restriction ordinances; club
    membership restrictions; deed restrictions
Reynolds, William H.
    about, 13, 100–101, **101**
    advertisements placed by, **113**
    Dean Alvord and, 62
    Frank Bailey and, 16, 101
    legal difficulties of, 111, 114
    Neponsit Realty Company and, 222, 274*n*14
    on transportation and Long Island development,
      103–104
    See also Dreamland; Kirby, Petit & Green; Lido
      Beach; Long Beach; Montauk Theatre
Rialto, American Venice, 231
Richards, Mary, 41
Rickenbacker, Edward, 162, 264*n*12
Rickert, Charles H., 79, 92, 135
Rickert, Edward J.
    about, 78–79, 92
    homes of, **90**, 91, 98
    H. Stewart McKnight on, 132
    on Kensington, 93, **94**
    on property improvements, 96
Rickert, Helen, 92
Rickert and Findlay, 20
Rickert-Finlay Realty Company
    about, 78, 79–80, **79**
    Douglas Manor, 81–89, 98–99
    East River Heights, 80–81
    Kensington, 81, 82, 83, 88–89, 90–92, 93–98
    Norwood, 80–81
    saltwater swimming and, **93**
Ringwood, Thomas
    about, **167**
    on Carl Fisher, 166, 167
    home of, 158
    Miami Beach and, 152
    Montauk Beach and, 154, 155, 162
    Montauk Beach Company and, 165
    Montauk Beach Development Corporation and,
      164, 165, 265*n*58
    property restrictions and, 159
Riverside, Chicago, Illinois, 18, 21, 24, 25, **25**
Riverside Cemetery, Rochester, New York, 59–60, **60**
Riverside Cemetery Association, 59, 60
Riverside Improvement Company, 24
roads, 80, 82
    See also Long Island Motor Parkway
Robbins & Ripley, 157
Robinson, Harry E., 241
Rochester, New York, 58–60, **60**, 212
Rochester Union Advertiser, 60

Rockaway Hunting Club, 169, 174
Rockaways, 168–169
    See also Far Rockaway; Neponsit
Rockefeller, Nelson, 245
Rockefeller family, 195, 245
Rogers, Ginger, 10, 252*n*4 (Ch.1)
roller chairs, 110, 115
Roosen, Herman D., 255*n*35
Roosevelt, Kermit, 218
Roosevelt, Quentin, 44
Roosevelt, Theodore, 39, 42, 188
Roosevelt Field, 44, 45
Rosberg, C. F., 268*n*13
Rose, Joseph, 74
Roslyn Estates, 20, 63–65
    houses of, **65**
    master plans and maps, **64**
    street layouts, **65**
Roslyn Estates, Inc., 69
Rossiter, Clinton L., 255*n*52
Rossiter, Ehrick K., 173
Roth, Emery, 109
Roullier, Gustav A., 18, 53, 254*n*11 (Ch. 4)
rus in urbe, 24, 62
Russell, Walter, 248
Russell Sage Foundation, 15, 20, 188–189, 190, 193
Ruth, Babe, 138

Sage, Olivia S., 186, 188–189, 193
Sage, Russell, 186, 188
Sage Foundation Homes Company, 192, 193
sailboating. *See* boating
salary increases, as leisure opportunity, 11
sales brochures. *See* marketing strategies
Salisbury Golf Club, 38
Salisbury Links, 38
saltboxes, 244
Sammon, Peter, 274*n*19
Sandringham Colony, 109–110
sanitation, 30, 91
    See also cesspools; housing reform; utilities
Sappho, 82
Saturday Evening Post, 221
Savannah, Georgia, 22
Save New York Committee, 170
Saylor, Henry H., 42, 123
scarlet maples, 85
"Scarlet Scooter," 13, **13**
Schaaf, Margaret G., 259*n*1
Schenck, Edward, 169
Schenley Distributors, 178
schools. *See specific names*
school teachers, 52, **54**
Schuler estate, American Venice, 236
Schultze & Weaver
    design exhibitions of, 264*n*46, 265*n*87
    Flamingo Hotel, Miami Beach, 153
    Lido Beach Hotel, 114
    Montauk Manor, 157–158, **160**
    office designs, **166**, 266*n*90
Schwab, Charles M., 262*n*23
Sea Gate, 15
Seaside Park, 225
seaside parks, 105

Seawanhaka Corinthian Yacht Club, 11
Secatogue Indians, 119
Second Empire style architecture, 26, 33
Second Suburb: Levittown, Pennsylvania (Harris), 8
Setauket, New York, 240, 244, 277*n*34, 277*n*43, 277*n*47
Shadow K, **153**, 155, 160
The Shadows, 150, 152, 264*n*37
Shape & Bready, 92
Sharpe, H. C., 254*n*12 (Ch. 3)
Sheepshead Bay, 13
Shepard, Charles, 213
Shepherd's Neck village, 155, **156**, 158, 159, 167
Shields, Brooke, 263*n*58
Shields, Cornelius, 147, **147**, 261*n*2
Shields, Louis, 140, 147, 261*n*1–261*n*2
    See also Shields brothers
Shields, Paul V.
    about, 140, 147, **147**, 261*n*1–261*n*2, 262*n*24
    Grenwolde and, 144, 145, 146
    home of, 146–147, **146**, 263*n*53
    marketing strategies of, 141, 144, 146
Shields, Veronica G. B., 147, 263*n*52
Shields & Company, **142**, 147
Shields brothers, 140, 141
Shingle style architecture, 36, 155, 172
Shinnecock Hills, 18, 38, **63**
Shinnecock Hills & Peconic Bay Realty Company
    (SHPBRC), 62–63
Shinnecock Hills Golf Club, 11, 63
Shinnecock Inn, 63
shopping malls, 45
    See also Stony Brook Crescent Colonial Revival
        Shopping Center
Shore Gables, Plandome, 55, **56**, 254*n*13 (Ch. 4)
Shoreham, 198, 202–211
    advertisements, **204**
    houses, **203**, **205**, **206**, **207**, **208**, **209**, **210**
    post office and store, **205**
    Shoreham Estates versus, **211**
    street layouts, **203**, **210**
    See also Oak Ridge; Wardenclyffe
Shoreham Boat Club, 207
Shoreham Country Club, 207
Shoreham Estates, **211**
Shoreham Garden Club, 207, 208
Shoreham Inn, 199, **200**
Shoreham Overhang, 202
SHPBRC. *See* Shinnecock Hills & Peconic Bay Realty
    Company (SHPBRC)
silver maples, 86
Singer Manufacturing Company, 275*n*12
Skidmore Estate, 144, 262*n*23, 262*n*25–262*n*26
Slee, John, 118
Slee & Bryson, 123
Sloan, Robert, 178
Smith, Almeron, 52
Smith, Edgeworth, 217, 270*n*1 (Ch. 17), 273*n*55
Smith, George J., 268*n*5
Smith, R. A. C., 273*n*54
Smith, William "Tangier," 247
Smith's Point, 133
Smithtown Hunt, 242, 276*n*16
Smythe, Richard H.
    about, 241

Old Field South designs, 242, 243, **243**, 244, **244**
    Stony Brook Village and, 277*n*37
snobbery, 141, 146, 243
    See also "desirable" people
Snowden, James H., 152
social activities and social organizations. *See specific*
    clubs
Society for the Preservation of Long Island
    Antiquities (SPLIA), 7, 239, 252*n*1 (Ch. 2)
socioeconomic opportunities for leisure, 11
S. Osgood Pell Company, 52
Soundview Golf Course, 135, 138, 139
Southern Colonial style architecture, 91
Southern State Parkway, 235
South Shore, 18–19, 104
    See also American Venice; Brightwaters;
        Rockaways; Woodmere
South Side Railroad, 168
South Side Sportsmen's Club, 46
Southwestern Oil and Steamship Company, 79
Spanish Baroque style architecture, 153
Spanish Colonial style architecture, 182, 268*n*13
Spanish style architecture
    Bayberry Point, 47, 51
    Garden City, 41, 43
    Great Neck Estates, 260*n*34
    Kensington, 90
    Laurelton, 62, 102
    Lido Beach, 114
    Long Beach, 108, 109, 115
    Montauk Beach, 158
    Plandome Heights, 57
    Woodmere, 173
Spaulding Construction Company, 241, 242
SPLIA. *See* Society for the Preservation of Long
    Island Antiquities (SPLIA)
sports and sportsman pursuits, 11, 46
    See also recreation; *specific sports*
Spring Grove Cemetery, Cincinnati, 59
spruce trees, 85
Stadelman, H., 260*n*34
stained glass windows, 33, 34
Stanlaws, Penrhyn, 248, 250
Stanton, Elizabeth C., 206
Star Island, 152, 158, 264*n*40
Star Island casino, **163**
Star Island Club, 265*n*76
Star Island Yacht Club, **164**, 167
State University of New York at Stony Brook, 240
    See also Stony Brook University
Stearns, John G., 46
Stebbins, George L., 179
Steinway Piano Company, 178
Stern, B. E., 178
Sterner, Frederick J., 17, 64, 67, **69**
Stevenson, Richard W., 170
Stewart, Alexander T.
    about, 26, **26**, 32–33
    bust of, 45
    homes of, 26, 30
    See also Garden City
Stewart, Anita, 127, **128**
Stewart, Cornelia C., 26, **26**, 32, 33, 34, 35
Stewart, Lucille, 127

Stewart, Robert, 27, 30
Stewart Arms Inn, Garden City, 36
Stewart Avenue Mall, Garden City, 41
Stickley, Gustav, 17, 41, 89, 202
St. John's University, 184
St. Joseph's Church, Garden City, 39
St. Mary's Cathedral School for Girls, Garden City, 34, **35**, 45
stock market crash (1929). *See* economic depressions and recessions
Stony Brook Community Fund, 277*n*39
Stony Brook Crescent Colonial Revival Shopping Center, 240, 243, 244, 245, **245**
Stony Brook Railroad, 240
Stony Brook University, 277*n*49–278*n*49
Stony Brook Village, 240, 244–245, 277*n*34, 277*n*37
Stony Brook Yacht Club, 242
storm sewers, 271*n*26
storm water drainage, 208
Stowe, Harriet Beecher, 23
St. Paul's School, Garden City, 33–34, **34**, 45
Strathmores, 8
Strauch, Adolph, 59
street lamps, **190**
strikes, 123
St. Therese of Lisieux Roman Catholic Church, 158
St. Thomas Episcopal Church, Bellerose, 76
Sturges & Hill, 47
Sturman, Sue, 272*n*49
Suburban Construction Company, 69–70
suburban real estate development
    Alvord as standard in, 71
    Carrère on, 15
    Long Island as a niche in, 13
    in present day Garden City, 45
    tools for managing, 20
    trends affecting, 73
subways, 12, 80, 117, 118
Success, 104, 108
Suffolk County, 21, 239, 276*n*63
Suffolk County Land Company, 205
Suffolk Improvement Company, 240, 241, 276*n*3
    See also Old Field South; Stony Brook Village
sugar maples, 29, 85
summer rental costs, 31, 49, 51
Sunday, William "Billy," 185
Sunnyside Gardens, 25, 194
Sunrise Highway, 235
Sunwood, Old Field, 240
Supper Club on Star Island, 158
Swasey, W. Albert, 114
sweet gum trees, 85
swimming, **93**, **94**, 95, **95**, **96**, **98**
    See also bathing pavilions
Swiss chalets, 61, **61**, 202, **203**
sycamore trees, 85

Tagliabue, Charles J., 201, 208, 209
Talbot, H. R., 110
Tangiers drawbridge, **249**
Tangiers Manor, 247–248
Tangiers Manors Administration Building and Clubhouse, **249**, **250**
Tangiers Manors Corporation, 247, **249**

Tappan, Robert, **156**, 158, **160**
Tarbell, Gage E., 11, 39–40, 41, 42
tax evaluations, 35
Taylor-Storm Realty, 254*n*15 (Ch. 4)
T. B. Ackerson Company
    on development speed, 119, 127–128
    marketing strategies of, 120, 122–123, 126, 258*n*9
    offices of, 118, **126**, 258*n*19
    as residence, 258*n*18
    standards of, 117–118
    start of, 116
Teignmouth Hall, Belle Terre Estates, 67, 68, **69**
telephone overcharges, 177
telephone services, **215**
    See also utilities
Tenement House Committee, 188
Tenement House Department, New York City, 188, 190
tennis. *See specific clubs and venues*
Tennis Court, **14**, 15, 17, 19
terra incognita, 11
Tesla, Nikola, 200, **201**
Tesla Science Center, 200, **201**
"thatched" roofs, 145, **146**, 172
This Salubrious Spot (Wolfe), 17
Thomas, A. J., 158
Thom McAn, 276*n*1
Thompson, LaMarcus A., 8
Thompson & Frohling, 183
Thompson Park, 8
Thoreau, Henry David, 23
Thorne, Francis B., 254*n*12 (Ch. 3)
Thorne family farm, 132, 134
Thorne mansion, Great Neck Estates, 134, 135, 139, 261*n*42
Thornewood, Great Neck Estates, 133, 260*n*26
Three Village Inn, 244
Three Villages, 240, 245
Tiffany, Louis C., 46–47, 187
"Tige," 115
tiger-tail trees, 85
Tillion & Tillion, 216, **218**, 272*n*45
Timpson, James L., 178
Title Guarantee and Realty Associates, 16
Title Guarantee and Trust Company, 16, 222
Tjaden, Olive F., 178, 268*n*31
"tobacco houses," 57
tobacco industry, 56
To-morrow: A Peaceful Path to Real Reform (Howard), 25, 189
Tomper, George V., 254*n*20
Tooker, E. Post, 18, 67, 255*n*56
Tooker and Marsh, 67
Toonerville Folks, 221
topography conformation
    Beacon Hill, 215
    Douglas Manor, 84
    Garden City, 28
    Great Neck Estates, 133
    Munsey Park, 196
    Plandome, 53
    South Shore, 18
    Woodmere, 171
topography consternation, 208

towers, 116, 126, **126**, 200, **201**
Town & Country, 161, 206
Town of Babylon, 239, 275*n*10–275*n*11
Town of Hempstead, 27, 105, 106, 178
Town of North Hempstead, 196
Townsend, Adelaide, 82
train lines. *See* railroads; subways; trolley lines
transatlantic ports, 148, 162
transportation
   in 19th century Long Island, 11
   as a marketing strategy, 126
   revolution in, 12–13, 80, 82, 180
   See also air travel; auto travel; intermodal travel
     opportunities; railroads; subways
Travis, Walter J., 38, 40
trees. *See specific type*
"The Trees of Douglas Manor" (Griffith), 84
trolley lines, 39, 109, 214, 222
   See also intermodal travel opportunities
Trowbridge, Alexander, 194
Trow's New York Directory (1909), 268*n*19
Trumbauer, Horace, 215
Tubby, William, 39
tuberculosis cure reward, 92
Tuchs, E. R., 134
Tudor Revival style architecture, 53, 75, 90, 216,
   217, 221
Tudor style architecture
   Belle Terre Estates, 67
   Garden City, 43, **44**
   Great Neck Estates, 134, 260*n*36
   Great Neck Villa Estates, 144
   Grenwolde, 146
   Jamaica Estates, 182, **185**
   Montauk Beach, 167
   Prospect Park South, **62**
   Roslyn Estates, **65**
   Shepherd's Neck village, **156**
   Woodmere, 174
   See also modified Tudor style architecture
tulip trees, 85
Tuttle, Calvin, 73
Tuxedo of the Seaside. *See* Bayberry Point
Tuxedo Park, 19, 181
   See also Belle Terre Estates
Tuxill, Carl, 218
Tuxill, Charles E.
   about, 212, **213**, 218, 271*n*6, 272*n*37
   homes of, 273*n*57, 273*n*58
   marketing strategies of, 214, 216
   offices of, 212, **213**, 218, 273*n*58
   See also Beacon Hill
Tuxill, Ethel, 273*n*67
Tuxill, Frank, 212, 216, 273*n*57
Tuxill, Wilfred, 212
Tuxill, William, 270*n*1 (Ch. 17)
Tuxill Realty Company, 212, 215, 216, 270*n*1 (Ch. 17),
   271*n*6
Tuxill Square, Auburn, New York, 212, 270*n*2 (Ch. 17)
Tweed Ring, 26, 27
Tyndall, Robert, 264*n*12, 265*n*52

Union Castle Steamship Company, 136
Union Mortgage Company, 255*n*46

United Holding Company, 72, 74, 75
Unjohn & Conable, 268*n*13
Upham, Donald, 206
Upham, Elizabeth, 202
Upham, Jabez B., 199, 201
Upham, Richard D., 205, 206, **208**
upper class families, 11
   See also "desirable" people; wealthy population
urban life versus residential park appeal, 10
U.S. Army, 166
U.S. Army Air Corps, 230
Use of Deed Restrictions in Subdivision Development
   (Monchow), 16
U.S. Mortgage & Trust, 216
utilities. *See* buried utilities
Utopia (More), 22
utopian schemes, 22–23, 25
Utterback, J. David, 273*n*68

Valentine, Benjamin E., 176
Vanderbilt, Cornelius, 112
Vanderbilt, William K., Jr., 13, 38, 62, 68, 184
Vanderbilt Cup Race, 38, 39
Vanderbilt Improvement Company, 60
van Duyne, Lewis, 204
Van Siclen, George W., 179
Van Wyck house, Douglas Manor, 87, **87**
Vaux, Downing, 18, 63, **63**
   See also Olmsted, Vaux, and Withers
Veiller, Lawrence, 188
Venetian American Properties, Inc., 238, 239
Venetian Community Builders Corp., 276*n*53
Venetian Holding Corp., 276*n*54
Venetian Home Builder, 238
Venice, as landscape inspiration, 18–19, 46, 47, 112,
   120
   See also American Venice
Venice Community House and Yacht Club, 238,
   276*n*58
Vick, James, 254*n*6 (Ch. 5)
Viemeister, August L., 65, 255*n*46
village incorporation, 15–16, 20
Village of Old Field, 240, 276*n*4
Villa La Pietra, Florence, Italy, 89
Villa Park Association, 133, 135
Villa Vizcaya, Miami, 89
Vitagraph Studios, 56, 127, **128**
Vivian, Henry A., 47
Vogue, 161
Vredenburgh, Watson, 268*n*22
Vreeland, Walter F., 144, 145, 146, **146**, 262*n*21,
   262*n*24–262*n*25

Wainwright, Louden S., Sr., 179
Walker, A. Stewart, 266*n*96
Walker, Frances, 199
Walker, Herbert H., 199
Walker & Gillette, 158, **164**, 266*n*96
Wampage Shores, 8
Wanser & Lewis, 247
Ward, LeRoy, 134, 138
Warden, James S., 198, 199, **199**
Wardenclyffe, 199–201, 202, 206
   advertisements, **204**

master plans and maps, **201**
    street layouts, **201**
    See also Shoreham
Wartime Housing Committee, 187
Washburn, H. J., 52
water features, 19, **19**, 64, **65**
    See also American Venice; Bayberry Point
waterfront access, **143**, **144**, 145, 223
    See also private beaches
waterfront lots, 18
waterfront ownership, 88
waterfront parks, 93–95, **93**, **94**, 97, 98
waterfront rights, 146, 214, 232
    See also common ownership
watersheds, 177, 268*n*28
water sports. *See* boating; recreation; swimming
water supply, 30, **31**, 44, 52, 67
waterworks, **31**
Watson Engineering Company, 262*n*35
Watts, A. Macdonald, 268*n*19
Wave Crest, 15
Wawapek Farm, 186
wealthy population, 91, 92, 104–105, 112, 138, 153
Webb, Albert, 152, 159
Webb, Dave, **163**
Webb, Richard, 157, 158, **163**
Weeks, Robert D., 187
Weil, Samuel, 175
Weir, J. Alden, 248
Weiss, Marc, 15
Wesmoreland, 78
West Rockaway Land Company, 222
Wethey, Charles E., 216, 272*n*48–272*n*49
White, Stanford, 35, 36, 38, 148, 162, 200
    See also McKim, Mead & White
"White City," 13–14
white-collar workers, 8, 75
white oak trees, 84
Whitney, Gertrude V., 184
Whitney, Harry P., 68, 184
Whitney, Henry, 229
Whitney Museum of American Art, 184
Whitson, A. U., 270*n*1 (Ch. 17)
Whittlesey, C. E., 174
Widener, P. A. B., 48
Widewater, Old Field, 240
Williams, Timothy, 255*n*52
Williamsburg Bridge, 39
Willowdale Terrace, 271*n*19
windmill house, **158**
Windsor Land Company, 72
Winthrop, John, 22, 252*n*6 (Ch. 2)
Withers, Frederick. *See* Olmsted, Vaux, and Withers
Withers, John T., 254*n*15 (Ch. 4)
Wodehouse, P. G., 10
Wohseepee Park, 122
Wolfe, Kevin, 17
women, 15, 38, 75
    See also Marsh, Helen

Wonderland, 56
Wood, Arthur W. B., 157, **158**, **165**
Wood, Gar, 264*n*12
Wood, Samuel, 168, 169
Woodemere Club, 176
Woodhull, John J., 199
Woodhull, Sylvester M., 199
Woodmere, 52, 53, 168–179
    houses, **171**, **173**, **174**, **175**, **177**
    lake, **171**
    picture postcards, **174**
    street layouts, **178**
Woodmere Academy, 174, 175
Woodmere Club, **176**, 178, 268*n*22, 268*n*23
Woodmere Improvement Society, 178
Woodmere Land Association, 174, 177, 268*n*19
Woodmere Land Improvement Company, 169
Woodmere Realty Company, 175, 176, 177, 178
Woodruff, Timothy L., 14, 39, 40, 41, **43**, 181, 184
Woodsburgh, 168, 170, 174
Woodsburgh (Woodmere subdivision), 174, 178–179
Woodsburgh Pavilion, 168, **169**, 170
Woodville Farms, **201**, **202**
Woodville Landing, 198–199, 200, 202
worker houses, **29**, 30, 155–156, 190
workers, 24
    See also construction crews; white-collar workers
working class population. *See* housing reform;
        Industrial Revolution
Works Progress Administration (WPA), 219–220
The World, 105
World Columbian Exposition, Chicago, 14, 48
World War II preparations, **114**, **157**, **160**, **164**, 166,
    166
WPA. *See* Works Progress Administration (WPA)
Wright, Frank Ayres, 173
Wright, Frank Lloyd, 17, 75, 134, 138, **139**
Wright, Joseph S., 169
Wurtsboro, New York, 218
Wyandance, Grand Sachem, 229
Wynn, Ed, 138

yachts and yacht clubs
    Carl Fisher and, 150, **153**, 155, 160
    Cornelius Shields and, 147
    William Douglas and, 82
    See also boating; *specific clubs*
yellowwood trees, 85
Yewell, John F., 220–221, **221**, 273*n*66–273*n*68
YMCA, Brooklyn, 65
YMCA, Rochester, New York, 58–59
Young, Victor, 138
Young & French, 158

Ziegler, Henry, 178
Zoar, Ohio, 23
zoning, 20, 185, 269*n*28
    See also building restriction ordinances; deed restric-
        tions; village incorporation